RELATIVISM

RELATIVISM
A CONTEMPORARY ANTHOLOGY

EDITED, WITH AN INTRODUCTION, BY

MICHAEL KRAUSZ

Columbia University Press   New York

Columbia University Press
Publishers Since 1893
New York   Chichester, West Sussex
Copyright © 2010 Columbia University Press
All rights reserved

Library of Congress Cataloging-in-Publication Data
Relativism : a contemporary anthology /edited, with an introduction, by Michael Krausz.
p. cm.
Includes bibliographical references and index.
ISBN 978-0-231-14410-0 (cloth : alk. paper)
ISBN 978-0-231-14411-7 (pbk. : alk. paper)
1. Relativity. I. Krausz, Michael. II. Title.

BD221.R429   2010
149—dc22
2009051340

Columbia University Press books are printed on permanent and durable acid-free paper.
This book is printed on paper with recycled content.

Printed in the United States of America

References to Internet Web sites (URLs) were accurate at the time of writing. Neither the
author nor Columbia University Press is responsible for URLs that may have expired or
changed since the manuscript was prepared.

Contents

PART III. Moral Relativism, Objectivity, and Reasons

PART IV. Relativism, Culture, and Understanding

Foreword

Relativism commits itself to the thought that we are not only culturally constrained in our beliefs but also that, as Clifford Geertz once said, "it's culture all the way down." In turn, many critics of relativism think that relativism is a form of skepticism that collapses into subjectivism.

We do not flinch when the anthropologist tells us that some cultures are "guilt cultures" and others are "shame cultures"; but many of us flinch when Pascal says that truth is different north and south of the Pyrenees, precisely because we think that saying "that's true" means that it is true for everyone and anyone. Many of the essays in this volume ask where we should draw the line between the banality that the world looks different from different perspectives and the unacceptable suggestion that we can say exactly what we like about it.

The authors in this volume invite us to ask how attached we are to the hardness of hard facts and to anchoring a hard ideal of truth to them. We are then led to consider the likelihood that the so-called hard sciences do not deal in facts whose hardness is unchallengeable, and then to consider anxieties about moral relativism. The essays consider the thought that human beings communicating with one another and understanding how and why the world looks so different to different peoples has value—not always in the hope of establishing commonality of vision but in the hope of enlarging the circle of our human sympathies.

Readers of this invaluable volume will have come to understand a great deal about the multiple varieties of epistemological, ontological, and moral relativism, and about the intellectual motivations of anthropologists, physicists, logicians, and ordinary persons. Nobody could read these essays without learning not only a great deal about relativism but also a great deal about how to do philosophy, period.

Alan Ryan
Warden, New College, Oxford University

Preface

This volume contains thirty-three essays. Nine new works were commissioned especially for it, and twenty-four others are reprinted from previous publications. Some of them were published in two earlier volumes by Notre Dame University Press: *Relativism: Cognitive and Moral* (1982), edited by Jack Meiland and Michael Krausz, and *Relativism: Interpretation and Confrontation* (1989), edited by Michael Krausz.

I extend grateful thanks to Wendy Lochner, senior executive editor at Columbia University Press, who, throughout the process, has been extremely encouraging and helpful; to Christine Mortlock, assistant editor at the press, for her attentive support; to the anonymous referees and advisors who offered valuable guidance; to Lydia Goehr and Gregg Horowitz for bringing the idea of this volume to the attention of the publishers; to Bryn Mawr College's Center for International Studies and Bryn Mawr's Office of the Provost for providing financial support for editorial assistance and copyright fees; to Notre Dame University Press for permission to include materials from the 1982 and 1989 volumes, and to others who granted copyright permissions. Details for each of the reprints can be found on the first page of each of those chapters. Finally, I am grateful to Lorraine Kirschner for her steadfast secretarial and moral support, and to Elizabeth D. Boepple, without whose tireless and expert assistance this volume could not have been produced.

RELATIVISM

Introduction

MICHAEL KRAUSZ

How can the earth be in motion according to one coordinate system and be stationary according to another? How can the shortest distance between two points be a straight line in one geometry and not in another? How can an act be just according to one value system and terrorist according to another? How can polygamy be good in one culture and bad in another? How can an individual-based morality be appropriate in one society and inappropriate in another? How can harming one's enemies be right in one morality and wrong in another? How can an artwork be beautiful for one person and ugly for another? Such questions often prompt relativistic responses.

Relativism is characteristically defined as the dual thesis that (1) truth, goodness, or beauty, for example, are relative—relative to some frame of reference; and (2) no absolute standards to adjudicate between competing reference frames exist. But what exactly does relativism assert? Does relativism apply to all domains of inquiry? Does it apply to claims of truth, goodness, and beauty, or to some but not all such values? Does it apply to what there is, or to our knowledge of what there is? What counts as a reference frame? How should we understand confrontation between pairs of reference frames? Are reference frames inter-translatable? Is mutual understanding between them possible? What does the claim of relativism oppose?

Part I provides a conceptual map of possible relativisms and outlines a brief history of the idea of relativism. Part II discusses types of relativisms, indicating some self-referential inconsistencies, the fabrication of facts, the place of relativism in the philosophy of science, non-bivalent versions of relative true, requirements to make relativism coherent, a strategy to deflate the very possibility of relativism, the relation between truth and convention, the idea of a conceptual scheme, the persistence of facts, targets of an anti-relativist argument, and a reconciliation between realism and relativism. Part III discusses varieties of moral relativism, their limits and grounds, the coherence of moral relativism, relationships between facts and values, grounds for understanding alien morals, the possibility of objectivity without absolutism, taste as an example of a coherent relativism, and the relation between moral relativism and moral realism. Part IV considers characteristic reactions to relativism, solidarity without relativism, the possibility of understanding without translatability, the nature of criticism internal to a culture, a way to overcome relativism, understanding cultures and selves without relativism or ethnocentrism, the point of cross-cultural conversations without the hope of agreement, relativism and the social construction of persons, the idea of relativism in the context of poststructuralism, and the pertinence of relativism for feminism. Here, closely following the words of their authors, are synopses of the essays that follow.

Michael Krausz suggests that within relativism no fewer than five sorts of variables can be identified: With respect to what reference frames (conceptual, cultural, historical, etc.) could relativism apply? With respect to what domains (cognitive, moral, aesthetic, etc.) could it apply? With respect to what level (ontic, epistemic) could it apply? With respect to what values (truth, reasonableness, goodness, praiseworthiness, beauty, etc.) could it apply? With respect to what variety of absolutism (objectivism, foundationalism, universalism) could its negations apply? We shall discover that relativism is not one doctrine; a myriad of relativisms exists. So the question, "Who is right, the relativist, absolutist, or neither?" should be preceded by, "Which relativism—with regard to which sort of reference frame, domain, level, value, or in opposition to which sort of absolutism?"

Maria Baghramian notes that the history of relativism spans twenty-five hundred years and testifies to its longevity and influence. She distinguishes between four relativistic schools of thought: cultural relativism, conceptual relativism, social constructionism, and postmodernism. Baghramian provides an historical account that draws upon the philosophies of Protagoras, Plato, Aristotle, Sextus Empiricus, Michel de Montaigne, Charles Montesquieu, Immanuel Kant, Johann Gottfried Herder, Georg Wilhelm Friedrich Hegel, Friedrich Nietzsche, Wilhelm Dilthey, W. V. O. Quine, Nelson Goodman, Paul

Feyerabend, Thomas Samuel Kuhn, Michel Foucault, Jacques Derrida, Donald Davidson, William James, and others.

Maurice Mandelbaum outlines subjective, objective, and conceptual relativism, claiming that all are self-refuting in the same way. Relativists contradict themselves by saying all statements are relatively true while relying on the absolute truth of some statements to prove their point. Mandelbaum extends his argument by noting that the relativist must take statements that express *evidence* for relativism to be true in some absolute sense while claiming that all statements are true only in a relativistic sense.

Nelson Goodman emphasizes the conventionality of the distinction between fact and convention, asking questions such as, "How can divergent diagrams or versions be of the same fact, the same world?" They must either be of no world or of different worlds. There must be many worlds if any. According to Goodman, facts are conventional as is the distinction between fact and convention. But the line between fact and convention is not capricious. Where one draws the line depends upon one's stance, and while a stance may be taken anywhere, it is not arbitrary.

Nancy Cartwright reviews relativisms in contemporary philosophy of science at the ontological, epistemological, and normative levels, locating their roots in the problems of induction and underdetermination, which threaten the claims of science to have a rational structure. Epistemic virtues are widely invoked to 'save' science from relativism, but these have only shaky claims to the title 'epistemic'; they are not precise enough to fix what is acceptable. The separate motives to picture contemporary science as a highly rational enterprise and to 'tell it like it is,' can either serve or conflict with each other. What is acceptable in science is always relative to a choice of goals; truth is just one among them. Even taking truth as the natural goal, the sole arbitrator of acceptability is otiose because we cannot directly determine what is true.

Joseph Margolis's moderate or 'robust relativism' opposes all familiar forms of skepticism, nihilism, anarchism, and irrationalism, compatible with nonrelativistic theories of truth. It opposes theories that do not apply nonrelativistic truth-values to all domains of inquiry. Robust relativism defends the formal availability of truth-like values. Judgments that would yield incompatible or contradictory judgments on a nonrelativistic or bipolar model of truth do not do so on this model. Margolis holds that the ontology of different sectors of the causal world is such that a relativistic theory is as reasonable as a nonrelativistic theory.

John MacFarlane seeks to make sense of relativism about truth, holding that it is the view that truth is relative to contexts of use and to contexts of assessment. Accordingly, he affirms that (1) to be a relativist about truth is to allow that its truth-value might vary with the context of assessment and of use; and (2) making sense of relativism requires understanding what committing to the truth of an assessment-sensitive sentence or proposition would constitute. The philosophical challenge is to explain what 'truth relative to a context of assessment' means. MacFarlane discusses arguments necessary to defend the claim that a sentence or proposition is assessment-sensitive.

Donald Davidson argues that the very idea of a conceptual scheme is incoherent because such coherence requires the coherence of the idea of an alternative conceptual scheme. But this idea also is incoherent. If it is translatable into the first conceptual scheme, it is not 'alternative,' and if not thus translatable, nothing intelligent can be said to distinguish it from the first. Since grounds for distinguishing a conceptual scheme from an alternative conceptual scheme do not obtain, the distinction collapses, and with it the coherence of the very idea of a conceptual scheme and of most forms of relativism.

Hilary Putnam presses for the possibility of relativism by arguing that the assumption that an interpreter's language needs to be singular is mistaken. An interpreter need not have only one language in which truth conditions can be given for every sentence in every language he claims to understand. Such interpreters may have more than one 'home' conceptual scheme; translation may be governed by several sets of constraints. On Putnam's view, conceptual relativity does not disappear upon inquiry into the meanings of conceptual alternatives.

Simon Blackburn questions the strength of Davidson's attack on conceptual schemes. Conceptual schemers who emphasize the contingent factors that shape our minds need not be wedded to Davidson's 'organize' metaphor invoked when speaking about schemes as (putative) categories or organizing structures of language. Instead, post-Kantian conceptual schemers are more likely to describe a conceptual repertoire as 'shaping' experience. They play a role in determining the form it takes. Further, the conceptual schemer is not deterred if we cannot 'verify' what the alien is saying or which truths aliens embrace.

Paul Boghossian observes that the traditional objection against global relativism is that any relativistic thesis needs to commit to the existence of some absolute truths. Yet a global relativism asserts that no absolute truths exist. Although Boghossian agrees with this traditional objection, he disagrees with the traditional argument by which it is defended, supporting a stronger argument instead. The global relativist faces a dilemma: either the argument that only relative facts exist does not succeed, or it consists in the claim that we should so reinterpret utterances such that they express 'infinitary' propositions we can neither express nor understand. Boghossian concludes that we must allow that some objective, mind-independent facts exist.

Harvey Siegel calls attention to the complex ways in which relativistic claims and arguments for or against them interact. The traditional argument raises concerns about the apparent incoherence of the assertion and defense of relativistic theses. Siegel suggests that Boghossian's complaint against the traditional argument does little to disarm or neutralize it. Instead, Siegel views Boghossian's formulation to be a minor variant of the traditional incoherence objection. Indeed, the strength of Boghossian's new argument for the incoherence of relativism rests on the strength of the traditional incoherence argument.

Akeel Bilgrami notes that discussions of realism and relativism often proceed as if these are starkly opposed doctrines, but that on one classical understanding of 'realism' and 'relativism,' the two doctrines share philosophical assumptions. The paper advances a distinct position, at once 'realist' and 'pragmatist.' That only one of two contradictory beliefs can be 'right' is a realist idea but one that allows us to embrace a more intuitively satisfying epistemology, in which we need never deny that we seek truth in inquiry, that we achieve it occasionally, or hold a pervasive diffidence about our beliefs.

Gilbert Harman opposes absolutists in moral theory who believe that what persons ought to do is independent of anything to which they might have agreed. He affirms that different people are subject to different moral demands depending on customs, practices, conventions, values, and principles they accept. He focuses on 'inner judgments,' moral judgments that imply that the agent whose action is being judged has reasons to do or to avoid that which the judgment asserts it ought to do or avoid. Harman says that an agent has a pertinent reason when he or she is a party to an agreement with others. In claiming that inner judgments make no sense apart from an agreement, he implies that no absolutely true moral code exists apart from human agreement, which renders inner judgments correct.

Bernard Williams holds that there is truth in ethical relativism. He distinguishes between real and notional confrontation. There is a real confrontation between two systems of belief at a given time if there is a group at that time for whose persons each of the two systems is a real option. Notional confrontation differs from real confrontation in that at least one of the considered systems of belief does not present a real option to them. The distinction between real and notional confrontation coheres with two propositions, both of which are true: that we must have a form of thought, not relativized to our existing system, for thinking about other systems of concern to us; and we can recognize that many systems may exist, which have insufficient relation to our concerns for our judgments to have any grip on them, while admitting that other persons' judgments—those for whom they were a real option—might get a grip on them.

David Wong observes that there is a kind of moral disagreement that poses special difficulties for universalism. This kind of disagreement evokes the complex reaction of moral ambivalence, in which one comes to appreciate the other side's viewpoint to the extent that it destabilizes one's sense of the unique rightness of one's own judgments. This experience involves both the recognition of sharing values with the other side and of having differing interpretations of these values or of placing different priorities on them in relation to other values. Wong explains how an explanation of moral ambivalence is furnished by a nuanced relativism that constrains the range of adequate moralities but denies that there is a single true morality. Wong agrees, therefore, with one implication of moral relativism as it is usually defined: that there is no single true morality.

Catherine Elgin argues that the acceptability of factual or evaluative sentences derives from its place in a system of considered judgments in reflective equilibrium. Something right relative to one acceptable system may be wrong relative to another. So several answers to a given question may be right, but not every answer or action is right. If many things are right, many more remain wrong. The demarcation of facts rests on considerations of value and evaluations are infused with considerations of fact. So factual judgments are not objective unless value judgments are, and value judgments are not relative unless factual judgments are. Tenable judgments of both kinds are at once relative and objective.

David Wiggins inventories five senses of relativity in moral philosophy. They concern (1) the rightness or wrongness of acts or practices and the specification of circumstances and context; (2) 'right' or 'wrong' as relational predicates and the specification of the moral system or society for which ethical predicates are indexed; (3) truth and falsehood as predicated on moral judgments relative to a system of moral assessment; (4) the acquisition of the sense of truth and falsity by a sensibility to certain particular features in any given act, person, or situation; and (5) the substance of disputants' understanding of the question of what one ought to do. Wiggins suggests that relativities (4) and (5) combine to constitute a key challenge of relativity.

David Lyon notes that the threat of logical incoherence arises when a relativistic theory implies that two conflicting moral judgments are equally valid. He refines the threat by distinguishing between the content of a moral judgment and making the judgment. A judgment's being false and justifying the making of it is not necessarily paradoxical. Therefore, if the moral relativist only implied that different people might be equally justified in making conflicting judgments, moral relativism would not be in jeopardy. In contrast, Lyons finds incoherent the suggestion of some moral relativists that the content of a single moral judgment can itself be simultaneously valid and invalid. He concludes that a truly relativistic moral theory would best concern itself with the content of moral judgments, not with one's making them.

Gopal Sreenivasan observes that, in practice, anthropologists rarely rely upon intertranslation when learning an alien culture, and young children never do. Instead, both groups resort to a process of 'going native.' By focusing on the structure of 'thick descriptions,' Sreenivasan distinguishes between understanding a language and radically interpreting it. If alien thick descriptions feature prominently in the language of another society, we may find that we understand their ethical outlook but still reject it. Sreenivasan argues that we can imagine an alien language that articulates an ethical outlook but which we could not radically interpret. Our inability to radically interpret this language still need not prevent us from understanding it.

Thomas Nagel offers a view of realism about values in terms of a distinctive view of objectivity. Realism about values is the view that propositions about what gives us reasons for action can be true or false independent of how things appear to us, and we can hope to discover the truth by transcending appearances, subjecting them to critical assessment. What we aim to discover by this method is not, however, a new aspect of the external world, called value. By stepping outside ourselves, constructing and comparing alternatives, we can reach a new motivational condition at a higher level of objectivity. Then the possibility opens for recognition of values and reasons that are independent of personal perspective, which has force for persons who can view the world impersonally as a place that contain them.

Crispin Wright rejects global relativism. He considers, though, whether relative truth is locally coherent. He shows that there is no point to trying to resolve disagreements that arise from an expression of different, permissibly idiosyncratic tastes. Nobody is wrong. They should just agree to disagree. According to true relativism, disputants can both be right even when they understand the claim in the same way, and even though they make incompatible judgments about it. No absolute facts exist regarding personal taste. Truth in that regard depends upon a stance, standard, or set of affective dispositions. The same claim can be true for one and false for the other.

Russ Shafer-Landau characterizes the master argument for moral relativism as maintaining that all moral requirements are contingent on personal commitments and that such requirements entail excellent reasons for action; reasons for action, in turn, depend on personal commitments for their existence. Shafer-Landau asserts that this argument is unsound. Accordingly, we should not succumb to relativistic temptations. He resists 'practical instrumentalism'—the view that the only reasons that can exist are so-called hypothetical reasons. Such reasons are in some way ancillary to the achievement of one's commitments, such as cares, desires, wants, and goals. If practical instrumentalism is true, then no categorical reasons—ones that obtain independent of their relation to an agent's commitments—can exist. But, Shafer-Landau argues, categorical reasons for action do exist, and so practical instrumentalism is false.

Clifford Geertz observes that the decentering of any perspective as the one absolutely true one does not necessitate the disastrous consequences many anti-relativists fear. He notes that what the relativists want us to worry about is provincialism—the danger that our perceptions will be dulled and our sympathies narrowed by the overvalued acceptance of our own society. What the anti-relativists want us to worry about is a kind of spiritual entropy in which everything is as significant and insignificant as everything else; there anything goes. Geertz finds provincialism altogether the more real concern so far as what actually goes on in the world.

Richard Rorty affirms that relativism is the epithet misapplied to pragmatism by realists. He urges that the issue of relativism should be placed within a larger discourse about how reflective human beings try to give sense to their lives. According to the way of objectivity one attaches oneself to something which can be described without reference to any particular human beings. According to the way of solidarity one does not ask about the relation between the practices of the chosen community and something outside that community. For Rorty, those who wish to ground solidarity in objectivity are realists, and those, like Rorty, who wish to reduce objectivity to solidarity, are pragmatists.

Alasdair MacIntyre distinguishes between translatability and understanding, and claims that one can understand two cultures without being able to translate between them. MacIntyre holds that bilingual people must be able to do this to determine what is not translatable from one culture to another. Just as untranslatability does not entail a limit on understanding, understanding does not entail translatability. MacIntyre's argument undercuts Davidson's claim that the coherence of the idea of a conceptual scheme or an alternative conceptual scheme is a matter of translatability.

Martha Nussbaum and Amartya Sen distinguish two ways in which traditional values may be undermined: object failure obtains when the objects of valuation treasured by a traditional value system become more difficult to obtain and sustain as a result of material change; value rejection obtains when the holds those values have on subjects is weakened. They argue that evaluation and criticism of tradition must be internal, using resources taken from within human history and human experience. Since cultures usually contain a plurality of voices and much active debate, sufficient resources for criticism can frequently be found without moving outside the culture in question. But any culture is part of a larger community; its communications with and responses to this larger world become a part of its 'internal' resources.

Jitendra Mohanty finds ethnography useful for phenomenology. He resists a radical incommensurability between conceptual frameworks and their correlative worlds. He argues that no opposition exists between diversity and unity. Rather than being a preexistent metaphysical entity, unity is being worked out in a gentle and tolerant, not a violent or imperious, way. Even for two world-noemata so far removed that any communication between them would seem impossible, a series of intervening world-noemata may still link and overlap the initial pair. This presupposes that each noematic world is not a fully holistic system; otherwise, for one to share part of its contents with another would be impossible. Thus communication is achievable.

Charles Taylor addresses the question of theorizing about very different societies. He argues that understanding is inseparable from criticism, but this in turn is inseparable from self-criticism. We cannot get an adequate explanatory account of other societies until we understand their self-definitions, which may be different enough from ours to force us to extend our language of human possibilities. Explanatory sciences of society are logically and historically dependent on self-definitions. They are logically dependent because a valid account must take the subject as an agent, and historically dependent because, within any given culture, the languages of social science are developed out of and nourished by the languages of self-definition, which have grown within it.

Anthony Appiah argues that even if the form of relativism that claims moral disagreements across cultures are sometimes rationally irresolvable is true, discussing normative issues with people from other cultures is still a valuable exercise. What moves people is often not an argument from a principle or a long discussion about values but, instead, a gradually acquired new way of seeing things. He urges that we discuss normative questions with people in other places not to achieve agreement but to foster familiarity. Understanding does not require agreement, and risk of disagreement about values should not deter us. If agreement is not the only goal, then the difficulties in arriving at agreement may not matter so much.

Amélie Rorty affirms that moral and political principles cannot be derived from the concept of personhood because that concept is socially and politically constructed. The defining characteristics of persons are set by primary practices and privileged actions. The epistemological difficulties on which relativists focus are compatible with the existence of genuine intercultural communication. Rorty's view makes vulnerable only those forms of relativism that disallow the possibility of intercultural communication. At issue is the holism of culture: the degree of overlap between the institutions and practices that define different cultures.

David Hoy contrasts pluralism and monism as regards interpretation with pluralism and monism as regards the world. He argues that pluralism as regards both contrasted cases is not a form of relativism. Hoy observes that hermeneutical and poststructuralist philosophers argue that what counts as the "world" is a function of how it is understood. In this way they court relativism. Since Heidegger and Gadamer, hermeneutics has espoused that everything is a matter of interpretation. Interestingly, in his later writings Jacques Derrida distances himself from relativism. He affirms that he is not opposed to a kind of universalism. Derrida contemplates the goal of philosophy as a projected universal, as an infinite process of universalization.

Lorraine Code urges that feminists may share a strategic advantage in "coming out" as relativists. She suggests that reasons why feminists often view relativism negatively derive from the prohibitions that structure hegemonic epistemological practice, not from the "natural" dictates of reason and the logic of inquiry or the practical consequences of occupying a relativist position. Anti-relativism underestimates the deliberative, negotiative, cooperative, contestatory aspects of knowledge production, suppressing the situatedness, the recognition of which informs feminist and other postcolonial projects. It makes too little of how knowledge claims are produced, negotiated, validated, or discredited in ongoing discussion. In contrast, a relativist position amounts, initially, to refusing the prohibitions that have shaped the epistemology of the Anglo-American mainstream.

The essays in this volume illustrate the significance and range of relativistic doctrines. They exhibit its varieties and rehearse its virtues and vices. They reflect a wide range of attitudes toward relativism, and deploy diverse philosophical orientations and idioms. They indicate the close relationships between relativism and neighboring philosophical issues. The divisions between the four interrelated parts cannot be strict, for views about relativism as to truth, for example, inevitably affect views about relativism as to moral, aesthetic, or other values. Regardless of the large number of essays included here, no such collection can claim comprehensiveness. The essays invite students and professionals alike to grapple with one of the most intriguing, enduring, and far-reaching philosophical problems of our age.

Orienting Relativism | **PART I**

Mapping Relativisms 1

MICHAEL KRAUSZ

I. AN INITIAL DEFINITION

Relativism claims that truth, goodness, or beauty is relative to a reference frame, and no *absolute* overarching standards to *adjudicate* between competing reference frames exist. This is only a preliminary definition, for it conceals no fewer than five sorts of variables couched in the following questions: With respect to what *reference frames* (conceptual, cultural, historical, etc.) could it apply? With respect to what *domains* (cognitive, moral, aesthetic) could it apply? With respect to what *level* (ontic, epistemic) could it apply? With respect to what *values* (truth, reasonableness, goodness, praiseworthiness, beauty) could it apply? With respect to what *variety of absolutism* (objectivism, foundationalism, universalism) could its negations apply?

I shall address these questions presently. It is already apparent, however, that, given the many types of reference frames, domains, levels, values, and negated varieties of absolutism, no one relativism but a myriad of relativisms can be conceived. Rather than argue for any particular variety of relativism—or absolutism, for that matter—my aim in this chapter is to show the relations between varieties of relativism and to articulate distinctions and strategies that they or their absolutist counterparts may deploy.

II. CONTRASTS BETWEEN RELATIVISM AND ABSOLUTISM

First let us consider some contrasts between relativists and absolutists. Relativists hold that several incompatible non-converging reference frames, in terms of which we perceive and understand the world, could exist. At the boundaries of pertinent reference frames, where grounds for evaluation unique to those frames exhaust themselves, we have no absolutist way to adjudicate between contending frames. No absolute frame-neutral grounds for adjudicating between frames exist. For the relativist, where standards of evaluation are exhausted at the bounds of reference frames, the search for pertinent absolute standards makes no sense. Global relativists urge that for all reference frames, no absolute standards for adjudication exists. Local relativists urge that for only some reference frames such absence exists.

In contrast, some absolutists worry that denying absolute standards will result in arbitrariness, anarchism, or nihilism. With no absolute standards, we would have no worthwhile goal of inquiry. By ruling out absolute truth, for example, we rule out the possibility of progress in knowledge. Without absolute standards, we could not distinguish between unenlightened and enlightened, backward from advanced, true from false, moral from immoral, beautiful from ugly.

An absolutist might charge that the relativist claim—that no absolute, overriding adjudicating standards exist—is not enough to unseat the absolutist program. For the absolutist may urge perseverance: 'keep looking for those standards.' Accordingly the absolutist might insist that to make the relativist claim compelling, the relativist would need to show that the absolutist program *in principle*—under any circumstances—*cannot* result in success. Yet for the relativist to accept this stronger requirement would verge on the contradictory. For the relativist is committed to making no such claim of principle. The best that a relativist could hope for—from within some reference frame—is to show that the absolutist program might be implausible, unlikely to succeed, issue hollow promises, or other such dissuasions. The relativist cannot rise to the absolutist's challenge for a frame-independent argument against the absolutist—which indeed satisfies relativists because they regard such absolutist demands as inappropriate. Thus what would count as a compelling argument for relativism or absolutism would itself be contentious between absolutists and relativists.

Often absolutists presume that relativists must adopt absolutist argumentative purposes and then declare relativism to be refuted when relativists fail to satisfy those purposes. But giving reasons or arguments can have different purposes. When relativists give reasons or offer arguments to the absolutist, they need not try to convince the absolutist. Relativists may give reasons or arguments to present their views in an ordered way to promote better understanding of their view. The relativist might deploy ampliative reasons, as I call them, in contrast to determinative reasons. Ampliative reasons provide rationales for embracing a view without having the aim to convince another to embrace the same view. Determinative reasons aim to convince someone that they should embrace a particular belief. In turn, one who resists the distinction between ampliative and determinative reasons might insist that reasons as such are meant to convince someone of a belief. Without the motivation to convince someone to adopt or modify a belief, ampliative reasons appear to be no reasons at all.

Absolutists might argue that the diversity of frames could show up only if such diversity were frame-independent. They might argue that relativists cannot even assert relativism without first transcending it. To affirm that truth, goodness, or beauty are frame-relative, for example, we must 'rise above' frame-relativity altogether. In this way an absolutist might argue that relativism actually presupposes absolutism. But this argument is invalid because frame-diversity may be noted within some more general reference frame. It does not follow that the relativist must rise above frame-dependence *as such*. Relativists would need only to transcend their immediate reference frames to note the diversity of reference frames generally. It does not follow that the relativist must rise above 'reference-framedness' per se or that 'rising above' entails frame-independence.

Yet while some 'meta-frame' may rise above certain lower-level reference frames, the question arises: What status should we attach to the possibility that there might be a single 'imperial' meta-frame that is itself a frame without a competitor, a frame of all frames? For the relativist, this is an anomaly, for, as our initial definition of relativism suggests, relativism concerns the non-adjudicability of more than one non-converging competing reference frame. If only one imperial reference frame exists, the relativist's central question of adjudication does not arise. I shall return to this issue when discussing reference frames in relation to certain suggestions of Immanuel Kant.

The relativist could argue that any would-be absolute standard would reflect the biases of the absolutist's home culture. Further, whichever standard the absolutist might advance would be arbitrary or contentless: arbitrary because it would invite further justification leading to a regress whose cut-off 'cap' would arbitrarily be supposed to be self-justifying, and contentless because it would have to be too general and vague to be informative. Relativists could hold that we need no absolute standards to have the only sort of knowledge for which we could reasonably hope, namely, local knowledge. What knowledge we have and may be improved upon is inevitably local, and its standards can only be local.

Relativists sometimes affirm that members of one culture are not entitled to interfere with the cultures of others. One community should not impose its values on another. Doing so would reflect our cultural biases. Culture-neutrality does not exist. Further, cultural intervention or imposition amounts to ethnocentrism. We should not judge other cultures in our terms. Instead, we should understand other cultures in terms of their values and beliefs.

Yet to ground the relativist's injunction not to intervene in another's culture in absolutist terms would be contradictory. The relativist might reply that such an injunction could be grounded in relativist rather than absolutist terms, and that the injunction is reasonable according to local standards. In turn, the absolutist might counter that such relativist grounds would be too weak to be compelling.

A defense of relativism might involve two sorts of approaches. A relativist might seek to demonstrate the implausibility of absolutism or the plausibility of the relativist program. Yet someone might be impressed with arguments against absolutism without actually endorsing relativism. One might agree that the absolutist's demand for frame-independent arguments is unrealistically high, yet still find that arguments *for* relativism remain uncompelling.

Accordingly the denial of relativism does not entail absolutism. We could deny relativism and deny absolutism. A global skeptic who denies the possibility of knowledge altogether (the self-inconsistency of this claim not withstanding) would fall into this class. An ineffabilist mystic would also fall into this class. The distinction between relativism and absolutism is not exhaustive. Also, the strength with which one may embrace relativism or absolutism may vary according to their varieties. Different attitudes may be adopted with respect to the variables that define relativism. Indeed, as we shall see, depending upon the varieties of relativism or absolutism one adopts, relativism and absolutism need not be exclusive.

III. WHAT RELATIVISM IS NOT

Before considering more specific varieties of relativism, let us consider what it is not. Relativism is not fallibilism, the view that, at any stage of inquiry, a person may hold false beliefs. Accordingly a person could endorse an absolutist notion of truth, for example, and still be a fallibilist.[1] While an absolutist could unpack the idea of a false belief in terms of a mismatch or discordance between a statement and a frame-independent state of affairs, the relativist could account for false belief in terms of a mismatch between a statement and facts as fabricated within a reference frame. Either way, neither relativism nor absolutism has a special claim on fallibilism.

Relativism is not the same as the claim of diversity. Relativism does begin with the observation of the diversity of beliefs and practices embedded in different cultures, for example. It claims further that truth or rightness does not extend beyond the reach of pertinent reference frames. Yet the diversity of beliefs and practices is also compatible with absolutism. Absolutists seek to evaluate or rank diverse beliefs and practices embedded in different cultures according to absolutist standards.

Relativism is not pluralism. Pluralism, as here defined, affirms that for a given reference frame a distinct subject matter, object of interpretation, or world exists. A pluralist could hold that for any scientific paradigm, for example, another world exists.[2] In contrast, relativism requires that, with respect to the *same* subject matter, *competing* reference frames exist. If a systematic plurality of subject matters answered to different reference frames, then pertinent frames could not compete. They would be talking past one another. Competition between reference frames requires that they address the same thing.

For example, Thomas Kuhn says, "There is, I think, no theory-independent way to reconstruct phrases like 'really there'; the notion of a match between the ontology of a theory and its 'real' counterpart in nature now seems to me illusive in principle."[3] He says, further, "The transition from Newtonian to Einsteinian mechanics illustrates with particular clarity the scientific revolution as a displacement of the conceptual network through which scientists view the world" (102). Accordingly Kuhn verges on the pluralist view when he adds, "Two groups, the members of which have systematically different sensations on receipt of the same stimuli, do *in some sense* live in different worlds" (193). Kuhn's remarks hint that if different paradigms employ different concepts to structure their subject matter, they cannot be about the same subject matter. But to preserve competition between reference frames, relativists need to reject the pluralist assumption that difference in concepts mandates difference in subject matter.

Relativism is not synonymous with subjectivism—the 'me-here-now' view that truth, rightness, or beauty is relative to a single person's present reference frame—which is but one form of relativism. Since not all reference frames are subjectivist, not all forms of relativism are subjectivist.

Relativism is not ineffabilism, sometimes called mysticism, the view that an indescribable undifferentiable realm, independent of reference frames, exists. According to this view, communicative resources inherently falsify the nature of such a realm. The ineffabilist might claim that languages or symbol systems are inherently dualistic. For languages or symbol systems must implicate such distinctions as subject versus object or self versus other. What exists before the application of frames is not dualistic. Ineffabilism is a kind of realism without expressibility about the nature of an undifferentiable order. In contrast, relativism holds that the values it invokes (truth, for example) are assertoric. While they are local and frame-dependent, they remain assertoric.

IV. BACK TO THE VARIABLES OF RELATIVISMS

I turn now to examine more closely the variables of relativism mentioned in my opening questions. Those variables are reference frames, domains, levels, values, and absolutisms negated. When combined in different ways, they yield myriad relativisms.

Reference Frames

Reference frames come in many varieties, depending upon specific interests and purposes of diverse thinkers. They may include situations or contexts. They may include conceptual schemes, conceptual frameworks, paradigms, symbol systems, systems of thought, systems of beliefs, practices, world-versions, languages, discourses, linguistic frameworks, points of view, perspectives, standpoints, worldviews, horizons, forms of life, codes, or norms. Reference frames may include cultures, tribes, communities, countries, civilizations, societies, traditions, historical periods, religions, races, or genders. They may include groups or individuals. This list is neither exhaustive nor exclusive.

Some of these varieties of reference frames overlap; others do not. Some of their boundaries are easily delineable; others are not. Sometimes we can easily distinguish what is inside and what is outside a reference frame; sometimes we cannot. The boundaries between Hindu and Buddhist traditions are vague, while those between Medieval, Renaissance, and Baroque periods are indeterminate. Boundaries between guilt and shame cultures are difficult to delineate. A person may be relativistic with respect to conceptual schemes, for example, but not with respect to tribes. A person may be relativist with respect to civilizations but not with respect to individuals. Some relativisms are 'global' applying to all reference frames. Others are 'local' applying only to some.

Relativists rely upon the idea—derived from a much-modified suggestion that Immanuel Kant advances—that what we experience takes on form in virtue of reference frames. They assert that many possible admissible reference frames exist. What different peoples experience reflects different individuable 'objects' as shaped by different reference frames. (For present purposes I use the term 'objects' in a generic sense, as a placeholder for all individuable existents, including processes. Further, I define objectivism in terms of frame-independence, thus allowing for individuable objects and for a non-individuable holistic realm.)

Kant's constructivist insight is sometimes adduced as the basis for asserting the multiplicity of reference frames. Yet Kant asserts that necessary and universal conditions for the possibility of experience exist. He urges that the mind organizes and imposes concepts or categories on sensory data and determines the form taken by our experience of the world. The mind provides basic concepts with which it organizes and interprets experience. So the world as we know it displays an order that the mind constructs. Spatial, temporal, and causal orders are manifestations of the logical structure of all possible forms of judgment.

Kant forecloses the relativist claim that the content of experience is relative to one of numerous possible reference frames. For the logical structure of all possible forms of judgment is basic and unique. Were Kant to have allowed that forms of judgment were non-basic and multifarious, his constructivist insight—again, that the structure of the world as we experience it is imported into that experienced world by our perceptual and cognitive processes—would have made room for the possibility of an *irreducible diversity* of reference frames. But he grants no such allowance, for the pertinent processes are necessary and universal.

At the same time, according to Kant, the individuation of particular experienced objects follows upon rather than precedes the constructivist resources for the possibility of experience at all. No individuable frame-independent objects can exist. Kant's necessary and universal resources are not sufficient to individuate particular objects. This, in turn, means that such resources are not sufficient to adjudicate between reference frames. While adjudication can proceed only after their transcendental possibilities have been granted, such possibilities alone are not enough for adjudication.

Put otherwise, even if Kant is right that the structure of the world as we experience it is imported into that experienced world by our perceptual and cognitive resources, we would still not have the resources necessary to adjudicate between reference frames. All that Kant's resources would provide are the conditions necessary for us to experience the world at all. While Kant's categories may be necessary and universal for the possibility of experiencing objects as the objects that they come to be, it does not follow that those categories determine the characteristics that individuate them or the conditions that adjudicate between admissible and inadmissible objects of knowledge. Recall that relativism denies that absolutist grounds exist to *adjudicate* between pertinent reference frames. So a relativist could even accept Kant's transcendental necessities and universalities and still maintain relativism where it counts, namely, with regard to individuable objects, including individuated reference frames.

In turn, Donald Davidson famously argues for the incoherence of the very idea of a conceptual scheme. If he is right, a relativism that deploys the idea of a conceptual scheme is incoherent. But even if Davidson is right, how wide-ranging his conclusions are remains an open question; that is, whether to be vulnerable to his arguments, all the varieties of reference frames I have mentioned are—in a sufficiently strong logical sense—cognates of conceptual schemes remains moot. Does the absence of criteria to individuate one would-be conceptual scheme with regard to another entail the same absence with regard to one or another religion, one or another historical period, and so on? If these reference frames are not cognates of conceptual schemes, Davidson would have to provide supplemental arguments with regard to such other sorts of reference frames. That assumes that, in the first place, his arguments against the idea of conceptual schemes are sound.

If the idea of a conceptual scheme—along with other cognates of reference frames—is coherent, we should distinguish between two senses of relative truth. The first sense holds that a statement is true relative to one frame and false relative to another frame. This threatens to lead to a contradiction. The second sense holds that a statement is true in one frame and (from the vantage point of the first frame) inexpressible—*hence neither true nor false*—in another frame. If the two frames are not translatable, a statement true in one frame may not even be expressible in the other frame. This second sense of relativism might avoid the threat of contradiction exhibited in the first sense.[4]

Domains

Next, let us consider the question of domains to which relativisms might apply. One might be relativist with respect to all domains or with respect to some designated domains. Thus a relativist might be *global* or *local*. For present purposes I distinguish between cognitive, moral, and aesthetic domains. My immediate purpose is to indicate a relativist's reach, global or local. Cognitive relativism asserts that a statement is true or false (reasonable or unreasonable, justifiable or unjustifiable) relative to a particular reference frame. Moral relativism asserts that an action is morally right or wrong (good or bad, virtuous or vicious, praiseworthy or blameworthy) relative to a particular reference frame. Each culture, moral relativism urges, develops the moral standards it finds acceptable. We cannot judge actions executed in one culture by the moral standards of another culture. Similarly aesthetic relativism affirms that an artwork or an experience is beautiful or ugly, sublime or not sublime, satisfying or unsatisfying, relative to a reference frame.

Depending upon our purposes and interests, we may divide domains in other ways, of course, such as formal studies (logic, mathematics, or computational studies), natural sciences, social sciences, humanities, and the arts. Or we could divide domains according to some departmental disciplines such as mathematics, physics, chemistry, biology, economics, sociology, anthropology, law, politics, history, philosophy, religion, languages and literatures, art, or music, and so on. According to such a departmental scheme, an individual could be a relativist with respect to law, history, religion, languages and literatures, art, or music but absolutist with respect to mathematics or physics, for example.

An individual might mix and match these domains with regard to their relativist standing. Each arrangement would require independent arguments. For example, legal relativism would hold that an act is criminal or not criminal (liable or not liable) relative to a reference frame. A religious relativist would hold that a person or text is holy or unholy (righteous or unrighteous) relative to a reference frame. One might embrace either legal or religious relativisms, for example, without embracing relativism in mathematics or physics. In turn, an individual could divide domains in terms of modes of experience. For example, in an adverbial mode, R. G. Collingwood proposes that we should understand art, religion, science, history, and philosophy (in that dialectical order) as forms of experience.[5] In any event, one might affirm relativism with respect to some domains—however those domains are construed—and absolutism with regard to other domains.

Returning to our initial scheme of domains, assuming that each domain is distinct and not reducible to another (admittedly this assumption is arguable)— for example, that moral or aesthetic domains are not reducible to the cognitive domain—here (without prejudice as to their plausibility) are their permutations: (1) cognitive relativism, moral relativism, aesthetic relativism; (2) cognitive relativism, moral absolutism, aesthetic relativism; (3) cognitive relativism, moral absolutism, and aesthetic absolutism; (4) cognitive relativism, moral relativism, and aesthetic absolutism; (5) cognitive absolutism, moral relativism, aesthetic relativism; (6) cognitive absolutism, moral relativism, aesthetic absolutism; (7) cognitive absolutism, moral absolutism, aesthetic relativism; (8) cognitive absolutism, moral absolutism, and aesthetic absolutism.

Levels

Relativism may be taken to apply at the *ontic* or the *epistemic* level. The distinction between the two levels may be superimposed upon each of the permutations generated by the domains just considered. A relativist at the ontic level embraces the relativity of objects to reference frames, such as virtues or vices being relative to a religious tradition. A global relativist at the ontic level affirms that *all* objects are frame-dependent. A local relativist at the ontic level affirms that only *some* objects are frame-dependent. In turn, a relativist at the epistemic level embraces the relativity of our knowledge of objects to reference frames. A global relativist at the epistemic level affirms that our knowledge of all objects is frame-dependent, and a local relativist at the epistemic level affirms that our knowledge of only some objects is frame-dependent.

The distinction between ontic and epistemic allows a variety of combinations: (1) ontic absolutism and epistemic absolutism; (2) ontic absolutism and epistemic relativism; (3) ontic relativism and epistemic absolutism; and (4) ontic relativism and epistemic relativism. The superimposition of the global/local distinction regarding domains can further complicate these permutations. For example, one might embrace the possibility that in the religious domain ontic absolutism and epistemic relativism obtains. (I shall return to this example shortly.) But in economics, monetary value exists relative to a reference frame, and our knowledge of such value is relative to a reference frame.

Yet the distinction between ontic and epistemic levels is contentious, thus complicating the permutations that assume its validity. For example, if we have no access to 'the world' as it might be, unperceived, we cannot compare our descriptions of the world with the world itself. At best we have access to the world only through some description or depiction of it. We can know the world only as conceptualized in one way or another. Therefore, when we seek to compare a description of the world to the world itself, we are comparing our description with the world as conceptualized—as already described. We are comparing our description of the world only to another description or conceptualization of the world. The most that can be established in this way is a relationship between the two descriptions, not a relationship between our description and the world-as-it-is-in-itself. Thus one might conclude that the notion of 'the world,' the world-in-itself, is of no use in inquiry. Correspondingly one might argue that the distinction between ontic and epistemic levels is of no use in inquiry.

The view according to which no world apart from our descriptions exists (call this view 'atheist') can be distinguished from the view according to which the notion of such a world can serve no use in inquiry (call this view 'agnostic'). The agnostic view does not deny that a frame-independent world exists but recommends that we should not invoke it in our inquiries. An absolutist might counter that to posit the notion of a frame-independent world to help make sense of our inquiries *is* useful, for without it we would have no point in pursuing those inquiries.

Values

Recall that relativisms may invoke different values such as cognitive truth, moral goodness, or aesthetic beauty. These values are typically taken in a bivalent way. The cognitive values of truth and falsehood, for example, are bivalent. Truth and falsity are mutually exclusive. Yet cognitive values may also be multi-valued. Reasonableness and unreasonableness, aptness and inaptness, or appropriateness and inappropriateness, for example, are not mutually exclusive. Accordingly two opposed or incongruent judgments may—as regards justifying or warranting grounds—be reasonable, appropriate, or apt. Thus a hypothesis may be true and reasonable, true and unreasonable, false and reasonable, false and unreasonable, and so on. Incongruent but not contradictory moral values, such as praiseworthiness and un-praiseworthiness or fairness and unfairness, may apply to a given action. Aesthetic values, such as beauty and ugliness or convincing and unconvincing, may apply to a given artwork, for example.

While some values are typically associated with particular domains—beauty, with respect to the aesthetic domain, for example—they may also apply to other domains. One might affirm that a given solution to a mathematical or scientific problem is beautiful, for example, or that moral or aesthetics claims may be true. Therefore no necessary connection exists between particular domains and corresponding values; they are not co-extensive, although they may overlap.

Absolutisms a Relativist Might Negate:
Objectivism, Foundationalism, or Universalism

When speaking about the varieties of absolutism that a relativist might negate, I adopt the metaphor of possible strands, some or all of which may comprise an absolutist's rope. Those strands include a kind of objectivism, foundationalism, or universalism. (The kinds will become apparent presently.) An absolutist rope comprises all or some of the mentioned strands. A strong relativism will negate all of them; a strong absolutism will affirm them all. A weaker relativism will negate only some of them; a weaker absolutism will affirm only some. The weaker versions incorporate both relativist and absolutist strands. Again, depending upon the variety of absolutism or relativism adopted, absolutism and relativism need not be exclusive.

Note that when I use the terms 'objectivism,' 'foundationalism,' 'universalism,' or versions thereof that a relativist may negate, I use them as terms of art; some measure of legislation is inevitable. For example, according to my usage, objectivism is a matter of frame-independence. In this sense objectivism should not be confused with intersubjectivity, or with fairness, disinterestedness, detachedness, evenhandedness, impartiality, neutrality, or the like—all of which could also be construed in frame-relative ways. Objectivism in my frame-independent sense is sometimes called realism.

As it pertains to relativism, the idea of objectivism as frame-independence requires a qualification. Frame-independence may apply to individuable or countable objects. Alternatively, as in Kant's *noumenon*, Anaximander's *apeiron*, or Hinduism's *Atman* or *Brahman*, frame-independence may apply to a non-individuable or non-countable 'holistic' realm. Only the first individuable application bears on the question of relativism, for only the first application could have the resources to *adjudicate* between reference frames. Saying with Kant or Anaximander, for example, that a non-individuable holistic order exists would be of no praxial use to rank one reference frame over another. It cannot determine whether Einsteinian mechanics is better than Newtonian mechanics, for instance. It cannot tell us whether a shame culture or a guilt culture answers to a putative moral fact of the matter. So, when arguing against relativists, absolutists could plausibly appeal to objectivism if they appeal only to an objectivism of the individuable kind. Regarding adjudication, whether a non-individuable holistic order exists is immaterial, because it could not do the work of adjudication that the absolutist would require. Whereas objectivism as frame-independence applies to both individuable and holistic claims, only individuable objectivism applies in the debate between relativists and absolutists. For that debate turns on the idea of the possibility of adjudication between reference frames.

Objectivism in its individuable sense holds that countable states of affairs exist independent of reference frames. These states of affairs may be cognitive, moral, or aesthetic. Ontically speaking, objectivism affirms that sticks and stones, for example, exist as such irrespective of reference frames. Correspondingly, at its epistemic level and in its individuable sense, objectivism affirms that if they hold, pertinent beliefs do so on grounds independent of any reference frame. The statement 'sticks and stones exist' is true, because sticks and stones do exist irrespective of reference frames. By contrast, non-objectivism in its ontic sense holds that individuable objects are frame-relative. They are mereologically variable. Thus whether the earth is stationary or in motion is frame-relative. That the shortest distance between two points is a straight line is frame-relative. Yet an ontic non-objectivism with respect to individuable objects does not entail that *nothing* exists independent of reference frames, only that individuable objects are frame-relative. Such a view still leaves open the possibility that Kant's holistic noumenon could exist.[6] Of course, an individuable objectivist might add that some theory of perception or some account of epistemic access to pertinent objects is required. Otherwise adjudication could not proceed.

Now consider our second strand of absolutism, foundationalism. At the ontic level, foundationalism asserts that whatever exists can be reduced to one most basic, unanalyzable, ultimate constituent. Drawing upon the pre-Socratic idea of an arché, I shall refer to such a condition as *archic*. At its ontic level, foundationalism holds that objects in designated domains reduce to archic conditions. For example, Thales of Miletus holds that all objects are composed of, and reducible to, water. Democritus holds that objects are reducible to atomic constituents, themselves irreducible. At the epistemic level, knowledge of such a condition can be captured by first principles that are incapable of further analysis. Such principles are self-justifying. At its epistemic level, foundationalism presupposes that there must be a terminus to any stage of justification, without which there would be an infinite regress. It posits a self-evident bedrock condition of self-justification. In its global variant foundationalism holds that archic grounds hold for all domains. In its local variant foundationalism holds that archic grounds hold for some but not all domains. Foundationalism is sometimes called essentialism.

At the ontic level, foundationalism denies what I call polymorphism—the view that continued levels of analysis or magnification will reveal ever further constituents of pertinent phenomena. Polymorphism denies that a most basic rock bottom reference frame exists. The nature and number of objects depend upon the reference frames one invokes. While sticks and stones exist as such in the reference frame of middle-sized objects, they do not exist as such at the molecular or the cellular level. Yet what might exist before the application of frames is not a most basic dough-like constituent capable of subdivision. Even Kant's noumenal realm, though predating individuable objects, is not a most basic constituent waiting to be cut up according to different reference frames.

Now let us consider the third strand of absolutism, a kind of universalism. At the ontic level, universalists hold that objects (cognitive, moral, or aesthetic) obtain for all peoples at all times and in all cultures. Such objects are either frame-independent or frame-dependent. They are either objective or nonobjective. In the moral domain, for example, universalists hold that human rights exist for all peoples. Non-universalists at the ontic level hold that some objects exist only for some peoples at some times in some cultures. Some sins, for example, exist for some people but not for others. At its epistemic level, universalism asserts that peoples at all times and in all cultures could agree about cognitive, moral, or aesthetic claims. For example, all peoples can agree that on earth, under normal conditions, all unsupported bodies drop at a fixed rate. At the epistemic level, non-universalists hold that some particular beliefs need not hold for peoples in all times and cultures. They could argue that, at the epistemic level, incommensurability between reference frames blocks universalism. Those of shame cultures (for example, traditional Japan), for example, cannot fully understand those of guilt cultures (for example, contemporary America), and vice versa. At the epistemic level, non-universalists may conclude that the search for a universal language is futile. At the epistemic level, a non-universalist could affirm that there could be no universal cognitive, moral, or aesthetic principles for all peoples at all times in all cultures.

At the epistemic level, a universalist might counter that even to know that two reference frames are incommensurable requires their being intelligible to someone to make the comparison—hence universalism. But this argument is invalid. From the possibility that some persons can compare pairs of reference frames, it does not follow that all peoples are capable of making such comparisons. Further, from the possibility that such frames are comparable—that is, set side-by-side—it does not follow that they may be ranked according to some absolute standard.

I distinguish between universalism as an existential claim from universalism as a regulative principle. The existential universalist claim asserts that universal commensurating resources exist. The regulative universalist claim asserts that it is useful to conduct one's inquiries *as if* the existential condition exists—without actually assuming that it does. We might overcome cross-cultural antagonisms, for example, if we adopt universalism as a regulative principle, even if we do not embrace universalism in its existential version. Thus progressively more general conditions for cross-cultural conversations might be fostered.

I also distinguish between two kinds of universalism—foundational and non-foundational. Foundational universalism holds that all peoples share some common characteristics by virtue of what—irreducibly and ultimately—it is to be a human being. Non-foundational universalism holds that all peoples share common characteristics without presuming that they do so by virtue of what—irreducibly and ultimately—it is to be a human being. Foundational universalism is a claim of necessity, whereas non-foundational universalism is a claim of contingency.

Consider two examples of these universalisms. First, all persons have biological mothers. This example would amount to a foundational universalism if it were tied to the claim that having a biological mother is an inherent, intrinsic, or ultimate feature of being human. Yet a non-foundational universalist might urge that the fact that all persons have biological mothers is contingent and—considering possible developments in human cloning—could be otherwise. Next consider the proposition that all cultures have and appreciate music of some sort. This example would similarly amount to a foundational universalism were it tied to the claim that having and appreciating music is an inherent, intrinsic, or ultimate feature of being human. Depending upon circumstances, this characteristic could be otherwise. Universal commonality alone does not amount to a foundational universalism. Further, foundationalism need not be universalist at all.

One might urge that foundational universalism explains the contingent fact of the universal instantiation of characteristics that all peoples might share, that we need foundational universalism to explain commonality. Without foundational universalism, the commonality of shared characteristics might appear miraculous. But it is an open question whether such commonality without foundational universalism is miraculous. Evolution theory appears to explain universality of shared characteristics without foundational universalism. Thus universalism appears not to require foundationalism.

Let us collect our findings. Objectivism does not entail foundationalism; frame-independence does not entail archism. Objectivism does not entail universalism; frame-independence does not entail universal sharability. Foundationalism does not entail objectivism; archism may be frame-dependent. Foundationalism does not entail universalism; foundationalism may apply locally and not globally. Finally, universalism does not entail objectivism; that which is shareable by all peoples need not be frame-independent. Universalism does not entail foundationalism; that which is shareable by all peoples need not be archic.

Here, then, are the possible combinations, in some or all domains at one or both levels: (1) objectivism, foundationalism, and universalism; (2) non-objectivism, foundationalism, and universalism; (3) objectivism, foundationalism, and non-universalism; (4) non-objectivism, non-foundationalism, and universalism; (5) objectivism, non-foundationalism, and non-universalism; (6) non-objectivism, foundationalism, and non-universalism; (7) objectivism, non-foundationalism, and universalism; and (8) non-objectivism, non-foundationalism, and non-universalism.

Consider an aesthetic case to which objectivism, foundationalism, or universalism might apply. For example, some say that the geometric proportions exhibited in the cross-section of the chambered nautilus shell exemplify aesthetically perfect proportions, formalized in the Fibonacci number series. In that series—1, 2, 3, 5, 8, 13, 21 ...,—starting with 3, any number is the sum of the previous two numbers. The aesthetic objectivist takes the series as embodying a perfect proportion independent of reference frames. In contrast, non-objectivists of this kind hold that the series is frame-dependent. Whether frame-independent or dependent, the foundationalist takes the series to be rock bottom, unanalyzable, and self-evident. The non-foundationalist denies such basicality. Whether objectivist or non-objectivist, foundational or non-foundational, universalists regard applications of the series as universally available, whereas non-universalists deny such universality.

Accordingly, with respect to a given domain, and maintaining the distinction between ontic and epistemic levels, here are the permutations between objectivism, foundationalism, and universalism: (1) ontic objectivism and epistemic objectivism; (2) ontic objectivism and epistemic non-objectivism; (3) ontic non-objectivism and epistemic objectivism; (4) ontic non-objectivism and epistemic non-objectivism; (5) ontic foundationalism and epistemic foundationalism; (6) ontic foundationalism and epistemic non-foundationalism; (7) ontic non-foundationalism and epistemic foundationalism; (8) ontic non-foundationalism and epistemic non-foundationalism; (9) ontic universalism and epistemic universalism; (10) ontic universalism and epistemic non-universalism; (11) ontic non-universalism and epistemic universalism; and (12) ontic non-universalism and epistemic non-universalism. Regarding their admissibility, each would require independent arguments.

By way of illustration, how might these permutations apply in the religious domain? (1) At the ontic level one might affirm the objective existence and nature of God, and at the epistemic level affirm that the existence and nature of God is knowable (or can be revealed) independent of any frame. (2) At the ontic level one might affirm the objective existence and nature of God, and yet at the epistemic level deny the possibility of objective knowledge of them. (3) At the ontic level one might deny the objective existence and nature of God, and yet at the epistemic level affirm that one can have objective knowledge about them (call this the atheist view). (4) At the ontic level one might deny the objective existence and nature of God, and at the epistemic level assert that we can have no objective knowledge of it. (5) At the ontic level one might affirm the foundational existence and nature of God, and at the epistemic level affirm the foundational knowledge of such existence and nature. (6) At the ontic level one might affirm the foundational existence and nature of God, but at the epistemic level affirm a non-foundational knowledge of the existence and nature of God. (7) At the ontic level one might deny the foundational existence and nature of God, and yet at the epistemic level affirm the foundational knowledge of the existence and nature of God. (8) At the ontic level one might affirm a non-foundational existence and nature of God, and at the epistemic level affirm the non-foundational knowledge of the existence and nature of God. (9) At the ontic level one might affirm that God exists for all peoples, and at the epistemic level affirm that all peoples can know God's existence and nature. (10) At the ontic level one might affirm the universal existence and nature of God, and yet at the epistemic level deny that all peoples can know God. (11) At the ontic level one might deny that God exists for all people (that is, God exists for some persons only), and yet at the epistemic level affirm that for whomever God exists, God is universally knowable. (12) At the ontic level one might affirm that God does not exist for all peoples, and at the epistemic level affirm that God is not knowable to all peoples. These permutations of objectivism, foundationalism, and universalism as they apply in the religious domain may overlap in many ways. Again, regarding their plausibility, each of them would require independent arguments. Finally, an ineffabilist mystic will reject all these permutations, for they are couched in sentential terms. Ineffabilism asserts the inexpressibility of the existence and nature of God.

V. ON THE PUTATIVE SELF-CONTRADICTION OF RELATIVISM

Now consider the most influential argument against relativism, which holds that relativism is self-contradictory or self-refuting. The charge of self-contradiction is often taken to be decisive. Let us revisit this argument against relativism in light of the varieties of absolutism and their relativist negations. The assertion that relativism is absolutely true appears to be self-contradictory. Yet if we unpack the varieties of relativism in terms of the varieties of absolutism that they negate, we see that—whatever other arguments to which they may be vulnerable—some relativisms need not be self-contradictory. *For the negation of objectivism, foundationalism, or universalism—in whatever versions—is not self-contradictory.* In other words, the negation of objectivism (the view that a frame-independent order of reality exists—whether it be individuable or holistic—or that we can know it) is not self-contradictory. Likewise, the negation of foundationalism (the view that one most basic unanalyzable constituent of what there is exists, or that the comprehension of such a condition can be captured by first principles incapable of further analysis) is not self-contradictory. In turn, the negation of universalism (the view that there are objects for all peoples or that all peoples can come to know them) is not self-contradictory. So if we conceive of relativism as a negation of one or more of the strands of the rope of absolutism, relativism is not self-refuting.

VI. CONCLUSION

In sum, a relativist must specify pertinent variables in which it applies: reference frames, domains, levels, values, and variety of absolutism negated. The strongest relativist position will be global, asserting itself across the board. The strongest absolutist position will also be global. Other positions may combine variables in moderating or conciliatory ways. Accordingly, I suggest that we should defer the question "Who is right—the relativist, the absolutist, or neither"—and first ask, "Which relativism?" For, as we have seen, relativism is no one doctrine.

NOTES

This chapter draws upon the absolutist trichotomy between objectivism, foundationalism, and universalism that, in another form, first appears in Rom Harré and Michael Krausz, *Varieties of Relativism* (Oxford: Blackwell, 1996), chap. 1. It also draws upon introductions in *Relativism: Cognitive and Moral*, ed. Jack Meiland and Michael Krausz (Notre Dame, Ind.: University of Notre Dame Press, 1982); and *Relativism: Interpretation and Confrontation*, ed. Michael Krausz (Notre Dame, Ind.: University of Notre Dame Press, 1989). I am indebted to Rom Harré, Joseph Margolis, and Bernard Harrison for many fruitful exchanges about relativism. For their helpful comments, I thank Andrew Brook, Jane Geyer, John Gibson, Edward Grippe, Patricia Hanna, Mark Harris, Christine Koggel, Michael McKenna, Peter Lamarque, Paul Thom, Mary Wiseman, David Wong, and Alison Wylie.

1. Karl Popper, "On the Sources of Knowledge and Ignorance," in *Conjectures and Refutations* (London: Routledge and Kegan Paul, 1963).

2. Micheal Krausz, *Rightness and Reasons: Interpretation in Cultural Practices* (Ithaca, N.Y.: Cornell University Press, 1993), 57–60. For a contrasting sense of pluralism, see David Hoy, "One What? Relativism and Poststructuralism" (this volume, chap. 32).

3. Thomas Kuhn, *The Structure of Scientific Revolutions*, 2nd ed. (Chicago: University of Chicago Press, 1970), 206.

4. Chris Swoyer, "True For," in *Relativism: Cognitive and Moral*, ed. Jack Meiland and Michael Krausz (Notre Dame, Ind.: University of Notre Dame Press, 1982), 84–108.

5. R. G. Collingwood, *Speculum Mentis or the Map of Knowledge* (Oxford: Clarendon Press, 1924).

6. For a triadic rather than a dyadic treatment (involving world, practices, and propositions), see Patricia Hanna and Bernard Harrison, *Word and World: Practice and the Foundations of Language* (Cambridge: Cambridge University Press, 2004).

A Brief History of Relativism

MARIA BAGHRAMIAN

I. INTRODUCTION

Writing a history of relativism, and a brief one at that, poses particular challenges, as the blanket term 'relativism' does not stand for a unified doctrine with
more or less discrete boundaries or intellectual genealogy. Relativism is not one
but several loosely interconnected doctrines developed and shaped in response
to a variety of philosophical concerns, and unified more by what they deny—
absolutism, universalism, and monism—than what they endorse. The varieties
of relativism are customarily individuated in terms of their domains—hence the
customary distinction between ontic, cognitive, moral, and aesthetic relativisms—or their objects, for example, relativism about science or law or religion;
each variety has a distinct, if occasionally overlapping, history.[1]

In recent decades four schools of thought with strong relativistic tendencies
have been influential in academia and beyond. The doctrine of cultural relativism, inspired by the work of social anthropologists, where it is argued that there
can be no such thing as a culturally neutral criterion for adjudicating between
conflicting claims arising from different cultural contexts, has become one of
the best known forms of relativism and has shaped not only the theoretical
framework of the social sciences but also the ethical and political outlooks of
many nonspecialists.

Conceptual relativism, a more narrowly delineated form of relativism, where ontology is relativized to conceptual schemes, scientific paradigms, or categorial frameworks, has been influential among a number of philosophers from the analytic tradition. It has also shaped the work of philosophers of science such as Thomas Samuel Kuhn and Paul Feyerabend. The underlying rationale for this form of relativism is the belief that the world does not present itself to us ready-made or ready carved; instead, we supply the different, at times incompatible, ways of categorizing and conceptualizing it. The extreme form of this approach is social constructionism, where it is claimed that reality—objects, entities, properties, and categories—is not simply out there to be discovered by empirical investigation or observation only; rather, it is constructed through a variety of norm-governed, socially sanctioned cognitive activities such as interpretation. Social constructionism has relativist consequences insofar as it claims that different social forces lead to the constructions of different 'worlds' and there is no neutral ground for adjudicating between them.

Finally, Postmodernism is arguably the most potent source of the popularity of relativism today. The movement is identified with relativism because of its mistrust of claims to objectivity, denial of universal conceptions of rationality, and rejection of the role of truth and reason as courts of appeal.

Different stories may be told about the philosophical pedigree of each of these strands of relativism, but all these stories begin with the Ancient Greeks.

II. THE BEGINNINGS

We can detect an increasing awareness of diversity in cultural beliefs and habits foreshadowing relativism in Greek thought from the fifth century B.C.E. Herodotus (ca. 485–430 B.C.E) provides accounts of the variability of customs and habits in Persia and India, and argues that if people were asked to name the best laws and customs, they would name their own; for as Pindar had said, 'custom' is the king of all.[2] Euripides (ca. 485–ca. 406 B.C.E.) shocked his audiences when one of his characters, discussing incest with his sister, announces that no behavior is shameful if it does not appear so to those who practice it.[3] Xenophanes (ca. 570–475 B.C.E.) went even further by arguing that different people have different conceptions of God: "Ethiopians say that their gods are black and snub-nosed, while the Thracians say that theirs are blue-eyed and red-haired." Indeed, he argues, "if cows, horses, and lions had hands, and were able to draw with their hands and do the work men do, horses would draw images of gods like horses and cattle like cattle."[4]

Protagoras of Abdera (ca. 490–420 B.C.E.), however, is considered the first official voice of relativism when he proclaims: "man is the measure [*metron*] of all things [*chremata*]: of the things which are that they are, and of the things which are not, that they are not."[5] Plato reports the dictum in *Theaetetus*, and Sextus Empiricus tells us that it was the opening passage of Protagoras's treatise *Truth* (*Alētheia*). Plato interprets Protagoras as meaning: "Each thing appears [*phainesthai*] to me, so it is for me, and as it appears to you, so it is for you—you and I each being a man,"[6] and gives the example of the same wind feeling cold to one person and hot to another. Sextus also introduces the topic of conflicting appearances and attributes to Protagoras the view that truth is whatever appears to each individual.

It is difficult to know what variety of relativism, if any, Protagoras was defending.[7] But Plato appears to attribute alethic relativism—that truth should be relativized to a framework or perspective—to Protagoras. "Man is the measure," being the opening statement of a treatise on truth, lends further credence to this interpretation. Plato also emphasizes the social and ethical dimensions of Protagorean relativism by attributing to him the view: "what may or may not fittingly be done, of just and unjust, of what is sanctioned by religion and what is not; and here the theory may be prepared to maintain that whatever view a city takes on these matters and establishes as its law or convention, is truth and fact for that city. In such matters, neither any individual nor any city can claim superior wisdom."[8]

The history of relativism is simultaneously a history of the attempts to refute it. Nowhere is this more evident than in the case of Protagoras, who speaks to us today only through the writings of his critics. It is a testament to the significance of Protagoras's work that Plato devotes two dialogues to his views and constructs painstaking arguments to refute them. In *Theaetetus*, he advances a sequence of arguments against 'Man is the measure,' known as turning about or reversal [*peritropē*'] to demonstrate the contradiction inherent in relativism. The argument, a model for numerous attempts to show that relativism is self-refuting, famously culminates in the conclusion:

> Most people believe Protagoras's doctrine to be false.
> Protagoras believes his doctrine to be true.
> By his own doctrine, Protagoras must believe that his opponents' view is true.
> Therefore, Protagoras must believe that his own doctrine is false.[9]

Plato's argument, as it stands, is damaging only if we assume that Protagoras is at least implicitly committed to the truth of his doctrine for everyone, that he smuggles the self-refuting assumption that truth is absolute after all. There has been much discussion as to whether Plato is entitled to impute this assumption to Protagoras.[10] What is beyond dispute, however, is that Plato initiated a particular line of argument against relativism that remains popular to this day.

Protagorean relativism casts its negative shadow on Aristotle's work as well. In Book I of *Metaphysics*, Aristotle argues that relativism is tantamount to the denial of the principle of noncontradiction; if man is the measure of all things, then different people would assign the value true or false to the same assertion, rendering it both true and false. Such a move, however, contravenes the principle of noncontradiction, the most certain of all basic principles and a presupposition of all thought and speech.[11] The relativist, Aristotle argues, assumes that every utterance and its negation are true by the measure of its utterer. Therefore the relativist is unable to make a meaningful statement, and even the very expression of relativism is meaningless since it does not exclude its denial. The relativist, then, by attaching the relativizing clause to all statements, makes contradictions in principle impossible. By so doing, all discourse is rendered devoid of content. Aristotle's criticism of Protagoras, not unlike Plato's, is based on an implicit and, from the relativist's perspective, question-begging use of a nonrelativized truth predicate. Protagoras advocates the legitimacy of (1) P is true for F1; and (2) not-P is true for F2; and (1) and (2) are not mutually contradictory. However, Aristotle's discussion of the principle of noncontradiction, in refutation of Protagoras, was one of the first and finest instances of engaging in philosophy of logic and remains influential to our day.

Despite Plato and Aristotle's criticisms, Protagoras's influence survived into the Hellenistic period in the work of the Pyrrhonian Skeptics in particular, who used 'Man is the measure' to strengthen their claims for skepticism. Sextus Empiricus, the most influential Pyrrhonian, reports:

> Protagoras has it that human beings are measure of all things, of those that are that they are, and of those that are not that they are not. By 'measure' he means the standard, and by 'things' objects; so he is implicitly saying that human beings are the standard for all objects, of those that are that they are and of those that are not that they are not. For this reason he posits only what is apparent to each person, and thus introduces relativity. Hence he is thought to have something in common with the Pyrrhonists.[12]

Sextus bases his 'Relativity Mode' (Mode 3 of the Ten Modes of skepticism) on Protagoras. He argues that judgments and observations are relative to the person who makes them, to their context, and to the object being observed. The example he gives is that of the right and left, which can be established only in relation to other objects. The conclusion Sextus derives is, "since we have established in this way that everything is relative [*pros ti*], it is clear then that we shall not be able to say what existing objects is like in its own nature and purely, but only what it appears to be like relative to something. It follows that we must suspend judgment about the nature of objects" (PH I 140). Sextus's Tenth Mode of skepticism, the Mode from variations in customs and laws, bears greater similarities to the modern understanding of relativism, where he lists the habits, beliefs, and laws of different people to argue that "since so much anomaly has been shown in objects by this mode too, we shall not be able to say what each existing object is like in its nature, but only how it appears relative to a given persuasion or law or custom and so on" (PH I 163).

One of the difficulties in constructing an intellectual history of relativism is to decide how closely we could map our current understanding of it onto earlier ones. For instance, among classical and medieval philosophers, we find a conflation of the ideas of relativism and relativity. Relativism, as currently understood, is the claim that what is true or false, right or wrong, logical and rational, is relative to a culture, belief system, conceptual scheme, or the psychological makeup of different people. Sentences expressing relational properties, such as taller, shorter, to the left of, to the right of, on the other hand, could be assigned non-relativized or absolute truth-values and do not support relativists' claims.[13] Many Greek philosophers, however, include in their discussions of relativism the idea of 'things relative to something' (*tapros ti*) meaning something is what it is in relation to other things, that it has no sui generis but only relational properties. This conflation of the two senses of 'relative' is evident when, among instances of relativity, Sextus lists not only beliefs and sense experiences but also signs and causes; he argues, "we shall not be able to say what each object is like in its nature but we shall be able to say how it appears relative to a given persuasion or law or custom and so on." He explains further, "an existing object appears to be such and such relative to the subject judging and to the things observed with it."[14]

The boundaries between relativism and skepticism were also often blurred. Sextus, for instance, bases his arguments on data that may appear to favor relativism; but the conclusions he draws support skepticism. Like Plato, Sextus believes that Protagean relativism is self-refuting for, "if every appearance is true, it will be true also, being in accordance with an appearance, that not every appearance is true, and thus it will become a falsehood that every appearance is true" (HP 389–390). Pyrrhonism, in contrast, is not susceptible to the self-refutation argument, as it does not commit itself to the truth of any of the contested judgments but chooses to suspend belief on all such matters. Despite these differences, notable similarities exist between Pyrrhonian skepticism and some contemporary approaches to relativism, particularly when Sextus argues for non-naturalism and relativism in ethics, and claims, "there is nothing good or bad by nature, for if good and bad exists by nature, then it must be either good or bad for everyone. But there is nothing which is good or bad for everyone in common; therefore, there is nothing good or bad by nature" (HP 29).

The discovery of Pyrrhonian skepticism and the publication, in 1562, of a Latin edition of the *Outlines of Scepticism* by the French scholar Henri Etienne had a profound impact in shaping modern philosophy and its sensibilities. In the modern era, skepticism and relativism, which had been ignored for almost fifteen centuries, once more became live philosophical topics.

III. RELATIVISM IN MODERN PHILOSOPHY

The most notable proponent of skepticism and relativism in the early modern period is Michel de Montaigne (1533–1592), whose work is the most significant link between the relativism and skepticism of the ancients and the various relativistic doctrines developed by modern philosophers.[15]

Montaigne uses the argument for schemas, made familiar by the Pyrrhonian skeptics in support of relativism and skepticism. Like Sextus, he points out that, with regard to changes in our bodily and emotional conditions, one and the same judgment may appear true to us on one occasion and false on another. Therefore no absolute truths on such matters exist. He also cites the diversity of opinion on scientific issues—for instance, the Ptolemaic astronomers' disagreement with Cleanthes or Nicetas and the Copernican claims that the earth moves—as evidence that we are not in a position to make well-grounded choices between conflicting scientific claims. How do we know that a millennium hence, another theory will not be offered, which would replace existing ones? Foreshadowing nineteenth-century discussions of non-Pythagorean geometries, he argues that even the allegedly most certain of sciences can be doubted, since alternative systems of geometry, such as in Zeno's, can be sketched.[16]

Encounters with new peoples and worldviews spurred debates on universalism and relativism in early modern philosophy as they had done for the ancient Greeks and would do again for twentieth-century social anthropologists. Montaigne relies on accounts of recently discovered faraway cultures to argue that there are no universal laws of human behavior and no innate human nature. In a highly provocative essay on the habits of the cannibals, he proclaims that there is nothing "savage or barbarous about those peoples, but that every man calls barbarous anything he is not accustomed to; it is indeed the case that we have no other criterion of truth or right-reason than the example and form of the opinion and customs of our own country."[17] He connects this last point to the Tenth Mode of Sextus and concludes that, given the diversity of moral, legal, and religious behavior, ethical relativism is the only possible position. Unlike Sextus, however, Montaigne does not distinguish clearly between relativism and skepticism. He seems to think that the two philosophical attitudes are fundamentally the same.

Montaigne was a major influence in the development of the French Enlightenment, which heralded the emergence of the modern scientific outlook and secular humanism. Contemporary postmodernist relativists condemn the Enlightenment for its faith in universal norms of rationality, but at least some strands of the Enlightenment bear the unmistakable signs of a nascent relativism. A strong interest in distant cultures of the New World and a call for tolerance toward other creeds and peoples marks the writing of key Enlightenment figures such as Voltaire (1694–1778), Diderot (1713–1784), and Montesquieu (1689–1755). The abundance of still fresh accounts of travelers charting unknown territories and peoples led to the construction of idealized versions of their exotic cultures and a valorization of their beliefs and outlooks—or what Todorov calls 'exoticism,' a tendency that foreshadows the ethical outlook of the cultural relativists of our time.[18] These authors were also the first to explore the idea of viewing one's culture from an outsider's point of view and using this external perspective as a vehicle to criticize local customs and norms.[19]

For instance, Diderot, in his "Supplement to the Voyage of Bougainville," tells us that the Tahitian is mild, innocent, and happy, whereas civilized people are corrupt, vile, and wretched; the natives live according to customs and rules that vary greatly from the Western ones. They do not possess private property or operate their affairs based on egalitarian principles, and they exercise sexual freedom not accepted in 'civilized societies.'[20] Diderot is opposed to the European mission of civilizing the natives. Despite his belief that a common human nature is the foundation of transcultural norms of morality, he advocates the relativistic-sounding maxim to be "monks in France and savages in Tahiti. Put on the costume of the country you visit, but keep the suit of clothes you will need to go home in" (228).

Montesquieu's Persian Letters presents a further instance of this proto-relativism. In this fictional conversation and correspondence between Persian visitors to Europe and their friends and relations in Persia, Rical, one of the two characters, echoing Xenophanes, says, "it seems to me, Uzbek, that all our judgments are made with reference covertly to ourselves. I do not find it surprising that the Negroes paint the devil sparklingly white and their gods black as coal." He concludes that if "triangles had a god, they would give it three sides."[21] The Enlightenment is particularly important in the story of relativism for fostering an intellectual climate inimical to ethnocentrism. The need for tolerance and respect for other cultures and beliefs is frequently used as a key justification for cultural relativism. The Enlightenment prepared the ground for this attitude of tolerance by turning alien cultures, habits, and perspectives into central areas of literary and philosophical concern.

Contemporary relativism paradoxically also owes its origins to prominent strands of the Counter-Enlightenment of the eighteenth century and the ensuing Romantic movement of the nineteenth century. Giambattista Vico (1668–1744), prominent above all for his anti-Cartesianism, Johann Georg Hamann (1730–1788), Johann Gottfried Herder (1744–1803), and Wilhelm von Humboldt (1767–1835) introduced the idea that an understanding of cultural outlooks and norms is possible only within their historical contexts. Hence they opened the way for a historicized and situational interpretation of cognitive and moral systems. Vico's views were influential on the development of a relativist approach to history. R. G. Collingwood's historicism, which is frequently but arguably mistakenly identified with relativism, is an example of this influence.[22] Hamann, to take another example, was a precursor of modern relativism in two senses: first, he initiated what Isaiah Berlin calls "the great romantic revolt, the denial that there was an objective order, a *rerum natura*, whether factual or normative, from which all knowledge and all values stemmed, and by which all action could be tested."[23] This romantic revolt in turn has inspired philosophers with relativistic instincts from Nietzsche to contemporary postmodernists. Second, Hamann's views on language foreshadow contemporary epistemic and linguistic relativism. He maintained that language is the "instrument and criterion of reason" and the source of all the confusions and fallacies of reason. Furthermore, the rules of rationality are embedded within languages "whose only warrant is custom, tradition and use." [24]

Similarly, Humboldt sees language as the medium through which the collective spirit of a people manifests itself. "Language is, as it were, the outer appearance of the spirit of a people, the language is their spirit and the spirit their language; we can never think of them sufficiently as identical."[25] Every language has an inner linguistic form or distinctive essence that shapes the thinking and the 'world picture' of its speakers. Language provides a conceptual framework for its users for thinking about the world. Different linguistic communities each bring their own possibly unique framework to bear on their ontological and metaphysical commitments. Despite a gap of two centuries, the distance separating von Humboldt and modern-day linguistic relativists such as Edward Sapir and Benjamin Lee Whorf is negligible.

Hamann directly influenced Herder, another major figure in the Counter-Enlightenment. With an intellectual attitude reminiscent of contemporary postmodernism, Herder saw the rational, universal, and scientific civilization—the Enlightenment—as the enemy.[26] According to Herder, different historic periods demonstrate different tastes and preferences in ethics and aesthetics; we are not in a position to rank them or objectively choose between them. His leaning toward historicism, which is a form of cultural relativism, is evident in the following passage:

> Could it be that what a nation at one time considers good, fair, useful, pleasant, and true it considers at another time bad, ugly, useless, unpleasant, false?—And yet this happens! ... one observes ... that ruling customs, that favorite concepts of honor, of merit, of what is useful can blind an age with a magical light, that a taste in these and those sciences can constitute the tone of a century, and yet all this dies with the century.[27]

The Counter-Enlightenment played a significant role in the work of Hegel, Nietzsche, and Dilthey, who in turn represent the intellectual force behind various strands of contemporary relativism.

Only during the mid-nineteenth century did we encounter the first use of the terms 'relativism' and 'relativity.' John Grote, in his *Exploratio Philosophica* (1865), is often credited with coining the term. He says, "The notion of the mask over the face of nature is ... what I have called 'relativism.' If 'the face of nature' is reality, then the mask over it, which is what theory gives us, is so much deception, and that is what relativism really comes to."[28] Around the same time William Hamilton advocated what John Stuart Mill calls the "doctrine of relativity of our human knowledge," according to which there can be no unconditional knowledge, for all knowledge lies between two contradictory inconceivables. Interestingly, Grote's brother, the historian and philosopher George Grote, in his monumental history of Greece and Greek philosophy, complains about the injustice of Plato's negative portrayal of Protagoras and identifies 'the principle of relativity,' laid down by Protagoras with the more contemporary relativism of Hamilton and others.[29] The Victorian relativists, like many who came later, received their inspiration not from the ancients but from German philosophers of the eighteenth and nineteenth centuries.

IV. THE ROOTS OF CONTEMPORARY RELATIVISM

The four main contemporary relativistic views outlined in the first section of this chapter primarily stem from the work of Kant, Hegel, and Nietzsche.

Kant and the Many Worlds We Make

Kant famously argued that although the very possibility of thought requires the assumption that the noumenal world and the world of the 'thing in itself' exists, we are not in a position to grasp it directly through our perceptions alone, for "what objects may be in themselves, and apart from all this receptivity of our sensibility, remains completely unknown to us."[30] The world we know—the phenomenal world—is grasped by our senses, but our worldly apprehensions are invariably mediated through 'forms of intuition' or the 'categories' that are the necessary elements of all knowledge. The raw data of our sensory experiences are organized and made intelligible by the concepts such as space and time, and the categories of understanding such as cause, unity, and substance. Without these a priori categories, experience itself would be impossible. "But though our knowledge begins with experience, it by no means follows that all arises out of experience. For on the contrary, it is quite possible that our empirical knowledge is a compound of that which we receive through impressions, and that which the faculty of cognition supplies from itself . . . independent of experience, and even of all sensuous impressions" (B1). The forms of our experiences provide the very framework within which all thinking becomes possible; they are a priori and necessarily universal. Our experiences of the world, and their descriptions, are subject to the laws of these a priori categories, which are the preconditions of all actual and possible experiences.

Kant's thinking on metaphysics and ethics was far removed from relativism. However, his distinction between raw experiences and the conceptual principle for organizing them introduced the possibility that a variety of equally acceptable incompatible schemes of organization could exist to which ontology is relativized. During the nineteenth century, naturalist interpretations of Kant's scheme-content distinction by the physiologist von Helmholtz and the psychologist Wundt turned the Kantian a priori into the psychological or physiological categories, and hence contingent preconditions of human knowledge.[31] For this very reason Husserl blames Kant, more than any other philosopher, for psychologism and relativism. He argues that nothing in Kant's work prevents us from thinking that the Kantian table of categories could vary in different species or even individuals.[32]

Conceptual relativism is what Grote had in mind when he introduced the term 'relativism,' a way of thinking about ontology that found its full expression in the twentieth century in the writings of neopragmatists Quine, Goodman, and Putnam. Classical pragmatists, in the earlier part of the twentieth century, renewed the Kantian dualism of scheme and content. William James, for instance, argued that we cannot make sense of the idea of a reality presented to us already formed, for the so-called reality is, at least in part, constructed through the very attempts to describe it. James writes, "Although the stubborn fact remains that there is a sensible flux, what is true of it seems from first to last to be largely a matter of our own creation."[33] Furthermore, we cannot single out a unique set of descriptions as superior to all others. Foreshadowing Quine, James writes:

> There is nothing improbable in the supposition that analysis of the world may yield a number of formulae, all consistent with the facts. In physical science different formulae may explain the phenomena equally well—the one-fluid and the two-fluid theories of electricity, for example. Why may it not be so with the world? Why may there not be different points of view for surveying it, within each of which all data harmonize, and which the observer may therefore either choose between, or simply cumulate one upon another?[34]

Quine's notorious thesis of ontological relativity echoes James when it advances the view that numerous incompatible but equally adequate translation manuals can be constructed for any given language, each delivering a different ontological commitment. According to Quine, ontology, or the theory of what there is, is always relative to a language or conceptual scheme, for there are no facts independent of a theory or language or so-called manual of translation to determine one's ontological commitments.

Quine's thesis relies on what has become known as the Quine-Duhem thesis of underdetermination of theory by data, or the claim that any set of empirical data can support more than one plausible theory. Consequently rival hypotheses may be equally justified by the same set ofobservations. In constructing a scientific hypothesis, the evidence available is not adequate for deciding in favor of a unique system or, as Quine puts it, "Physical theories can be at odds with each other and yet compatible with all possible data even in the broadest sense. In a word, they can be logically incompatible and empirically equivalent."[35]

Quine was quite clear in his rejection of more extreme forms of relativism—cultural relativism and relativism about truth in particular—however, the Quine-Duhem thesis was central in shaping Paul Feyerabend's version of relativism and the less overtly relativistic tendencies of Thomas Kuhn. Feyerabend's democratic relativism—the view that different societies may look at the world in different ways and regard different things as acceptable—is rooted in the thesis of underdetermination insofar as it defends the view, "for every statement, theory, point of view believed (to be true) with good reason there exist arguments showing a conflicting alternative to be at least as good, or even better."[36] Feyerabend believes that privileging one conception of truth, rationality, or knowledge in the name of scientific objectivity runs the risk of imposing a repressive worldview on members of other cultural groupings who do not share the same assumptions or intellectual framework. He sees his brand of relativism as a plea for intellectual and political tolerance and a denunciation of dogmatism in science and in politics, "It says that what is right for one culture need not be right for another."[37]

On the opposite side of the debate on relativism, Donald Davidson also sees the distinction between scheme and content dualism largely responsible for the popularity of the heady but ultimately empty doctrine of relativism. He argues that the very idea that there are diverse and mutually incompatible conceptual schemes, an idea that is at the core of relativism, hinges on the hypothesis of incommensurability or untranslatability between languages. But contra Kuhn and Feyerabend, Davidson thinks incommensurability is not a genuine possibility, because we count something as a language or conceptual scheme only if it is translatable into ours. The idea of a language forever beyond our grasp is incoherent by virtue of what we mean by a system of concepts. So a worldview governed by a paradigm or conceptual scheme radically different from ours will necessarily turn out to be very much like our own.[38]

Nelson Goodman's 'Worldmaking,' an even more radicalized form of conceptual relativism, has been influential in the development of recent relativist trends in social constructionism, science studies, and sociology of knowledge.[39] The driving idea behind Goodman's worldmaking suggests that our categories and conceptual schemes not only carve up the world but also, in an important sense, create or construct the world. We are actively engaged in making a world when, for instance, we make constellations by picking out and putting together certain stars rather than others, or when we make stars and planets by drawing certain boundaries rather than others. It makes no sense to talk about a preexisting world prior to these human carvings, because nothing in nature dictates whether the sky should be marked off into constellations or other objects. Furthermore, the worlds we construct would vary with the different conceptual tools we bring into play, tools shaped by our social background, cultural settings, and context-bound interests.[40]

The Strong Programme of Barry Barnes and David Bloor,[41] and 'science studies,' influenced by Bruno Latour, take the Kantian insights into its most extreme by arguing that scientific facts, and even reality, are not simply 'out there' to be discovered by the scientists, through their experiments or observations. Instead, they are constructed via interactive norm-governed processes and practices such as negotiations, interpretations, and manipulation of data. As Latour and Woolgar put it, "Our point is that 'out-there-ness' is the consequence of scientific work rather than the cause."[42] Even bacteria were 'invented' and not discovered, as was commonly assumed, through the practices of the nineteenth-century scientists. Although they do not dispute the existence of a world or a reality independent of us, they insist that 'scientific facts' and 'scientific truths' are the products of socially sanctioned norms and practices that emerge out of social and conceptual practices and their construction is guided by projects that are of cultural, economic, or political importance. In their hands, the anti-realist insight inspired by Kant, that we do not have access to a world uncontaminated by our concepts, becomes a fully fledged relativist position barely distinguishable from postmodernism.

Hegelian Historicism and Contemporary Cultural Relativism

Like Kant, Hegel, the towering figure of nineteenth-century philosophy, could not be characterized as relativist. Hegelianism, however, which itself was influenced by the Counter-Enlightenment through its emphasis on the historical dimension of human reason and understanding, gave rise to the idea that different histories, rather than the transcendental absolute idea of history, shape human understanding and knowledge in distinct ways.

Hegelian historicism had a crucial influence on Marxist and neo-Marxist historical relativism and the relativistic hermeneutics of Wilhelm Dilthey (1833–1911) and his followers. According to Engels's brand of relativism, truth and falsity have absolute validity only within an extremely limited sphere. Not only ethics, which varies greatly from society to society, but also even logic cannot give us conclusive truths and do not deal with unassailable universal principles. Different social systems, with their varying modes of production—feudal aristocracy, the bourgeoisie, and the proletariat—give rise to unique beliefs and practices, and therefore knowledge claims, especially those concerning the historical or human sciences, are "limited to an apprehension of the pattern and the effects of certain forms of society and of the state that exist only at a particular time and for a particular people and that are by their very nature transitory."[43] Although Marxist relativism is most readily identifiable with historical and cultural relativisms, it has also shaped the thinking of postmodernist philosophers and social scientists such as Michel Foucault. Furthermore, it has had a role in the advent of social constructivism through the work of the Russian psychologist and social constructivist Lev Vygotsky (1896–1934), an important figure in the development of social constructionism and the sociology of knowledge, who, in turn, was strongly influenced by Marxist and Humboldtian approaches to culture and language.[44]

In a manner reminiscent of Herder and Hamann, Dilthey argues that each nation is a self-contained unit with its own 'horizon,' that is, a characteristic conception of reality and system of values. The Hegelian 'objective *Geist*,' or collective spirit, manifests itself through texts and other uses of language, and so is available for study, but only by way of subjective, intuitive, empathetic understanding. Therefore the methods of the natural sciences are completely inappropriate for the study of the human realm. According to Dilthey's 'historical relativism,' comparisons of views and perspectives held in different periods show the relativity and contingency of all historical convictions. Ironically those beliefs that present themselves as unconditional and universal—metaphysical and religious systems, in particular—more than all others carry the imprint of their historical conditions and consciousness. Different historical epochs produce different values or norms, each presenting itself as unconditional and universal. By acquiring historical consciousness, we become aware of the conflicts between these supposedly unconditional and hence universal values and discover their historical contingency. However, for Dilthey, relativism does not lead to a free-for-all cognitive anarchy, because "the historical consciousness of the finitude of every historical phenomenon . . . and of the relativity of every kind of faith, is the last step toward the liberation of mankind." Hence, the one nonrelative 'truth': for although metaphysical systems are historically relative, historical relativism as a noncontingent philosophical proposition is not. The discovery of its truth leads to liberation from dogmatism and ensures continuous creativity.[45]

Dilthey's views directly influenced Franz Boas, the founder of cultural anthropology, who attended Dilthey's lectures in Berlin, and Ruth Benedict, the anthropologist responsible for popularizing cultural relativism, who cited Dilthey in her 1934 *Patterns of Culture*.[46] Boas saw cultural relativism as an antidote to the then prevailing evolutionary theories of culture advocated by Charles Taylor and James G. Frazer, which placed Western societies in the highest echelons of the development of human civilization and 'primitive' tribes in its early stages. Boas countered the ethnocentrism of the early anthropologists by arguing that the "data of ethnology prove that not only our knowledge but also our emotions are the result of the form of our social life and of the history of the people to whom we belong,"[47] Cross-cultural comparisons and ranking, of the type that evolutionary anthropologists advocated, are baseless. Through the work of Edward Westermarck, Margaret Mead, and Melville J. Herskovits, cultural relativism not only became the orthodoxy in social anthropology but also shaped popular contemporary views on relativism in the moral and social domains.

Nietzsche and Postmodernism

Nietzsche is possibly the most influential single philosopher of relativism in recent history. His writing directly and indirectly influenced many varieties of contemporary relativism but, most notably, foreshadowed and shaped key ideas of postmodernism. Nietzsche agrees with Kant that we are incapable of unmediated knowledge of the world or the 'thing in itself', but radicalizes this Kantian view by rejecting the distinction between the noumenal and the phenomenal world. This distinction has no coherent basis because to draw it is to presuppose the very thing Kant ruled out: the possibility of separating what the mind contributes to the world and what is in the world. All reports of so-called facts are statements of interpretation and could always be supplemented or replaced by other interpretations: "The world with which we are concerned is false, that is it is not a fact but a fable and approximation on the basis of a meager sum of observations; it is 'in flux' as something in a state of becoming, as a falsehood always changing but never getting near the truth: for—there is no 'truth.'"[48]

All the Kantian categories, such as cause, identity, unity, and substance, arise from language. Language, however, is not the simple means of describing what there is. Instead, it imposes its own interpretation or 'philosophical mythology' on our thoughts. All our conceptions and descriptions, even those in physics, the purest of all sciences, are "only an interpretation and arrangement of the world (according to our own requirements, if I may say so!)—and not an explanation of the world."[49] Descriptions of reality, claims to knowledge, and moral judgments are inevitably made from a certain standpoint or perspective, and hence cannot be representations of what is really out there. "There is only a perspective seeing, only a perspective knowing."[50] Our perceptions and our understanding of the world are partial in two different senses. We can only see the world, literally and metaphorically, from a particular angle. Furthermore, our perceptions and conceptions are colored by our values and desires. No one perspective can occupy a privileged position for there are no true or objective perspectives, only perspectives that prevail at any given time in history. We cannot appeal to any facts or standards of evaluation independent of their relation to the perspectives we have; we can do little more than insist on the legitimacy of our own perspective and try to impose it on other people. Nietzsche's perspectivism, if not identical to relativism, comes quite close to it.

Nietzsche's influence is evident in the postmodernist movement's questioning of the very possibility of objective norms, truth, reason, and justification. The key ideas of postmodernism were propagated by a number of post-structuralist

French philosophers during the 1970s. Prominent among them were Michel Foucault, Jacques Derrida, and Jean François Lyotard. The postmodernists trace their intellectual genealogy to the historicism of Hegel, the radical politics of Marx, Heidegger's phenomenology, and Saussurian linguistics. Above all, Nietzsche's iconoclasm, his rejection of realist and foundationalist conceptions of truth and objectivity, conjoined with his perspectivism, proved to be a continued source of inspiration for postmodern thought. Like Nietzsche, postmodernists scorn the quest for universal values, cognitive and moral. They see it as a manifestation of the will to power masquerading as objectivity. They reject the Enlightenment as an authoritarian movement and a formative ideology of Western imperialism and colonialism. Postmodernism, on the other hand, is presented as an ally in the fight for emancipation from tyrannies of all sorts.

Nowhere is Nietzsche's imprinting of postmodern thinking clearer than in Michel Foucault's thesis that all claims to knowledge and truth are disguised power relationships. The will to truth is always bound up with particular political (social, cultural, economic) hegemonies. Philosophers discussing traditional ideas of truth inevitably share the presuppositions of such power structures, for they are inevitably located within the nexus of particular social relations. Since Nietzsche, Foucault argues that we have come to realize that "truth is undoubtedly the sort of error that cannot be refuted because it was hardened into an unalterable form in the long baking process of history."[51]

Foucault historicizes, and in that sense relativizes, truth and knowledge by claiming that each society has its regime of truth, its 'general politics' of truth. Each society, or locus of power, generates its own truths and moral imperatives and with different historical and political periods these claims to power, and hence claims to knowledge and truth, take different forms.[52]

Since the 1980s postmodernism has become a dominant theoretical approach in literary theory, sociology, social anthropology, cultural studies, feminist theories, and more. Although not many postmodernists evoke the term 'relativism' in expounding their views, the relativistic implications of their Nietzschean outlook is evident to their critics, if not to them.[53]

Relativism, unlike many other influential philosophical ideas, has often met with opprobrium, if not dismissive contempt, by professional philosophers. It is, however, a testament to its longevity and influence that this brief sketch of its history spans a period of twenty-five hundred years and evokes the names of so many philosophical giants, from Plato and Aristotle to Kant and Hegel.

NOTES

1. For a more detailed historical account of relativism, see Maria Baghramian, *Relativism* (New York: Routledge, 2004). See also Michael Krausz, "Mapping Relativisms" (this volume, chap.1); Rom Harré and Michael Krausz, *Varieties of Relativism* (Oxford: Blackwell, 1996), chap. 1.

2. Herodotus, *The History*, bk. 3, trans. D. Grene (Chicago: University of Chicago Press, 1988), chap. 38.

3. Euripides, *Andromache*, in *The Sophists*, ed. W. K. C. Guthrie (Cambridge: Cambridge University Press, 1971), 173–176.

4. Clement of Alexandria, *Stromateis*, 7 22 1 and 5 109 3, in *The Sceptics*, ed. R. J. Hankinson (London: Routledge, 1995), 31–32.

5. Plato, *Theaetetus*, 152a 1–3, in *Complete Works*, ed. John M. Cooper and D. S. Hutchinson, trans. M. J. Levett, rev. Myles Burnyeat (Indianapolis: Hackett, 1997).

6. Ibid., 152a 6–8. This passage is likely a direct quotation from Protagoras's *Truth*, as the same passage also appears in Plato's *Cratylus*, 386a. Aristotle and Sextus Empiricus also use examples of conflicting sensory experiences in their restatements of Protagoras's position.

7. For discussions of alternative interpretations of the Protagorean doctrine, see Baghramian, *Relativism*, chap. 1; and Mi-Kyoung Lee, *Epistemology after Protagoras: Responses to Relativism in Plato, Aristotle* (Oxford: Oxford University Press, 2005).

8. Plato, *Theaetetus*, 172a 2–6.

9. Ibid., 169–171. See also M. F. Burnyeat, "Protagoras and Self-Refutation in Later Greek Philosophy," *Philosophical Review* 85, no. 1 (1976): 44–69; and Lee, *Epistemology after Protagoras*, for detailed reconstructions of Plato's argument.

10. For examples, see Burnyeat, "Protagoras and Self-Refutation in Later Greek Philosophy."

11. Aristotle, *Metaphysics*, bk. I, 1011b, in *The Works of Aristotle Translated into English*, vol. 8, trans J. A. Smith and W. D. Ross (Oxford: Clarendon, 1908).

12. Sextus Empiricus, *Outlines of Pyrrhonism*, trans. J. Annas and J. Barnes (Cambridge: Cambridge University Press, 1994), PH II 216–217.

13. For a useful discussion of this topic, see J. Annas and J. Barnes, *The Modes of Skepticism: Ancient Texts and Modern Interpretations* (Cambridge: Cambridge University Press, 1985), 130–145.

14. Sextus Empiricus, *Outlines of Pyrrhonism*, HP 163, 167.

15. Montaigne was not the only philosopher of the period to discuss relativism. For instance, in *Les Dialogues de Guy de Brués, contre les nouveux Academiciens* (1557), de Brués presents the skeptics Baif and Auber, adducing arguments in favor of relativism

based on the diversity of human opinions. They conclude that ethical and legal views are mere beliefs and hence do not have the absolute or universal authority of genuine knowledge claims. See Richard Popkin, *The History of Scepticism* (Oxford: Oxford University Press, 2003). In conversation, Popkin expressed the view that no philosopher in this period made a firm distinction between relativism and skepticism.

16. Montaigne was writing in the shadow of the heretic Giordano Bruno, who posited the existence of an infinite number of worlds and speculated about recurrent incarnations; he was burned at the stake for his views.

17. Michel de Montaigne, "On Cannibals," in *Essays* (London: Penguin, 1991).

18. T. Todorov, *On Human Diversity*, trans. C. Porter (Cambridge, Mass.: Harvard University Press, 1993).

19. Descartes also was aware of the diversity in religious beliefs; for instance, he mentions that the Hurons in Canada believe that God is a tree or a stone. However, he thinks that this shows that all human beings have an innate and universal idea of God.

20. D. Diderot, "Supplement to Bougainville's 'Voyage,'" in *Rameau's Nephew and Other Works*, trans. J. Barzum and R. H. Bowen (New York: Doubleday, 1956), 183–239.

21. C. De Secondat Montesquieu, *Persian Letters*, trans. C. J. Bretts (London: Penguin, 1821/1973), lix.

22. T. Modood, "The Later Collingwood's Alleged Historicism and Relativism," *Journal of the History of Philosophy* 27 (1989): 101–125.

23. I. Berlin, *Three Critics of the Enlightenment: Vico, Hamann, Herder*, ed. H. Hardy (Princeton, N.J.: Princeton University Press, 2000), 354.

24. J. G. Hamann, *Hamann's Socratic Memorabilia. A Translation and Commentary*, trans. and ed. James C. O'Flaherty (Baltimore: Johns Hopkins University Press, 1967).

25. W. von Humboldt, *On Language*, ed. M. Losensk, trans. P. Heath (Cambridge: Cambridge University Press, 1992).

26. A. Kuper, *Culture: The Anthropologists' Account* (Cambridge, Mass.: Harvard University Press, 1999), 7.

27. J. G. Herder, *Philosophical Writings*, ed. M. N. Foster (Cambridge: Cambridge University Press, 2002 [1766]), 256.

28. J. Grote, *Exploratio Philosophica: Rough Notes on Modern Intellectual Science* (Cambridge: Deighton, Bell, 1865), I.xi, 229.

29. C. Herbert, *Victorian Relativity: Radical Thought and Scientific Relativity* (Chicago: University of Chicago Press, 2001).

30. I. Kant, *Critique of Pure Reason*, trans. N. Kemp Smith (London: Macmillan, 1929), A 26/B42.

31. M. Kusch, *Psychologism* (London: Routledge, 1995), 327.

32. E. Husserl, *Prolegomena to the Logical Investigations* (London: Routledge, 2001), 132.

33. William James, *Pragmatism: A New Name for Some Old Ways of Thinking* (Cambridge, Mass.: Harvard University Press, 1975), 398.

34. William James, *The Will to Believe* (Cambridge, Mass.: Harvard University Press, 1979), 66.

35. W. V. O. Quine, "On the Reasons for Indeterminacy of Translation," *Journal of Philosophy* 67, no. 6 (1970): 178–183, 179.

36. P. Feyerabend, *Science in a Free Society* (London: Verso, 1987), 59, 76.

37. Ibid., 85. Feyerabend's relativism diverges strongly from Popper's views, which involved accepting a version of dualism of scheme and content but condemning relativism as a key component of modern irrationalism. See *The Myth of the Framework: In Defence of Science and Rationality* (London: Routledge, 1994).

38. Donald Davidson, *Inquiries into Truth and Interpretation* (Oxford: Oxford University Press, 1984).

39. Nelson Goodman, "Just the Facts, Ma'am!" (this volume, chap. 4).

40. For reasons of space, this account leaves out the significant role of Richard Rorty's brand of relativism, which he paradoxically calls 'ethnocentrism.'

41. Barry Barnes and David Bloor, "Rationalism and the Sociology of Knowledge," in *Rationality and Relativism*, ed. Martin Hollis and Steven Lukes (Cambridge, Mass.: MIT Press, 1982).

42. B. Latour and S. Woolgar, *Laboratory Life: The Construction of Scientific Facts* (Princeton, N.J.: Princeton University Press, 1986), 180.

43. Friedrich Engels, *Anti-Düring, 1886*, in *Ethical Relativism*, ed. J. Ladd (New York: University Press of America, 1985), 18.

44. L. S. Vygotsky, *Mind in Society* (Cambridge, Mass.: Harvard University Press, 1978).

45. W. Dilthey, *Introduction to the Human Sciences*, trans. R. J. Betanoz (London: Harvester, 1988).

46. Ruth Benedict, *Patterns of Culture* (New York: Houghton Mifflin, 1934).

47. F. Boas, "The Aims of Ethnology," in *Race, Language, and Culture* (New York: Free Press, 1940), 636.

48. F. Nietzsche, *The Will to Power*, trans. W. Kaufmann and R. J. Hollingdale (New York: Vintage, 1968), §616.

49. F. Nietzsche, *Beyond Good and Evil*, trans. W. Kaufmann (New York: Vintage, 1996 [1886]), §14. The similarities to a social constructivist view of science are unmistakable.

50. Nietzsche, *Will to Power*, §540.

51. M. Foucault, "Nietzsche, Genealogy, History," trans. D. Bouchard and S. Sherry, in *Language, Counter-Memory, Practise*, ed. D. Bouchard (Ithaca, N.Y.: Cornell University Press, 1977), 143.

52. M. Foucault singles out the Renaissance, the Classical Age (seventeenth and eighteenth centuries), and the Modern Age (nineteenth and twentieth centuries) as three key historical periods where distinct conceptions of knowledge or 'epistemes' and what counts as true were produced, in "Truth and Power," in *The Nature of Truth*, ed. M. P. Lynch (Cambridge, Mass.: MIT Press, 2001), 14.

53. See, for instance, A. Sokal and J. Bricmont, *Intellectual Impostures* (London: Profile Books, 1998).

Relativism, Truth, and Knowledge | **PART II**

Subjective, Objective, and Conceptual Relativisms

3

MAURICE MANDELBAUM

Frequently, throughout the history of modern philosophy, it has been held that although claims to knowledge can be adequately defended against relativistic arguments, judgments of value cannot. Positions of this type were widely accepted in Anglo-American philosophy during the last half century. To be sure, some philosophers have, at all times, attacked such a dichotomy, holding that arguments similar to those, which justify a rejection of relativism, are mistaken in both spheres. Recently, however, there has been an attack on the same dichotomy from the opposite direction. An increasing number of philosophers have accepted positions that lead to a relativization of judgments of fact as well as of judgments of value. This tendency has many independent roots, and those who accept it in one form or another may hold antithetical positions on a variety of other issues. I shall, therefore, not attempt to disentangle the presuppositions, which underlie contemporary relativistic theories of knowledge, though I shall indicate some of them in passing. Rather, I shall confine myself to showing that an acceptance of relativism in the theory of knowledge frequently—and perhaps always—involves a prior commitment to nonrelativistic interpretations of at least *some* judgments concerning matters of fact. Consequently, whatever may be the case with respect to judgments of value, epistemological relativism may be said to be self-limiting.[1]

I

In order to proceed with the argument, it will be necessary to identify what various forms of 'relativism' have in common. The most basic common denominator appears to be the contention that assertions cannot be judged true or false in themselves, but must be so judged with reference to one or more aspects of the total situation in which they have been made. The aspects of a particular assertion's context with respect to which it is treated as relative may be of various types; I shall single out three such types for discussion. The first holds that any assertion must be viewed in relation to the beliefs and attitudes of the particular individual making the assertion. As a consequence, one cannot speak of the truth or falsity of an assertion *simpliciter*: what should be understood is that the assertion is 'true (or false) for him or for her.' A relativism of this type may best be described as *subjective relativism*, the truth being relative to characteristics of the person making the assertion. Though a relativism of this sort has sometimes been accepted with respect to judgments of value (as uses of the *de gustibus* maxim remind us), it has rarely been applied in a wholesale manner when the truth or falsity of judgments of fact is at issue.

A second type of relativism is that which has been characterized as *objective relativism*. It takes as its point of departure the undoubted fact that whenever a person makes an assertion there is some reason for his making that assertion; further, it appeals to the fact that whenever an assertion is made, the person making that assertion occupies some particular position, or point of view, with reference to that with which his assertion is concerned; finally, it points out that any assertion refers only to some and not other aspects of that with which it is concerned. These three components in the knowledge relationship are not likely to be wholly independent of one another. A person's purposes will often determine with which aspects of an object he is concerned, and his purposes frequently depend upon the specific relationship in which he stands to that particular object. Consequently (the objective relativist argues), the truth of what is asserted cannot be judged independently of the context in which the assertion is made: all assertions are relative to the purposes of whoever makes the assertion, the point of view from which his judgment is made, and the aspect of the object with which he is concerned. While this leads an objective relativist to deny that assertions are either true or false *simpliciter*, his position is not identical with that of a subjective relativist. Unlike the subjective relativist, he would deny that what is taken to be true or false is primarily a function of the beliefs and attitudes of the particular person making the assertion: rather, it is relative to the nature of the total context in which the assertion is made. Also, unlike the subjective relativist, an objective relativist claims that such judgments will be concurred in by others who are similarly placed and share the same concerns. Thus, he claims that knowledge can be said to be objective in spite of its being relative to a particular context.

A third general form of relativism is that which I shall term *conceptual relativism*. Like objective relativism, it holds that judgments concerning matters of fact are to be interpreted with reference to the context in which they are made, not with reference to the individual who makes them. That which is relevant for a conceptual relativist is not, however, the individual's purposes or interests, nor the particular relationship in which he stands to the objects with which his judgments are concerned; rather, what is relevant is taken to be the intellectual or conceptual background which the individual brings to his problems from the cultural milieu to which he belongs. A relativism of this type has been brought to the forefront of attention by aspects of Wittgenstein's later work, by Benjamin Lee Whorf, by T. S. Kuhn, and more recently by Richard Rorty, among others. I shall attempt to show that in its appeal to what may be termed culture-bound interpretations of matters of fact, this type of relativism must rely on data which are not to be interpreted as themselves being culture-bound. In this case, as in the others, I shall argue that those who attempt to establish relativism make claims that involve what I have elsewhere termed 'the self-excepting fallacy,' that is, the fallacy of stating a generalization that purports to hold of all persons but which, inconsistently, is not then applied to oneself.[2]

Let us first take the case of subjective relativism, and consider it briefly. A subjective relativist puts forward the claim that the judgments of fact, which are made by others, are always relative to their own interests, attitudes, and biases as these are reflected in antecedently held commitments or beliefs. Not only does he make this claim, but also he attempts to support it by evidence. Yet, in order to do so, he must assume that he himself actually knows the interest, attitudes, and biases of others, and that, in addition, he knows that their assertions would have been significantly different had it not been for these particular interests, attitudes, and biases. Thus, when a historical relativist such as Charles A. Beard offers evidence in favor of his relativism by analyzing the role of bias in the historical writings of others, he fails to take seriously the fact that if his thesis were universally true, it would also apply to his own analysis, thus destroying the evidence on which it was based.

To be sure, evidence *can* be gathered to show that there are many cases in which one can only understand why a person asserted what he did—and why he presumably took his assertion to be true—by understanding that his assertion was related to his own particular interests, attitudes, and biases. What must not be overlooked, however, is that evidence of this sort is only convincing so long as it is not itself interpreted relativistically, as a consistent subjective relativist would be forced to interpret it. Nor could a subjective relativist escape this criticism by appealing to some general Protagorean or Carneadean thesis instead of actual instances in which an individual's judgments are distorted: such general theses are only convincing insofar as they are assumed to follow from psychological or ontological premises. Such premises, however, must be taken to be true in a sense other than the only sense, which the subjective relativist ascribes to the concept of truth.

II

It is a less simple matter to single out the difficulties in objective relativism, but such difficulties nonetheless exist. I shall discuss them under three heads: first, with respect to the role of interest or purpose in judgments concerning matters of fact; second, with respect to the influence of the standpoint of the observer on the judgments he makes; and, third, the consequences which follow from the fact that any judgment is selective, dealing only with particular features or aspects of the object or situation judged. While there is in each case an element of truth in the contentions of the objective relativist, the conclusions, which are claimed to follow from these facts, will not successfully withstand scrutiny.

The term 'objective relativism' was coined by Arthur E. Murphy in 1927, in an article entitled "Objective Relativism in Dewey and Whitehead."[3] As one notes in that article, what was most characteristic of the position was a belief that events and relationships, not objects, are the ultimate constituents of what there is. However, as the term suggests, it was on the epistemological consequences held to follow from this ontological position that attention was primarily focussed.[4] It is with these epistemological consequences that I shall here be concerned.[5]

No one, I take it, would be likely to deny that every judgment concerning a matter of fact issues from a situation in which the person making that judgment has an interest or a purpose related to that with which his judgment is concerned. One should, however, distinguish two ways in which such interests can presumably come into play. On the one hand, whatever is an object of knowledge may interest a person because it is instrumentally connected with some state of affairs that he would like to bring about or avoid; in such cases his present interest in the object depends upon a further purpose which is of interest to him. On the other hand, a person may presumably be interested in an object for no reason other than that it does in fact interest him. In that case, his activity with respect to that object need not be said to be lacking in purpose; the purpose, however, will be one of appreciating, or exploring, or understanding, or explaining the particular object or state of affairs in which he is interested. Of course, these two basic types of interest need not be mutually exclusive: an individual's purposes in any situation may be of both types, and both may be simultaneously present. What the objective relativist underemphasizes, overlooks, or sometimes even denies, is that there are these two possible relations between an individual's interests and that with which his judgments are concerned; in the account of knowledge most characteristic of objective relativists, only the instrumental relationship, and not an interest in the object for its own sake, is stressed.[6]

In any case of Dewey at least, the objective relativist's stress on this aspect of judgments can be accounted for in terms of his acceptance of an instrumental view of mind. It is clear, however, that anyone holding such a view does so with the intention of claiming that this view is true independently of his own interests and purposes. Pushing this contention a step further, it may plausibly be argued that one reason why Dewey accepted as instrumental theory of mind was that he believed it to be demanded by evolutionary theory. As his famous essay on the influence of Darwinism on philosophy makes clear, Dewey derived great support for his own philosophic views from that which was revolutionary in Darwin's thought. At the same time, it was only because he regarded Darwin's theory as true, independently of the use to which he could put it, that Dewey could in fact use it in this way. In fact, in order to accept Darwin's theory as true, the only instrumental function that had to be attributed to it was that it had permitted Darwin and others to understand and explain a wide variety of facts with which biologists, paleontologists, philosophers, and theologians were concerned. Thus, it is my contention that the view of the knowledge relationship stressed by objective relativists such as Dewey ultimately depends on regarding *some* assertions concerning matters of fact as true or false independently of any further uses to which those assertions can be put.

I now turn to consider the second aspect of the objective relativist's thesis: that judgments of matters of fact are always relative to the standpoint of the person judging. Here the notion of 'a standpoint' can be conceived in either of two ways: temporally or spatially. Those objective relativists who have been primarily concerned with historical knowledge, rather than with sense perception, have emphasized the relativity of our judgments with respect to *when* they are made, whereas those who have been primarily concerned with sense perception, or with analogues to it, have frequently placed greater emphasis on the fact that different observers, looking at the same object, do so from different points of view. Yet, no sharp line is to be drawn between these two approaches. Objective relativists are also apt to use the concept of 'a point of view' in at least a metaphorical sense when dealing with historical knowledge; similarly, temporal factors may be taken into account in discussions of sense perception when, for example, objective relativists refer to the epistemological implications of the Doppler effect, or to those entailed by the finite velocity of light. Regardless of whether they emphasize the implications of temporal or of spatial relations, objective relativists hold that differences in standpoints are objective facts, and that they influence every judgment that it is possible for anyone to make. Whether this claim is consistent with an acceptance of relativism, as I have defined it, is what I propose to examine.

With respect to the influence of the temporal factor on judgments of the past, those objective relativists who are concerned with historical knowledge may stress either of two ways in which such influences are brought to bear. Each, however, depends on the fact that selection and interpretations are essential to the writing of history. The first and less radical of these arguments consists in the claim that what dominates the selection and interpretation of the past by those writing history in the present is to be found in present interests, *and* that those events on which interest will be focused are events which the historian sees as in some way continuous with his present. Consequently, as the present changes, so will interpretations of the past.[7] This argument is flawed. It fails to take into account the basis on which historians are led to accept, reject, or modify the work of other historians. Even if one were to accept the fundamental premise of the argument—that historians are only interested in the past insofar as they see it as continuous with their present—it would be inconsistent with the ways in which historians actually assess the accounts of both their contemporaries and their predecessors. For example, historical accounts are criticized for claiming continuities among events which evidence fails to substantiate; furthermore, they are even more severely criticized for having neglected those aspects of the past, which are discontinuous with what is characteristic of the historian's present. In short, it is in relation to accumulated evidence deriving from many sources, and not in relation to the historian's own present, that the works of past and present historians are actually judged. That this is so should not be surprising: the very notion of taking something as *evidence* involves treating it as not being self-referential, but as pointing beyond itself. Thus, even a historian who may be exceptionally immersed in present concerns treats the evidence on which his account is based as referring not to his own situation but to something which occurred in the past. When later historians subsequently assess the reliability of his account, it is in relation to all the evidence at their disposal, and not merely in terms of whatever evidence his own situation led him to use. Thus, if an objective relativist is to take seriously criticism as it is practiced in the historical profession, he will have to enlarge his theory, allowing some assertions to be true or false with reference to accumulated evidence rather than in relation to the particular historical conditions out of which they arose. Since objective relativists such as Dewey and Randall do not in their own historical writings seem to deny that one interpretation of the past is better warranted than another, their actual critical practice is not consistent with the form of relativism they espouse.[8]

The second and more radical argument which objective relativists derive from the purported influence of a temporal factor on historical judgments rests on the claim that, in fact, the past itself undergoes significant change through what later develops. This thesis rests on the contention that what is incipient in any event cannot be recognized until the future unrolls, and the connections between that event and its consequences become apparent. As Randall said, "the history the historian will write, and the principle of selection he will employ, will be undergoing continual change, because the histories things themselves possess are continually changing, always being cumulatively added to. With the occurrence of fresh events, the meaning and significance of past events is always changing."[9] Therefore, a historian who attempts to write contemporary history is not likely to hit upon an adequate interpretation of the events with which he deals, since he will be too close in time to those events to grasp their actual outcomes. Nor will the work of later historians prove to be more acceptable, since ever-new consequences of the past will continue to appear in the future.[10] Therefore, contrary to fact, each historical inquiry will have to be evaluated with reference to its own standpoint only; as Randall said, "knowledge is 'objective' only *for* some determinate context: it is always knowledge of *the* structure and relations essential *for* that context. In historical knowledge, the context is always a teleological and functional one, pointing to a structure of means and ends, of 'means for' or 'relative *to*' ends and eventuations."[11]

Once again, we must ask whether these assertions are to be applied to the contentions of the objective relativist himself. What obviously underlay Randall's thesis was a set of metaphysical assumptions, which can be described as a modernized form of Aristotelianism. Randall, however, does not ask whether one is to view his acceptance of these assumptions as relative to his own historical situation. In that case, what would follow from them would presumably have to undergo change as the historical situation in philosophy changes. Yet, Randall defines metaphysics as "the investigation of existence as existence, an inquiry distinguished from other inquiries by a subject-matter of its own, the general characters and the ultimate distinctions illustrated and exhibited in each specific and determinate kind of existence and existential subject-matter."[12] Given that definition, one has a right to expect that such inquiries uncover a set of categories, which are objective, not only in the sense that they are nonarbitrary, but also as denominating the pervasive features of whatever exists. Randall, himself, assuredly believed that his metaphysical categories were, in principle, capable of doing this, since it was only because of his insistence that process is the ultimate metaphysical category, and that the world involves a pluralism of processes, that (like Dewey and Whitehead) he initially accepted objective relativism. Yet, if objective relativism were to be applied to this metaphysical position it would undercut that position's claim to being true in any nonrelative sense. Once again, then, it should be apparent that even though it is always possible to show that *some* assertions are indeed relative to the interests, purposes, and historically conditioned circumstances of those who assert them, not all assertions can consistently be interpreted in this way.

At this point an objective relativist might abandon a temporalistic interpretation of what constitutes the standpoint to which judgments are relative (except perhaps in the case of historical judgments), and might instead appeal to the analogy of spatial location to indicate that to which every judgment is relative. He might then hold that just as objects appear to be of different shapes when viewed from different perspectives, or of different sizes when viewed from different distances, so the truth of any factual judgment is relative to the point of view from which that object is seen. In metaphysical propositions, for example, one philosopher might stress mobility and change whereas another might stress relative permanence, and both might be correct if that which is judged does, in fact, have both aspects: each judgment would then be true relative to those features of the object to which the judgment had reference. As McGilvary said in the opening sentences of his Carus Lectures, "Every philosophy is the universe as it appears in the perspective of a philosopher. It is a *Welt angeschaut* and not *die Welt an und für sich*."[13] This statement, taken alone, may appear as a relatively innocuous truism, but its consequences, as McGilvary developed them, were radical; and it was with these consequences that his book as a whole was concerned. In his case, as in the case of Randall, one finds that underlying his perspectival relativity there was a fundamental metaphysical thesis. He stated this thesis as follows: "Every particular in the world is a member of a context of particulars and is what it is only because of its context; and every character any member has, it has only by virtue of its relations to other members of that context" (17). He then interpreted this as implying that "in a world of nature any 'thing' at any time is, and is nothing but, the totality of the relational characters, experienced or not experienced, that the 'thing' has at that time in whatever relations it has at that time to other 'things'" (30).

From this it followed as a corollary that "every character which any thing has at any time it has only as it is a term of some relation in which at that time it stands to some other thing" (36). I do not believe that these metaphysical doctrines can be rendered harmless by turning McGilvary's own perspectival theory against them; unlike Randall's temporalistic version of objective relativism, McGilvary's perspectivism does not undercut his own metaphysical claims. Nevertheless, there are important difficulties in his theory, which must be brought to light.

One such difficulty is that to which Lovejoy continually referred in his attack on objective relativism: that the doctrine dissolves the object (whatever it is) into a set of perspectival views. Therefore, two persons standing in different relations to what is ostensibly one and the same object will not be encountering the same object at all. Where that is the case, their views could not be said to be contradictory, and the question of whether any of these diverse views is more correct than any other is not a question that should arise. To this, McGilvary would presumably have answered through appealing to his basic realistic postulate: that we are living organisms, and that there is presented to us in sense experience a real world in which each of us does and must live.[14] While an appeal of this type would not have satisfied Lovejoy, who would have insisted (and rightly, I believe) that such a contention presupposes knowledge which is not restricted to the knower's own standpoint,[15] let us grant that McGilvary's realistic assumption provides an escape from the danger than when two people claim to know a particular object, what they know is not in any sense the same object. Even so, a difficulty remains. Since the characters possessed by any object are in all cases claimed to be dependent on its relations to other objects, and since these relations vary indefinitely, it will possess many characteristics that will appear to be incompatible. The same railroad tracks will be parallel and convergent, the surface of the same coin will be both circular and elliptical, depending on the position in which a percipient organism stands (or might stand) in relation to it. The same person may be kind or cruel, the same object a piece of brass or a work of art, the same drug curative or poisonous, depending on what experiences define the characteristics of the object with which we are concerned. None of this need be troublesome so long as we find ways to explain why it is that the same object can take on characteristics that appear to be antithetical. This, however, involves offering explanations that appeal to differences between the various relations in which that object stands to other objects. Such explanations could not be given were our knowledge limited to the relations directly existing between these objects and ourselves. We must also know how they affect other persons, and how they affect other objects. This is the sort of knowledge which, for example, we acquire through physical and physiological optics; that knowledge is neutral with respect to any one perspective, and through it we are in a position to explain the differences in perception which depend upon perspectival differences. Similarly, the physics of acoustics serves to explain why a train's whistle sounds as it does when the train is approaching and sounds differently as it recedes. In these explanations of the Doppler effect, a standpoint is adopted, which is free of these differing perspectival views, neither of which is adopted, though both are explained. Nor would one be entitled to take the perspective of the train's engineer as authoritative if one could not, through a knowledge of physics, reconcile what is given from his perspective with what is given from each of the other two points of view. Or, to choose an example of a different sort, it is necessary for us to gain non-perspectival knowledge of the characteristics of human beings in order to explain why some particular person may be kind to some and cruel to others, or kind under one set of circumstances and cruel under others. In order to made sense of his actions, we must somehow place ourselves within the perspective of that person himself, or we shall not understand how such contrary characteristics are elicited by different situations. The striving to justify this sort of transcendence of one's *own* perspective is evident even among some of the strongest defenders of perspectivism, as is evident both in Karl Mannheim's essay, "*Wissenssoziologie*,"[16] and in George Herbert Mead's paper, "The Objective Reality of Perspectives."[17]

Both Mannheim and Mead in fact assumed that the theorist can escape the limitations of his own perspective, and this is but another example of what I have termed the self-excepting fallacy.

I come now to the third aspect of the objective relativist's position, the fact that every judgment is selective, and does not fully mirror all that an observer viewing an object is actually in a position to see. Thus, the knowledge we have of any object is limited not only by the position we occupy with respect to that object, but it is also limited by the focus of our interest on one rather than another of its characteristics. It is on this basis that the objective relativist argues that the object as we know it is not knowledge of what it may be like independently of us, but only what it is like for and to us.

In order to draw this conclusion from the undoubted fact that our attention is always selective, the objective relativist must assume that if we could simultaneously discern all of the characteristics of any object, no one of them would be exactly like what we take it to be when viewed independently of the others. This is surely not always the case. I may, for example, be so situated that I, at first, can see only one surface of an object, but when, later, I am able to view it from other angles, my conception of that surface may not have had to undergo change. Nor is this sort of independence of one characteristic of an object from its other characteristics always confined to simple cases of this sort. In coming to know a person, for example, I may first be struck by some trait, such as his shyness, and may only later come to discover that he is also exceptionally bright. While the fact that I know him to be bright as well as being shy will round out my picture of the person, and will provide additional insight into his character, this will not alter my view that he is in fact exceptionally shy, nor will my awareness of his shyness conceal the fact that he is exceptionally bright. To be sure, it is often the case that various characteristics possessed by a person, or by an object, are so related that if one were to attempt to describe one of these characteristics independently of its relations to the others that description might be not only inadequate but positively misleading. The existence of such cases does not, however, establish the objective relativist's thesis, since what they involve is a *correction* of the original judgment, not merely the substitution of one judgment for another. That which entitles one to view them as corrections is the fact that what has changed is not the relationship between the observer and that which he is observing; rather, it is the observer's discernment of a previously unrecognized relationship *within* the object itself.

An objective relativist might be inclined to challenge such an answer, asking why one should hold that the discernment of this relationship can be said to have yielded a more adequate view of the object, rather than merely a different one. To this there is, I believe, an obvious answer. While all objective relativists hold that judgments are relative to a particular standpoint, they do not hold that all are equally worthy of credence. For example, although a judgment regarding the past is made with reference to the relationships between that past and the present, not all judgments, which purport to refer to the past, are taken to be equally reliable: only those which refer to what did actually exist in the past are to be accepted.[18] Thus, even though every judgment is made from some point of view, and deals with only some aspects of an object which is seen from that point of view, it is not with reference to its point of view that we discriminate among judgments. Instead, we are forced to appeal to whatever judgments issue from a point of view, which permits an observer to discern whatever qualities the object itself possesses. Thus, objective relativists, no less than those holding other epistemological positions, will have to appeal to tests, which decide what characteristics particular objects do in fact possess. This involves an abandonment of the assumption that objects possess characteristics only insofar as they are seen from certain points of view, and with respect to certain purposes.

III

We now turn to a consideration of the even more radical thesis of conceptual relativism.[19] While its background is complex, one can isolate three convergent streams of influence which have been of special importance in establishing the widespread acceptance it enjoys today. The first stems from developments within the philosophy of science; the second from problems of method in the *Geisteswissenschaften*; the third from the ways in which certain perceptual phenomena, and also data drawn from comparative linguistics, have often been interpreted. I shall briefly—and admittedly inadequately—identify each of these factors.

With respect to the first, since the last quarter of the nineteenth century, it has increasingly come to be recognized that scientific explanations are not uniquely determined by the observations from which they may have been derived, nor from those which are used as confirmatory evidence for them. While this conviction was an essential feature in the otherwise divergent views of Mach, Poincaré, and Duhem, among others, it failed to forestall the acceptance of the epistemological foundationalism, which was characteristic of logical positivism. The acceptance of that form of foundationalism was, however, shaken by Quine's "Two Dogmas of Empiricism," in which it was claimed that in conflicts between observations and a theory it is not necessarily the theory that must be abandoned. Instead, these conflicting observations may be reinterpreted in terms of an alternative theory. In addition, logical positivism had been committed to drawing a sharp distinction between observational terms and theoretical terms, but that distinction came under increasingly severe attack, also serving to undermine the foundationalism characteristic of the positivist's position.

With respect to the second of the influences, a cognate issue arose in connection with the interpretation of texts, and also in connection with the interpretation of the character of a person or a historical period. Ast, Schleiermacher, and Dilthey identified this problem as the 'hermeneutic circle.'[20] The apparent circularity in interpretation arises because one can presumably only interpret any given portion of a text in terms of the whole of which it is a part, but one is only in a position to interpret that whole through experiencing its individual parts. Thus, the interplay of part and whole in all interpretations of texts, and in interpreting the character of persons or of historical periods, parallels the interplay of observation and theory in interpretations of nature. Here, too, the search for a rock bottom and unassailable foundation of facts, on which interpretation is supposedly based, is lacking.

In addition to the problems ostensibly posed by the hermeneutic circle, the thought of those who were concerned with the methods of the *Geisteswissen-*

schaften was often deeply affected by subjective relativism, and sometimes by that form of objective relativism, which stresses the role of ideological factors in determining the content of our systems of knowledge. In either case, it was claimed that whatever individual facts could be objectively established would be insufficient to determine the account in which they were included. Instead, it was held that these facts were fitted into a structure, which depended on the values, which the inquirer himself had brought to the materials with which he sought to deal. Once again, this parallels the position of conceptual relativism when applied to the sciences: interpretations do not emerge directly from the facts in any given situation; rather, the facts cited are those which conform to some accepted interpretation.[21]

Turning now to the impact of psychology and comparative linguistics, we may note that conceptual relativism has been fostered by interpretations placed on our perception of reversible figures, such as the duck-rabbit figure made familiar through Wittgenstein's use of it; in addition, it has been fostered by the uses to which data derived from comparisons between Indo-European languages and Native American languages have been put by Whorf and by others.

First, with respect to the question of the epistemological significance of reversible figures, one can see that if one takes such figures as paradigmatic of what occurs in all sense perception, one would be tempted to accept conceptual relativism. It is, for example, natural to say when describing what one sees when one looks at the duck-rabbit figure that one sees it as a duck, or else as a rabbit. Similarly, in the reversible cube figure, one can describe what one sees as a cube seen from above, or as a cube seen from below. In such cases the same visual figure is seen in either of two ways, and each is no less legitimate than the other. Thus, what is directly presented to our sense organs does not uniquely determine in what ways we may describe it. When these cases are taken as paradigmatic for the analysis of perceptual experience (as they have been by such conceptual relativists as Hanson and Kuhn), attention is focused on the question of 'seeing *as*', rather than on whatever is involved in the act of seeing itself. As a consequence, in many instances philosophic interest has been diverted from those traditional epistemological questions which had their roots in analyses of the specific conditions which are responsible for different persons (or for the same person at different times), attributing different properties to the same object. Many contemporary philosophers (unlike Locke, Berkeley, and Hume) would regard all such empirically oriented questions as lying wholly outside philosophical analysis. As a consequence, they are unlikely to ask in what ways reversible figures differ from nonreversible figures. However, unless it can be shown that there are no epistemologically relevant differences between reversible and nonreversible figures, it is odd to take the former as paradigmatic for analyses of perception generally.[22]

Furthermore, a blanket use of the concept 'seeing as' conceals difficulties. It is perfectly normal to say that one sees the duck-rabbit figure first 'as a duck' and then 'as a rabbit.' It is sometimes also perfectly normal to use the locution 'seeing as' in cases in which one is not referring to reversible figures. For example, one can say that the astronomer looking at a photographic plate sees a point of light 'as a star.' However, there is no parallel between that case and what occurs with respect to reversible figures, except that the same locution has been used. In looking at the photographic plate, the astronomer can simultaneously recognize what he sees 'as a point of light' and also 'as a star,' but what he sees is not a reversible figure. Rather, that which is seen can be described in either of two ways, each of which is equally applicable *at the same time*.[23] In a reversible figure, on the contrary, what I see at any one time is *either* a rabbit or a duck, not both. I do not see a rabbit, which I also recognize to be a duck, nor a duck, which I can equally well describe as a rabbit. Given this difference in the two types of case, the mere fact that the same locution is used does not justify the analogy, which N. R. Hanson, T. S. Kuhn, and others, have drawn between reversible figures and the observational data used in the sciences.[24]

Having considered, and rejected, the ways in which reversible figures have recently been used in support of conceptual relativism, I now turn to a comparable argument that has its source in comparative linguistics. The most striking instance of epistemological conclusions being drawn from this source is Benjamin Lee Whorf's hypothesis that all natural languages include an implicit metaphysics, and that how the world appears to those using a language reflects the metaphysics contained in its grammatical structure. To choose merely one example of his formulation of this point, I shall cite the following:

> The background linguistic system (in other words, the grammar) of each language is not merely a reproducing instrument for voicing ideas but rather is itself the shaper of ideas, the program and guide for the individual's mental activity, for his analysis of impressions, for his synthesis of his mental stock in trade. . . . The categories and type that we isolate from the world of phenomena we do not find there because they stare every observer in the face; on the contrary, the world is presented as a kaleidoscopic flux of impressions which has to be organized by our minds—and this means largely by the linguistic systems in our minds.[25]

Whorf's thesis was based on an analysis of differences in the grammatical structure of different languages, with reference, for example, to factors such as whether there are tenses representing past, present, and future in the language; or, to choose another example, whether or not sentences in the language are formed in terms of subject and predicate. That there are significant differences of this sort in the structure of different languages cannot be questioned. What must not be overlooked, however, is that the illustrations used by Whorf show that, in spite of linguistic differences, users of different languages in many cases refer to precisely the same objects and activities. For example, his illustrations in "Science and Linguistics" show that persons using Shawnee and persons using English are equally able to refer to cleaning a gun with a ramrod. Similarly, as is evident in his paper on "Language and Logic," it is possible in both the English and Nootka languages to refer to inviting people to a feast, though the grammatical structure of the two sentences is wholly different.

Nor is this situation confined to cases in which two alternative languages refer to relatively isolable objects or activities. As Whorf's own translations indicate, precisely the same situation obtains in those cases in which he seeks to deny that it does—for example, in how the world of nature is viewed by those using different languages. Comparing the views of nature of the Apache with those which ostensibly depend on the structure of Indo-European languages, he said, "The real question is: What do different languages do, not with artificially isolated objects but with the flowing face of nature in its motion, color, and changing form; with clouds, beaches, and yonder flight of birds? For as goes our segmentation of the face of nature, so goes our physics of the cosmos."[26] Then, speaking of the Apache, he continues, "Such languages, which do not paint the separate-object picture of the universe to the same degree as do English and its sister tongues, point toward possible new types of logic and possible new cosmical pictures." Yet, even though Whorf was brought up on Indo-European languages, with the logic of his thinking presumably dependent on the grammatical structure of these languages, he was able to understand how nature appeared to the Apache. In short, as a linguist, he was not bound by his own grammar, but stood outside both his own language and theirs. In doing so he was not only able to understand both languages, but was able, using English, to explicate the world-views implicit in other languages. It follows, then, that conceptual relativism, as represented by Whorf, is not universally applicable: at least he and other linguists are not entrapped within it.

And how, we may ask, does the linguist escape? It is, I submit, because he takes statements made in each language to be referential, and in each case seeks to establish that to which they refer. If it were the case that every statement in a language received its meaning solely through other expressions used within that language, each language would be self-enclosed, and no equivalence of meaning between statements in any two languages could be established. Thus, contrary to fact, neither Whorf nor anyone else could effect even a rough translation from one language to another. What breaks the circle is a recognition of the intentionality inherent in all uses of language, and the possibility of offering ostensive definitions of the meanings of many words, phrases, and sentences which occur in a given language. It is on these foundations that any person must ultimately rely when learning a language. It is only later, after having acquired knowledge of two or more languages, that anyone is in a position to compare their lexicons, grammatical structures, and modes of expression. Such comparisons are of interest, and perhaps suggest that those who use a particular language will be likely to single out for attention aspects of the environment which may not so readily be noticed by those whose language possesses a very different form. Conceptual relativism, however, goes beyond a recognition that this may be the case. In its linguistic form, it holds that the influence of language on thought is so pervasive and so compelling that, insofar as it is a question of truth or falsity, one cannot legitimately compare statements made in one language with those made in another; the truth of each must be assessed within the framework provided by the conceptual system implicit in the structure of the language used. In short, paraphrasing Kuhn, one might say that the Whorfian hypothesis contends that different languages are incommensurable, for they serve to structure different worlds. It is *this* contention that must be rejected.

As we have seen, if the Whorfian thesis were accepted without limitation, Whorf himself would have been unable to draw the contrasts he drew between different languages: in order to draw them he initially had to assume that the same objects and activities were being referred to in both languages. Therefore, it cannot be the case that how the world appears to those who speak a particular language is in *all* respects determined by the language they speak. While varying grammatical forms may lead to varying ways of classifying objects and relating them to one another, languages presuppose a world of extra-linguistic objects to which the speakers of a language refer. Since, however, it is possible to refer to the same aspects of this world when using radically different languages (as Whorf's own practice established that one can), it cannot be maintained that those whose thought is expressed in different languages do not share a common world.

As we shall now see, objections of a similar sort can be raised when Kuhn speaks of scientific theories, which are based on different paradigms as being incommensurable because they structure different worlds. To be sure, his thesis is less all-embracing than was Whorf's, for he confined his attention to what occurs within science, thus excluding any discussion of the more general world-pictures.[27] Furthermore, in speaking of scientific theories, he explicitly acknowledged that historians of science *are* in a position to compare these theories (just as linguists are in a position to compare languages); he also held that scientists themselves are able to do so. Nevertheless, he held that merely being able to recognize the point of view from which another theory was formulated does not serve to establish true communication between those holding different theories.[28] Although he then outlined various stages in a process of persuasion, which could lead from the acceptance of an old paradigm to the adoption of a new one, he nevertheless insisted that, in the end, it is only through a 'gestalt-switch,' that is, a 'conversion,' that the new comes to be established.

In this discussion, and throughout his analyses of scientific procedures, Kuhn was forced to assume that rival theories do in fact include reference to some of the same sets of facts, although placing different interpretations on them.[29] Were this not the case, there would be no conflict whatsoever between them: they would in no sense be *rival* theories, since each would pass the other by, without contact. That there is, in fact, rivalry concerning the proper interpretation of the same data was acknowledged by Kuhn when he said, "Before the group accepts it, a new theory has been tested over time by the research of a number of men, some working within it, others within its traditional rival."[30] Nevertheless, he placed relatively little emphasis on this stage in scientific conflicts. While he would surely admit that particular conflicts are sometimes resolved by an appeal to further facts, as is the case when hypotheses of limited generality are tested, what he emphasized were those clashes in which differences between an old and a new interpretation of many of the same data rested on the use of basically different conceptual frameworks. To the question of how such differences can be adjudicated, Kuhn's answer is that they cannot be: one theory simply supplants the other. In this connection, he quotes Planck's dictum: "A new scientific theory does not triumph by convincing its opponents and making them see the light, but rather because its opponents eventually die, and a new generation grows up that is familiar with it."[31]

It cannot be denied that there usually is a deep, ingrained conservatism in those who uphold an earlier theory, but it is nevertheless also necessary to account for the fact that those in the new generation convert to the new theory. As I have indicated, Kuhn uses terms such as 'gestalt-switch' and 'conversion' to indicate the change that occurs when a revolution has taken place, but this treatment of the mechanisms needed for such a change are not, I believe, adequately analyzed.[32] To be sure, he stresses the role of anomalies in the normal science of the preceding period, but such anomalies only arise because the world of nature does not in all respects conform to what the theory had originally anticipated. Consequently, if a new theory is able, without strain, to incorporate what were formerly regarded as anomalies, and especially if the new interpretation of them constitutes an important component within the new theory, that fact alone would explain much of its appeal. What this indicates, however, is that scientific theories are not to be considered as self-enclosed systems; rather, each claims to depict and explain features of the world, which are what they are, independently of it. This point is not, of course, in any sense novel; it is perhaps for that reason that Kuhn failed to place any emphasis on it. Had he done so, however, his account of what is involved in scientific inquiry, and how scientific change occurs, would have been far less radical than it now appears to be.[33] As I shall next indicate, in his account of what makes one scientific theory more acceptable than another, Kuhn did, in fact, appeal to the way the world is, but since he failed to make such appeals clear and explicit, the most striking feature of his position is his claim that alternative scientific theories are incommensurable.

As examples of passages in which an appeal is made to the world as it is, independently of theory, consider the following: "Successive paradigms tell us different things about the population of the universe and about the population's behavior."[34] Also, Kuhn acknowledges that scientific theories 'attach to nature' at various points.[35] Furthermore, in discussing pre-revolutionary and post-revolutionary paradigms, he holds that even in the case of those who accept differing paradigms "both their everyday and most of their scientific world and language are shared."[36] To be sure, although each of these statements suggests that no scientific theory is wholly self-enclosed, in the same passages Kuhn immediately qualifies his statements in ways which stress the interpretive role played by an accepted theoretical framework. For example, the different things we learn from different theories reflect the structure of the theory, not merely what is found in nature; similarly, while all scientific theories 'attach to nature' at some points, there may be large interstices between these points which can only be filled by theory, and will be differently filled by different theories; finally, while there may be much that is shared by those who accept differing theories, the acceptance of one rather than another way of interpreting what is experienced depends not on an appeal to nature but on how rival theories structure nature.[37]

Faced by what appear to be these conflicting strains in Kuhn's epistemology, I suggest that it is enlightening to turn to what he says concerning the criteria to be used in evaluating any scientific theory. In a previously unpublished lecture, now found in *The Essential Tension*, he lists five such criteria, which, as he says, "play a vital role when scientists must choose between an established theory and an upstart competitor. Together with others of much the same sort, they provide the shared basis for theory choice."[38] I shall quote his characterizations of these criteria, at least three of which—and perhaps all five—contain an implicit appeal to facts which are theory-independent. In order to direct attention to this aspect of these criteria, I shall italicize those phrases which I take to be most significant in this respect. Kuhn says:

> First, a theory should be accurate: within its domain, that is, consequences deducible from a theory should be in demonstrated *agreement with the results of existing experiments and observations*. Second, a theory should be consistent, not only internally or with itself, but also with currently accepted theories applicable to *related aspects of nature*. Third, it should have broad scope: in particular, a theory's consequences should extend far beyond the particular observations, laws, or subtheories it was initially designed to explain. Fourth, and closely related, it should be simple, bringing order to phenomena that in its absence would be individually isolated and, as a set, confused. Fifth, ... a theory should be fruitful of new research findings; it should, that is, *disclose new phenomena or previously unnoticed relationships among those already known*.

Kuhn does not intend this list to be exhaustive, and he is insistent that it should not be interpreted as providing an algorithm capable of unambiguously determining which of two theories is to be granted precedence. In this connection he points out that these criteria are imprecise, and that individuals may differ as to how they apply them in particular cases; furthermore, in particular cases there may be conflict between them. Consequently, he does not regard them as *rules* to be followed, but rather as *values* which guide, but do not dictate, the choices scientists make.[39]

With this one can have no quarrel, but it is worth noting that there are a number of passages which show that Kuhn does not actually regard each of these criteria as equally fundamental.[40] For example, he frequently stresses *accuracy*. Yet, accuracy is a relational attribute: there must be something (presumably observations of one sort or another) with respect to which a theory is judged to be accurate or lacking in accuracy; yet Kuhn does not specify what this is. To pursue this point, we may note that among the passages which stress accuracy, some single out the importance of quantitative formulations;[41] others stress accuracy of prediction, which Kuhn characterizes as being "probably the most deeply held value."[42] In fact, he holds that if one substracts 'accuracy of fit to nature' from the list of criteria, "the enterprise may not resemble science at all, but perhaps philosophy instead."[43] With respect to accuracy we may also note that Kuhn claims "with the passage of time, scientific theories taken as a group are obviously more and more articulated. In the process, they are matched to nature at an increasing number of points and with increasing precision."[44] Finally, it is important to recall that in discussing scientific change, Kuhn emphasized the role of anomalies in preparing the way for paradigm shifts. An anomaly, however, only exists when observations are apparently at odds with what an otherwise entrenched theory would lead one to expect: in short, at such points the theory ceases to be accurate. If, however, a theory were to be treated as wholly self-enclosed, there actually would not be anything to designate as an anomaly.

It is at this point that one can see the tension, and indeed the vacillation, within Kuhn's epistemology. On the one hand, his criteria are, as he says, "all standard criteria for evaluating the adequacy of a theory"; otherwise, he tells us, he would have discussed them more fully in *The Structure of Scientific Revolutions* (322). On the other hand, however, the standard interpretation of these criteria falls within what Kuhn called 'the traditional epistemological paradigm,' which emphasizes the fundamental character of observation in scientific procedures, whereas Kuhn himself argues that observation is *not* foundational since it is always theory-laden. This tension can be concretely illustrated in contrasting two possible interpretations of the criterion of accuracy, as Kuhn formulates it. As we have seen, he said that accuracy demands "consequences deducible from a theory should be in demonstrated agreement with the results of existing experiments and observations." To interpret this passage one must, however, know what are to be taken as '*the results*' of an experiment or observation. If these 'results' are how an experiment or observation is interpreted when seen from the point of view of an antecedently accepted theory, then they cannot serve as an adequate test of that theory. It is only if they are initially taken to be neutral with respect to alternative theories that they provide a test for those theories. According to Kuhn's epistemology, however, no observation or experiment is in fact theoretically neutral.

How is one to escape this dilemma? The answer, I suggest, lies in considering what led Kuhn into it. On the one hand, he did not wish to deny or fundamentally reinterpret the standard criteria actually used by scientists in theory-choice, and these criteria include, among other elements, a reliance on the role of observation and experiment in confirming a theory. On the other hand, he insisted that the foundationalist epistemology of the positivistic interpretation of scientific procedures failed to do justice to the ways in which theory-construction can alter the *significance* of the supposedly 'hard data' that observation and experiment supply. However, these two theses are not, in themselves, incompatible. What led Kuhn so to regard them was his acceptance of the view that 'observation' is never controlled by that which is observed, but depends upon the prior experience of the observer, and that, as a consequence, seeing is never merely *seeing*, but is always '*seeing as*.' He derived this view from an unqualified acceptance of conclusions drawn from various psychological experiments, which he mistakenly identified with Gestalt psychology,[45] and from the faulty assumption that reversible figures furnish reliable clues to what occurs in perception generally. If, however, one were to abandon these psychological assumptions, a rejection of positivistic foundationalism would be entirely compatible with ascribing to observation and experiment a role no less important than that ascribed to them by the positivist tradition.

The path to this reconciliation lies in an acceptance of the now familiar view that in a scientific theory what is to be confirmed is the theory itself, not its individual components, taken individually. But how is one to test a theory taken as a whole? To attempt to match each of two theories, taken as wholes, with 'the way the world is' would be futile if both theories were relatively comprehensive in what they included.[46] This was the sort of difficulty which Kuhn stressed: each scientific theory had its own way of organizing its data, and each differed from the other in how it did so. Nevertheless, one can test a theory as a whole in a way other than attempting to *test* it *as a whole*. Every theory includes observational elements, and also holds that these elements are related to one another in certain definable ways: the theoretical aspect of a theory lies precisely in this—in the relations it ascribes to the observations and experiments included within it. Therefore, one can test the adequacy of a theory as a whole by attempting to show whether or not the ascribed connections among observables, as deducible from the theory, do or do not exist; and whether their relations have been accurately determined. In addition, of course, a theory is tested through seeking out new observational or experimental data, which, if the theory were true, could be immediately absorbed by it, or which, alternatively, would call for adjustments in it. If absorption or adjustments were to fail, this would ultimately lead to abandonment of the theory.

Although crudely drawn, this picture, I submit, is consistent with what was fundamental in traditional views of theory-confirmation, but does not involve the foundationalism which Kuhn attributed to positivistic philosophies of science. In this respect, it admits what Kuhn attempted to establish: that no set of observational or experimental data, taken individually, can either falsify or adequately confirm a scientific theory. Yet, unlike Kuhn's position with respect to that point, it does not commit one to the view that scientific theories can successfully resist the impact of new observational and experimental data. If a view such as that which I propose were to be accepted, it would follow that even the most comprehensive scientific theories are not to be construed as self-enclosed systems, with the acceptance of one rather than another resting solely—or even largely—on sociological and psychological factors. Instead, the chief factor inducing scientific change would be located in those further inquiries that uncover relationships in nature which previous inquiry had failed to reveal.

It is, then, my contention that what is generally taken to be Kuhn's position, and what he tends to emphasize in that position, is not ultimately tenable. As in the case of Whorf and others, the conceptual relativism which he apparently sought to establish was not established; like Whorf, he was forced to relate alternative conceptual systems to various points of contact with what lay outside those systems, and it was with respect to that which was thus 'outside' that the systems themselves were interpreted and judged. If what I have briefly suggested concerning the role of observational and experimental data in confirming scientific theories is sound, that which was held in common by Mach, Poincaré, and Duhem with respect to the role played by theory in the sciences need not be taken as establishing conceptual relativism. What I have suggested concerning the relation of whole and part in confirmation procedures in the domain of science can, in my opinion, also be applied to the so-called hermeneutic circle. Consequently, I believe that issues concerning interpretation within the *Geisteswissenschaften* do not pose a unique sort of problem, but that is another question that I cannot here address.

NOTES

1. I attempted to establish a similar point with respect to skepticism regarding the senses, in *Philosophy, Science, and Sense-Perception* (Baltimore: Johns Hopkins University Press, 1964), chap. 3.

2. Maurice Mandelbaum, "Some Instances of the Self-Excepting Fallacy," *Psychologische Beiträge* 6 (1962): 383–386.

3. Arthur E. Murphy, "Objective Relativism in Dewey and Whitehead," *Philosophical Review* 36 (1927): 121–144, reprinted, along with "What Happened to Objective Relativism?" in *Reason and the Common Good* (Englewood Cliffs, N.J.: Prentice Hall, 1963).

4. The same may be said with respect to E. B. McGilvary's Carus Lectures, *Toward a Perspective Realism* (La Salle, Ill.: Open Court, 1956). Murphy wrote an extended review of McGilvary's book in *Journal of Philosophy* 54 (1959): 149–165. He was sympathetic but critical and reiterated his belief that objective relativism is untenable.

5. As the example of C. D. Broad illustrates, one can accept the ontological thesis underlying objective relativism but not accept its supposed epistemological consequences.

6. This parallels a criticism made by Arthur O. Lovejoy with reference to the application of objective relativism to historical studies. See "Present Standpoints and Past

History," *Journal of Philosophy* 36 (1939): 477–489. For his more extended criticism of objective relativism, see *The Revolt against Dualism* (Chicago: Open Court, 1930), esp. chaps. 3, 4.

7. For example, J. H. Randall says, "A 'history' thus always involves the relation between an outcome in a present, and the past of that present. It will have both a determinate 'focus' in a 'present,' and a past from which that focus selects what has a bearing on that particular history" (*Nature and Historical Experience* [New York: Columbia University Press, 1958], 36).

8. In an essay on Hobbes, Dewey wrote, "It is the object of this essay to place the political philosophy of Hobbes in its historical context. The history of thought is peculiarly exposed to an illusion of perspective. Earlier doctrines are always getting shoved, as it were, nearer our own day" (*Studies in the History of Ideas* [New York: Columbia University Press, 1918], 1:236). Yet, in the *Journal of Philosophy* in 1938, he espoused what would appear to be a diametrically opposed position, which is reiterated in *Logic: The Theory of Inquiry* (New York: Holt, 1938), where he says, "Historical inquiry … is controlled by the dominant problems and conceptions of the period in which it is written" (236).

With respect to the relation between Randall's theory and his practice, one may note that in "Controlling Assumptions in the Practice of American Historians" (written with George Haines), the position of objective relativism was stated as follows: "Knowledge can be objective only *for* a determinate context; it is always a knowledge of the relations essential for that context." However, only five sentences later, we find the following: "It is the aim of this essay to illustrate [that thesis] in terms of the principles of selection and interpretation *actually employed* by certain of the major historians of the last two generations" (*Theory and Practice in Historical Study: A Report of the Committee on Historiography*, Bulletin 54 [New York: Social Science Research Council, 1946]; emphasis added). In short, it was assumed possible to discover the controlling assumptions actually employed by other historians, not how such assumptions appear to later historians from the point of view of their own controlling assumptions. A few pages later we also find the following: "These salient facts of the institutional development of the historical profession in the United States have been emphasized, because they provide the framework indispensable for understanding the assumptions and principles of selection American historians have actually employed" (27). Once again, Randall's own practice seems not to have been covered by the principle of objective relativism that he held to be universally true.

9. Randall, *Nature and Historical Experience*, 39. As is well known, the same point is stressed in G. H. Mead, *Philosophy of the Present* (Chicago: Open Court, 1932). A similar view, though based on entirely different metaphysical presuppositions is to be found in F. H. Bradley, "What Is the Real Julius Caesar?" in *Essays on Truth and Reality* (Oxford: Clarendon Press, 1914). We may also note that Bergson held that the future alters the past, as when he said, "Nothing hinders us today from associating the romanticism of the

nineteenth century to that which was already romantic in the classicists. But the romantic aspect of classicism is only brought [about] through the retroactive effect of romanticism once it has appeared. If there had not been a Rousseau, a Chateaubriand, a Vigny, a Victor Hugo, not only should we never have perceived, but *there would never really have existed* any romanticism in the earlier classical writers" (*The Creative Mind* [New York: Philosophical Library, 1946], 23).

10. Randall, *Nature and Historical Experience*, 42.

11. Ibid., 60–61; cf. 54. For another statement of the position held by objective relativists, see *Theory and Practice in Historical Study*, 22–23.

12. Randall, *Nature and Historical Experience*, 144.

13. McGilvary, *Toward a Perspective Realism*, 1.

14. Ibid., 15. Though McGilvary did take note of Lovejoy's *Revolt against Dualism*, his only extended discussion of Lovejoy concerned the interpretation of Einstein's theory of relativity, not Lovejoy's criticism of objective relativism. See *Toward a Perspective Realism*, chap. 10.

15. Lovejoy, *Revolt against Dualism*, 120.

16. Reprinted as an appendix to Karl Mannheim, *Ideology and Utopia: An Introduction to the Sociology of Knowledge* (New York: Harcourt, Brace, 1936), esp. 270–272.

17. Edgar Sheffield Brightman, *Proceedings of the Sixth International Congress of Philosophy: Harvard University, Cambridge, Massachusetts, United States of America, September 13–17, 1926* (New York: Longmans Green, 1927), 75–85.

18. In this connection, we may quote Randall, adding italics to signal the points at which reference is made to the actual past, not its continuity with the present: "'Objective relativism' means concretely: The history of anything is *what has happened* and becomes relevant in the envisaged past of that thing. The understanding of that history consists in looking backward from a 'focus,' *tracing the continuities or persistences of materials to be found in that history, uncovering the operations of the various factors and processes that have in the past modified and reconstructed those materials,* and understanding those modifications in terms of the best scientific knowledge available today" (*Nature and Historical Experience*, 61).

19. I have been unable to determine when, and by whom, this term was first used, but one source, which has doubtless contributed to the frequency of its recent occurrence, is to be found in Donald Davidson, "On the Very Idea of a Conceptual Scheme," *Proceedings and Addresses of the American Philosophical Association* 47 (1973–1974): 5–20 (this volume, chap. 8). In the various uses to which the term has been put, there have been some variations in its extension, but so far as I am aware, it has in all cases been used to refer to positions which strongly resemble one another.

20. Richard E. Palmer, *Hermeneutics* (Evanston, Ill.: Northwestern University Press, 1969).

21. For a recent example of this point of view in historiography, see Wolfgang J. Mommsen, "Social Conditioning and Social Relevance," *History and Theory* 17, no. 4 (1978): 22.

22. The oddity here does not depend on the fact that reversibility occurs less frequently than non-reversibility. Rather, one should note that reversibility as it occurs in vision does not occur in any of the other sense modalities; it is thus a doubtful example to use as a paradigm for what is involved in all cases of perceiving. One should also note that it is extremely difficult to construct reversible figures. Unless one comes upon them by chance, one must, in fact, understand the general principles underlying visual organization, *and be able to negate them*, in order to construct such figures. Finally, we may note that those optical illusions which have, in the past, been regarded as most important for epistemology, have *not* been reversible figures. This is readily intelligible. Epistemologically important illusions are always, at the time, experienced as veridical; we later find that they conflict with other perceptual experiences, which were also regarded as veridical. In the case of reversible figures, however, no comparable conflict is engendered: we simply see that the figure *is* reversible, that it can be seen in either of two ways, neither of which need be taken to be better justified than the other. If we are puzzled by such figures, we are only puzzled as to why they are in fact reversible. For a similar point, see Israel Scheffler, "Vision and Revolution: A Postscript on Kuhn," *Philosophy of Science* 39 (1972): 372.

23. Similar situations obtain with respect to touch and to our other sense modalities. I can, for example, designate what I hold in my hand as being a solid, cylindrical object, or as being my pen; I can say that I hear a train or that I hear a train's whistle, etc. Both descriptions are in these cases (as in the photograph of a star) applicable at the same time, and there is not the involuntary alteration in them that is to be found in reversible figures.

24. N. R. Hanson, *Patterns of Discovery* (Cambridge: The University Press, 1958), chap. 1; T. S. Kuhn, *The Structure of Scientific Revolutions*, 2nd enl. ed., *International Encyclopedia of Unified Science*, vol. 2:2 (Chicago: University of Chicago Press, 1970), 85, 111, 126ff.

25. Benjamin Lee Whorf, "Science and Linguistics," in *Language, Thought, and Reality*, ed. J. B. Carroll (Cambridge, Mass.: Technology Press of Massachusetts Institute of Technology, 1956), 212–213. Whorf recognizes a possible exception to the view that language structures experience, found in our experience of space. However, Whorf held that even in this case our *concepts* of space (Newtonian space, Euclidean space) are linked to other language-dependent concepts. See "Relation of Habitual Thought and Behavior to Language," in *Language, Thought, and Reality*, 158ff. Whether there are other aspects of experience not directly tied to linguistic structures remains an open question. My criticism of the Whorfian hypothesis suggests that there may be, but my argument will not

presuppose that there are. Kuhn also accepts the assumption that the world is originally presented as being without structure, as being—in William James's phrase—"a bloomin', buzzin' confusion" (*Structure of Scientific Revolutions*, 113).

26. Benjamin Lee Whorf, "Languages and Logic," in *Language, Thought, and Reality*, 240–241.

27. Not all who have adopted Kuhnian concepts have been equally restrained. Kuhn acknowledges having received early stimulation from Whorf's theory, but mentions no special indebtedness to him (*Structure of Scientific Revolutions*, vi). Whorf is mentioned, but noncommittally, in T. S. Kuhn, *The Essential Tension: Selected Studies in Scientific Tradition and Change* (Chicago: University of Chicago Press, 1977), 258.

28. Kuhn, *Structure of Scientific Revolutions*, 202–203.

29. Kuhn rejects this phraseology, which he associates with "the traditional epistemological paradigm." Instead of referring to what occurs in a scientific revolution as providing a new *interpretation* of some of the same facts that had been included within the theories of the previous periods, he describes what happens as the opening up of a new world: a seeing of different things than had previously been seen. See *Structure of Scientific Revolutions*, 111, 120–123, 150. Since, as Kuhn acknowledges (150), he has not yet worked out the epistemological consequences of this position (which he formulates chiefly in metaphors), I shall continue to speak of facts and their interpretation. However, the argument which follows does not, I believe, rest on my use of this terminology. Hanson also rejected any dichotomy between facts and their interpretation in *Patterns of Discovery*, chap. 1

30. Kuhn, *Essential Tension*, 332.

31. Quoted in Kuhn, *Structure of Scientific Revolutions*, 151. For Kuhn's comparable analysis, see *Essential Tension*, 203.

32. Maurice Mandelbaum, "Note on T. S. Kuhn's *Structure of Scientific Revolutions*," *The Monist* 60 (1977): 442–452.

33. Kuhn acknowledged that no new and adequate epistemological paradigm has as yet developed; therefore, he found that he was unable wholly to give up the traditional one. On the other hand, he also found himself unable to accept it (*Structure of Scientific Revolutions*, 126). As I shall later suggest, his dilemma was not inescapable.

34. Kuhn, *Structure of Scientific Revolutions*, 103.

35. Kuhn, *Essential Tension*, 290.

36. Kuhn, *Structure of Scientific Revolutions*, 201.

37. In this connection Kuhn says, "There is, I think, no theory-independent way to reconstruct phrases like 'really there'; the notion of a match between the ontology of a theory and its 'real' counterpart in nature now seems to me illusive in principle" (ibid., 206).

38. Kuhn, "Objectivity, Value Judgment, and Theory Choice," in *Essential Tension*, 332.

39. Ibid., 322–325, 330–331. Kuhn also spoke of the criteria used by scientists as 'values' (*Structure of Scientific Revolutions*, 184–186). It is of interest that he held that criteria such as accuracy "do much to provide a sense of community to natural scientists as a whole," and he considered such criteria as being "relatively, though not entirely, stable from one time to another and from one member to another in a particular group" (185).

40. At the end of the same essay, Kuhn adds a parenthetical remark concerning the application of the five criteria to problems of theory-choice, saying, "Accuracy and fruitfulness are the most immediately applicable, perhaps followed by scope. Consistency and simplicity are far more problematic" (*Essential Tension*, 339).

41. For example, Kuhn, *Structure of Scientific Revolutions*, 153ff., 185.

42. Ibid., 185; cf. Kuhn, *Essential Tension*, 222ff., 331ff.

43. Kuhn, *Essential Tension*, 331. For another instance in which he uses the locution of a fit between a theory and facts, see Kuhn, *Structure of Scientific Revolutions*, 147.

44. Kuhn, *Essential Tension*, 289. As is well known, Kuhn wrestled repeatedly with the problem of whether progress occurs in science. The interpretation of his views on this matter is not of primary importance for the present discussion. However, he consistently holds that the theories of successive periods become "vastly more powerful and precise" than those of their predecessors (30; cf. 288–289). What he *rejects* is that such growth is continuous, and that it is incrementally cumulative, suffering no losses when one paradigm is given up for another. What he does *not* reject is that changes over time represent long-term gains—not stasis, mere alteration, nor retrogression.

45. Mandelbaum, "Note on T. S. Kuhn's *Structure of Scientific Revolutions*."

46. This point has already been stressed in W. V. O. Quine, "Two Dogmas of Empiricism," where he signalized it in the following striking fashion: "Physical objects are . . . convenient intermediaries—not by definition in terms of experience, but simply as irreducible posits comparable, epistemologically to the gods of Homer. For my part I do, *qua* lay physicist, believe in physical objects and not in Homer's gods; and I consider it a scientific error to believe otherwise. But in point of epistemological footing the physical objects and the gods differ only in degree and not in kind" (*From a Logical Point of View* [Cambridge, Mass.: Harvard University Press, 1953], 44). Kuhn acknowledges a debt to this essay (*Structure of Scientific Revolutions*, vi). For Quine's later statement of his position, which would appear to be less extreme, see *Word and Object* (Cambridge, Mass.: MIT Press, 1960), chap. 1 (esp. sec. 5, 6), and chap. 2 (esp. sec. 7, 10).

"Just the Facts, Ma'am!"   **4**

NELSON GOODMAN

The terms 'convention' and 'conventional' are flagrantly and intricately ambiguous. On the one hand, the conventional is the ordinary, the usual, the traditional, the orthodox as against the novel, the deviant, the unexpected, the heterodox. On the other hand, the conventional is the artificial, the invented, the optional as against the natural, the fundamental, the mandatory. Thus we may have unconventional conventions (unusual artifices) and conventional nonconventions (familiar facts). The two uses of 'convention' are not only different but almost opposite—yet not quite so; for to say that something is usual carries some suggestion that there are less usual alternatives; and what is mandatory, without alternatives, is usual.

Philosophers have been primarily concerned with convention as fabricated form imposed on uninterpreted content. Sometimes they aim at clearing away artifice to discover pure fact, sometimes simply at distinguishing the contributions of convention and of content. But the conventional as the usual, the habitual, cannot be dismissed as merely a popular usage that occasions frequent confusion, for it plays a major role in some theoretical contexts. For instance, in a

Nelson Goodman, "Just the Facts, Ma'am!" was originally published in *Relativism: Interpretation and Confrontation* (Notre Dame, Ind.: Notre Dame University Press, 1989), pp. 80–85. Reprinted here with permission of the author. All rights reserved.

recent paper on literary theory the author writes: "In this essay, 'conventions' refers to *manifestations of shared practices*."[1] But I shall begin by considering convention as contrasted with content, the conventional as the optional or artificial as contrasted with the mandatory or factual.

Consider the motion of the moon. The moon rotates in that its orientation to the sun changes in a certain regular way, but it is fixed on its axis in that its orientation to the earth never changes. Does it rotate or not, then? Well, Yes and No. If that seems self-contradictory, we like to say that the moon rotates relative to the sun but not relative to the earth. But this is a somewhat deceptive way of speaking; for to say that something 'moves relative to' something else is not to impute any motion to it at all. To say that the moon rotates relative to the sun is entirely compatible with saying that the sun revolves about a fixed moon. And to say that the moon does not rotate relative to the earth is entirely compatible with the earth's revolving about a rotating moon, as well as with saying that both earth and moon remain at rest. So perhaps to avoid giving a false impression, one should say simply that different aspects of the moon face the sun at different times; and that the same aspect of the moon faces the earth at all times. No more about rotation, rest, revolution, no more indeed about motion. Motion disappears from the realm of fact. And that should have been expected from the start, when the question 'Does the moon rotate or not?' is answered by 'That depends upon what we take as frame of reference.' It depends upon what we do; we *make* the moon rotate or stand still. Motion is optional, a matter of convention, of fabrication imposed upon what we find.

But, then, what *is* found? The size and shape of the moon vary, it seems, according to the speed and direction of its motion. Thus since motion is a matter of convention, so are size and shape, and these, also, must be subtracted from fact. And, of course, any description in terms of the sun, moon, earth, etc., is conventional in that there are alternative equally legitimate versions in terms of other concepts. Organization into these familiar units, like the organization of stars into constellations, is optional.[2] All fact threatens to evaporate into convention, all nature into artifice.

You are likely not to go along with this but to protest: "How can there be no fact, no content, but only alternative ways of describing nothing? Surely there must be something that is described, however many different ways there are of describing it. There must be some line between what there is and how we describe it."

Quite so. The two statements about the moon are alternatives in that they describe something in common: that they are about the same objects, that they agree with certain observations, measurements, and principles, that they are in some way descriptive of the same facts. Yet these objects, observations, measurements, principles are themselves conventional; these facts are creatures of their descriptions. Two versions are 'of the same facts' to the extent that they share some terms, comprise some identical or kindred concepts, can be translated into one another. All convention depends upon fact, yet all fact is convention.

Is the distinction between convention and fact, then, indispensable but meaningless? Rather, I think the distinction is itself conventional. That, of course, is meaningless if the distinction between convention and fact is meaningless. And if all facts are conventions and all conventions are facts, how can the distinction be meaningful, especially for a hard-boiled extensionalist?

Consider for a moment the terms 'immediate predecessor' and 'immediate successor' as applied to the integers, or to the clockwise series of minute marks on a watch face. Every integer, or every mark, is both an immediate predecessor and an immediate successor, yet the distinction between immediate predecessor and immediate successor does not vanish. For they are not categorical terms sorting a realm into different classes, but relational terms. So also for the terms 'rest' and 'motion.' They do not sort bodies into classes; all bodies are at rest and in motion. And so also for 'conventional' and 'factual.' They do not sort statements or versions into classes but relate versions to each other.

In other words, two terms that apply to exactly the same things may have parallel compounds that apply to very different things. The pairs of terms just discussed are cases of what I have elsewhere explained as difference in meaning through difference in secondary extensions. Although all centaurs are unicorns and all unicorns are centaurs, simply because there are no centaurs and no unicorns, still 'centaurs' and 'unicorns' differ in meaning in that certain parallel compounds of them are not coextensive; for example, not all centaur pictures (or descriptions)—indeed very few—are also unicorn pictures or descriptions.[3] Likewise, while immediate predecessor and immediate successor are coextensive because both apply to all integers, still 'immediate predecessor of the integer 5' and 'immediate successor of the integer 5' name very different things. Again, while all bodies are both in motion and at rest, 'moves relative to the earth' and 'is at rest relative to the earth' do not apply to all the same things. And while 'factual' and 'conventional' are coextensive, applying to all versions, 'factual relative to version V' and 'conventional relative to version V' are not.

If we are asked under what circumstances an integer is immediate successor to another, we can readily reply that the immediate successor is that integer plus one. But if we are asked to explain under what circumstances one of two bodies moves relative to another, we may say, for the sun and the earth, for example, 'If the sun is fixed, the earth moves; if the sun moves, the earth is fixed.' But the apparent conditionalization in the two clauses is specious. Compare such a sentence as 'If the black horse wins, I'm rich; if the white horse wins, I'm broke,' where each antecedent is true or false according to which horse wins. In contrast, since unrelativized statements of motion are incomplete, the antecedents 'the sun is fixed' and 'the sun moves' are vacuous. We cannot determine whether the earth moves or is fixed by finding out whether the sun is fixed or moves, for the sun and the earth and all other bodies are both fixed and moving. A slightly different, familiar formulation runs: 'On the assumption that the sun is fixed, the earth moves; on the assumption that the sun moves, the earth is fixed.' Plainly this is no better, for the 'assumptions,' like the antecedents before, are vacuous. All this may not dispel a dogged conviction that nevertheless, in some sense or other, if the sun is taken as fixed, the earth moves, while if the sun is taken as moving, the earth is fixed. Putting it this way may seem to be going from bad to worse. For what does 'taken as' mean? We cannot take hold of the sun or the earth and keep it still or give it a push to get it moving. And how can taking one body as fixed or moving make another revolve or stop? But when 'taken as' is read as 'plotted as' (under a given system) and associated adjustments are made, we have something like 'When the sun is plotted as a point, the earth is to be plotted as a surrounding closed curve; when the sun is plotted as a closed curve, the earth is to be plotted as a surrounded point.' 'Plotting' may be broadened here to include mathematical or verbal description. The faults of our former proposals vanish. Apparent talk of motion turns out to be talk of diagrams, descriptions, mathematical functions, versions.

Diagrams or other versions under a given system, differing only through what is taken as fixed, are alternatives, optional, conventional. Furthermore, a system of plotting whereby whatever is taken as fixed is shown as a point, and whatever is taken as moving is shown as a path, is itself conventional—one among alternative systems, each admitting various versions.

But what has become of 'the facts'? What are all these versions versions of? You may feel like the inspector in the radio series who tires of talk and keeps insisting "Just the facts, ma'am!" But all that can be done to comply with a demand to say what the versions are versions *of* is to give another version. Each version tells what 'the facts' are, but the several versions are at odds with each other. How can the earth at the same time stand still, revolve around the sun, and move in countless other ways? How can divergent diagrams or versions be of the same facts, the same world? They must be either of no world or of different worlds. There must be many worlds if any.

That may suggest to you that we have taken leave, if not of our wits, at least of everyday experience and ordinary discourse. Let's get back to solid ground. A friend of mine was stopped by an officer of the law for driving fifty-six miles an hour. She argued, "But officer, taking the car ahead of me as fixed, I was not moving at all." "Never mind that," replied the officer, "You were going fifty-six miles an hour along the road, and (as he stamped his foot) this is what is fixed." "Oh, come now, officer; surely you learned in school that this road as part of the earth is not fixed at all but is rotating rapidly eastward on its axis. Since I was driving westward, I was going slower than those cars parked over there." "O.K., lady, I'll give them all tickets for speeding right now—and you get a ticket for parking on the highway."

Where does this leave us? If everything is the way it is taken to be, and anything can be correctly taken in all sorts of opposing ways, are we condemned to chaos? No. For despite Bruno, and the speeder's sophistry, the officer was of course right in the first place. Although nothing is absolutely fixed or moving, and although whether it is fixed or how it moves depends upon how it is taken, that in turn depends upon context, circumstances, purpose. Where cars on the highway are concerned, the earth is taken as fixed, and the ticket for speeding is deserved. In other contexts the earth is rotating and revolving; we use an alternative version.

Almost always some *stance* or other is adopted. Merely noting that many alternative versions can be constructed does not provide us with any. We have to hold some things steady for a while as a working basis. Along with the recognition that there is no fixed distinction between fact and convention must go the recognition that nevertheless there is almost always *some* distinction or other between fact and convention—a transient distinction drawn by the stance adopted at the time. Adoption of a stance, as we have seen, turns a relational term into a categorical one: designation of an integer as origin divides the class of integers into origin, an immediate predecessor, an immediate successor, and all other integers; designation of certain bodies as fixed may sort other bodies into the fixed and the moving; designation of certain statements as mandatory may classify other statements as mandatory or optional. A shift in stance effects a re-sorting. The Copernican revolution constituted such a shift. It did not so much change cosmology to fit the facts as transform the facts by changing stance from earth to sun.

Although a stance may be taken anywhere, and shifted often and without notice, it is not arbitrary. Most of our stances and shifts of stance are habitual, instilled by practice. We commonly take the earth as fixed in describing the motion of a plane, but on an airplane we automatically take the plane as fixed in describing the motions of the cabin crew. Where a choice of stance is more deliberate, it may involve complex considerations of simplicity, convenience, suitability to context, efficacy for a purpose, and accessibility by those we must communicate with. Taking the tip of a fly's wing as fixed in describing the motion of bodies in the solar system would presumably fail on all these counts.

In sum, I have been arguing such obvious points as that there is no firm distinction between fact and convention, but that that distinction is very important; that the line between fact and convention shifts often and may be drawn anywhere but is not capricious; that when a convention (as option) becomes a convention (as the usual), it thus tends to become factual; and that rather than the facts determining how we take them, how we take them determines the facts—but that we had better be careful how we take them.

In a recent review of Italo Calvino's novel *Mr. Palomar*, Michael Wood puts it more poignantly:

A fact is what won't go away, what we cannot *not* know, as Henry James remarked of the real. Yet when we bring one closer, stare at it, test our loyalty to it, it begins to shimmer with complication. Without becoming less factual, it floats off into myth. Mr. Palomar looks at the sky, the lawn, the sea, a girl, giraffes, and much more. He wants only to observe, to learn a modest lesson from creatures and things. But he can't. There is too much to see in them, for a start. . . . And there is too much of himself and his culture in the world he watches anyway: the world is littered with signs of our needs, with mythologies.[4]

Readers wanting more particular applications of what I have been saying should have no trouble working some out. Getting the facts straight is easy enough so long as we bear in mind that the facts are paradoxical.

NOTES

1. Steven Mailloux, "Rhetorical Hermeneutics," *Critical Inquiry* 11 (1985): 638n.5.

2. See, further, Nelson Goodman, *Of Mind and Other Matters* (Cambridge, Mass.: Harvard University Press, 1984), 40–42.

3. Nelson Goodman, *Problems and Projects* (Indianapolis: Bobbs-Merrill, 1972), 221–238.

4. Michael Wood, "Theory with a Wife," *London Review of Books*, October 3, 1985, 17.

Relativism in Philosophy of Science 5

NANCY CARTWRIGHT

I. INTRODUCTION

Relativism in current philosophy of science is driven by the twin problems of induction and underdetermination, which threaten claims that science has a rational structure. Tensions are created by two separate motives: first, to picture contemporary science as a supremely rational enterprise, possibly our most successful epistemic activity; second, to 'tell it like it is,' which can either serve or conflict with the first motive. Conflict here has real bite. Scientists feel threatened or angry in the face of claims that real practice is not rational. Those who propound views about rationality must be seriously disturbed if science does not meet their standards.

Relativisms cluster along two main axes: those that oppose scientific realisms and those that oppose claims that science is/can/should be value-free. For each node on one of these axes, there are a variety of proposals on offer about what the disputed aspect of science is supposed to be relative to. The most common are concepts and methods, models and theories, aims and purposes, cultural and socioeconomic viewpoints, kinds of negotiation or critical discussion, historical location, and kinds of epistemic, moral, political, and aesthetic values. As usual, the debates occur at different levels: the ontological—there are no truths of the kind in dispute; the epistemological/methodological—there may be such truths but we do not have reasonable access to them; and the normative or descriptive—whether there are such truths and whether we are able to learn them. This is not what science ought to be doing, or not what science is, in fact, doing.

In all discussions of relativism, it is easy to slip between levels, especially in contemporary philosophy of science where issues are frequently framed with the term 'accept': What are the standards that make a claim or practice acceptable in science? This can mean: 'What characterizes the kinds of claims we would like to admit in science?' 'What are the standards we should use in admitting claims and practices?' 'What are the standards we do use?'

The natural starting point for discussion might be the ontological level. In addition, there with truth, we can ask whether scientific truths are relative and, if so, what are they relative to, and in what sense. But the truths that concern science are usually thought of as hidden—Nature's secrets. That is why we need special experimental and mathematical techniques, the care and precision that characterize modern science, to unearth them. But can the carefully honed methods of science give sufficient warrant for accepting its results? This question provides the seedbed for relativism about science.

II. INDUCTION, OVERDETERMINATION, AND THE SHIP OF LIFE

Hardly anyone disputes that science is and should be in the business of building outward from claims and practices that are already accepted and that have some established reliability to new claims and practices that can be used reliably in new situations. So David Hume's problem of induction is immediate. There are, Hume argued, no methods whose reliability can be defended in a noncircular way for going from what is known to what is unknown. The problem invites a general solution: just suppose that Nature's truths are accessible by this or that favored methods of investigation. Hume and John Stuart Mill both discussed a solution of this form for the method of simple induction (i.e., infer that unobserved cases will be like observed ones): some kind of principle of the uniformity of nature. The solution suggests a fundamental relativism: scientific practices and claims are acceptable relative to the assumption that Nature is uniform in the appropriate way or, for more sophisticated methods, relative to the assumption that Nature does appropriately underwrite the method.

Presumably, though, Nature either is or is not uniform in the requisite manner, or does or does not have the appropriate structure to vindicate a given method for inferring the unknown from the known. So it seems the method is either reliable or not, *simpliciter*. No relativism here, certainly not at the ontological level. But principles like these, so the standard arguments go from Hume onward, cannot have a noncircular basis. So our entitlement to count the method reliable is relative to an unsupported *assumption*, as in consequence is our entitlement to any claims we infer with the method.

Call this 'epistemological' if you will, but there is far more at stake than whether our beliefs are mistaken. Consider Otto Neurath's famous remark that in constructing knowledge claims we are like sailors who must repair their ship at sea, never able to put in to dry dock to build from solid ground. Neurath worried not just about the quality of the planks available, but about the plan for how to use them. There are, he claimed, no properly rationally grounded scientific methods to guide the new construction: Evidence neither confirms nor disconfirms hypotheses; at best it 'shakes' them. For him, the decision to accept a new knowledge claim is always relative—relative to a 'free' judgment, a judgment rising out of experience, thought, and inherited practices and beliefs, but not licensed by a properly grounded method, in the end a kind of 'plumping.'[1]

Neurath's is not a Kantian worry that we cannot ever grasp the 'real' noumenal world but will always live in the world of experience. His worry is about how we can survive in the world of experience. The concern is not that we may fail to build a ship that matches the original plan of the master builder but that we may not be able to build a ship that is seaworthy. Neurath's relativism threatens not just the truth of our new knowledge claims, but the effectiveness of the practices we base on them.

The problem of 'underdetermination' opens a similar road to relativism. If scientific hypotheses are to say anything new, there will always be a number of incompatible hypotheses compatible with all facts already accepted. So taught Pierre Duhem,[2] W. V. O. Quine,[3] and many others. What makes one of these hypotheses more acceptable than the others? Nelson Goodman's 'new riddle of induction,'[4] which has plagued science since its start, is a special case of underdetermination. What are the correct concepts to use in making inductive inferences? In studying falling bodies, medieval physicists focused on the rate of change of velocity with *distance fallen* (dv/dx). We make more reliable predictions from dv/dt. Or, in a Euclidean space, which is approximated by the space around us, where we have traditionally made our observations, bodies traverse Euclidean straight lines. Modern physics teaches that they will not do so in curved geometries. The appropriate concept for projecting from the observed to the unobserved is that of a 'geodesic'—the shortest distance between two points in the geometry.

At the ontological level, again perhaps there is no relativism. There is only the question of whether a given hypothesis involving the concepts it uses is true or false, *simpliciter*. Matters are different at the epistemological level. There are two main kinds of 'solutions' to the problem of underdetermination on offer, and both have been accused of falling into relativism.

First, employ some additional factual claims and use what Clark Glymour describes as 'bootstrapping': given the 'background' assumptions, the known facts logically imply the hypothesis.[5] This seems to be the method employed in Francis Everritt's Gravity Probe experiment to test the general theory of relativity.[6] The theory implies that a gyroscope should be caused to precess from coupling with the space-time curvature. To design the gyroscopes and get them into space took twenty-five years. But the setup was so carefully engineered with such voluminous knowledge of what else can cause precession that when the Gravity Probe gyroscopes precessed, nothing but coupling with the space-time curvature could have been responsible.

One may then say that the coupling hypothesis is acceptable *relative to* these background assumptions that already use a specific choice of concepts. This seems to amount to the dual claims that the space-time coupling is true if the background assumptions are true and that a belief in its truth is well grounded if the background assumptions are well grounded. Since these are factual claims, that may not seem a serious problem—probably they are indeed well grounded. It matters greatly that they should be well grounded, for there are many examples where the same fact can count either as strong evidence for a hypothesis or strong evidence against it depending on what background assumptions are made.

But worries about relativism to these claims escalate if, as would be the case on standard reconstructions, these background assumptions must include general claims whose grounding seems problematic: Nothing causes a precession except a torque; every precession must have a cause; all sources of torque are controlled for in the experiment. Some of these—like 'every precession has a cause'—are so fundamental and grand that they might get labeled as 'metaphysical' to mark the impossibility of confirmation by standard empirical procedures (independent of worries about how well grounded these procedures are in themselves). This label is backed up by the suspicion that if we trace the cairn of support back stone by stone, we are likely to encounter assumptions clearly eschewed by even mild Positivists as metaphysical, such as 'every event has a cause.' It is hard to be confident about the seaworthiness of our boat if its safety is relative to claims like this.

Consider as a second example the randomized controlled trial (RCT), widely regarded as the 'gold standard' for testing causal claims in the human sciences, especially in medicine. Various proofs are available that in an ideal RCT, a higher probability of the effect in the treatment group than in the control group deductively implies that the treatment causes the effect in the experimental population. Proofs, of course, require premises. One premise is that in the ideal RCT 'confounding' factors are distributed in the same way in the treatment and control groups. (Real RCTs famously use random assignment to try to make this likely.)

Further premises are necessary to connect causality with probability. This can be done through the probabilistic theory of causality, which also undergirds the powerful Bayesian network method for causal inference. On the probabilistic theory, an earlier event-type, C, causes a later, E, just in case C increases the probability of E once all 'other' causes of E simultaneous with C are taken into account. The idea is that once other reasons for E to be probabilistically dependent on C are eliminated, the dependence must be due to Cs causing E. Clearly this presupposes that probabilistic dependencies must have causal explanations. This is again a grand claim. As before, as we look down through the cairn of support for claims about treatment efficacy, we encounter assumptions near the base that have not been subjected to the kinds of careful empirical investigation we demand in science.

The second way of resolving underdetermination is by appeal to various 'virtues' that acceptable claims or practices should have, or certain aims they should meet, where, of course, the virtues themselves may be 'relative': different virtues matter for different occasions, different scientists, different sciences, different uses, and different agenda. Those who are keen to keep values and local agenda out of science, to 'rescue' science from relativism, often pick a subset of these virtues as special for science, generally labeled 'epistemic' virtues. These include, usually first and foremost, compatibility with already accepted fact. Further, these include simplicity, unifying power, precise novel prediction, fruitfulness, coherence with other accepted hypotheses and theories, practical usefulness, explanatory power, and survival of critical public scrutiny.[7] In addition, specific disciplines may add subject-specific virtues. In physics, for example, one may demand that theories be renormalizable or satisfy certain high-level symmetry principles.

III. WHERE IS THE EPISTEME IN EPISTEMIC VIRTUES, AND HOW MUCH HELP ARE THEY ANYWAY?

The label epistemic matters since it is often supposed that relativizing scientific practices to epistemic virtues is not pernicious, not contrary to the spirit of science. Whereas relativizing to other kinds of values is. But in what sense do any of these earn the label 'epistemic,' which suggests that they conduce to knowledge or to truth? If the phenomena in a domain are complex or diverse, why should choosing the simplest claim or the one that unifies the most help in arriving at true claims? We may suppose that truth and our favorite epistemic virtues march hand-in-hand, but that looks to be one of those grand 'metaphysical' assumptions not confirmed by the detailed scrutiny demanded of proper scientific claims.

Beyond this, there are other worries about how far epistemic virtues can fend off relativism. First, they are vague, so do not provide real grounds for choice. Attempts to make them more precise seem to require further metaphysical assumptions to back them up. Second, to the extent that they do have grip on a particular claim or practice, it is not guaranteed that they all point in the same direction. There seems no natural hierarchy or weighting scheme among them. Third, it seems that without what look to be very arbitrary definitions, they will not narrow the options to a single choice, so the problem of underdetermination remains.

Once the issue of epistemic virtues is raised, even the demand that acceptable claims be compatible with already known facts comes into question. Imre Lakatos famously maintained that every theory is born, refuted, and stays that way all its life. We should not be aiming for true theories, he urged, but those that get a sufficient number of the known facts right and are progressive.[8] Others urge that theories be good at problem solving,[9] that they produce correct predictions about targeted phenomena,[10] or that they be the ones best suited to serve democratically chosen aims.[11] So, for many, the truth of a claim is not a trumping virtue. What is acceptable in science is always relative to a choice of goals, with truth just one among many we might embrace. This naturally escalates the problem one step. Are some goals legitimate in science and others not? What are the grounds for legitimacy?

Even if truth is taken to be the natural goal, the sole arbitrator of what is acceptable, it is otiose as a guideline for what we *should* accept, because we cannot directly tell what is true. That is why even staunch truth advocates engage in laying out other more readily ascertainable characteristics to aid in the quest for truth. This brings us back to the idea of epistemic virtues and their problems. Since it seems unlikely that the epistemic virtues, whatever their defense, can be honed fine enough to provide judgments about specific claims and practices, what fills in the gap? Standard answers include other values—political, moral, cultural, aesthetic; personal and group motives, fair and foul; local cultural and scientific practices; tacit knowledge; plumping; charisma; money; available technologies.

Now we have reached the point at which the question arises as to how the sciences do settle on what to accept and how various epistemic virtues and other values should blend. Contemporary history and sociology of science abound with studies of what was actually going on as particular scientific results and practices stabilized.[12] What was the material and cultural environment in which the stabilization occurred, who spoke to whom, what kinds of techniques/ideas/equipment were available, and so forth? These can describe well what did, in fact, resolve the underdetermination problem. But it seems to leave the scientific result relative to the historical accidents of what was happening where and how it developed.

For many this outcome is welcome. It paints science as a human activity, not a magic tunnel to the basic truths of the universe. For others, it is totally unacceptable. Science can not only help build a boat seaworthy enough to keep us afloat in life, but it can also build the right boat. Something about scientific practice, when done assiduously, honestly, and continuingly, brings the accepted claims of science ever closer to the truth. Their actual acceptance at any time may be relative to facts about their origins, but if the history goes as it should, they will also approach the truth. They will be not only accepted but also accept*able*, judged by the standard of truth, taken as the virtue that trumps all others.

Those who believe that science gets closer and closer to the truth face two main challenges. The first is to explain this notion of 'closer to,' especially across scientific revolutions. Consider: Aristotelian physics has a totally different conception of the universe from that of Newton, and Newtonian physics a totally different conception from the physics of Einstein. In what sense do the central theoretical claims get closer to the truth as we go from one to another? Second, what are the scientific methods that get to the truth and how can we defend that they do so? Attempts to answer these two questions are still the meat of the philosophy-of-science debate, both writ large, across the sciences, and writ small, within the small corners of specific disciplines.

IV. ARE ALL SCIENTIFIC TRUTHS RELATIVE?

Induction and underdetermination plague our decisions about what to accept in science; the relativisms to which they give rise are at the epistemological level. Is there place for relativism at the ontological level, especially with respect to the kinds of truths science investigates, assuming it is sometimes in the business of looking for truths?

Start with scientific truth in general. Two related lines of thought suggest a 'yes' answer, lines of thought that can capture the imagination but are difficult to explicate. The first is that all truths of interest in science are relative to a perspec-

tive or point of view. All qualities in Nature are in some sense secondary qualities, like colors or tastes. Just as one might argue that what is true of the world for
a bat is different from what is true for a human, what is true from one scientific
perspective is not true from another. The difficult task is to explain what a scientific perspective consists of. This, too, is one of the salient topics about which
philosophers of science argue,[13] and to which feminist epistemology has made a
special contribution.[14]

If all features of the world are like secondary qualities, truth will be relative
to perspective. There are a number of similar-sounding but less radical accounts
that are at base not relativist, often formulated in terms of 'aspects.' A scientific theory/model/treatment can never give a *complete* image of the phenomena
studied. We study only some aspects or other, and at some 'level' of coarse grain-
ing. The truths that are acceptable in a particular study are ipso facto relative to
the choice of aspect and level. This, however, is not a relativism at the ontological
level so long as the aspects pick out features that are supposed really to be there.
Incompleteness of description, even if inevitable, does not generate the serious
ontological relativisms that perspectivism does.

The second line of thought leading to relativism about scientific truth in
general is a bowdlerized Kantianism, that Nature is a kind of undifferentiated sea
that demands a conceptual scheme before it gives rise to truths. Yet, it seems, not
any conceptual scheme will do: some do—perhaps only one? Some do not allow
for the emergence of claims and practices that pass scientific tests for acceptability. Consider Neurath. He would talk only about the world of our experiences,
but that world seems to consist of '*Ballungen*'—loose clusters with vague edges
(like a '*Ballungsgebeit*' or metropolitan area).[15] These can, however, for various
purposes, be represented by the kinds of precise concepts we use in science,
though different ones for different purposes. Or consider Duhem. He can plausibly be read as claiming that Nature is qualitative; the quantities of science are
just abstract symbols we use to represent it.[16]

This particular source of relativism has a venerable tradition in the social
sciences. Max Weber, for instance, argued that the study of society could not be
a science because the concepts with which we should be concerned in that study
do not name precise quantities figuring in regular laws.[17] Supposing—as is not
uncommon—that these precise quantities are what really exist in Nature, truths
in social science are in trouble at the ontological level. If they are true at all, it
must be relative to something. Often the underlying idea appears to be that they
are relative, in some way or another, to that which we human beings are responsive. We group the 'true' features of Nature together to assign concepts where no
proper referent exists in Nature. Here values and purposes are likely to play a

significant role, and plumping of the Neurath style may be inevitably involved if there are no strict rules in the offing for how the assignment is done.

Consider, for instance, attempts to operationalize the important social concept of poverty. Should poverty be taken as an absolute concept or as a relative measure and, if relative, relative to what? One standard approach defines poverty in a targeted society as having less than two-thirds the median income there. But are individuals or households judged to be poor? Surely children in rich households are not poor. Within households, do we demand that a family of seven, including elderly grandparents and small children, have seven times two-thirds the median income? The first thing to notice is that there seems no natural or 'scientific' way to settle these questions. Second, the ways we settle them will give rise to very different poverty figures and count different individuals as poor—thus advantaging some individuals and disadvantaging others in the face of attempts to help poor persons.[18]

Perhaps this does not seem so surprising with respect to poverty. Consider then *price*, which figures prominently in economic theory. To calculate real price we need an index of inflation. How shall we calculate that? Many goods have increased in quality so that owning them now provides more utility than before. But many people cannot afford the new higher-quality goodsat all; or the goods are available at reasonable cost in suburban outlets, which require cars for access. Veterans' benefits are usually pegged to inflation indices. But the recent suggestions of the American Boskin Commission on how to treat quality improvement in calculating inflation does not consider that veterans who need the benefits cannot afford cars.[19] So, is there a proper quantity, price, that figures in true economic relations, or is every version of this concept relative, either consciously constructed relative to purpose or willy-nilly serving one moral/political aim rather than another with no ontological or scientific justification for doing so?

V. SCIENTIFIC REALISMS AND ANTI-REALISMS

It may seem natural to some to take practically anything that science talks about as a good candidate for existing in reality.[20] But much of philosophy of science has been in the business of stripping reality of one thing or another, leaving only some favored set of things as really there. The basic divide is between those who take the science—or favored bits of the science—as right and the rest as, at best, relative, and, at worse, chimerical or nonsensical; and those who do the reverse.

Wilfrid Sellars distinguished between the scientific and the manifest image.[21] The manifest image involves the concepts with which we have been in the habit

of responding to the world, refined but not discarded since the dawn of humanity. The scientific image involves the concepts that science uses to describe the
world. These, so say scientific 'realists,' describe what is really there (at least when
science is done at its best). The others involve true descriptions only when they
can be reduced to those of science (and, in general, it should not be supposed
that this is possible). The concepts of so-called folk psychology are a special
target nowadays, with the demand for the reduction of features of the mind to
those of the brain a special case. If the terms of folk psychology do not reduce to
those of a proper science, then if they are truths at all, they must be relative. We
might suppose them to be relative to perspective or experience, but for a staunch
reductionist it is hard to see what there can be for them to be relative to.

Similar considerations apply to various other reductionisms, like that of
chemistry or biology to physics, or of group characteristics to those of individuals or of the macro to the micro. Failing strict reduction, for those who think that
only one kind or level of phenomena is basic, the other kinds or levels, it seems,
can only be true relatively. The task is to explain what these truths can be relative
to, and how. The alternative looks to be that we talk nonsense when we use these
non-reducible concepts, which is itself not very palatable given how reasonable
our discussions often seem.

Oppositely, there are those who are suspicious about the scientific world
picture. Perhaps only claims about what is observable are true, *simpliciter*, or are
acceptable without relativization. Often the motivation is some version of the
problem of induction: it is hard to see what the license can be for moving beyond
what we can be sure about from our own observation.

Others take issue with specific kinds of scientific claims, or—more
usually—admit only certain kinds. Causal talk has been one main target. Rudolf
Carnap urged that many things that are expressed in the material mode—that is,
many claims that surface appearances are about the world—are more correctly
construed in the formal mode, as about our representations.[22] So to claim that
x causes y can mean roughly that y is deducible from x within our best theories.
Causation thus becomes relative to theory or, as others might have it, to our
choice of model.[23] Others take causation to be relative to what we can manipulate[24] or to a range of situations across which the regular association between
the so-called cause and so-called effect remains stable.[25] Others even more radically maintain that what we single out as causes is fixed by prejudice or political
agenda.

Laws are another favorite target. I argue that we have insufficient empirical
warrant for most of our abstract high-level laws, such as the fundamental laws of
physics.[26] Our warrant is far better for long, complicated, detailed claims about

very specific systems in specific circumstances. The more general our law claims, the more they try to encompass, the shakier they become. What is acceptable at the abstract level then becomes relative to a choice among a variety of desiderata, including the so-called epistemic virtues. This does not necessarily make the acceptability of either theoretical entities or theoretical features of the world (for example, the quantum state of a SQUID) relative.

Others despair of high-level laws because they have been replaced repeatedly as we have reconceptualized the world. But this need not lead to complete relativism about them. Rather, many look for something about the laws that is retained across conceptualizations. Currently one favorite is the structure or relations represented in laws, which may be true independent of conceptualization or acceptable across reconceptualizations even if the contents, the very features that figure in the structure, are not.[27]

These are but examples. Realisms versus anti-realisms are hot topics nowadays. Philosophers and scientists alike declare themselves realists or anti-realists about broad scientific categories such as entities,[28] laws,[29] mechanisms,[30] causes,[31] fields,[32] mathematical structures,[33] groups and institutions,[34] or minds.[35] They debate equally about very subject-specific topics such as the acceptability of concepts of group selection,[36] strings,[37] utility,[38] or the natural level of unemployment.[39] In each case, relativism lurks as a solution to account for why talk of the flawed category might nevertheless be acceptable.

An alternative is to call into question the very idea of scientific acceptance. What is it and where is it? Science, I would argue, is just a conglomerate of people, practices, techniques, materials, technologies, books, journal articles, lab notebooks, lectures, professional meetings, funding bodies, conversations, and the like. Is a particular claim acceptable? Or accepted? That depends on the context and the purpose. Are we trying to solve a specific scientific problem ourselves? Then much of what matters are the claims and techniques of which we are master. Or, are we recommending where a student should go to graduate school—to work with a group that supposes this rather than that about strings or about selection or about how to model the economy? This decision depends a lot on where funding is, what the students' capabilities are, and what are their aspirations and work habits. If we are sitting on a funding council, our considerations about what to 'accept' will be different, and different yet again if we are dispensing funds earmarked for 'blue skies' research. Shall we use a particular assumption in building our bridge or rocket or auction? Costs and benefits, safety and responsibility loom large here.[40] In each case, the acceptability of the scientific claim or practice is relative, but relative in a myriad of different ways in a myriad of different contexts.

Many will find this extreme relativism unpalatable. They long for an encyclopedia in which is written all and only what science accepts or should accept, at least for the nonce, or even, ideally, just what is true or significant and true. But who will do the peer review on this encyclopedia, and how?

NOTES

Thanks to Fernando Morett for his help. Also note that references herein are samples to help the reader get started and are not meant to be comprehensive.

1. N. Cartwright, J. Cat, and T. Ubel, *Otto Neurath: Philosophy Between Science and Politics* (Cambridge: Cambridge University Press, 1996).

2. Pierre Duhem, *The Aim and Structure of Physical Theory* (Princeton, N.J.: Princeton University Press, 1982 [1906]).

3. W. V. O. Quine, *From a Logical Point of View* (Cambridge, Mass.: Harvard University Press, 1953).

4. Nelson Goodman, *Fact, Fiction, and Forecast* (Cambridge, Mass.: Harvard University Press, 1986).

5. Clark Glymour talks about the facts implying an *instance* of the hypothesis on which an induction is then performed. But many scientific methods can be reconstructed in the stronger way I describe.

6. C. Will, "Relativity at the Centenary," *Physics World*, January 2005, 27–32; J. D. Fairbank, B. S. Deaver Jr., C. W. F. Everitt, and P. F. Michelson, *Near Zero: New Frontiers of Physics* (New York: Freeman, 1988).

7. Thomas Samuel Kuhn, *The Structure of Scientific Revolutions* (Chicago: University of Chicago Press, 1970); H. Longino, *Science as Knowledge* (Princeton, N.J.: Princeton University Press, 1990); E. McMullin, *The Social Dimensions of Scientific Knowledge* (Notre Dame, Ind.: University of Notre Dame Press, 1992).

8. I. Lakatos, *The Methodology of Scientific Research Programmes* (Cambridge: Cambridge University Press, 1978).

9. L. Laudan, "A Problem Solving Approach to Scientific Progress," in *Scientific Revolution*, ed. I. Hacking (Oxford: Oxford University Press, 1981).

10. M. Friedman, *Essays in Positive Economics* (Chicago: University of Chicago Press, 1953) and other instrumentalists.

11. P. Kitcher, *Science, Truth, and Democracy* (New York: Oxford University Press, 2003).

12. C. Smith and N. M. Wise, *Energy and Empire: A Biographical Study of Lord Kelvin* (Cambridge: Cambridge University Press, 1989); H. Chang, *Inventing Temperature: Measurement and Scientific Progress* (New York: Oxford University Press, 2008); H. Collins,

Changing Order: Replication and Induction in Scientific Practice (Chicago: University of Chicago Press, 1985); H. Collins and T. Pinch, *The Golem: What Everyone Should Know about Science* (Cambridge: Cambridge University Press, 1993); P. Galison, *How Experiments End* (Chicago: University of Chicago Press, 1987); S. Shapin and D. Schafer, *Leviathan and the Air Pump: Hobbes, Boyle, and the Experimental Life* (Princeton, N.J.: Princeton University Press, 1985).

13. R. N. Giere, *Scientific Perspectivism* (Chicago: University of Chicago Press, 2006).

14. S. Harding, *The Science Question in Feminism* (Ithaca, N.Y.: Cornell University Press, 1986), and *Feminism and Methodology: Social Science Issues* (Bloomington: Indiana University Press, 1987); Noretta Pinnick, Cassandra L. Koertge, and Robert F. Almeder, *Scrutinizing Feminist Epistemology: An Examination of Gender in Science* (New Brunswick, N.J.: Rutgers University Press, 2003).

15. Cartwright, Cat, and Uebel, *Otto Neurath*.

16. Duhem, *Aim and Structure of Physical Theory*.

17. Max Weber, "Objectivity," in *The Methodology of Social Sciences*, ed. and trans. E. A. Shils and H. A. Finch (Glenco, Ill.: Free Press, 1949).

18. A. B. Atkinson, *Poverty in Europe* (Oxford: Blackwell, 1998).

19. J. Reiss, *Error in Economics* (Oxford: Routledge, 2007).

20. A. Fine, *The Shaky Game* (Chicago: University of Chicago Press, 1986).

21. W. Sellars, *Science, Perception, and Reality* (London: Routledge and Kegan Paul, 1963).

22. R. Carnap, *Philosophy and Logical Syntax* (London: Kegan Paul, 1935).

23. P. Suppes, "A Probabilistic Theory of Causality," *Acta Philosophica Fennica* 24 (1970); J. Heckman, "Econometrics, Counterfactuals, and Causal Models" (Keynote address, International Statistical Institute, Seoul, Korea, 2001).

24. P. Menzies and H. Price, "Causation as a Secondary Quality," *British Journal for the Philosophy of Science* 44 (1993): 187–203.

25. J. Woodward, *Making Things Happen* (Oxford: Oxford University Press, 2004).

26. N. Cartwright, *How the Laws of Physics Lie* (Cambridge: Cambridge University Press, 1983).

27. J. Worrall, "Structural Realism: The Best of Both Worlds," in *The Philosophy of Science*, ed. D. Papineau (Oxford: Oxford University Press, 1996); James Ladyman, "Science, Metaphysics and Structural Realism," *Philosophica* 67 (2002): 57–76.

28. I. Hacking, *Representing and Intervening* (Cambridge: Cambridge University Press, 1983).

29. D. M. Armstrong, *What Is a Law of Nature?* (Oxford: Blackwell, 1983); M. Tooley, *Causation* (Oxford: Clarendon Press, 1987); F. Dretske, "Laws of Nature," *Philosophy of Science* 44 (1977): 248–268.

30. C. F. Craver and W. Bechtel, "Mechanism," in *Philosophy of Science: An Encyclopedia*, ed. S. Sarkar and J. Pfeifer (New York: Routledge, 2006); P. Machamer, L. Darden, and C. Carver, "Thinking About Mechanisms," *Philosophy of Science* 67 (2000): 1–25.

31. For anti-realism, see Wolfgang Spohn, "Bayesian Nets Are All There Is to Causal Dependence," in *Stochastic Causality*, ed. Maria Carla Galavotti, Patrick Suppes, and Domenico Costantini (Stanford: CSLI, 2001); for realism, see Cartwright, *How the Laws of Physics Lie*.

32. M. Hesse, *Forces and Fields* (Edinburgh: Thomas Nelson, 1961).

33. S. Shapiro, *Thinking about Mathematics* (New York: Oxford University Press, 2000); M. D. Resnick, *Mathematics as a Science of Patterns* (New York: Oxford University Press, 2000).

34. M. Gilbert, *On Social Facts* (Princeton, N.J.: Princeton University Press, 1989); P. Sheeby, *The Reality of Social Groups* (Aldershot: Ashgate, 2006); R. Grafstein, *Institutional Realism: Social and Political Constraints on Rational Actors* (New Haven, Conn.: Yale University Press, 1992).

35. S. Hampshire, *Spinoza and Spinozism* (Oxford: Clarendon Press, 2005); P. M. Churchland, *Matter and Consciousness* (Cambridge, Mass.: MIT Press, 1988).

36. E. Sober, *The Nature of Selection* (Chicago: University of Chicago Press, 1993); S. Okasha, *Evolution and Levels of Selection* (New York: Oxford University Press, 2006).

37. L. Smolin, *The Trouble with Physics* (New York: Mariner, 2006).

38. A. Sen, "Rational Fools: A Critique of the Behavioral Foundations of Economic Theory," *Philosophy and Public Affairs* 6, no. 4 (1977): 317–344.

39. J. Reiss, "Natural Economic Quantities and Their Measurement," *Journal of Economic Methodology* 8, no. 2 (2001): 287–311.

40. H. Douglas, "Rejecting the Ideal of Value Free Science," in *Value-Free Science: Ideal or Illusion?* ed. H. Kincaid, J. Dupre, and A. Wylie (New York: Oxford University Press, 2007).

The Truth About Relativism   **6**

JOSEPH MARGOLIS

Any would-be defense of relativism must make its way against ingrained prejudice, ignorance of logical options not often exercised, the fatal support of historically hopeless theories that monopolize the popular sense of the label, and the sheer difficulty of fixing the full significance of what a viable account would entail. It requires a good dose of patience and a sense of what is missing in standard accounts of truth-claims. The bare bones of every relativism that has survived all the charges of self-contradiction, conceptual anarchy, nihilism, irrelevance, palpable falsehood, and even recovery within an ampler anti-relativism, features two essential doctrines: (1) that, in formal terms, truth-values logically weaker than bipolar value (true and false) may be admitted to govern otherwise coherent forms of inquiry and constative acts, and (2) that substantively, not merely for evidentiary or epistemic reasons, certain sectors of the real world open to constative inquiry may be shown to support only such weaker truth-values. That is all.

It is true that doctrines (1) and (2) do not exhaust all potentially interesting forms of relativism—for example, relativisms confined to the management of

Reprinted from "The Truth About Relativism," originally published in Michael Krausz, ed., *Relativism: Interpretation and Confrontation* (Notre Dame, Ind.: Notre Dame University Press, 1989) with permission of the author. © Joseph Margolis.

truth-claims under various contingent limitations regarding the state of knowl-edge. But such theories, like theories of probabilistic judgments relativized to shift-ing evidentiary concessions, are easily reconciled with strongly anti-relativistic accounts of empirical truth-claims. It is also true that (1) and (2) cannot, by them-selves, define a full-blooded relativism. Given the unfavorable climate of opinion, however, it would not be a bad idea to introduce a rationale for supporting (1) and (2)—or for supporting either one alone—to encourage the development of all sorts of relativisms that are needlessly battered by the usual charges mentioned. Our strategy, therefore, will be confined to showing (section I) a lacuna regarding bivalence and *tertium non datur* (in effect, alternative views regarding the scope of excluded middle) essential to the defense of (1); to showing (section II) how the application of one of the most influential analyses of the predicate 'true,' the application of a Tarskian-like theory of truth to natural language or to the lan-guage of natural inquiry, obscures both the lacuna charged and the need for an independent analysis of the nature of the empirical domain to which a Tarskian-like (or any other similarly extensional) account is to be applied (bridging [1] and [2]); and to showing (section III) what is involved in distinguishing relativisms that depend on substantive views of the nature of particular sectors of reality (domains suited to empirical inquiry) from those merely confined to cognitive limitations of one sort or another (the distinctive feature of [2]).

The account that follows is essentially strategic, therefore. It lays the ground for relativistic theories distributed over particular empirical domains, but it does not pretend to supply any single such theory. It cannot even pretend to have established doctrines (1) and (2).[1] It is meant primarily to offer a defense of the viability of relativistic theories and to indicate the direction in which the most ramified theories are bound to go. It is certainly not meant to advance the most radical forms of relativism that have been advocated. It would be impossible in any case to assess the prospects of such theories within the span of this paper. The burden of what follows is, then, no more than the thesis that standard views of a realist inquiry and science cannot convincingly preclude versions of the moderate relativism here espoused. Whether more radical options would also be defensible is a question left unanswered. But the intended gain, if confirmed, would certainly be a handsome one.

I

In Robert Stalnacker's recent account of propositions and of their role in devel-oping an adequate theory of beliefs and of intentionality in general, the following thesis is advanced: "A proposition is a function from possible worlds into truth-values." Stalnacker goes on to say, by way of explanation, "There are just two truth-values—true and false. What are they: mysterious Fregean objects, properties, relations of correspondence and noncorrespondence? The answer is that it does not matter what they are: there is nothing essential to them except that there are exactly two of them."[2] Stalnacker does not pause to link truth-values to the processes of actual inquiry or the resolution of scientific and metaphysical questions: he says, "these questions are concerned less with truth itself than with belief, assertion, and argument, and with the relation between the actual world and other possible worlds." (2) Perhaps. But might it not be a substantive matter regarding truth-values that: (a) their number cannot be determined independently of particular inquiries into particular sectors of the world, and (b) relative to particular such inquiries, their number cannot convincingly be fixed as two?

In fact, Stalnacker nearly concedes the point in an extremely candid and telling way in attempting to strengthen a realism with regard to counterfactuals, context-dependence, and a possible-worlds reading of intentionality—against the encroachments of anti-realism. We shall shortly be able to trade very profitably on his careful remarks in this regard. So let us have them before us:

> The interests, projects, presuppositions, culture, and community of a speaker or writer provide resources for the efficient expression of content, but they also provide something more fundamental: they provide resources which contribute to the construction of content itself. Content, I have been suggesting, can be represented as a subset of some set of possible states of the world.... But if the space of possible states of the world itself, the way it is possible to distinguish one possible state from another, is influenced by the situations and activities of the speakers (or more generally, the agents) doing the distinguishing, then we have a kind of context-dependence that infects content itself and not just the means used to express it.... I think this is right.... But it is no retreat from a reasonable realism to admit that *the way we describe the world*—the features and aspects of reality that we choose to focus our attention on—is not entirely dictated by the reality we purport to describe. However we arrive at *the concepts we use to describe the world*, so long as there is something *in* the world in virtue of which our descriptions are true or false, the realist will be vindicated. (152–153, emphasis added)

Here we must notice that Stalnacker means to *restrict* the 'constructive' feature of descriptions or knowledge to the 'content' of such descriptions (or to the way we 'express' them), but he nowhere frontally considers that the real world as we inquire into it cannot be disjunctively segregated from our would-be descriptions of it. It is true that he criticizes Bas van Fraassen's thesis that "scientific *propositions* are not context-dependent in any essential way." But at that very point Stalnacker remarks that he himself assumes "that context-dependence is a matter of the relation between expressions and their content."[3]

Now, this is simply unsupported and quite arbitrary, peculiarly so in the context, for instance, of attempting to offset Michael Dummett's anti-realism (regardless of the merits of Dummett's position). For *if* there is no way to support a pertinent realism except *within* the framework of the indissolubility of realist and idealist elements, or of something like a minimal Kantianism (without Kant's 'objectivist' claims), or of some form of anti-realism in the sense of admitting concessions in the direction of decidability (though not necessarily Dummett's extreme view of that), or of something like what Hilary Putnam has recently dubbed the 'internalist' view of science (again, without subscribing to Putnam's many variant themes), then Stalnacker *could* not restrict context-dependence to descriptive *expressions*: context-dependence would affect *what we take the real world to be,* and in that case the naive assurance "so long as there is something in the world in virtue of which our descriptions are true or false" would not hold at all.

To concede this much is *not* (necessarily) to retreat from realism or to endorse any extreme version of anti-realism. But it is certainly to concede either that it is not the case that "there are just two truth-values—true and false" or that it is the case that we are unable to say how many we will *need* without prior attention to what we take *the world we are able to inquire into* to be like. It is essential to relativism, it should be said, that we cannot always reasonably claim that there are just two truth-values and that, in particular sectors of inquiry, it is more reasonable to claim that the truth-values or truth-like values we need are logically weaker than the bipolar pair—but not merely (if we are to hold to realism) because of limitations restricted to the cognitive resources of human investigators.[4]

Michael Dummett's anti-realism is a little surprising, once this distinction is in place. For Dummett opposes what *he* calls the 'realist' view: "the belief [bivalence, excluded middle] that for any statement there must be something in virtue of which either it or its negation is true: it being only on the basis of this belief that we can justify the idea that truth and falsity play an essential role in the notion of the meaning of a statement, that the general form of an explanation of meaning is a statement of the truth-conditions."[5] Since the anti-realist interprets 'capable of being known' as 'capable of being known *by us*,' the anti-realist is himself a *realist* (and the realist may be conceded to hold a defensible position) just insofar as both restrict the 'realist interpretation' to "those statements, [only] which are in principle effectively decidable." [6] The upshot is that Dummett only appears to retreat from a bipolar pair of truth-values in giving up bivalence. For he gives up bivalence in order to disqualify realism (or what Putnam has dubbed 'metaphysical realism'),[7] but he is not at all prepared to give up *tertium non datur*—"the principle that, for no statement, can we ever rule out both the possibility of its being true and that of its being false, in other words, the principle that there can be no circumstances in which a statement can be recognized as being, irrevocably, neither true nor false [excluded middle restored after deciding decidability]."[8] In effect, this is to draw Stalnacker and Dummett closer to one another's sense of realism (though not necessarily to one another's specific views about the realist import of given kinds of statements, for instance, counterfactuals). In a way, therefore, the same weakness noted in Stalnacker's account reappears in Dummett's—in a different guise. For Dummett never explains *why*, if the realist view of truth (in effect, bivalence) fails because it is 'spurious,' because it supposes that the truth-values of *any* statement may (for all we know) be decidable by beings whose cognitive capacities exceed our own, the serious *anti-realist* objection might not, relative to a particular domain, extend to bipolar truth-values themselves—to the equally spurious assurance that *tertium non datur* will always (may we say 'irrevocably'?) obtain. Clearly, Dummett (not unlike Stalnacker) must segregate the question of decidability and the question of reality. But that is an illicit, unmotivated maneuver: illicit, because it must be open to discovery *what* the actual conditions are on which claims *are* decidable; unmotivated, because the anti-realist scruple has not been brought to bear on *tertium non datur* itself.

Finally, and very simply, Dummett had objected to F. P. Ramsey's 'redundancy theory of truth,' that is, the thesis that 'is true' is 'an obviously superfluous addition' to an asserted proposition.[9] Dummett's objection, however, focuses only on the fact that Ramsey has left no room for the anti-realist complaint. But there is a deeper reason Ramsey's thesis is inadequate: it may just be that for a particular sector of inquiry the redundancy theory is actually false; the truth-like values it will support may be logically weaker than the bipolar pair.

There you have the charge. Neither Stalnacker nor Dummett nor Ramsey has actually bothered to consider that the viable claims of *determinate sectors of inquiry* may not support—*anywhere along a continuum from realism to anti-realism—bipolar truth-values* (or, effectively, *tertium non datur* or an *adjusted version of excluded middle*).

Relativism obliges us to retreat from bipolar truth-values or *tertium non datur*—but *not* globally, not indiscriminately, not on an all-or-nothing basis. Relativism is a logical thesis, an alethic thesis, applied piecemeal. It could not be a reasonable thesis if it did not resist the kind of disjunctions Stalnacker and Dummett favor (Stalnacker: between 'reality' and our expressed descriptions of reality; Dummett: between the decidability of our statements and what, apart from their decidability, decidability cannot fail to reveal about reality thus addressed). In a word, a serious relativism fitted to the actual inquiries of the sciences, ontology, methodology, interpretation, appraisal and evaluation, and more, *cannot fail to presuppose that in no respect is the world distributively, cognitively transparent*, sufficiently transparent, either in advance of or subsequent to establishing decidability, to be able to install bipolar values everywhere.

II

There are two very large substantive constraints on all seriously engaged speculations regarding the truth-values (or truth-like values) suited to a given domain of inquiry. They are of rather different sorts, but they must be brought to bear jointly on such strong claims as those of Stalnacker, Ramsey, and Dummett. One stems (in our own time) from Alfred Tarski's *metametatheoretical* discussion of truth; the other, from the generally convergent finding of recent Western philosophy repudiating all cognitive transparency. Relativism is the beneficiary of the intersection of these two currents. The convergence intended yields the protean finding that there is no realism suited to rigorous inquiry that can escape the limitation that the world we inquire into is not *cognitively* accessible in any way that would support a disjunction between *it* and whatever *we* identify as the world we inquire into. That is the idealist face every realist torso must expose if it cannot claim perfect transparency. It is also in a way the important theme of nearly every contemporary philosophy of science: we may inquire into an independent world, but we cannot state its nature as it is independently of our inquiries.[10]

This is what is implicitly denied or unacknowledged in Stalnacke and Dummett's disjunctions: we cannot relegate the open, unsystematizable consequences of context-dependence to the mere cultural *expressions* of our science without affecting the demarcation of the structures of the world we examine; and we cannot encumber the claims of our science in the name of *decidability*, while assuring ourselves in advance that no decidable claims can fail to accord with the formal features of bipolar truth-values. We cannot convincingly support the cognitively blind assurance that the real world cannot but accord with certain logical doctrines—largely formal, largely uninterpreted, largely untested—that assure us *a priori* that only research programs congruent with those doctrines could possibly be viable or productive.

In an intriguing sense these and related claims are due, perhaps a little indirectly, to a misreading or misapplication of Tarski's well-known account of truth or of similar purely formal theories of truth. Certainly, both Stalnaker's and Dummett's disjunctions are loosely analogous with Tarski's distinction between the concept of logical consequence and the criterion of deducibility.[11] But Tarski addresses the issue only in formal terms suited to the arithmetic of natural numbers, and himself admits the material difficulty of adequately sorting disjunctively logical and extralogical terms. Without the extension of Tarski's kind of analysis to the whole of that part of natural language that is needed in the pursuit of the empirical sciences (if that makes sense), it would be quite impossible to vindicate either Stalnaker's or Dummett's disjunctions. Tarski quite openly concludes, we may be "compelled to regard such concepts as 'logical consequence,' 'analytical statement,' and 'tautology' as relative concepts which must, on each occasion, be related to a definite, although in greater or less degree arbitrary, division of terms into logical and extralogical. The fluctuation in the common usage of the concept of consequence would—in part at least—be quite naturally reflected in such a compulsory situation." (120) Correspondingly, Tarski was quite convinced that his semantic conception of truth was not, in general, suited to the 'whole' of the language used in the empirical sciences.[12]

It has been said, for instance by Hilary Putnam, that 'true' on Tarski's theory "is, amazingly, a *philosophically neutral* notion. 'True' is just a device for 'semantic ascent': for 'raising' assertions from the 'object language' to the 'meta-language,' and the device does not commit one epistemologically or metaphysically."[13] But the fact is that Tarski's complete conception *fits* certain formalized languages only. Either, then, Putnam has prized apart the 'bare' concept from its 'application' or else he has divided Tarski's theory pointlessly and against Tarski's own purpose. One *can* distinguish between Tarski's bare 'definitional' notion of 'true' and the actual 'structural-descriptive' rule or canon for determining the truth of distributed object-language sentences. But doing that would deprive the definitional element itself of any substantive bearing on the *actual sentences* of a functioning science. For instance, one could hold (on Dummett's summary) that, "for any sentence A, A is [materially] equivalent to ⌐It is true that A⌐, or to ⌐S is true⌐, where S is a [metalinguistic] ('structural-descriptive') name for A."[14] But *if* we separate the two notions, Putnam would be right in treating Tarski's equivalence thesis as 'philosophically neutral' only in the undesirably strong sense that it had no philosophical bearing at all in an *epistemically* pertinent regard; for what would be the point of introducing provision for a structural-descriptive name for A if, in doing so, we had to concede no information about the nature of the relevant descriptions of such distributed sentences? On the other hand, *if* such descriptions did conform with what Tarski offers as the extensionally regimented descriptions suitably fitted *to* the interpreted formal languages he actually examines, then: first of all, the notion would no longer be philosophically neutral (it obviously would favor a global extensionalism), and, secondly, it (the complete notion) would require, to be theoretically vindicated, an independent argument about the properties of the pertinent language of science—which Tarski, confessedly, nowhere provides. It is Dummett's point that "Rejection of the principle of bivalence [every statement is either true or false] when not accompanied by rejection of *tertium non datur* [no statement is neither true nor false] does not lead to any conflict with the equivalence thesis." But it is also Dummett's point (against Ramsey's redundancy thesis) that since the Tarskian truth-definition "is *not* an expansion of the object-language," we cannot *apply* the predicate 'true' to the sentences of an object-language (any object-language)—in accord with the truth-definition—"if we do not yet understand the object-language . . . [that is, if we do not have] a grasp of the meaning of each such sentence" in virtue of which 'true' can be distributively applied (xx–xxi).

The point is that if Tarski's conception of truth—that is, the entire conception, including provision for the metalinguistic structural description of distributed object-language sentences—fits the formalized languages Tarski claims it fits, then it does so on the strength *of an actual analysis of such languages*. It is not construed by Tarski to be an *a priori* matter. Hence, if it is to be extended to natural languages, then, on Tarski's view, it must be suitably justified by an analysis of those languages as well. *If* the Tarskian definition of truth (without the structural-descriptive account) is 'philosophically neutral,' then it is neutral because it is vacuous, *because it affirms no object-language/metalanguage relationship and because it imposes no constraint on any material equivalence between object-language and metalinguistic sentences*. It may well capture some profound common intuition about truth, but it could hardly (then) be said to capture such an intuition along the lines of the equivalence thesis. Anyone who supposed it would automatically do that would have to be extraordinarily sanguine about extensionalism—and would in any case be open to empirical challenge and possible defeat. Hence, it does not really matter that Tarski's definition invokes bipolar truth-values, for it was meant all along for languages that conformed sufficiently closely to the formal languages that serve as Tarski's paradigms, and there it *is* the appropriate choice. Therefore, no incompatibility exists between subscribing to Tarski's conception and insisting that, for particular domains of inquiry, we should (should have to) introduce truth-values logically weaker than the bipolar pair.

In fact, if theories of truth are viewed empirically, then there are at least two distinct sources of contention vis-à-vis Tarski's conception: first, that truth-values logically weaker than bipolar values may be required in particular domains (the formal concession essential to relativism), and, second, that for either bipolar or logically weaker values or both, sentences true or justified with regard to the actual features of a given domain of inquiry may not satisfy Tarski's provisions for their 'structural' description (an ontological claim that, however minimal in other respects, is not in the least inhospitable to relativism).

Donald Davidson (the effective custodian of all efforts to extend Tarski's account to empirical disciplines) is quite explicit about "treating theories of truth as empirical theories," though he obviously means this more in terms of (what he calls) 'Convention T,' the 'structural-descriptive' account, than in terms of the suitability of restricting the range of bipolar values.[15] Thus he says, answering one of his critics:

> Of course, my project does require that all sentences of natural languages can be handled by a T-theory, and so if the intensional idioms resist such treatment, my plan [the grand plan of Davidson's philosophy] has foundered. It seems to be the case, though the matter is not entirely simple or clear, that a theory of truth that satisfies anything like Convention T cannot allow an intensional semantics, and this has prompted me to try to show how an extensional semantics can handle what is special about belief sentences, indirect discourse, and other such sentences.[16]

Davidson's admission shows very nicely the underground linkage between limiting extending the scope of bipolar truth-values by analogy with Tarski's analysis of certain formal languages and supporting an ontology that eschews all cognitive transparency, along lines favoring a pragmatized holism and the indissoluble symbiosis of realist and idealist elements.[17] For there can be no doubt that the prospects of a sturdy and substantive relativism positively depend on such philosophical policies as: (1) rejecting transparency, (2) advocating scientific holism, and (3) acknowledging the indissolubility of realist and idealist themes within the scope of (1) and (2). If we continued along these lines, emphasizing, for instance, (4) the historical contingency of inquiry itself, and (5) the context-dependence of inquiry under the condition of being unable to fix the absolute context of all context-dependence (relative to all possible worlds, say, or to synthetic *a priori* truths)—if we continued thus we should have admitted just the conditions under which 'an intensional semantics' would be least likely to be suppressed or eliminated. Projects like Davidson's would then 'founder' (as Davidson admits), and a robust relativism would either be required or strongly favored. The irony is that Davidson *is* quite well committed to (1)–(5), and yet he comes extraordinarily close to advocating on *a priori* grounds the extension of Tarski's strategy to the empirical disciplines (in fact, to the whole of natural language). The issue is a tricky one, but its resolution definitely bears on rescuing relativism. For in demonstrating the impossibility of vindicating on purely formal grounds a bipolar model for all empirical domains—in particular, in demonstrating that no formalism of Tarski's sort (as Tarski himself clearly foresaw) could vindicate either the universal applicability of bipolar values or a thoroughly extensional treatment of every empirical domain (which would entail bipolarity)—we effectively demonstrate that the relativistic account cannot be precluded for particular inquiries. So the issue invites a bit of patience regarding Davidson's important attempt to extend a Tarskian-like model to natural languages.

Davidson's would-be extension is actually not easy to defend. Its weakness, in fact, serves to expose a characteristic double prejudice against relativistic truth-values and a strong intensionalism that would be hospitable to relativism.

But that extension is not easy to defend. There is, in fact, a certain conceptual slippage in Davidson's argument—that cannot fail to recall Putnam's hearty claim about the 'amazing' philosophical neutrality of Tarski's conception of truth. For consider that when he sketches the extension of 'Convention T' to natural languages, Davidson candidly observes:

> I suggest that a theory of truth for a language [as we want a theory to do] does ... give the meanings of all independently meaningful expressions on the basis of an analysis of their structure. And ... a semantic theory of a natural language cannot be considered adequate unless it provides an account of the concept of truth for that language along the general lines proposed by Tarski for formalized languages.[18]

Here Davidson advocates Convention T as a *criterion* of the adequacy of theories of truth. The point of his proposal is, however, not entirely clear. It definitely risks being equivocal. For there is a sense in which the appeal to Tarski is merely an appeal to *some* (as yet unspecified) metalinguistic description of the structural properties of object-language sentences, in virtue of which the truth of such sentences can be shown to depend on the structure and structural relations among their constituent parts. It is, perhaps, in this sense that Davidson warns us that "to seek a theory that accords with Convention T is not, in itself at least, to settle for Model T logic or semantics [that is, Tarski's own full strategy]." Convention T, in the skeletal form I have given it, makes no mention of extensionality, truth functionality, or first-order logic. It invites us to use whatever devices we can contrive appropriately to bridge the gap between sentence mentioned and sentence used. Restrictions on ontology, ideology, or inferential power find favor, from the present point of view, only if they result from adopting Convention

T as a touchstone. "What I want to defend is the Convention as a criterion of theories, not any particular theories that have been shown to satisfy the Convention in particular cases [Tarski's own application, say], the resources to which they may have been limited."[19] On this first line of advocating Convention T, then, emphasis is placed on preferring or favoring structural-descriptive ways of linking the extension of the truth of particular (object-language) sentences to those very sentences rather than on relying (hence, on giving their meanings thereby) on any other approach to managing that relationship. Davidson does not (here) deny the power of Tarski's example: it is only that he does not trade on its own particular strategies; on the contrary, here he proposes a more general overview by means of which to demonstrate the superiority of Tarski's full account over all others. But how does he do this?

The apparent argument is simplicity itself. Let someone say [Davidson observes] "There are a million stars out tonight" and another reply, "That's true," then nothing could be plainer than that what the first has said is true if and only if what the other has said is true. . . . We have learned to represent these facts by sentences of the form: "The sentence 'There are a million stars out tonight' is true if and only if there are a million stars out tonight." Because T-sentences (as we may call them) [sentences of the biconditional form just illustrated] are so obviously true, some philosophers have thought that the concept of truth, at least as applied to sentences, was trivial. But that's not so. T-sentences don't . . . show how to live without a truth predicate; but taken together, they do tell what it would be like to have one. For since there is a T-sentence corresponding to each sentence of the language for which truth is in question, the totality of T-sentences exactly fixes the extension, among the sentences, of any predicate that plays the role of the words "is true." From this, it is clear that although T-sentences do not define truth, they can be used to define truth predicatehood: any predicate is a truth predicate that makes all T-sentences true. (65) Look at this a little more carefully, however. When T-sentences are constructed to capture the sense of narratives like the story of the million stars—when they 'are so obviously true'—they are meant to be trivially true; they are *not* meant to affirm a material equivalence between object-language sentences and metalinguistic sentences formed by any (as yet unspecified) structural analysis of those sentences, that thereby gives "the truth conditions of the described sentence[s]."[20] On that reading (the second reading of the equivocation remarked) T-sentences are hardly 'obviously true.' Putnam's (and Davidson's) claim could only refer to the vacuous thesis ('obviously true') that *if*, in stories like the million-stars story, in asserting "There are a million stars out tonight" one is affirming that there are (that it is true that there are), then the corresponding T-sentence is ('obviously') true as well. But that is to say that in the original irresistible vignette *nothing is said or intended regarding relations between object-language and metalanguage,* certainly not anything regarding any (specified or unspecified) structural-descriptive analysis of object-language sentences in virtue of which their truth-conditions are given.

No. The irresistible vignette *may* capture a profound intuition about truth. Such a vignette *is* 'philosophically neutral.' It *may* reasonably be said to be the intuition on which Tarski constructs his account. But the latter (the strong extensionalized account suited to certain formalized languages), *and* its extension to natural languages (Davidson's project), *and* the import of using Tarski's (so-called) Convention T as a *criterion* of the adequacy of theories of truth (without yet invoking Tarski's own strongly extensionalized program) *are definitely not philosophically neutral.* The statement of these three theses is certainly not obviously true. So Davidson shifts ground considerably when, with all his cautions, he finally affirms:

> The reason Convention T is acceptable as a criterion of theories is that (i) T-sentences are clearly true (preanalytically)—something we could recognize only if we already (partly) understood the predicate 'is true,' and (ii) the totality of T-sentences fixes the extension of the truth predicate uniquely. The interest of a theory of truth, viewed as an empirical theory of a natural language, is not that it tells us what truth is in general, but that it reveals how the truth of every sentence of a particular L [a particular language] depends on its structure and constituents.[21]

Here it is obvious that Davidson must be equivocating on the meaning of 'T-sentences' in giving his reasons for supporting Convention T: in (i), T-sentences must, to be 'clearly true (preanalytically),' take the trivial form of the first reading of Tarski's strategy; and in (ii) T-sentences must accord with an extension of Tarski's own strategy (which Tarski never intended and actually believed unworkable) or else must involve some suitably strong analogue of Tarski's own strategy (recalling Davidson's caveat about not adopting prematurely 'Model T logic or semantics'). In any case, it is certainly not clear that either in general (by some as yet unspecified structural descriptive canon fitted to Convention T) or specifically as an extension of Tarski's own canon, the criterion offered in (ii)—that "*the totality of T-sentences fixes the extension of the truth predicate uniquely*"—could be shown to be true, could be shown to be sufficiently promising to support an empirically responsible claim that it is true, or could be so characterized that we would even have a reasonable sense of *how to proceed to show that it was true*—or to show, for that reason, that the truth-values logically weaker than the bipolar pair could never be empirically vindicated (on doctrine 1).

This is the sense in which Davidson's claim is effectively, must be, an *a priori* claim, despite all his insistence on treating the theory of truth as an empirical question. Apart from his own frank admission of numerous details that we cannot yet be sure would support the extension of Tarski's strongly extensionalized canon,[22] there is the stunningly plain fact that to the extent Davidson subscribes (as he apparently does) to Quine's holism, to the extent he admits the historicized and contextualized nature of natural language, to the extent he subscribes to our constraints (a)–(e), it is simply impossible for him to profess (ii) *on empirical grounds*.[23]

Davidson actually calls a theory of truth, that is, "a theory that satisfies something like Tarski's Convention T" (where he simply appeals to "a canonical description of a sentence of *L*" without insisting on Tarski's own canon—but also without refusing its use), 'absolute': "to distinguish [it, he says] from theories that (also) relativize truth to an interpretation, a model, a possible world, or a domain. In a theory of the sort I am describing, the truth predicate is not defined, but must be considered a primitive expression."[24] But in the *empirical* sense in which the theory proposed is to be fitted to natural language, subscribing to (a)–(e), or even to a good part of that set, effectively commits one to relativizing determinations of truth-conditions, even if the predicate 'true' is not itself treated relationally. Davidson himself makes the essential admission: "'absolute' truth goes relative when applied to a natural language."[25] But it does so, surely, in just that sense in which criterion (ii) regarding testing the adequacy of any theory of truth cannot be shown to be effective, cannot eliminate an 'intensional semantics,' and cannot preclude the need to retreat (in particular domains of inquiry) from bipolar truth-values to logically weaker values. In this sense no extension of a Tarski-like strategy could, *empirically*, disallow a substantive relativism. This, then, confirms the sense in which relativism is favored by the intersection of neutralizing Tarskian-like programs for the empirical sciences and exploiting the ramified import of the developing philosophical repudiation of all forms of cognitive transparency. But it also prophesies increasing concessions regarding intentional complications in the analysis of any theory of science and serious inquiry. That is, the failure of Davidson to vindicate a Tarskian-like program for natural languages is not Davidson's fault. It is merely a symptom of the impossibility of settling *a priori*, by formal means alone, the adequacy of (a) an extensional model for natural languages, and (b) the adequacy of a bipolar model of truth-values for any particular sector of inquiry (whether in accord with bivalence or *tertium non datur*).

III

There is no need for a developed relativism if transparency obtains. On that condition any relativism signifies merely provisional limitations in the cognitive powers of human investigators. A substantive relativism requires that the scientific description of the 'independent' physical world (that is, the real world as it is independent of human inquiry) be an artifact of a cognitive competence that is at once justifiably realist in its claims about that independent world and incapable in principle of being extricated from the preformative conditions of the historical existence of human investigators—whether conceptual, doxastic, conative, institutional, praxical, ideological, tacit, programmatic, or critical conditions. It must, in short, manifest—symbiotically—both realist and idealist aspects. It may be that Kantianism in its strict form preserves a version of transparency (or what effectively functions as a surrogate for transparency); at the same time it fuses the realist and idealist features of an apt science. That, presumably, is what Husserl objected to in Kant, in charging Kant with 'objectivism'.[26] An analogous charge has been leveled of course against Husserl as well, given his obsessive search for the apodictic, his transcendental solipsism, and his sense of the apparent privilege of the phenomenological method.[27] In that spirit we may employ the pejorative epithet 'logocentrism' for any theory that fixes, in the absence of, or even specifically in opposition to, pretensions of transparency, a privileged constraint on any reasonably productive (or realist) science within the bounds of a realist/idealist fusion. Thus, in the analytic tradition there can be no doubt that Quine's extreme extensionalism—particularly its a priori repudiation of intentionality (and consequent intentional complications)[28] must count as a most influential form of logocentrism in the absence of (in opposition to, in fact) all forms of transparency. This is the same sense in which the global a priori insistence on bipolar truth-values, in Stalnacker and Dummett, and the union of that thesis, *via* Tarski, with a subtle version of Quine's extensionalism, as in Davidson, are here construed as forms of logocentrism. The fact is that doctrines of these sorts preclude any substantive relativism. It is an irony, therefore, as well as a clear sign of a profound incoherence, that Quine is the champion both of a draconian extensionalism that precludes an empirically exploratory relativism along intentional lines and of a pragmatized holism that entails a pervasive relativism.

The principle benefit, as far as the fortunes of relativism are concerned, of the realist/idealist symbiosis under conditions precluding transparency and logocentrism is simply that relativism can no longer be restricted to the contingencies of cognitive accident and limitation. That is, the contribution of relativism cannot be exhausted by considerations of probabilizing evidence, or of ambiguity, or vagueness, or of deliberately heuristic or idiosyncratically constructed schemata, or interpretations, or the like. On the argument, relativism, a robust or substantive relativism, answers to the general finding that *we cannot uniquely fix the structures of reality just at the point at which we are reasonably justified in treating our cognitive claims in realist terms.* There are many ways in which this charge could be fleshed out. But the following may serve as the barest hints of substantive possibilities going beyond (but hardly precluding) mere epistemic limitations. For example, ontic commitment, construed in accord with Quine's holist insistence on indeterminacy of translation and inscrutability of reference, cannot fail to support relativism. (§§15–16) Again, if cultural phenomena are real and exhibit intensionally complex intentional features, despite Quine's repudiation of intentionality, (§15) then it becomes impossible to disallow interpretive complexities from affecting our being able to identify descriptively unique, or at least convergent and compatible, real structures within the cultural world—for reasons that cannot be confined to mere evidentiary considerations. Again, if cultural phenomena, artworks for instance, actually possess intentional structures, then we cannot draw a principled demarcation between the properties such phenomena possess and properties that can only be imputed to such phenomena.[29] Again, if high-level theories in the physical sciences are radically underdetermined by observational data, if there are good reasons (causal reasons involving strategic experiments or technological inventions) for regarding as real theoretical entities postulated in ways that also serve to explain observed regularities, and if explanatory laws are idealizations from, even distortions of, phenomenological regularities or laws, then, for reasons that exceed epistemic worries, there can be no way of precluding relativistic accounts of such entities.[30] These four lines of inquiry, all concerned with determining what there (really) is or what the properties of what there is (really) are, are certainly among the more salient options that a moderate relativism would claim to accommodate. They indicate that a merely formal extensionalism, even a formal physicalism, could not convincingly preclude the relativistic option, and that any enrichment of such an account by admitting the intentional complexities of the cultural world is bound to strengthen its hand. But our concern here is to indicate, without actually elaborating, the full sense in which the question of relativism is a substantive and not merely a formal matter (the point of our having distinguished, at the start of this paper, between doctrines 1 and 2).

Notice that the physical sciences are themselves enterprises that, precisely in positing an 'independent physical world,' fall within the inquiries of culturally encumbered human investigators. Clearly, the social and historical world of man cannot intelligibly be construed as separable, even in principle, from the investigative aptitudes of reflexive inquirers; although to say that is not to preclude pertinent notions of objective confirmation and validity with regard to the human sciences; it is only to insist that in the space of human culture there can be no initial disjunction between the epistemological and the ontological. There is none in the physical sciences either; but there is often said to be one (extensionalism), and there *is* a systematic function assigned the notion of an 'independent physical world' *within* the space of the other that cannot even in principle (or at least so we are here claiming) be matched in the human sciences.[31] Relativism, then, is nothing less than the attempt to recover within realist terms whatever forms of objectivity may be secured for any science or comparable inquiry in which, for reasons affected by the impossibility of uniquely fixing the real structures of this or that sector of things, we are obliged to retreat to truth-like values logically weaker than bipolar values.

Nevertheless, relativism has a bad name. Its ancient form, Protagoreanism, is a philosophical scandal: not, let it be said, because Protagoras's thesis cannot be given a coherent reading, but because almost no one wishes to. Paul Feyerabend offers these tantalizingly brief sentences in introducing his collected *Philosophical Papers*: "The reader will notice that some articles [included] defend ideas which are attacked in others. This reflects my belief (which seems to have been held by Protagoras) that good arguments can be found for the opposite sides of any issue."[32] Feyerabend associates this belief with what he calls 'democratic relativism,' which to many, may suggest only a sense of conceptual thrift and an unwillingness to lose potential contributions made by fringe or minority groups. But Feyerabend's view is actually closer to attacking the logocentrism of privileged traditions (under what, notably, as in Putnam's criticisms,[33] are would-be idealist constraints on scientific realism). Hence, when, subverting the hegemony of Western science (Western 'rationalism'), Feyerabend observes, "*They simply take it for granted that their own traditions of standard construction and standard rejection are the only traditions that count,*"[34] he is speaking not merely of intellectual tolerance but surely also as a relativist committed to the thesis we have just formulated—the structures of reality cannot be fixed either in terms of transparency or logocentric privilege (*a priori*, privileged traditions)—and as one committed as well to the thesis that *that* is a reasonable reading of Protagoras.

This may be a way of understanding sympathetically the ancient report that Protagoras "was the first to say that there were two contradictory arguments about everything."[35] It suggests regarding his famous maxim, "Of all things the measure is Man, of the things that are, that they are, and of the things that are not, that they are not" (125), that Protagoras should be construed as anticipating modern forms of incommensurabilism (or a retreat from bipolar truth-values) rather than as merely subscribing to the anciently assigned doctrine that every opinion is true and every opinion false. The latter is usually pressed even today, as, for instance, quite straightforwardly by W. H. Newton-Smith.[36] In that form, it is simply a hopelessly stupid thesis. We may then identify 'ancient' relativism (Protagoreanism) as the stupid doctrine that any and every state-ment is both true and false, while at the same time we reserve for ourselves the right to construe Protagoras's own view as requiring a retreat from the global adequacy of bipolar values and a shift, under that constraint, toward a form of incommensurabilism.

The pity is we have lost Protagoras's work. There is an ancient report that the Athenians destroyed all the copies of Protagoras's book. Plato's *Protagoras* is certainly at least in part a parody for his own purpose and Aristotle's refutation of Protagoras in the *Metaphysics* could, on the standard argument regarding the law of contradiction, be offset if Protagoras had meant to retreat from bipolar values. (So read, Protagoras's maxim would afford a nice counter to that of Parmenides.)[37] In any case, there is a way of attempting to salvage even the ancient form of rela-tivism. (Also, to put matters this way helps, as we shall see, to give form to the notion that relativism is much more flexible than ordinarily admitted.)

The principle modern form is, surprisingly, almost as inexplicit as Protag-oreanism. It is usually termed *incommensurabilism* and is formulated chiefly (and disadvantageously) by the opponents of those said to advance the thesis—in particular, against Thomas Kuhn and Paul Feyerabend. Incommensurabilism *begins* at least with the conceptually innocuous truism that not all measures are mutually commensurable (in the sense, for instance, in which the hypot-enuse of an isosceles right triangle is incommensurable with its side), although that is no reason for believing that incommensurable measures are not, sever-ally, capable of being successfully applied *and* of being jointly intelligible, even comparable, to the same rational agent.[38] Incommensurabilism acquires color as a form of relativism only when, one way or another, it extends to what may be called 'conceptual relativity,' that is, accords with the thesis that—under the preformational conditions of historical existence or under the conditions of adhering to different theories, different research projects, different paradigms, different modes of training, orientation, and the like (or both)—different inves-tigators (located either synchronically or diachronically) are, on the available evidence, often unable to incorporate an adequate and coherent picture of one another's conceptions within the terms of reference of their own. The emphasis here is on distinctly finite, real-time constraints in attempting to effect such coherence. But it emphatically is not skeptical about the intelligibility of such divergent conceptions.

So construed, incommensurabilism is not a principled position but an empirical phenomenon that yields a certain relativity of inquiry and the results of inquiry that, over time, may, in principle, be overtaken distributively. The opponents of incommensurabilism, however, take its contemporary advocates to be advancing a very strong principled thesis—a thesis, in fact, that is either incoherent or unnecessarily (and unconvincingly) skeptical. As with Protagoreanism, therefore, it is the better part of strategy to seek to recover a viable form of incommensurabilism from the excesses of its overzealous opponents.

Two lines of argument have been pursued. One distinctly treats incommensurabilism as the 'new relativism' and takes it to be tantamount to 'skepticism, historicism, and nihilism' (as notably by Richard J. Bernstein);[39] the other treats incommensurabilism as flatly incoherent and self-defeating (as notably by Donald Davidson).[40] On Bernstein's view, the objectivist is committed to "some permanent, ahistorical matrix or framework" for resolving all cognitive questions; the relativist denies that there is such a framework and *thereupon* draws the skeptical conclusion.[41] The incommensurabilist thesis is, therefore, the denial of objectivism construed as disallowing the adjudication of all truth-claims. Bernstein does *not* advocate returning to objectivism. He means merely to urge either that the rejection of that doctrine does not lead to relativism or skepticism or that there may be a form of incommensurabilism that does not lead to the relativist or skeptical conclusion. But he never explains how this is possible, and the relativist, sympathetic with incommensurabilism, *may* simply retreat from the global adequacy of bipolar values *and thereby separate relativism from skepticism*.[42] Bernstein himself apparently believes that the ongoing 'tradition' of inquiry somehow preserves the path by means of which unique or very strongly convergent resolutions of contending truth-claims can be counted on to be effected. But this itself is an obvious form of logocentric assurance—one we may christen 'traditionalism,' one in fact strenuously advocated (but not seriously defended or methodologically specified) by Hans-Georg Gadamer (whom Bernstein professes to follow) and by Charles Taylor.[43]

The second counterstrategy (Davidson's) leads us to consider the tenability of 'conceptual relativism,' the thesis (on Davidson's reading) that *we* are able to individuate plural conceptual schemes different from our own because of *their* partial or total untranslatability into *our* conceptual scheme.[44] The argument is intended as a reductio specifically against Kuhn and Feyerabend. But the truth of the matter is that we have no clear idea how to establish *untranslatability* (nor does Davidson) when we have merely encountered an actual failure of translation of a suitably stubborn and pervasive kind. So 'conceptual relativism' may well be an excessive and incoherent claim, as Davidson avers. But a *moderate* incommensurabilist (certainly Kuhn in his more careful moments, possibly even Feyerabend despite his deliberate provocations) may affirm no more than 'conceptual relativity' (as characterized above: sustained failure of translation under real-time conditions). He may then go on to reject 'conceptual relativism' (Davidson's impossibly difficult untranslatability thesis) and to lead the first option in the direction of a principled argument, as by: (1) denying (what Bernstein terms) the objectivist thesis (which, in an obvious sense, Davidson is logocentrically committed to, by way of his reading of Tarski's semantic conception); (2) affirming some form of the realist/idealist symbiosis; and (3) concluding that, under the actual contingencies of historical inquiry and existence, we can never ensure escaping some range of (moderate) incommensurability. This is all the relativist needs to ensure the recovery of the incommensurabilist thesis as a valid form of relativism not in the least skewed toward skepticism or nihilism. That thesis is certainly not internally incoherent. Within the analytic tradition of the philosophy of science perhaps Ian Hacking is as reasonable an advocate of this sort of relativism as any,[45] though it is also fairly assigned to Kuhn and Feyerabend.

Nevertheless, relativism does not achieve its strongest formulation in Protagoreanism and incommensurabilism, though it may avail itself of their resources. What we may now characterize as a *robust* or moderate relativism is a substantive thesis about constraints on truth-values in distributed sectors of inquiry due to (what may be generously construed as) empirical evidence that those sectors (but not necessarily every sector) cannot reasonably support truth-claims in terms of bipolar values. On the argument we must fall back to logically weaker, many-valued claims (as of plausibility, reasonableness, aptness, and the like) if we are to salvage a measure of objectivity with respect to the inquiries of those sectors. Such a retreat may be required, for instance, in advancing claims about explanatory theories and laws in the physical sciences,[46] or about reference to theoretical entities through changing theories,[47] or about ontological schemes of 'what there is.'[48] If the concession is required here, it is a foregone conclusion that it will be required in historical studies, in interpretation, in the social and human sciences, in criticism, and in appraisal and evaluation as well.

The skeleton of the relativist argument, then, is extraordinarily simple. It posits the nearly trivial (but not unimportant) thesis that we may introduce by fiat any consistent logical constraints we care to admit on the truth-values or truth-like values particular sets of claims or claims in particular sectors of inquiry may take. We may, by fiat alone, deny to a given sector the power of pertinent claims or judgments to take bipolar truth-values (or, acknowledging an asymmetry between 'true' and 'false,' the power to take the strong value 'true'); and then, by introducing logically weaker values, we may admit claims or judgments to be evidentially supported or supportable even where, on a bipolar model of truth-values but not now, admissible judgments would yield incompatible or contradictory claims. We may simply abandon excluded middle or *tertium non datur*. On the new model, such judgments could be said to be 'incongruent,' and a suitable discipline could be provided for their confirmation and disconfirmation. At the same time, on the strength of relevance considerations certain other logically undesirable possibilities could easily be precluded (in probabilistic contexts, for instance, it would be undesirable to deny that "Nixon probably knew about Watergate in advance and did not know about Watergate in advance" was a contradiction, even though "There is a probability that Nixon knew about Watergate in advance and a probability that Nixon did not know about Watergate in advance" would normally not be construed as self-contradictory).[49]

The essential point is that the formal (relativistic) characterization of truth-like values *appropriate* to particular sectors of inquiry (i) need not be logically incoherent or self-contradictory, (ii) effectively capture the salvageable themes of Protagoreanism and incommensurabilism and more, and (iii) may be formulated so as to accommodate the salient philosophical convergences of our own time. The rest of the argument really concerns how to show, in given sectors of inquiry, that a relativistic thesis is as reasonable as, or more reasonable than, any program of scientific *objectivity*—not committed to transparency or logocentric privilege—that still insists (in the manner of Stalnacker, Dummett, and Davidson, and so many others) that "there are just two truth-values."[50]

The strongest substantive reason for advocating relativism rests, as we have seen, with the finding that we cannot uniquely fix the structures of reality just where we are justified in insisting on the objective and realist import of our cognitive claims. That finding draws strength from arguments in favor of the realist/idealist symbiosis of science, a pragmatized holism, a moderate incommensurabilism, a historicized context-dependent sense of human inquiry and existence, the impossibility of totalizing the conditions of cognition, and the general rejection of transparency and logocentrism. It needs to be said as well that since relativism is to be promoted in a piecemeal and distributed way, there is no incompatibility in managing, within one science, both bipolar claims and the logically weaker claims here advocated; for it is certainly clear that inquiries that promote relativistic values depend on a *theory* of bipolar values even where they retreat from the use of such values. Also, of course, there is no reason to deny that relativistic programs readily accommodate comparative judgments of merit or force, notions of progress, rigorous evidence, and the like. In short, relativism is expressly opposed to skepticism and nihilism. There are no areas of inquiry usually cast in bipolar terms that are adversely affected by replacing such values with relativistic values. The reason for the substitution, wherever applied, would rest with an argument that the bipolar model was too strict for the domain in question; in effect, the evidence would itself be straightforwardly empirical.

It is extraordinary, therefore, how little must be adjusted in order to make room for a viable relativism—and how extensive its scope may arguably be. It may take a limited evidentiary form if one insists, but its principal force rests with substantive claims about the real structure of this or that sector of inquiry. Any latitude regarding that structure—in physical as well as cultural terms—along, say, the four lines of reasoning sketched just above or in accord with the realist/idealist symbiosis, the rejection of cognitive transparency, the artifactual nature of whatever, within inquiry, we take to be real, or the impossibility of closure in realist terms, is bound to favor the pertinence of relativistic claims.

Relativism, then, is the thesis, at once alethic and metaphysical, that particular sectors of reality can only support, distributively, incongruent claims, that is, claims that on a bipolar model, but not now, would confirm incompatible or contradictory judgments and claims. To forestall misunderstanding, it may be mentioned again that relevance constraints may always be introduced to disallow unwanted contradictions even within the space of relativistic truth-values; that relativism itself is fully compatible with extensionalism and physicalism but is also hospitable to the intentional complexities of human culture; that no *bona fide* inquiries are adversely affected merely by introducing relativistic values; that the use of relativistic values is entirely reconcilable with the use of bipolar values; and that judgments of scientific progress or of the comparative force of opposed claims, or judgments of comparative value, are entirely eligible within the space of relativistic values. Where applicable, bipolar values quite understandably take precedence over relativistic values. But relativistically, judgments of greater or lesser epistemic force need not be disjunctively construed.

So relativism is clearly coherent and viable and, on the strength of substantive arguments, may well be favored in one domain or another.

NOTES

1. The ramified account on which the present argument depends is given in Joseph Margolis, *Pragmatism Without Foundations: Reconciling Realism and Relativism* (Oxford: Blackwell, 1986), and *Science Without Unity: Reconciling the Human and Natural Sciences* (Oxford: Blackwell, 1987).

2. Robert C. Stalnacker, *Inquiry* (Cambridge, Mass.: MIT Press, 1984), 2.

3. Ibid., 151; also see Bas C. van Fraassen, *The Scientific Image* (Oxford: Clarendon Press, 1980), 134–137.

4. The full argument regarding realism and anti-realism is given in Margolis, *Pragmatism Without Foundations*, pt. 2, especially with regard to van Fraassen, Dummett, and Putnam.

5. Michael Dummett, "Truth," in *Truth and Other Enigmas* (Cambridge, Mass.: Harvard University Press, 1978), 14.

6. Ibid., 24; I have italicized 'realist.'

7. Hilary Putnam, *Meaning and the Moral Sciences* (London: Routledge and Kegan Paul, 1978).

8. Dummett, preface to *Truth and Other Enigmas*, xxx.

9. E. P. Ramsey, "Facts and Propositions," in *Foundations of Mathematics*, ed. Richard B. Braithewaite (London: Routledge and Kegan Paul, 1931), 143.

10. Thomas S. Kuhn, *The Structure of Scientific Revolutions*, 2nd enl. ed. (Chicago: University of Chicago Press, 1970), Postscript, 1969.

11. Alfred Tarski, "On the Concept of Logical Consequence," in *Logic, Semantics, Metamathematics: Papers from 1923 to 1938*, 2nd ed., ed. John Corcoran, trans. J. H. Woodger (Indianapolis: Hackett, 1983).

12. Alfred Tarski, "The Concept of Truth in Formalized Languages," in Corcoran, *Logic, Semantics, Metamathematics*, and "The Semantic Conception of Truth," in *Semantics and the Philosophy of Language*, ed. Leonard Linsky (Urbana: University of Illinois Press, 1952).

13. Hilary Putnam, "Reference and Truth," in *Philosophical Papers* (Cambridge: Cambridge University Press, 1983), 3:76.

14. Dummett, preface to *Truth and Other Enigmas*, xx.

15. Donald Davidson, "Introduction," in *Inquiries into Truth and Interpretation* (Oxford: Clarendon, 1984), xiv.

16. Donald Davidson, "Reply to Foster," in *Inquiries into Truth and Interpretation*, 176.

17. That is, of course, always conceding that 'ontologies' need not be committed to transparency—contrary to the fashionable charge in Richard Rorty, *Philosophy and the Mirror of Nature* (Princeton, N.J.: Princeton University Press, 1979).

18. Donald Davidson, "Semantics for Natural Languages," in *Inquiries into Truth and Interpretation*, 55; see also "Truth and Meaning," in ibid., 35.

19. Donald Davidson, "In Defense of Convention T," in *Inquiries into Truth and Interpretation*, 68.

20. One of the most recent formulations of 'Convention T' is given in Donald Davidson, "Reality Without Reference," in *Inquiries into Truth and Interpretation*, 215.

21. Ibid., 218.

22. See, for instance, Davidson, "Truth and Meaning," 35–36.

23. See the perceptive remarks of Ian Hacking, *Why Does Language Matter to Philosophy?* (Cambridge: Cambridge University Press, 1975), 154–155.

24. Davidson, "Reality Without Reference," 215–216.

25. Davidson, "In Defense of Convention T," 75.

26. Edmund Husserl, *Phenomenology and the Crisis of Philosophy*, trans. Quentin Lauer (New York: Harper & Row, 1965).

27. This marks a substantial part of the thrust of Derrida's early work, though it is as much addressed to Kant as to Husserl. See Jacques Derrida, *Speech and Phenomena*, trans. David B. Allison (Evanston, Ill.: Northwestern University Press, 1973).

28. W. V. Quine, *Word and Object* (Cambridge, Mass.: MIT Press, 1960), §45.

29. This is an issue on which both Monroe Beardsley's new critical conception and E. D. Hirsch's romantic hermeneutic conception of literature utterly fail to exclude relativism. See, for instance, Monroe C. Beardsley, *The Possibility of Criticism* (Detroit: Wayne State University Press, 1970), esp. "The Authority of the Text"; E. D. Hirsch Jr., *The Validity of Interpretation* (New Haven, Conn.: Yale University Press, 1967); and Joseph Margolis, *Art and Philosophy* (Atlantic Highlands, N.J.: Humanities Press, 1980), chap. 6.

30. See, for instance, Nancy Cartwright, *How the Laws of Physics Lie* (Oxford: Clarendon Press, 1985); and Ian Hacking, *Representing and Intervening* (Cambridge: Cambridge University Press, 1985).

31. Carl G. Hempel, "Studies in the Logic of Explanation," in *Aspects of Scientific Explanation* (New York: Free Press, 1965), 263.

32. Paul K. Feyerabend, *Realism, Rationalism, and Scientific Method, Philosophical Papers* (Cambridge: Cambridge University Press, 1981), 1:xlv.

33. Hilary Putnam, "Two Conceptions of Rationality," in *Reason, Truth, and History* (Cambridge: Cambridge University Press, 1981).

34. Paul K. Feyerabend, "Historical Background: Some Observations on the Decay of the Philosophy of Science," in *Problems of Empiricism, Philosophical Papers* (Cambridge: Cambridge University Press, 1981), 2:28–29.

35. Kathleen Freeman, *Ancilla to the Pre-Socratic Philosophers* (Oxford: Blackwell, 1948), 126.

36. W. H. Newton-Smith, *The Rationality of Science* (London: Routledge and Kegan Paul, 1981), 34–37.

37. Mario Untersteiner, *The Sophists*, trans. Kathleen Freeman (Oxford: Blackwell, 1954), 50n.18; also Untersteiner's effort at reconstructing Protagoras, in chap. 3, pt. 3.

38. Perhaps the clearest expression of this view is given in Thomas S. Kuhn, "Theory-Change as Structure-Change: Comments on the Sneed Formalism," *Erkenntnis* 10 (1976), where the triangle case is given.

39. Richard J. Bernstein, *Beyond Objectivism and Relativism* (Philadelphia: University of Pennsylvania Press, 1983), 79, 2ff.

40. Donald Davidson, "On the Very Idea of a Conceptual Scheme," in *Inquiries into Truth and Interpretation* (this volume, chap. 8).

41. Bernstein, *Beyond Objectivism and Relativism*, 8.

42. This is the argument of Margolis, *Pragmatism Without Foundations*, chap. 3.

43. Charles Taylor, "Philosophy and Its History," in *Philosophy in History*, ed. Richard Rorty, Jerome B. Schneewind, and Quentin Skinner (Cambridge: Cambridge University Press, 1984).

44. Davidson, "On the Very Idea of a Conceptual Scheme," 197–198.

45. Ian Hacking, "Language, Truth, and Reason," in *Rationality and Relativism*, ed. Martin Hollis and Steven Lukes (Cambridge, Mass.: MIT Press, 1982).

46. Cartwright, *How the Laws of Physics Lie*.

47. Putnam, Lecture 2 (The John Locke Lectures 1976), in *Meaning and the Moral Sciences*.

48. This is surely the essential point of Quine's notion of 'ontological relativity.' See W. V. Quine, "Ontological Relativity," in *Ontological Relativity and Other Essays* (New York: Columbia University Press, 1969).

49. Margolis, *Pragmatism Without Foundations*, pt. 1.

50. It is fashionable but completely unjustified to construe relativism as committed to treating 'truth or rational acceptability as subjective,' as Putnam does ("Two Concepts of Rationality," 123). At best it is the result of a conventional reading of Protagoras; at worst it is a cryptic reference to the arbitrary skepticism of incommensurabilism.

Making Sense of Relative Truth

7

JOHN MACFARLANE

The goal of this paper is to make sense of relativism about truth. There are two key ideas. (1) To be a relativist about truth is to allow that a sentence or proposition might be assessment-sensitive: that is, its truth-value might vary with the context of assessment as well as the context of use. (2) Making sense of relativism is a matter of understanding what it would be to commit oneself to the truth of an assessment-sensitive sentence or proposition. Analytic philosophers tend to regard relativism about truth as hopelessly confused, easily refuted, and even a sign of deficient intellectual character. This attitude is not entirely unreasonable. Proponents of relativism have focused much more on *motivating* their doctrine than on making sense of it, or even stating clearly what it is to be a relativist about truth. But if relativists have underestimated the difficulties here, their opponents have overestimated them. It is possible to make good sense of relativism about truth—or so I hope to show.

In the first part of this paper, I will try to say exactly how the relativist's position should be stated. Relativism about truth, I will argue, is the view that truth (of sentences or propositions) is relative not just to contexts of use but also to *contexts of assessment*. The philosophical challenge is to explain what this talk of

Reprinted from John MacFarlane, "Making Sense of Relative Truth," *Proceedings of the Aristotelian Society*, 105 (2005), 321–339. Reprinted by courtesy of the Editor of the Aristotelian Society © 2005.

'truth relative to a context of assessment' *means*. In the second part of the paper, I will meet this challenge—not by giving a definition (that is not how one should expect to illuminate fundamental concepts like truth), but by giving assessment-relative truth a role to play in a normative account of assertion. My account will settle precisely what one has to argue in order to defend the claim that a certain sentence or proposition is assessment-sensitive.

I. STATING THE POSITION

One might think that being a relativist is just a matter of relativizing truth to some parameter. But it is not that simple. Many relativizations of truth are entirely orthodox. In model theory, we talk of sentences being true relative to a model and an assignment of values to the variables, and in formal semantics we talk of sentences being true relative to a speaker and time, or more generally (following Kaplan[1]) a context of use. To my knowledge, no one has ever accused Tarski and Kaplan of being relativists for making use of these relativized forms of truth!

Sometimes relativism is presented as a thesis about sentence *tokens*: particular inscriptions or acoustic blasts. But even a sentence token can have different truth-values on different occasions of use. When I leave my office for a quick errand, I put an old yellow Post-it note with a token of I'll be back in a minute on my door. Usually, this sentence token expresses a truth, but sometimes I get sidetracked and it expresses a falsehood.

Here the relativist might appeal to a distinction between sentence tokens and utterances. An utterance (in the sense relevant here) is an *act*. If I use my Post-it note to announce that I will be back in a minute, my act counts as one utterance; if I do the same thing the next day, that is another utterance, using the same sentence token as a vehicle. The relativist thesis might be put this way: one and the same utterance or assertion can be true, relative to X, and false, relative to Y. This sounds more like a controversial thesis.

But there is something a bit odd about calling utterances or assertions, in the 'act' sense, true or false at all. We characterize actions as correct or incorrect, but not as true or false. We say "His aim was true," but not "His aim*ing* was true," and it sounds equally funny to say, "That speech act was true" or "What he did in uttering that sentence was true." This suggests that when we say "His assertion was false" or "That was a true utterance," we are using 'assertion' and 'utterance' to refer to what was asserted or uttered, not to the act of asserting or uttering.[2] Characterizing relativism as a thesis about the truth of assertions or utterances in the 'act' sense looks like a category mistake.

Similar considerations apply to the identification of *beliefs* as the things whose truth is 'relative.' 'Belief' is ambiguous in much the same way as 'assertion.' It can be used to refer to a *state* of a subject (Joe's *believing* that newts are a kind of reptile) or to what is believed (that newts are a kind of reptile). When we say, "Joe's belief is true," we are talking about the content of his belief, not the belief-state. That is why we can paraphrase "Joe's belief is true" as "What Joe believes is true," but not as "Joe is in a true state."

All of this suggests that the relativist doctrine should be stated as a claim about the truth of the things that are believed and asserted: propositions. Accordingly, Max Kölbel has suggested that, "A relativism is not tame, if it involves the claim that the truth of propositions (or contents) of some kind can be relative, i.e., has the form (RP) For any *x* that is a proposition of a certain kind *K*, it is relative to *P* whether *x* is true."[3] But by this criterion, just about everyone who uses propositions in formal semantics would count as a non-tame relativist. For it is standard practice to relativize proposition truth to a *circumstance of evaluation*: typically a possible world, but in some frameworks a world and a time, or even a world and a standard of precision.[4] The proposition that dodos are extinct in 2004 is true in the actual world, but there are possible worlds relative to which the very same proposition is false. Surely that does not vindicate relativism in any interesting sense.

Here it may seem tempting to say: "A *real* relativist is someone who takes proposition truth to be relative to some *other* parameter, in addition to worlds and possibly times."[5] But this kind of response would miss the point. It's not the *kind* of parameter that matters, but how it's treated. We could even relativize proposition truth to an *aesthetic standards* parameter without being relativists about truth in any interesting sense! Suppose we took the predicate 'beautiful' to express a property whose extension varies not just with time and world but also with an aesthetic standard. We would presumably then say that the proposition expressed by:

(1) Helen was beautiful at the beginning of the Trojan War

has truth-values only relative to a world *and* an aesthetic standard. Would this make us relativists? Not all by itself. It depends on how the aesthetic standards parameter is treated in the definition of (sentence) truth at a context. An aesthetic absolutist might treat it this way:

Aesthetic absolutism: *S* is true at a context of use *C* iff there is a proposition *p* such that:

(a) *S* expresses *p* at *C*, and

(b) *p* is true at the world of *C* and the One True Aesthetic Standard.

According to aesthetic absolutism, whether (1) is true at a context of use is completely independent of the speaker's (or anyone else's) aesthetic standards. The truth of (1) is no more 'relative' than the truth of any other tensed claim.

Why would an aesthetic absolutist *bother* relativizing propositional truth to an aesthetic standard? For the same kinds of reasons that led Kaplan to relativize propositional truth to times.[6] She might have independent semantic reasons for taking qualifiers like 'on any standard' to be propositional operators. Propositional operators need a parameter to shift: just as modal operators shift the world parameter and temporal operators shift the time parameter, so these putative operators would shift the aesthetic standards parameter. I am not advocating this treatment of 'on any standard'; I am merely pointing out that there might be good reasons for introducing a parameter of propositional truth that gets set to a constant value in the definition of truth at a context. (Indeed, that is precisely how actualists treat the world parameter.)

Alternatively, one might look to the context of use to fix a value for the aesthetic standards parameter:

Aesthetic contextualism: S is true at a context of use C iff there is a proposition p such that:

(a) S expresses p at C, and

(b) p is true at the world of C and the aesthetic standards of the speaker at C.

This is a kind of relativism about beauty, perhaps, but not about truth. There is always an absolute answer to the question, Is S true at C? or Did A utter S truly?

How would one have to treat the aesthetic standards parameter in order to be a relativist about truth? Here is my suggestion: the parameter would have to be initialized not by a constant (as in aesthetic absolutism) or by a feature of the context of use (as in aesthetic contextualism), but by a feature of the context in which the speech act (or other use of the sentence) is being *assessed*. In order to state the relativist's position, then, we must employ the doubly contextual predicate 'true at context of use C_U and context of assessment C_A' in place of the familiar 'true at context of use C.' By a 'context of assessment,' I mean simply a concrete situation in which a use of the sentence is being *assessed*. We perform speech acts, but we also assess them; so, just as we can talk of the context in which a sentence is being used, we can talk of a context (there will be indefinitely many) in which a use of it is being assessed. Using this notion, we can articulate a radical aesthetic relativism:

Aesthetic relativism: S is true at a context of use C_U and context of assessment C_A iff there is a proposition p such that:

(a) S expresses p at C_U, and

(b) p is true at the world of C_U and the aesthetic standards of the assessor at C_A.

This formulation does, I think, capture what the relativist is after. Whether we can make any sense of the doubly contextual truth predicate to which it appeals is another question, to which we will soon turn.

First, however, it will be useful to fix some terminology. I will call a sentence *use-sensitive* if its truth-value varies with the context of use (keeping the context of assessment fixed), *assessment-sensitive* if its truth-value varies with the context of assessment (keeping the context of use fixed), and *context-sensitive* if it is either use-sensitive or assessment-sensitive. Similarly, I will call a sentence *use-indexical* if it expresses different propositions at different contexts of use (keeping the context of assessment fixed), *assessment-indexical* if it expresses different propositions at different contexts of assessment (keeping the context of use fixed), and *indexical* if it is either use-indexical or assessment-indexical.

Although indexicality and context sensitivity are often conflated, it is important to distinguish them. A sentence can be use-sensitive without being use-indexical: consider, for example:

(2) The number of AIDS-infected babies born in Oakland in 2004 is 65.

Although (2) is use-sensitive—its truth at a context of use depends on the *world* of the context—it is not use-indexical: it expresses the same proposition at every context of use.[7] Use indexicality and use sensitivity can come apart because the context of use plays two distinct roles in determining the truth-value of a sentence at a context, as can be seen from Kaplan's definition of sentence truth at a context: "If c is a context, then an occurrence of [a sentence] Φ in c is true iff the content expressed by Φ in this context is true when evaluated with respect to the circumstance of the context."[8] First, the context of use helps determine which proposition is expressed. But because this proposition has truth-values only relative to circumstances of evaluation, we must appeal to the context of use a second time to fix the relevant circumstance of evaluation (what Kaplan calls 'the circumstance of the context'). In a sentence that is use-sensitive but not use-indexical, context plays no role at the first step but still has an effect on truth-value at the second.[9]

For the same reason, assessment sensitivity need not be due to assessment indexicality. According to the version of aesthetic relativism presented above, for example, (1) is assessment-sensitive but not assessment-indexical. We do not need to allow that the propositional content of an assertion might vary from one assessor to another in order to make sense of relative truth.

The concepts of use sensitivity and assessment sensitivity can be applied to propositions as well as sentences. If it seems odd to characterize a *proposition* as context-sensitive, remember that not all context sensitivity is due to indexicality. (2) is use-sensitive not because it expresses different propositions at different contexts of use, but because the proposition it expresses is itself use-sensitive: this proposition can be truly asserted at some contexts but not at others. I will say that a *proposition* is true at a context of use C_U and context of assessment C_A just in case it is true at the circumstance of evaluation determined by C_U and C_A.[10] (The relation of 'determination' will vary from one semantic theory to another: in the aesthetic relativist's semantics, for example, the circumstance of evaluation determined by C_U and C_A will be composed of the world of C_U and the aesthetic standards of the assessor at C_A, while in the aesthetic contextualist's semantics, it will be composed of the world of C_U and the aesthetic standards of the speaker at C_U.) I will call a proposition *use-sensitive* if its truth-value varies with the context of use (keeping the context of assessment fixed), and *assessment-sensitive* if its truth-value varies with the context of assessment (keeping the context of use fixed).

We are now in a position to state the relativist's position in its full generality. *Relativism about truth* is the view that there is at least one assessment-sensitive sentence. If we restrict the domain to natural languages, or to some particular language, we get a thesis that is at least partly empirical, while if we broaden it to all conceivable languages, we get a thesis that might be settled *a priori*. Two further subdivisions are useful. An *expressive relativist* holds that there is at least one assessment-indexical sentence, while a *propositional relativist* holds that there is at least one assessment-sensitive proposition. In what follows, I will focus on propositional relativism, which seems to me more promising in its applications.

II. WHAT DOES IT MEAN?

We have stated the relativist's thesis. But do we really understand it? We cannot understand it unless we grasp what is meant by 'true at context of use C_U and context of assessment C_A,' and it is not clear that we do. For it is not clear that the concept of truth *admits* of relativization to assessors. If 'true' as it occurs in 'true for X' is just the ordinary, non-relative truth predicate, then it is unclear what 'for X' adds, unless it is just 'and X believes this.' On the other hand, if the occurrence of 'true' in 'true for X' is like the 'cat' in 'cattle,' then the relativist needs to explain what 'true for X' means and what it has to do with truth, as ordinarily conceived.[11]

Relativists often try to meet this challenge by giving a *definition* of truth that makes its relativity plain. If truth is idealized justification, then it might reasonably be thought to be assessor-relative, since ideal reasoners with different starting beliefs or prior probabilities might take the same ideal body of evidence to support different conclusions. Similarly, if truth is defined pragmatically, as what is good to believe, then it might also be assessor-relative, insofar as different things are good for different assessors to believe. But although these coherentist and pragmatic definitions of truth capture the 'relative' part of 'relative truth,' I do not believe they capture the 'truth' part. Indeed, for familiar reasons, I doubt that the concept of truth can be usefully illuminated by a definition in terms of more primitive concepts.[12]

Of course, the relativist semanticist can give a formal definition of 'true at context of use C_U and context of assessment C_A' that fixes its extension over a particular class of sentences and contexts. But such a definition would not answer the challenge, for reasons Michael Dummett made clear in his classic paper "Truth."[13] Dummett pointed out that a set of T-biconditionals or a recursive definition of 'true in *L*' cannot simultaneously explain the meanings of the expressions of *L and* the meaning of 'true in *L*.' Thus, if our aim is to explain the meanings of expressions by showing how they contribute to the truth conditions of sentences containing them, we must have a grasp of the concept of truth that goes beyond what a Tarskian truth definition tells us. On Dummett's view, this grasp consists (at least in part) in our knowledge that the central convention governing the speech act of assertion is to assert only what is true.

Two things are worth noting here. First, if Dummett is right, then it is not just the relativist who owes an explication of the significance of her truth predicate. The absolutist owes one as well—at least if she is to use this predicate in semantics. Second, Dummett's proposed explication does not take the form of a definition. Instead, it is a description of the role 'true' plays in a broader theory of language use: specifically, an account of the speech act of assertion. These two points suggest a strategy for the relativist: start with such an explication of truth (one that is acceptable to the non-relativist), then find a job for contexts of assessment in this framework. Having done this, the relativist should be able to say to the absolutist: "If you can make sense of your absolute truth predicate, you should be able to make sense of my relative one, too, and to see why it deserves to be called a *truth* predicate."

The strategy is, I think, a promising one. But if we try to execute it by generalizing Dummett's explication of truth as the conventional aim of assertion, we immediately run into difficulties—difficulties that may explain why so many philosophers have dismissed relative truth as unintelligible. There are three ways in which we might connect the aim of assertion with doubly contextual truth:

(1) *Relativize the aim of assertion to contexts of assessment*: Relative to context C_A, assertion is governed by the convention that one should assert at context C_U only what is true relative to context of use C_U and context of assessment C_A.

(2) *Quantify over contexts*: One should assert at C_U only what is true at context of use C_U and *some/most/all* contexts of assessment C_A.

(3) *Privilege one context of assessment* (the one occupied by the asserter at the moment of utterance): One should assert at C_U only what is true at context of use C_U and context of assessment C_U.

But none of these options will help us understand assessment-relative truth. Option (1) just replaces one unexplicated relativization with another. Conventions supervene on patterns of mutual belief and expectation among the participants in a practice.[14] So the only way conventions can be assessment-relative is if facts about the participants' mental states are assessment-relative. An explication of assessment-relative truth that presupposes an understanding of assessment-relative *facts* is not going to get us very far.

Option (2) is at least intelligible, but it does not serve the relativist's purposes. It is too easy to assert something that is true at *some* context of assessment, and if we require truth at *every* context of assessment, the resulting norm will forbid asserting *anything* assessment-sensitive. 'Most' seems the best choice of quantifier, but there is something arbitrary about it; majority rule looks misplaced here. Nor is it clear what 'most' means in this context, if, as seems likely, there are infinitely many possible contexts of assessment. More seriously, option (2) leaves room for the anti-relativist to respond by saying:

What you call 'truth at some/all/most contexts of assessment' and identify with the aim of assertion is what I call 'truth (*simpliciter*).' But I fail to see what you mean by 'true at context of assessment C.' Suppose there are only three possible contexts of assessment: C_1, C_2, and C_3. What is the practical difference between being true at C_1 and C_2 but not C_3 and being true at C_2 and C_3 but not C_1? Nothing you have said discriminates between these possibilities, so I still lack any understanding of the difference.

Option (3) is the choice of most relativists who have considered the matter at all.[15] If a single context of assessment is to be privileged as that relative to which one should assert only truths, it seems reasonable that it should be the context one occupies when making the assertion. But a version of the previous objection applies here as well. Option (3) gives a significance to 'true at context of use C_U and context of assessment C_A' only for the special case where $C_U = C_A$, and not for arbitrary C_U and C_A. As a result, it cannot help us to understand assessment sensitivity. Suppose two rival semantic theories, T_1 and T_2, agree about the truth-value of S at a context of use C_U and context of assessment C_A whenever

$C_U = C_A$, but disagree about the truth-value of *S* at C_U and C_A for at least some context pairs such that $C_U = C_A$. According to T_1, *S* is assessment-sensitive, while according to T_2, it is not (figure 7.1).

The relativist ought to have something to say about how these theories differ from each other in practice and how one might decide between them. But if all we're told is that the aim of assertion is to assert something that is true as assessed from the context of use, we cannot discern any practical difference between T_1 and T_2.

It might be protested that although the difference between T_1 and T_2 does not manifest itself as a difference in the norms for asserting *S*, it manifests itself as a difference in the norms for asserting that particular utterances of *S* are 'true.' For example, T_1 and T_2 disagree about whether it would be correct for a speaker at context C_1 to call an utterance of *S* at C_3 'true.' But this reply puts the cart before the horse. It is important to distinguish the monadic predicate 'true,' which is just another word in the language being studied, from the three-place predicate 'true at context of use ... and context of assessment,' which the semanticist uses in describing the language. It would be mad to explain the main semantic predicate in our meta-language by appealing to the use of an *object-language* expression whose meaning we are describing using that very predicate. And what happens if the language we are studying does not contain 'true' or its equialent? Do we then lose our grip on the significance of relative-truth ascriptions?[16]

I think we must conclude that there is no prospect of generalizing the Dummettian conception of truth as the aim of assertion in a way that makes assessment-relative truth intelligible. But it would be too hasty to conclude from this that relative truth talk is incoherent. We have only explored one approach to explicating truth talk (Dummett's), and we might reject this approach for reasons that have

T_1

	$C_A =$		
	C_1	C_2	C_3
$C_U =$ C_1	*T*	*T*	*F*
$C_U =$ C_2	*T*	*T*	*F*
$C_U =$ C_3	*T*	*F*	*F*

T_2

	$C_A =$		
	C_1	C_2	C_3
$C_U =$ C_1	*T*	*T*	*T*
$C_U =$ C_2	*T*	*T*	*T*
$C_U =$ C_3	*F*	*F*	*F*

Figure 7.1. T_1 and T_2.

nothing to do with assessment sensitivity. After all, truth is not the *only* thing we are conventionally understood to be aiming at in making assertions. We also expect assertions to be warranted by what the asserter knows and relevant to the conversational setting in which they occur. Moreover, we expect asserters to be sincere: to assert only what they believe. So truth can hardly be singled out as *the* conventional aim of assertion. It is not even obvious that it is *a* conventional aim of assertion. An insincere assertion that happens to be true seems a more flagrant violation of the norms for assertion than a sincere (and warranted) one that happens to be false. Perhaps assertion aims at truth only indirectly, by aiming at the sincere expression of *belief*, which aims in turn at truth.

The claim that belief 'constitutively' aims at truth is on firmer ground: it is arguable that a cognitive state that did not aim at truth would not count as a belief at all.[17] We might accordingly try to understand truth as the condition for the correctness of beliefs. The problem is that (as with assertions) there are many dimensions along which beliefs might be assessed as correct or incorrect. If you have patiently gathered the evidence and it overwhelmingly favors not-*p*, there is an important sense in which it would be incorrect for you to believe that *p*, even if *p* happens to be true. But there is also a sense in which your belief that *p* would be correct. One might try to distinguish the two senses of correctness at issue here— perhaps as 'subjective' and 'objective,' or as 'epistemic' and 'representational,'—but it is hard to see how this could be done without invoking the notion of truth. It seems unlikely, then, that one could get a grip on the concept of truth just by being told that truth is the aim of belief, or the norm for correct belief.

How, then, *should* we understand the significance of truth talk in semantic theorizing? I think Dummett is right that our grip on truth comes from an understanding of its relation to assertion. But where Dummett focused on the norms *for* making an assertion, I propose we focus on the normative *consequences* of making an assertion. An assertion (even an insincere one) is a *commitment to the truth* of the proposition asserted.[18] It might be thought that this idea is just as inimical to relative truth as Dummett's. Just as it doesn't make sense to aim to speak truth if truth is relative, so (one might suppose) it doesn't make sense to commit oneself to the truth of a proposition if truth is relative.[19] But that's not clear—partly because it's not clear what it *means* to be committed to the truth of a proposition. How, exactly, does one honor or violate such a commitment? What is one committed to *doing*? I want to suggest that when this is spelled out in a plausible way, we can make very good sense of 'commitment to truth' even if truth is assessment-relative.

Here are three things that might be thought to constitute the 'commitment to truth' one undertakes in making an assertion:

(W) Commitment to withdraw the assertion if and when it is shown to have been untrue.

(J) Commitment to justify the assertion (provide grounds for its truth) if and when it is appropriately challenged.

(R) Commitment to be held responsible if someone else acts on or reasons from what is asserted, and it proves to have been untrue.

Everyone should be able to agree that assertoric commitment includes at least (W). Imagine someone saying: "I concede that what I asserted wasn't true, but I stand by what I said anyway." We would have a very difficult time taking such a person seriously as an asserter. If she continued to manifest this kind of indifference to established truth, we would stop regarding the noises coming out of her mouth as assertions. We might continue to regard them as expressions of beliefs and other attitudes (just as we might regard a dog's whining as an expression of a desire for food). We might even find them useful sources of information. But we would not regard them as commitments to truth, and hence not as assertions.

There will be less agreement about (J). Brandom has argued that assertoric commitment includes (J) as well as (W),[20] but this may be over-generalizing from seminar-room assertions to assertions in general. Suppose someone were to say: "You've given some very good reasons to doubt the truth of what I asserted. I have nothing to say in answer to your objections, yet I continue to stand by my claim." She would not be playing the game of assertion the way philosophers play it, but perhaps philosophers do not get to set the rules here. We would surely take her assertions less seriously than we would if she were responsive to reasons. But would we cease treating her as an asserter at all? That is not so clear.

What about (R)? Asserting is a bit like *giving one's word* that something is so, and our reactions to assertions that turn out to have been untrue can resemble our reactions to broken promises. We feel a legitimate sense of grievance, especially if we have acted on what we were told. Suppose someone tells you that there will be a talk by an interesting celebrity at a nearby university. You cancel some appointments and spend considerable time and energy getting there—but there is no talk. You expect that when you confront your informant, she will apologize profusely. Even if she has an excuse (perhaps there was a typo in the schedule), she will accept some measure of responsibility. You will be shocked if she says: "You actually *acted* on my assertion? Well, that's not my problem. It's up to *you* to sort out what's worth taking seriously." But why does this response sound so wrong? After all, it *is* up to us whether to believe what we are told, and we don't expect our informants to be infallible. A plausible answer (though not the only one) is that part of what it is to make an assertion is to accept partial responsibility for the accuracy of what one says.

Suppose we understand the assertoric 'commitment to truth' in terms of some combination of (W), (J), and (R). Can we understand what it would be to commit oneself to the truth of an assessment-sensitive proposition? That is, can we find plausible construals of (W), (J), and (R) in a framework that relativizes truth to contexts of assessment as well as contexts of use?

(W) talks of the asserted proposition being 'shown to have been untrue.' Untrue, relative to which context of use and context of assessment? The relevant context of use is obviously the context in which the proposition was asserted. But what about the context of assessment? There are four natural options:

(1) Quantify over contexts of assessment: the proposition must be shown to be untrue relative to the context of use and *some/all/most* contexts of assessment.

(2) The relevant context of assessment is the context in which the proposition was asserted (= the context of use).

(3) The relevant context of assessment is the context in which the putative refutation is being given.

(4) The relevant context of assessment is the context in which the asserter is evaluating the putative refutation.

It should be plain from our parallel discussion of the aim of assertion that the first two options will not help make sense of assessment sensitivity. They imply that for any given assessment-sensitive proposition, there will be a systematically related assessment-invariant proposition whose assertion results in exactly the same commitments. But unless we can see some difference in practice between asserting an assessment-sensitive proposition and asserting a related assessment-invariant one, we lack a real understanding of assessment sensitivity.

Only the third and fourth options give an essential and ineliminable role to contexts of assessment. They differ on what a successful refutation must establish: while the fourth option demands proven untruth relative to the *asserter's* context, the third looks to the *challenger's* context. The third option can be ruled out, I think, as too damaging to the integrity of a single person's body of assertions. If I withdraw some of my assertions because they are untrue relative to Bob's context and others because they are untrue relative to Marie's, I may end up with a body of assertions that is incoherent and reflects no one's point of view. This would be a bit like letting a bush be pruned by several gardeners with radically different conceptions of how it should look: the little that remained would not satisfy any of them. It demands too much of asserters to give every challenger the home stadium advantage.

I conclude that the relativist should construe (W) along the lines of the fourth option, which privileges contexts the asserter occupies, while still allowing the relevant context of assessment to diverge from the context of use:

(W*) In asserting that p at C_1, one commits oneself to withdrawing the assertion (in any future context C_2) if p is shown to be untrue relative to context of use C_1 and context of assessment C_2.

There should be no worries about the intelligibility of (W*). Logically, it is no more complex than a commitment to refill the pitcher (at any future time t) if it is shown to be empty (at t). And it reduces to the original (W) when p is not assessment-sensitive.

It should now be clear how we must generalize (J). Since (W*) requires that an assertion be withdrawn when it is proven untrue relative to the asserter's current context of assessment, the justification demanded by (J*) must consist in grounds for the truth of the asserted proposition relative to this same context:

(J*) In asserting that p at C_1, one commits oneself to justifying the assertion when the assertion is appropriately challenged. To justify the assertion in a context C_2 is to provide grounds for the truth of p relative to context of use C_1 and context of assessment C_2.

For similar reasons, we must construe (R) as follows:

(R*) In asserting that p at C_1, one commits oneself to accepting responsibility (at any future context C_2) if on the basis of this assertion someone else takes p to be true (relative to context of use C_1 and context of assessment C_2) and it proves to be untrue (relative to C_1 and C_2).

Let's take stock. We began with the worry that we did not really *understand* the relativist's doubly contextual truth predicate, 'true at context of use C_U and context of assessment C_A.' To assuage this worry, we decided, it would not be necessary to give an informative definition of this predicate in conceptually simpler terms (since not even the absolutist can do *that*): it would be enough to describe the predicate's role in a larger theory of meaning. We have now done just this. We have given an account of assertoric commitment that settles just what one is committing oneself to in asserting an assessment-sensitive proposition. By doing this, I suggest, we have made relativism about truth intelligible.[21]

But is relativism *true*? The weakest relativist position we distinguished in Section I was the claim that there is at least one assessment-sensitive sentence in some conceivable language. We have already said enough to vindicate this claim. We can certainly imagine a language in which the word 'beautiful' works as described by the aesthetic relativist (from Section I): just imagine that its speakers use sentences containing 'beautiful' to undertake the commitments implied by (W*), (J*), and (R*), together with the relativist's semantics. (Some philosophers may hold that English is such a language.) Even if you think it would be rash or irresponsible to undertake such open-ended commitments, it seems at least conceivable that speakers might do so, and that they might have a conventional linguistic way of doing so. So the weakest form of relativism about truth would seem to be true.[22]

A stronger, more interesting thesis is that some of the things *we* say and think are assessment-sensitive. We have not established that, but we have at least shown what such a claim would imply and what evidence might count for or against it. To defend an assessment-sensitive semantics for a particular class of sentences, one would have to adduce evidence about the norms for defending and withdrawing assertions made using those sentences. I think that quite a good case can be made for the assessment sensitivity of the future tense, epistemic modals, knowledge attributions, predicates of personal taste, and other constructions, but I cannot argue that here.[23]

NOTES

I am grateful to audiences at Harvard, Princeton, Santa Barbara, and San Diego for useful feedback on ancestors of this paper. This research was supported in part by an ACLS/Andrew W. Mellon Fellowship for Junior Faculty and a University of California at Berkeley Humanities Research Fellowship.

1. D. Kaplan, "Demonstratives: An Essay on the Semantics, Logic, Metaphysics, and Epistemology of Demonstratives and Other Indexicals," in *Themes from Kaplan*, ed. J. Almog, J. Perry, and H. Wettstein (Oxford: Oxford University Press, 1989).

2. Y. Bar-Hillel, "Primary Truth Bearers," *Dialectica* 27 (1973): 303–312, esp. 304.

3. M. Kölbel, *Truth Without Objectivity* (London: Routledge, 2002), 119.

4. For recent discussions of what is at stake in choosing between these alternatives, see M. Richard, introduction to Part I, and N. Salmon, "Tense and Intension," in *Time, Tense, and Reference*, ed. A. Jokić and Q. Smith (Cambridge, Mass.: MIT Press, 2003); and Jeffrey C. King, "Tense, Modality, and Semantic Value," *Philosophical Perspectives* 17 (2003): 195–245. The debate turns on the logic of propositional attitude reports and on the proper treatment of tenses and expressions like 'strictly speaking,' not on issues concerning relativism.

5. For this kind of response, see R. Nozick, *Invariances: The Structure of the Objective World* (Cambridge, Mass.: Harvard University Press, 2001), 19, 307n.7.

6. Kaplan, "Demonstratives," 502–504.

7. There are worlds in which sentences orthographically identical with (2) have completely different meanings, or no meanings at all. But when we ask what proposition a sentence expresses relative to a context of use, we are asking about the sentence with its actual meaning.

8. Kaplan, "Demonstratives," 522; for a formal version, see 547.

9. Distinguishing these two roles for context helps illuminate what is at stake in the debate between 'eternalists' (like Salmon and Richard) and 'temporalists' (like Kaplan). The issue is whether the time of utterance affects the truth values of tensed sentences in the first way (by determining which proposition is expressed) or the second (by determining how it is to be evaluated).

10. This assumes that a context of use and context of assessment will always determine a unique circumstance of evaluation. There are some semantic applications for which that restriction is too limiting. A more general formulation would replace 'the circumstances of evaluation determined by CU and CA' with 'all the circumstances of evaluation compatible with CU and CA.'

11. J. Meiland, "Concepts of Relative Truth," *The Monist* 60 (1977): 568–582. Meiland's own explication of 'true for X' as 'corresponds to reality for X' just pushes the problem back a level. The absolutist can object that her understanding of 'correspondence to reality' leaves no room for an added 'for X.'

12. D. Davidson, "The Folly of Trying to Define Truth," *Journal of Philosophy* 94 (1997): 263–278.

13. M. Dummett, "Truth" (1959), in *Truth and Other Enigmas* (London: Duckworth, 1978).

14. D. Lewis, *Convention* (Cambridge, Mass.: Harvard University Press, 1969).

15. Kölbel, *Truth Without Objectivity*, 125; A. Egan, J. Hawthorne, and B. Weatherson, "Epistemic Modals in Context," in *Contextualism in Philosophy: Knowledge, Meaning, and Truth*, ed. G. Preyer and P. Peter (Oxford: Oxford University Press, 2005).

16. M. Dummett, *Frege: Philosophy of Language*, 2nd ed. (Cambridge, Mass.: Harvard University Press, 1981), 320–321. The issues here are subtle, in part because in a language that contains any assessment-sensitive expressions, the predicate 'true' must also be assessment-sensitive.

17. B. Williams, "Deciding to Believe," in *Problems of the Self* (Cambridge: Cambridge University Press, 1973).

18. See, for example, J. R. Searle, *Expression and Meaning* (Cambridge: Cambridge University Press, 1979), 12, though the idea is ubiquitous.

19. M. F. Burnyeat argues that the Protagorean relativist is thwarted by "the commitment to truth absolute which is bound up with the very act of assertion" ("Protagoras and Self-Refutation in Plato's *Theaetetus*," *Philosophical Review* 85 [1976]: 172–195, esp. 195).

20. R. Brandom, "Asserting," *Noûs* 17 (1983): 637–650, and *Making It Explicit: Reasoning, Representing, and Discursive Commitment* (Cambridge, Mass.: Harvard University Press, 1994).

21. Once we have come to understand the relativist's doubly contextual truth predicate through reflection on its connection with assertion, we can employ it in our theories of the propositional attitudes and speech acts other than assertion without worrying that our use of it is completely unconstrained.

22. There are no worries about self-refutation here, because we may suppose ourselves to be describing the 'relativistic' language in a meta-language devoid of assessment sensitivity.

23. For some arguments, see Kölbel, *Truth Without Objectivity*, and "Faultless Disagreement," *Proceedings of the Aristotelian Society* 104 (2004): 53–73; J. MacFarlane, "Future Contingents and Relative Truth," *Philosophical Quarterly* 53 (2003): 321–336, and "The Assessment Sensitivity of Knowledge Attributions," in *Oxford Studies in Epistemology*, ed. Tamar Szabó Gendler and John Hawthorne (Oxford: Oxford University Press, 2005); M. Richard, "Contextualism and Relativism," *Philosophical Studies* 119 (2004): 215–242; and Egan, Hawthorne, and Weatherson, "Epistemic Modals in Context."

On the Very Idea of a Conceptual Scheme

8

DONALD DAVIDSON

Philosophers of many persuasions are prone to talk of conceptual schemes. Conceptual schemes, we are told, are ways of organizing experience; they are systems of categories that give form to the data of sensation; they are points of view from which individuals, cultures, or periods survey the passing scene. There may be no translating from one scheme to another, in which case the beliefs, desires, hopes and bits of knowledge that characterize one person have no true counterparts for the subscriber to another scheme. Reality itself is relative to a scheme: what counts as real in one system may not in another.

Even those thinkers who are certain there is only one conceptual scheme are in the sway of the scheme concept; even monotheists have religion. And when someone sets out to describe 'our conceptual scheme,' his homey task assumes, if we take him literally, that there might be rival systems.

Conceptual relativism is a heady and exotic doctrine, or would be if we could make good sense of it. The trouble is, as so often in philosophy, it is hard to improve intelligibility while retaining the excitement. At any rate, that is what I shall argue.

Originally published as Donald Davidson, "On the Very Idea of a Conceptual Scheme," *Proceedings and Addresses of the American Philosophical Association* 47 (1973–1974): 5–20, copyright granted by American Philosophical Association, all rights reserved.

We are encouraged to imagine we understand massive conceptual change or profound contrasts by legitimate examples of a familiar sort. Sometimes an idea, like that of simultaneity as defined in relativity theory, is so important that, with its addition, a whole department of science takes on a new look. Sometimes revisions in the list of sentences held true in a discipline are so central that we may feel that the terms involved have changed their meanings. Languages that have evolved in distant times or places may differ extensively in their resources for dealing with one or another range of phenomena. What comes easily in one language may come hard in another, and this difference may echo significant dissimilarities in style and value.

But examples like these, impressive as they occasionally are, are not so extreme but that the changes and the contrasts can be explained and described using the equipment of a single language. Whorf, wanting to demonstrate that Hopi incorporates a metaphysics so alien to ours that Hopi and English cannot, as he puts it, 'be calibrated,' uses English to convey the contents of sample Hopi sentences. Kuhn is brilliant at saying what things were like before the revolution using—what else?—our post-revolutionary idiom. Quine gives us a feel for the 'preindividuative phase in the evolution of our conceptual scheme,' while Bergson tells us where we can go to get a view of a mountain undistorted by one or another provincial perspective.

The dominant metaphor of conceptual relativism, that of differing points of view, seems to betray an underlying paradox. Different points of view make sense, but only if there is a common coordinate system on which to plot them. Yet the existence of a common system belies the claim of dramatic incomparability. What we need, it seems to me, is some idea of the considerations that set the limits to conceptual contrast. There are extreme suppositions that founder on paradox or contradiction; there are modest examples we have no trouble understanding. What determines where we cross from the merely strange or novel to the absurd?

We may accept the doctrine that associates having a language with having a conceptual scheme. The relation may be supposed to be this: if conceptual schemes differ, so do languages. But speakers of different languages may share a conceptual scheme provided there is a way of translating one language into the other. Studying the criteria of translation is, therefore, a way of focussing on criteria of identity for conceptual schemes. If conceptual schemes are not associated with languages in this way, the original problem is needlessly doubled, for then we would have to imagine the mind, with its ordinary categories, operating with a language with *its* organizing structure. Under the circumstances, we would certainly want to ask who is to be master.

Alternatively, there is the idea that *any* language distorts reality, which implies that it is only wordlessly if at all that the mind comes to grips with things as they really are. This is to conceive language as an inert (though necessarily distorting) medium independent of the human agencies that employ it; a view of language that surely cannot be maintained. Yet if the mind can grapple without distortion with the real, the mind itself must be without categories and concepts. This featureless self is familiar from theories in quite different parts of the philosophical landscape. There are, for example, theories that make freedom consist in decisions taken apart from all desires, habits, and dispositions of the agent; and theories of knowledge that suggest that the mind can observe the totality of its own perceptions and ideas. In each case, the mind is divorced from the traits that constitute it; a familiar enough conclusion to certain lines of reasoning, as I said, but one that should always persuade us to reject the premises.

We may identify conceptual schemes with languages, then, or better, allowing for the possibility that more than one language may express the same scheme, sets of intertranslatable languages. Languages we will not think of as separable from souls; speaking a language is not a trait a man can lose while retaining the power of thought. So there is no chance that someone can take up a vantage point for comparing conceptual schemes by temporarily shedding his own. Can we then say that two people have different conceptual schemes if they speak languages that fail of intertranslatability?

In what follows, I consider two kinds of case that might be expected to arise: complete, and partial, failures of translatability. There would be complete failure if no significant range of sentences in one language could be translated into the other; there would be partial failure if some range could be translated and some range could not (I shall neglect possible asymmetries). My strategy will be to argue that we cannot make sense of total failure, and then to examine more briefly cases of partial failure.

First, then, the purported cases of complete failure. It is tempting to take a very short line indeed: nothing, it may be said, could count as evidence that some form of activity could not be interpreted in our language that was not at the same time evidence that that form of activity was not speech behavior. If this were right, we probably ought to hold that a form of activity that cannot be interpreted as language in our language is not speech behavior. Putting matters this way is unsatisfactory, however, for it comes to little more than making translatability into a familiar tongue a criterion of languagehood. As fiat, the thesis lacks the appeal of self-evidence; if it is a truth, as I think it is, it should emerge as the conclusion of an argument.

The credibility of the position is improved by reflection on the close relations between language and the attribution of attitudes such as belief, desire and intention. On the one hand, it is clear that speech requires a multitude of finely discriminated intentions and beliefs. A person who asserts that perseverance keeps honor bright must, for example, represent himself as believing that perseverance keeps honor bright, and he must intend to represent himself as believing it. On the other hand, it seems unlikely that we can intelligibly attribute attitudes as complex as these to a speaker unless we can translate his words into ours.

There can be no doubt that the relation between being able to translate someone's language and being able to describe his attitudes is very close. Still, until we can say more about *what* this relation is the case against untranslatable languages remains obscure.

It is sometimes thought that translatability into a familiar language, say English, cannot be a criterion of languagehood on the grounds that the relation of translatability is not transitive. The idea is that some language, say Saturnian, may be translatable into English, and some further language, like Plutonian, may be translatable into Saturnian, while Plutonian is not translatable into English. Enough translatable differences may add up to an untranslatable one. By imagining a sequence of languages, each close enough to the one before to be acceptably translated into it, we can imagine a language so different from English as to resist totally translation into it. Corresponding to this distant language would be a system of concepts altogether alien to us.

This exercise does not, I think, introduce any new element into the discussion. For we should have to ask how we recognized that what the Saturnian was doing was *translating* Plutonian (or anything else). The Saturnian speaker might tell us that that was what he was doing, or rather, we might for a moment assume that that was what he was telling us. But then it would occur to us to wonder whether our translations of Saturnian were correct.

According to Kuhn, scientists operating in different scientific traditions (within different 'paradigms') 'live in different worlds.' Strawson's *The Bounds of Sense* begins with the remark that "It is possible to imagine kinds of worlds very different from the world as we know it."[1] Since there is at most one world, these pluralities are metaphorical or merely imagined. The metaphors are, however, not at all the same. Strawson invites us to imagine possible non-actual worlds, worlds that might be described, using our present language, by redistributing truth values over sentences in various systematic ways. The clarity of the contrasts between worlds in this case depends on supposing our scheme of concepts, our descriptive resources, to remain fixed. Kuhn, on the other hand, wants us to think of different observers of the same world who come to it with incommensurable systems of concepts. Strawson's many imagined worlds are seen (or heard)—anyway described—from the same point of view; Kuhn's one world is seen from different points of view. It is the second metaphor we want to work on.

The first metaphor requires a distinction within language of concept and content: using a fixed system of concepts (words with fixed meanings) we describe alternative universes. Some sentences will be true simply because of the concepts or meanings involved, others because of the way of the world. In describing possible worlds, we play with sentences of the second kind only.

The second metaphor suggests instead a dualism of quite a different sort, a dualism of total scheme (or language) and uninterpreted content. Adherence to the second dualism, while not inconsistent with adherence to the first, may be encouraged by attacks on the first. Here is how it may work.

To give up the analytic-synthetic distinction as basic to the understanding of language is to give up the idea that we can clearly distinguish between theory and language. Meaning, as we might loosely use the word, is contaminated by theory, by what is held to be true. Feyerabend puts it this way:

> Our argument against meaning invariance is simple and clear. It proceeds from the fact that usually some of the principles involved in the determinations of the meanings of older theories or points of view are inconsistent with the new ... theories. It points out that it is natural to resolve this contradiction by eliminating the troublesome ... older principles, and to replace them by principles, or theorems, of a new ... theory. And it concludes by showing that such a procedure will also lead to the elimination of the old meanings.[2]

We may now seem to have a formula for generating distinct conceptual schemes. We get a new out of an old scheme when the speakers of a language come to accept as true an important range of sentences they previously took to be false (and, of course, vice versa). We must not describe this change simply as a matter of their coming to view old falsehoods as truths, for a truth is a proposition, and what they come to accept, in accepting a sentence as true, is not the same thing that they rejected when formerly they held the sentence to be false. A change has come over the meaning of the sentence because it now belongs to a new language.

This picture of how new (perhaps better) schemes result from new and better science is very much the picture philosophers of science, like Putnam, Feyerabend, and historians of science, like Kuhn, have painted for us. A related idea emerges in the suggestion of some other philosophers, that we could improve our conceptual lot if we were to tune our language to an improved science. Thus both Quine and Smart, in somewhat different ways, regretfully admit that our present ways of talking make a serious science of behavior impossible. (Wittgenstein and Ryle have said similar things without regret.) The cure, Quine and Smart think, is to change how we talk. Smart advocates (and predicts) the change in order to put us on the scientifically straight path of materialism; Quine is more concerned to clear the way for a purely extensional language. (Perhaps I should add that I think our *present* scheme and language are best understood as extensional and materialist.)

If we were to follow this advice, I do not, myself, think science or understanding would be advanced, though possibly morals would. But the present question is only whether, if such changes were to take place, we should be justified in calling them alterations in the basic conceptual apparatus. The difficulty in so calling them is easy to appreciate. Suppose that in my office of Minister of Scientific Language I want the new man to stop using words that refer, say, to emotions, feelings, thoughts and intentions, and to talk instead of the physiological states and happenings that are assumed to be more or less identical with the mental riff and raff. How do I tell whether my advice has been heeded if the new man speaks a new language? For all I know, the shiny new phrases, though stolen *from* the old language in which they refer to physiological stirrings, may in his mouth play the role of the messy old mental concepts.

The key phrase is: for all I know. What is clear is that retention of some or all of the old vocabulary in itself provides no basis for judging the new scheme to be the same as, or different from, the old. So what sounded at first like a thrilling discovery—that truth is relative to a conceptual scheme—has not so far been shown to be anything more than the pedestrian and familiar fact that the truth of a sentence is relative to (among other things) the language to which it belongs. Instead of living in different worlds, Kuhn's scientists may, like those who need Webster's dictionary, be only words apart.

Giving up the analytic-synthetic distinction has not proven a help in making sense of conceptual relativism. The analytic-synthetic distinction is, however, explained in terms of something that may serve to buttress conceptual relativism, namely the idea of empirical content. The dualism of the synthetic and the analytic is a dualism of sentences some of which are true (or false) both because of what they mean and because of their empirical content, while others are true (or false) by virtue of meaning alone, having no empirical content. If we give up the dualism, we abandon the conception of meaning that goes with it, but we do not have to abandon the idea of empirical content: we can hold, if we want, that *all* sentences have empirical content. Empirical content is, in turn, explained by reference to the facts, the world, experience, sensation, the totality of sensory stimuli, or something similar. Meanings gave us a way to talk about categories, the organizing structure of language, and so on; but it is possible, as we have seen, to give up meanings and analyticity while retaining the idea of language as embodying a conceptual scheme. Thus in place of the dualism of the analytic-synthetic we get the dualism of conceptual scheme and empirical content. The new dualism is the foundation of an empiricism shorn of the untenable dogmas of the analytic-synthetic distinction and reductionism shorn, that is, of the unworkable idea that we can uniquely allocate empirical content sentence by sentence.

I want to urge that this second dualism of scheme and content, of organizing system and something waiting to be organized, cannot be made intelligible and defensible. It is itself a dogma of empiricism, the third dogma. The third, and perhaps the last, for if we give it up it is not clear that there is anything distinctive left to call empiricism.

The scheme-content dualism has been formulated in many ways. Here are some examples. The first comes from Whorf, elaborating on a theme of Sapir's. Whorf says that:

> language produces an organization of experience. We are inclined to think of lan-
> guage simply as a technique of expression, and not to realize that language first of all
> is a classification and arrangement of the stream of sensory experience which results
> in a certain world-order.... In other words, language does in a cruder but also in
> a broader and more versatile way the same thing that science does.... We are thus
> introduced to a new principle of relativity, which holds that all observers are not
> led by the same physical evidence to the same picture of the universe unless their
> linguistic backgrounds are similar or can in some way be calibrated.[3]

Here we have all the required elements: language as the organizing force, not to be distinguished clearly from science; what is organized, referred to variously as 'experience,' 'the stream of sensory experience,' and 'physical evidence'; and finally, the failure of inter-translatability ('calibration'). The failure of inter-translatability is a necessary condition for difference of conceptual schemes; the common relation to experience or the evidence is what is supposed to help us make sense of the claim that it is languages or schemes that are under consideration when translation fails. It is essential to this idea that there be something neutral and common that lies outside all schemes. This common something cannot, of course, be the subject *matter* of contrasting languages, or translation would be possible. Thus Kuhn has recently written:

Philosophers have now abandoned hope of finding a pure sense-datum language ...
but many of them continue to assume that theories can be compared by recourse to a
basic vocabulary consisting entirely of words which are attached to nature in ways that
are unproblematic and, to the extent necessary, independent of theory ... Feyerabend
and I have argued at length that no such vocabulary is available. In the transition from
one theory to the next words change their meanings or conditions of applicability in
subtle ways. Though most of the same signs are used before and after a revolution e.g.
force, mass, element, compound, cell—the ways in which some of them attach to nature
has somehow changed. Successive theories are thus, we say, incommensurable.[4]

'Incommensurable' is, of course, Kuhn and Feyerabend's word for 'not intertranslatable.' The neutral content waiting to be organized is supplied by nature.

Feyerabend, himself, suggests that we may compare contrasting schemes by
"choosing a point of view outside the system or the language." He hopes we can
do this because "there is still human experience as an actually existing process"
independent of all schemes.[5]

The same, or similar, thoughts are expressed by Quine in many passages:
"The totality of our so-called knowledge or beliefs ... is a man-made fabric
which impinges on experience only along the edges.... total science is like a
field of force whose boundary conditions are experience.... As an empiricist I
... think of the conceptual scheme of science as a tool ... for predicting future
experience in the light of past experience."[6] And again:

We persist in breaking reality down somehow into a multiplicity of identifiable and
discriminable objects. ... We talk so inveterately of objects that to say we do so
seems almost to say nothing at all; for how else is there to talk? It is hard to say how
else there is to talk, not because our objectifying pattern is an invariably [sic] trait of
human nature, but because we are bound to adapt any alien pattern to our own in
the very process of understanding or translating the alien sentences.[7]

The test of difference remains failure or difficulty of translation, "to speak of that
remote medium as radically different from ours is to say no more than that the
translations do not come smoothly" (25). Yet the roughness may be so great that
the alien has an "as yet unimagined pattern beyond individuation" (24).

The idea is, then, that something is a language, and associated with a conceptual scheme, whether we can translate it or not, if it stands in a certain relation
(predicting, organizing, facing or fitting) to experience (nature, reality, sensory
promptings). The problem is to say what the relation is, and to be clearer about
the entities related.

The images and metaphors fall into two main groups: conceptual schemes (languages) either *organize* something, or they *fit* it (as in "he warps his scientific heritage to fit his ... sensory promptings").[8] The first group contains also *systematize, divide up* (the stream of experience); further examples of the second group are *predict, account for, face* (the tribunal of experience). As for the entities that get organized, or which the scheme must fit, I think again we may detect two main ideas: either it is reality (the universe, the world, nature), or it is experience (the passing show, surface irritations, sensory promptings, sense data, the given).

We cannot attach a clear meaning to the notion of organizing a single object (the world, nature, etc.) unless that object is understood to contain or consist in other objects. Someone who sets out to organize a closet arranges the things in it. If you are told not to organize the shoes and shirts, but the closet itself, you would be bewildered. How would you organize the Pacific Ocean? Straighten out its shores, perhaps, or relocate its islands, or destroy its fish.

A language may contain simple predicates whose extensions are matched by no simple predicates, or even by any predicates at all, in some other language. What enables us to make this point in particular cases is an ontology common to the two languages, with concepts that individuate the same objects. We can be clear about breakdowns in translation when they are local enough, for a background of generally successful translation provides what is needed to make the failures intelligible. But we were after larger game: we wanted to make sense of there being a language we could not translate at all. Or, to put the point differently, we were looking for a criterion of languagehood that did not depend on, or entail, translatability into a familiar idiom. I suggest that the image of organizing the closet of nature will not supply such a criterion.

How about the other kind of object, organizing it? Much the same difficulties recur. The notion of organization applies only to pluralities. But whatever plurality we take experience to consist in—events like losing a button or stubbing a toe, having a sensation of warmth or hearing an oboe—we will have to individuate according to familiar principles. A language that organizes *such* entities must be a language very like our own.

Experience (and its classmates like surface irritations, sensations and sense data) also makes another and more obvious trouble for the organizing idea. For how could something count as a language that organized *only* experiences, sensations, surface irritations or sense data? Surely, knives and forks, railroads and mountains, cabbages and kingdoms also need organizing.

This last remark will no doubt sound inappropriate as a response to the claim that a conceptual scheme is a way of coping with sensory experience; and

sentence to which we are strongly attached on a community basis, we may be tempted to call this a difference in schemes; if we decide to accommodate the evidence in other ways, it may be more natural to speak of a difference of opinion. But when others think differently from us, no general principle, or appeal to evidence, can force us to decide that the difference lies in our beliefs rather than in our concepts.

We must conclude, I think, that the attempt to give a solid meaning to the idea of conceptual relativism, and hence to the idea of a conceptual scheme, fares no better when based on partial failure of translation than when based on total failure. Given the underlying methodology of interpretation, we could not be in a position to judge that others had concepts or beliefs radically different from our own.

It would be wrong to summarize by saying we have shown how communication is possible between people who have different schemes, a way that works without need of what there cannot be, namely a neutral ground, or a common coordinate system. For we have found no intelligible basis on which it can be said that schemes are different. It would be equally wrong to announce the glorious news that all mankind—all speakers of language, at least—share a common scheme and ontology. For if we cannot intelligibly say that schemes are different, neither can we intelligibly say that they are one.

In giving up dependence on the concept of an uninterpreted reality, something outside all schemes and science, we do not relinquish the notion of objective truth—quite the contrary. Given the dogma of a dualism of scheme and reality, we get conceptual relativity, and truth relative to a scheme. Without the dogma, this kind of relativity goes by the board. Of course, truth of sentences remains relative to language, but that is as objective as can be. In giving up the dualism of scheme and world, we do not give up the world, but reestablish unmediated touch with the familiar objects whose antics make our sentences and opinions true or false.

NOTES

1. Peter Strawson, *The Bounds of Sense* (London: Methuen, 1966), 15.

2. Paul Feyerabend, "Explanation, Reduction, and Empiricism," in *Scientific Explanation, Space, and Time: Minnesota Studies in the Philosophy of Science*, ed. Herbert Feigl and Grover Maxwell (Minneapolis: University of Minnesota Press, 1962), 3:82.

3. Benjamin Lee Whorf, *Language, Thought, and Reality: Selected Writings of Benjamin Lee Whorf*, ed. J. B. Carroll (New York: Wiley, 1956), 55.

4. Thomas Kuhn, "Reflection on My Critics," in *Criticism and the Growth of Knowledge*, ed. I. Lakatos and A. Musgrave (Cambridge: Cambridge University Press, 1970), 266–267.

5. Paul Feyerabend, "Problems of Empiricism," in *Beyond the Edge of Certainty: Essays in Contemporary Science and Philosophy*, ed. R. G. Colodny and Norwood Russell Hanson (Englewood Cliffs, N.J.: Prentice Hall, 1965), 214.

6. W. V. O. Quine, "Two Dogmas of Empiricism," in *From a Logical Point of View: 9 Logico-Philosophical Essays* (Cambridge, Mass.: Harvard University Press, 1961), 42, 44.

7. W. V. O. Quine, "Speaking of Objects," in *Ontological Relativity, and Other Essays* (New York: Columbia University Press, 1969), 1.

8. Quine, "Two Dogmas of Empiricism," 46.

9. These remarks are defended in my "True to the Fact," in "Symposium: Truth, Sixty-Sixth Annual Meeting of the American Philosophical Association Eastern Division," *Journal of Philosophy* 66, no. 21 (1969): 748–764.

10. Alfred Tarski, "The Concept of Truth in Formalized Languages," in *Logic, Semantics, Metamathematics: Papers from 1923–1938* (Oxford: Clarendon Press, 1956).

On Davidson's Refutation of Conceptual Relativism

HILARY PUTNAM

The 'internal realism' I have defended[1] has both a positive and a negative side. Internal realism denies that there is a fact of the matter as to which of the conceptual schemes that serve us so well—the conceptual scheme of commonsense objects, with their vague identity conditions and their dispositional and counterfactual properties, or the scientific-philosophical scheme of fundamental particles and their 'aggregations' (i.e., their mereological sums)—is 'really true.' Each of these schemes contains, in its present form, bits that are 'true' (or 'right') and bits that will turn out to be 'wrong' in one way or another—bits that are right and wrong *by the standards appropriate to the scheme itself*—but the question "Which kind of 'true' is really Truth?" is one that internal realism rejects.

A simple example[2] will illustrate what I mean. Consider 'a world with three individuals (Carnap often used examples like this when we were doing inductive logic together in the early nineteen fifties), x_1, x_2, x_3.' How many *objects* are there in this world?

Reprinted from Hilary W. Putnam, "Truth and Convention: On Davidson's Refutation of Conceptual Relativism," in *Dialectica*, Volume 41, no. 1–2, pp. 69–77. Copyright, 1987, Blackwell Publishing Company. All rights reserved. Used by permission of the publisher.

Well, I *said* "consider a world with just three individuals" didn't I? So mustn't there be three objects? Can there be nonabstract entities, which are not 'individuals'?

One possible answer is "No." We can identify 'individual,' 'object,' 'particular,' and so on and find no absurdity in a world with just three objects which are independent, unrelated, 'logical atoms.' But there are perfectly good logical doctrines which lead to different results.

Suppose, for example, like some Polish logicians, I believe that for every two particulars there is an object which is their sum. (This is the basic assumption of 'mereology,' the calculus of parts and wholes invented by Lesniewski). If I ignore, for the moment, the so-called null object, then I will find that the world of 'three individuals' (as Carnap might have had it, at least when he was doing inductive logic) actually contains *seven* objects:

WORLD 1	WORLD 2
x_1, x_2, x_3	$x_1, x_2, x_3, x_1 + x_2$
	$x_1 + x_3, x_2 + x_3, x_1 + x_{2+3}$
(A world à la Carnap)	('Same' world à la Polish logician)

Some logicians (though not Lesniewski) would also say that there is a 'null object,' which they count as a part of every object. If we accepted this suggestion and added this individual (call it o), then we would say that Carnap's world contains *eight* objects.

Now the classic metaphysical realist way of dealing with such problems is well known. It is to say that there is a single world (think of this as a piece of dough) which we can slice into pieces in different ways. But this 'cookie-cutter' metaphor founders on the question "What are the 'parts' of this dough?" If the answer is that $x_1, x_2, x_3, x_1 + x_2, x_1 + x_3, x_2 + x_3, x_1 + x_{2+3}$ are all the different 'pieces,' then we have, not a *neutral* description, but rather a *partisan* description—just the description of the Warsaw logician! And it is no accident that metaphysical realism cannot really recognize the phenomenon of conceptual relativity—for that phenomenon turns on the fact that the *logical primitives themselves, and in particular the notions of object and existence, have a multitude of different uses rather than one absolute 'meaning.'*

An example, which is historically important, if more complex than the one just given, is the ancient dispute about the ontological status of the Euclidean plane. Imagine a Euclidean plane. Think of the points in the plane. Are these *parts* of the plane, as Leibniz thought? Or are they 'mere limits,' as Kant said?[3]

If you say, in *this* case, that these are 'two ways of slicing the same dough,' then you must admit that what is a *part* of space, in one version of the facts, is an abstract entity (say, a set of convergent spheres—although there is not, of course, a *unique way* of construing points as limits) in the other version. But then you will have conceded that which entities are 'abstract entities' and which are 'concrete objects,' at least, is version-relative. Metaphysical realists to this day continue to argue about whether points (space-time points, nowadays, rather than points in the plane or in three-dimensional space) are individuals or properties, particulars or mere limits, and so on. My view is that God himself, if he consented to answer the question "Do points really exist or are they mere limits?" would say, "I don't know"; not because his omniscience is limited, but because there is a limit to how far questions make sense.

One last point before I leave these examples: *given* a version, the question "How many objects are there?" has an answer, namely, "three" in the case of the first version ('Carnap's World') and "seven" in the case of the second version ('The Polish Logician's World'). Once we make clear how we are using 'object' (or 'exist'), the question "How many objects exist?" has an answer that is not at all a matter of 'convention.' That is why I say that this sort of example does not support cultural relativism. Of course, our concepts are culturally relative, but it does not follow that the truth or falsity of what we say using those concepts is simply 'determined' by the culture. But the idea that there is an Archimedean point (or a use of 'exist' inherent in the world itself) from which the question "How many objects *really* exist?" makes sense is an illusion.

Nor does it help, in general, to talk about 'meanings' or 'truth conditions.' Consider again the two sentences (I am referring to the same example as before):

(1) There is an object, which is partly red and partly black.
(2) There is an object, which is red, and an object, which is black.

Observe that (2) is a sentence, which is true in both the Carnapian and the Polish logician's version if, say, x_1 is red and x_2 is black. (1) is a sentence which is true in the Polish logician's version. What is its status in the Carnapian version?

Let me introduce an imaginary philosopher, whom I will call Prof. Antipode. Professor Antipode is violently opposed to Polish mereology. He talks like this:

I know what you are talking about if by an object you mean a car, or a bee, or a human being, or a book, or the Eiffel Tower. I even understand it if you refer to my nose or the hood of my car as 'an object.' But when philosophers say that there is an 'object' consisting of *the Eiffel Tower and my nose*, that is just plain crazy. There simply is no such object. Carnap was talking just fine when he said to you 'consider a world with just three objects'—I ignore Carnap's regrettable tendency to what he called 'tolerance'—and it is crazy to suppose that every finite universe contains all the objects those Poles would invent, or, if you please, 'postulate.' You cannot create objects by 'postulation' any more than you can bake a cake by 'postulation.'

Now, the language Carnap had in mind (we were working together on inductive logic at the time, and most often the languages we considered had only one-place predicates) probably did not contain a two-place predicate for the relation 'part of,' but even if it did, we can imagine Professor Antipode denying that there is any object of which x_1 and x_2 are both 'parts.' If there were such an object, "it would have to be different from both of them," he would say (and here the Polish logician would agree), "and the only object different from both of them in the world you showed us is x_3. But x_3 does not overlap with either x_1 or x_2. Only in the overheated imagination of the Polish logician is there such an additional object as $x_1 + x_2$." If we add 'Part Of' to Carnap's little language, so that sentence (1) can be expressed in it, thus:

(3) $(Ex)(Ey)(Ez)$ (y is Part Of x & z is Part Of x & Red(y) & Black(z)),

then, true to his anti-Polish form, Professor Antipode will say that this sentence is false. "Whether you say it in plain English or in fancy symbols," he growls, "if you have a world of three non-overlapping individuals, which is what Carnap described, and each is wholly red or wholly black, which is what Carnap said, then there cannot be such a thing in that world as an 'object which is partly red and partly black.' Talking about the 'mereological sum of x_1 and x_2,' makes no more sense than talking about 'the mereological sum of my nose and the Eiffel Tower.'"

Professor Antipode, it will be seen, is a staunch metaphysical realist. He *knows* that only some objects are parts of other objects, and that to say that for *every* pair of objects there is an object of which they both are parts (which is an axiom of mereology) is just 'rubbish.' (In the world Carnap imagined (1) is false and (2) is true, and there is the whole story.)

Carnap himself would have taken a very different attitude, Carnap was a conceptual relativist (that is, in part, what his famous Principle of Tolerance is all about), and he would have said that we can choose to make (1) false (that is, we can choose to talk the way Professor Antipode talks) *or* we can choose to make (1) true—to talk as the Polish logician talks. There is even—and this is very important—a way in which we can have the best of both worlds. We keep

Carnap's version as our official version (our 'unabbreviated language'); we refrain from adding Part Of as a new primitive, as we did before, but we introduce Part Of as a *defined* expression (as 'abbreviated language', or, as Quine often puts it, as a *façon de parler*). This can be done, not by giving an *explicit* definition of Part Of, but by giving a scheme which translates the Polish logician's language into Carnap's language (and such a scheme can easily be given in a recursive way, in the case of the kind of first order language with finitely many individuals that Carnap had in mind). Under such a scheme, (1) turns out to say no more and no less than (2).

To verify this, assuming that 'red' and 'black' are predicates of Carnap's language, observe that the only way a Polish logician's object—a mereological sum—can be partly red is by containing a red atom, and the only way it can be partly black is by containing a black atom. So if (1) is true in the Polish logician's language, then there is at least one red atom and at least one black atom—which is what (2) says in Carnap's language. Conversely, if there is at least one black atom and at least one red atom, then their mereological sum is an 'object' (in the Polish logician's sense) which is partly red and partly black.

While the formal possibility of doing this—of 'interpreting' the Polish logician's version in Carnap's version—is easy to establish as a result in mathematical logic, the philosophical significance of this fact, of the interpretability of the second language in the first, is more controversial. An objection—an objection to the idea that this kind of interpretability supports conceptual relativity in any way—might come from a philosopher who pursues what is called 'meaning theory.' Such a philosopher might ask, "What is the point of treating (1) as an abbreviation of (2) if it does not, in fact, have the same *meaning* as (2)?" Meaning theorists who follow Donald Davidson might argue that while (1) and (2) are 'mathematically equivalent' (if, like the Polish logician, and unlike Professor Antipode, we are willing to count the axioms of mereology as having the status of logical or mathematical truths), still, sentence (2) is not a sentence one would ordinarily offer as an explanation of the truth-conditions of sentence (1); or at least doing so would hardly be in accordance with what is called 'translation practice.' And a 'meaning theory,' it is said, must not correlate just *any* extensionally or even mathematically correct truth-conditions with the sentences of the language the theory describes; the sentence used to state a truth condition for a sentence must be one that might be correlated with that sentence by 'translation practice.' Whatever one is doing when one invents reductive definitions that enable one to explain away talk about 'suspicious' entities as a mere *façon de parler*, it obviously is not simply 'radical translation.'

One suggestion as to what one *is* doing comes from a classic article by Quine. In "On What There Is,"[4] he suggested that the stance to take in a case such as the one I have been describing—in a case in which one language seems more useful than another, because it countenances entities which (although philosophically 'suspicious') enable us to say various things in fewer words, and in which the at first blush 'richer' language is formally interpretable in the at first blush 'poorer' language—might be to say (a stance Professor Antipode might adopt):

> Sentence (1), asserting as it does the existence of mereological sums, is literally false. But if one wants to go on talking like the Polish logician while rejecting his undesirable ontological commitments, one can do that. One can responsibly take the view that the Polish logician's story is only a useful make-believe, and yet employ its idioms, on the ground that each of the sentences in that idiom, whatever its 'meaning,' *can* be regarded—by fiat, if you like—as merely a convenient abbreviation of whatever sentence in the 'unabbreviated language' it is correlated with be the interpretation scheme.

To give another example, one long familiar to students of mathematical philosophy, Frege and Russell showed that number theory is interpretable in set theory. This means that if one wants to avoid ontological commitments to 'unreduced numbers' (to numbers as objects over and above sets)—and if one does not mind commitment to *sets!*—one can treat every sentence of number theory, and, indeed, every sentence in the language which uses a number word, as a mere abbreviation for another sentence, one which quantifies over sets, but not over any such entities as 'numbers.' One need not claim that the sentence of number theory and its translation in set theory have the same 'meaning.' If they do not, so much the worse for our intuitive notion of a 'number'! What this kind of interpretation—call it *reductive interpretation*—provides is evidence against the real existence of the unreduced entities, as anything over and above the entities countenanced by the language to which we are doing the reducing. The moral we should draw from the work of Frege and Russell is not that there is a conceptual *choice* to be made between using a language which countenances only sets and one which countenances set *and* numbers, but that—unless the numbers are in fact identical with the set with which we identified them—there is no reason to believe in the existence of numbers. Talk of numbers is best treated as a mere *façon de parler.* Or so Quine maintains.

It is easy to see why Professor Antipode should like this line. In the case of the two versions we have been discussing, the reductive interpretation is syncategorematic, that is, it interprets sentence (1) (and likewise any other sentence of Carnap's language) as a whole but does not identify the individual words in (1) with individual words and phrases in (2); nor does it identify 'mereological sums' with any objects in the language to which the reducing is being done. (1), as a whole, is 'translated' by (2) as a whole, but the noun-phrase 'object which is partly red and partly black' has no translation by itself. In this case the moral of the translation—the moral if Professor Antipode imitates Quine's rhetoric—is slightly different. We cannot say *either mereological sums are identical with the entities with which we identified them or they do not really exist* (because the 'translation', or relative interpretation of the Polish logician's language in Carnap's language, did not identify 'mereological sums' with *anything*, it just showed how to translate sentences about them syncategorematically). The moral is rather, *mereological sums do not really exist, but it is sometimes useful to talk as if they existed.* Of course Professor Antipode would be delighted with *this* moral!

I do not mean to give the impression that the possibility of reducing entities away by a formal translation scheme is always decisive evidence that they do not really exist according to Quine. Sometimes we have the choice of either doing without one batch of entities, call them the *A* entities, or doing without another batch, call them the *B* entities—the reduction may be possible in either direction. In such a case, Occam's razor does not know who to shave! Or the reducing language may itself seem suspicious (some people think *sets* are very suspicious entities). But when the reducing language (the *prima facie* 'poorer' language) is one we are happy with, and the reduction does not go both ways, it is clear that Quine regards this as very strong evidence for denying the real existence of the unreduced entities.

Carnap, on the other hand, rejected the idea that there is 'evidence' against the 'existence' of numbers (or against the existence of numbers as objects distinct from sets). He would, I am sure, have similarly rejected the idea that there is evidence against the 'existence' of mereological sums. I know what he would have said about this question: he would have said that the question is one of a choice of a language. On some days it may be convenient to use what I have been calling 'Carnap's language' (although he would not have *objected* to the other language); on other days it may be convenient to use the Polish logician's language. For some purposes it may be convenient to regard the Polish logician's language of mereological sums as 'primitive notation', in other contexts it may be better to take Carnap's language as the primitive notation and to regard the Polish logician's language as 'abbreviations', or defined notation. And I agree with him.

It will be seen that there are a number of different stances one could take to the question of the *relation* between (1) and (2). One could say:

(a) The two sentences are mathematically equivalent.

(b) The two sentences are logically equivalent.

(c) The two sentences are neither logically nor mathematically equivalent.

(d) The first sentence is false and the second true (Professor Antipode's position).

(e) The two sentences are alike in truth, value, and meaning.

(f) The two sentences are alike in truth, value, and unlike in meaning.

(g) The second sentence can be used as an abbreviation of the first, but this is really just a useful 'make believe.'

My own position—and my own internal realism—is that there is no fact of the matter as to which of *these* positions is correct. Taking the original dispute up into the 'metalevel' and reformulating it as a dispute about the properties—mathematical or logical equivalence, synonymy, or whatever—of linguistic forms does not help. None of these notions is well defined enough to be a useful tool in such cases. Suppose, for example, I follow the apparently innocent route pioneered by Donald Davidson and say that the test for meaning is to see what we get when we construct a theory of language which is (1) recursively presented (in the style of a Tarskian truth-definition) and (2) in accord with translation practice. Obviously, I shall have to admit that it violates standard translation practice to give (2) as a translation of (1).[5] This settles the truth-value of (e) above: (e) is false whether the sentences be alike or unlike in truth-value, since they are not the same in meaning.

Suppose we follow Davidson farther and accept the central Davidsonian tenet that if I regard a sentence in an 'alien language' as meaningful (and I claim to know what it means), then I must be able to give (or would be able to give if I were sufficiently self-conscious about my knowledge) a *truth-condition* for that sentence in my 'own' language (one, which follows from a 'meaning theory', which is in conformity with the 'constraints on translation practice'). If my 'own' language is Carnap's, and we accept it that *no* 'truth-condition' for (1) stateable in Carnap's language will satisfy the constraints on translation practice any better than (2) did, then the conclusion is forced: the Polish logician's language is *meaningless*. We have arrived at a strong metaphysical result from what looked like a bit of ordinary language philosophizing (aided with a bit of Tarskian semantics) about the notion of 'meaning'!

Of course, we might simply adopt the Polish logician's language as our own language to begin with. But what we cannot do, according to Davidson, is regard both choices as genuinely open.

It seems to me that the very assumption that there is such a thing as the radical interpreter's 'own' language—one language in which he can give the truth conditions for *every* sentence in *every* language he claims to be able to understand—is what forces the conclusion. As long as one operates with this assumption, conceptual relativism will seem unintelligible (as it does to Davidson).[6] But if one recognizes that the radical interpreter himself may have more than one 'home' conceptual scheme, and that 'translation practice' may be governed by more than one set of constraints, then one sees that conceptual relativity does not disappear when we inquire into the 'meanings' of the various conceptual alternatives: it simply reproduces itself at a metalinguistic level!

NOTES

1. H. Putnam, *Reason, Truth, and History* (New York: Cambridge University Press, 1981).

2. This example comes from H. Putnam, *The Many Faces of Realism* (LaSalle, Ill.: Open Court, 1987).

3. "*Dem mathematischen Punkte, der einfach, aber kein Teil, sondern bloss die Grenze eines Raumes ist*" (*Kritik der rein en Vernunft*, B470); note also the flat statement "*Nun besteht der Raum nicht aus einfachen Teilen, sondern aus Raumen*" (ibid., B463). Both remarks occur on the 'Antithesis' side of the Second Antinomy.

4. W. V. Quine, "On What There Is," in *From a Logical Point of View* (Cambridge, Mass.: Harvard University Press, 1953).

5. For example, even the truth-functional connectives are not preserved if we 'translate' (1) as (2).

6. D. Davidson, "The Very Idea of a Conceptual Scheme," in *Truth and Interpretation* (Oxford: Oxford University Press, 1984) (this volume, chap. 8).

Conceptual Schemes | 10

SIMON BLACKBURN

We confront the idea of the Other: the person or persons whose minds are shaped so differently—by language, experience, culture or beliefs—that interpretation and understanding are baffled by them. Their entire way of thinking is different. The same stimuli provoke entirely different reactions. The world as they apprehend it is different from the world as we apprehend it. Here the 'diversity of subjectivities' [...] engulfs so much that mutual understanding is impossible. Their whole 'conceptual scheme' is different. Pessimists see this as bedeviling everyone, as in the Yorkshire saying, "All the world's queer except thee and me. And even thee's a little queer." Attempts to understand others, they say, are exercises of power: We impose upon Them. By interpreting them our way, we annex them, colonize them, trample on their difference, and force them into our own mould. Not so, reply optimists. We can join hands, find ourselves in them, obtain a 'fusion of horizons,' partake of a common humanity.[1]

Here, very clearly, a political edge creeps into our reflections. If we are pessimistic about mutual understanding, then divisions are inevitable, and we must contour our politics around them. Perhaps men cannot understand women, the

Reprinted from "Historians and Others," chap. 8, in *Truth: A Guide* (Oxford: Oxford University Press, 2005). By permission of Oxford University Press.

East cannot understand the West, and our period cannot understand any previous period. Perhaps classes can only fight, and we are left with a divisive, uncomprehending politics of identity. Nowhere is the immediate political and moral impact of ideas more obvious, or potentially more depressing.

Some help is to hand. In one of the most discussed papers in recent philosophy, a head-on attack on the relativist tradition from Protagoras to Immanuel Kant and Friedrich Nietzsche, Donald Davidson argued influentially that the kind of difference that is imagined here should not trouble us. The others are supposed not to share our 'conceptual scheme,' but, Davidson argued, the role allocated to conceptual schemes in these pessimistic scenarios is incoherent: "Conceptual relativism is a heady and exotic doctrine, or would be if we could make good sense of it. The trouble is, as so often in philosophy, it is hard to improve intelligibility while retaining the excitement."[2] Davidson points out that examples designed to soften us up to accept the idea of massive diversity are not all that compelling. The issue is one of translation, for, Davidson argues, the enterprise of understanding the thoughts of another is the same as the enterprise of finding our own words for those thoughts, or in other words translating the others' words into our own. But typically this goes well enough, for in spite of whatever differences we find, it turns out that we can say in our own terms what the others think. And, Davidson claims, this is not an accident for, when it comes to interpretation, "We cannot make sense of total failure." This brings him to the first statement of the argument: "It is tempting to take a very short line indeed: nothing, it may be said, could count as evidence that some form of activity could not be interpreted in our language that was not at the same time evidence that that form of activity was not speech behavior" (185).

This sounds shockingly complacent, and Davidson himself draws back a little "as fiat the thesis lacks the appeal of self-evidence." It certainly does. It sounds like the imposition of a kind of linguistic imperialism, whereby anything that cannot be said in late-twentieth-century American terms doesn't make sense at all. More precisely, we might worry about the implicit verificationism—the philosophically unpopular idea that possibilities that we cannot verify as obtaining cannot be real possibilities at all. And we might worry even more about the kind of verification that is demanded, namely translation back into our own language. For this to seem wholly arbitrary, we have only to consider the enterprise of learning to understand something or someone by expanding and changing our own conceptual repertoires. When someone joins a university physics department, he verifies that his teachers make sense not by translating what they say back into terms he brings with him, but by discovering new vocabularies, new theories and new ways of understanding the new phenomena to which he is also introduced.

Nevertheless, Davidson promises us an argument for his conclusion, and the subsequent pages of his paper are dense with points that build up to one. He supposes that when we talk of conceptual schemes, we picture a division between 'scheme and content.' The empirical content of a thought is explained by reference to "the facts, the world, experience, sensation, the totality of sensory stimuli, or something similar." And the 'scheme' is presented as the 'categories,' 'the organizing structure of language,' and so on. "I want to urge that this second dualism of scheme and content, of organizing system and something waiting to be organized, cannot be made intelligible and defensible. It is itself a dogma of empiricism ... perhaps the last, for if we give it up it is not clear that there is anything distinctive left to call empiricism" (189).

[Davidson] continues his assault on the idea of a conceptual scheme by showing that in the writings of many conceptual schemers the dominant metaphors fall into two distinct groups:

> conceptual schemes (languages) either *organize* something, or they *fit* it ... the first group contains also *systematize, divide up* (the stream of experience); further examples of the second group are *predict, account for, face* (the tribunal of experience). As for the entities that get organized, or which the scheme must fit, I think again we may detect two main ideas: either it is reality (the universe, the world, nature) or it is experience (the passing show, surface irritations, sensory promptings, sense data, the given). (191)

Davidson's plan is to undermine each metaphor. His first argument therefore is against the idea of a scheme 'organizing' experience. He reasonably points out that only pluralities (like the shoes in a closet) get organized: "If you were told not to organize the shoes and shirts, but the closet itself, you would be bewildered" (192). He concedes that a language may contain predicates (terms that apply to different things, such as common adjectives) that are not matched by those in another language, but points out that this possibility itself depends on there being enough in common between the two languages to make it clear that they are talking about the same things (they share an ontology, in philosophical jargon). You and I might organize the same closet differently, but we are each alike dealing with shoes and shirts.

If we turn to the idea of language organizing experience, the same point applies: "Whatever plurality we take experience to consist in—events like losing a button or stubbing a toe, having a sensation of warmth, or hearing an oboe—we will have to individuate according to familiar principles. A language that organizes *such* entities must be a language very like our own" (192).

He also dryly points out that language cannot be supposed *only* to organize experience (sensations, sense data, and so on). "Surely knives and forks, railroads and mountains, cabbages and kingdoms also need organizing."

Before evaluating this attack on the 'organizing' metaphor, we will briefly turn to the other prong, where Davidson attacks the idea of sentences of language 'fitting' things, or 'facing the tribunal of experience.' He urges, again reasonably, that what the metaphors in this group come down to is the idea of the sentences of a language being *true*. And then:

> Nothing, however, no *thing*, makes sentences and theories true: not experience, not surface irritations, not the world, can make a sentence true. *That* experience takes a certain course, that our skin is warmed or punctured, that the universe is finite, these facts, if we like to talk that way, make sentences and theories true. But this point is put better without mention of facts. The sentence "My skin is warm" is true if and only if my skin is warm. Here there is no reference to a fact, a world, an experience, or a piece of evidence. (194)

As far as this point goes, Davidson is at one with minimalism about truth. There is nothing general or abstract to say about truth. You give me a sentence, and provided it locates a definite issue, I will say what makes it true, but only in the very terms that the sentence provides, or more accurately, using a translation of them into my own language. There is no general answer to the question: what makes French sentences true? But if we are given an intelligible candidate, there will be an answer, only not one that refers to any of the grandiose notions whose use Davidson is attacking. What makes the French sentence "*La neige est blanche*" true? It is true if, and only if, snow is white.

Davidson claims that this much minimalism undermines any attempt to 'divorce' the notion of truth from the notion of translation.[3] It prevents us, he thinks, from making use of any notion of 'true but untranslatable.' Of course, in a particular context I may suppose some foreign sentence to be true although I cannot myself translate it. But I can envisage a translation, and only that would enable me to identify the content of the sentence, and thereby to tell what would count as its truth.

The scope and ambition of Davidson's paper are breathtaking, but is the attack on conceptual scheming actually as strong as it appears? There are several reasons for doubt. Perhaps the most obvious is that by attacking the utility of notions such as 'fitting experience' Davidson seems to detach language too far from the detailed, piecemeal procedures of verification that are part and parcel of our lives. He is eventually left only with the unconvincing substitute of covering our beliefs with a snowy mantle of truth, leaving their particular and individual footing in experience of no importance (hence the claim to have destroyed any final allure of empiricism).

And each side of the argument seems to have holes in it. First, conceptual schemers who emphasize the contingent factors that shape our minds need not by any means be wedded to the 'organize' metaphor. In fact, it is a particularly crude parody of their position; it indeed implies an underlying commonality, possession of the same experience, waiting like the same shoes in the closet, ready to be organized one way or another. But that is appropriate only for the Humean or Lockean theory, stuck with the Myth of the Given. PostKantian conceptual schemers are far more likely to use the different metaphor of our conceptual repertoire shaping or *molding* our experience, or in other words playing a role in determining the form it takes. Consider, for instance, the change that occurs when one begins to recognize patterns of speech in the hitherto chaotic noise of foreign talk, or begins to hear the melody in what was previously a welter of noise produced by a jazz musician. We should agree with Davidson that it is not appropriate to talk as if the experience before the change, and the experience after it, contain the same ingredients differently organized. But we should agree with conceptual schemers that there has been a change going right down to experience itself. Things sound different after the change. In these cases the change, it is true, is not really effected by shifts of language or theory. Fundamentally, it is experience that shapes experience. But that affords no argument that we must all have ended up in the same place, or even all ended up in some place from which we can, by ordinary processes of understanding, get to any other place. We can certainly hope to do so, but we may fail, just as some of us will never understand physics, or for that matter, jazz.

The other prong of Davidson's argument attempts to undermine conceptual scheming with thoughts drawn from minimalism about truth. But it is hard to see it as doing any better. We can accept the minimalist premise that no 'thing' makes sentences true, or perhaps more cautiously that it is philosophically useless to say that any 'thing' does, just as it may be harmless, but philosophically useless, to think of truth in terms of correspondence with the facts. It is also true, of course, that I cannot say what makes an alien sentence true unless I can say what it means. But neither of those points gets us near to denying the possibility of a massive dissociation between two minds, each of which has locked on to different versions of the world. To the conceptual schemer it is no objection that we cannot 'verify' what the alien is saying or which truths he may have cottoned on to; it is simply part of the position that this may be so.[4]

However, we can concede this much to Davidson: even if the bare possibility of untranslatable difference is left, there is not very much that we can actually do with it. Faced with more-or-less incomprehensible aliens, our only possible approach is to soldier on, doing what we can to share their perspective and to understand the world as they see it. If we seem unable to do so, it may be sad to reflect that we may never know whether it was their failure to manage any kind of thinking, or our failure to get on all fours with them, that was the problem. But we should not cheer ourselves up by a blithe certainty that it must have been the former.

NOTES

1. Optimists include Hans Georg Gadamer; pessimists look to Derrida or Foucault.

2. Donald Davidson, "On the Very Idea of a Conceptual Scheme," in *Inquiries into Truth and Interpretation*, 2nd ed. (Oxford: Oxford University Press, 2001), 183 (this volume, chap. 8).

3. I say 'this much minimalism' because officially Davidson denied that he was a minimalist. He shared a great deal with the idea, however, and at this point it is the overlap that matters.

4. I urge that Davidson may have misled himself here by a mistaken reading of Tarski, in Simon Blackburn, *Spreading the Word* (Oxford: Oxford University Press, 1984), chap. 7. Since the argument is somewhat technical, and subsidiary to the main theme of this chapter, I shall not repeat it here.

PAUL A. BOGHOSSIAN

I. RORTY'S RELATIVISTIC CONSTRUCTIVISM

With special reference to the problem of conceptual competence, Rorty writes:

> people like Goodman, Putnam and myself—people who think that there is no description-independent way the world is, no way it is under no description—keep being tempted to use Kantian form-matter metaphors. We are tempted to say that there were no objects before language shaped the raw material (a lot of ding-an-sichy, all content-and-no-scheme stuff). But as soon as we say anything like this we find ourselves accused (plausibly) of making the false causal claim that the invention of 'dinosaur' caused dinosaurs to come into existence—of being what our opponents call 'linguistic idealists'.[1]

If, however, we are not to understand the construction of facts on this Kantian cookie-cutter model, according to which our concepts cut boundaries into the

Reprinted from "Relativizing the Facts," *Fear of Knowledge: Against Relativism and Constructionism* (Oxford, Clarendon Press, 2006), pp. 42–57. By permission of Oxford University Press. (Footnotes have been converted to endnotes to provide consistency of format in the volume.)

'raw material' of the world, thereby causing there to be such things as dinosaurs, how then are we to understand it?

Here is what Rorty has to say (it will prove useful to quote him at some length):

> none of us anti-representationalists have ever doubted that most things in the universe are causally independent of us. What we question is whether they are representationally independent of us. For X to be representationally independent of us is for X to have an intrinsic feature (a feature that it has under any and every description) such that it is better described by some of our terms rather than others. Because we can see no way of deciding which descriptions of an object get at what is 'intrinsic' to it, as opposed to merely its 'relational', extrinsic features (e.g., its description-relative features), we are prepared to discard the intrinsic-extrinsic distinction, the claim that beliefs represent, and the whole question of representational independence or dependence. This means discarding the idea of (as Bernard Williams has put it) "how things are *anyway*," apart from whether or how they are described.
>
> [My critics seem] to think that neither I nor anyone else would feel any "serious temptation to deny that the claim . . . 'There are no chairs in this room' will be true or false in virtue of the way things are, or the nature of reality." But I do, in fact, feel tempted to deny this. I do so because I see two ways of interpreting 'in virtue of the way things are.' One is short for 'in virtue of the way our current descriptions of things are used and the causal interactions we have with those things.' The other is short for '*simply* in virtue of the way things are, quite apart from how we describe them.' On the first interpretation, I think that true propositions about the presence of chairs, the existence of neutrinos, the desirability of respect for the dignity of our fellow beings, *and everything else* are true 'in virtue of the way things are.' On the second interpretation, I think that *no* proposition is true 'in virtue of the way things are.' (86–87)

Although it is not easy to make sense of everything in this passage, the basic idea seems to be this.[2] On the cookie-cutter model, we literally make it the case that certain facts obtain that there are giraffes, for example—by describing the world in terms of the concept *giraffe*. But this is to buy in on the Kantian play with form and content and to court the problems about the relation between mind and reality outlined above.

The right way to think about the matter, rather, is to regard all talk about facts as just so much talk about how things are according to some theory of the world—or 'language game,' as Rorty sometimes puts it, using Wittgenstein's metaphor. No sense can be made of the idea that reality is a certain way in and of itself. And no sense can be made of the idea that the mind causes the world to be a certain way, through its use of descriptions. The only notion we can make sense of is that of the world's being a certain way *according* to some way of talking about it, *relative* to some theory of it.[3]

Now, we need to understand better this idea of a proposition's being true only relative to a theory, and not just true simpliciter, and we shall turn to that in a moment. But I think we are already in a position to see that, if Rorty's idea were cogent, it would help significantly with the three problems we outlined for fact-constructivism.

Suppose we may never claim that some propositions are simply true but only that they are true relative to this or that way of talking. The ways of talking themselves can't be said to be truer than one another, or more faithful to the way things are in and of themselves than one another, because there is no way things are in and of themselves. There is just one way of talking as opposed to another.

Does that imply that one can talk anyway one pleases, that there are no constraints on which descriptions of the world to adopt? Well, yes and no. Reality as it is in itself won't stand in the way of our talking one way as opposed to another, since there is no such thing as reality as it is in itself.

As Rorty explains, however, that does not mean that all ways of talking will be on a par; we will prefer some ways of talking to others, for pragmatic reasons. We will prefer some ways of talking to others because some of these ways will prove more *useful* to us in satisfying our needs. In ordinary life, when we simply claim something to be true, what we mean (or anyway ought to mean) is that it is true relative to *our* preferred way of talking, a way of talking that we will have adopted because it has come to seem so useful to us.

Now, notice that according to our way of talking, most aspects of the world are causally independent of us and antedate our existence. As Rorty puts it:

> Given that it pays to talk about mountains, as it certainly does, one of the obvious truths about mountains is that they were here before we talked about them. If you do not believe that, you probably do not know how to play the language games that employ the word 'mountain.' But the utility of those language games has nothing to do with the question of whether Reality-as-It-Is-in-Itself, apart from the way in which it is handy for human beings to describe it, has mountains in it.[4]

It is, therefore, correct, on Rorty's view, to say that we do not make the mountains and that they existed before we did; those are claims that are licensed by a way of talking that we have adopted. However, that does not mean that it is just plain true that there are mountains independently of humans; it never makes sense to say that anything is just plain true. All we can intelligibly talk about is what is true according to this or that way of talking, some of which it pays for us to adopt. That takes care of the problems of causation and conceptual competence.

It might help to understand Rorty's view here, by thinking of it on analogy with what we would say about truth in a fiction. We all know that the characters in a novel are constructions of the author. But within the novel, the characters are not thought of as being constructed (except possibly by their parents). They are thought of, rather, as real people, with real biological origins.

Thus, it is true, according to the fiction *The Amazing Adventures of Kavalier and Clay*, that Joseph Kavalier was a Jew who fled from Nazi-occupied Prague, and that his parents died at the hands of the Nazis.[5]

Similarly, the Rortian constructivist thinks that once we decide upon a given theory of the world that includes the description 'There are mountains' (as the author decides upon his various characters), it is true according to that theory that mountains are causally independent of us, and that they existed before we did.

Rorty's relativistic constructivism also provides a smooth solution to the problem of disagreement. Just as it can be true according to one fiction that P and true according to another fiction that not-P, so there is no difficulty accommodating the fact that it may pay for one community to, for example, affirm the existence of immaterial souls, and pay for another community to reject them. Since:

It's true according to C1's theory T1, that there are X's

in no way contradicts:

It's true according to C2's theory T2, that there are no X's,

the views are not in competition with each other and the problem of disagreement simply disappears.

Going relativistic, then, seems to help with all three of the seemingly insuperable problems we uncovered for fact-constructivism in the previous chapter. And it is hard to see what else could help. If fact-constructivism is to work at all, then, it looks as though it *has* to assume this relativistic Rortian form.

In particular, it looks as though there can be no solution to the problem of disagreement without resorting to relativization. This is a general lesson for constructivist views, even for those, unlike the one currently under discussion, which are restricted to local domains and are not meant to apply to all facts.

Take any unrelativized proposition P and any two communities C1 and C2. So long as the constructions in question are socially contingent, so that it is possible that C2 constructs the fact that not-P, even while C1 constructs the fact that P, there can be no question of our saying that C1 constructed the fact that P. Any such view would immediately violate the principle of non-contradiction. Rather, the most that any such constructivist view will be able to say is that C1 constructed the relativized fact:

According to C1: P

or something along similar lines.

Contemporary would-be constructivists, it seems to me, even those working within the analytic tradition, have paid insufficient attention to this point.[6]

II. RELATIVISMS LOCAL AND GLOBAL

Rorty's postmodernist brand of global relativism harks back to Protagoras' famous pronouncement: "Man is the measure of all things."[7] Historically, though, the most influential relativistic theses have been directed at *specific* domains, at truth in *morality*, for example, or *aesthetics*, or *etiquette*. It will prove useful to pause for a bit and examine how we should construe them.[8]

Take the important case of morality. Imagine Eliot uttering the sentence:

(1) "It was wrong of Ken to steal that money."

The moral relativist begins with the observation there are no facts in the world, which could make such an absolute judgment true. No act is ever simply morally right or morally wrong. Let us put this by saying that a moral relativist begins by endorsing the thesis of *moral non-absolutism*:
Moral Non-Absolutism:

(2) There are no absolute moral facts, which can confirm absolute moral judgments.

Now, any thinker who endorses moral non-absolutism faces a choice. He must say what he proposes to do about our ordinary moral utterances, given that he has come to endorse a view about them, which implies that all such utterances are uniformly false.

The response of the moral nihilist is to advocate abandoning moral discourse altogether. His view is that the discovery that there are no absolute facts of the required kind renders the discourse of morality useless, in much the way that one might think that the putative discovery that there is no God renders religious discourse irremediably useless.

The moral expressivist, on the other hand, attempts to hang onto moral discourse by attempting to construe moral utterances so that they are taken to express not judgments but rather the speaker's affective states of mind. Thus, a moral emotivist will construe Eliot's saying

"It was wrong of Ken to steal that money."

as saying roughly:

(3) "Boo, to Ken's stealing that money!"

Since saying Boo! to someone's doing something is not to say anything that could be either true or false, it no longer matters that there are no facts to validate the truth of moral utterances.

The moral relativist disagrees both with the moral nihilist and with the moral expressivist. By contrast with the moral nihilist, the moral relativist advocates retaining moral discourse; and by contrast with the moral expressivist, he advocates retaining the appearance that moral utterances express truth-apt judgments. His solution is to recommend that we so construe moral utterances that they report not on the sorts of absolute fact that have been conceded not to obtain, but on the sorts of *relational* fact that no one disputes. A reasonable first stab at formulating the relativist's recommendation might look something like this:

Moral Relationism (first stab):

If Eliot's moral judgment is to have any prospect of being true, we must not construe his utterance of:

"It was wrong of Ken to steal that money."

as expressing the claim:

"It was wrong of Ken to steal that money,"

but rather as expressing the claim:

(4) *"According to moral framework M, it was wrong of Ken to steal that money."*

This reasonable first stab must soon give way to a small but important modification. The point is that in making his utterance, Eliot was *endorsing* a view about

Ken's stealing that money, whereas a merely relational judgment like (4) is just a logical statement about the relation between the moral framework M and the judgment that it was wrong of Ken to steal that money. Even someone who disagreed with Eliot that it was wrong of Ken to steal that money could agree with (4).

To see that, consider George. George is not inclined to say that it was wrong of Ken to steal that money because George does not accept moral code M but rather a different moral code, M*, according to which it was not wrong of Ken to steal that money. Still, George could agree that, *according to M*, it was wrong of Ken to steal that money.

To accommodate this point, then, we must modify the relationist clause so that it makes reference to the speaker's *acceptance* of the particular moral framework to which he must, according to relativism, relativize his moral claims, thus:

Moral Relationism:

If Eliot's moral judgment is to have any prospect of being true, we must not construe his utterance of:

"It was wrong of Ken to steal that money."

as expressing the claim:

"*It was wrong of Ken to steal that money,*"

but rather as expressing the claim:

(5) "*According to moral framework M, that I, Eliot, accept, it was wrong of Ken to steal that money.*"

Finally, in order to emphasize that there is nothing that privileges any one of these moral frameworks over any of the others, the relativist typically adds a clause saying as much:

Moral Pluralism:

There are many alternative moral frameworks, but no facts by virtue of which one of them is more correct than any of the others.

Moral relativism, then, is the combination of moral non-absolutism, moral relationism and moral pluralism, all three theses now suitably generalized.

Moral Relativism

(6) There are no absolute moral facts which can confirm absolute moral judgments.

(7) If S's moral judgments are to have any prospect of being true, we must not construe his utterances of the form:

"It is wrong of P to A."

as expressing the claim:

"*It is wrong of P to A,*"

but rather as expressing the claim:

"*According to moral framework M, that I, S, accept, it is wrong of P to A.*"

(8) There are many alternative moral frameworks, but no facts by virtue of which one of them is more correct than any of the others.

Now, Rorty's global relativism is an attempt to generalize such a relativistic conception to *all* domains. As he puts it, there are many alternative schemes for describing the world, none of which can be said to be more faithful to the way things are in and of themselves, for there is no way things are in and of themselves.

Of course, some of these theories will be more useful to us than others, and so we will accept some but not others. Those that we accept will naturally be more salient to us as we make claims about the world. So we go around saying:

"There are giraffes"

not:

"There are giraffes according to a theory that we accept."

Nevertheless, it is not, and cannot, *simply* be true that there are giraffes (just as Rorty says that it cannot *simply* be true that there are chairs in this room); at best what's true is that there are giraffes according to a way of talking that we find it useful to accept.

Global Relativism about Facts:

(9) There are no absolute facts of the form, p.

(10) If our factual judgments are to have any prospect of being true, we must not construe utterances of the form:

$$\text{``}p\text{''}$$

as expressing the claim:

$$\text{``}p\text{''}$$

but rather as expressing the claim:

"According to a theory, T, that we accept, p."

(11) There are many alternative theories for describing the world, but no facts by virtue of which one is more faithful to the way things are in and of themselves than any of the others.

III. REJECTING GLOBAL RELATIVISM: THE TRADITIONAL ARGUMENT

Philosophers have long suspected that a global relativism about facts is a fundamentally incoherent position. A local relativism about a specific domain—moral relativism, for example—may not be particularly plausible; but it seems coherent. In contrast, many philosophers have held that a relativism gone global makes no sense. Why not?

The rough idea behind this oft-repeated traditional objection is that *any* relativistic thesis needs to commit itself to there being at least *some* absolute truths; yet what a global relativism asserts is that there are *no* absolute truths. Hence, a global relativism is bound to be incoherent.

I agree with this traditional objection—though I do not agree with the traditional argument by which it is defended.

The traditional argument is elegantly rendered by Thomas Nagel (Nagel uses the words 'subjective' and 'objective' in place of my 'relative' and 'absolute,' respectively):

the claim "Everything is subjective" must be nonsense, for it would itself have to be either subjective or objective. But it can't be objective, since in that case it would be false if true. And it can't be subjective, because then it would not rule out any objective claim, including the claim that it is objectively false. There may be some subjectivists, perhaps styling themselves as pragmatists, who present subjectivism as applying even to itself. But then it does not call for a reply, since it is a report of what the subjectivist finds it agreeable to say. If he also invites us to join him, we need not offer any reason for declining since he has offered us no reason to accept.[9]

According to this traditional argument, then, the global relativist is caught on the horns of a dilemma. Either he intends his own view to be absolutely true, or he intends it to be only relatively true, true relative to some theory or other. If the former, he refutes himself, for he would then have admitted at least one absolute truth. If the latter, we may just ignore him, for then it is just a report of what the relativist finds it agreeable to say.

Relativists are prone to dismissing self-refutation arguments of this sort as clever bits of logical trickery that have no real bearing on the issues at hand. That attitude, I think, is a mistake. It is always a good idea to ask how some very general view about truth, knowledge, or meaning applies to itself; and few things could be more damaging to a view than to discover that it is false *by its own lights*. Having said that, however, it has to be noted that it is not clear that this particular self-refutation argument is sound, for it is not clear that it follows from the concession that relativism is itself to be true only relative to a theory, that it is just a report of what the relativist 'finds it agreeable to say.' Perhaps relativism is true relative to a theory that it pays for us all to accept, relativists and non-relativists alike.

For this reason, then, I am not impressed with the traditional argument for the claim that global relativism is self-refuting. There is, however, a stronger argument to the same effect.

IV. REJECTING GLOBAL RELATIVISM: A DIFFERENT ARGUMENT

The global relativist maintains that there could be no facts of the form:

(12) There have been dinosaurs

but only facts of the form:

(13) According to a theory that we accept, there have been dinosaurs.

Well and good. But are we now supposed to think that there are absolute facts of this latter form, facts about which theories we accept?

There are three problems for the relativist who answers "yes" to this question. First, and most decisively, he would be abandoning any hope of expressing the view he wanted to express, namely that there are no absolute facts of any kind, but only relative facts. Instead, he would end up expressing the view that the only absolute facts there are, are facts about what theories different communities accept. He would be proposing, in other words, that the only absolute facts there are, are facts about our *beliefs*. And this would no longer be a global relativism.

Second, this would be a very peculiar view in its own right, for it's hard to believe that there is a difficulty about absolute facts concerning mountains and giraffes, but none concerning what beliefs people have. This seems to get things exactly the wrong way round. It is the mental that has always seemed most puzzling to philosophers, not the physical—so much so, indeed, that many of them have been driven to rejecting facts about the mental outright, eliminating them from their conception of what the world contains. Philosophers who advocate doing this are called 'eliminativists,' and it is perhaps just a little ironic that one of the most influential early eliminativists was Richard Rorty himself.[10]

Finally, the relativist is not driven to his position by the peculiar thought that facts about the mental are somehow in better shape than facts about the physical; if that were his motivation, he would owe us a very different sort of argument from the one to which he typically appeals. It would have to be an argument not about the mysteriousness of absolute facts as such, but about the mysteriousness of absolute facts about the physical in particular, in contrast with those concerning the mental. But that is not at all what the global relativist has in mind. His initial thought, rather, is that there is something incoherent about the very possibility of an absolute fact, whether this concerns physical facts or mental facts or normative facts.

It is, therefore, not really a viable option for the relativist to answer "yes" to the question we posed: are there absolute facts of the kind described in (13)? But what would it mean to answer "no"?

If it isn't simply true that we accept a theory according to which there have been dinosaurs, then that must be because that fact itself obtains only relative to a theory that we accept. So, the thought must be that the only facts there are, are of the form:

> According to a theory that we accept, there is a theory that we accept and according to this latter theory, there have been dinosaurs.

And, now, of course, the dialectic repeats itself. At each stage of the looming regress, the relativist will have to deny that the claim at that stage can be simply true and will have to insist that it itself is true only relative to a theory that we accept.

The upshot is that the fact-relativist is committed to the view that the only facts there are, are infinitary facts of the form:

> According to a theory that we accept, there is a theory that we accept and according to this latter theory, there is a theory that we accept and ... there have been dinosaurs.

But it is absurd to propose that, in order for our utterances to have any prospect of being true, what we must mean by them are infinitary propositions that we could neither express nor understand.

The real dilemma facing the global relativist, then, is this: either the formulation that he offers us does not succeed in expressing the view that there are only relative facts; or it consists in the claim that we should so reinterpret our utterances that they express infinitary propositions that we can neither express nor understand.

In a sense, this difficulty should have been obvious from the start. Our grip on relativistic views derives from our grip on local relativisms—relativistic views of such specific domains as the polite and the moral. Local relativisms, however, explicitly commit themselves to the existence of absolute truths: what they claim is that judgments in a given domain have to be relativized to a parameter if they are to have absolute truth conditions. Once they are so relativized, though, they then *do* have absolute truth conditions and so are capable of absolute truth or falsity. As a result, they do not offer us a model for how we might escape commitment to absolute truth as such.

V. CONCLUSION

There are two ways to try to implement the thought that all facts are constructed: cookie-cutter constructivism and relativistic constructivism. Both versions face decisive difficulties. The cookie-cutter version succumbs to the problems with causation, conceptual competence, and disagreement. And the relativistic version faces a decisive dilemma: either it isn't intelligible or it isn't relativism.

We have no choice but to recognize that there must be some objective, mind-independent facts. This argument, of course, doesn't tell us all by itself which facts obtain and which ones don't; nor does it tell us, of the facts that do obtain, which ones are mind-independent and which ones aren't.

But once we see that there is no general philosophical obstacle to acknowledging mind-independent facts, we also see that we have been given no reason for supposing that those facts aren't just the ones we always took them to be—facts about dinosaurs, giraffes, mountains, and so forth.

NOTES

1. Richard Rorty, *Truth and Progress* (New York: Cambridge University Press, 1998), 90.

2. Rorty's exegesis is a notoriously tricky matter. So think of me as making the following claim: if there is anything in Rorty's writings, which will help the fact constructivist with the problems we have uncovered, it is the view I am attributing to him.

3. Ian Hacking seems to have a similar idea in mind when he writes, "The world is so autonomous, so much to itself, that it does not even have what we call structure in itself. We make our puny representations of the world, but all the structure of which we can conceive lies within our representations" (*The Social Construction of What?* [Cambridge, Mass.: Harvard University Press, 1999], 85).

4. Richard Rorty, "Does Academic Freedom Have Philosophical Presuppositions: Academic Freedom and the Future of the University," *Academe* 80, no. 6 (1994): 57.

5. Michael Chabon, *The Amazing Adventures of Kavalier and Clay* (New York: Picador USA, 2000). For the suggestion that this analogy might be helpful in explaining Rorty's view, I am grateful to Nishiten Shah.

6. For an example of a contemporary constructivism about morality, see Christine Korsgaard, *The Sources of Normativity* (Cambridge: Cambridge University Press, 1996).

7. By 'global' I mean 'inclusive of all subject matters,' rather than 'applying everywhere on the globe.'

8. I will develop one especially influential way of formulating a relativistic view of a particular domain—an approach I will call 'thoroughgoing relativism.' It begins with, but somewhat modifies, Gilbert Harman's fine discussion of moral relativism in his contribution to Harman and Judith Jarvis Thomson, *Moral Relativism and Moral Objectivity* (Cambridge: Blackwell, 1996). There are at least two other approaches to the formulation of local relativism in the literature. One—which starts from the idea that a relativistic view of a given domain consists in the claim that in that domain we can have true contradictions—I regard as hopeless. Another approach, which I call 'absolute relativism,' I will discuss briefly in chapter 6 [reference to original publication].

9. Thomas Nagel, *The Last Word* (Oxford: Oxford University Press, 1997), 15.

10. See, for instance, Richard Rorty, "Mind-Body Identity, Privacy, and Categories," *Review of Metaphysics* 19 (1965): 24–54.

Targets of Anti-Relativist Arguments **12**

HARVEY SIEGEL

Paul A. Boghossian's "Relativizing the Facts" argues against a particular form of relativism, one based on Richard Rorty's defense of 'fact-constructivism.'[1] I applaud Boghossian's conclusion and many of his arguments. Nevertheless, I argue that anti-relativists like Boghossian and me need to exercise care in individuating our anti-relativist arguments and the targets of those arguments. I suggest that the relations between the Rortian version of relativism that Boghossian criticizes and other versions of relativism, and the relations between Boghossian's arguments and other familiar anti-relativist arguments—especially those first articulated by Plato—are more complex than they might at first appear.

Boghossian's discussion targets Rorty's version of fact-constructivism which, he says, "is tailor-made to get around the three problems we have just raised for constructivism" (41): "the problems of *causation* (how can our descriptions cause the existence of things like mountains, the existence of which appears to antedate ours?); *conceptual competence* (how can we coherently hold that the existence of things like electrons is dependent on our descriptions, given that part of the concept of electron is that their existence is independent of us?); and *disagreement* (given the contingent nature of social needs, interests, and activities, how can fact-constructivism avoid violating the Law of Non-Contradiction (How could it be the case both that the world is flat (the fact constructed by pre-Aristotelian Greeks) *and* that it is round (the fact constructed by us)?)" (40, emphasis in original) Rorty's fact-constructivism attempts to get around these problems by going *relativistic*: all talk of facts and 'the way the world is' must be understood as relative to a theory, language game, or way of talking. On this view, facts like 'electrons exist and have negative charges' and 'giraffes have long necks' are facts only relative to our language/way of talking, which are in turn shaped by our contingent needs, interests, and activities; there are no facts independent of our descriptions.

This view helps resolve the three problems just mentioned, Boghossian claims, because it does not rely on there being any 'basic worldly dough'—any way the world is in itself, independently of our descriptions—and so on a distinction between it and our contingent ways of carving it up (44–47). Boghossian suggests that such relativization is the only way to solve these problems: "If fact-constructivism is to work at all, then, it looks as though it *has* to assume this relativistic Rortian form" (47, emphasis in original). But Boghossian argues that Rortian relativism is untenable. According to this untenable view:

Global Relativism about Facts:

(1) There are no absolute facts of the form, p.

(2) If our factual judgments are to have any prospect of being true, we must not construe utterances of the form:

$$\text{"}p\text{"}$$

as expressing the claim:

$$\text{"}p\text{"}$$

but as expressing the claim:

"According to a theory, T, that we accept, p."

(3) There are many alternative theories for describing the world, but no facts by virtue of which one is more faithful to the way things are in and of themselves than any of the others (52, renumbered, emphasis in original).

Boghossian considers 'the traditional argument' (52) according to which this view is untenable because incoherent, and finds that argument wanting; he offers another argument in its place. Let us look at these in turn.

According to Boghossian, the traditional argument concludes that the kind of relativism here addressed (global relativism about facts) is incoherent because "*any* relativistic thesis needs to commit itself to there being at least *some* absolute truths; yet what a global relativism asserts is that there are *no* absolute truths" (53, emphasis in original). He quotes a version of the argument given by Thomas Nagel, according to which (making the substitutions of 'absolute' for 'objective' and 'relative' for 'subjective') the relativist's assertions—that "there are no absolute facts of the form, p" for the *Global Relativist about Facts*, or "there are no absolute truths or absolute standards of justification" for the traditional epistemological relativist—are caught on the horns of a dilemma: either they are offered as absolute truths, in which case the relativist, in offering them, contravenes her relativism; or they are offered as relative truths, in which case they fail to challenge the absolutism they are meant to deny. Either way, according to the traditional argument, the case for relativism fails.

Nagel's argument actually aims at establishing the incoherence of *subjectivism* rather than relativism:

> the claim that "Everything is subjective" must be nonsense, for it would itself have to be either subjective or objective. But it can't be objective, since in that case it would be false if true. And it can't be subjective, because then it would not rule out any objective claim, including the claim that it is objectively false. There may be some subjectivists, perhaps styling themselves as pragmatists, who present subjectivism as applying even to itself. But then it does not call for a reply, since it is a report of what the subjectivist finds it agreeable to say. If he also invites us to join him, we need not offer any reason for declining since he has offered us no reason to accept.[2]

Boghossian reports that he "agree[s] with this traditional objection—though I do not agree with the traditional argument by which it is defended."[3] He rejects the traditional argument because "it is not clear that it follows from the concession that relativism is itself to be true only relative to a theory, that it is just a report of what the relativist 'finds it agreeable to say'. Perhaps relativism is true relative to a theory that it pays for us all to accept, relativists and non-relativists alike."[4]

I agree with Boghossian that Nagel's argument for the incoherence of subjectivism is relevantly similar to the traditional Platonic argument for the incoherence of relativism. But I do not think that Boghossian's objection to that traditional argument is compelling. To see why, we need only ask of the key claim articulated on the relativist's behalf—that it is possible that "relativism is true relative to a theory that it pays for us all to accept"—whether it is true, or asserted by the critic on behalf of the relativist to be true, relatively or absolutely. Here the dilemma that Plato raised for the relativist re-arises with full force. Either the critic is asserting as an absolute truth that this is possible, in which case relativism is contravened, or the critic is asserting it as a relative truth—"According to theory T, that I accept, it is possible that relativism is true relative to a theory that it pays for us all to accept"—in which case it fails seriously to challenge the absolutism it is meant to contest and the absolutist remains free to ignore it. The problem for the relativist, according to the traditional, Platonic anti-relativist, is that relativists find themselves in an intolerable bind when asked about the status of their claim that "it is possible that relativism is true relative to a theory that it pays for us all to accept, relativists and non-relativists alike." Either they assert this claim 'absolutistically,' in which case they contravene their relativism; or they assert it only 'relativistically,' in which case their absolutist opponent is free to ignore it. The problem the traditional argument raises for the relativist concerns the apparent incoherence of the *assertion and defense* of relativistic theses[5]—including the claim concerning the possibility that relativism is true relative to a theory that it pays for us all to accept. If so, Boghossian's complaint against the traditional argument does little to neutralize that argument.

Boghossian's new argument for relativism's incoherence goes as follows: The relativist denies that there are facts of the form "There have been dinosaurs," but accepts that there could be facts of the form "According to a theory that we accept, there have been dinosaurs." Are facts of the latter form absolute, according to the relativist? If the relativist answers "yes," he faces three problems: "First, and most decisively, he would be abandoning any hope of expressing the view he wanted to express, namely that there are no absolute facts of any kind, but only relative facts. Instead, he would end up expressing the view that the only absolute facts there are, are facts about what theories different communities accept."[6] In doing so, he contravenes his relativism by acknowledging the existence of absolute facts, namely those concerning our beliefs, and "this would no longer be a global relativism" (55). Second, it is a "peculiar view in its own right," because "it's hard to believe that there is a difficulty about absolute facts concerning mountains and giraffes, but none concerning what beliefs people have. This seems to get things exactly the wrong way round" (55). Third, answering "yes" seems to go against the thought that typically motivates the relativist, since "his initial thought . . . is that there is something incoherent about the very possibility of an absolute fact, whether this concerns physical facts or mental facts or normative facts" (55).

These three difficulties appear to provide quite compelling reasons for rejecting the version of relativism that flows from the "yes" answer. But the first seems to be at most a minor variant of the problem with relativism noted by the traditional Platonic argument. The second appears to be relevant at best to a quite different metaphysical issue concerning the relative stability or fundamentality of physical versus mental facts. The third appears to amount, like the first, to a variant of the traditional argument. That is, the first and third problems offer but variants of the traditional objection to epistemological relativism, depending as they do on difficulties attending the apparently necessarily 'absolutistic' assertion and defense of a relativistic thesis, whereas the second addresses a worthy but different target.

If the "yes" answer is untenable, what of the "no" answer? Boghossian argues that it leads to an infinite regress, according to which the relativist who answers "no":

> is committed to the view that the only facts there are, are infinitary facts of the form: According to a theory that we accept, there is a theory that we accept and according to this latter theory, there is a theory that we accept and ... there have been dinosaurs. But it is absurd to propose that, in order for our utterances to have any prospect of being true, what we must mean by them are infinitary propositions that we could neither express nor understand. (56)

This does indeed seem absurd. Boghossian concludes: "The real dilemma facing the global relativist [about facts], then, is this: either the formulation that he offers us does not succeed in expressing the view that there are only relative facts; or it consists in the claim that we should so reinterpret our utterances that they express infinitary propositions that we can neither express nor understand" (56). The newness of Boghossian's argument is highlighted by its leading to this dilemma rather than the more familiar one raised by the traditional argument concerning the relative or absolute status of the relativist's claim that truth (or justification) is relative.

Boghossian's new argument against the coherence of relativism succeeds, I think, as an argument against the Rorty-inspired *Global Relativism about Facts*—which "harks back to Protagoras," according to Boghossian (47)—that we have considered thus far. It appears to be a different argument than the traditional one, in that it leads to a different dilemma for the relativist, although it seems in the end to be no more than a minor variant of the traditional 'incoherence' objection first leveled against the relativism captured by Protagoras's *homo mensura* (man is the measure) and challenged by philosophers from Plato to Nagel. It should also be noted that Rorty has taken considerable pains to distance himself from the latter sort of relativism—a fact Boghossian never mentions.[7] Aimed at the Protagorean view concerning truth or rational justification—at which the traditional objection is usually aimed—the new argument is in considerable part misdirected. Addressed to Rortian global relativism about facts, that argument is powerful. But the Plato/Nagel-type anti-relativist arguments Boghossian's new argument is meant to replace are directed in part at a quite different target. In addition, his diagnosis of the success of the new argument—that it shows that "our grip on [global] relativistic views derives from our grip on local relativisms ... [which] explicitly commit themselves to the existence of absolute truths"[8]—is very much in line with the traditional objection that relativists cannot defend their view except by presupposing and relying on the very sort of absolute truth that their relativism is meant to reject. The strength of Boghossian's new argument for the incoherence of relativism (that global relativism relies, despite itself, on "the existence of absolute truths") seems clearly enough to rest on the strength of the traditional Platonic incoherence arguments.[9] Boghossian's discussion is hampered by its failure to address the complexities just noted concerning the targets of the anti-relativist arguments and the similarities and differences among those arguments.

Similar things can be said of Boghossian's treatment of epistemic relativism—relativism concerning rational justification. His discussion of epistemic relativism begins with a brief explication of the Galileo/Bellarmine dispute, using this case as a running example to discuss Rorty's "constructivist/relativist view of justified belief," according to which "there are no absolute facts about what justifies what." Rather, there are "fundamentally different *epistemic systems*—fundamentally different 'grids' for determining "what sorts of evidence there could be for statements about the movements of planets. In addition, there is no fact of the matter as to which of their systems is 'correct.'"[10] As with the Rortian view of facts, on the Rortian view, justification is relative to such systems and ways of talking about evidence and justification. There is no non-question-begging way to establish the 'absolute' strengths/weaknesses of such systems: "If our judgments about what it's 'rational' to believe are to have any prospect of being true, we should not claim that some belief (for example, Copernicanism) is justified absolutely by the available evidence (for example, Galileo's observations), but only that it is justified relative to the particular epistemic system that we have come to accept" (62–63). Since there is no fact of the matter concerning the correctness of such epistemic systems, we should be relativists about justification.

Consider the example: How might we show that Robert Bellarmine is incorrect when he denies that Galileo's observations justify Copernicanism? Showing that this follows from our fundamental epistemic principles will cut no ice, since Bellarmine will reject some subset of those principles, advancing one (*Revelation*) in its place that we, in turn, reject. The dispute is ultimately one concerning alternative epistemic *systems* and their respective fundamental principles. Could it be shown that any such principle is justified? Boghossian says, "To show ...

that our system is correct and theirs wrong, we would have to *justify* the principles of our system over theirs, we would have to offer them some *argument* that demonstrated the objective superiority of our system over theirs. But any such argument would require using an epistemic system, relying on the cogency of some epistemic principles and not others" (77, emphasis in original). Because we think our system is correct, we would use it, and Bellarmine would, for the same reason, use his. Though not inevitable, it is 'very likely' that each system of principles would "decide in favor of themselves and against the other practice" (77). In this case, "we will have two self-supporting practices that are at odds with each other. Will we have shown anything substantive; could we really claim to have demonstrated that our principles are correct, and theirs not? Is either one of us in a position to call the other 'wrong'?" (77).

If not:

> the relativist's argument goes through. The most that any epistemic practice will be able to say, when confronted by a fundamentally different, genuine alternative, self-supporting epistemic practice, is that it is correct by its own lights, whereas the alternative isn't. But that cannot yield a *justification* of the one practice over the other, without begging the question. If the point is to decide which of the two practices is better than the other, self-certification is not going to help. Each side will be able to provide a *norm-circular* justification of its own practice; neither side will be able to provide anything more. With what right, then, could either party claim to have a superior conception of rational or justified belief? (79–80, emphasis in original)

Boghossian does not actually think that this argument of the relativist succeeds. He begins to address it critically by taking up the matter of norm-circularity. He considers Nagel's defense of the norm-circular defense of reason on the grounds that challenges to it presuppose reason's legitimacy by demanding reasons for or against it, so that "the appeal to reason is implicitly authorized by the challenge itself."[11] He concedes that Nagel's defense works against the skeptic who challenges reason itself, but denies that this helps against Rorty's relativist, because the problem of norm-circularity "is not in the first instance a challenge to reason itself, but a challenge to the objective validity of specific forms of reasoning."[12] Neither Galileo nor Bellarmine skeptically challenge reason itself; instead, they challenge each other's fundamental epistemic principles and seemingly cannot defend their own as objectively superior to their opponents' principles, since both they and their opponents can defend their principles only norm-circularly.

Boghossian is, I think, too easy on Rorty here. The question facing Rortian epistemic relativists is whether their 'at best norm-circular' thesis is in any way objectively superior, epistemically, to the alternative absolutist thesis. The standard Platonic objection to relativism appears to apply with full force here. Rorty's argument concludes that no fundamental epistemic principle is objectively better or worse than any other, because such principles can be justified at most norm-circularly, and such justification cannot establish objective epistemic merit. Does this argument itself depend upon any such principles? If yes, since they can be justified only norm-circularly, that conclusion seems to be established not 'absolutely,' but only relatively to those principles, in which case Rorty's opponent has no reason to embrace them. If no, then this relativism is contravened. It is not at the level of the Galileo/Bellarmine dispute, but at the meta-level at which Rorty's argument against norm-circular justification is reflexively applied to itself, that the traditional objection is forceful.

Boghossian reconsiders the 'traditional refutation' of relativism considered earlier, this time reformulated to address relativism concerning epistemic justification rather than fact constructivism (52–84). As before, he again finds fault with 'the subjectivist horn' of the dilemma posed by the refutation. As above, Boghossian's reply on behalf of the relativist does not succeed. The argument offered by the 'objectivist' (as Boghossian labels the relativist's opponent) has a better formulation than the one Boghossian gives: if the relativist is *taking issue* with the objectivist/absolutist and offering and defending a position that he takes to be superior to his opponent's position, which defense ought rationally to persuade his opponent, he has given up his relativism; if not, he fails to challenge (as opposed to disagree with) that opponent's position.

Boghossian's characterization of epistemic relativism—according to which "the relativist's central thought is that particular epistemic judgments are *uniformly false*" (85, emphasis in original)—does not capture the traditional, Protagoras-inspired character of the view, according to which 'particular epistemic judgments' are not 'uniformly false,' but *relatively* true or false (or, justified or unjustified). Does it capture Rorty's version? On this point, I defer to Boghossian and other Rorty scholars. But as Boghossian has characterized it, the Rortian epistemic relativist does *not* allow us "to *accept* absolute *general* judgments about what justifies what" (87, emphasis in original). Instead, Rorty's relativist insists that we relativize such judgments to epistemic systems. Rortian relativists accept the deliverances of their epistemic systems, but at the same time fully recognize that those deliverances enjoy no higher epistemic status than the deliverances of alternative systems. They do not take them to enjoy any sort of absolute justificatory status, but realize that acceptance of them is arbitrary in the sense that they flow from systems which cannot themselves be non-question-beggingly defended. Consequently, 'accept' is a misleading term to characterize the view:

as such a relativist, Rorty 'accepts' the judgments that flow from his epistemic system, but he recognizes that they are no more justified, absolutely, than the incompatible judgments that flow from alternative systems. If he is consistent, he recognizes that that recognition is likewise no more justified, absolutely, than those that flow from alternative systems. This appears to make his view vulnerable to the traditional objection that relativists are incapable of defending their view without giving it up.

In any case, a more direct response to the allegedly problematic status of norm-circularity appears to be more effective in rebutting the 'norm-circular justification only' type of relativism on the table. It begins by noticing that not all norm-circular justifications are alike. Consider *Revelation* ("For certain propositions p, including propositions about the heavens, believing *p* is *prima facie* justified if *p* is the revealed word of God as claimed by the Bible" [69]): When Galileo challenges it, and Bellarmine responds by claiming that its justificatory status depends upon the principle's being *revealed*, Galileo seems well within his rights when he charges Bellarmine with begging the question by presupposing the legitimacy of the principle being challenged.

Now consider another principle, *Reason*, according to which epistemic principles are justified to the extent that they enjoy adequate support from objectively good reasons. (I immediately grant that *Reason* needs to be stated far more carefully to be taken seriously as a candidate fundamental epistemic principle.) There is a striking difference between *Revelation* and *Reason*: whereas Galileo can challenge the former without presupposing it, apparently the latter cannot be challenged in that way. Challenging *Reason* (like challenging any other putative principle) amounts to claiming that there is no good non-question-begging reason to accept it. This challenge stands or falls on the identification of such good, non-question-begging reasons—the challenger presupposes, in offering the challenge, that it is possible in principle for such reasons to be identified, and further, that if such reasons were forthcoming, the challenge would be met and defeated. The challenger is thus committed, in launching the challenge, to the challenged principle. Such a principle—indeed, the possibility of such a principle—stands as a direct counter-example to the Rortian 'norm-circular justification only' view. It demonstrates anew Plato's insight that that view cannot coherently be asserted and defended.

My discussion has been unduly compressed; there is unfortunately insufficient space to treat the details of Boghossian's complex discussion here.[13] To briefly conclude: my intention here has not primarily been to advance anti-relativistic arguments, although I have done that. Neither has it been to criticize Boghossian's discussion, which I think is generally quite powerful, though I have done that, too. My primary purpose has rather been to call attention to the complex ways in which different relativistic claims, and different arguments for and against them, interact, and to urge care on all sides.

NOTES

This paper is a revised version of a portion of Harvey Siegel, "Review of Paul Boghossian, *Fear of Knowledge: Against Relativism and Constructivism,*" *Notre Dame Philosophical Reviews* (January 2007), retrieved from http://ndpr.nd.edu/review.cfm?id=8364, (accessed June 11, 2008). I am grateful to Gary Gutting and the *Notre Dame Philosophical Reviews* for permission to use that earlier material here. Thanks to John Biro, Edward Erwin, Colin McGinn, and especially Paul Boghossian for helpful comments and advice on the original review.

1. Paul Boghossian, *Fear of Knowledge: Against Relativism and Constructivism* (Oxford: Oxford University Press, 2006), chap. 4 (this volume, chap. 11).

2. Nagel's argument concerns the alleged subjectivity of *reason* and of *judgment*, not of facts. See *The Last Word* (Oxford: Oxford University Press, 1997), 13–15, quote at 15.

3. Boghossian, *Fear of Knowledge*, 53.

4. Ibid., 54 (internal citation from Nagel).

5. Harvey Siegel, *Relativism Refuted: A Critique of Contemporary Epistemological Relativism* (Dordrecht: Kluwer, 1987), 6–9, and "Relativism," in *Handbook of Epistemology*, ed. I. Niiniluoto, M. Sintonen, and J. Woleński (Dordrect: Kluwer, 2004), 747–780, esp. 748.

6. Boghossian, *Fear of Knowledge*, 54.

7. For references and brief discussion, see Siegel, *Relativism Refuted*, 767–768.

8. Boghossian, *Fear of Knowledge*, 56.

9. Boghossian's failure to distinguish from among these different sorts of relativism and the arguments for and against them, and failure to dip more deeply into the literature on both, weakens his otherwise strong discussion. For extensive references, see Siegel, *Relativism Refuted* and "Relativism."

10. Boghossian, *Fear of Knowledge*, 62 (emphasis in original, internal citations from Rorty).

11. Nagel, *Last Word*, 24, cited in ibid., 81. Nagel argues that this presupposition renders the challenge to reason 'unintelligible' (ibid.). In my view, this is a mistake. The presupposition shows not that the challenge is unintelligible but rather that it contains within itself the seeds of the dispute's resolution in reason's favor. See Harvey Siegel, *Rationality Redeemed? Further Dialogues on an Educational Ideal* (New York: Routledge, 1997), chap. 5.

12. Boghossian, *Fear of Knowledge*, 82.

13. Harvey Siegel, "Review of Paul Boghossian, *Fear of Knowledge: Against Relativism and Constructivism*," *Notre Dame Philosophical Reviews* (January 2007), retrieved from http://ndpr.nd.edu/review.cfm?id=8364 (accessed June 11, 2008).

Realism and Relativism 13

AKEEL BILGRAMI

Discussions of realism and relativism often proceed as if these are starkly opposed doctrines. I want to begin by observing that on one, by now classical, understanding of those terms ('realism,' 'relativism'), the two doctrines in fact *share* some rather conspicuous philosophical assumptions. If that is really so, then there may be another doctrine, which is neither of these, since it opposes these shared assumptions. And, of course, therefore—as in so much of philosophy—a question will arise of any such position, whether it is to be most illuminatingly classified under a different name altogether, or whether, by the very way in which such a position comes to light, one is given the right to say that there was something not quite inevitable about the initial classification of doctrines and that there is instead a more illuminating non-arbitrary reclassification in which the position can without prejudice claim for itself at least one of the initial terms—in this case, 'realism'—though of course not any longer in the classically understood sense of that term. This sort of dialectical situation is common in philosophy, when distinctions among doctrines are

Reprinted from "Realism and Relativism," *Noûs*, 36, Supplement: Philosophical Issues, 12, Realism and Relativism (2002), pp. 1–25, with permission of Wiley Publishers, Columbia University Press.

drawn, contested, and redrawn. I must apologize at the outset for producing yet another paper in philosophy of this rather routine sort.

The paper aims at advancing the cause of such a distinct position, a position properly describable as at once 'realist' and 'pragmatist,' but unlike current positions held by fellow critics of classical realism (such as, say, Davidson and Putnam and Rorty), providing a more credible and appealing epistemology than they do.

This position, which I am describing as both realist and pragmatist, will be contrasted in this paper with two other realist doctrines, which owe in one way or another to Cartesian conceptions of reality and truth. The first, which will be discussed in section I, I will call 'classical realism,' and it is the one which shares some assumptions with the doctrine of relativism. By questioning those assumptions, an argument against both classical realism and relativism will be presented there. The second I will call the 'residual Cartesian realism' and it is the position that some contemporary critics of classical realism, such as Davidson, have embraced, and it will be discussed in Sections II and III of the paper. The pragmatism espoused in the paper gets most fully motivated by way of contrast with this second realist doctrine. Finally, I will be arguing, in Section IV, that the realist element in this pragmatism is initially hidden from view primarily because, at first sight, it seems as if it really is a doctrine that must imply relativism rather than realism, but a closer look at the argument provided in Section I against relativism makes clear that no such thing is implied.

I

Let's then begin with the relations between realism and relativism. First, realism. The standard and by now classical characterization of it, often discussed under the label 'the absolute conception of reality' owes to Descartes, and is intimately tied to the sort of radical skepticism that he thought possible in his early *Meditations*.[1] On the basis of arguments invoking the deliberately exaggerated idea of our comprehensive deception by dreams or by malign intervention, Descartes argued for the possibility that all the propositions by which we purport to describe reality (and therefore all our beliefs) are false, and this last was supposed to indicate the idea of a reality that was superlatively independent and therefore wholly ulterior to and remote from our knowing powers and wholly beyond the power of the propositions we employ, to describe. Thus a reality unconstrained and 'absolute' in its very conception.

Key to such a realism, as we have just seen, is the conclusion that it is possible that all our beliefs can be false. Familiar modem versions of this ideal of realism have expressed it with more scientific glosses of the fictional intervention, which makes such comprehensive error possible: mad scientists manipulating brains-in-vats.

Next, relativism. In his brilliant and celebrated paper, "On the Very Idea of a Conceptual Scheme," Donald Davidson argues that conceptual relativism is the doctrine that the truth of beliefs or of propositions is relative to a point of view or, as he calls it following Kuhn and others, relative to a 'conceptual scheme,' and he says that this idea of relativism is coherent only if one can make sense of the idea that different points of view have no common coordinate system on which they can be plotted.[2] If differences of conceptual schemes always *do* have such an underlying common coordinate system, then that undermines the point of seeing them as 'different' and, in turn, undermines the very idea of a conceptual scheme.[3] If that is undermined, there is no scope for relativization of truth to anything, and therefore no relativism. So relativism, the idea that there are radically different conceptual schemes to which truth must be relativized, requires the idea that there can be conceptual schemes *without* a common coordinate system on which they can be plotted. Davidson then adds that this latter idea, in turn, can only amount to one of two things. It can mean: (1) there are subjects with beliefs expressible in language, which when their language is interpreted, they turn out to be such that they have mostly false beliefs, by the lights of the interpreter. Or it can mean (2) there are subjects with beliefs expressible in language, and whose beliefs the interpreter grants to be mostly true, but whose language is not interpretable. Davidson argues against both possibilities, and in doing so claims to have repudiated relativism.

But before elaborating the arguments, I want to remark on the proximity in which (1) stands to the characterization given earlier of the standard, and by now classical, doctrine of realism. If relativism as a doctrine turns on the intelligibility of the idea mentioned in (1); i.e., the idea of mostly false beliefs, and realism as a doctrine turns on the intelligibility of the idea of wholly false beliefs, then if the latter condition (wholly false beliefs) held, so would the former (mostly false beliefs). That brings to the surface the large and conspicuous assumption *shared* by what are always presented as two *opposed* doctrines. Both relativism and realism assume that someone's beliefs can be mostly or wholly false. (I will further below deal with the protest that relativism is defined by the idea of beliefs which are false by the lights of an interpreter, whereas realism is defined by the idea of beliefs which are false, *simpliciter*.)

So far I have said that only (1) is shared by both realist and relativist. But, in fact (2), the other defining feature of relativism, can also be seen to figure in the kind of realism we are discussing. Let me bring this out by looking at Davidson's argument.

The argument against (1) rests on his familiar claim that interpreting some-one to have any false beliefs requires that a background of true beliefs also be attributed to him. Thus, for instance, it is not possible to interpret someone as believing (what, let's say, by our—the interpreters'—lights, is false) that there are ghosts, without also interpreting him as at least believing (what, let's say, by our—the interpreters'—lights, is true) that people die. This is so because otherwise it would put into doubt that we were right in the initial belief we interpreted him as having, viz., the belief that it is *ghosts* that there are.[4] (Of course, it is not denied that there might be other false beliefs too that might be involved in identifying the initial false belief about ghosts, but Davidson's point is that intelligibility of interpretation requires that somewhere in this burgeoning network of intercon-nected beliefs required to identify these false beliefs, there will be beliefs that, by the interpreters' lights, are true.) To repeat, this argument therefore establishes that all our beliefs cannot be false, by claiming to show that for any to be false, some others must be true.

The argument presupposes that what is true is determined by what the inter-preter believes, what he or she takes to be true. And it might be claimed that this is not a realist way of proceeding, in the first place. The realist is always going to ask, why might not the interpreter herself have things completely wrong? True and false by the interpreter's lights, he might say, is not true and false. Davidson's response will be that if it is the case that the interpreter has things completely wrong, she will have to be *interpreted* as having beliefs that are completely false, and this will have to be so by some (other) interpreter's lights. But he has already shown by his argument discussed above that if she is interpreted at all, she can-not be interpreted to be completely wrong in this way. Thus, no one can fail to share beliefs with all others, so long as they are interpretable one by the other. It is therefore not really possible or interesting according to Davidson to try and pull apart the notion of 'false' beliefs from the notion of 'unshared' beliefs between interpreter and speaker (nor, by the same token, 'true' beliefs from 'shared' beliefs).

And it is here that the question then arises: were we even to grant that if someone is interpreted at all, they must come out as having many true beliefs, what if someone is simply not interpretable by another, what if he is completely opaque. This is just (2) above. So by a brisk dialectic, (2) is also shown to be implicated in any notion of realism which takes (1) or the possibility of comprehensive error as an assumption.

Davidson argues against this possibility of exploiting (2) to shore up (1), by saying that even God, an omniscient Being and Interpreter, would have to interpret someone as having true beliefs. Being omniscient, He cannot fail to know what someone believes and says, so He cannot find anyone opaque and uninterpretable as (2) suggests, and yet if He is genuinely interpreting, He must (as the original argument goes) find the agent being interpreted to have true beliefs by his lights. Thus (1) is still false. So uninterpretability cannot be a way of objecting to the conclusion that every agent has true beliefs, if he or she has any false ones.[5]

This is not a good argument, as it stands. The trouble with this appeal to an omniscient interpreter to repudiate the difficulty raised by invoking (2) to counter the original argument against (1) is that the appeal is exploiting two somewhat contradictory ideas. On the one hand, such an interpreter is defined as knowing everything including what everyone believes; on the other hand, the argument requires that He interpret to know another's beliefs. If He knows everything, He ought not to be required to interpret to know, it might rightly be protested. And it's not as if interpretation is in the end what *underlies* what He does know, as it is, according to Davidson, in our (ordinary mortals') case when two speakers know the same language and do not explicitly interpret one another. When I, an English speaker, know what my English-speaking wife means and believes, I do not have to carry out the sort of interpretation (radical interpretation) which, according to Davidson, requires that I make her come out as having many true beliefs. But all the same, it is Davidson's (and Quine's) point that radical interpretation underlies what we know about our fellow English speakers in such cases. As Quine once said, "radical translation begins at home." But the omniscient Interpreter is *not* like us in this regard; His sort of knowledge is *defining* of him, and unlike as between speakers of the same natural language, interpretation does not implicitly underlie what he knows without explicit interpretation. So there is something suspect about Davidson's appeal to both omniscience and underlying radical interpretation in the same argument.

A better argument (one which modifies the argument Davidson actually gives) against those who invoke uninterpretability in this way would be to say something different. In fact it is the only response an anti-relativist and anti-classical realist can give to someone who invokes uninterpretability to come to a relativist or classical realist conclusion. The response is: if someone is completely opaque, then all that shows is that we *should keep trying to interpret him*. The idea that someone is known to be a thinker with thoughts and is in principle not interpretable needs some sort of impossibility theorem to support it. Without such an impossibility theorem, there is no instruction to give, but keep trying.

Impossibility *theorem* there perhaps is not, but we could simply have Cartesians saying (as Tom Nagel does say) that it is *conceivable* that there is a sort of super-knower who knows all truths, and he is to us as we are to nonhuman animals.[6] We simply do not have anything like the conceptual repertoire that he has, the conceptual repertoire to get things right. So he is not interpretable by us at all. And if that is conceivable, it is also conceivable that we have things completely wrong because our concepts are too impoverished to get them right. But the possibility that we get things completely wrong is just the possibility claimed by (1). Thus again (2) very quickly comes to nest with (1) by providing support for what (1) claims, viz., it is possible that all our beliefs are false, and providing support therefore for a defining condition of classical realism. Proof of this lies in what Nagel is asking us to conceive. It's not as if what he is asking us to conceive is like some ordinary matter of conceiving someone being more ignorant than others (what I am to an advanced physicist, say). He is not asking us to conceive that we know some of the things that the super-knower knows, but he knows a lot more, just as I know some of the things that an advanced physicist knows, but she knows a lot more. That would not be of any consequence to a philosophical issue. Rather, what he asks us to conceive is that our relation to the super-knower is quite literally analogous to what animals are to us, where none of the concepts deployed by the super-knower to think and describe the world accurately are learnable by us, given our limitations. Such a super-knower obviously would not be interpretable by us. His beliefs, which *ex hypothesi* truly describe reality, are such that we do not share any of them. Thus we may grant to Davidson that interpretation requires shared beliefs and concepts but insist that not every thinker is interpretable by us. In particular, such a super-knower is not. Hence, Davidson's argument via the demands of interpretation is ineffective, and the claim (1) above, viz., that all of our beliefs can be false, still haunts us. The Nagelian fantasy underlying (2) shows how (2) can be used to support (1), and in fact must be used to support (1), if (1) is to hold up against the modified Davidsonian argument just given.

Davidson might persist and say that it is quite unclear that we have any right to say that it is thoughts exactly, or beliefs, that this super-knower has, if we do not share any beliefs or concepts at all with him. The idea of thoughts or beliefs is *our* idea, he might say. We are supposed to be using the idea, and we don't even know what it is we mean when we attribute thoughts to the super-knower. What we mean by this idea, by 'thoughts,' is something that emerges in our notion of interpreting others, and that is precisely what, we are told by this Nagelian fantasy, we cannot do with the super-knower.

But the Nagelian response to this might simply be to say: "Yes, we do know what we mean when we say the super-knower has thoughts or beliefs, which we cannot interpret at all. We mean that he has intentional states of mind that are the sorts of things that are capable of being true and false, that have truth conditions; it's just that we do not know what his thoughts are." The suggestion, then, is that we give a criterion for what a thought or belief is (a truth-value bearing state of mind), but we insist that we cannot detect, in this case of the Nagelian super-knower, that the criterion applies. It is in principle undiscoverable that this criterion applies to such a creature, but that should be no bar to supposing that it *does* apply to him. To demand that one must, in principle, be able to discover that the criterion applies before we can suppose that it does apply is to make a question-begging anti-realist demand, one precisely being opposed by the classical realist and the absolute conception of reality presupposed by Descartes.

At last, then, the presupposition in Descartes that is being questioned by the (modified) Davidsonian argument is now out in the open. In Davidsonian terms, the presupposition emerges via semantic ascent. An absolute conception of reality is a conception of reality which may be accurately described in the thoughts or sayings of someone who, for all we know, is not interpretable by us at all, even in principle; and to deny that he has thoughts because we cannot interpret him is to give up on the realist assumption that for applicability of the criterion by which we define what a thought is, there need be no demand that we in principle be able to discover that it applies or fails to apply. In particular, we may not know whether it applies or fails to apply to the super-knower, but it may nevertheless be the case that it does apply to him, that he does have thoughts.

The point of interest in this way (via semantic ascent) of bringing out the Cartesian assumption of the 'absolute' conception of reality, is that this conception is (at least implicitly) poised to stand in opposition to the main conclusion of Wittgenstein's extended remarks on the impossibility of a private language. Wittgenstein's conclusion was precisely that we do not have a concept or meaning if we do not in principle have any idea when it is correct to apply it and when it is not. In the case of the super-knower's thoughts, we are being told just what Wittgenstein wants to rule out, that we have a right to say that he has thoughts even though (*ex hypothesi*) we could never detect that this is a correct or incorrect application of the term 'thought' to him.[7]

And notice one final thing. What Wittgenstein wanted to rule out is the intelligibility of the idea of meaning or thoughts that are not publicly available in principle to another (and therefore in particular unavailable to the Davidsonian interpreter) and the idea of such undiscoverable thoughts is just a *special instance* of a more general idea, the idea of a reality that is in principle unknowable—Descartes' absolute conception of reality. The thesis of the principled publicness of thought and the thesis known as anti-realism (or at any rate an anti-classical realism) are related to each other as species to genus.

This discussion began by pointing out how *relativism* might be characterized by a commitment to either (1) or (2). It then tried to show that (1) is an assumption of *realism* as well, and then, with just a little dialectic, that (2) also supports, and indeed must support, realism, if (1) is to support it. Thus both relativism and classical realism share two large assumptions. Finally, a somewhat modified and fortified Davidsonian strategy against these assumptions (1) and (2) was shown to be effective so long as one took for granted the publicness of thought.

However, because, as we just saw, the denial of the publicness of thought and language is just a special case of the assumptions of classical realism, there is no non-question begging way of showing that meanings and thoughts are public, i.e., without denying (1) and (2) which realism and relativism take for granted. And equally there is no non-question begging way for the realist and relativist to show that it is wrong to demand that thoughts and meanings be public, i.e., to show it without assuming their own (1) and (2).

I rather suspect that for all the highly sophisticated philosophy that has been expended on it, this is the situation (the question-beggingness on both sides) we have always been in, in our discussions of this entire subject. What we have here (and have always had) is an abiding impasse in philosophy, one of the largest and most vexing of its perennial frustrations.

But recognition of the impasse need not put an end to philosophizing in this region. Given the impasse, we can turn to other philosophical tasks, taking one or other side on the dispute and thereby frankly and openly begging the question in one or other direction. If in taking one side of the dispute, interesting and fresh explorations with attractive conclusions emerge, then adopting that side of the dispute will have paid off, and to that extent would in retrospect seem a justified and non-arbitrary decision. The rest of this paper will from this point on assume, with Wittgenstein, that thought and meaning are public, and that therefore both relativism and realism in the classical sense are operating with two untenable assumptions, i.e., (1) and (2).

Having done this, it will now address the following question. Taking it that *relativism* has definitively and *unsurvivably* been repudiated by the untenability of (1) and (2) which define it, is there any notion of *realism* which *does survive* the untenability of (1) and (2) which also defines *it*? The untenability of (1) and (2) has shown that the 'absolute' conception of reality in the classical picture is wrong, and for that to have been shown means we have admitted into our conception of reality some elements which do not make it quite so absolute, which do not allow it to be so ulterior to our epistemological status as believers and inquirers. So the question is, how shall we think of this surviving realism, if there is one, such that it squares with a credible epistemology?

II

In my dialectic so far, classical realism (and relativism) are supposed to have been repudiated by an argument which undermined an assumption which they both share, viz., that it is possible that all our beliefs are false. It is interesting to note that in Descartes himself there is *another* conception of realism (a 'residual' Cartesian realism, let's call it) which turns not on this assumption at all, but another, one which generates a different form of skepticism than the radical and comprehensive one expressed by the assumption just undermined by the Davidsonian argument. It is a realism that unfortunately *Davidson himself*, and many other philosophers today who like him are critical of classical realism, quite readily accept. Let me state this residual Cartesian realist position in this section, and argue against it in the next.

In Descartes' early *Meditations*, the driving thought is that nothing in our experiences gives us the epistemological right to claims to knowledge of the external world. But the force of this thought is split by [Descartes'] own argument to generate two quite different forms of skepticism, each of which presupposes somewhat different realist ideas. The first takes the form of claiming that, given the absence of this epistemological right, *all* our beliefs about the external world might be false, and hence we lack knowledge of the external world. The second form of skepticism about the external world (the one I want to now focus on) concludes (from the arguments of the same text) that *no given* belief about the external world can be firmly claimed to be true and to amount to knowledge.

The second is different from the first because it is possible to grant the second skepticism and not grant the first. If the first form of skepticism were true, then of course the second would also be true. If all our beliefs about the external world might be false, then any given one might be false. But it is often thought that things are not so obvious the other way round. If any given belief about the external world might always be false, despite our best epistemological efforts, it is still thought arguable that it does not follow from this that all our beliefs about the external world could be false.

Any strategy opposing the first form of skepticism (while granting the second form of skepticism) about the external world, therefore, needs to show that the passage from the idea that any given belief of ours about the external world might fail to be knowledge to the idea that all our beliefs about the external world might so fail, is illicit. The second form of skepticism, however, will only be countered if for any given belief about the external world we are able to show that it can be claimed to amount to knowledge. The thought, "Well, we are happy to allow that any given belief about the external world is not knowledge but that does not mean that all are not" does not even take up the difficulty, as it is seen by the second form of skepticism. It concedes it at the outset.

We have in Section I of this paper looked at the realism underlying the first form of skepticism in Descartes, and called it 'classical realism.' What notion of realism underlies the second form of skepticism? It does not assume (1) and (2) which define 'classical' realism. Rather it is just the idea of a notion of truth, which is such that *we can never know which of any (empirical) belief of ours is true.* This is different from (1) because it can grant that some, and very likely many, of our beliefs are true, and in fact Davidson's argument against (1) is supposed to have established that. It only claims that truth is such, that we never know when in particular we have attained it, even if we know that many of our beliefs are true. It is, to coin a phrase, 'an epistemologically blind' notion of truth. And it defines a realism distinct from the classical one that the modified Davidsonian argument of the last section has rejected. Nothing in that argument, nothing about the publicness of thought and meaning, can help to show that this form of realism is wrong. And it better not do so, because as I said Davidson himself has explicitly embraced this epistemologically blind notion of truth and the realism it points to, describing it as the 'objectivity of truth.'[8] In doing so, Davidson has not really gotten out of the clutches of an essentially Cartesian picture, and has merely convinced himself that he has by focusing on only one form of skepticism and realism in Descartes—the classical one which he successfully rejects by the argument of the last section.

In the rest of this paper, I want very briefly to argue for two things. First, that this other notion of truth (and the 'residual' realism it entails) is quite as bad as 'classical realism,' even if it does not fall afoul of the same argument as given in Section I. It is quite as bad because it generates an equally unsatisfactory epistemology. Having argued this I want to briefly sketch an alternative position on realism and the objectivity of truth, one that might properly be regarded as 'pragmatist,' and I want to claim—returning to a point made in the first section—that if Davidson has been right to reject relativism by his argument there, then that very same argument gives him the space to occupy this much more credible epistemology rather than the quite different space he in fact occupies in embracing this epistemologically blind notion of truth and its residual Cartesian realism.

III

A view of truth and realism, which has it that we can never know when one of our beliefs is true, does not encourage a plausible epistemology for a very simple reason. It makes truth fall outside of the targets of inquiry. Truth is no longer something we can aim for, not something we can intend to attain. This is not because such a view makes truth impossible to attain. If it did that, it would obviously remove truth from the targets of inquiry since we cannot intend to attain what we know it is impossible to attain. But it's because of something almost as bad. Though it allows that truth is possible to attain, and in fact though it is even compatible with the Davidsonian position (discussed in Section I) that it is not only possible but that it will and must be attained in the case of most of our beliefs, it nevertheless remains that it makes us blind as to when we have attained it. We never can tell or know which of our beliefs is true. We can never know when it is in any particular case that we have attained the truth. Under such circumstances, inquiry into or the search for truth would always be like sending a message in a bottle out to sea, making all success in the search something like a fluke or a bonus, something over which we have no control. What sort of notion of inquiry into truth is that? What kind of an epistemology is that? Why would one even set up truth as a goal, under such circumstances?

It is for this reason that pragmatists balk at such a realist conception of truth, even if it is less extreme than the classical realist conception discussed in Section I. From the pragmatist point of view it is still caught up in retrograde ways with elements of Cartesian skepticism, not the ones which give rise to classical realism, but close cousins of it, and generative of an equally unattractive skepticism, if a somewhat different one.

I've mentioned the pragmatists, but notice that once we see things this way, once we see clearly that this realism is connected with Cartesian skepticism of this second variety, we can see that its not just pragmatism but certain well-known responses to this variety of skepticism, owing to G. E. Moore, J. L. Austin, and Wittgenstein, which can be counted as opponents of such a realism as well. Moore famously claimed that there *are* particular beliefs and statements (his example was the belief about the presence of one's hand under certain routinely obtaining circumstances) which are such that they are not susceptible to this variety of skepticism, and so presumably that there is no question of not know-ing that they are true, when they are. I will return to Austin and Wittgenstein a little later. I mention all this only to make clear that there is nothing novel or eccentric about opposing the widespread commitment to such a realist notion of truth, and it is not merely done by a fringe of pragmatists. An opposition to it is implied by a long cast of opponents of a certain variety of skepticism, with which this realist notion of truth is closely linked.

All the same 'pragmatism' remains a good label for making explicit the metaphilosophy involved in one's dissatisfaction with a notion of truth which yields an epistemology in which truth cannot be a goal of inquiry—for such a notion makes truth fall outside of what can make a difference to *practice*. It is the pragmatists who have always from the outset proposed that what does not make a difference to practice does not make a difference to philosophy. At any rate, given our interests in this paper, it does not make a difference to episte-mology. We have seen that this realist notion of truth makes truth fall outside of the aims of inquiry, and inquiry is the one general practice which is central to epistemology.

In saying that bad Cartesian epistemologies may be opposed by stressing practice, as pragmatists do, and by seeing inquiry as the central practice of epis-temology, I am doing two different things.

First, I am assuming that philosophy itself is not an inquiry, in the requisite sense. Thus it won't do to say that the logical possibility of any given empiri-cal belief of ours being false (on the basis of Cartesian hypotheses about evil demons and brains in vats) is relevant to and makes a difference to *some* sort of inquiry, *philosophical* inquiry. The point about invoking practice was to bring in, as a criterion for what is good philosophy, the concept of inquiry as a cognitive practice, relevance to which will be crucial in judging what is good *in philosophy* and in epistemology in particular. Hence, to then say that philosophy itself is an inquiry would be to altogether miss the point of setting up such a criterion. (There may also be reasons, quite apart from the point—missing just mentioned, reasons familiar from Wittgenstein, for resisting the idea that philosophy is an inquiry. For Wittgenstein philosophers did not engage in inquiry any more than they engaged in what ordinary people think about in their ordinary reflection. Both inquiry as scientists pursue it, and the plain thought of ordinary people uncontaminated by philosophy, are to be distinguished from the sort of thing philosophy is, the sort of thing which encourages all sorts of confusions and dis-tortions and misrepresentations of what goes on in 'inquiry' properly so called as well as in ordinary thought. Philosophy thus stands *apart* both from ordinary reflection and from inquiry, and should not be thought of as a case or a version of one of these. And to this we can add that once we see traditional philosophy in this light—as the source of confusion by adopting a mode of thinking, whose confusions arise *because* it departs from both our ordinary responses and from inquiry, properly so-called—we might then fruitfully do what pragmatists suggest: propose a criterion which constrains philosophy so as to minimize these confusions, viz., "Don't admit anything that does not make a difference to inquiry." (Wittgenstein himself made other proposals, having more to do with the charms of ordinary language, about which I am much more skeptical and about which we need not concern ourselves here.)

Second, in stressing practice as I have, I am not avowing those crude forms of pragmatism which take it that truth must be characterized in terms of practices and values that are *not cognitive* practices and values, but rather practices which essentially involve the *applications* of cognitive and theoretical conclusions (such as, say, in engineering or medicine) and therefore values that speak to the *usefulness* of our theoretical and cognitive pursuits in some sort of *practical* terms. That is a caricature of pragmatism, no doubt encouraged by some reckless remarks of some pragmatists, but by no means compulsory for those embracing a pragmatist epistemology in order to respond to one of the essentially Cartesian versions of realism, as we are.[9] The strategy of the response we are pursuing shuns this caricature by bringing to center stage *only* the *cognitive* practice of inquirers, and claims that any characterization of the notion of truth and of philosophical doctrines such as realism should restrict itself to what does make a difference to inquiry so conceived, i.e., merely as a cognitive practice.

How, then, may one do better by way of characterizing truth in a way that retains its direct relevance to the goals of inquiry, so conceived? (Some care is being taken to use the word 'characterizing' instead of 'defining.' One can happily join those who think that 'truth' cannot be deemed, as we shall see later, and still make the claim that it characterized in such a way that it remain a goal of inquiry.)[10]

Truth remains a goal of inquiry only if there is no place to doubt the truth of beliefs on grounds that are *general* and *purely philosophical* in ways that Descartes made famous and familiar. Comprehensive illusion or dream, intervening malign genies or mad scientists, are all hypotheses contrived to conclude only this: it is logically possible that any particular (empirical) belief of ours is false. But inquirers are not moved by logical possibilities. They are only moved if some reason or evidence is offered for doubting some *particular* belief on particular grounds relevant to *that* belief.[11] The logical possibility of a particular empirical belief being false is something it shares with all such beliefs, and so that possibility lacks the particularity of grounds for doubt that move the inquirer. Fanciful hypotheses about malign genies and brains-in-vats, for which there is no particular ground in any particular case, can be wheeled in to make vivid the logical possibility of the falsehood of empirical belief *in general*. The inquirer may grant such a possibility and proceed exactly as she would have proceeded anyway. It makes no difference to her, qua Inquirer.

Some efforts at going beyond Cartesian style arguments and the notion of truth it presupposes, have not, in the end, avoided the problem in Descartes that we are discussing.

Putnam, for instance, who is sensitive to the point that we must stress the role of inquiry in characterizing truth, tries to do better than the conception presupposed by Descartes, but he so *idealizes* the notion of inquiry in the characterization that it is not clear that the notion of truth which emerges *can* make any difference to practice as it is carried out in any *actual* inquiry. For Putnam, truth becomes the omnibus deliverance of inquiry in the ideal limit, inquiry at the end of time, so any given inquirer at any actual given time and point of inquiry will just as surely worry, not now perhaps about the logical possibility of being wrong in holding any of his (empirical) beliefs, but about the possibility that any of the beliefs he now holds will be judged false in the ideal limit of inquiry. The fact is, however, that such a generalized doubt about the truth of one's beliefs is just as bad as the Cartesian doubt, since it cannot make a difference to inquiry at any given actual point of time.

Apart from Putnam's unsatisfactory version of the appeal to pragmatism, there is another strategy, which also tries to show that any given belief may be false without appealing to malign interventions or comprehensive dreams. It looks instead to meta-inductive arguments to make the case. But these strategies too are bootless. It is bootless to try to make the case by saying that we have been wrong in the past, so we are very likely to be wrong in at least some of the beliefs we currently hold. Even if, on the basis of this argument, an inquirer conceded the claim that some of her beliefs are bound to be false, that preface-paradoxical concession would still not be a concession to anything that made a difference to her inquiry. Unless she had evidence or grounds to think any *particular* belief or set of beliefs were put into doubt, she would proceed with inquiry just as before. Thinking that *some* beliefs (in the general sense of 'some or other' beliefs) are bound to be false would make no odds. What beliefs she took to be certain, the inquirer would continue to take to be certain and proceed with inquiry without any doubt about these, without any anxiety or concession at all that they might be false, even if she conceded on meta-inductive grounds that some of her beliefs are bound to be false.

So far I have been making negative remarks about Descartes and some other ways of thinking of truth, which fall short of the pragmatist conception as I am presenting it. To turn to a more positive set of remarks about this pragmatist conception now, let's first just declare that our doubt-free beliefs would possess the property, *truth*. We can then, as a perfectly accurate description of the procedure of inquiry, point out that taking these beliefs for granted, inquirers look at other states of mind about which they are not certain ('hypotheses'), but which it is the point of inquiry to ascertain whether they are to be included in the set of beliefs which possess this property of truth or to discard them as not belonging there. (It may be all right to call these other states of mind 'beliefs' as well, but we would then need to be very careful to distinguish between two senses of 'belief,' one of which possesses the property of truth and the other which merely takes the form of supposals and hypotheses and conjectures, the question of whose truth is inquiry's large and governing motivation to answer. Confusion, however, may best be avoided by calling them something different, simply 'hypotheses' and not 'beliefs.')

A picture of the relations between truth and belief and inquiry along these lines would find no need to say with Davidson (and puzzlingly Rorty,[12] even though he has long declared himself a pragmatist) that truth is not a goal of inquiry because it is not something we know we have achieved in any particular case. We *do* know when we have achieved it, and where we do, we proceed to take for granted these beliefs that possess truth, and use them as a standard and guide in our inquiries about other states of mind such as hypotheses. Such a picture was well stated by Quine and he explicitly mentions it as a picture that departs from Descartes: "Unlike Descartes, *we own and use* our beliefs of the moment. . . . Within our own totally evolving doctrine, we can judge *truth*."[13]

If we *do* know we have achieved truth when we have, and if we *can* make it a goal of inquiry, a crucial question arises as to how we should think of its *objectivity*. Doesn't the objectivity of truth require precisely that it must be divorced altogether from our epistemic reach and become, just as Davidson says, something that is beyond us to know if we have achieved it?

It is notorious that notions such as objectivity, just as much as 'realism,' are multiply understood. And so the question is, can this pragmatist position we are promoting claim for its understanding of truth, the property of 'objectivity,' as it is understood in at least some senses of the term?

Here is a sense in which we certainly can. A Tarskian T-sentence (say, "Hanse has accepted a bribe" is true if and only if Hanse has accepted a bribe), even for this pragmatist position, still captures something central about the notion of truth. What is that? I have said that the idea of taking beliefs (as opposed to hypotheses) for granted in inquiry is just the familiar idea of a background theory which provides the standard by which we judge truth in a particular case or by which we assess a hypothesis on the question of its truth. Quine was clear about this point too, and in the same passage as the one quoted earlier says:

> It is rather when we turn back into the midst of an actually present theory . . . that we can and do sensibly speak of this or that sentence as true. . . . To say that the statement "Brutus killed Caesar" is true or that "The atomic weight of sodium is 23" is true, is in effect simply to say that Brutus killed Caesar, or that the atomic weight of sodium is 23. [Here Quine in a footnote explicitly cites Tarski and his T-sentences for a way of developing this point] . . . the truth of attributions are made from the point of view of the same surrounding body of theory.

When the surrounding body of theory or beliefs is doing its work, what does the Tarskian T-sentence of (as Quine puts it) "this or that sentence" capture? It captures the fact that something *correct* is going on, something *true* is stated by the sentence "Hanse has accepted a bribe," if Hanse has indeed accepted a bribe. The appeal to Tarski therefore is not, as it is sometimes thought, an appeal to something bland and insubstantial regarding truth. This is because, if what I have just said about them is right, it is not something bland and insubstantial that is being stated by such T-sentences. It's not as if some mere syntactic device of removing quotations is all that is effected, nor as others think, something merely of a piece with bringing to light that the predicate 'is true' has the function of summarizing the unspoken detail packed into such statements as "Whatever Plato said is true." T-sentences cannot possibly be insubstantial in this way, if the kind of *correctness* they capture, the kind of correctness involved in uttering the sentence "Hanse has accepted a bribe" when Hanse has accepted a bribe, is just the correctness that *inquiry aims for*. It thus has the full prestige and normativity of 'substantial' truth. The fact that disquotation can be understood as capturing something as substantial as the goal of inquiry is proof that there is nothing insubstantial in this way of characterizing truth.

Now, it must be admitted of course that if the ideal of the objectivity of truth is one in which the correctness involved goes *beyond* the kind of correctness which I have just identified as being captured in T-sentences, then Davidson will be justified in sticking with his own picture of the relation between truth, belief, and inquiry, i.e., that inquiry does not have the truth of beliefs as a goal. What would that more demanding correctness be? Presumably it would be something like this: the normative (normative, because of the word 'correct' used above in characterizing the role of T-sentences) relatedness of our beliefs to things in the world would have to be a relatedness of our beliefs to things, *not* as they figure in our world view, but quite *independent* of our world view. Such an independence of the things to which our beliefs are related in this correctness relation would explain why (for Descartes, Davidson, and many others) we do *not* have any grip on when we have attained truth in any particular case.

I am assuming instead with Quine (Quine explicitly says this in the first quotation from him above) and others (such as McDowell, from one of whose fine essays I have taken the phrase "normative relatedness of our beliefs to things as they figure in our world view")[14] that this sort of independence is exactly what is being rejected by the idea that we *use* our own beliefs as a standard in inquiry. To say we use them in this way is just to say that they constitute the world view within which specific beliefs (or hypotheses) are judged (or assessed) for truth. It is quite crucial to understand that Quine in his talk of such *use* of our beliefs and McDowell in his talk of truth as a normative relatedness of our beliefs (or sentences) to things *as they figure in our world view* are making the same point in their different ways. Here is the relation between their two ways of making the point. It is because we think of *our beliefs* as providing the standard of *truth* in inquiry, that the sentence we employ on the right hand side of a T-sentence refers to things as they figure *in our world view*, and not independent of our world view.

What sort of *independence* remains, once we *reject* the idea that truth is a normative relatedness of our beliefs to things *independent* of our worldview? This is a question that Davidson and many others caught up in a realism still moored to elements in Descartes are bound to ask us. How can there be any independence, they will ask, if the standard of correctness comes from our beliefs themselves? (This question is a cousin of a host of complaints usually sounded against pragmatist epistemologies—and also in a slightly different form against Moorean, Austinian, Wittgensteinian epistemologies—complaints such as "In stressing inquiry, this pragmatism has stressed the inquirer's point of view, but how can *truth* be characterized from a point of view? It is the point of truth that it is independent of points of view" and "Isn't what is being offered by pragmatists just a theory of *belief*, or at most belief justified by inquiry?" It cannot therefore be a characterization of the notion of *truth* or of the doctrine of *realism*, notions and doctrines which must go beyond belief, however justified belief may be by inquiry.)

In answering the original question about independence we will have said something relevant to all these related complaints. The answer to the question about independence is this. The standard of correctness provided by our beliefs in inquiry is such that we know that, were we to suppose that we judge something true which is not dictated by these standards, we would be wrong to do so. If an inquirer believes that Hanse has accepted a bribe, if this particular belief meets the standards of correctness that are dictated by the background beliefs in use in inquiry, then the inquirer will say that were he to believe otherwise he would believe something false. The correctness involved here thus does meet a requirement of independence from belief (though not all requirements obviously, in particular not ones motivated by the Cartesian picture we are opposing) because it makes clear that the truth of this belief would not be threatened at all, if he believed its opposite. That (opposite) belief would be false. Inquiry's standards of correctness make that independence-conferring outcome perfectly available.

When I wrote some of these things in a recent essay,[15] Rorty responded by saying that I am trying to *define* truth in terms of beliefs that we as inquirers hold to be certain, and recoiled from the thought not only because he thinks it is the wrong definition, but because it is wrong to think that one can define truth. But I nowhere claimed then, nor do I now claim, that I am defining truth. I could not possibly have been defining truth in terms of belief in saying the sorts of pragmatist things I said, since presumably if truth were *defined* in terms of one's beliefs, then something like the Euthyphro scenario would hold. Our beliefs would not be tracking the truth, but rather they would be determining what is true. But no such idea of non-tracking or non-independence follows from what I said. "Truth is what inquirers believe," if it is intended as a *definitional* slogan, would imply that inquirers believe *all the truths there are*. That absurd and extreme conclusion is indeed anti-realist, and it is what follows from taking truth to be *defined* in terms of belief. But not only is the pragmatist happy to grant that inquirers are massively ignorant of any number of the indefinite number of truths there are, he insists on it. So if this absurd and extreme conclusion does not follow from what I did say, (viz., roughly that what inquirers believe—as opposed to hypothesize—is true and known to be true by them, and it sets the standard by which their inquiries are carried out, and specific truths are then judged) then that is proof that I was not deeming truth at all. I, along with Quine and McDowell, for the reasons I am giving, rather than define truth, are merely characterizing it in terms of a kind of normative relatedness of our beliefs to things as they figure 'in our world view.' In doing so, we are all characterizing a substantial notion of truth, a normative notion, a goal of inquiry, and not merely a 'minimalist' notion with no substantialist aspirations. Moreover, as I've been saying, that the normative relatedness is to things as they figure '*in our world view*' does not undermine the idea of the objectivity of truth, the idea of the independence of truth from belief. However, it is independence only in the sense carried by disavowing the absurd anti-realist conclusion that we have just seen to be implied by the claim that doubt free beliefs (or a 'worldview') *define* truth. And it is also independence in the somewhat stronger sense mentioned in the previous paragraph. That such notions of independence should not be even stronger, i.e., that truth should *not* be characterized as a kind of normative relatedness to things that are *independent of our world view*, may of course disappoint those who are still barking around the Cartesian kennel even after having come out of it, as Davidson and Rorty are with their ideal of the objectivity of truth. But an epistemology in which truth remains a goal of inquiry and continues to provide a norm and a goal which we know to be fulfilled when it is fulfilled, is a gain that should more than compensate for a disappointment along those lines.

The weaker independence just expounded which pragmatism provides still makes clear that no idealism is entailed by these pragmatist ideas, ideas which are present too in figures such as Moore, Austin, and Wittgenstein.

I said something about Moore earlier, and promised to say more about Austin and Wittgenstein. Let me conclude this section by saying something about these antecedents and allies, before returning in the next section to conclude with some remarks again about the initial theme of the relation between realism and relativism.

Austin, like Moore, presents his opposition to the realism we are rejecting by criticizing the notion of knowledge that its implied variety of skepticism in Descartes promotes. He says: "The expression 'When you know, you can't be wrong' is perfectly good sense. You are prohibited from saying 'I know it is so, but I may be wrong.' This conveys in terms of the concept of knowledge, rather than truth, the shortcomings of the epistemology which has it that we never know when one of our beliefs is true."[16] Austin also says a little later "Being aware that you may be mistaken doesn't mean merely being aware that you are a fallible human being; it means that you may be mistaken in this case."[17] We have been making this point by saying that being aware that one is fallible in general but not being aware of (having any evidence of) any actual fault in any particular case makes no difference to inquiry, and therefore is of no interest to practice, in the only sense of practice that is relevant to epistemology.

Wittgenstein is a trickier case. He too thinks that there are some beliefs which we take for granted in inquiry, and whose truth is something quite secure, and we do not ever think that we may be wrong in believing them or that they may be false. He calls these 'hinge' propositions For instance, he says "the *questions* that we raise and our *doubts* depend on the fact that some propositions are exempt from doubt, are as it were, like hinges on which those turn. That is to say that it belongs to the logic of our scientific investigations that certain things are *indeed* not doubted."[18] This is the point we have been making when we said that there are, broadly speaking, two relevant kinds of cognitive states of mind, beliefs and hypotheses, and scientific investigation targets the latter and in doing so takes for granted the former in the background as providing the standard by which the investigation is carried out. Without beliefs, we would not know how to assess the deliverances of such investigation. And what provides the standard (our beliefs) is something we 'own and use' and is not something we can doubt or think *might* be false (in any interesting epistemological sense, as opposed to a logical sense). So the notion of 'hinge' propositions (what in this paper I am simply calling 'beliefs,' as opposed to hypotheses) is very much present in the picture of epistemology presented as an alternative in this section to the residual Cartesian epistemology presented in Section II.

Wittgenstein, however, goes on to spoil the good point I have cited above by adding that hinge propositions are never questionable or revisable, that they involve some notion of necessity, at least of a conventional kind, if not some other. That further thought is not a pragmatist thought. Just because a hinge proposition cannot be doubted on the basis of *general* philosophical grounds of the sort found in the early *Cartesian Meditations*,[19] just because the logical possibility of their being false does not translate into an epistemically interesting possibility, in no way suggests that they cannot be revised if *particular* evidence against any particular one of them comes in. They are not abiding and necessary truths just because they are used as a standard during inquiry. So though I am taking Wittgenstein to be an antecedent of this pragmatism in having seen the importance of not doubting what we use in inquiry, while we are using it, his conception of the propositions or beliefs we do not doubt is not the same as the one being presented here because for him they are—not revisable at all on the basis of evidence, not the *sort of things* which can be revised on the basis of evidence. Thus hinges for him are not empirical beliefs at all, not beliefs such as "Here is a hand," "the earth is round," etc. They are much more general, and apparently in some sense or other, necessary truths, such as "there is a material world."[20] On the picture presented here, the hinges of inquiry are all of the ordinary and scientific empirical beliefs (such as the two mentioned above) which we do not doubt and take for granted in the ordinary circumstances in which we find ourselves. But these latter are certainly revisable under extraordinary circumstances, if specific evidence comes in against their credibility for the inquirer.

The revisability of the 'hinges' of inquiry, therefore, is central to a pragmatist epistemology which rejects the residual Cartesian realism we are considering. And so a few questions about revisability arise which must be considered now. Since some of these questions relate importantly to the topic of relativism, which is one half of the subject of this paper, I conclude now by a brief discussion of relativism and realism again.

IV

I have said two things that are perfectly compatible: first, that an inquirer's beliefs are true and are fully known by her to be true and are used by her as standards relevant in her inquiry regarding hypotheses; and, second, that an inquirer's beliefs are revisable by her. As Quine says in the same passage cited earlier, "Within our own evolving doctrine, we can judge *truth . . . subject to correction*, but that goes without saying" (my emphasis).

The possibility of correction does not spoil the idea that it is *truth* we are possessed of earlier, before the revision. Austin too says this explicitly in the same essay cited earlier.[21] But somebody may question this, arguing that something like relativism follows from the pragmatism I am espousing. And in fact, Quine's remark is explicitly made by him in the context of the worry that, if we say that we do possess the truth in our body of beliefs, and know ourselves to do so, and *use* those beliefs in the ways I have been stressing, then someone may think that this must inevitably lead to relativism. He asks, "Have we now so lowered our sights as to settle for a relativistic doctrine of truth, rating the statements of each theory as true for that theory and brooking no higher criticism?" And he replies with some of the words I have cited before, "Not so. The saving consideration is that we continue to take seriously our own particular . . . theory. . . . Unlike Descartes, we own and use our beliefs of the moment. . . . Within our own totally evolving doctrine, we can judge truth. . . . subject to correction, but that goes without saying."

But we are moving too quickly here, and a serious difficulty posed by revision for the pragmatism we are espousing must be addressed before Quine's reply can stick.

What is it exactly that is happening when one revises a doctrine (or some part of a doctrine) that is said to be possessed of (and known to be possessed of) the property of truth? We are, of course, judging p at one time, and not-p at a later time. And, it is also, of course, from the point of view of the doctrine at one time that p is judged true, and from the point of view of the revised doctrine at a later time that not-p is judged true. But, given the pragmatism sketched in the last section, shouldn't this amount to saying that the *truth* of the judgments is relative to the doctrines of the earlier and later time respectively, i.e., just what relativism says? In other words, since, for the pragmatism sketched, it was so urgent to say that inquirers' beliefs actually *possess* the property of truth, and are not merely thought to do so by the inquirers, is there not a threat that it will fall into saying that both p and not-p are *true*? And is not the intolerability of saying that only removed by making pragmatism pass over into relativism? The whole point of relativism is to be unperturbed by the disagreement over *truth* between two believers, relativizing the truth of the disagreed upon belief to each of their points of view. It allows that each is right (not merely thinks himself right). But each is only right relative to their doctrine.

The problem before us is that the pragmatist position being espoused here seems to imply that two people or (taking the case of revision) one person at different times, who hold contradictory beliefs, both have truth on their side. If an inquirer's beliefs held with certainty (unlike his hypotheses) are not epistemically segregated from truths, then it would seem that something like this *is* implied. But that (like any contradiction) is intolerable, and can only be made tolerable if the truth of the relevant belief of each inquirer is relative to his current doctrine. (It should be obvious that it is intolerable not in the sense that there is irrationality of any kind when *two* people make contradictory claims. So it's not really from the point of view of the notion of *rationality* that one is driven to find it intolerable, but rather from the point of view of the notion of truth. *Truth*, because it is the world which cannot be such that both are right.)

Notice what is happening here. Everyone, both the pragmatist and his opponents, may well agree that truth is *judged* relative to the current doctrine. But his opponents are saying that when the pragmatist of Section III above claimed that there was to be no epistemological segregation of confident judgment (belief) from truth, he was saying much more than this innocuous thing which all may agree upon. He was saying not merely that truth is *judged* relative to the current doctrine, but that *truth* is relative to the current doctrine. It is this last which is (the despised) relativism. In being committed to the idea that we never know when any belief of ours is true, this opponent of pragmatism has no such relativist worries pressing on his position, since he thinks that confident judgment does not amount to truth itself, and so he can without any such worries grant that we *judge* truth relative to our current doctrine, without granting that *truth* is relative to it.

Is there really a worry here for the pragmatist which his opponent avoids? Quine denies that there is any such worry in the quoted passage, claiming that, even for the pragmatist, revision is perfectly compatible with the idea that truth is not relative at all. On what grounds can he claim this? He does not mention any grounds, and seems to think it obvious—as he says in the quotation above, 'it goes without saying.' But he was perhaps wrong to make it seem so obvious, as if no philosophy or argument was necessary to show it. To show it, it will be necessary to return to some of the points made in Section I.

What has to be shown to stave off relativism is that in those cases when two inquirers contradict one another on some matter (or when a verdict at a later inquiry-stage contradicts the verdict of an earlier inquiry-stage), *it is every bit as bad* and intolerable as when the same inquirer contradicts himself at one and the same stage of his inquiry. Every bit as bad, in the sense that in those cases too we want to say that only one of the contradictory beliefs is true. But how may *a pragmatist* give herself the right to say this? Her opponent can easily give himself the right by saying that since belief (or confident judgment of truth) and truth are *epistemologically segregated*, only one of these two contradictory verdicts is right, even though these inquirers, or inquirer-stages, *do not know which*. It's just this way of thinking about truth, a way of thinking that is happy with the idea of 'do not know which,' that pragmatism has been complaining about in the last section, in the critique of residual Cartesian realism. It does not seem so easy for her therefore to give herself the same right. If she insists that contradiction is just as bad in these cases as it is in the single inquirer at a single stage of inquiry, she would seem to be abandoning the pragmatist *denial* of such a segregation which had been argued for in section III.

Let's deal with this problem in two stages. First, notice that the pragmatist is certainly not abandoning the denial of the segregation we argued for in Section III if she says that it is intolerable that the *same* inquirer at the *same stage* of inquiry contradicts himself. Even the opponent of pragmatism will grant that nothing pragmatist is being abandoned when the pragmatist says that. What this opponent is insisting, however, is that the case of two inquirers and the case of revision, i.e., of two inquiry-stages, are not like the case of the same inquirer at the same stage of inquiry. In these cases, the opponent of pragmatism will insist that the pragmatist is not in a position to say that contradiction is intolerable without abandoning the pragmatism. And the opponent will claim that the only way the pragmatist can get out of this is by saying that the truth of each contradictory belief or judgment is relative to a different doctrine, so they are not in the end contradictory. Pragmatism thus implies relativism, the opponent will say. So the pragmatist has to find an argument to show that these cases are in fact, in all important and relevant respects, just like the case of the single inquirer at a single stage of inquiry.

And so we move to the second stage, and this paper's punch line. That these other cases are just like the single inquirer at a single stage of inquiry is indeed the *entire point* of Davidson's argument against the very idea of a conceptual scheme which was presented in Section I. I will not rehearse the argument here which was presented there in detail, but merely recall that the argument's conclusion was that the very idea of a conceptual scheme does not make any sense at all. So there is *nothing* to which truth can be relativized. It is the precise force of this argument therefore that two people contradicting one another, or two inquiry-stages contradicting one another, is *quite as bad* (from the point of view of truth, that is, and not rationality) as one inquirer contradicting himself at the same stage of inquiry. The argument has this force because it has shown that two inquirers or two inquirer-stages and their body of beliefs *cannot be elevated to two 'conceptual schemes'* where conceptual schemes are just the sorts of things that lack a coordinate system underlying them. If the argument presented at length in Section I showed that there is always such an underlying coordinate system, then there are no conceptual schemes to which truth can be relativized. And the pragmatist, *appealing also to just this argument*, may insist that his position does not entail that he must deny the intolerability (from the point of view of truth) of two inquirers or two inquiry stages contradicting each other. He can, just as much as the realist with antipragmatist and residual Cartesian inclinations, insist that only one of these contradictory claims is right.

The upshot is that when it is reported that two inquirers or two inquirer-stages *confidently judge* respectively that p and not-p, relative to their doctrines or background sets of beliefs, there is no scope to make this harmless report slide into the quite different and relativistic point that the *truth* of p and not-p is relative to their respective doctrines or background sets of beliefs. Such a slide is blocked, despite the fact that the pragmatist denies the segregation of confident judgment from truth, because the pragmatist has now (by Davidson's argument) been given the resources to say that only one of these two contradictory beliefs of the two inquirers or inquirer-stages is right, just as much as he has the resources to say it of two contradictory beliefs of one inquirer at a single stage of inquiry. The doctrines or sets of beliefs of these two inquirers or inquirer-stages do not and cannot amount to two conceptual schemes. There is nothing therefore to which the truth of p and not-p can be relativized. One *could* express the thought we have arrived at by saying that the pragmatist has been given the resources to say that only one of them is right because since there are no 'different' conceptual schemes, they are both part of a single conceptual scheme, just as much as the single inquirer at one and the same stage of inquiry is part of a single conceptual scheme. All inquirers, all inquirer-stages, are part of a single conceptual scheme. Therefore, contradiction within one inquirer, contradictory judgments by two inquirers, contradictory judgments issuing out of revision made by an inquirer from one stage of his inquiry to the next, are all just as intolerable from the point of view of truth. But Davidson's preferred way to say it is to say something slightly different. He does not say that there is always only one conceptual scheme. He instead says: if there are no *different* conceptual schemes, there are *no* conceptual schemes. The very idea of a conceptual scheme is mistaken. However one says it, the outcome is the same anti-relativist one.

The idea that one should always insist that one of two contradictory beliefs is right is of course a *realist* idea that we have arrived at by appending Davidson's *anti-relativist* argument to pragmatism. But it's a realist idea which, unlike the classical realist idea and the residual Cartesian realist idea, allows us to embrace a more intuitively satisfying epistemology, an epistemology in which one need never deny that we seek truth in inquiry, nor deny that we achieve it from time to time, nor go around with a pervasive diffidence (diffidence, in the sense captured in "we never know when any given belief of ours is true") about the beliefs (as opposed to hypotheses) one has. In other words, a realism by which each of two disagreed inquirers can say *as realists*, "Only one of us is right," and then *as pragmatists* add from the corners of their mouth, but with no diffidence at all, "And I am."

Summing up, then, where does all this leave us on the question of realism and relativism? It is the claim of [this section of the paper] that if the *classical* realism of Descartes' absolute conception of reality (along with relativism, with which it shares a crucial assumption) was successfully refuted by the argument presented in Section I, then the second and residual form of Cartesian realism presented in Section II cannot claim any advantage over the far more attractive pragmatist realism (more attractive because it promotes a more credible epistemology) presented in Section III. This is because the only reason to think that it might have any advantage over the pragmatist version of realism is that the latter seemed susceptible to a kind of relativism. But since it was precisely the force of the argument of Section I that it not only refuted classical realism but also refuted at the same time the kind of relativism with which it shares a crucial assumption, that advantage is illusory. The pragmatist can appeal to that argument, as we have just done in the present section, to show that no such relativism threatens her, despite her rejection of the residual Cartesian realism of Section II.

It is a pity that Davidson does not see the force of his own argument, presented in Section I, as allowing him the space to occupy a far more plausible epistemology than the residual Cartesian one that he rests with. He is happy to rest with the thought that not all our beliefs can be false, thinking that that is enough to keep the Cartesian skeptic at bay. He therefore aggressively asserts that once we have established that not all our beliefs can be false, we must add that we never know which ones among them are true. Truth, of this kind, is still realist truth of course, if not quite that of the absolute conception of reality. In embracing it, Davidson completely neglects the fact that a quite distinct and just as crippling skeptical Cartesian position is entailed by it, a skepticism which remains unhurt by his argument presented in Section I, a skepticism which Moore, Austin, Wittgenstein, and the pragmatists are all resisting, the one which says that we are never given the right to claim that any particular belief amounts to knowledge, even if we have the general right to the general claim that we have a great deal of knowledge. But he need not have gone on to assert this residual Cartesian position. If I am right in this last section, *his own argument* with its combined and integrated force against classical realism *and* relativism allows him to assert an alternative position, a pragmatism, with no concessions to Cartesian skepticism of any variety, with no concessions—despite appearances—to relativism of any sort, and moreover a position (as was shown in Section III) which may properly also call itself a 'realism' because it satisfies basic realist demands, once they are shorn off from extreme and gratuitous Cartesian notions of the sort of independence truth and reality are supposed to have from our position as inquirers.

I have singled out Davidson for the most discussion because it is particularly ironic and frustrating that someone who has provided an argument against relativism which makes no appeal to Cartesian realism of any variety in the course of giving the argument, someone who has provided therefore an argument which helps us see that in opposing relativism we do not have to embrace any realism of a sort that implies an unattractive epistemology, should then have failed to arrive at a much more satisfying realism, a realism that integrates itself with a far more attractive epistemology. But it's not just Davidson, Putnam, Rorty, and all the other philosophers who are opposed to one or other versions of Cartesian epistemology and the realisms they presuppose, should all prize such an integration that pragmatism in this form provides. Yet, as I said earlier, Putnam ties truth to unnecessarily idealized conceptions of warranted assertibility, and Rorty has given up the idea that truth is in any sense a goal of inquiry, seeking to replace it by notions of justification and warranted assertibility. None of those options seem necessary or attractive, once this pragmatist version of realism comes to light.

NOTES

1. Rene Descartes, *Meditations on First Philosophy*, trans. John Cottingham (Cambridge: Cambridge University Press, 1986).

2. Donald Davidson, "On the Very Idea of a Conceptual Scheme," in *Inquiries into Truth and Interpretation*, 2nd ed. (Oxford: Oxford University Press, 2001), 183 (this volume, chap. 8).

3. Donald Davidson, *Inquiries into Truth and Interpretation* (Oxford: Oxford University Press, 1984).

4. It would seem that there is an element of analyticity presupposed in the argument, at the point where one assumes a certain sort of connection between the very notion of

ghosts and the belief that people die. But some weaker connection than the despised analyticity may be just as good to work the trick (and, in fact, there had better be one since Davidson has himself denied any truck with analyticity.) Perhaps it is enough that for the initial belief that there are ghosts to be properly attributed, it's not so much that any specific defining belief is also required to be attributed in each and every case where that belief is attributed to an agent in interpretation. Different agents may have different concepts of what a ghost is (of what the term 'ghost' means) and so there is no canonical belief or set of beliefs defining of ghosts. To stretch this point a little further, particular agents may have different concepts of what a ghost is at different times of speaking. Thus, the concept may differ from person to person, even from occasion to occasion, and so there is no analyticity, merely highly localized and idiolectical use of words and deployment of concepts. *But still* some background of true beliefs (by the interpreters' lights) is required to be attributed to identify any given agent's belief about any particular sort of thing (such as ghosts) at any given time, and that is enough to ward off the comprehensive skepticism.

5. This argument is given in a subsequent paper, "The Method of Truth and Metaphysics," in Davidson, *Inquiries into Truth and Interpretation* (1984).

6. Thomas Nagel, *The View from Nowhere* (New York: Oxford University Press, 1986), chap. 6.

7. Ludwig Wittgenstein, *Philosophical Investigations* (Oxford: Blackwell, 1953). Because the point in Davidson emerges by semantic ascent, it seems to say something higher-order than what is usually found in Wittgenstein, but the philosophical significance is the same. In Wittgenstein, the point is usually expressed by saying that a particular thought or the meaning of any particular term must be such that the criterion for its attribution or use is something we can tell has been applied correctly when it has been. Because of the semantic ascent involved in Davidson's reply to the idea of a super-knower, it's not any particular thought or meaning of which this philosophical point is made but about the application of the criteria for the term 'thought' (or 'meaning') itself.

8. Donald Davidson, "Truth Rehabilitated," in *Rorty and His Critics*, ed. Robert Brandom (Oxford: Blackwell, 2000).

9. In Davidson, "Truth Rehabilitated," Davidson's characterization of pragmatism comes close to this caricature. The pragmatism being sketched in the present paper by contrast is ignoring a host of what I, in the text above, have called 'reckless' remarks made by pragmatists over decades which encourage this caricature. In doing so it is really going back to the pragmatism to be found in Peirce's classic paper "The Fixation of Belief," *Popular Science Monthly*, November 1877, 1–15. That extraordinarily profound paper has been an inspiration for the sort of pragmatism that has come over decades to be associated with Columbia's Philosophy Department (which was—lest it's forgotten—for years John Dewey's department) thanks to the determined advocacy of Isaac Levi, who has himself shaped a highly original philosophy of belief revision out of it. I am happy to see this

paper of mine and others I have been writing on the subject over the years as contributing in minor ways to the propagation of what might as well be called 'Columbia Pragmatism' against a range of other less attractive epistemologies in the field. My debt to this paper by Peirce and to Levi should be apparent to those who have read them.

10. Rorty in his reply to my "Is Truth a Goal of Inquiry? Rorty and Davidson on Truth," in Brandom, *Rorty and His Critics*, suggests that I had tried to define truth in that essay. See below for more on this misreading.

11. A certain amount of holism may enter, of course, which would make one doubt a number of implied beliefs if evidence is encountered against anyone. But this would still be different from the logical possibility of empirical beliefs being false, giving rise to doubts of a general and comprehensive kind regarding all such beliefs.

12. In "Is Truth a Goal of Enquiry? Davidson vs. Wright," *Philosophical Quarterly* 45, no. 180 (1995): 281–300, Rorty quite fails to see the attractions of the pragmatism being presented here, and, like Davidson, is happy to give up the idea (an idea that is preserved in the pragmatism being presented here) that truth is a goal of inquiry. See also his "Universalty and Truth," in Brandom, *Rorty and His Critics*.

13. W. V. Quine, *Word and Object* (Cambridge, Mass.: MIT Press, 1960), 24–45; emphasis added.

14. John McDowell, "Towards Rehabilitating Objectivity," in Brandom, *Rorty and His Critics*.

15. See my "Is Truth a Goal of Inquiry?" and Rorty's reply, "Reply to Bilgrami," in the same volume.

16. There may be a temptation to drive a wedge between knowledge and truth here, allowing that Austin is right about knowledge but disallowing us our criticism of Davidson and Rorty on truth. This wedge would be based on some separation of the concept of knowledge from that of truth, a move that I think should be regarded with great suspicion, a suspicion which I will not articulate now.

17. J. L. Austin, "Other Minds," in *Philosophical Papers* (New York: Oxford University Press, 1960), 98.

18. Ludwig Wittgenstein, *On Certainty*, ed. G. E. M. Anscombe and G. H. von Wright (Oxford: Blackwell, 1969).

19. Edmund Husserl, *Méditations cartésiennes: Introduction á la phénoménologie* (Paris: Librairie Armand Colin, 1931).

20. Crispin Wright, "Facts and Certainty," *Proceedings of the British Academy* 71 (1985): 429–472.

21. See the discussion of "goldfinches" in Austin, "Other Minds," 88–89.

Moral Relativism, Objectivity, and Reasons | **PART III**

Moral Relativism Defended | **14**

GILBERT HARMAN

My thesis is that morality arises when a group of people reach an implicit agreement or come to a tacit understanding about their relations with one another. Part of what I mean by this is that moral judgments—or, rather, an important class of them—make sense only in relation to and with reference to one or another such agreement or understanding. This is vague, and I shall try to make it more precise in what follows. But it should be clear that I intend to argue for a version of what has been called moral relativism.

In doing so, I am taking sides in an ancient controversy. Many people have supposed that the sort of view, which I am going to defend, is obviously correct—indeed, that it is the only sort of account that could make sense of the phenomenon of morality. At the same time there have also been many who have supposed that moral relativism is confused, incoherent, and even immoral, at the very least obviously wrong.

Most arguments against relativism make use of a strategy of dissuasive definition; they define moral relativism as an inconsistent thesis. For example, they define it as the assertion that (1) there are no universal moral principles and (2)

Gilbert Harman, "Moral Relativism Defended," in *The Philosophical Review*, Volume 84, no. 1, pp. 3–22. Copyright, 1975, Cornell University Press. All rights reserved. Used by permission of the publisher.

one ought to act in accordance with the principles of one's own group, where this latter principle, (2), is supposed to be a universal moral principle.[1] It is easy enough to show that this version of moral relativism will not do, but that is no reason to think that a defender of moral relativism cannot find a better definition.

My moral relativism is a soberly logical thesis—a thesis about logical form, if you like. Just as the judgment that something is large makes sense only in relation to one or another comparison class, so too, I will argue, the judgment that it is wrong of someone to do something makes sense only in relation to an agreement or understanding. A dog may be large in relation to Chihuahuas but not large in relation to dogs in general. Similarly, I will argue, an action may be wrong in relation to one agreement but not in relation to another. Just as it makes no sense to ask whether a dog is large, period, apart from any relation to a comparison class, so too, I will argue, it makes no sense to ask whether an action is wrong, period, apart from any relation to an agreement.

There is an agreement, in the relevant sense, if each of a number of people intends to adhere to some schedule, plan, or set of principles, intending to do this on the understanding that the others similarly intend. The agreement or understanding need not be conscious or explicit; and I will not here try to say what distinguishes moral agreements from, for example, conventions of the road or conventions of etiquette, since these distinctions will not be important as regards the purely logical thesis that I will be defending.

Although I want to say that certain moral judgments are made in relation to an agreement, I do not want say this about all moral judgments. Perhaps it is true that all moral judgments are made in relation to an agreement; nevertheless, that is not what I will be arguing. For I want to say that there is a way in which certain moral judgments are relative to an agreement but other moral judgments are not. My relativism is a thesis only about what I will call 'inner judgments,' such as the judgment that someone ought not to have acted in a certain way or the judgment that it was right or wrong of him to have done so. My relativism is not meant to apply, for example, to the judgment that someone is evil or the judgment that a given institution is unjust.

In particular, I am not denying (nor am I asserting) that some moralities are 'objectively' better than others or that there are objective standards for assessing moralities. My thesis is a soberly logical thesis about logical form.

I. INNER JUDGMENTS

We make inner judgments about a person only if we suppose that he is capable of being motivated by the relevant moral considerations. We make other sorts of judgment about those who we suppose are not susceptible of such motivation. Inner judgments include judgments in which we say that someone should or ought to have done something or that someone was right or wrong to have done something. Inner judgments do not include judgments in which we call someone (literally) a savage or say that someone is (literally) inhuman, evil, a betrayer, a traitor, or an enemy.

Consider this example. Intelligent beings from outer space land on Earth, beings without the slightest concern for human life and happiness. That a certain course of action on their part might injure one of us means nothing to them; that fact by itself gives them no reason to avoid the action. In such a case it would be odd to say that nevertheless the being ought to avoid injuring us or that it would be wrong for them to attack us. Of course, we will want to resist them if they do such things and we will make negative judgments about them; but we will judge that they are dreadful enemies to be repelled and even destroyed, not that they should not act as they do.

Similarly, if we learn that a band of cannibals has captured and eaten the sole survivor of a shipwreck, we will speak of the primitive morality of the cannibals and may call them savages, but we will not say that they ought not to have eaten their captive.

Again, suppose that a contented employee of Murder, Incorporated, was raised as a child to honor and respect members of the 'family' but to have nothing but contempt for the rest of society. His current assignment, let us suppose, is to kill a certain bank manager, Bernard J. Ortcutt. Since Ortcutt is not a member of the 'family', the employee in question has no compunction about carrying out his assignment. In particular, if we were to try to convince him that he should not kill Ortcutt, our argument would merely amuse him. We would not provide him with the slightest reason to desist unless we were to point to practical difficulties, such as the likelihood of his getting caught. Now, in this case it would be a misuse of language to say of him that he ought not to kill Ortcutt or that it would be wrong of him to do so, since that would imply that our own moral considerations carry some weight with him, which they do not. Instead we can only judge that he is a criminal, someone to be hunted down by the police, an enemy of peace loving citizens, and so forth.

It is true that we can make certain judgments about him using the word 'ought.' For example, investigators who have been tipped off by an informer and who are waiting for the assassin to appear at the bank can use the 'ought' of expectation to say, "He ought to arrive soon," meaning that on the basis of their information one would expect him to arrive soon. And, in thinking over how the assassin might carry out his assignment, we can use the 'ought' of rationality to say that he ought to go in by the rear door, meaning that it would be more rational for him to do that than to go in by the front door. In neither of these cases is the moral 'ought' in question.

There is another use of 'ought' which is normative and in a sense moral but which is distinct from what I am calling the moral 'ought.' This is the use which occurs when we say that something ought or ought not to be the case. It ought not to be the case that members of Murder, Incorporated, go around killing people; in other words, it is a terrible thing that they do so.[2] The same thought can perhaps be expressed as "They ought not to go around killing people," meaning that it ought not to be the case that they do, not that they are wrong to do what they do. The normative 'ought to be' is used to assess a situation; the moral 'ought to do' is used to describe a relation between an agent and a type of act that he might perform or has performed.

The sentence "They ought not to go around killing people" is therefore multiply ambiguous. It can mean that one would not expect them to do so (the 'ought' of expectation), that it is not in their interest to do so (the 'ought' of rationality), that it is a bad thing that they do so (the normative 'ought to be'), or that they are wrong to do so (the moral 'ought to do'). For the most part I am here concerned only with the last of these interpretations.

The word 'should' behaves very much like 'ought to.' There is a 'should' of expectation ("They should be here soon"), a 'should' of rationality ("He should go in by the back door"), a normative 'should be' ("They shouldn't go around killing people like that"), and the moral 'should do' ("You should keep that promise"). I am, of course, concerned mainly with the last sense of 'should.'

'Right' and 'wrong' also have multiple uses; I will not try to say what all of them are. But I do want to distinguish using the word 'wrong' to say that a particular situation or action is wrong from using the word to say that it is wrong *of someone* to do something. In the former case, the word 'wrong' is used to assess an act or situation. In the latter case it is used to describe a relation between an agent and an act. Only the latter sort of judgment is an inner judgment. Although we would not say concerning the contented employee of Murder, Incorporated, mentioned earlier that it was wrong *of him* to kill Ortcutt, we could say that *his action* was wrong and we could say that it is wrong that there is so much killing.

To take another example, it sounds odd to say that Hitler should not have ordered the extermination of the Jews, that it was wrong of him to have done so. That sounds somehow 'too weak' a thing to say. Instead we want to say that Hitler was an evil man. Yet we can properly say, "Hitler ought not to have ordered the extermination of the Jews," if what we mean is that it ought never to have happened; and we can say without oddity that what Hitler did was wrong. Oddity attends only the inner judgment that Hitler was wrong to have acted in that way. That is what sounds 'too weak.'

It is worth noting that the inner judgments sound too weak not because of the enormity of what Hitler did but because we suppose that in acting as he did he shows that he could not have been susceptible to the moral considerations on the basis of which we make our judgment. He is in the relevant sense beyond the pale and we therefore cannot make inner judgments about him. To see that this is so, consider, say, Stalin, another mass murderer. We can perhaps imagine someone taking a sympathetic view of Stalin. In such a view, Stalin realized that the course he was going to pursue would mean the murder of millions of people and he dreaded such a prospect. However, the alternative seemed to offer an even greater disaster—so, reluctantly and with great anguish, he went ahead. In relation to such a view of Stalin, inner judgments about Stalin are not as odd as similar judgments about Hitler. For we might easily continue the story by saying that, despite what he hoped to gain, Stalin should not have done so. What makes inner judgments about Hitler odd, 'too weak,' is not that the acts judged seem too terrible for the words used but rather that the agent judged seems beyond the pale—in other words beyond the motivational reach of the relevant moral considerations.

Of course, I do not want to deny that for various reasons a speaker might pretend that an agent is or is not susceptible to certain moral considerations. For example, a speaker may for rhetorical or political reasons wish to suggest that someone is beyond the pale, that he should not be listened to, that he can be treated as an enemy. On the other hand, a speaker may pretend that someone is susceptible to certain moral considerations in an effort to make that person or others susceptible to those considerations. Inner judgments about one's children sometimes have this function. So do inner judgments made in political speeches that aim at restoring a lapsed sense of morality in government.

II. THE LOGICAL FORM OF INNER JUDGMENTS

Inner judgments have two important characteristics. First, they imply that the agent has reasons to do something. Second, the speaker in some sense endorses these reasons and supposes that the audience also endorses them. Other moral judgments about an agent, on the other hand, do not have such implications—they do not imply that the agent has reasons for acting that are endorsed by the speaker.

If someone S says that A (morally) ought to do D, S implies that A has reasons to do D and S endorses those reasons—whereas if S says that B was evil in what B did, S does not imply that the reasons S would endorse for not doing what

B did were reasons for B not to do that thing. In fact, S implies that they were not reasons for B.

Let us examine this more closely. If S says that (morally) A ought to do D, S implies that A has reasons to do D, which S endorses. I shall assume that such reasons would have to have their source in goals, desires, or intentions that S takes A to have and that S approves of A's having because S shares those goals, desires, or intentions. So, if S says that (morally) A ought to do D, there are certain motivational attitudes M which S assumes are shared by S, A, and S's audience.

Now, in supposing that reasons for action must have their source in goals, desires, or intentions, I am assuming something like an Aristotelian or Humean account of these matters, as opposed, for example, to a Kantian approach which sees a possible source of motivation in reason itself.[3] I must defer a full-scale discussion of the issue to another occasion. Here I simply assume that the Kantian approach is wrong. In particular, I assume that there might be no reasons at all for a being from outer space to avoid harm to us; that, for Hitler, there might have been no reason at all not to order the extermination of the Jews; that the contented employee of Murder, Incorporated, might have no reason at all not to kill Ortcutt; that the cannibals might have no reason not to eat their captive. In other words, I assume that the possession of rationality is not sufficient to provide a source for relevant reasons, that certain desires, goals, or intentions are also necessary. Those who accept this assumption will, I think, find that they distinguish inner moral judgments from other moral judgments in the way that I have indicated.

Ultimately, I want to argue that the shared motivational attitudes M are intentions to keep an agreement (supposing that others similarly intend). For I want to argue that inner moral judgments are made relative to such an agreement. That is, I want to argue that, when S makes the inner judgment that A ought to do D, S assumes that A intends to act in accordance with an agreement which S and S's audience also intend to observe. In other words, I want to argue that the source of the reasons for doing D which S ascribes to A is A's sincere intention to observe a certain agreement. I have not yet argued for the stronger thesis, however. I have argued only that S makes his judgment relative to *some* motivational attitudes M which S assumes are shared by S, A, and S's audience.

Formulating this as a logical thesis, I want to treat the moral 'ought' as a four-place predicate (or 'operator'), 'Ought (A, D, C, M),' which relates an agent A, a type of act D, considerations C, and motivating attitudes M. The relativity to considerations C can be brought out by considering what are sometimes called statements of *prima facie* obligation, "Considering that you promised, you ought to go to the board meeting, but considering that you are the sole surviving relative, you ought to go to the funeral; all things considered, it is not clear what you ought to do."[4] The claim that there is *this* relativity, to considerations, is not, of course, what makes my thesis a version of moral relativism, since any theory must acknowledge relativity to considerations. The relativity to considerations does, however, provide a model for a coherent interpretation of moral relativism as a similar kind of relativity.

It is not as easy to exhibit the relativity to motivating attitudes as it is to exhibit the relativity to considerations, since normally a speaker who makes a moral 'ought' judgment intends the relevant motivating attitudes to be ones that the speaker shares with the agent and the audience, and normally it will be obvious what attitudes these are. But sometimes a speaker does invoke different attitudes by invoking a morality the speaker does not share. Someone may say, for example, "As a Christian, you ought to turn the other cheek; I, however, propose to strike back." A spy who has been found out by a friend might say, "As a citizen, you ought to turn me in, but I hope that you will not." In these and similar cases a speaker makes a moral 'ought' judgment that is explicitly relative to motivating attitudes that the speaker does not share.

In order to be somewhat more precise, then, my thesis is this. 'Ought (A, D, C, M)' means roughly that, given that A has motivating attitudes M and given C, D is the course of action for A that is supported by the best reasons. In judgments using this sense of 'ought,' C and M are often not explicitly mentioned but are indicated by the context of utterance. Normally, when that happens, C will be 'all things considered' and M will be attitudes that are shared by the speaker and audience.

I mentioned that inner judgments have two characteristics. First, they imply that the agent has reasons to do something that are capable of motivating the agent. Second, the speaker endorses those reasons and supposes that the audience does too. Now, any 'Ought (A, D, C, M)' judgment has the first of these characteristics, but as we have just seen a judgment of this sort will not necessarily have the second characteristic if made with explicit reference to motivating attitudes not shared by the speaker. If reference is made either implicitly or explicitly (for example, through the use of the adverb 'morally') to attitudes that are shared by the speaker and audience, the resulting judgment has both characteristics and is an inner judgment. If reference is made to attitudes that are not shared by the speaker, the resulting judgment is not an inner judgment and does not represent a full-fledged moral judgment on the part of the speaker. In such a case we have an example of what has been called an inverted-commas use of 'ought.'[5]

III. MORAL BARGAINING

I have argued that moral 'ought' judgments are relational, 'Ought (A, D, C, M);' where M represents certain motivating attitudes. I now want to argue that the attitudes M derive from an agreement. That is, they are intentions to adhere to a particular agreement on the understanding that others also intend to do so. Really, it might be better for me to say that I put this forward as a hypothesis, since I cannot pretend to be able to prove that it is true. I will argue, however, that this hypothesis accounts for an otherwise puzzling aspect of our moral views that, as far as I know, there is no other way to account for.

I will use the word 'intention' in a somewhat extended sense to cover certain dispositions or habits. Someone may habitually act in accordance with the relevant understanding and therefore may be disposed to act in that way without having any more or less conscious intention. In such a case it may sound odd to say that he *intends* to act in accordance with the moral understanding. Nevertheless, for present purposes I will count that as his having the relevant intention in a dispositional sense.

I now want to consider the following puzzle about our moral views, a puzzle that has figured in recent philosophical discussion of issues such as abortion. It has been observed that most of us assign greater weight to the duty not to harm others than to the duty to help others. For example, most of us believe that a doctor ought not to save five of his patients who would otherwise die by cutting up a sixth patient and distributing his healthy organs where needed to the others, even though we do think that the doctor has a duty to try to help as many of his patients as he can. For we also think that he has a stronger duty to try not to harm any of his patients (or anyone else) even if by so doing he could help five others.[6]

This aspect of our moral views can seem very puzzling, especially if one supposes that moral feelings derive from sympathy and concern for others. But the hypothesis that morality derives from an agreement among people of varying powers and resources provides a plausible explanation. The rich, the poor, the strong, and the weak would all benefit if all were to try to avoid harming one another. So everyone could agree to that arrangement. But the rich and the strong would not benefit from an arrangement whereby everyone would try to do as much as possible to help those in need. The poor and weak would get all of the benefit of this latter arrangement. Since the rich and the strong could foresee that they would be required to do most of the helping and that they would receive little in return, they would be reluctant to agree to a strong principle of mutual aid. A compromise would be likely and a weaker principle would probably be accepted. In other words, although everyone could agree to a strong principle concerning the avoidance of harm, it would not be true that everyone would favor an equally strong principle of mutual aid. It is likely that only a weaker principle of the latter sort would gain general acceptance. So the hypothesis that morality derives from an understanding among people of different powers and resources can explain (and, according to me, does explain) why in our morality avoiding harm to others is taken to be more important than helping those who need help.

By the way, I am here only trying to *explain* an aspect of our moral views. I am not therefore *endorsing* that aspect. And I defer until later a relativistic account of the way in which aspects of our moral view can be criticized 'from within.'

Now we need not suppose that the agreement or understanding in question is explicit. It is enough if various members of society knowingly reach an agreement in intentions—each intending to act in certain ways on the understanding that the others have similar intentions. Such an implicit agreement is reached through a process of mutual adjustment and implicit bargaining.

Indeed, it is essential to the proposed explanation of this aspect of our moral views to suppose that the relevant moral understanding is thus the result of *bargaining*. It is necessary to suppose that, in order to further our interests, we form certain conditional intentions, hoping that others will do the same. The others, who have different interests, will form somewhat different conditional intentions. After implicit bargaining, some sort of compromise is reached.

Seeing morality in this way as a compromise based on implicit bargaining helps to explain why our morality takes it to be worse to harm someone than to refuse to help someone. The explanation requires that we view our morality as an implicit agreement about what to do. This sort of explanation could not be given if we were to suppose, say, that our morality represented an agreement only about the facts (naturalism). Nor is it enough simply to suppose that our morality represents an agreement in attitude, if we forget that such agreement can be reached, not only by way of such principles as are mentioned, for example, in Hare's "logic of imperatives,"[7] but also through bargaining. According to Hare, to accept a general moral principle is to intend to do something.[8] If we add to his theory that the relevant intentions can be reached through implicit bargaining, the resulting theory begins to look like the one that I am defending.

Many aspects of our moral views can be given a utilitarian explanation. We could account for these aspects, using the logical analysis I presented in the previous section of this paper, by supposing that the relevant 'ought' judgments presuppose shared attitudes of sympathy and benevolence. We can equally well explain them by supposing that considerations of utility have influenced our implicit agreements, so that the appeal is to a shared intention to adhere to those agreements. Any aspect of morality that is susceptible of a utilitarian explanation can also be explained by an implicit agreement, but not conversely. There are aspects of our moral views that seem to be explicable only in the second way, on the assumption that morality derives from an agreement. One example, already cited, is the distinction we make between harming and not helping. Another is our feeling that each person has an inalienable right of self-defense and self-preservation. Philosophers have not been able to come up with a really satisfactory utilitarian justification of such a right, but it is easily intelligible on our present hypothesis, as Hobbes observed many years ago. You cannot, except in very special circumstances, rationally form the intention not to try to preserve your life if it should ever be threatened, say, by society or the state, since you know that you cannot now control what you would do in such a situation. No matter what you now decided to do, when the time came, you would ignore your prior decision and try to save your life. Since you cannot now intend to do something later which you now know that you would not do, you cannot now intend to keep an agreement not to preserve your life if it is threatened by others in your society.[9]

This concludes the positive side of my argument; that, what I have called inner moral judgments, is made in relation to an implicit agreement. I now want to argue that this theory avoids difficulties traditionally associated with implicit agreement theories of morality.

IV. OBJECTIONS AND REPLIES

One traditional difficulty for implicit agreement theories concerns what motivates us to do what we have agreed to do. It will, obviously, not be enough to say that we have implicitly agreed to keep agreements, since the issue would then be why we keep *that* agreement. And this suggests an objection to implicit agreement theories. But the apparent force of the objection derives entirely from taking an agreement to be a kind of ritual. To agree in the relevant sense is not just to say something; it is to intend to do something—namely, to intend to carry out one's part of the agreement on the condition that others do their parts. If we agree in this sense to do something, we intend to do it and intending to do it is already to be motivated to do it. So there is no problem as to why we are motivated to keep our agreements in this sense.

We do believe that in general you ought not to pretend to agree in this sense in order to trick someone else into agreeing. But that suggests no objection to the present view. All that it indicates is that *our* moral understanding contains or implies an agreement to be open and honest with others. If it is supposed that this leaves a problem about someone who has not accepted our agreement—"What reason does *he* have not to pretend to accept our agreement so that he can then trick others into agreeing to various things?"—the answer is that such a person mayor may not have such a reason. If someone does not already accept something of our morality it may or may not be possible to find reasons why he should.

A second traditional objection to implicit agreement theories is that there is not a perfect correlation between what is generally believed to be morally right and what actually is morally right. Not everything generally agreed on is right and sometimes courses of action are right that would not be generally agreed to be right. But this is no objection to my thesis. My thesis is not that the implicit agreement from which a morality derives is an agreement in moral judgment; the thesis is rather that moral judgments make reference to and are made in relation to an agreement in intentions. Given that a group of people have agreed in this sense, there can still be disputes as to what the agreement implies for various situations. In my view, many moral disputes are of this sort. They presuppose a basic agreement and they concern what implications that agreement has for particular cases.

There can also be various things wrong with the agreement that a group of people reach, even from the point of view of that agreement, just as there can be defects in an individual's plan of action even from the point of view of that plan. Given what is known about the situation, a plan or agreement can in various ways be inconsistent, incoherent, or self-defeating. In my view, certain moral disputes are concerned with internal defects of the basic moral understanding of a group, and what changes should be made from the perspective of that understanding itself. This is another way in which moral disputes make sense with reference to and in relation to an underlying agreement.

Another objection to implicit agreement theories is that not all agreements are morally binding—for example, those made under compulsion or from a position of unfair disadvantage, which may seem to indicate that there are moral principles prior to those that derive from an implicit agreement. But, again, the force of the objection derives from an equivocation concerning what an agreement is. The principle that compelled agreements do not obligate concerns agreement in the sense of a certain sort of ritual indicating that one agrees. My thesis concerns a kind of agreement in intentions. The principle about compelled agreements is part of, or is implied by, our agreement in intentions. According to me it is only with reference to some such agreement in intentions that a principle of this sort makes sense.

Now it may be true our moral agreement in intentions also implies that it is wrong to compel people who are in a greatly inferior position to accept an agreement in intentions that they would not otherwise accept, and it may even be true that there is in our society at least one class of people in an inferior position who have been compelled thus to settle for accepting a basic moral understanding, aspects of which they would not have accepted had they not been in such an inferior position. In that case there would be an incoherence in our basic moral understanding and various suggestions might be made concerning the ways in which this understanding should be modified. But this moral critique of the understanding can proceed from that understanding itself, rather than from 'prior' moral principles.

In order to fix ideas, let us consider a society in which there is a well established and long-standing tradition of hereditary slavery. Let us suppose that everyone accepts this institution, including the slaves. Everyone treats it as in the nature of things that there should be such slavery. Furthermore, let us suppose that there are also aspects of the basic moral agreement which speak against slavery. That is, these aspects together with certain facts about the situation imply that people should not own slaves and that slaves have no obligation to acquiesce in their condition. In such a case, the moral understanding would be defective, although its defectiveness would presumably be hidden in one or another manner, perhaps by means of a myth that slaves are physically and mentally subhuman in a way that makes appropriate the sort of treatment elsewhere reserved for beasts of burden. If this myth were to be exposed, the members of the society would then be faced with an obvious incoherence in their basic moral agreement and might come eventually to modify their agreement so as to eliminate its acceptance of slavery.

In such a case, even relative to the old agreement it might be true that slave owners ought to free their slaves, that slaves need not obey their masters, and that people ought to work to eliminate slavery. For the course supported by the best reasons, given that one starts out with the intention of adhering to a particular agreement, may be that one should stop intending to adhere to certain aspects of that agreement and should try to get others to do the same.

We can also (perhaps—but see below) envision a second society with hereditary slavery whose agreement has no aspects that speak against slavery. In that case, even if the facts of the situation were fully appreciated, no incoherence would appear in the basic moral understanding of the society and it would not be true in relation to that understanding that slave owners ought to free their slaves, that slaves need not obey their masters, and so forth. There might nevertheless come a time when there were reasons of a different sort to modify the basic understanding, either because of an external threat from societies opposed to slavery or because of an internal threat of rebellion by the slaves.

Now it is easier for us to make what I have called inner moral judgments about slave owners in the first society than in the second. For we can with reference to members of the first society invoke principles that they share with us and, with reference to those principles, we can say of them that they ought not to have kept slaves and that they were immoral to have done so. This sort of inner judgment becomes increasingly inappropriate, however, the more distant they are from us and the less easy it is for us to think of our moral understanding as continuous with and perhaps a later development of theirs. Furthermore, it seems appropriate to make only non-inner judgments of the slave owners in the second society. We can say that the second society is unfair and unjust, that the slavery that exists is wrong, that it ought not to exist. But it would be inappropriate in this case to say that it was morally wrong of the slave owners to own slaves. The relevant aspects of our moral understanding, which we would invoke in moral judgments about them, are not aspects of the moral understanding that exists in the second society. (I will come back to the question of slavery below.)

Let me turn now to another objection to implicit agreement theories, an objection which challenges the idea that there is an agreement of the relevant sort. For, if we have agreed, when did we do it? Does anyone really remember having agreed? How did we indicate our agreement? What about those who do not want to agree? How do they indicate that they do not agree and what are the consequences of their not agreeing? Reflection on these and similar questions can make the hypothesis of implicit agreement seem too weak a basis on which to found morality.

But once again there is equivocation about agreements. The objection treats the thesis as the claim that morality is based on some sort of ritual rather than an agreement in intentions. But, as I have said, there is an agreement in the relevant sense when each of a number of people has an intention on the assumption that others have the same intention. In this sense of 'agreement,' there is no given moment at which one agrees, since one continues to agree in this sense as long as one continues to have the relevant intentions. Someone refuses to agree to the extent that he or she does not share these intentions. Those who do not agree are outside the agreement; in extreme cases they are outlaws or enemies. It does not follow, however, that there are no constraints on how those who agree may act toward those who do not, since for various reasons the agreement itself may contain provisions for dealing with outlaws and enemies.

This brings me to one last objection, which derives from the difficulty people have in trying to give an explicit and systematic account of their moral views. If one actually agrees to something, why is it so hard to say what one has agreed? In response I can say only that many understandings appear to be of this sort. It is often possible to recognize what is in accordance with the understanding and what would violate it without being able to specify the understanding in any general way. Consider, for example, the understanding that exists among the members of a team of acrobats or a symphony orchestra.

Another reason why it is so difficult to give a precise and systematic specification of any actual moral understanding is that such an understanding will not in general be constituted by absolute rules but will take a vaguer form, specifying goals and areas of responsibility. For example, the agreement may indicate that one is to show respect for others by trying where possible to avoid actions that will harm them or interfere with what they are doing; it may indicate the duties and responsibilities of various members of the family, who is to be responsible for bringing up the children, and so forth. Often what will be important will be not so much exactly what actions are done as how willing participants are to do their parts and what attitudes they have—for example, whether they give sufficient weight to the interests of others.

The vague nature of moral understandings is to some extent alleviated in practice. One learns what can and cannot be done in various situations. Expectations are adjusted to other expectations. But moral disputes arise nonetheless. Such disputes may concern what the basic moral agreement implies for particular situations; and, if so, that can happen either because of disputes over the facts or because of a difference in basic understanding. Moral disputes may also arise concerning whether or not changes should be made in the basic agreement. Racial and sexual issues seem often to be of this second sort; but there is no clear line between the two kinds of dispute. When the implications of an agreement for a particular situation are considered, one possible outcome is that it becomes clear that the agreement should be modified.

Moral reasoning is a form of practical reasoning. One begins with certain beliefs and intentions, including intentions that are part of one's acceptance of the moral understanding in a given group. In reasoning, one modifies one's intentions, often by forming new intentions, sometimes by giving up old ones, so that one's plans become more rational and coherent—or, rather, one seeks to make all of one's attitudes coherent with each other.

The relevant sort of coherence is not simply consistency. It is something very like the explanatory coherence which is so important in theoretical reasoning. Coherence involves generality and lack of arbitrariness. Consider our feelings about cruelty to animals. Obviously these do not derive from an agreement that has been reached with animals. Instead it is a matter of coherence. There is a *prima facie* arbitrariness and lack of generality in a plan that involves avoiding cruelty to people but not to animals.

On the other hand, coherence in this sense is not the only relevant factor in practical reasoning. Another is conservatism or inertia. A third is an interest in satisfying basic desires or needs. One tries to make the least change that will best satisfy one's desires while maximizing the overall coherence of one's attitudes. Coherence by itself is not an overwhelming force. That is why our attitudes towards animals are weak and wavering, allowing us to use them in ways we would not use people.

Consider again the second hereditary slave society mentioned above. This society was to be one in which no aspects of the moral understanding shared by the masters spoke against slavery. In fact that is unlikely, since there is *some* arbitrariness in the idea that people are to be treated in different ways depending on whether they are born slave or free. Coherence of attitude will no doubt speak at least a little against the system of slavery. The point is that the factors of conservatism and desire might speak more strongly in favor of the *status quo*, so that, all things considered, the slave owners might have no reason to change their understanding.

One thing that distinguishes slaves from animals is that slaves can organize and threaten revolt, whereas animals cannot. Slaves can see to it that both coherence and desire oppose conservatism, so that it becomes rational for the slave owners to arrive at a new, broader, more coherent understanding, one which includes the slaves.

It should be noted that coherence of attitude provides a constant pressure to widen the consensus and eliminate arbitrary distinctions. In this connection it is useful to recall ancient attitudes toward foreigners, and the ways people used to think about 'savages,' 'natives,' and 'Indians.' Also, recall that infanticide used to be considered as acceptable as we consider abortion to be. There has been a change here in our moral attitudes, prompted, I suggest, largely by considerations of coherence of attitude.

Finally, I would like to say a few brief words about the limiting case of group morality, when the group has only one member; then, as it were, a person comes to an understanding with himself. In my view, a person can make inner judgments in relation to such an individual morality only about himself. A familiar form of pacifism is of this sort. Certain pacifists judge that it would be wrong of them to participate in killing, although they are not willing to make a similar judgment about others. Observe that such a pacifist is unwilling only to make *inner* moral judgments about others. Although he is unwilling to judge that those who do participate are wrong to do so, he is perfectly willing to say that it is a bad thing that they participate. There are of course many other examples of individual morality in this sense, when a person imposes standards on himself that he does not apply to others. The existence of such examples is further confirmation of the relativist thesis that I have presented.

My conclusion is that relativism can be formulated as an intelligible thesis, the thesis that morality derives from an implicit agreement and that moral judgments are in a logical sense made in relation to such an agreement. Such a theory helps to explain otherwise puzzling aspects of our own moral views, in particular why we think that it is more important to avoid harm to others than to help others. The theory is also partially confirmed by what is, as far as I can tell, a previously unnoticed distinction between inner and non-inner moral judgments. Furthermore, traditional objections to implicit agreement theories can be met.

NOTES

Many people have given me good advice about the subjects discussed in this paper, which derives from a larger study of practical reasoning and morality. I am particularly indebted to Donald Davidson, Stephen Schiffer, William Alston, Fredrick Schick, Thomas Nagel, Walter Kaufmann, Peter Singer, Robert Audi, and the editors of the *Philosophical Review*.

1. Bernard Williams, *Morality: An Introduction to Ethics* (New York: Harper & Row, 1972), 20–21; Marcus Singer, *Generalization in Ethics: An Essay in the Logic of Ethics, with Rudiments of a System of Moral Philosophy* (New York: Knopf, 1961), 332.

2. Thomas Nagel has observed that often, when we use the evaluative 'ought to be' to say that something ought to be the case, we imply that someone ought to do something or ought to have done something about it. To take his example, we would not say that a certain hurricane ought not to have killed fifty people just on the ground that it was a terrible thing that the hurricane did so but we might say this if we had in mind that the deaths from the hurricane would not have occurred except for the absence of safety or evacuation procedures which the authorities ought to have provided.

3. For the latter approach, see Thomas Nagel, *The Possibility of Altruism* (Oxford: Oxford University Press, 1970).

4. Donald Davidson, "Weakness of Will," in *Moral Concepts*, ed. Joel Feinberg (Oxford: Oxford University Press, 1969).

5. R. M. Hare, *The Language of Morals* (Oxford: Oxford University Press, 1952), 164–168.

6. Philippa Foot, "Abortion and the Doctrine of Double Effect," in *Moral Problems: A Collection of Philosophical Essays*, ed. James Rachels (New York: Harper & Row, 1971).

7.   R. M. Hare, *The Language of Morals* (Oxford: Oxford University Press, 1963), and *Freedom and Reason* (Oxford: Oxford University Press, 1963).

8. Hare, *Language of Morals*, 18–20, 168–169.

9. Thomas Hobbes, "Of the First and Second Natural Laws, and of Contracts," pt. 1, chap. 14, in *Leviathan* (Oxford: Oxford University Press, 1957), inter alia.

BERNARD WILLIAMS

This chapter tries to place certain issues in the discussion of relativism, not to deal with any one of them thoroughly. It is concerned with any kind of relativism, in the sense that the questions raised are ones that should be asked with regard to relativistic views in any area, whether it be the worldviews of different cultures, shifts in scientific paradigms, or differences of ethical outlook. A machinery is introduced which is intended to apply quite generally. But the only area in which I want to claim that there is truth in relativism is the area of ethical relativism. This does not mean that I here try to argue against its truth in any other area, nor do I try to pursue any of the numerous issues involved in delimiting the ethical from other areas.

I. CONDITIONS OF THE PROBLEM

A. There have to be two or more *systems of belief* (Ss) which are to some extent self-contained. No very heavy weight is put on the propositional implications of

Originally published as Bernard Williams, "The Truth in Relativism," *Proceedings of the Aristotelian Society* 75 (1975), pp. 215–228. Reprinted by courtesy of the Editor of the Aristotelian Society © 1975.

the term 'belief', nor, still less, is it implied that all relevant differences between such systems (let S1, S2, stand for examples from now on) can be adequately expressed in propositional differences: the extent to which this is so will differ with different sorts of examples. Any application of this structure will involve some degree of idealization, with regard to the coherence and homogeneity of an S. There is more than one way in which these characteristics may be imposed, however, and difference in these affects the way (perhaps, the sense) in which the resultant S is an idealization.

The characteristics may be involved in the very identification of the Ss: thus two synchronously competing scientific theories may be picked out in part in terms of what bodies of beliefs hang together. But even in this case the Ss will not just be intellectual items constructed from the outside on the basis of the harmony of their content: there will in fact be bodies of scientists working within these theories (research programs, etc.) and seeking to impose coherence on them. If failures in imposing coherence were to be regarded as *a priori* impossible, the structure of description in terms of various Ss would lose a great deal of explanatory value.

In the case of alien cultures, the identification of an S may be effected initially through other features (geographical isolation and internal interaction of a group of persons), and the coherence of the S operate rather as an ideal limit for the understanding of the group's beliefs. This idea is, in fact, problematical, at least if taken as indicative of understanding in any objective sense: one comprehensible, and surely plausible, hypothesis is that no group of human beings will have a belief system which is fully coherent. The demand operates, nevertheless, as a constraint on theory-construction about the group, since the data will even more radically underdetermine theory if room is left for indeterminate amounts of incoherence within the S which theory constructs.

The problems of relativism concern communication between S1 and S2, or between them and some third party, and in particular issues of preference between them. It is worth noticing that quite a lot is taken for granted in the construction of the problem-situation already, in the application of the idea of there being a plurality of different Ss. Thus it is presupposed that persons within each S can understand other persons within that S; also that persons receive information in certain ways and not others, are acculturated in certain ways, etc. It may be that some forms of relativism can be shown to be false by reference to these presuppositions themselves: not on the ground (which would prove nothing) that the *genesis* of the ideas such as 'a culture', like that of 'relativism' itself, lies in a certain sort of culture, but on the ground that the *application* of a notion such as 'a culture' presupposes the instantiation in the subject-matter of a whole set of relations which can be adequately expressed at all only via the concepts of one culture rather than another (e.g., certain notions of causality). Any relativism which denied the non-relative validity of concepts involved in setting up its problem at all would be refuted. This aspect of the matter has received some attention;[1] I shall not try to take it further here.

B. S_1 and S_2 have to be *exclusive of one another*. That this should in some sense be so is a necessary condition of the problems arising to which relativism is supposed to provide an answer; indeed, it can itself be seen as a condition of identifying S_1 and S_2, in any sense relevant to those problems.

Suppose, for example, that two putative Ss constituted merely the history or geography of two different times or places: then evidently they are not Ss in the sense of the problem, because they can merely be conjoined.

A much harder question, however, is raised by asking what are the (most general) conditions of two Ss excluding one another. The most straightforward case is that in which S_1 and S_2 have conflicting consequences, a condition which I shall first take in the form of requiring that there be some yes/no question to which consequence C_1 of S_1 answers "yes" and consequence C_2 of S_2 answers "no." Under this condition S_1 and S_2 have to be (at least in the respect in question) *comparable*.

The questions to which relativism is supposed to give an answer may be raised by the case of conflicting consequences, but relativism will not stay around as an answer to them unless something else is also true, namely, that the answering of a yes/no question of this sort in one way rather than the other does not constrain either the holder of S_1 or the holder of S_2 to abandon respectively the positions characteristic of S_1 and S_2 (and of the difference between them). If this further condition does not hold, there will be a straightforward decision procedure between S_1 and S_2, and relativism will have been banished. In the scientific case, the possibility of this condition holding, granted that C_1 and C_2 are consequences of S_1 and S_2, lies in the possibility that the consequence follows from the system only using material peripheral to the system and to its most characteristic positions: the situation is the much-discussed one in which theory is underdetermined by observation.

However, if theory is radically underdetermined by observation, can it be required that Ss are even to this modest degree comparable? Thus, in the spirit of one fashionable line of argument, if every observation statement is theory-laden and all theory-ladenness displays meaning-variance, then it is unclear how there can be one yes/no question which stands in the required relation to S_1 and S_2. Here it is important to see how little is implied by there being conflicting consequences of S_1 and S_2. All that is required is that there be *some* description of a possible outcome, which description is acceptable to both S1 and S2, and in terms of which a univocal yes/no question can be formed: it may well be that there are other descriptions of what is (in some sense) the same event which are noncomparable. If this minimal requirement is not satisfied, severe problems are likely to follow, particularly in the case of scientific theories, for the original description of the Ss. We lose control on the notion of observation, concerning which it is said that it underdetermines theory; and we lose the descriptions of certain passages in the history of science which are the subject and in some part the motivation of these accounts (roughly it looks as though not only the choice of a replacement paradigm, but the occasion of the choice, might emerge as entirely socially determined, as though a chief determinant of the alteration of scientific theory were boredom).

However it may be with scientific theories, it would perhaps be unwise to exclude, at least at the beginning of the argument, the possibility of systems so disparate that they were not, in terms of conflicting consequences, comparable at all: some social anthropologists have given accounts of the Ss of traditional (pre-scientific) societies in terms which seem to imply that they are quite incommensurable with the Ss of modern, scientific societies. I shall not go into the question of whether such accounts could be true.[2] The issue is rather, if such accounts were true, what content could be left to the idea that the traditional and the scientific Ss were exclusive of one another—as surely everyone, including these social anthropologists, would say that they were. Here it looks as though the only thing to be said is that, in ways which need to be analyzed, it is impossible to live within both Ss. Accepting this vague idea, we can indeed continue to use, at a different level, the language of conflicting consequences, since if it is impossible to live within both S1 and S2, then the consequences of (holding) S1 include actions, practices, etc., which are incompatible with those which are consequences of (holding) S2.

I do not take this to be a very illuminating assimilation, since the variation required in the interpretation of 'consequence' remains unexplained. But it does harmlessly help to handle a wider range of cases without constant qualification; and it does, more than that, positively bring out one thing—that even in this limiting case (which I shall call that of *incommensurable exclusivity*), there has to be something which can be identified as the *locus* of exclusivity, and hence is not from every point of view incommensurable. This *locus* will be that of the actions or practices which are the consequences of living within S1 or S2. Another light will be shed on them when we turn, next, to broadly ethical cases.

In ethical cases (taken in a broad sense), the conditions of conflict come out, obviously enough, differently from the form they take with, for instance, scientific theories. The simplest case is that of conflict between answers which are given to yes/no questions, which are practical questions, questions about whether to do a certain thing. Now such a question might be a general, or type, action question, asking whether a certain type of thing was to be done in a certain type of situation. In this case, the relevant formulation is that it is possible for S1 to answer "yes" to such a question while S2 answers "no" to it; this is parallel to two theories yielding conflicting predictions, but without the question yet being raised of one or the other actually being borne out in fact. We get a structure resembling the occurrence of an actual observation only when we move to an idea of a particular token action question, as asked by a particular agent in a particular situation. Here the practical question *gets answered* in actual fact; and this occurrence of course trivially satisfies the conditions: the fact that a given question gets answered in this sense in a way which conflicts with, say, the consequence of S1 does not constrain a holder of S1 to abandon his position (he may say that the agent was wrong so to decide). What actually is done trivially underdetermines systems of belief about what ought to be done.

Action decisions are not the only possible site of conflicting consequences in the ethical case: various forms of approval, sentiment, etc., can equally come into it. With these, but also with action-descriptions, difficulties can, once more, arise about the satisfaction of the comparability condition. This condition is easily satisfied under, for example, Hare's theory, which is strongly analogous to a positivist philosophy of science, in regarding an ethical outlook or value system (theory) as consisting of a set of principles (laws) whose content is totally characterized by what imperatives (predictions) they generate. But on any more complex view, very severe problems of comparability arise. Here again, we can appeal to the weak requirement, which was made in the theory case: that there be some description of the action (say) in terms of which a univocal yes/no question can be formulated. Thus it is certainly true and important that marriage to two persons in a polygamous society is not the same state or action as bigamy in a monogamous society, nor is human sacrifice the same action as murder in the course of armed robbery. But there may well be descriptions such that a univocal yes/no question can be formed for each of these examples, and S1 and S2 differ in their answers. There can be, that is to say, system-based conflict: two persons can be in a conflict situation, which can be characterized as their giving opposed answers to the same question of action, approval, etc., and be motivated to this by their value system (this is to exclude quarrels inspired by motivations themselves not sanctioned by the value system).

The line I have sketched for describing cases (if there are any) of incommensurable exclusivity implies that for every pair of Ss which are incommensurably exclusive, there must be some action, practice, etc., which under some agreed description will be a locus of disagreement between the holders of the Ss. If this condition is not met, it is unclear what room is left for the notion of exclusivity at all and hence for the problems of relativism.

II. VARIATION AND CONFRONTATION

With regard to a given kind of S, there can be both diachronic and synchronic variation. In the history and philosophy of science, anthropology, etc., there is room for a great deal of discussion about the interrelations of and the limitations to these kinds of variation. There is, for instance, the question of whether certain synchronic variations represent certain diachronic ones, i.e., whether certain cultural variations in one place are survivals of what was an earlier culture elsewhere (do the Hottentots have a Stone Age culture?). Again, the definition of a certain class of Ss can limit variation: thus the range within which something can count as a *scientific theory* is a well known matter of dispute, as is the question whether the use of such restrictions to delimit what is counted as diachronic variation (to constitute, that is, a history *of science*) is merely a matter of *ex post facto* evaluation. (The matter takes on a different aspect with respect to synchronic variation at the present time, in view of the existence of a unified and institutionalized international scientific culture.)

In many, if not all, cases of diachronic variation, it is an important fact that a later S involves consciousness of at least its neighboring predecessor (though not necessarily, of course, in terms which the predecessor, or again S's successors, would assent to). There are very important issues at this point about the writing of 'objective' cultural history, but I do not intend to take them on. In fact, I propose from this point on to ignore cases in which S2 arises in a way which involves some conscious relation with S1, and to consider only those in which mutual awareness can be regarded as, in principle, a development independent of the existence of S1 and S2. While this simplification is a drastic one, it will do for present purposes.

Under this simplification, let us now consider some possible relations, or lack of them, between S1 and S2. There is, first, the primitive situation in which S1 and S2 exist in ignorance of one another. After that, there are cases in which at least one of S1 and S2 encounters the other: either directly, in the case in which persons who hold one of the Ss encounter persons who hold the other, or indirectly, when persons holding one merely learn of the other.

Some such encounters, I shall call *real confrontations* (the term 'confrontation' is not meant to carry all the implications it has in contemporary politics).

For any S, there has to be something which counts as assenting to that S, fully accepting it, living within it, etc.—*whatever* it is, in each sort of case, for an S of that sort to be *somebody's* S: I shall call this relation in general 'holding.' There is a real confrontation between S1 and S2 at a given time if there is a group at that time for whom each of S1 and S2 is a real option; this includes, but is not confined to, the case of a group which already holds S1 or S2, for whom the question is one of whether to *go over* to the other S. *We shall come back shortly to the question of what a 'real option' is.*

Contrasted with this situation is that of notional confrontation.[3] Notional confrontation resembles real confrontation in that there are persons who are aware of S1 and S2, and aware of their differences; it differs from it in that at least one of S1 and S2 do not present a real option to them. S1 and S2 can of course be in both real and notional confrontation, but not with respect to the same persons at the same time. S1 and S2 can be in notional confrontation without ever having been in real confrontation: for example, if no one comes to know of both S1 and S2 until at least one of them has ceased to represent real options. Again, S1 and S2 can be in real confrontation without ever being in notional confrontation: e.g., if no one ever thinks of one of them after the hour of its struggle (presumably unsuccessful) with the other.

What is it for an S to be a real option? In accordance with the starting point that Ss belong to groups (which is not to deny that they are held by individuals, but to assert that they are held by individuals in ways which require description and explanation by reference to the group), the idea of a real option is meant to be a social notion. S2 is a real option for a group if either it is their S or it is possible for them to go over to S2; where going over to S2 involves, first, that it is possible for them to live within, or hold, S2 and retain their hold on reality, and, second, to the extent that rational comparison between S2 and their present outlook is possible, they could acknowledge their transition to S2 in the light of such comparison.[4] Both these conditions use concepts which imply that whether a given S is a real option to a given group at a given time is, to some extent at least, a matter of degree: this consequence is not unwelcome.

Something must be said in explanation of each of these conditions: let me take the second first. The purpose of this is to ensure that the question of whether an S is a real option is not just (granted the satisfaction of the first condition) a matter of such things as the state of psychological technology: we do not want to say that an eccentric scientific theory is a real option for a group of scientists because they could be drugged or operated upon in such a way that they emerged believing it. To the extent that S1 and S2 are comparable, do expose themselves to experiment which can tend to favor one over the other, etc., these methods of assessment are what are to count in the consideration of the accessibility of S2 from S1. Whether something is a real option is a social question, but one rooted in as much rationality as is available on the given type of issue.

In the limiting case of incommensurable exclusivity, this condition will have virtually no effect: there will be little room in such a case for anything except conversion. But even conversion had better be something which can be lived sanely: and this is the force of the first condition. To speak of people who have accepted S2 'retaining their hold on reality' is to imply such things, as that it is possible for S2 to become their S, and for them to live within S2, without their engaging in extensive self-deception, falling into paranoia, and such things. The extent to which that is so depends in turn, to some degree, on what features of their existing social situation are held constant under the assumption of their going over to S2. Thus S2 may not be realistically possible for a group granted features of their present social situation, but it might be if those features were changed. The question of whether S2 is, after all, a real option for them then involves the question of whether those features could be changed.

It is neither a necessary nor a sufficient condition of an S's being a real option for a group that they think that it is a real option. It is not a sufficient condition, because they may be ill-informed, unimaginative, un–self-aware, optimistic, etc., about what it would be like for them to try to live within that S (and this may not be just a personal, but a social or political mistake). It is not a necessary condition, because they may not have realized what possibilities going over to that S would offer them: the psychology of conversion, of course, relates to this matter. I regard the question of whether a given S is a real option for a given group at a given time as basically an objective question. Of course, people may differ about such questions as what is included under 'a hold on reality', and also, notoriously, about what degree of rational comparability can be displayed by Ss of a given kind. In terms of the present structure, such disagreements may well affect what range of Ss those people will regard as real options, for themselves or others.

In this sense many Ss, which have been held, are not real options now. The life of a Greek Bronze Age chief, or a mediaeval Samurai, and the outlooks that go with those, are not real options for us: there is no way of living them. This is not to say that reflection on those value-systems may not provide inspiration for thoughts about elements missing from modern life, but there is no way of taking on those Ss. Even Utopian projects among a small band of enthusiasts could not reproduce *that* life: still more, the project of re-enacting it on a societal scale in the context of actual modern industrial life would involve one of those social or political mistakes, in fact a vast illusion. The prospect of removing the conditions of modern industrial life altogether is something else again—another, though different, impossibility.

In this connection, it is important that there are asymmetrically related options. Some version of modern technological life and its outlooks has become a real option for members of some traditional societies, but their life is not, despite the passionate nostalgia of many, a real option for us. The theories one has about the nature and extent of such asymmetries (which Hegelians would ground in asymmetries of both history and consciousness) affect the views one takes of the objective possibilities of radical social and political action.

III. RELATIVISM

Suppose that we are in real confrontation with some S. Then there will be some vocabulary of appraisal—'true-false,' 'right-wrong,' 'acceptable-unacceptable,' etc.—which will be deployed, and essentially deployed, in thought and speech about this confrontation. The ways in which it is deployed, and the considerations it is geared into, will of course differ with the type of S in question—for instance, with the degree of comparability that obtains between Ss of this type; but whatever these differences, in speaking of a 'vocabulary of appraisal,' I refer only to those expressions which can *at least* be used to express one's own acceptance or rejection of an S or an element of an S. Such a vocabulary is essentially deployed in reflective thought within situations of real confrontation, since in reflection one has to be able to think, and articulate one's feelings, about the different Ss which are a real option for one, and to organize what is to be said in favor or against a given S becoming one's own; and since Ss are things held or accepted, not just conformed to, what has to be said in favor of or against a given S must have some footing in the appraisal of its content.

We can also use this vocabulary about Ss which stand in merely notional confrontation with our own. For some types of S, however, the life of the vocabulary is largely confined to cases of real confrontation, and the more remote a given S is from being a real option for us, the less substantial seems the question of whether it is 'true,' 'right,' etc. While the vocabulary can no doubt be applied without linguistic impropriety, there is so little to this use, so little of what gives content to the appraisals in the context of real confrontation, that we can say that for a reflective person the appraisal questions do not, for such a type of S, and when it is standing in purely notional confrontation, genuinely arise.

We can register that the S in question is not ours, and that it is not a real option for us; there is indeed quite a lot we can say about it, and relevantly to our concerns—thus certain features of an alien way of life, for instance, can stand to us symbolically as emblems of conduct and character to which we have certain attitudes in our own society: in much the same way, indeed, as we can treat works of fiction. The socially and historically remote has always been an important object of self-critical and self-encouraging fantasy. But from the standpoint I am now considering, to raise seriously questions in the vocabulary of appraisal about this culture considered as a concrete historical reality will not be possible for a reflective person. In the case of such Ss, to stand in merely notional confrontation is to lack the relation to our concerns which alone gives any point or substance to appraisal: the only real questions of appraisal are about real options.

To think that the standpoint I have just sketched is the appropriate standpoint towards a given type of Ss is, in a recognizable sense, to hold a relativistic view of such Ss; relativism, with regard to a given type of S, is the view that for one whose S stands in purely notional confrontation with such an S, questions of appraisal of it do not genuinely arise. This form of relativism, unlike most others,[5] is coherent. The truth in relativism—which I shall state, not argue for—is that for ethical outlooks at least this standpoint is correct.

This form of relativism (as a structure—its application to any particular type of S will always of course be a further question) is coherent because unlike most other forms it manages, in the distinction between real and notional confrontation, to cohere with two propositions both of which are true: first, that we must have a form of thought not relativized to our own existing S for thinking about other Ss which may be of concern to us, and to express those concerns; but, second, we can nevertheless recognize that there can be many Ss which have insufficient relation to our concerns for our judgments to have any grip on them, while admitting that other persons' judgment could get a grip on them, namely, those for whom they were a real option.

Most traditional forms of relativism have paid insufficient respect to the first of these propositions. The simplest form merely seeks to relativize the vocabulary of appraisal, into such phrases as 'true for us,' 'true for them.' It is well known that these formulations do not work, and in particular cannot represent the basic use of the vocabulary in real confrontations. This view could be said to reduce the entire vocabulary of appraisal to expressions for the description of confrontation. Related to this is the view in ethics, which I have elsewhere called 'vulgar relativism,'[6] the view which combines a relativistic account of the meaning or content of ethical terms with a nonrelativistic principle of toleration. This view is not hard to refute; it was perhaps worth discussing, since it is widely held, but to dispose of it certainly does not take us very far. We can perhaps now see that view more clearly. What vulgar relativism tries to do is to treat real confrontations like notional confrontations, with the result that it either denies that there are any real confrontations at all, or else brings to bear on them a principle which is inadequate to solve them, and is so because, while it looks like a principle for deciding between real options, it is really an expression of the impossibility or pointlessness of choosing between unreal options.

Opposed to these kinds of views, is that which represents the use of the vocabulary of appraisal as solely that of expressing (not stating) that an S is or is not the speaker's own. For such a view (consider, for example, the pure redundancy or 'speech-act' view of 'true') the issues which have concerned relativists evaporate—there is no way of expressing them. But equally, what has rightly concerned relativists evaporates, and we lose hold on the second truth which the present account is designed to accommodate. The distinction among Ss, between those which are and those which are not the speaker's own, is by no means the most significant in this area. The assumption that it is, is something that the discarded forms of relativism, and the evaporating view which apparently stands opposed to them, seem to have in common.

With those types of S for which relativism is not true, it is not that there is no distinction between real and notional confrontations, but that questions of appraisal genuinely arise for Ss in notional confrontation. But if that is so, then the status of those Ss will reveal itself also in the relevant criteria for distinguishing real and notional confrontations, the considerations that go into determining that a given S is or is not a real option for a given group at a given time. This is important for the case of scientific theories. Phlogiston theory is, I take it, not now a real option; but I doubt that that just means that to try to live the life of a convinced phlogiston theorist in the contemporary Royal Society is as incoherent an enterprise as to try to live the life of a Teutonic knight in 1930s Nuremburg. One reason that phlogiston theory is not a real option is that it cannot be squared with a lot that we know to be true.

These considerations, if pursued, would lead us to the subject of realism. One necessary (but not sufficient) condition of there being the kind of truth I have tried to explain in relativism as applied to ethics, is that ethical realism is false, and there is nothing for ethical Ss to be true of—though there are things for them to be true to, which is why many options are unreal. But scientific realism could be true, and if it is, relativism for scientific theories must be false.

NOTES

1. See, e.g., Steven Lukes, "Some Problems about Rationality," *European Journal of Sociology* 8 (1967), reprinted in *Rationality*, ed. B. R. Wilson (Oxford: Oxford University Press, 1970), and "On the Social Determination of Truth," in *Modes of Thought: Essays on*

Thinking in Western and Non-Western Societies, ed. R. Horton and R. Finnegan (London: Faber, 1973).

2. For an illuminating discussion, see Robin Horton, "Levy-Bruhl, Durkheim, and the Scientific Revolution," in Horton and Finnegan, *Modes of Thought*.

3. The terminology of "real" and "notional" was suggested by John Henry Newman and Charles Frederick Harrold, *An Essay in Aid of a Grammar of Assent* (New York: Longmans, Green, 1947).

4. "They" does not mean "each and every one of them": the problem is a familiar one in the description of social phenomena. There are other difficulties which will have to be overlooked, connected with the very simple use made of the notion of a *group*—e.g., that it ignores the case of persons who could adopt a different S if they belonged to a different group.

5. For a different kind of relativist view which avoids the standard errors, see Gilbert Harman, "Moral Relativism Defended," *Philosophical Review* 84 (1975): 3–22.

6. Bernard Williams, "An Inconsistent Form of Relativism," in *Morality: An Introduction to Ethics* (New York: Harper & Row, 1972), chap. 3.

DAVID B. WONG

I. INTRODUCTION

'Moral relativism' is overwhelmingly used in the popular media as a term of condemnation, frequently of scorn or derision. In Anglophone moral philosophy, the tactics are employed in a more genteel fashion. Introductory ethics textbooks typically portray the view as an extreme variety of subjectivism or thoroughgoing conventionalism, which holds that a person's (or a group's) accepting that something is right makes it right for that person (or group). Rarely does someone try to formulate a nuanced or plausibly motivated version of relativism. Generations of philosophy professors award the role of the howling pack of relativists to confused students in their Introduction to Philosophy classes or, more recently, to literary theorists. Professors who condescend to the dogmatic relativism of their students seldom question their own reflexive universalism.

I am among the handful of philosophers willing to be associated with relativism. The version I defend constitutes an alternative to the universalist view that a single true morality exists and the easily quashed view that any morality is as good as any other. My alternative agrees with one implication of relativism, namely, that no single true morality exists. However, my view, which I call 'pluralistic relativism,' recognizes significant limits on what can count as a true morality. In this essay, I sketch one crucial part of the argument for pluralistic relativism.[1] This part starts with moral difference and disagreement, the implications of which are often at the center of debates between relativists and universalists.

Moral universalism has perennially suffered from attacks based on disagreement over moral values. Yet universalists correctly point out that the mere fact of disagreement, even apparently irresolvable disagreement over significant or fundamental matters, does not differentiate morality from other bodies of belief concerning, say, history and the sciences, typically judged to be true or false in a nonrelative manner.

One kind of moral disagreement does pose special difficulties for universalism. This kind of disagreement evokes the complex reaction of moral ambivalence. We experience it when we see that reasonable and knowledgeable people could have made different judgments from the ones we would have made about these conflicts. We come to understand and appreciate the other side's viewpoint with the result that our sense of the unique rightness of our judgments gets destabilized.

I do not claim that all intelligent and reasonably informed people experience this phenomenon of moral ambivalence. I only claim that some do, and that this requires explanation. Some who feel no moral ambivalence will claim they are right not to feel it. My position is that they overlook the complexity and plurality of moral truth.

II. MORAL VALUE PLURALISM AND VALUE CONFLICT

Moral value pluralism makes moral ambivalence possible: there exists a plurality of basic moral values, where such values are not derivable from or reducible to other moral values. I use 'value' here to include types of obligations and duties, as well as morally desirable ends. The denial of pluralism—theoretical commitments to the supremacy of one or another value—dominates the history of modern Western moral philosophy. Moral value monism cannot possibly be conclusively refuted, but we can find good reason to find it unpersuasive.

The nature and source of moral claims and obligations appear to be diverse and resistant to reduction. Consider Thomas Nagel's classification of five different sources of value: first, specific obligations to other people or institutions, which depend on some special relation to the person or institution in question; second, constraints on action deriving from general rights that everyone has, such as the right to freedom from assault or coercion; third, utility, the effects of what one does on everyone's welfare; fourth, perfectionist ends or values, such as the intrinsic value of scientific or artistic achievements; and fifth, commitment to one's projects and undertakings.[2] We should also consider other sources of value that Nagel does not mention, such as those having to do with different normative stances human beings might take toward the natural world. But Nagel's list constitutes a fairly comprehensive view of the diverse array of what there is to value.

One reason why each kind of value appears to be irreducibly basic is that deep tensions stand between the projects of realizing all of them. To take a well-known theme from Isaiah Berlin, we can envision no utopia in which the maximal realizations of these different sorts of value are made compatible with one another.[3] Therefore, if a morality prescribes a set of values to be realized or observed in human life, it must specify priorities to govern cases of conflict between these values. For example, specification of governing priorities is crucial when honoring individual rights conflicts with promotion of social utility, or when an obligation based on friendship, kinship, or some other kind of special relation conflicts with honoring a right based on someone's humanity or with the promotion of social utility. In coming to a similar conclusion, anthropologist Ruth Benedict found virtues to appreciate in radically different ways of life. She asserted the unlikelihood "that even the best society will be able to stress in one social order all the virtues we prize in human life." [4] If no one culture could possibly avoid sacrificing some things that human beings prize, while emphasizing other things, then a plurality of different cultures could provide legitimate satisfaction and sustenance to human beings and in that sense be worthy of respect.

III. EXAMPLES OF VALUE CONFLICTS GIVING RISE TO MORAL AMBIVALENCE

Value conflicts giving rise to moral ambivalence can occur within a single society, and within a single rich and complex moral tradition. For example, the source of disagreement in the United States over the moral permissibility of abortion seems not so much to be a difference in the ultimate moral principles held by opposing sides as a difference over the applicability of a commonly held principle requiring the protection of human life and partly a difference over the relative weight to be given to another widely held principle requiring the protection of individual autonomy. Serious disagreement remains as to how to balance individual rights versus utility, for example, where the security of many people against terrorism could be increased at the cost of curtailing the rights of a few.

Another key value difference underlying many moral disagreements is the contrast between two types of moralities, one having at its center the rights persons have purely as individuals and the other having at its center the duties arising from the value of community (which covers relationships to particular others as well as to groups of varying sizes). In the first type of morality, individuals are seen as having interests that need to be defended against others. Rights have come to be conceived in the West as owed to individuals independent of their potential contributions to any community. Consequently, a central kind of right protects against interference from others.

Let me associate the value of 'autonomy' with these ideas that rights have an independent justification apart from the individual's contribution to community and that rights are needed to protect the individual's morally legitimate interests in case of conflict with communal interests. In communally oriented moralities, duties arising from the individual's relationships (for example, under Confucian morality the duties of filial piety) occupy a central place. To hold such a morality is to hold that the individual's good is interdependent with the community's good.

This contrast is consistent with the value of community being a part of Western moral traditions. These traditions are distinct in the centrality they accord to notions of autonomy and individual rights, not by the absence of these other values. When values of relationship and autonomy conflict in the West, people evince a comparatively greater tendency to give priority to autonomy. Autonomy and community often function as counterpoints *to each other*, in that one value is asserted against the other value because it is seen as addressing the liabilities of asserting the other value strongly. Autonomy gets asserted against the sort of collective responsiveness to individual need that can be a great benefit of community when that responsiveness turns into the liability of oppressive suffocation or an alienating exclusion of those who fall from good standing. On the other side, community gets asserted against the barriers to intervention afforded by autonomy when this benefit blocks responsiveness to need.

The United States' moral tradition, I believe, exhibits this kind of dynamic between autonomy and community. Compared to many Asian traditions, it gives far greater priority to rights as the expression of individual autonomy, but the presence of the value of community is real even if it is relatively recessive. Much of the appeal of communitarian critiques of the United States' tradition lies in its pointing to the receding nature of community and alleged result of decreasing responsiveness to individual need.

The identity of a culture is partly defined by the values that are most salient and serve as counterpoints to others. A shared culture consists in this dynamic configuration of values, but the configuration typically leaves a significant degree of openness and ambiguity in how conflicts between values are to be resolved. This is one important reason why moral ambivalence exists not only across different moral traditions but also within a single moral tradition. Values derive much of their force from their correspondence to compelling human needs. But because the human psyche is many-sided and not typically a harmonious whole, uncertainty and fluctuation will always surface as to how the needs and corresponding values are to be balanced against each other.

To illustrate how moral ambivalence can arise from the sort of conflict involving values that serve as counterpoints to each other, let me focus on two Confucian values, the first of which is *xiao*, usually translated as 'filial piety.' It is a common feature of many cultures that holds people should honor their father and mother. At the same time, the Confucian tradition is unusual in the stringency of its duties to parents.

The *Analects* 2.7 identifies the requirements of *xiao* as going beyond providing parents material support when they are elderly. More fundamentally, it directs that we should show *jing*, often translated as 'reverence,' originally conceived as an attitude of devotion people should have when sacrificing for ancestors. The scope of duties to parents includes taking care of the body one has received as a gift from them. One student of Confucius is portrayed in the *Analects* 8.3 as gravely ill and near death. He bids his students to look at his hands and feet, and through quoting from the *Book of Poetry*, alludes to the idea that he has been striving to keep his body intact as a duty to his parents. Only now, near death, can he be sure of having fulfilled this duty to parents. This idea of keeping our body intact as a duty of gratitude to parents has remained a central idea in Chinese culture.

Why is *xiao* so central a virtue in the Confucian ethic? One reason is its centrality to the development of ethical character. We learn respect for others first for those within our family. Another reason is the need to express gratitude to those who have given us life and nurture.

In *Analects* 17.21 a student protests that the traditional three-year period of mourning for deceased parents is too long. Confucius replies by asking whether this student had not received three years' worth of love from his parents. The virtue and its rationale have analogues in American culture. We can recognize the themes of gratitude, the need to reciprocate in some fashion for great gifts received, and the conception of family relationships as pivotal in the development of character. Such similarities of theme, however, seem to underdetermine the centrality of filial piety and the stringency of its duties in Confucianism and in the larger traditional Chinese culture. Though we Americans recognize such rationales for filial piety, we generally do not accord it nearly as central a place in the catalogue of moral virtues, nor do we conceive its duties to be so stringent. However, Americans, taking the Confucian perspective, might come to have an inkling that it makes sense. They might be able to imagine themselves reasonably taking that path that they have not, in fact, taken.

The second key Confucian value is that placed on harmonious relationships as a central part of the ethical life, again illustrated by the *Analects* on adults' relation to their parents. The strong Chinese preference for *he* (harmony) emerges in 2.6, where the Master advises that we should give parents no cause for anxiety except for illness. In 4.18, where Confucius considers occasions on which our opinions as to what is right or best can conflict with our parents' wishes, we should remonstrate with our parents gently. The value placed on harmony does not require silence in the face of genuine disagreement with superiors. Indeed, the Confucian tradition celebrates scholar-intellectuals who say to the ruler's face what they think about the ruler's actions (this sort of moral autonomy is central to the Confucian ethic). Harmony is one of the ends to be served by such frankness. Harmony is the legitimate reconciliation of the potentially conflicting interests of members of a group. When a ruler fails to accomplish such reconciliation, advisers must say so.

The rationale for harmony lies, in part, simply in the satisfaction of participating in a common project with others, of belonging, of having a place that others recognize and appreciate. Another part of the rationale is that someone must have authority to settle conflicts. Human beings have yet to invent a society without having to designate such authority and to inculcate some degree of respect for it. This does not mean that conflicts are to be settled arbitrarily or based on the whims of those who have authority. Ideally such persons exercise their responsibilities by reconciling interests and obtaining consensus on what is best for everyone. The reasons for preferring harmony thus conceived are quite intelligible, but these reasons underdetermine the degree of preference for it that is manifest in the culture. For example, informal negotiation involving interaction and reconciliation between contending parties is still the traditional way of resolving business disputes in China. Informal mediation committees operate to resolve disputes at the grassroots rural village and urban neighborhood levels, and Chinese courts encourage mediation between contending parties even after litigation procedures have begun.

Some preference for harmony exists in American moral traditions. American culture, after all, embraces a significantly diverse range of subcultures that manifest a high degree of preference for harmony. These subcultures include Chinese-American and other Asian-American subcultures, and Latino and Mexican-American subcultures. The different subcultures of European descent in American society have, in the past, demonstrated a stronger preference for family harmony and cooperation within levels of community than they do now. This internal diversity helps make Confucian values intelligible as a path that we could, and in some cases have, taken.

IV. WHY MORAL AMBIVALENCE MAKES TROUBLE FOR UNIVERSALISM

Conflicts characterized by moral ambivalence constitute a challenge for universalist moral theories that assert a single true morality. The dominant response in universalist theory has rested on denying the underlying phenomenon of moral value pluralism. Much of the work of Kantians and utilitarians, for example, is aimed at showing that the apparently irreducible and potentially conflicting sources of value are reducible to one source, whether it is the goal of promoting the greatest happiness or respect for rational natures. Consider one such conflict. Philosophers working from the impersonal perspective, from which our actions must be rooted in the recognition that no person is more or less morally important than any other person, have tried to subsume special duties under that perspective. They argue that impersonal values are best fulfilled through the recognition and performance of these obligations.

Peter Railton attempts to subsume special obligations to family under a sophisticated act consequentialism by arguing that some goods are reliably attainable only if people have certain enduring motivational patterns, traits, or commitments (such as those which involve acting for the good of loved ones) that sometimes override acting for the best. He argues that people's overall contribution to human welfare would be less, in the end, if they were not morally permitted to strive for goods that could only be achieved in emotionally intimate relationships. Such relationships sometimes require channeling resources to intimates that we could have channeled toward many strangers in great need. Railton argues that we ought to give people moral permission to strive for such goods because otherwise they might become "more cynical and self-centered,"[5] and therefore contribute less to the overall good.

How many of us truly believe that the rightness of taking special care of our children should depend on making the case that everyone would be better off if we did such things? How many of us think that that is the *reason* caring for our children is right? While Railton's theory recognizes special relationships as goods, it makes the rightness of claiming them for ourselves depend on whether doing so ultimately promotes such goods for all. But the claims generated by our moral ties to family members and particular others such as friends seem more basic than this. Their pull on us appears to be independent of their justifiability by reference to the goal of promoting impersonal good. On the other hand, when we take the impersonal perspective and are not especially concerned to show how that perspective justifies every moral value we hold dear, we see as unjustifiable many of the mundane acts of care and devotion we direct to particular others. The unjustifiability emerges when we compare what is at stake for those close to us to what is at stake for millions of people elsewhere in the world: life itself, and some small measure of human dignity in the face of brutality and degradation.[6]

Denials of moral value pluralism run up against the widespread sense that different value claims often require different kinds of justification. Recognizing the reality of moral ambivalence involves denying a strong form of value commensurability that many philosophers have asserted: that all values can be justified on the basis of a single kind of value and that this single kind of value establishes a scale for resolving value conflicts.

Other attempts to deal with this conflict stop short of assuming moral value monism and attempt to show that definite priorities between the plural values can be established. Samuel Scheffler has distinguished two moral ideals that correspond to this conflict. On one hand, the 'Ideal of Humanity' carves out a space for us to live our lives and makes only a moderate demand on us to meet the needs of others. On the other hand, the 'Ideal of Purity' requires us to act from the impersonal viewpoint from which our lives are no more important than the lives of other human beings. The Ideal of Humanity, he argues, has 'broader and deeper' roots in our morality. It better fits our belief in the legitimacy of a space to live our own lives. Very rarely, he claims, does anyone question our right to have this space, except when we purchase luxuries that could have gone to meet desperate need. Further, he argues, living our lives generates personal relationships that in turn generate special duties. So the space of moral permission that Humanity carves out for the individual inevitably generates its own duties. Finally, Scheffler argues that the Ideal of Humanity can accommodate to some extent the Ideal of Purity, but not vice versa. From the perspective defined by the first, we can regard the second as a supererogatory ideal.[7]

Scheffler cannot claim that our special duties weigh in favor of the Ideal of Humanity *and* that we can view Purity as supererogatory—not if our special duties can override duties of Purity (for example, if the duty to care well for our children does override duties to devote most of our resources to the care of many other children in the world in desperate need).[8] On the other hand, if our impersonal duties to others override our special duties to particular people, then the primacy of Humanity appears implausible. People *do* question our right to live our lives, and not just when our purchase of luxuries is in question. We help ourselves to goods hardly essential to human life, or even to a decent minimum, and some have questioned whether we ought to do so when others are in desperate need. We should expect such questioning in a moral tradition with deep roots in early Christianity, with its radical challenge to material comfort and to partiality. The problem is that our tradition contains strains of thought corresponding to both ideals, and no compelling, deeper rationale for subordinating one to the other presents itself. Recognizing the reality of moral ambivalence involves denying another form of value commensurability asserted by many philosophers: that a single correct way to establish priorities between irreducibly plural values exists.

V. A SKETCH OF HOW CONSTRAINED RELATIVISM CAN ACCOUNT FOR MORAL AMBIVALENCE

Moral ambivalence suggests that different moralities have values in common but that we can experience profound uncertainty about how to balance these values when they come into conflict. We need to explain the sense of commonality *and* the sense of a multiplicity of diverging paths from those commonalities. Here, succinctly, is the explanation I have defended at some length elsewhere.[9] On my naturalistic approach, morality is not about moral properties that are *sui generis* or an irreducible part of the fabric of the world, but a cultural invention that has interpersonal and intrapersonal coordination functions in human life. The interpersonal function is to promote and regulate social cooperation. The intrapersonal function is to foster a degree of ordering among potentially conflicting motivational propensities, including self- and other-regarding motivations; this ordering serves to encourage people to become constructive participants in the cooperative life and to live worthwhile lives. The potential for tensions between these functions exists (being a constructive cooperator may sometimes come at some cost to living a worthwhile life, at least by some important measures of such a life). How a morality deals with these tensions is in part what distinguishes it from other moralities.

The content of moral norms is constrained not only by the functions they must fulfill but also by the nature of the beings they govern. This nature includes a diverse array of motivational propensities plausibly considered to be innate to most human beings (not all because polymorphism of psychological traits is a plausible result of the evolution of a species of complex organisms).

Alongside their instincts for self-preservation, most members of the human species have the capability to care for kin, a willingness to engage in mutually beneficial practices of cooperation with others if they show a similar willingness, a willingness to punish those who violate the agreements and norms that make cooperative practices possible (even when the expenditure of resources to punish cannot be justified on the grounds of pure self-interest), and some degree of altruistic concern for nonrelated others. Human beings developed all these capacities because they were fitness-enhancing in an inclusive sense, a conclusion that much of the latest work in evolutionary theory supports.[10] Human beings, then, were selected in the course of their biological evolution to have a diverse array of innate psychological tendencies that can potentially come into conflict with one another if they do not have ways of regulating and tempering the expression of these tendencies. Moral norms, as a subset of human culture, play a large part in this structuring of motivation for the sake of intrapsychic order within the individual and for the sake of social cooperation among individuals.

The human capability to regulate the self through cultural norms coevolved with biological traits. Some of these evolved biological traits might prepare us to regulate ourselves through culture: for example, the disposition to follow the majority or to emulate the most successful members of one's group.[11] Such traits prepare human beings to follow norms that do not simply require behavior that is cooperative with and considerate of the interests of others, but also norms that encourage, strengthen, and direct the sorts of feelings and desires that make people promising partners in social cooperation.

Morality's functions, plus the nature of the beings it governs, constrain the content of its norms. Different moralities must share some general features if they are to perform their functions of coordinating beings that have particular kinds of motivations. The shared general features account for the commonalities experienced in moral ambivalence. The diverging paths experienced in moral ambivalence arise from the fact that the constraints only *place boundaries on* the range of moralities that adequately fulfill the coordinating functions, but they do not select only one specific morality.

For an example of what must be shared, consider the strength of self-regarding motivations in most human beings. This must be considered when moral norms are being established or evaluated for adequacy, not only to accommodate these motivations but also to provide outlets for their expression consistent with the expression of other-regarding motivations. By making other-regarding behavior less costly, moralities can increase the degree to which individuals feel they can afford to indulge their concerns for others. Norms of reciprocity that require a return of good for good received play a crucial role in such reconciliation of motivations. The need to reconcile self- and other-concern appears first in family relationships. Across widely different cultures, people recognize duties to respect and honor parents and others whose roles involve raising and nurturing the young. Performance of such duties constitutes a kind of return of good for good. Sometimes the return is similar to the original good, as in the case of children's care of aged parents. Most other times, however, the return is a good fitting to the nature of our relationship to those who have cared and nurtured: obedience and receptiveness to what is taught, for example. Perfectly selfless parents might not need such reinforcement, but profoundly ambivalent beings might not be able to do without it. Norms of reciprocity help to specify and to regulate and sustain many of the special relationships that form a central portion of human life (a life both cooperative and worthwhile). Our being cooperative creatures, who regularly engage in small-scale relationships over extended periods, accounts for one of the most important commonalities that feed into moral ambivalence.

At the same time, human beings are utterly remarkable among earthly creatures in their capability to engage in social cooperation on a very large scale and to cooperate within large groups that interact with other large groups. Obvious advantages are associated with this capability for large-scale cooperation in terms of the specialization of labor made possible, and the exchange and sharing of complementary resources and goods. Morality plays a role in promoting and regulating relationships that constitute and emerge from such large-scale cooperation. Impersonal duties are especially pertinent in dealing with relationships with strangers whom we may never know individually or encounter on single occasions. Consider rights we recognize strangers to have, even though we may never have benefited from association with them directly or indirectly.

Widespread and common features of human motivation and of cooperative life account for widespread and common values such as special and impersonal duties toward others. Obviously, such features are quite general and could be specified very differently in more specific norms and practices. Norms that spell out when we are to reciprocate, for what kind of benefit, and how we are to do so can vary quite widely. Which rights are recognized, and their specific content, can also vary significantly. Furthermore, a variety of relative priorities between special and impersonal duties is consistent with moralities fulfilling their functions of intra- and interpersonal coordination. For the sake of providing specific guidance, cultures will favor some ways of further specifying and prioritizing these duties relative to each other over others. For example, in traditional Chinese culture, filial piety, the duties of special relationships, and reciprocity receive enormous emphasis as compared with the mainstream of contemporary American culture, where autonomy and rights play a much larger role. But when we encounter other ways and come to understand what might lead people to find satisfaction and meaning in them, we might become puzzled by having to recognize the reasonableness of those other ways. The result is moral ambivalence. A Chinese student of mine, who has lived in the United States for some years, observed that when he speaks in English he thinks one way about moral matters, but when he speaks in Chinese he disagrees with his English-speaking self.

VI. SUMMARY AND CONCLUSIONS

Let me briefly clarify my position vis-à-vis other positions that have been contrasted with relativism. I have focused on relativism as the denial of the universalistic view that a single true morality exists. As Michael Krausz points out in his contribution to this volume,[12] relativism is not only contrasted with universalism but also can be opposed to objectivism in its individuable sense, defined as the view that a way can be found to adjudicate between the reference frames in relation to which claims about truth, beauty, and goodness are made. His conception of objectivism holds that the basis of adjudicating between reference frames must be something that exists independently of those frames.

My pluralistic relativism partly supports objectivism thus defined, but only partly. The constraints on moralities provided by their functions and human nature do provide a way to adjudicate between reference frames in relation to which moral claims about goodness, rightness, and duty are made. However, the adjudication is only partial and does not identify a single reference frame as the correct one. My view does not hold that the basis for adjudicating between moral reference frames exists independently of those frames, because part of the common content of those frames is that moralities have the intra- and interpersonal functions. These functions are part of the content because human beings invent moralities as having these functions (it is possible, therefore, that a group of human beings could have no morality at all if they do not undertake to cooperate with one another, but I doubt it would last very long as a *group*). Given that moralities have these functions, certain objective constraints apply to judging what can be a true morality. Consider an analogy: no bridges would exist without the reference frames within which human beings conceive of structures that span bodies of water or deep depressions in the terrain for the purpose of traversing them. However, *once these functions are in place*, constraints arise on what constitutes an adequate bridge (for example, that bridges must be made of materials of sufficient strength and durability; given particular materials, bridges must be designed and constructed in circumscribed ways). These constraints apply independently of human invention.

Analogously, no moralities would exist without the reference frames within which human beings conceive moralities with the functions that define them. But once these functions are in place and are conjoined with the 'material' of human nature, constraints arise on what constitutes an adequate morality that applies independently of human invention. Whether a morality objectively fulfills its functions depends on the nature of widespread human propensities that exist whether or not they are recognized under a particular 'frame.'

Finally, Krausz points out that relativism can be contrasted with foundationalism, defined as the view that self-justifying first principles exist, which are the basis for justifying other claims within a domain of knowledge. My approach, because it is naturalistic, rejects foundationalism, which is partly characterized by the tenet that nothing is immune from revision in response to new experience and the theory change that may result.

This essay has sketched part of a long story that must be told in favor of a nuanced version of relativism. Opponents of relativism should recognize that such nuanced versions exist and should take the responsibility for telling their own long counter-stories.

NOTES

1. This essay is based on my *Natural Moralities: A Defense of Pluralistic Relativism* (New York: Oxford University Press, 2006), introduction, chaps. 2–3.

2. Thomas Nagel, "The Fragmentation of Value," in *Mortal Questions* (Cambridge: Cambridge University Press, 1979), 128–131.

3. Isaiah Berlin, "Two Concepts of Liberty," in *Liberty: Incorporating Four Essays on Liberty*, ed. Henry Hardy (Oxford: Oxford University Press, 2002), 212–217.

4. Ruth Benedict, *Patterns of Culture* (New York: Penguin, 1934), 229.

5. Peter Railton, "Alienation, Consequentialism, and Morality," *Philosophy and Public Affairs* 13 (1984): 159.

6. Peter Singer articulates the classic defense of this point of view in "Famine, Affluence, and Morality," *Philosophy and Public Affairs* 1 (1972): 229–243.

7. Samuel Scheffler, *Human Morality* (New York: Oxford University Press, 1992).

8. Scheffler provides a subtle discussion of such possible conflicts in "Families, Nations, and Strangers" and "Relationships and Responsibilities," both in *Boundaries*

and Allegiances: Problems of Justice and Responsibility in Liberal Thought (Oxford: Oxford University Press, 2001).

9. Wong, *Natural Moralities*, chaps. 2–3.

10. On the selection mechanism for altruism toward kin, see W. D. Hamilton, "The Genetical Evolution of Social Behavior," *Journal of Theoretical Biology* 7 (1964): 1–52. On the mechanism for selecting a willingness to cooperate with others if they show willingness to cooperate, see Robert Trivers, "The Evolution of Reciprocal Altruism," *Quarterly Review of Biology* 46 (1971): 35–56. For a theory of 'group selection' as the mechanism behind concern for nonkin, see Elliott Sober and David Wilson, *Unto Others: The Evolution and Psychology of Unselfish Behavior* (Cambridge, Mass.: Harvard University Press, 1998); for another theory emphasizing the role of sexual selection in altruism, see Geoffrey Miller, *The Mating Mind* (New York: Anchor Books, 2000). For evidence supporting the existence of non–self-interested willingness to punish and reward others who cooperate, see Herbert Gintis, *Game Theory Evolving* (Princeton, N.J.: Princeton University Press, 2000).

11. Robert Boyd and Peter J. Richerson, *Culture and the Evolutionary Process* (Chicago: University of Chicago Press, 1985); Peter Richerson and Robert Boyd, *Not by Genes Alone: How Culture Transformed Human Evolution* (Chicago: University of Chicago Press, 2005).

12. Michael Krausz, "Mapping Relativisms" (this volume, chap. 1).

CATHERINE Z. ELGIN

Fact and value purport to be polar opposites: facts being absolute, material, objective, and impersonal; values relative, spiritual, subjective, and personal; facts being verifiable by the rigorous, austere methods of science; values being subject to no such assessment. The facts, they say, don't lie. So every factual disagreement has a determinate resolution. Whether barium is heavier than plutonium is a question of fact, and whatever the answer, there are no two ways about it. Values, if they don't precisely lie, are thought perhaps to distort. So evaluative disputes may be genuinely irresolvable. Whether, for example, a Van Gogh is better than a Vermeer might just be a matter of opinion. And on matters like these, everyone is entitled to his own opinion. Such is the prevailing stereotype.

I believe that stereotype ought to be rejected, for it stifles our understanding of both fact and value. Far from being poles apart, the two are inextricably intertwined: the demarcation of facts rests squarely on considerations of value, and evaluations are infused with considerations of fact. So factual judgments are not objective unless value judgments are, and value judgments are not relative unless

Originally published in *Relativism: Interpretation and Confrontation*, Michael Krausz, ed. (Notre Dame, Ind.: University of Notre Dame Press, 1989), and reprinted in Catherine Z. Elgin, *Between the Absolute and the Arbitrary* (Ithaca, N.Y.: Cornell University Press, 1989). Reprinted here with permission of the author. All rights reserved.

factual judgments are. I want to suggest that tenable judgments of both kinds are at once relative and objective.[1]

First, let's look at the facts. When we proclaim their independence from and indifference to human concerns, we forget that we are the ones who set and enforce the standards for what counts as a fact. We stipulate, "a thing cannot both be and not be"; or "no entity is without identity"; or "whatever is, is physical." In effect, we decree that whatever fails to satisfy our standards hasn't got what it takes to be a fact.

At the same time, we arrange for our standards to be met. We construct systems of categories that settle the conditions on the individuation of entities and their classification into kinds. Thus, for example, we devise a biological taxonomy according to which a Dachshund is the same kind of thing as a Doberman, but a horse is a different kind of thing from a zebra.

For all their clarity, scientific examples may mislead. We are apt to think that constructing a biological taxonomy is simply a matter of introducing terminology for what is already the case. Then prior to our categorization Dachshunds and Dobermans were already alike; horses and zebras, already different. The problem is that any two things are alike in some respects and different in others. So likeness alone is powerless to settle matters of categorization. In classing Dachshunds and Dobermans together, horses and zebras apart, we distinguish important from unimportant similarities. That is, we make a value judgment.

The selection of significant likenesses and differences is not, in general, whimsical. It is grounded in an appreciation of why a particular classificatory scheme is wanted, and this, in turn, depends on what we already believe about the subject at hand. If our goal is to understand heredity, for example, it is reasonable to group together animals that interbreed. Then despite their obvious differences dachshunds and Dobermans belong together, and despite their blatant similarities horses and zebras belong apart.

More general considerations come into play as well. If our system is to serve the interests of science, the cognitive values and priorities of science must be upheld. Membership in its kinds should be determinate and epistemically accessible. There should be no ambiguity and no (irresolvable) uncertainty about an individual's membership in a kind. The classification should be conducive to the formulation and testing of elegant, simple, fruitful generalizations and should perhaps mesh with other scientific classifications of the same and adjacent domains. In constructing a system of categories suitable for science, then, we make factual judgments about what the values of science are and how they can be realized.

Science streamlines its categories in hopes of achieving exceptionless, predictive, quantitative laws. Narrative has quite different ends in view, being concerned with the particular, the exceptional, the unique. So schemes suited to narrative enterprises exhibit different features from those suited to science. Scientific vices—ambiguity, imprecision, immeasurability, and indeterminacy—are often narrative virtues.[2] The complex characterization of the emotional life that we find, for example, in the novels of Henry James, requires a baroque conceptual scheme whose involuted categories intersect in intricate and subtle ways. And equally complex categories may be required to achieve the sort of understanding that biographers, historians, psychoanalysts, and serious gossips strive to achieve.

A category scheme provides the resources for stating various truths and falsehoods, for exhibiting particular patterns and discrepancies, for drawing specific distinctions, for demarcating conceptual boundaries. Purposes, values, and priorities are integral to the design. They constitute the basis for organizing the domain in one way rather than another. And the acceptability of any particular scheme depends on the truths it enables us to state, the methods it permits us to employ, the projects it furthers, and the values it promotes. Together these constitute a system of thought. A failure of the components to mesh undermines the system, preventing it from doing what it ought to do.

We design category schemes with more or less specific purposes in mind and integrate into the scheme such values and priorities as we think will serve those purposes. But the values that our schemes realize are not always or only the ones we intend to produce. Some are simply mistakes; others, inadvertent holdovers from prior systems; yet others, unintended by-products of features we intentionally include. When pregnancy and aging are classified as medical conditions, they come to be considered and treated as diseases or disabilities—as deviations from a state of health. If Marx is right, the values of the ruling class are invisibly embedded in the social and economic categories of a society. And my students are convinced that a fundamental truth is revealed by the fact that witchcraft comes just after philosophy in the Library of Congress classification system.

As a first approximation, facts are what answer to true sentences. And different systems produce different truths. It is a truth of physics, not of botany, that copper is lighter than zinc. This alone does not lead to relativity, for such systems may complement one another or be indifferent to one another. Relativity emerges when systems clash—when what is true according to one system is false according to another. Evolutionary taxonomy so groups animals that crocodiles and lizards are close relatives; crocodiles and birds, distant ones. Cladistic classification shows crocodiles and birds to be close; crocodiles and lizards distant. Each system divulges some affinities among animals and obscures others. Neither invalidates the other. So whether it is a fact that crocodiles and lizards are closely related depends on a choice of system. According to one system any violation of the law is a crime; according to another only serious violations— felonies—are crimes. So whether spitting on the sidewalk is a crime depends on which system is in use.

According to one medical classification, health is the absence of disease; according to another, health is the absence of disease or disability. So whether a congenital defect renders a person unhealthy depends on which system is in effect. A single domain can be organized in a multitude of ways, while different schematizations may employ a single vocabulary. So under one schematization a given sentence—say, "Spitting on the sidewalk is a crime"—comes out true; under another it comes out false. Truth then is relative to the system in effect.

Still, facts are objective. For once the system is in place, there is no room for negotiation. Events that are simultaneous relative to one frame of reference are successive relative to another. But it is determinate for each frame of reference whether given events are successive or simultaneous. Similarly, although some psychologistic systems consider neuroses to be mental illnesses and others do not, once a system is chosen there is a fact of the matter as to whether a compulsive hand washer is mentally ill.

Such objectivity might seem spurious if we can switch frameworks at will. What is true according to one framework is false according to another. So can't we simply choose our facts to fit our fancy? There are at least two reasons why we can't. The first is that rightness requires more than truth.[3] We need to employ an appropriate framework—one that yields the right facts. For example, the fact that someone went to Choate neither qualifies nor disqualifies him for a federal judgeship. So a classification of candidates according to their secondary schools is inappropriate, even if it would enable us to choose the candidate we want. Correctness requires that the facts we appeal to be relevant. Psychoanalytic categories are powerless to settle the issue of criminal insanity because they mark the wrong distinctions. People who cannot be held criminally liable for their actions are supposed to be, in some important respect, different from the rest of us. And the categories in question reveal no difference. For they characterize everyone's behavior in terms of motives and desires the agent can neither acknowledge nor control. So the facts that psychoanalytic theory reveals do not suit the purposes of the criminal court: they do not discriminate the class of criminally insane. Rightness of categorization thus depends on suitability to a purpose. And an aspiring lepidopterist whose collection consists of larvae seems to have missed the point. Lepidopterists concentrate on mature forms—they collect butterflies, not caterpillars. Although biologists class butterflies and caterpillars together, butterfly collectors do not. Rightness here requires fit with past practice. The fellow fails as a lepidopterist because he employs radically nontraditional categories in selecting specimens for his collection.

Moreover, even though we construct the categories that fix the facts, we cannot construct whatever we want. If we take the notion of construction seriously, this will come as no surprise. Although we make all manner of inventions, we can't make a nonfattening Sacher Torte, a solar-powered subway, or a perpetual-motion machine. And although we design programs that endow computers with amazing abilities, we can't get a computer to translate a natural language or compute the last digit in the decimal expansion of π.

Some of these incapacities are irremediable; others will eventually be overcome. My point in mentioning them is to emphasize that construction is something we do, and we can't do everything we want. Our capacities are limited, and our aspirations often interfere with one another. So there is no reason to think that we can convert any fantasy into fact by designing a suitable system. Plainly we cannot.

In constructing a political system, for example, we'd like to maximize both personal liberty and public safety. We'd like, that is, to arrange for as many actions as possible to fall under the predicate 'free to ...' and as many harms as possible to fall under the predicate 'safe from ...' But we can't maximize both at once. The cost of security is a loss of liberty, and the cost of liberty, a risk of harm. With the freedom to carry a gun comes the danger of getting shot. So we have to trade the values of liberty and safety off against each other to arrive at a system that achieves an acceptable level of both.

In constructing a physicalistic system, we'd like all the magnitudes of elementary particles to be at once determinate and epistemically accessible. But this is out of the question. For although we can measure either the position or the momentum of an electron, we can't measure both at once.

In building a system of thought we begin with a provisional scaffolding made of the (relevant) beliefs we already hold, the aims of the project we are embarked on, the liberties and constraints we consider the system subject to, and the values and priorities we seek to uphold. We suspend judgment on matters in dispute. The scaffolding is not expected to stand by itself. We anticipate having to augment and revise it significantly before we have an acceptable system. Our initial judgments are not comprehensive; they are apt to be jointly untenable; they may fail to serve the purposes to which they are being put or to realize the values we want to respect. So our scaffolding has to be supplemented and (in part) reconstructed before it will serve.

The considered judgments that tether today's theory are the fruits of yesterday's theorizing. They are not held true come what may but are accorded a degree of initial credibility because previous inquiry sanctioned them. They are not irrevisable, but they are our current best guesses about the matter at hand. So they possess a certain inertia. We need a good reason to give them up.[4]

System-building is dialectical. We mould specific judgments to accepted generalizations, and generalizations to specific judgments. We weigh considerations of value against antecedent judgments of fact. Having a (partial) biological taxonomy that enables us to form the generalization 'like comes from like'—that is, progeny belong to the same biological kind as their parents—we have reason to extend the system so as to classify butterflies and caterpillars as the same kind of thing. Rather than invoke a more superficial similarity and violate an elegant generalization, we plump for the generalization and overlook obvious differences.

Justification is holistic. Support for a conclusion comes, not from a single line of argument, but from a host of considerations of varying degrees of strength and relevance. What justifies the categories we construct is the cognitive and practical utility of the truths they enable us to formulate, the elegance and informativeness of the accounts they engender, the value of the ends they promote. We engage in system building when we find the resources at hand inadequate.[5] We have projects they do not serve, questions they do not answer, values they do not realize. Something new is required. But a measure of the adequacy of a novelty is its fit with what we think we already know. If the finding is at all surprising, the background of accepted beliefs is apt to require modification to make room for it, and the finding may require revision to be fitted into place. A process of delicate adjustments occurs, its goal being a system in wide reflective equilibrium.[6]

Considerations of cognitive value come into play in deciding what modifications to attempt. Since science places a premium on repeatable results, an observation that cannot be reproduced is given short shrift, while one that is readily repeated may be weighted so heavily that it can undermine a substantial body of theory. And a legal system that relies on juries consisting of ordinary citizens is unlikely to favor the introduction of distinctions so recondite as to be incomprehensible to the general public.

To go from a motley collection of convictions to a system of considered judgments in reflective equilibrium requires balancing competing claims against one another. And there are likely to be several ways to achieve an acceptable balance. One system might, for example, sacrifice scope to achieve precision; another trade precision for scope. Neither invalidates the other. Nor is there any reason to believe that a uniquely best system will emerge in the long run.

To accommodate the impossibility of ascertaining both the position and the momentum of an electron, drastic revisions are required in our views about physics. But which ones? A number of alternatives have been suggested. We might maintain that each electron has a determinate position and a determinate momentum at every instant, but admit that only one of these magnitudes can be known. In that case, science is committed to the existence of things that it cannot, in principle, discover. Or we might contend that the magnitudes are created in the process of measurement. Then an unmeasured particle has neither a position nor a momentum, and one that has a position lacks momentum (for the one measurement precludes the other). Physical magnitudes are then knowable because they are artifacts of our knowledge-gathering techniques. But from the behavior of particles in experimental situations nothing follows about their behavior elsewhere. Yet a third option is to affirm that a particle has a position and affirm that it has a momentum, but deny that it has both a position and a momentum. In that case, however, we must alter our logic in such a way that the conjunction of individually true sentences is not always true. That science countenances nothing unverifiable, that experiments yield information about what occurs in nature, that logic is independent of matters of fact—such antecedently reasonable theses are shown by the findings of quantum mechanics to be at odds with one another. Substantial alterations are thus required to accommodate our theory of scientific knowledge to the data it seeks to explain. Although there are several ways of describing and explaining quantum phenomena, none does everything we want. Different accommodations retain different scientific desiderata. And deciding which one to accept involves deciding which features of science we value most and which ones we are prepared, if reluctantly, to forego. "Unexamined electrons have no position" derives its status as fact from a judgment of value—the judgment that it is better to construe magnitudes as artifacts of measurement than to modify classical logic, or commit science to the truth of claims it is powerless to confirm, or to make any of the other available revisions needed to resolve the paradox.

Pluralism results. The same constellation of cognitive and practical objectives can sometimes be realized in different ways, and different constellations of cognitive and practical objectives are sometimes equally worthy of realization. A sentence that is right according to one acceptable system may be wrong according to another.

But it does not follow that every statement, method, or value is right according to some acceptable system. Among the considered judgments that guide our theorizing are convictions that certain things—for example, affirming a contradiction, ignoring the preponderance of legal or experimental evidence, or exterminating a race—are just wrong. Such convictions must be respected unless we find powerful reasons to revise them. And there is no ground for thinking that such reasons are in the offing. So it is not the case that anything goes.

Senses of Moral Relativity   **18**

DAVID WIGGINS

The term of art 'relativity' sounds so many different bells in moral philosophy that it will be well to make a brief inventory of its senses and single out the sense or senses that are most relevant here.

(1) Among the first and oldest things there are to mean by relativity is the claim that no act or practice can be assessed as right or wrong, good or bad, etc., without the full specification of circumstances and context (and even, in some versions, the identity of agents). This position could be called contextualism and might be attributed to Aristotle. In Aristotle, it very readily consists with the idea that there is a unitary morality that can find expression in a variety of different acts in a variety of different contexts. This is an undogmatic form of objectivism. Modern versions of the position offer what is still one of the most coherent responses to the facts about ethical diversity.

(2) At the other extreme, there is the position that maintains that 'right' or 'wrong,' 'good' or 'bad,' are really relational predicates requiring supplementation not by context or circumstances but by the specification of the moral system or society for which ethical predicates are indexed. Such a position makes

Originally published as "Moral Cognitivism, Moral Relativism, and Motivating Moral Beliefs," *Proceedings of the Aristotelian Society* (1991), sec. IX–X, pp. 72–77. Reprinted by courtesy of the Editor of the Aristotelian Society © 1991.

disagreement between different moral systems strictly impossible. What seem like rival views of a given act or practice simply attribute different but (it now seems) compossible properties to that act or practice. Squeezing out all inter-systematic disagreement, as it does, this position is too silly (as it stands) to threaten anything.

(3) Somewhat similarly, it has sometimes been maintained that the properties of truth and falsehood as predicated of moral judgments are really relative to a system of moral assessment, so that the sentence "Harming one's enemies is wrong" could be true relative to Christian morality and false relative to ordinary pre-Christian Greek morality. But this, too, is a quite unsuitable position from which to make the attack on cognitivism. There is nothing for the words 'relative to pre-Christian morality' to mean in the combination 'true relative to pre-Christian morality', except of course 'according to pre-Christian morality.' And then all that is being said is that *according* to pre-Christian morality, it is true that harming one's enemies is wrong. This relativizes nothing.

What we learn from these failures of formulation ((2) and (3), I mean), is to look for subtler ways in which something might be relative to an ethical system. Relativism (2) and Relativism (3) sought to establish difference in extension by dint of crude distortions of sense. What is really needed perhaps is to discover a relativity of sense that is already theoretically uncontroversial and then try to discover some relativity in reference or extension, if there is one, that is *consequential* on that relativity of sense. Versions (4) and (5) attempt this.

(4) Consider the sense of a value-predicate. On the subjectivist account, we grasp the sense of such a predicate by acquiring a sensibility all parties to which respond in a particular way to certain particular features in what they notice in any given act, person or situation. (Contrast this sort of relativity with the relativity or relationality mentioned in versions (1), (2), (3)). There are then two reasons for finding relativity at the level of the sense of value-predicates. First, on the subjectivist account, value predicates cannot be elucidated otherwise than by reference to the responses that the properties that they introduce call for or make appropriate. But if a moral or aesthetic sensibility comprises responses keyed to associated properties, and these moral or aesthetic properties are demarcated only by reference to responses they make appropriate, then the sense of a predicate standing for a property begins by being fixed only correlatively to that response. Secondly, although the sensibility that links value property and response will be eagerly propagated by its participants and I will aim for universality (will seek, not without mutual adaptation, to take over the thoughts of all it comes into contact with), it cannot be assumed that it will actually attain universality. So until such time as it attains that, it may be important in the case

of any given value-predicate, taken in a certain given sense, to be prepared to make any effort that it takes to strive to enter into the sensibility that conditions that sense.

(5) Finally, then, if what you attribute by a value term can depend not only on (e.g.) a reference class (good when appraised *as an f*) or on circumstances (see relativity (1)) but also, more fundamentally, on the nature of the sensibility that conditions the sense of the value term; and if the reference and extension of a predication involving the term depend at least in part on that sense so conditioned: then (if all this holds) there is the possibility of a fifth and quite unsurprising kind of relativism. This says (however plausibly or implausibly) that, in spite of the fact that disputants with different sensibilities can nominally or formally agree that what is at issue in some argument is (say) 'whether one ought to acquiesce in the institution of slavery' or 'whether one ought to try to harm one's enemies'—in spite, that is, of disputants seeming to mean the same by 'one ought to' or the words translated so—the eventual conclusion that anyone will come to will depend on what is distinctive in the *substance* of their understanding of the question of what one ought to do. That substance is not guaranteed to be the same by its being agreed that 'ought' is the best rendering of the thoughts they are thinking.

Relativities (4) and (5) combine to constitute the real challenge of relativity. I think that the cognitivist response to the challenge will best take the form of distinguishing at least three kinds of difference of opinions that may be exemplified by the moral convictions of parties apparently, potentially or actually in dispute.

Verdict of Incommensurability. It may seem in a certain sort of given case that the disputants (who may or may not know of one another's existence and may not actually argue) are caught up in such utterly different forms of life and civilization— that their expectations and presumptions are so different—that any semblance of agreement on the sense of the question what one ought to do or what is good is only a semblance. Because the standards of correctness implicit in their respective norms are so utterly different, the reference and the extension of the words that they use cannot be expected to be the same. The reference and extension may differ even though one cannot improve on an interpretation that interprets all the parties as claiming this or that is what they 'ought' to do. Let it be noted that this form of relativism, which may remind the reader of various claims entered by Peter Winch, does not threaten cognitivism as such. (Whatever else it may threaten.) For here at least, the difference between the disputants is too great for them even to arrive at a point where they really disagree; and the fact of their seeming to disagree cannot count against the cognitivist expectation that there will be convergence in belief among those who *do* understand the same thing.

Counsel of Perseverance. On the other hand, it may seem in a given case that there really is a common question that the disputants are addressing, that the disagreement between them is non-trivial, but that their initial disagreement is best explained by a difference in their starting points, a difference they could overcome. If that is how things seem, then a philosopher can begin by trying to make explicit any relativity to circumstances that may be discovered within the content of the question on which they disagree. Once that has been attempted, it may still appear that there is a disagreement of substance. But this disagreement does not imply that it is senseless to urge that the matter be deliberated further and argued *à outrance*. For under the present diagnosis of the situation, we may want to say that it simply does not matter that at the outset the parties' understandings are conditioned by different sensibilities. For surely they can try to overcome that by any means that may come to hand. What is more, before they continue argument on the level of reasons, they must sometimes interrogate one another and themselves about the *aetiology* of their beliefs. Once they understand that better, then, despite the difference in their starting points, surely one or the other or both parties can still arrive at an improved sensibility that is the proper inheritor of the sensibility they began with. If so, why can they not arrive at an improved standard of correctness?[1] Insofar as our philosophical response to disagreement is to urge perseverance with the matter in hand as a substantive moral or social question, we have still not abandoned the Aristotelian idea that (at least as regards substantial questions) a unitary morality can be found beneath the visible diversity of practices. An account of morality that begins by grounding the phenomenon in human sensibility and in the contingency of particular desires that arise from practices at particular times and places can postulate an *initial* relativity of morality to that sensibility, but then (in a manner in some ways anticipated by David Hume himself) make room for what is central to any given morality to surmount this condition. Of course, unless a fully formed universal notion of rationality exists in advance of the attempt to surmount—unless there is a notion of practical rationality which is more than something immanent in actual norms and practices, more than Aristotelian—there is no guarantee (*pace* Immanuel Kant) that morality can always or everywhere transcend its starting point. Equally, though, no limit needs to be set in advance. For the effect of morality's attaining a better understanding of itself along the lines suggested by Hume is not to identify that clear limit but to make room for both possibilities, our capacity to transcend in one case and our inability to transcend in another case. (See relativisms (1) and (3).) The cognitivist need not make predictions, except to urge in general terms (and to try to show in particular cases) that, for the central core of morality, perseverance is the proper counsel.

Finding of Underdetermination. So much for cases where we may reasonably persevere. In other cases, on the other hand, even though there *is* the appearance of a common question, disagreement may appear inexpugnable. Relativization to circumstances does not help. Relativization to *ethos* represents distortion. And there is no manifest possibility of any winning set of considerations ever being mustered. In this case, the disagreement between the two parties may be real yet represent, in a certain sense that has interested Bernard Williams, a purely notional confrontation. It may represent a choice between alternatives such that it could never be a real option for an upholder of one option to live the other. And it may seem that there is no standpoint from which this choice could ever be deliberated truly practically. If so, and if, where practical reason idles, it is point-less to look to it for a practical verdict, then—insofar as we persist in attributing to the disputants a common understanding of what is meant by the question of what one ought to do about this or that—well, indeterminacy or underdetermi-nation is revealed in the reference and extension of certain moral words (under-stood in this way) or in certain combinations of them (so understood).[2]

NOTES

1. With some disagreements, it may eventually appear that the question is not so much one of morality as one of ethos, and that the disputants can be content to leave mat-ters at that. See [the section] "Finding of Underdetermination" below. For the distinction of morality and ethos, see Aurel Kolnai, "Moral Consensus," *Proceedings of the Aristote-lian Society* 70 (1969–1970): 93–120.

2. For a ramified treatment of the present article, see David Wiggins, "Objectivity in Ethics," in *Ethics: Twelve Lectures on the Philosophy of Morality* (Cambridge, Mass.: Harvard University Press, 2006), chap. 11, 325–356.

Ethical Relativism and the Problem of Incoherence

DAVID LYONS

It is natural to suppose that 'ethical relativism' names a single type of theory that either makes good sense or none at all. Opponents of relativism may, therefore, be expected to argue that it is an incoherent doctrine. Some have done so, understanding it as the combination of blatantly inconsistent claims. Recently, Gilbert Harman has objected to such a strategy of 'dissuasive definition' and has shown its inadequacies by developing a theory that is recognizably relativistic while lacking any obvious inconsistencies.[1] It may therefore seem as if ethical relativism is immune to such charges and can continue to demand our respect.

I agree with Harman that relativistic theories do not uniformly lapse into incoherence, but there nevertheless remain reasons for suspecting many relativistic theories of being untenable—reasons not of accidental formulation but rooted deeply in certain ways of thinking about morality. As a consequence, whole classes of relativistic theories may well prove to be incoherent.

In this paper, I shall explore the nature and extent of one important threat of incoherence to ethical relativism. I shall sketch the source of that particular threat, I shall show how relativistic theories differ in their vulnerability to it, and

David Lyons, "Ethical Relativism and the Problem of Incoherence," in *Ethics*, Volume 86, pp. 107–121. Copyright, 1976, University of Chicago Press. All rights reserved. Used by permission of the publisher.

remains to be seen whether the conflicting judgments that he is then committed to endorsing are related in a coherent manner.

In the second place, I wish to separate the issues as far as possible, and so I do not wish to discuss right now (what will be discussed later) whether relativism can be saved if we suppose that apparently conflicting judgments are not really incompatible in the relevant, troublesome cases. Right now we wish to see what difference it might make for a relativist to deny that the relevant conflicting judgments are true, while he nevertheless regards them as logically incompatible. To put the point another way, we wish to see how relativism can fare when it accepts as far as possible the relevant logical appearances—for example, the apparent incompatibility of certain moral judgments that he may wish simultaneously to endorse.

To see what this possibility amounts to, we must shift our focus slightly. What becomes crucial here is not so much the lack of truth-values as the character of the relativist's appraisal of moral judgments. Within a noncognitive moral theory, he refrains from endorsing them as true. Is there then a way of endorsing conflicting moral judgments, which maintains the spirit of relativism and yet avoids incoherence? I shall argue to the contrary. I shall show, first, how a clearly coherent position that seems relativistic on the surface forsakes relativism entirely. I shall indicate what must be done to transform such a theory into a form of ethical relativism and suggest why that may be impossible. Finally, I shall show how a clearly relativistic theory developed within the present guidelines generates apparently unintelligible results. I will not show that a coherent form of relativism within the current guidelines is impossible, but I will give reasons for supposing that the prospects are not encouraging.

It would be difficult to imagine how to proceed if we did not have Hare's ethical theory to serve as the basis for discussion. At any rate, it seems at first to meet our requirements. Hare regards moral judgments as 'prescriptions' for action[10] and so does not construe them as either true or false. Nevertheless, he takes the apparent logic of moral discourse quite seriously, and he offers an apparently relativistic theory of justification.

It seems fair to say that Hare's analysis of the logic of moral discourse is committed to preserving and explaining most of the logical phenomena, save what seems most intimately connected with the notions of truth and falsity. Hare would seem to regard Alice and Barbara's conflicting judgments about Claudia's proposed abortion as logically incompatible, because he believes that such relations are not restricted to the realm of 'factual' assertions. Hare tries to account for these phenomena not despite, but rather by means of, his specific noncognitive theory. Thus, the essential meaning of a moral judgment is alleged to be (something like) its prescriptive force, such as the condemnation of Claudia's proposed abortion (by Alice) or the withholding of such condemnation (by Barbara). The relevant relations between such utterances are held to be substantially the same as the relations between an assertion and its denial. But the details (and of course the soundness) of Hare's theory are not at issue here. The main point is that he wishes to preserve the relevant logical phenomena—to treat such judgments as conflicting in the strictest logical sense.

Hare believes, furthermore, that moral judgments can be justified by subsuming them under general principles from which they can be derived when suitable assumptions are made about the facts. One's judgment can be faulted—shown to be unjustified—if such support is unavailable. But a defense is only as good as the support that is offered. Unless one can show not only that one's factual assumptions are reasonable but also that one's basic moral principles are not arbitrary, it would be implausible to speak of justifying moral judgments. It is therefore important that, on Hare's view, even one's basic principles are subject to a kind of rational criticism. It will suffice for our purposes to note here Hare's original suggestions about such criticism (for his later elaborations do not affect the relevant points).

One must consider the 'consequences' of a (basic) principle and the 'way of life' it represents and make a 'decision of principle' whether to accept or reject it. If one accepts a principle under those conditions, one's decision is justified: it is neither 'arbitrary' nor 'unfounded,' Hare says, because "it would be based upon a consideration of everything upon which it could possibly be founded."[11]

The upshot seems to be a form of appraiser relativism, for moral principles are supposed by Hare to have universal scope, and those emerging from decisions of principle can conceivably diverge. As Hare fully recognizes, whether or not a principle can pass the sort of test he describes is a psychological fact about a given person. The relevant dispositions of individuals can vary, so that two persons might make decisions of principle with differing results (for example, one condemning abortion, the other condoning it); their principles could then be applied most rigorously in conjunction with the same set of true factual beliefs about an action (Claudia's proposed abortion, for example) to obtain what in Hare's view would be fully justified moral judgments, which could not be faulted in any way, though they conflicted.

Does this show that an appraiser theory can endorse logically incompatible judgments without lapsing into incoherence? I believe not. If we interpret Hare's theory of justification in the most natural way, its limited claims hardly deserve to be called 'relativistic' (they seem in fact to be perfectly innocuous), while a truly relativistic reinterpretation yields a theory that is difficult to understand, if it is at all intelligible.

Hare's theory of justification seems to concern the conditions under which a person can be justified in making or maintaining a moral judgment. It says nothing whatsoever about the judgment itself (its content). Thus, on Hare's theory, Alice can be justified in judging Claudia's proposed abortion to be wrong, and Barbara can simultaneously be justified in judging Claudia's proposed abortion not to be wrong; but Hare's theory speaks only of their judging, not of the contents of their judgments—that is, that Claudia's abortion would be wrong and that Claudia's abortion would not be wrong.

There is nothing especially 'relativistic' about a theory which acknowledges the possibility that two individuals can be justified in making their respective judgments, even when the judgments themselves are (regarded as) logically incompatible. Consider a case outside ethics. Alice might be justified in predicting rain tonight while Barbara is justified in predicting none, because justification here is 'relative' (in a perfectly innocuous sense) to such things as evidence and reasons, which two people do not necessarily share. Hare may be understood as claiming that justification in morals is similarly 'relative' (so far, in this same perfectly innocuous sense) to individuals' 'decisions of principle.' But that alone is not ethical relativism, because it is compatible with all that an antirelativist might ever desire. Consider Alice and Barbara's conflicting weather predictions once more. They may both be justified; but one is correct and the other incorrect, regardless of their justifications; that is to say, either it will or will not rain tonight. The parallel supposition in ethics is perfectly compatible with Hare's theory of justification in morals as we have so far construed it. Hare's theory tells us nothing at all about the validity of the judgments themselves. For all we have said so far, it may be the case that Alice's judgment (that is, that Claudia's proposed abortion would be wrong) is correct and that Barbara's conflicting judgment is consequently incorrect.

Now, it may be observed that Hare seems also to believe that moral judgments cannot be, as it were, 'objectively' appraised—that they cannot be correct or incorrect independently of the justification one may have for making them. Indeed, his reasons for this belief seem partly to underlie his theory of justification. Hare maintains that 'factual' judgments cannot guide conduct, while moral judgments do. He also maintains that moral judgments here have (something like) an imperatival character or component, and he assumes that factual judgments must be expressed in the indicative mood. He then argues that 'imperatives' cannot be deduced from 'indicatives' alone, which he therefore takes as implying that moral judgments cannot be deduced from factual considerations. From this, he infers that moral judgments are logically independent of the facts. One must take account of the facts when making moral judgments, but one must also appeal to (imperative-like) general principles. When one arrives at basic principles, arbitrariness is avoided by the sort of rational reflection that is involved in making decisions of principle. Thus, Hare seems to say, the most that we can possibly do by way of appraising moral principles is to subject them to such personal criticism. And this, he believes, is not negligible. It entitles us to talk quite seriously of 'justification.'

I wish to maintain, however, that we are not obliged to accept this more radical position, even if we endorse a noncognitive conception of more discourse like Hare's. In the first place, Hare's line of reasoning to his more radical position is fallacious. Hare begs a crucial question by assuming that 'factual' judgments must be understood in the indicative while moral judgments must be assimilated to the imperative. This bias seems based on Hare's unwarranted assumption that 'factual' judgments, and generally judgments that are properly expressed in the indicative mood, cannot be guides to action. Most important, Hare fails to consider seriously the possibility of logically sound nondeductive arguments from factual premises to moral conclusions. So, Hare has not shown (or even given us any reason to believe) that moral judgments are independent of the facts and cannot be objectively appraised for that (or some other) reason. I have no idea how that might be shown.

In the second place, Hare's noncognitive conception of moral discourse does not seem to preclude the possibility that moral judgments are 'objectively' correct or incorrect. It is clear that both Bentham and J. S. Mill, for example, regarded moral judgments as objectively correct or incorrect. And there are good reasons for ascribing to them a noncognitive theory of moral discourse roughly like Hare's.[12] The difference is that they believe what Hare appears to deny—namely, that basic principles are objectively correct or incorrect. The result is not obviously untenable. But perhaps an analogy might help to suggest the possibility of such a position. It is not implausible to regard prudential judgments as objectively correct or incorrect, and this idea would seem to have no bearing on the question of whether prudential judgments require a noncognitive analysis. But if that can be said for prudential judgments, why not for moral judgments too?

In the third place, the idea of combining Hare's innocuously 'relativistic' theory of justification with the claim that moral judgments are not themselves objectively correct or incorrect is itself suspect. Consider what the resulting position would be like. One would be maintaining that Alice can be justified in judging that Claudia's proposed abortion would be wrong, but that the judgment itself—that Claudia's proposed abortion would be wrong—can be neither correct nor incorrect. The suggestion is dubious, partly because the very notion of 'relative' justification has its home among items, which can be appraised in objective terms (such as weather predictions). Indeed, we seem to get an understanding of what is meant by justifying one's judgments in that 'relative' sense partly by contrasting it with objective appraisal of the judgment itself. It is unclear whether the idea of 'relative' justification has any proper application, any reasonable interpretation, outside such a context.

The usual suggestions that it does are based on the notion that the best we can do always counts as justification. That idea is endorsed by Hare when he says that a 'decision of principle' can be regarded as justified "because it would be based upon a consideration of everything upon which it could possibly be founded." This is much too indulgent, for it would oblige us to regard any totally unjustifiable assertion as completely justified! (This is especially embarrassing to Hare, since he recognizes no good, logically respectable arguments from factual premises to moral principles; thus he seems to encourage the endorsement of principles that are not only without foundation but also indistinguishable, on his own account of justification, from totally unjustifiable positions.)

To transform Hare's theory into a truly relativistic position, therefore, one needs a good argument for denying that moral judgments themselves are objectively correct or incorrect plus an account of how the notion of 'relative' justification can nevertheless apply. I have never seen a plausible account of this matter, and I am uncertain, for the reasons indicated above, whether any such account is possible. Let us see if others can meet this challenge.

Meanwhile, I suggest that if we wish to see what a truly relativistic theory of justification would be like within the present guidelines, we must build upon Hare's theory quite differently. I shall use the materials provided by Hare, without suggesting that the results would meet with his approval.

Such a theory would concern the judgments themselves, not one's making or maintaining them. And here I am uncertain of what terms of appraisal to use. It seems misleading to adopt the term 'justified,' since it most naturally applies to the attitude rather than its object. And we cannot here, within the confines of noncognitivism, speak of truth. So I suggest that we use the term most favored by ethical relativists—'valid'—hoping it will have no misleading connotations.

The theory can be sketched as follows. More than one basis for moral appraisals is recognized, and these make it possible to validate conflicting moral judgments. For purposes of illustration, let us suppose that the bases are decisions of principle and that Alice and Barbara subscribe to differing principles, such that the judgment condemning Claudia's act is validated by Alice's principles while the withholding of such condemnation is validated by Barbara's principles. To avoid irrelevant complications, we assume further that Alice and Barbara each have internally consistent moral positions, in the sense that the principles attributable to one of them cannot be used to both validate and invalidate one of these judgments or to validate both of them.

Difficulties arise when we imagine the following sort of case. Suppose that Barbara's actual judgment, on this occasion, conflicts with the principles to which she would subscribe on due reflection. Her actual judgment is, therefore, held to be invalid. (This must be possible, or the theory would imply that all actual judgments are valid.) It is important now to see that, so far as such a theory is concerned, the actual judgments made by Alice and Barbara are identical in content; they have the same meaning. (On the particular theory we are using for purposes of illustration, they have the same meaning because they both condemn Claudia's abortion.) Now, the theory appraises judgments in respect to their contents and by reference to personal principles. But, since different persons' judgments can be identical in meaning, the standards that are invoked cannot, so to speak, tell the difference between one person's judgments and another's. So, whether the relativist likes it or not, Alice's principles can be used to appraise Barbara's judgments as well as her own, and vice versa. The upshot is that such a theory allows one and the same judgment (in respect of content) to be both valid and invalid. In the case we have just imagined, the judgment that Claudia's proposed abortion would be wrong is held valid because it accords with (or is derivable from) Alice's principles and invalid because it conflicts with Barbara's. But it is difficult to understand what this might mean—that such a judgment (the judgment itself, not someone's making it) is simultaneously both valid and invalid.[13]

One might expect the relativist here to try to relativize the notion of validity. But we are speaking of the contents of judgments, not someone's making them, so it is not clear how that might be done; the innocuously 'relative' notion of justification seems out of place, for example. It remains to be seen whether any sensible interpretation can be given to this paradoxical appraisal.

The foregoing arguments do not conclusively show that a truly relativistic theory, which accommodates most of the relevant logical phenomena, is impossible, but it strongly suggests that conclusion. I therefore tentatively conclude that relativism must reject the apparent logic of moral discourse and resort to more desperate theoretical measures.

V. RELATIVISTIC ANALYSES

Relativistic theories that are threatened by incoherence might try to avoid it by claiming that the relevant conflicting moral judgments are not really incompatible. This has, in fact, been suggested by anthropologists when they claim that to say that an act is wrong simply means that the act conflicts with certain norms.[14] On this approach, appraiser's-group relativism would be modified so that it understands Alice's utterance, "Claudia's proposed abortion would be wrong," to mean that Claudia's contemplated act conflicts with the norms of Alice's group while construing Barbara's assertion, "Claudia's proposed abortion would not be wrong," to mean that Claudia's act would not conflict with the norms of Barbara's group. Now, Alice and Barbara either belong to the same group or they do not. If they do, then the theory regards their judgments as incompatible, which accords with the logical appearances. The troublesome sort of case arises when Alice and Barbara belong to different groups whose respective norms disagree about abortion. The present theory would allow both Alice and Barbara's judgments to be true but denies that they are incompatible, since one judgment relates the act to one set of norms while the other judgment relates it to another set. In this way, such a theory can avoid endorsing inconsistencies.

Some of the consequences of such theories should not pass unnoticed. On the surface it appears that Alice and Barbara are disagreeing about Claudia's proposed abortion, saying incompatible things about it. But, according to this sort of theory, they are confused if they believe their judgments to be incompatible. In fact, the theory says, they are actually talking at cross-purposes.

And consider what the theory says when Alice and Barbara seem to agree about Claudia's proposed abortion, both saying it would be wrong or both denying that. It implies that Alice and Barbara must be understood as meaning different things, appearances notwithstanding.

An attempt might be made to reconcile such theories with our own views about what goes on in moral discourse by accounting for the perceived agreements and disagreements in terms of shared or conflicting attitudes that are expressed by such judgments. When Alice and Barbara disagree in their judgments, their difference is not propositional but rather attitudinal. They have, and their judgments express, different attitudes toward the act in question, one condemning the act (let us say) and the other refusing to condemn it. When they agree about the act, it is not that they make the same assertion but rather that they share an attitude toward the act, both condemning or both refusing to condemn it.

I do not wish to deny that attitudes are expressed by such judgments. The trouble with the suggestion is that Alice and Barbara's beliefs may be ignored. But their beliefs are essentially connected with the relevant attitudes, in that the condemnatory attitude expressed by the judgment that Claudia's act would be wrong either is, or is grounded upon, the belief that Claudia's act would be wrong. So we cannot account for agreement or disagreement in such cases without deciding how the relevant beliefs are to be analyzed. Such theories are then committed to analyzing the beliefs relativistically along the lines adopted in construing the corresponding utterances. This simply returns us to the original decision of such theories, to reject clear logical phenomena in favor of preserving relativism.

It seems reasonable to say that such a relativist has incurred a sizable debt of explanation and justification. He must give very good reasons why we should regard apparently conflicting judgments as compatible and apparently identical judgments as different, and he must presumably show that they require analysis in one particular relativistic way rather than another. But what reasons are actually given? So far as I can see, they are not clearly reasons for analyzing moral judgments in a certain way.

The anthropologists who suggest such relativistic analyses seem tacitly to reason as follows: When individuals in a given society judge conduct, they typically invoke prevailing standards. Therefore, what it means to call an act 'wrong' is that the act conflicts with the group's norms. This reasoning is painfully fallacious.

Harman suggests a different sort of argument for his relativistic analysis. His theory is limited to what he calls 'inner' moral judgments—the ones we make when we judge it right or wrong of a particular person to do something or that some particular person ought or ought not to do something. Harman allows that we might judge a certain type of act nonrelativistically, even when we relativistically judge such conduct as performed by a given person.

The relevant part of Harman's reasoning may be summarized as follows: He gives examples to show that, when we judge a person's conduct, we take into account that person's own attitudes. We do not invoke considerations which we believe would not count as reasons for him, would not move him or influence his decision. These considerations are closely connected, in Harman's view, with that person's own moral standards. Thus, we refrain from saying that it is wrong of someone to do a certain thing (or that he ought not to do it) if we believe that he would not be moved by the considerations that concern us, or that his action conforms to his own moral code, even when we are ready to condemn the sort of conduct he practices. Therefore (Harman seems to reason), judgments to the effect that it is wrong of someone to do something (or that he ought not to do it) make essential reference to—by their very meaning invoke—that person's own attitudes and moral standards.

This amounts, in effect, to an agent theory, so Harman does not seem (does not perhaps intend) to endorse conflicting moral judgments. Because it is a rare attempt to justify a relativistic analysis, however, it merits our attention.

What concerns me is that the data assumed by Harman could equally well be accounted for in other ways—for example, by reference to our substantive convictions about the pointlessness of advising a person when we think we cannot influence him and, more generally, the unfairness of judging a person for doing something (as opposed to judging the sort of act he performs viewed more abstractly) by standards other than his own. We have no clear reason for rejecting this alternative account in favor of Harman's theory about the meaning of the relevant class of judgments. So we have no good reason to reject the nonrelativistic logical phenomena as illusory.

I mention Harman's case because I believe it typical. Relativistic analyses are not supported in the way they need to be. Now, it may be asked what all this shows. Have I succeeded in suggesting any more than that such theories are unfounded and perhaps implausible? That would be far from showing them untenable because of their incoherence.

But the only clear reason that we seem to have for resorting to relativistic analyses of moral judgments is that this will save the vulnerable forms of relativism from the scrap heaps of incoherence. As I suggested earlier, a theory that avoids incoherence by arbitrary modifications, that lacks independent theoretical justification, cannot command our respect. My suggestion now is that similar considerations apply to theories that avoid incoherence through the same devices, not by deliberate design but, as it were, by luck or accident—for example, by fashionably formulating their claims as analyses of meaning, claims which, if formulated in other ways (which happen to be equally supported by the facts) would be untenable.

It looks as if relativism can be given a coherent gloss, even when it endorses conflicting moral judgments. But theories that avoid incoherence by such unjustified claims are, it seems, much worse than unfounded and implausible.

NOTES

1. Gilbert Harman, "Moral Relativism Defended," *Philosophical Review* 84 (1975): 3–22 (this volume, chap. 14).

2.   W. G. Sumner, *Folkways* (Boston: Ginn, 1940); M. J. Herskovits, *Man and His Works* (New York: Knopf, 1948), chap. 5, and *Cultural Anthropology* (New York: Knopf, 1955), chap. 19.

3. R. M. Hare, *The Language of Morals* (Oxford: Clarendon Press, 1952), and *Freedom and Reason* (Oxford: Clarendon Press, 1963).

4. For an emphatic presentation of such points in another connection, see Carl Wellman, "Emotivism and Ethical Objectivity," *American Philosophical Quarterly* 5 (1968): 90–92.

5. As Sumner makes clear and Herskovits implies, this does not mean that the norms themselves are beyond evaluation. Their approach to the norms is, in fact, broadly utilitarian and thus (in a significant sense) nonrelativistic. (Sumner seems to reason that the function of the norms is adaptation to the circumstances, that something is good insofar as it performs its function well, and thus that norms are good insofar as they are adapted to circumstances—in which case, he assumes, they serve societal welfare.) But the appraisal of conduct is treated as an independent matter, governed by existing norms. (Sumner seems to struggle with the tension here, tying 'immorality' to conformity and yet praising enlightened dissent.)

6. I am here ignoring the possibility that some norms of a group may themselves conflict.

7. One could eliminate this feature of the theory, for example, by invalidating 'cross-cultural' judgments. But for our purposes we can ignore this possibility.

8. Harman's theory, so far as it goes (it concerns only one type of judgment about conduct), has the basic features of an agent theory, since it allows no more than one set of values (to which one is a tacit subscriber) to govern one's conduct.

9. And the relations between social groups, such as economic exploitation, suggest how naive is the assumption that prevailing social norms serve 'societal welfare.'

10. As Hare seems to recognize (*Language of Morals*, 20–24), this characterization ignores half of our possible judgments of conduct, such as Barbara's judgment that Claudia's proposed abortion would not be wrong, which is by no means a 'prescription' or imperatival. But Hare's general idea could be expanded into a more adequate theory, as Bentham, for example, was aware. See David Lyons, *In the Interest of the Governed* (Oxford: Clarendon Press, 1973), chap. 6.

11. Hare, *Language of Morals*, 69.

12. For Bentham, see *In the Interest of the Governed*, chap. 6; for Mill, one must begin with his *System of Logic*, bk. 6, chap. 12. Neither writer will seem unambiguous to modern readers; there are textual grounds for the standard view of them as ethical 'naturalists.' I am only suggesting a possible interpretation that seems interestingly compatible with their antirelativism.

13. The foregoing argument does not, in fact, require that the two judgments have precisely the same meaning. It would suffice if they were so related that their respective negations were logical contraries. But to regard them as identical is to respect the logical appearances as fully as possible.

14. See, for example, Sumner, *Folkways*, sec. 439; and Ruth Benedict, "Anthropology and the Abnormal," in *Value and Obligation*, ed. R. B. Brandt (New York: Harcourt, Brace & World, 1961), 457.

GOPAL SREENIVASAN

I. INTRODUCTION

On the face of it, anthropology offers to acquaint us with a rich variety of different cultures and mores. Many of us are familiar, even if only secondhand, with reports from the field of alien goings-on among the Azande or the Yanomamo, for example. But really how different from ours are the various moralities on which ethnographers report? Can they be so different as to be 'incommensurable' with our morality, as is often claimed? If these moralities seem as alien as all that, what makes anyone so sure that the ethnographers have understood them properly in the first place?

I have no doubt that, on the whole, the ethnographers have got it right, and I take this to be the common-sense reaction. But it is one thing to accept a claim and quite another to defend it philosophically. In this chapter, I examine and reject a prominent philosophical strategy for maintaining a priori skepticism about the extent of the moral differences reported by ethnographers. The strategy is suggested by Susan Hurley and aims to exclude the possibility of incommensurability between ethical outlooks using Donald Davidson's famous argument against the very idea of a conceptual scheme.[1] I call it the Hurley-Davidson argument (HDA).

After I explain the HDA in section 2, my criticism follows in two parts. In section 3 I specify a language that cannot be 'radically interpreted,' in Davidson's sense. This provides the kind of case needed to test the HDA. The language contains alien thick descriptions, and I show that languages resist radical interpretation *when* mastering their thick descriptions requires that one appreciate the evaluative conception(s) from which these descriptions get their point(s). In section 4 I argue that we can nevertheless understand languages containing alien thick descriptions. On Davidson's account, *understanding* alien sentences requires that one's knowledge of their truth-conditions be expressible in one's own language. But this requirement for understanding a language turns out to be less demanding than Davidson's requirements for radically interpreting one. I argue that thick descriptions are sensitive to this differential in requirements, which explains how they can resist radical interpretation while remaining tractable to understanding. Our test case thereby becomes a counter-example.

II. THE HURLEY-DAVIDSON ARGUMENT

To begin, I should like to distinguish sharply between two relations that are often run together under the name of 'incommensurability.'[2] The first relation characterizes pairs of vocabularies or languages, typically languages that articulate different outlooks or theories. It applies when the languages are not intertranslatable. Translation is prevented because some terms in the first language have extensions that are not provided by any expression in the second. I shall designate pairs of languages that stand in this relation as *not intertranslatable.*

The second relation characterizes pairs of outlooks or theories directly. It applies when the outlooks recognize distinct considerations as determining the basis for choosing an outlook: in such circumstances, the proponents of the respective outlooks will appeal to different premises in defending their choice of outlook.[3] For simplicity, let me introduce *criteria* as a term of art to designate the considerations recognized within an outlook as determining the basis for choosing an outlook.[4] Competing outlooks *share* criteria if and only if criteria recognized within both outlooks are capable of vindicating one outlook or the other. The second relation may then be understood as the absence of shared criteria. I shall reserve the term *incommensurable* to designate pairs of competing outlooks that do not share criteria.

It is important to distinguish a failure of intertranslatability between languages from the absence of shared criteria between outlooks. For, while the first relation is more commonly associated with the term 'incommensurability,' it is actually the second relation that specifically threatens the rational resolution of disagreements between outlooks. The threat arises because it is unclear how any resolution of a disagreement between outlooks that do not share criteria could be appropriately accounted rational. Hence the strategy under discussion must exclude the possibility that a pair of ethical outlooks do not share criteria.

As is well known, Davidson argues on a priori grounds that failures of inter-translatability between languages are impossible. But unless the intertranslat-ability of languages in which different outlooks are articulated entails that those outlooks share criteria, Davidson's *conclusion* does not establish what is required here. Nevertheless, elements of Davidson's *argument* can be used to demonstrate, further, that outlooks must share criteria. Hurley suggests, more specifically, that this kind of demonstration can be given in the case of ethical outlooks. It will facilitate the discussion, however, if we begin with Davidson's original argument.

The primary aim of Davidson's paper, "On the Very Idea of a Conceptual Scheme," is to refute the doctrine of conceptual relativism, that is, the sugges-tion that "reality itself is relative to a scheme: what counts as real in one system may not in another."[5] Conceptual schemes, on Davidson's analysis, are (provi-sionally) identified with sets of intertranslatable languages. Hence, a failure of intertranslatability between languages turns out to be a necessary condition of any difference in conceptual schemes (185, 190). Davidson seeks to impugn the intelligibility of divergences in conceptual schemes by arguing against the pos-sibility of failures of intertranslatability. He distinguishes complete failures of intertranslatability from partial failures, dividing the course of his argument cor-respondingly. The bulk of his argument is devoted to the case of complete failure, defined as obtaining "if no significant range of sentences in one language could be translated into the other" (185).

But most important for our purposes is Davidson's argument against partial failures of intertranslatability. As he explains, partial failures introduce "the pos-sibility of making changes and contrasts in conceptual schemes intelligible by reference to the common part" (195). He rules out this possibility, however, on the basis of a theory of 'radical interpretation,' the exigencies of which afford no purchase to the identification of differences in conceptual schemes.

Radical interpreters have simultaneously to account for the psychologi-cal attitudes (beliefs, intentions, desires) and to interpret the speech of speak-ers of an alien language, with evidence that assumes nothing about either (196). In Davidson's view, the basic evidence for radical interpretation is the attitude of holding as true, directed at sentences. The following problem thus confronts radical interpreters: "If all we know is what sentences a speaker holds true, and we cannot assume that his language is our own, then we cannot take even a first step towards interpretation without knowing or assuming a great deal about the speaker's beliefs" (196). Being ignorant of their speech, we cannot know speakers' beliefs. Consequently, our only recourse, Davidson argues, is to assume general agreement on beliefs.

The upshot is to make the assumption of widespread agreement a precondition of radical interpretation. "We get a first approximation to a finished theory by assigning to speakers' sentences conditions of truth that actually obtain (in our own opinion) just when the speaker holds these sentences true" (196). Realizing this agreement in practice requires that the speaker of an alien language be accounted right in most matters—right, that is, by the interpreter's own lights: this is Davidson's famous principle of charity. Davidson's radical interpreters begin by establishing a systematic correlation between a massive set of sentences that speakers of the alien language hold true and sentences of their own language that they themselves hold true. On this basis, they construct a theory of truth for the alien language that maximizes, by their lights, the alien speakers' truth telling.[6] Radical interpreters complete their interpretation by hypothesizing that the canonical T-theorems of the theory they have constructed are translational.

Now before we consider how Davidson's argument bears on our question about incommensurability between outlooks, we should notice that it has a hidden premise. The argument is based upon certain claims about the requirements of radical interpretation. But these claims only apply to languages that can be radically interpreted. So no general conclusion about language follows unless all meaningful languages can be radically interpreted. Indeed, for Davidson's purposes, what must be true is that all meaningful languages can be radically interpreted *in the same language*. That is the hidden premise, albeit one that Davidson can perhaps be seen as affirming elsewhere: "All understanding of the speech of another involves radical interpretation."[7]

It is simply unclear what the argument for the hidden premise, thus understood, is supposed to be. It follows from this premise that at least one language exists in which all meaningful languages can be radically interpreted. Suppose English is such a language. Imagine that we are confronted by speakers of an alien candidate-language and that the sentences of this candidate-language have no truth-conditional paraphrases in English. In that case there will be no massive set of sentences held true by speakers of this candidate-language with which we can correlate English sentences that we hold true and that are also translational. Hence, the candidate-language will not be radically interpretable in English. Still assuming the hidden premise, it follows furthermore that the candidate-language is not a language after all. What the aliens appear to say is just meaningless.

But the inference licensed here will not withstand much scrutiny, at least not on Davidson's conception of what suffices for a candidate-language to be meaningful. As he observes elsewhere, "the [truth] definition works by giving necessary and sufficient conditions for the truth of every sentence, and to give truth-conditions is a way of giving the meaning of a sentence. To know the semantic concept of truth for a language is to know what it is for a sentence—any sentence—to be true, and this amounts, in one good sense we can give to the phrase, to understanding the language."[8]

We might capture this conception by noting that it recognizes the following condition as sufficient to secure the meaningfulness of a candidate-language, namely, that necessary and sufficient conditions for the truth of each of its sentences can be given. The critical point is that this places no restriction on the language *in which* the truth-conditions are to be given. Accordingly, to disqualify a candidate-language as meaningless, it would have to be established that truth-conditions for its sentences cannot be given in *any* language. But the most a failure radically to interpret some candidate-language in English could show is that the candidate-language's sentences cannot be given truth-conditions in English. It manifestly does not follow that they cannot be given truth-conditions in any language. So, even if the candidate-language's sentences cannot be given truth-conditions in English, it does not follow that they are meaningless. Yet that inference is licensed by the hidden premise.

Of course, it may be that the hidden premise can be defended on the basis of some other conception of meaningfulness. I shall not pursue that question here because it does not matter for present purposes if the hidden premise is false. If no language exists in which all meaningful languages can be radically interpreted, then Davidson's argument against partial failures of translatability is seriously impaired. But the relevance of his argument to the question of incommensurability survives more or less intact without the hidden premise. I have drawn attention to it here so that it will not distract us later.

The relevance of Davidson's argument lies in its ability to furnish the elements of a demonstration that any outlook articulated by a radically interpreted language shares criteria with the radical interpreter's own outlook. Granted a crucial assumption, this demonstration can also be extended to the more specific case of *ethical* outlooks.[9] Davidson furnishes two elements, although only one is distinctively Davidsonian: the idea that a radical interpreter must establish "a systematic correlation of sentences held true with sentences held true."[10] The generic element is a model of translation on which knowledge of the truth-conditions of a given alien sentence must be expressible in one's own language if one is to be able to translate that sentence. These elements may be combined as follows:

Consider the sentences in an alien candidate-language, Q, that articulate its associated ethical outlook. Call them QE. On the generic model of translation, translators of QE know what QE's truth-conditions are and their knowledge is expressible in their own language. If these translators have also succeeded in radically interpreting Q, then they will believe, furthermore, that the truth-conditions for a 'massive' set of sentences in Q actually obtain. This is just what 'radical interpretation' involves (on Davidson's account). Call this massive set of sentences the *base set*.[11] Successful radical interpreters of Q will thus, perforce, have judged that its base set is true. If we add the *crucial assumption* that enough of QE belongs to the base set,[12] it follows that successful radical interpreters of Q will have judged that the ethical outlook upheld by speakers of Q is (at least, largely) true.

Indeed, the basis on which they do so will be effectively equivalent to whatever basis speakers of Q themselves employ to judge the truth of their ethical outlook. For the truth-conditions that radical interpreters assign to the relevant sentences must be equivalent to those assigned by speakers of Q;[13] and the judgments radical interpreters make about whether they obtain must tally with those made by the speakers of Q. Moreover, since these truth-conditions are specified in their own language, the radical interpreters' judgment of the truth of the Q-speakers' ethical outlook is one that they render *in propria persona*.

In that case, however, there evidently exists a set of considerations that is at once recognized by radical interpreters and the speakers of the alien language alike and sufficient, by their lights, to vindicate the truth of a particular ethical outlook—and so, *a fortiori*, the rationality of adopting it—namely, the truth-conditions of QE together with the belief that these conditions obtain. But this is just to say that radical interpreters and the speakers of the alien language share criteria, in this case, criteria for ethical outlooks. QED.

I shall call this the *Hurley-Davidson argument* (HDA). Part of the point is to distinguish it from Davidson's own argument. At least in print, Davidson does not extend his argument to the ethical case, and thus need not accept this extension's crucial assumption. I call it the *Hurley*-Davidson argument, even though its details have been freely constructed, because it is Hurley who claims that Davidson's argument can be invoked to show, "alternative reason-giving concepts ... must be local alternatives; we cannot make sense of the possibility of an entirely alien scheme of reasons for action, without losing our grip on the very idea of intentional action. To be a reason for action just is to be one of our reasons, related to one another in roughly the ways they are."[14] She is, accordingly, committed to the crucial assumption.[15]

Like Davidson's original argument, the HDA only applies to languages that can be radically interpreted. It demonstrates that any ethical outlook articulated by a radically interpreted language shares criteria (that is, is commensurable) with the radical interpreter's own ethical outlook. But the commensurability thereby established is limited to ethical outlooks articulated by languages radically interpretable in the same language. So the strong conclusion that incommensurable ethical outlooks are impossible, which Hurley advocates above, can only be justified if *all* meaningful languages are radically interpretable in the same language: her strong conclusion requires Davidson's hidden premise.

Still a weaker, and nevertheless significant, conclusion can be drawn from the HDA without this hidden premise, namely, that mutual understanding between ethical outlooks guarantees that they share criteria. Two additional claims are required to reach this conclusion. First, knowledge of an alien sentence's truth-conditions, expressible in one's own language, is a necessary condition of understanding it. Second, if the sentences of an alien candidate-language have truth-conditions expressible in one's own language, then that candidate-language can be radically interpreted in one's own language.[16] It follows that any alien language one understands can be radically interpreted in one's own language.[17] Hence, if these claims are correct, the HDA implies that any ethical outlook (articulated by a language) one understands shares criteria with one's own.

III. THICK DESCRIPTIONS IMPEDE RADICAL INTERPRETATION

It may seem that a cogent argument against the possibility of understanding alien morals is therefore at hand: any alien language one understands can be radically interpreted in one's own language, and any ethical outlook articulated by a radically interpreted language shares criteria with the radical interpreter's own ethical outlook. Thus individuals confronted by an apparently alien ethical outlook will find one of two things. *Either* they will fail to understand the language in which it is articulated and so find the ethical outlook alien indeed, *or* they will understand the language but find that the ethical outlook is not that alien after all, as it shares criteria with their own. In neither case does anyone find an ethical outlook that remains alien once it has been understood.

As I said at the outset, this conclusion sharply conflicts with the apparent deliverances of anthropology. Furthermore, even this weaker version of the argument suggests that, as long as the antagonists truly understand each other, major disagreements between ethical outlooks will be rationally resolvable in principle because the contending outlooks will share criteria.

The weaker version of the HDA appears cogent because its additional claims are plausible. It is very plausible that understanding an alien sentence requires knowledge of its truth-conditions, expressible in one's own language. It is also plausible that an alien language can be radically interpreted in one's own language if its sentences have truth-conditions expressible in one's own language. Nevertheless, while it follows that any alien language one understands can be radically interpreted in one's own language, the resultant appearance of cogency is misleading.

I shall argue that understanding an alien language should be firmly distinguished from radically interpreting it. In principle, of course, the distinction is clear enough. On Davidson's own account, the intrinsic requirements imposed by understanding differ from those imposed by radical interpretation. In his view, the only intrinsic requirement on understanding an alien language is the necessity of knowing the truth-conditions of its sentences, expressible in one's own language. By contrast, there is at least one further intrinsic requirement on radically interpreting an alien language. To wit, one must establish a systematic correlation between a massive set of sentences held true by speakers of the alien language and sentences of one's own language that one holds true oneself.

However tempting, it is a mistake to think that these differing requirements are always jointly satisfied. My argument for this conclusion proceeds in two parts. To begin, I shall argue that we can imagine an alien language that articulates an ethical outlook, but which we could not radically interpret. I shall then argue that our inability radically to interpret this language still need not prevent us from understanding it. The burden of this part of the argument will be to show that having truth-conditions expressible in English, say, does not entail that the sentences of an alien language can be radically interpreted in English. Hence there could easily be cases in which Davidson's requirement on understanding an alien language was satisfied, while his further requirement on radically interpreting that language was not satisfied.

It will therefore emerge that understanding another ethical outlook is no guarantee that it shares criteria with one's own. At least in some cases, understanding another ethical outlook is perfectly consistent with rejecting it in large part. Although I focus on the weaker version of the HDA, I should perhaps emphasize that my criticism also refutes the stronger version. The weaker version asserts that any pair of ethical outlooks one understands will share criteria, while the stronger version asserts this and more, as it asserts that any pair of meaningful ethical outlooks shares criteria. So if the weaker version turns out to be false, then both versions are refuted at once.

Let me begin then. The argument will concentrate on so-called thick descriptions or concepts.[18] In anthropology and ethics, the term 'thick description' primarily designates descriptive terms the use of which carries culturally specific evaluative implications. Take 'courageous' as an example. Its descriptive content is something like *persevering in the face of danger*; and if an action open to one would be courageous, then one has a reason—though not necessarily a decisive one—to perform it.

In addition to being "both world-guided and action-guiding," as Williams puts it, thick descriptions also typically have some evaluative point; and when they do this bears on their extension.[19] The point of courageous, for example, is given by some conception—I shall not try to elucidate it—of what makes perseverance in the face of danger worthwhile. Whatever makes perseverance in the face of danger worthwhile is what provides one with a reason to act courageously, to applaud courageous behavior, and so on. Conversely, when there is no value in persevering in the face of a given danger, one has no reason to persevere. Perseverance under those circumstances cannot be courageous, then, since one always has some reason to act courageously. The extension of courageous is therefore sensitive to the evaluative conception from which it derives its point. It is only when perseverance in the face of danger *is* worthwhile—only when one has some good reason to persevere—that doing so is courageous.

Accordingly, where a thick description has an evaluative point, there will be a straightforward sense in which its extension *depends* upon the evaluative conception that provides the description's point: namely, satisfying an appropriate evaluative condition will be a necessary condition of an action's belonging to that extension. But in another sense, a thick description's extension might nevertheless be independent of the relevant evaluative conception. Let me explain.

For any given thick description with an evaluative point, there may be another description—a pure one, bereft of any evaluative element—with the same believed extension. In that case, the referents of the pure description would all have to satisfy the evaluative condition governing the thick description in question. It is possible, however, that all the referents of some pure description do satisfy this evaluative condition. Consider our example again. Perseverance in the face of danger is not always worthwhile; so some referents of 'perseverance in the face of danger' will not satisfy the evaluative condition governing courageous. But perhaps there is some more subtle, purely descriptive elaboration of perseverance in the face of danger that identifies all and only the conditions in which perseverance in the face of danger is worthwhile.[20] If there were some such pure description, there would be a sense in which the believed extension of courageous was independent of the evaluative conception that provides its point. One measure of this independence is that those who remain completely ignorant of what (we think) makes perseverance in the face of danger worthwhile could still master the believed extension of courageous.[21] Someone could do this by learning the hypothesized subtle elaboration of perseverance in the face of danger, since its extension would match the believed extension of courageous.

Now consider the following position, which I shall call the *descriptive equivalence thesis*. It holds that, *for every thick description, someone has or could acquire a pure description with the same believed extension.* I think this is a rather implausible thesis, though it has its defenders. It is certainly very demanding. It implies that, for every thick description, someone could master its believed extension while prescinding from the evaluative conception that provides its point.

I introduce the descriptive equivalence thesis because the HDA is only tenable if this thesis is true. I said the first part of my argument will show that there could be an ethical outlook articulated by an alien language we could not radically interpret. The ethical outlook is one in which alien thick descriptions feature prominently. I shall argue that we could not radically interpret every language containing alien thick descriptions *unless* the descriptive equivalence thesis were true.

The need to rely upon the descriptive equivalence thesis can be established as follows: Imagine a possible alien ethical outlook and its associated language, Q. Let us also entertain a number of assumptions:

(1) One does not understand Q. For example, Q may be, or may be part of, a natural language that one does not understand.

(2) Thick descriptions feature prominently in Q; and each has an evaluative point.

(3) None of the thick descriptions in one's own language has a believed extension matching that of any of Q's thick descriptions.

(4) The descriptive equivalence thesis is false.

Given these assumptions, one could not radically interpret many of Q's sentences. As we have seen, radically interpreting an alien language requires that one assign to a (massive) base set of its sentences truth-conditions that actually obtain in one's own view just when alien speakers hold the sentences true. Moreover, one's assignment has to yield a *systematic correlation* of sentences held true with alien sentences held true, otherwise the resultant interpretation will not count as a translation. But, if one's base set includes the sentences that feature at least one of Q's thick descriptions, no such correlation will emerge *unless* believed extensional equivalences for each of the featured alien thick descriptions are available within one's own language.[22] However, the availability of these equivalences is exactly what our assumptions rule out.

The possibility that a believed extensional equivalent for a given thick description in Q will be found among one's own thick descriptions is ruled out by the third assumption. I take it that rescinding this assumption is not open to us in the present context. It *is* possible that one of one's own thick descriptions will be the same as a given alien thick description. But unless this possibility is always widely realized with respect to the thick descriptions of any given alien language, there will be cases where the third assumption holds. Perhaps there can be no such cases. But that is the sort of fact, if it is one, that should emerge *from* the HDA, rather than being assumed at the outset.

What remains is the possibility that—by trial and error, or whatever other procedure radical interpreters employ to devise assignments of truth-conditions in their own language—the believed extension of a given thick description in Q can be matched by some construction from the purely descriptive resources of one's own language. This obviously requires there to be some pure description with the same believed extension as the given thick description. Even if the descriptive equivalence thesis is false, one's language might contain some such pure description by sheer coincidence.[23] But to enable a radical interpreter to exploit the possibility under discussion, this coincidence must obtain for each of Q's thick descriptions, where Q can stand for any number of imaginable alien languages. In that case, the descriptive equivalence thesis is basically true. So this possibility is ruled out by the fourth assumption.

To maintain that Q can always be radically interpreted—for any value of Q—we therefore have to assume the descriptive equivalence thesis. Of course, other theoretical positions are also committed to this thesis. On certain versions of non-cognitivism in ethics, for example—most notably, prescriptivism[24]—it is supposed that it will be possible to resolve any thick concept into two components, a purely descriptive component (a characterization of the facts independent of any evaluative outlook) and an attitudinal component (a characterization that colors these same facts in some appropriate manner). With prescriptivism, the prospect of resolving all thick descriptions in this fashion is founded on the claim that moral judgments are universalizable, where this means, in effect, that moral terms supervene on nonmoral terms (10–16, 21). But, as John McDowell has convincingly shown, the supervenience of evaluative classifications upon nonevaluative classifications does not suffice to establish that the prescriptivist's ambition can always be realized. To see this, let us distinguish between supervenience and *trackable supervenience*. Supervenience "requires only that one be able to find differences expressible in terms of the level supervened upon whenever one wants to make different judgments in terms of the supervening level."[25] Trackable supervenience requires, further, that exactly those items picked out by the supervening term can be grouped together (tracked) at the supervened upon level.

This idea can be illustrated by a variant of the Sesame Street exercise, "One of these things is not like the others." Consider the following actions described in nonevaluative terms, at the supervened upon level.

(1) NN advances along Juno beach with his rifle while other people shoot at him from the bluff above.

(2) NN remains where he is after someone tells him, "If you don't get out of my way, I am going to punch you."

(3) NN stands up when a woman enters the room at the Green Party conference.

(4) NN remains seated at the banquet while the band plays "God Save the Queen."

(5) NN remains seated at the banquet while the band plays "La Marseillaise."

(6) NN remains seated during the after-dinner dance.

Some of these statements describe an action that is courageous (in my book) and others describe an action that is not. We may suppose that courageous supervenes upon various nonevaluative terms. For its supervenience to be trackable, others must be able to identify which of (1)–(6) pick out an action in the extension of courageous (as I use it) without availing themselves of any information in evaluative terms (at the supervening level). In particular, they cannot avail themselves of any information about what (I think) makes perseverance in the face of danger worthwhile.

Even if no one could make the correct identification,[26] it would not follow that courageous (as I use it) does not supervene on nonevaluative terms. The crux of McDowell's argument is that supervenience does not entail trackable supervenience, since it imposes no requirement that "the set of items to which a supervening term is correctly applied need constitute a kind recognizable as such at the level supervened upon."[27] The descriptive equivalence thesis, however, does require trackable supervenience because, for every thick description, it requires some construction at the level supervened upon (a pure description) to track exactly those items thought to be picked out by the supervening term (the believed extension of the thick description). So the prescriptivist defense of the descriptive equivalence thesis is a failure.

To summarize the first part of my criticism of the HDA: We can imagine a language that articulates an alien ethical outlook in which thick descriptions feature prominently. For all languages of this kind to be radically interpretable in one's own language, the descriptive equivalence thesis must be true. But that thesis is quite dubious. We may therefore suppose that some languages that articulate alien ethical outlooks cannot be radically interpreted in one's own language.

IV. UNDERSTANDING WITHOUT RADICAL INTERPRETATION

My criticism is incomplete as it stands. The HDA's additional claims imply that any alien language one understands can be radically interpreted in one's own language. If that were true, its defenders could object that one *could not understand* a language in which alien thick descriptions feature prominently precisely because it could not be radically interpreted in one's own language. I shall therefore complete my criticism by refuting the HDA's second additional claim. To review, its additional claims are, first, that knowledge of an alien sentence's truth-conditions, expressible in one's own language, is a necessary condition of understanding it; and, second, that if the sentences of an alien language have truth-conditions expressible in one's own language, then that language can be radically interpreted in one's own.

I shall argue that sentences articulating an alien ethical outlook in which thick descriptions feature prominently can have truth-conditions expressible in one's own language, and one can know what they are, even though one still cannot radically interpret the sentences. Hence, at least as far as the HDA's first claim is concerned, there is no impediment to one's understanding this language. Radically interpreting an alien language should not be conflated, then, with understanding it.

Let 'Q' stand once more for the imagined alien language specified in the previous section. Recall, in particular, that none of Q's thick descriptions is the same as any of an *outsider's* own. Allow me the *provisional assumption* that outsiders can come to understand Q. I shall return to defend it presently. In coming to understand Q, the outsiders also come to understand, *pari passu*, its thick descriptions. The falsity of the descriptive equivalence thesis presents no obstacle to this process, as the outsiders are not here required to prescind from the ethical outlook that provides Q's thick descriptions with their evaluative point. Consequently, in coming to understand Q's thick descriptions, outsiders are at no point required to find pure descriptions with the same believed extension.

It follows that the process whereby outsiders come to learn Q's thick descriptions must consist in something other than translation into their own language, since *ex hypothesi* the outsiders' language does not already contain any of Q's thick descriptions. This fits the common observation that, in practice, anthropologists rarely rely upon intertranslation when learning an alien culture and young children never do.[28] Instead, both groups are said to resort to a process typically described as one of 'going native.'[29]

To learn Q's thick descriptions, outsiders will have to learn the ethical outlook to which they belong. There is no need to think that this outlook has to be learned *before* the thick descriptions are. We may suppose that the two are learned together. Naturally, in the course of going native, outsiders may discover that they reject various elements of the ethical outlook that provides Q's thick descriptions with their point. Most simply, they may discover that it includes various false beliefs. In such cases, mastering the use of Q's thick descriptions—specifically, comprehending the contribution made by certain false beliefs to the evaluative implications and believed extensions of particular thick descriptions—will require the outsiders to make believe, that is, to imagine as if the relevant beliefs were true.

For example, suppose Q is spoken by a tribe whose ethical outlook centrally includes a fierce communal pride. Underpinning their pride, say, is a belief in their inherent superiority. Suppose, further, that this pride is partly what gives a point to the tribe's practice of applying Q's thick description, 'plonk.' Calling things plonk is partly an expression of pride, and that some things are plonk is also a source of pride. It is a conceptual truth that if some*one* is plonk, then his or her interests count for no more than an animal's. Say the outsiders do not believe in the inherent superiority of this tribe. Whatever their belief on this matter, they must—if they are to master the use of plonk—know the role of the tribe's pride in the practice, as well as knowing what the tribe counts as an expression of pride, and what as a source of pride. It is plausible that the outsiders will sometimes have to imagine feeling the tribe's pride in the prevailing circumstances to decide whether the tribe would count something as a source of pride, and so would count some particular as plonk. That is, the outsiders will have to imagine as if they believed in the tribe's inherent superiority.

Suppose the outsiders have now understood Q and its thick descriptions. The critical question is whether they can construct correct truth-conditions, expressed in their own language, for sentences of Q featuring its thick descriptions. By hypothesis, recall, the outsiders' language contains no thick description identical to any of Q's. Hence, there is a sense in which their language lacks the resources to ensure that any description, expressed in its terms, of the conditions under which Q-sentences of the form "So-and-so is plonk" are true is also a description of conditions under which so-and-so's interests count for no more than an animal's. But that is exactly what is required if truth-conditions expressed in the outsiders' language are to be equivalent to

the truth-conditions sentences of this form have in Q. This lack can be remedied, however, if the outsiders can introduce a new term into their language—
call it 'plonk*'—that applies just when plonk applies and that implies, when
applied to individual humans, that their interests count for no more than
an animal's.[30]

I believe that the outsiders can introduce this new thick description (and
similar others) into their language. Naturally, to enable other speakers of their
language to learn them, the outsiders will also have to provide explanations of
(the relevant parts of) the ethical outlook articulated by Q. Thus, their introduction of plonk* must be accompanied by an explanatory rider that conveys the
role of the tribe's pride in the proper uses of plonk, its connection with a belief in
the inherent superiority of the tribe, the range of things that count as expressions
or sources of pride, and so on. If the tribe's understanding of pride is sufficiently
different from its own community's, the outsiders may also have to introduce a
further term to mark these differences. More generally, the outsiders may have
to introduce together, and interdefine, an entire gamut of new thick descriptions
(along with explanatory riders).

Alongside their pedagogic function, the outsiders' explanatory riders serve
to identify the *presuppositions* of using their new descriptions. They identify the
elements of the ethical outlook articulated by Q that one must accept either to
apply or not to apply Q's thick descriptions *in propria persona*. In our example,
making genuine assertions containing the term 'plonk' or 'plonk*' presupposes
that one believes in the inherent superiority of the Q-speaking tribe.[31] I have suggested that, on some occasions, deciding whether something is plonk requires
one either to accept that belief or to imagine as if one did. Q-speakers and outsiders may naturally differ in their respective attitudes toward this presupposition: while the former actually believe it is satisfied, the latter may only make
believe that it is. Unless *that* difference systematically interferes with one's ability
to determine whether something is plonk, there is no reason to deny that plonk*
can apply just when plonk does. If there is none, then once their own language
comes to contain new thick descriptions, such as plonk*, that correspond to Q's
thick descriptions, the outsiders plainly can assign correct truth-conditions,
expressed in their own language, to sentences featuring Q's thick descriptions.

I am now in a position to defend my provisional assumption that outsiders can come to understand Q. My defense is simply to observe that it is fully
consistent with the HDA's first additional claim, which was that knowledge of an
alien sentence's truth-conditions, expressible in one's own language, is a necessary condition of understanding it. Since outsiders can correctly assign truth-
conditions expressed in their own language to Q's sentences, the first additional

claim affords no basis for objecting to my provisional assumption. This is sufficient to show that it does not beg any questions in the present context.

I must still explain why the outsiders' understanding of Q, and ability to translate it into their own (enriched) language, does not entail that they could also *radically interpret* Q. To see why not, let us focus on the set of sentences in Q featuring at least one of its thick descriptions. Call this QT. It does not follow from having translated QT into their own language that the outsiders know that its sentences are actually true. Indeed, they might know that these sentences are false. The truth-conditions the outsiders assign to QT are expressed in terms of the new descriptions introduced into their own language, such as plonk*. They apply just when the corresponding thick descriptions in Q apply and have the same evaluative presuppositions the Q-descriptions have. But the outsiders' new descriptions do not require them—or, indeed, anyone—to believe that their presuppositions are satisfied (neither do the Q-descriptions, for that matter).

Say the outsiders believe that these presuppositions are *not* satisfied. Confronted with circumstances in which Q-speakers assert "So-and-so is plonk," the outsiders will accept—so long as Q-speakers are not making a local mistake about the believed extension of plonk—that there is a sense in which their assertion is correct: To wit, if the Q-speaking tribe were inherently superior, so-and-so would be plonk*. But the outsiders do not believe in the inherent superiority of this tribe. So, although they have assigned the correct truth-conditions—"So-and-so is plonk" is true if and only if so-and-so is plonk*—the outsiders do not believe that these truth-conditions ever actually obtain. Hence, they will treat "So-and-so is plonk," even in these circumstances, as false (or perhaps as undefined). Moreover, something similar can be said about the other sentences in QT.

Accordingly, outsiders who reject the presuppositions of genuine assertions containing Q's thick descriptions can never find themselves holding as true anything that translates the sentences in QT when they are held true by speakers of Q. In other words, outsiders could never correlate a translational sentence of their own language that they hold true with a sentence in QT that speakers of Q hold true. But that is exactly what Davidson requires (successful) interpreters of an alien language to do: systematically to correlate sentences of their own language that they hold true with a 'base set' of sentences held true by speakers of the alien language. It follows that our outsiders could never include QT in the base set of a successful radical interpretation of Q, which is to say that they could not radically interpret QT.[32] Yet, despite this, the sentences in QT have truth-conditions expressed in the outsiders' language. The HDA's second additional claim therefore contains a non sequitur. Having truth-conditions expressible in the outsiders' language does not entail that the sentences in QT can be radically interpreted by our outsiders.

This outcome is explained by two points. The first is that a thick description's presence in a sentence makes two distinct contributions to the truth-value of genuine assertions of that sentence. One contribution is made by the descriptive content of the thick description; and the other by the specific elements of the evaluative outlook presupposed by using that description. Thus, to revisit our old example, the truth-value of the assertion "Roger gave a courageous speech last week" depends *both* on (something like) whether Roger's speech-giving constituted perseverance in the face of some danger *and* on whether his perseverance was worthwhile. The second point, recapitulating our discussion in section 3, is that mastering the believed extension of a thick description requires one to suppose that its evaluative presuppositions are satisfied. Mastering the believed extension of courageous requires an observer to know what, as we think, makes perseverance in the face of danger worthwhile and to make believe in our conception.

It follows that, holding its believed extension fixed, a thick description's descriptive content only contributes to the truth of assertions in which it appears *when* its evaluative presuppositions also contribute, by local lights, to the (perceived) truth of those assertions.[33] To illustrate, suppose that (1) Roger's speech-giving last week did indeed constitute perseverance in the face of danger; but also that (2) on our conception, the danger in the face of which he persevered was not worthwhile. In that case, (1) contributes nothing, on our conception, to the truth of "Roger gave a courageous speech last week." An observer who divorced (1) from the (negative) contribution made by (2), and concluded, given (1), that Roger gave a courageous speech last week, would thereby mistake the believed extension of our thick description, courageous. To understand a particular thick description, one's truth-valuation of assertions in which it appears must—on pain of mistaking its believed extension—discount the contribution made by its descriptive content *unless* the contribution made by its evaluative presuppositions is positive, by local lights.

However, it does not follow that whenever the descriptive content of a thick description contributes to the truth of assertions in which it appears, then anyone who understands that description must regard the assertion as true. It is possible for the descriptive content of courageous to contribute to the truth of the assertion "Roger gave a courageous speech last week"—because, say, Roger's speech-giving last week constituted perseverance in the face of danger and, on our conception, his perseverance *was* worthwhile—even though its evaluative presuppositions actually contribute to the falsity of that assertion—because, say, perseverance in the face of danger is never worthwhile (or never for the reasons upheld on our conception). Understanding a thick description does not prevent anyone from recognizing this, or cases like it, and so is compatible with discriminating the distinct contributions an alien thick description makes to the truth-value of genuine assertions in which it appears.

Radical interpreters can fail to understand QT because, unlike outsiders who go native, they are *unable* to discriminate the same two contributions. Radical interpreters fix upon the attitude of 'holding as true' directed at alien sentences and attempt to match it with their own attitude of 'holding as true' directed at their own sentences. Given that this match must turn out to be translational and that the alien sentences contain thick descriptions, it is a necessary condition of there being any such match that *both the descriptive content and the evaluative presuppositions of the alien thick descriptions contribute to the perceived truth—by the radical interpreter's lights—of the alien assertions that contain them.* But this is not also a necessary condition of the alien thick descriptions being understood by an outsider. Hence, whenever the underlined condition fails to obtain, there will be a case in which QT can be understood by an outsider who still cannot radically interpret it. The coherence of this case forces us to distinguish firmly between understanding an alien language and radically interpreting it.

NOTES

1. Susan Hurley, *Natural Reasons* (Oxford: Oxford University Press, 1989); Donald Davidson, "On the Very Idea of a Conceptual Scheme," in *Inquiries into Truth and Interpretation* (Oxford: Clarendon, 1984) (this volume, chap. 8). By 'outlook,' I mean a reasonably self-contained system of belief.

2. Both relations came to prominence under that description as a result of Thomas S. Kuhn's well-known *The Structure of Scientific Revolutions*, 2nd ed. (Chicago: University of Chicago Press, 1970), 148–149. Kuhn refers to 'paradigms' where I have 'outlooks.' Neither of these relations has much direct connection with the most frequent use of 'incommensurability' as a technical term in *moral* philosophy, which refers to a relation between individual goods. See Joseph Raz, *The Morality of Freedom* (Oxford: Clarendon, 1986), chap. 13. We shall just have to ignore that third sense of the term.

3. Kuhn variously describes the considerations that the paradigms in question do not share as "standards [or] definitions of science" (*Structure of Scientific Revolutions*, 148) or as an "algorithm for theory-choice" (200).

4. This use of 'criteria' follows Charles Taylor, "Explanation and Practical Reason," in *The Quality of Life*, ed. M. Nussbaum and A. Sen (Oxford: Clarendon Press, 1993), to which I am also generally indebted.

5. Davidson, "On the Very Idea of a Conceptual Scheme," 183.

6. The greater the extent of the agreement thus established, the sharper is said to be the 'clarity and bite of declarations of difference.' In Davidson's view, however, the crucial point about these remaining differences is that a radical interpreter is in no position to classify them as differences in conceptual scheme as opposed to differences of opinion, or vice versa. "When others think differently from us, no general principle, or appeal to evidence, can force us to decide that the difference lies in our beliefs rather than in our concepts" (ibid., 197).

7. Donald Davidson, "Radical Interpretation," in *Inquiries into Truth and Interpretation*, 125.

8. Donald Davidson, "Truth and Meaning," in *Inquiries into Truth and Interpretation*, 24.

9. For reasons of economy, I shall omit the mediating step and simply present the demonstration in the specifically ethical version. It is not difficult to see how the more general version would proceed.

10. Davidson, "On the Very Idea of a Conceptual Scheme," 197.

11. Notice that this notion of a base set allows us to sidestep an important question that sometimes bedevils discussions of Davidson's argument, namely, the question of what counts as a 'massive' set of sentences. The point at issue here concerns a particular property of the sentences privileged in radical interpretation—that of being known by the radical interpreter to be true. Our concern is whether the subset of sentences QE has this property; and that can be settled simply by knowing whether QE belongs to the privileged set, that is, to the base set. It makes no difference in this context how massive the base set is.

12. I shall not attempt to motivate this crucial assumption independently. I only note that it is needed if the demonstration is to apply to ethical outlooks in particular. Later we shall see that there is an important range of cases in which the assumption cannot be true.

13. If this equivalence does not hold, then the required 'systematic correlation' will not have been achieved; alternatively, the radical interpreter's rendition of the relevant sentences will not count as a *translation*.

14. Hurley, *Natural Reasons*, 53.

15. Others clearly committed to this assumption include David Cooper, "Moral Relativism," *Midwest Studies in Philosophy* 111 (1978): 97–108; he, too, applies Davidson's argument to the ethical case, in order to exclude moral relativism. See also Samuel Fleischacker, *The Ethics of Culture* (Ithaca, N.Y.: Cornell University Press, 1994), 14–20; and Henry Richardson, *Practical Reasoning About Final Ends* (Cambridge: Cambridge University Press, 1994), 250–270, 277–279.

16. Since the weaker conclusion does not impugn the meaningfulness of candidate-languages one cannot radically interpret, I henceforth omit the prefix 'candidate-' unless Davidson's hidden premise is under discussion.

17. This provides a weaker interpretation of Davidson's claim that "all understanding of the speech of another involves radical interpretation" than the interpretation provided by the hidden premise ("Radical Interpretation," 125).

18. Clifford Geertz, *The Interpretation of Cultures* (New York: Harper & Row, 1973), first essay.

19. Bernard Williams, *Ethics and the Limits of Philosophy* (Cambridge, Mass.: Harvard University Press, 1985), 141.

20. I here ignore the point that perseverance in the face of danger might be worthwhile for reasons that have nothing to do with courage.

21. To master the believed extension of a thick description, someone has (roughly) to be able to apply it to all and only those aspects of the world to which it would be applied by those who believe the evaluative conception that provides its point.

22. This point is clearly illustrated by sentences of the form, "Such-and-such is F," where F represents one of Q's thick descriptions. The believed extensional equivalent for F need not itself be a simple expression.

23. Notice that even if this coincidence obtains, and radical interpreters thus have the believed extensional equivalent they need, there remains the problem of explaining how their pure description is (or is not) to end up *translating* Q's thick description. I shall not pursue this, as it is merely an exotic instance of a well-known challenge facing Davidson's account: namely, to explain how a theory of truth for a language that is also to serve as a theory of meaning avoids entailments such as "Snow is white" if and only if grass is green. See Davidson, "Truth and Meaning," 25–26nn.10–11.

24. R. M. Hare, *Freedom and Reason* (Oxford: Clarendon Press, 1963). What prescriptivism supposes is actually more general than this, but the difference is unimportant here.

25. John McDowell, "Non-Cognitivism and Rule-Following," in *Wittgenstein: To Follow a Rule*, ed. S. Holtzman and C. Leich (London: Routledge and Kegan Paul, 1981), 144–145.

26. I have in mind (1)–(4).

27. McDowell, "Non-Cognitivism and Rule-Following," 145.

28. See, e.g., Paul Feyerabend, "Consolations for the Specialist," in *Criticism and the Growth of Knowledge*, ed. I. Lakatos and A. Musgrave (Cambridge: Cambridge University Press, 1970), 222–225; Barry Barnes and David Bloor, "Relativism, Rationalism, and the Sociology of Knowledge," in *Rationality and Relativism*, ed. M. Hollis and S. Lukes (Oxford: Blackwell, 1982), 36–39; and Alasdair MacIntyre, *Whose Justice? Which Rationality?* (London: Duckworth, 1988), 374ff. Cf. Kuhn, *Structure of Scientific Revolutions*, 204.

29. Clifford Geertz, "From the Native's Point of View: On the Nature of Anthropological Understanding," in *Local Knowledge* (New York: Basic Books, 1983).

30. If this lack can be remedied—as I think it can—by the introduction of a new thick description, then there is another sense in which the outsiders' language *has* the resources—namely, whatever resources are needed to introduce the description in question—to ensure that a description, expressed in its terms, of the conditions under which Q-sentences of the form "So-and-so is plonk" are true is also a description of conditions under which so-and-so's interests count for no more than an animal's. Notice that, in that case, the HDA's first additional claim is less restrictive than it might otherwise seem. The claim is that knowledge of an alien sentence's truth-conditions, expressible in one's own language, is a necessary condition of understanding it. It still does not follow from the fact that the truth-conditions of an alien sentence cannot *now* be expressed in my language that the sentence cannot be understood by speakers of my language.

31. My example presents a case that is extremely simple in two important respects. First, the element of the alien ethical outlook that the outsiders reject is a single false belief. Second, the relation of the false belief to the use of the thick description is one of straightforward presupposition. This picture of the connection between thick descriptions and the evaluative outlook that sustains them is oversimplified in both respects. But it seems to me that the overly simple picture is nevertheless adequate to specify the relevance of thick descriptions to the project of radical interpretation, which is all that concerns me here. For a contribution to a more sophisticated understanding of this connection, see Allan Gibbard, "Thick Concepts and Warrant for Feelings," *Proceedings of the Aristotelian Society*, supplementary volume 66 (1992): 278–282.

32. If the fact that thick descriptions feature prominently in Q means that no set of sentences in Q excluding QT counts as 'massive', then it also follows that these outsiders could not successfully radically interpret Q.

33. I here ignore cases in which the locals make a mistake, by their own lights, in applying their evaluative conception.

THOMAS NAGEL

Objectivity is the central problem of ethics. Not just in theory, but in life. The problem is to decide in what way, if at all, the idea of objectivity can be applied to practical questions, questions of what to do or want. To what extent can they be dealt with from a detached point of view toward ourselves and the world? I want to defend the objectivity of ethics by showing how that standpoint alters and constrains our motives. The possibility of ethics and many of its problems can be best understood in terms of the impact of objectivity on the will. If we can make judgments about how we should live even after stepping outside of ourselves, they will provide the material for moral theory.

In theoretical reasoning objectivity is advanced when we form a new conception of reality that includes ourselves as components. This involves an alteration or at least an extension of our beliefs. In the sphere of values or practical reasoning, the problem is different. As in the theoretical case, we must take up a new, comprehensive viewpoint after stepping back and including our former perspective in what is to be understood. But here the new viewpoint will be not a new set of beliefs, but a new or extended set of values. We try to arrive at normative judgments, with motivational content, from an impersonal standpoint. We cannot use

Reprinted from Thomas Nagel, "Value," in *The View from Nowhere* (Oxford: Oxford University Press, 1986), chap. 8, sec. 1, pp. 138–143 by permission of Oxford University Press.

a nonnormative criterion of objectivity, for if values are subjective, they must be so in their own right and not through reducibility to some other kind of objective fact. They have to be objective values, not objective anything else.

Here as elsewhere there is a connection between objectivity and realism, though realism about values is different from realism about empirical facts. Normative realism is the view that propositions about what gives us reasons for action can be true or false independently of how things appear to us, and that we can hope to discover the truth by transcending the appearances and subjecting them to critical assessment. What we aim to discover by this method is not a new aspect of the external world, called value, but rather just the truth about what we and others should do and want.

It is important not to associate this form of realism with an inappropriate metaphysical picture: it is not a form of Platonism. The claim is that there are reasons for action, that we have to discover them instead of deriving them from our preexisting motives—and that in this way we can acquire new motives superior to the old. We simply aim to reorder our motives in a direction that will make them more acceptable from an external standpoint. Instead of bringing our thoughts into accord with an external reality, we try to bring an external view into the determination of our conduct.

The connection between objectivity and truth is therefore closer in ethics than it is in science. I do not believe that the truth about how we should live could extend radically beyond any capacity we might have to discover it (apart from its dependence on nonevaluative facts we might be unable to discover). The subject matter of ethics *is* how to engage in practical reasoning and the justification of action once we expand our consciousness by occupying the objective standpoint—not something else about action which the objective standpoint enables us to understand better. Ethical thought is the process of bringing objectivity to bear on the will, and the only thing I can think of to say about ethical truth in general is that it must be a possible result of this process, correctly carried out. I recognize that this is empty. If we wish to be more specific, all we can do is to refer to the arguments that persuade us of the objective validity of a reason or the correctness of a normative principle (and a given principle may be established in more than one way got at from different starting points and by different argumentative routes).

Perhaps a richer metaphysic of morals could be devised, but I don't know what it would be. The picture I associate with normative realism is not that of an extra set of properties of things and events in the world, but of a series of possible steps in the development of human motivation, which would improve the way we lead our lives, whether or not we will actually take them. We begin with a partial and inaccurate view, but by stepping outside of ourselves and construct-ing and comparing alternatives we can reach a new motivational condition at a higher level of objectivity. Though the aim is normative rather than descriptive, the method of investigation is analogous in certain respects to that of seeking an objective conception of what there is. We first form a conception of the world as centerless—as containing ourselves and other beings with particular points of view. But the question we then try to answer is not "What can we see that the world contains, considered from this impersonal standpoint?" but "What is there reason to do or want, considered from this impersonal standpoint?"

The answer will be complex. As in metaphysics, so in the realm of practi-cal reason the truth is sometimes best understood from a detached standpoint; but sometimes it will be fully comprehensible only from a particular perspec-tive within the world. If there are such subjective values, then an objective con-ception of what people have reasons to do must leave room for them.... But once the objective step is taken, the possibility is also open for the recognition of values and reasons that are independent of one's personal perspective and have force for anyone who can view the world impersonally, as a place that con-tains him. If objectivity means anything here, it will mean that when we detach from our individual perspective and the values and reasons that seem acceptable from within it, we can sometimes arrive at a new conception, which may endorse some of the original reasons but will reject some as false subjective appearances and add others.

So without prejudging the outcome—that is, how much of the domain of practical reasons can be objectively understood—we can see what the objectifying impulse depends on. The most basic idea of practical objectivity is arrived at by a practical analogue of the rejection of solipsism in the theoretical domain. Realism about the facts leads us to seek a detached point of view from which reality can be discerned and appearance corrected, and realism about values leads us to seek a detached point of view from which it will be possible to correct inclination and to discern what we really should do. Practical objectivity means that practical reason can be understood and even engaged in by the objective self.

This assumption, though powerful, is not yet an ethical position. It merely marks the place, which an ethical position will occupy if we can make sense of the subject. It says that the world of reasons, including my reasons, does not exist only from my own point of view. I am in a world whose character is to a certain extent independent of what I think, and if I have reasons to act it is because the person who I am has those reasons, in virtue of his condition and circumstances. The basic question of practical reason from which ethics begins is not "What shall I do?" but "What should this person do?"

This sets a problem and indicates a method of attacking it. The problem is to discover the form, which reasons for action take, and whether it can be described from no particular point of view. The method is to begin with the reasons that appear to obtain from my own point of view and those of other individuals, and ask what the best perspectiveless account of those reasons is. As in other domains, we begin from our position inside the world and try to transcend it by regarding what we find here as a sample of the whole.

That is the hope. But the claim that there are objective values is permanently controversial because of the ease with which values and reasons seem to disappear when we transcend the subjective standpoint of our own desires. It can seem, when one looks at life from outside, that there is no room for values in the world at all. So to say: "There are just people with various motives and inclinations, some of which they may express in evaluative language; but when we regard all this from outside, all we see are psychological facts. The ascent to an objective view, far from revealing new values that modify the subjective appearances, reveals that appearances are all there is: it enables us to observe and describe our subjective motives but does not produce any new ones. Objectivity has no place in this domain except what is inherited from the objectivity of theoretical and factual elements that play a role in practical reasoning. Beyond that it applies here with a nihilistic result: nothing is objectively right or wrong because objectively nothing matters; if there are such things as right and wrong, they must rest on a subjective foundation."

I believe this conclusion is the result of a mistake comparable to the one that leads to physicalism, with its attendant reductionist elaborations. An epistemological criterion of reality is being assumed which pretends to be comprehensive but which in fact excludes large domains in advance without argument.

The assumption is surreptitious, but natural. Values can seem really to disappear when we step outside of our skins, so that it strikes us as a philosophical *perception* that they are illusory. This is a characteristic Humean step: we observe the phenomenon of people acting for what they take to be reasons, and *all we see* (compare Hume's treatment of causality) are certain natural facts: that people are influenced by certain motives, or would be if they knew certain things.

We are continually tempted to reoccupy Hume's position by the difficulties we encounter when we try to leave it. Skepticism, Platonism, reductionism, and other familiar philosophical excesses all make their appearance in ethical theory. Particularly attractive is the reaction to skepticism, which reinterprets the whole field, ethics included, in completely subjective terms. Like phenomenalism in epistemology, this conceals the retreat from realism by substituting a set of judgments that in some way resemble the originals.

The only way to resist Humean subjectivism about desires and reasons for action is to seek a form of objectivity appropriate to the subject. This will not be the objectivity of naturalistic psychology. It must be argued that an objective view limited to such observations is not correct. Or rather, not necessarily correct, for the point is that an objective view of ourselves should leave room for the apprehension of reasons—not exclude them in advance.

They seem to be excluded in advance if the objective standpoint is assumed to be one of pure observation and description.[1] When we direct this sort of attention to what appears subjectively as a case of acting for reasons and responding to good and evil, we get a naturalistic account that seems to give the complete objective description of what is going on. Instead of normative reasons, we see only a psychological explanation.

But I believe it is a mistake to give these phenomena a purely psychological reading when we look at them from outside. What we see, unless we are artificially blind, is not just people being moved to act by their desires, but people acting and forming intentions and desires for reasons, good or bad. That is, we recognize their reasons *as reasons*—or perhaps we think they are bad reasons— but in any case we do not drop out of the evaluative mode as soon as we leave the subjective standpoint. The recognition of reasons as reasons is to be contrasted with their use purely as a form of psychological explanation.[2] The latter merely connects action with the agent's desires and beliefs, without touching the normative question whether he *had* an adequate reason for acting—whether he should have acted as he did. If this is all that can be said once we leave the point of view of the agent behind, then I think it would follow that we don't really act for reasons at all. Rather, we are caused to act by desires and beliefs, and the terminology of reasons can be used only in a diminished, nonnormative sense to express this kind of explanation.

The substitution of an account in which values or normative reasons play no part is not something that simply falls out of the objective view. It depends on a particular objective claim that can be accepted only if it is more plausible than its denial: the claim that our sense that the world presents us with reasons for action is a subjective illusion, produced by the projection of our preexisting motives onto the world, and that there aren't objectively any reasons for us to do anything—though of course there are motives, some of which mimic normative reasons in form.

But this would have to be established: it does not follow from the idea of objectivity alone. When we take the objective step, we don't leave the evaluative capacity behind automatically, since that capacity does not depend on antecedently present desires. We may find that it continues to operate from an external standpoint, and we may conclude that this is not just a case of subjective desires popping up again in objective disguise. I acknowledge the dangers of false objectification, which elevates personal tastes and prejudices into cosmic values. But it isn't the only possibility.

NOTES

1. Cf. G. E. M. Anscombe, "Causality and Determination," in *Metaphysics and the Philosophy of Mind: Collected Philosophical Papers* (Minneapolis: University of Minnesota Press, 1981), 137: "This often happens in philosophy; it is argued that 'all we find' is such-and-such, and it turns out that the arguer has excluded from his idea of 'finding' the sort of thing he says we don't 'find.'"

2. Donald Davidson, "Actions, Reasons, and Causes," in *Essays on Actions and Events* (Oxford: Oxford University Press, 1980).

Intuitionism, Realism, Relativism, and Rhubarb

22

CRISPIN WRIGHT

I. THE ORDINARY VIEW OF DISPUTES OF INCLINATION

Imagine that Tim Williamson thinks that stewed rhubarb is delicious and that I beg to differ, finding its dry acidity highly disagreeable. There is, on the face of it, no reason to deny that this is a genuine disagreement—each holding to a view that the other rejects. But it is a disagreement about which, at least at first pass, the Latin proverb—*de gustibus non est disputandum*—seems apt. It is, we feel—or is likely to be—a disagreement, which there is no point in trying to settle, because it concerns no real matter of fact but is merely an expression of different, permissibly idiosyncratic tastes. Nobody's wrong. Tim and I should just agree to disagree.

Call such a disagreement a *dispute of inclination*. The view of such disputes just gestured at—I'll call it the *Ordinary View*—combines three elements:

(1) that they involve genuinely incompatible attitudes (*Contradiction*);
(2) that nobody need be mistaken or otherwise at fault (*Faultlessness*); and

Reprinted from "Realism, Relativism, and Rhubarb," *Truth and Realism*, eds. Patrick Greenough and Michael P. Lynch (Oxford: Clarendon Press, 2006), pp. 38–60. By Permission of Oxford University Press. The endnotes have been reformatted to conform to the format of this volume.

(3) that the antagonists may, perfectly rationally, stick to their respective views even after the disagreement comes to light and impresses as intractable (*Sustainability*).

Assuming that there are indeed disputes as so characterized, it is, of course, an important and controversial issue how far they extend—whether, for example, certain differences of opinion about ethics, or aesthetics, or justification, or even theoretical science, come within range. But my question here is more basic: it is whether the three noted elements can be combined coherently—whether there *are* any disputes of inclination, as characterized by the Ordinary View, at all.

The question is given urgency by the fact that the four most salient alternatives to the Ordinary View all seem rebarbative or misconceived. There is, first, the *rampant realist* proposal—an analogue of the epistemic conception of vagueness. Rampant realism holds that there have to be facts of the matter which either Tim, or I, is missing. Rhubarb just has to be either delicious or not, so one of us has to be mistaken, even if there is no way of knowing who. Such a view is vulnerable to a charge of semantic and metaphysical superstition. It also arguably precludes Sustainability—the possibility of persisting in the dispute with rational integrity—since neither Tim, nor I, has the slightest reason to think that our own tastes reflect the putative real facts about deliciousness, once rampant—realistically conceived.

Realism need not be rampant. A more moderate realism might try to domesticate the relevant facts by attempting to construe them as, in one way or another, *response-dependent*—proposing, for instance, that what is delicious is what (a majority of) well-qualified judges find to be so. But this seems a misdirection too: for one thing, I don't think we really believe in 'well-qualifiedness' in *basic* matters of taste—that's the point of the Latin proverb. For another, the proposal promises no better than its rampant counterpart in accommodating Faultlessness and Sustainability.

Recoiling from these views, one may be tempted by the thought that perhaps no genuine dispute is involved after all. Perhaps the impression to the contrary is somehow an artifact of language. One—*expressivist*—version of that idea has it that we are misled by the indicative surface of the dispute: maybe Tim's avowal that rhubarb is delicious serves merely to give expression to the pleasure he takes in the stuff and is thus something with no properly negatable content; maybe my avowal to the contrary serves merely to give expression to my corresponding distaste for it. Such a proposal will face all the familiar difficulties in the philosophy of language, difficulties, for example, in accounting for routine conditional, disjunctive, tensed, and attitudinal constructions embedding such apparent indicative contents, which are faced by strict expressivist proposals in other areas, and to which many believe they have no satisfactory response.

An alternative strategy for denying that there is any genuine disagreement is to take the indicative appearances at face value, but hold that the contents in question are not really in conflict—for instance, that they are elliptical and that when the ellipsis is unpacked, the impression of incompatibility vanishes. It may be suggested, for instance, that Tim's view is properly characterized as being that rhubarb is delicious *by his standards*, and that I am saying that rhubarb is not delicious *by mine*. So we are talking past each other and may both well be right.

This suggestion is open to the charge that it distorts the meaning of what we intend to say when we give voice to judgments of taste. There is, for example, a challenge involved in the question: "If, as you say, rhubarb is delicious, how come nobody but you here likes it?" which goes missing if the proper construal of it mentions an explicit standard-relativity in the antecedent. So it looks as though a larger package will be called for, involving not just hidden constituents but an error-theory concerning our ordinary understanding of the relevant kinds of claim. A related consideration points out that, on our ordinary understanding, the explicitly standard-relativized kind of formulation represents a fall-back claim if the original, unqualified claim gets into difficulty—a puzzling phenomenon if they coincide in content.

There are other forms of semantic contextualism, of course, besides those which postulate ellipsis or hidden constituents. But the awkwardnesses just noted will remain on any such view. If Tim's and my differing tastes are sufficient, one way or another, to ensure that we express different concepts of the delicious in our respective assessments of rhubarb, and hence that there is no obstacle to our both being right, then why will we each be inclined to withdraw if suitably many others don't concur? Why doesn't the contextualist explanation of why my judgment is not in conflict with Tim's survive as a means to explain why I can be right *no matter how idiosyncratic my view*? And why fall back on an explicitly standard-relativized claim if the content of my original claim was already implicitly relativized?

Each of the four views canvassed—that there is a real but undetectable fact of the matter about whether rhubarb is delicious, that there is a real but response-dependent fact of the matter, that there is no real matter in dispute because no truth-evaluable content is involved, and that there is no real dispute because the contents involved are elliptical, or otherwise contextually distinct—each of these four views not merely involves compromise of one or more of the three components of the Ordinary View but seems open to additional objection. If we want to avoid metaphysical hypostasis, snobbery in matters of taste, unplayable philosophy of language, or misrepresentation of linguistic practice, then we should want the Ordinary View. So, it comes as an unpleasant surprise that it seems, under quite modest pressure, to collapse.

II. THE SIMPLE DEDUCTION

The collapsing argument is what in earlier work I dubbed the Simple Deduction.[1] It is disarmingly straightforward. The idea that there is genuine disagreement involved in the dispute goes with the idea that there is a genuinely indicative content, capable of featuring in attitudes and standing in relations of incompatibility to other such contents. Any such genuine content can also be *supposed*. So: suppose that rhubarb is delicious. Then I'm mistaken. But the Ordinary View has it that no one is mistaken (Faultlessness). So rhubarb isn't delicious. But then Tim is mistaken. So someone has to be mistaken after all. Contradiction precludes Faultlessness.

More explicitly:

1	(1) A accepts P	———	Assumption
2	(2) B accepts Not-P	———	Assumption
3	(3) A and B's disagreement involves no mistake (4) P	———	Assumption
4	(4) P	———	Assumption
2, 4	(5) B is making a mistake	———	2, 4
2, 3	(6) Not-P	———	4, 5, 3 Reductio
1, 2, 3	(7) A is making a mistake	———	1, 6
1, 2	(8) Not-[3]	———	3, 3, 7 Reductio

The occurrence of genuine disagreement seems to demand, by elementary and uncontroversial logical moves, the existence of mistakes.[2] Further, once that's recognized, it becomes impossible to see how Tim and I can persist in our disagreement with rational integrity. Apparently, one of us has to be mistaken. But if one of us is mistaken, how can we tell who? Isn't it just a conceit to think it has to be the other? So Sustainability is compromised too. Thus the three components in the Ordinary View fall apart.

Faced with this difficulty, the natural temptation for a proponent of the Ordinary View is to try to refine the second component—to qualify Faultlessness. Maybe it's too much to demand that there need be no mistake involved in the dispute. Maybe the most that can be asked is that there be no *epistemically blameworthy* mistake. Perhaps Faultlessness should be replaced by something like the idea that neither Tim, nor I, need have done anything which would have opened our opinions to proper suspicion when considered in isolation, by someone with no view on the matter in hand but otherwise as knowledgeable as you like. Or something like that.

But this suggestion doesn't really help. For one thing, part of the attraction of Faultlessness is that, while we want to acknowledge that there may be no settling a dispute of inclination, we precisely don't want that acknowledgment to commit us to the idea of potentially unknowable facts of the matter—that's why the rampant realist proposal strikes us as so bizarre. The rhetoric of 'no fact of the matter' expresses the natural, folk-philosophical view: such disputes are potentially irresolvable, we think, not because the facts in question can transcend our impressions but because the impressions themselves are in some way basic and constitutive; so when they conflict, there need be no further court of appeal. If that thought can be reconciled with the idea of truth at all, then truth—at least in matters of taste—had better be per se knowable. But then the Simple Deduction is easily emended to argue not just that Tim's and my disagreement must involve a mistake but that it must involve a cognitive shortcoming in the stronger sense proposed, since one of us fails to know something that can be known.[3]

And indeed, even if the Ordinary View can somehow avoid commitment to evidential constraint, the situation is still not stable. For the conclusion of the Simple Deduction, that there is a mistake—false belief—involved in any such dispute, still stands unchallenged, even if no cognitive blame need attach to either disputant. And now, since for all I can tell it may as well be me who has a false belief as Tim, and since Tim is in an analogous position, it still seems impossible to understand how it can be rationally acceptable for us to agree to differ and persist in our respective views. The threat to Sustainability is already posed by the concession that Faultlessness *in the weak sense* is precluded by Contradiction.

So far, I've not said anything about relativism. It may be thought that the Ordinary View—the suggestion of the possibility of genuine but fault free disagreements in which the protagonists are fully rationally entitled to persist in their conflicting opinions—is tantamount to relativism—specifically, to the idea that truth in the region of discourse in which the dispute is articulated should be viewed as relative to the differences in standard, or context, or whatever, which generate the disagreement in the first place. But this is not correct. Relativism, I want to suggest, is best viewed as a *theoretical attempt* to underwrite and reconcile the elements in the Ordinary View. It is a response to the problem, rather than merely a label for the amalgam of ideas, which gives rise to it. Whether it is an adequate, or theoretically attractive, response remains to be seen.

III. AN INTUITIONISTIC RESPONSE

First, I want to table a different response. The Simple Deduction—exploiting, be it noted, only the most elementary logic and placing no reliance on any distinctively classical moves—elicits a contradiction from the three assumptions, that Williamson believes that rhubarb is delicious, that Wright believes that rhubarb is not delicious, and that nobody is mistaken. The conclusion seems to be forced, accordingly, that somebody has to be mistaken in any genuine such dispute. But it's not forced. There is a distinctively classical move involved in the interpretation of the reductio as indicative that a mistake always has to be involved. Specifically, take the third assumption as that:

It is not the case that Williamson is mistaken and it is not the case that Wright is mistaken. Then to interpret the reductio as showing that someone must have made a mistake is to take it that the negation of that conjunction licenses us in concluding:

Either Williamson is mistaken or Wright is mistaken.

That's to make an inferential transition of the form:

$$\frac{\text{Not (Not A \& Not B)}}{\text{A V B}}$$

—a pattern whose classical validation demands elimination of double negations, and which is not in general intuitionistically valid.

Very well. But so what? How might sticking at the intuitionistically valid conclusion—the negated conjunction—put us in a position to accommodate the components in the Ordinary View, and to reconcile them with each other? And even if resisting the transition to the disjunction would help, how might intuitionistic restrictions sufficient to block the relevant de Morgan Law be motivated in the type of context at hand?

Let's consider the second question first. The key issue, as always, concerns the status of the principle of Bivalence for statements of the relevant kind. For since:

$$\text{Not (Not A \& Not B)}$$

is, by uncontroversial steps, equivalent to:

$$\text{Not Not (A V B),}[4]$$

the move at which it is being suggested we may balk is tantamount to double negation elimination for disjunctions. If this class of cases of double negation elimination is accepted, Excluded Middle will hold quite generally, since its own double negation may likewise be established by wholly uncontroversial steps. Thus assuming—as we may in this dialectical context[5]—that Excluded Middle rests upon Bivalence, the defensibility of the transition from the thesis that Tim and I cannot both be right to the uncomfortable claim that *someone in particular*—either Tim, or me—is mistaken about rhubarb, rests on the defensibility of Bivalence for claims like: "rhubarb is delicious."

In intuitionistic mathematics, the challenge to Bivalence is best seen as flowing from a combination of two claims: first an insistence on a form of evidential constraint—that truth in mathematics may not defensively be supposed to outrun decidability in principle by a certain loosely characterized class of constructively acceptable methods; second that, for any theory at least as rich as number theory, we possess no guarantee that any given statement is indeed decidable by such methods. Simply put: if Bivalence holds for Goldbach's conjecture—if either the conjecture or its negation is true—then, by evidential constraint, one or the other will be verifiable by intuitionistically acceptable methods. So since we do not, in our present state of information, know that either can be so verified, we do not, in our present state of information, have any right to claim that Bivalence holds for Goldbach's conjecture, nor therefore throughout number theoretic statements as a class.

The intuitionistic reservation about Bivalence is thus one of agnosticism. But it is not an agnosticism based on the specter of third possibilities—additional truth-values, or truth-value gaps. Rather, it is based on our inability to guarantee the possibility of knowledge, along with the thesis—held for independent reasons—that truth requires that possibility for the type of statement for which the validity of Bivalence is under review.

Either of these claims may of course be contested for a given class of statements. But both may seem attractive for each of two non-mathematical kinds of example, for which, accordingly, the validity of Bivalence may consequently come into question. One comprises those vague statements typified by predications of adjectives like 'red' and 'bald.' The other is precisely our present focus: judgments of taste and other matters of inclination. In both these cases, we are antipathetic to the idea that truth has no implication of ascertainability; but in both cases we are likewise uneasy with the suggestion that claims have to be decidable, one way, or the other. In the terminology I have used in earlier work, borderline cases of vague predications, and predications of concepts of taste, are, no less than mathematical statements like Goldbach's conjecture, liable to present *quandaries*: examples where we may be uncertain not merely what it may be correct to think but even whether there is any metaphysical space for knowledge, or all-things-considered *best* opinion, properly so-termed. These two pressures—evidential constraint and the potentiality for quandary—squeeze out an unqualified acceptance of Bivalence over the two classes of statements in question; but they put no pressure on a continued adherence to the law of non-contradiction. So we should not, in reasoning among these statements, rely on a logic which forces us to be insensitive to the distinction between them which, it appears, had better be made.

This comparison—between statements like Goldbach's conjecture, borderline predications of vague concepts and judgments of taste—has been misunderstood by at least one commentator[6] so further clarification may help. Undeniably, there is the following difference. While no one knows whether knowledge either of Goldbach's conjecture or its negation is metaphysically possible and—it is tempting to add—no one is really entitled to an opinion (contrast: a hunch) about the matter, borderline cases of vague predicates may quite unobjectionably give rise to weak, qualified opinions. And matters of taste, for their part, may give rise to strong ones. So what is the intended analogy between the three kinds of statements? What similarity is the notion of quandary meant to mark? The answer is: a similarity which is manifested by each of the three kinds of statement *as a class*. Sure, any particular statement of each of the three kinds in question is such that we cannot rule out the possibility of a competent determinate—positive or negative—view of it (though with statements about borderline cases of vague concepts we can, admittedly, rule out the possibility of a competent but *strong* view). But nor, in each of the three kinds of case, do we have any grounds for thinking that knowledge, or in all things considered best opinion, has to be possible *for every example*. In particular, while I may indeed have many opinions on matters of taste, and consider them competent, or even superior, I have to acknowledge that I know nothing, which ensures that a determinate knowledgeable or best opinion is possible about every matter of taste or inclination generally. That would be a guarantee that all disputes of inclination have a winner. We have no such guarantee.

There, then—in the combination of quandary and evidential constraint—is one kind of motivation for broadly intuitionistic reservations about classical logic in general, and about the (in my formulation above, implicit) final step in the Simple Deduction. If accepted, it allows us to stop short of letting the Simple Deduction conclude that someone has to be mistaken in any dispute of inclination—indeed in any dispute about a genuinely indicative content.

Maybe the foregoing train of thought is of most interest in a context in which the primary question is whether the intuitionists' ideas about the logic appropriate to mathematics can be generalized to other regions of discourse. Anything properly viewed as an extension of their ideas will have to involve *some* kind of play with evidential constraint, since that is the role, in the mathematical case, of their very *constructivism*. However, we should not overlook another, simpler, and perhaps yet more compelling line of reservation about Bivalence in the cases that concern us, which puts evidential constraint to one side. Reflect that the opinion that Bivalence holds, of necessity, throughout vague discourse is a commitment to holding that each vague predicate is associated with a property of absolutely sharply bounded extension as its semantic value. But for a very wide class of such expressions—including especially predicates of Lockean secondary qualities—we have no clear idea what kinds of properties these may be. Nor, in general, do we have any clear idea how the required semantic associations might have been established. A commitment to Bivalence holding of necessity in all such cases is a commitment to postulating a kind of arcane natural history of semantic relationships for which we have absolutely no evidence. And it's just the same with predications of taste. There is just the same semantic mystery, just the same puzzlement, in a wide class of cases, about the nature of the properties that would be fit to discharge the demanded role. What *is* deliciousness if it is to be possible for normally competent speakers, like Tim and me, to go so completely astray about it in a perfectly ordinary case? The idea that there is a mandate for unrestricted Bivalence is, one way or another, a commitment to philosophical obligations—perhaps rampant realist, perhaps response-dependence realist— which we simply do not know how to meet. Surely the mere idea that Tim and I hold contradictory opinions about rhubarb ought to impose no such obligations. The reductio carried out in the Simple Deduction properly takes us no further than to the conclusion that our opinions cannot both be true. It is classical logic that is responsible for muddying the distinction between that and the idea that one in particular of us is missing the real fact.

IV. CAN THE INTUITIONISTIC RESPONSE RESCUE FAULTLESSNESS AND SUSTAINABILITY?

As remarked, however, it is one question whether there is a well-motivated intuitionistic distinction to draw, in the service of stabilizing the Ordinary View, between the claim that Tim and I cannot both be right about rhubarb, and the claim that one of us in particular must be wrong. Even if so, it is a further question whether we thereby secure the means to say something effective in stabilizing the Ordinary View of disputes of inclination. The challenge was to harmonize the three ingredients—Contradiction, Faultlessness, and Sustainability. And the point hasn't gone away that if it is insisted that a dispute can be regarded as fault free only if it's open to us to suppose that each antagonist has a correct view, then a mere acceptance that the dispute is genuine—so involves contradictory opinions—precludes regarding it as fault free. *Punkt.*

The question, of course, is what, in regarding such a dispute as potentially fault free, we really intend to maintain. Well, each will have to examine their own preconceptions. But my own impression is that the principal point is to contrast the case with situations where, should attempts at resolution fail, the mere existence of a contrary opinion, no worse supported than one's own, is sufficient to put one at fault in persisting in one's view. That will be a characteristic of the rhubarb dispute once the Simple Deduction is allowed to establish the disjunctive conclusion: either Tim is mistaken or I am. As soon as it is accepted that one of us has to be mistaken, the fact that neither of us is able to make his opinion prevail ought to encourage the worry that the mistaken party could as well be him as his antagonist. And once one recognizes that, then it should seem at best pigheaded not to withdraw from one's initial opinion. If this is right, then the really important thing about the idea of fault free disagreement in such cases is actually its implication of Sustainability—its implication of the idea that the opinions in a dispute of inclination may justifiably be persisted in, even when it is clear that it is a stalemate.

This comes close to but is not quite the same thing as suggesting that the essence of the Ordinary View can be captured just by the first and third components—Contradiction and Sustainability. But that conclusion is not right. There are readily conceivable cases where Contradiction and Sustainability are satisfied but where there is—or may be, depending on one's view—no proper comparison with disputes of inclination. Consider, for instance, two rival scientific theories, which match in their empirical, explanatory, and other virtues, which are unsurpassed by any other extant theory, and for which we've yet to devise a crucial experiment. It is debatable whether it should be regarded as irrational for a supporter of either theory to persist in holding to it even after he becomes aware of the credentials of the other. After all, there is, by hypothesis, no sufficient reason to adopt the opposing view—there is, by hypothesis, parity of virtue. And merely to abandon either theory without putting anything in its place would mean restoring all the disadvantages, whatever they may be, of having no theory of the subject matter in question at all. In such a case, then, regarding the dispute as genuine and factual is quite consistent with Sustainability. If so, then even if the intuitionistic response can indeed save Sustainability—I will address that in a minute—the scientific example shows us is that we need something extra, *something* to play the role of Faultlessness, if we are to explain the difference between the two kinds of case. And we are still no wiser about what that extra might be, consistently with the Simple Deduction, nor about whether the intuitionistic setting can provide it.

The difference between the two kinds of case—rhubarb and the scientific theoretical disagreement—consists in the way in which Sustainability is supported. In the scientific example, there *is* reason to accept (at least if one is a scientific realist) the disjunctive claim: one theory or the other—and perhaps both—will be false to the facts. One in particular—perhaps both—of the rival theorists will be proposing a misrepresentation of Nature. And the point is then that, notwithstanding that consideration, there are nevertheless overriding *pragmatic* reasons, grounded in the desirability of having a theory in the first place, for each to persist in their respective views—so that we have Sustainability anyway. In the rhubarb dispute, by contrast, there is—according to intuitionistic proposal—no impartial reason to suppose that one disputant in particular—Tim, or I—is making a mistake; and it is *because there is no reason so to suppose* that we have Sustainability.

So the suggestion at which we arrive is this: disputes of inclination may indeed be stably characterized by ascribing to them versions of all three features proposed by the Ordinary View: they are genuine disputes in which conflicting opinions are held; they may be fault free; and they may be rationally sustained even after it becomes clear that they are stand-offs. The refinements we need to add are, first, that in disputes of inclination Sustainability is properly seen as grounded in Faultlessness; in disputes of fact, by contrast, Sustainability, where it occurs, is grounded otherwise—in the scientific theoretical example, for instance, it is grounded pragmatically. Second, Faultlessness needs to be interpreted not as something flatly inconsistent with genuine conflict—with Contradiction—but rather as something that resides in the unavailability of any impartial reason to make (the relevant analogue of) the disjunctive claim: to insist that there is fault somewhere. What counts against rationally sustaining a dispute, once debate is exhausted without producing a winner, is the thought, roughly, that someone is mistaken here and, for all that has emerged, "it could as well be me." Once it is granted that someone has to be mistaken, that thought locates a concern that rationally ought to occur to each of the antagonists. The concern may still not mandate withdrawal if, as in the scientific theory case, there are overriding reasons that license retaining a view. But—the crucial point—it does not get off the ground without independent reason for the disjunctive claim.[7] It is by refusing the disjunctive claim that the intuitionistic proposal rescues Sustainability, and grounds it on Faultlessness, with the latter now understood precisely as located in the shortfall between the negated conjunction—which, it is conceded on all hands, the Simple Deduction establishes—and the stronger disjunctive claim which is what it takes to implicate error on one side or the other.

This proposed way of developing the Ordinary View and staving off the threat posed by the Simple Deduction seems to me to be stable this far. The question is whether there is any serious additional cause for dissatisfaction with it.

V. A PROBLEM FOR THE INTUITIONISTIC RESCUE

The intuitionistic rescue reconciles Contradiction with Faultlessness by insisting that it is insufficient for a dispute to involve Fault, merely that it be a genuine dispute—genuinely involving contrary or contradictory opinions. Conflict of opinion—it is contended—suffices for the presence of a mistake only when Bivalence is guaranteed to hold for the discourse of the dispute; and that, it is argued, is something for which there is—in the cases which concern us—no guarantee.

Someone who is sympathetic to intuitionistic ideas is not likely to find this a particularly controversial application of them. And indeed I would suggest that this also makes for an argument in the opposite direction. Absent a better kind of proposal, the need to make sense of the Ordinary View, and the apparent impossibility of doing so in a classical framework, provides a powerful argument for sympathy with intuitionistic distinctions and for further work on them.

There is, however, a problem with the approach, which, if we are convinced that coherent provision must be made for the Ordinary View, threatens to force us to look further afield. Simply stated, it is this: since the Ordinary View is inconsistent with rampant realism, no justice can have been done to it by an account that is consistent with the possibility that rampant realism is correct. But the intuitionistic proposal merely leaves us in a position of agnosticism about that. The response to the Simple Deduction was to argue that there is no justification for the relevant transition of the form:

$$\frac{\text{Not (Not A \& Not B)}}{\text{A V B}}$$

Even granting the proposed interpretation of Faultlessness, that is merely to say that there is no extant justification for regarding either Tim, or me as having a mistaken opinion. But to say that *there's no justification* for regarding the dispute as involving a mistake is not to say that *it's not the case* that the dispute involves a mistake. Yet surely, the objection says, Faultlessness should involve the latter. Yet the latter—the negation of the disjunction—does entail, even intuitionistically, the negations of both disjuncts. And those, conjoined, are then inconsistent with the intermediate conclusion—the negated conjunction—which, everyone agrees, the Simple Deduction does establish (and indeed inconsistent in their own right).

So, a critic may contend, the intuitionistic rescue has not really saved Faultlessness in any intuitively sufficient sense. The most that has been saved is justification for our reluctance to *attribute* fault in relevant cases, consistently with acknowledging the Simple Deduction. This leaves it epistemically open that there is indeed a determinate fact of the matter in the rhubarb dispute, and indeed in such disputes in general, and hence that there is indeed a determinate fault on one side or the other. And that is exactly what we—most of us—are reluctant to believe. It is good if the intuitionistic proposal can save us from being forced to think it true just by elementary logic. But we would like to be in a position to think it false.

A supporter of the intuitionistic rescue may rejoin that it is no serious shortcoming in the proposal that it leaves us at most unsympathetically agnostic towards the rampant realist view of the dispute. After all, that, as it may seem, just is the extent of the justified position. The rampant realist view calls for the association of the predicate 'delicious,' understood as by both Tim and me, with a property that determinately applies or fails to apply to stewed rhubarb. We may not believe there is, as a matter of metaphysics, any suitable such property, much less that our linguistic practices somehow enthrone such a property as the *Bedeutung* of delicious. But come on: we do not *know* that these things are not so—not if knowing requires being in a position to prove it. The honest objection to rampant realism is not that we know that its presuppositions are not met but that there is not the slightest reason to regard it as true. If the preconceptions that underwrite the Ordinary View slur that distinction, they are not to be respected to the letter. We should stick to what we can justify.

This reply, though, only partially addresses the objection. Maybe we do not, strictly, know that rampant realism is false. But at the level of analysis displayed by the Simple Deduction, even with intuitionistic distinctions superimposed, the point remains that no space is left for a coherent belief that neither Tim, nor I, is mistaken in the original dispute. In particular, no way whatever has been offered of recovering a content for the idea that there is no 'fact of the matter' to be mistaken about. Even if we don't know that the rampant realist's insistence that there is indeed a fact of the matter is itself mistaken, it may yet be felt as a very serious limitation of the intuitionistic treatment if it does not, so far, allow us so much as to attach content to the idea of that mistake. The worst mistake of which we have been empowered to make sense is an epistemic mistake: one of lack of warrant—the unwarranted insistence that the world and the relevant concepts are bound to conspire to render true one of the disputed opinions or the other. But nothing has been said to explain how, or in what respect, rampant realism might be incorrect, rather than merely unjustified.

The intuitionistic rescue provides theoretically respectable houseroom for our reluctance to be press-ganged into realism by the Simple Deduction. But it does not offer—and it seems has no resources to offer—any account of what it would be for (rampant) realism to be, not merely not imposed, but false: a misrepresentation in its own right. Surely, it may be felt, a satisfactory account of disputes of inclination should explain how it is possible that this might be so, even if we are forced to grant that, in the end, we are not in a position to show, once and for all, that it is so.

VI. THE INTUITIONISTIC RESCUE RESCUED?

The objection may seem convincing. But, in fact, it runs together two distinct complaints and arguably derives some of its force from the conflation.

One complaint is that the intuitionistic rescue treats the transition from the conjunction:

It is not the case that neither Williamson nor Wright is mistaken.

to the disjunctive conclusion:

Williamson is mistaken or Wright is mistaken.

merely as a *non sequitur*, whereas someone who takes the Ordinary View will want to reserve space for the belief—even if conceded not to be a strictly *knowledgeable* belief—that the disjunctive conclusion is *incorrect*: that nobody need be mistaken. Since there is no provision within an intuitionistic framework for a coherent denial of the disjunction, it appears that the intuitionistic rescue cannot do justice to the Ordinary View. However, a second, distinct complaint is that the intuitionistic rescue cannot so much as provide for a coherent belief that *rampant realism* is false—even if it were granted that such disbelief would involve a degree of presumption. Since the Ordinary View is indeed inconsistent with rampant realism, the two complaints converge on the thought that the intuition-istic rescue cannot do justice to the Ordinary View. Nevertheless, the complaints are not the same—for the straightforward reason that denial of the disjunction is not required by the denial of rampant realism.

What are their relations? Well, rampant realism is—presumably—commit-ted to the disjunction; conversely, an acceptance that the disjunction follows just from the premise that Tim and I have contradictory views is, arguably, a com-mitment to rampant realism. But that is not to say that only a framework that provides for a coherent denial of the disjunction can provide for a coherent dis-belief in the metaphysical and semantic postulations of rampant realism. That would be true only if disbelief in rampant realism were a commitment to deny-ing the disjunction. But that cannot be correct: after all, both Tim and I accept the disjunction, presumably (since each thinks the other is mistaken)—but at most one of us is a rampant realist about matters of basic taste in desserts!

It is not—the point is—an acceptance of the disjunction *qua propositional content* that commits to rampant realism; it is an acceptance that its truth is ensured simply by the fact of Tim's and my respective views being contradicto-ries. In fact, anyone with a determinate—positive or negative—view on whether stewed rhubarb is delicious should accept the disjunction; no *philosophical* com-mitment is entrained. A philosophical commitment is entered into only when one regards the disjunction as imposed by the nature of the subject matter and the kind of content carried by claims of the kind in dispute. One may therefore reject a rampant realist—indeed, any form of realist—view about those matters without commitment to any particular attitude to the disjunction.

The second of the two complaints is accordingly misconceived. A supporter of the intuitionistic rescue is quite at liberty to *deny* rampant realism. It is not true that he can go no further than agnosticism about the point. He thereby denies that the truth of the disjunction is guaranteed in the way rampant realism supposes. The dialectical situation is, in fact, exactly analogous to that in the philosophy of mathematics, where the intuitionist may quite coherently—if he wishes—deny the Platonist metaphysics of a crystalline world of determinate mathematical structures, potentially conferring truth and falsity upon our mathematical state-ments in ways transcending all possibility of proof. That denial commits him to denying that Excluded Middle holds of necessity for reasons connected with that metaphysics. But it does not commit him to denying Excluded Middle itself, still less any instance of it. Rather, in the absence of justification for the principle of any other kind, he merely regards it as unacceptable.

The first complaint still stands, though: the thought that the intuitionis-tic rescue leaves no space for a coherent belief that neither Tim, nor I, is mistaken in the original dispute. The closest the intuitionistic rescue gets to this is in establishing a position from which it can be allowed that the presence of error is dictated neither by elementary logic and the contradictoriness of the attitudes involved nor—I have just argued—by the semantics and metaphysics of discourse of taste. So we save *a* negative modal claim: there doesn't have to be error for *those* reasons at least. But we don't, it seems, give sense to the idea that there doesn't have to be error *tout court*, nor therefore provide any possibility for someone coherently to believe that there *isn't* any error in the case in point. But wasn't that suggestion just the force of the Latin proverb? Recall that we initially glossed the Ordinary View with the words, "Nobody's wrong. Tim and I should just agree to disagree."

It is easy, of course, to dismiss the idea that there *is* any such coherent belief, stronger than any of the beliefs that the intuitionistic rescue can accommodate and still remaining to be made sense of. After all, Tim and I do disagree. So Tim must think, presumably, that my view is mistaken. And I must think that his is mistaken. So someone who thinks that nobody actually is mistaken is committed to disagreeing with us *both*—and so to regarding *everybody* as mistaken: Tim, I, and indeed themselves! If there is a way further forward, it must consist in finding the means to deny that Tim and I must both, in fact, regard the other's view as mistaken—this despite the fact that our views are genuinely contradictory. So in a certain sense, their contradictoriness notwithstanding, we have to agree that our views are not in conflict—that we do *not* disagree.

This extra step is inaccessible on the intuitionistic treatment, and it is unquestionably of interest to consider what kind of position could possibly accommodate an insistence on it while avoiding aporia. One may well think that, for all we have so far seen, the intuitionistic treatment delivers enough to rank as a satisfactory explication of the Ordinary View. But if there is a stable account which manages the extra step—which can somehow allow that while Tim and I have genuinely contradictory attitudes, neither of us need regard the other as mistaken—it may well be felt to offer progress.

VII. TRUE RELATIVISM

That is the prospectus that what I will call the *True Relativist* exegesis of the Ordinary View aims to fill. According to true relativism, it can be the case that Tim and I are both right even though we understand the claim that rhubarb is delicious in the same way, and even though we are making incompatible judgments about it. And the reason is because there are no absolute facts about taste—what it is true to say about taste depends upon a stance, or a set of standards, or a set of affective dispositions. The very same claim can be true for Tim and false for me—and that it is so can be something that is available to us both.

Familiarly, the idea that truth is *globally* relative—that some form of relativity is of the nature of truth—has often been held to implicate dialectical incoherence, or worse. Whatever the fact about that, our questions are more specific: whether relative truth is even *locally* coherent; whether, if so, it can accommodate each of Contradiction, Faultlessness, and Sustainability at all; and whether it can do so without undue metaphysical cost, and in particular in a way which allows for more robust understanding of Faultlessness than could be secured by the intuitionistic proposal—a way which allows for a consistent profession that Tim's and my views can both be correct.

Obviously, in order to accomplish the last of these things, true relativism has to have the means to block the Simple Deduction *before* it reaches the problematical line:

It's not the case that (it's not the case that Williamson is mistaken and it's not the case that Wright is mistaken).

It is clear how the attempt should be made. The true relativist must insist that, for statements of the kind that concern us, we may no longer validly infer from the supposition that P that someone who holds that not-P is making a mistake. A mistake will be implicated only if the judgment that not-P is held accountable to the same standards, or perspective, or whatever, that are implicated in the (hypothetical) supposition that P is true. Very simply: if P is true by one set of standards, or whatever the relativistic parameter is, and I judge it false by another, then what makes P true need not be something which, in judging that it is not true, I mistakenly judge not to obtain.

That, then, will be the *shape* of the true relativist response to the Simple Deduction. The question is whether it can be made sense of. There is a temptation to think that making sense of it is easier than it really is which we need to expose straight away. A philosopher seeking to stabilize the Ordinary View should not be interested in relativity—as a function of context of utterance, or whatever else—in the truth-conditions, and hence the truth-values, of *sentences*. The relativity that needs to be made out is relativity in the truth of *thoughts* or *propositions*. If we identify a proposition by its truth-conditions, the relevant form of relativity is relativity in the question whether *those very truth-conditions* are satisfied. Suppose that in the course of a medical procedure, a surgeon says of a scalpel that's been poorly prepared: "This instrument is dangerously blunt."

Later, when the instrument is about to be re-sharpened and sterilized, his assistant may warn an inexperienced orderly: "Watch out when you handle that—it's dangerously sharp." Granted, it would be crass to say that the surgeon and his assistant mean different things by 'sharp' and 'blunt' respectively. What is true is that there is a relativity of standard: the surgeon's needs require a much finer edge on the blade than would suffice to justify his assistant's subsequent warning.

A similar setup is illustrated by the kind of attributer-contextualist accounts of knowledge proposed by writers such as Keith DeRose and Stewart Cohen.[8] The point to note, however, is that the kind of relativity involved in these examples—plausible in the case of the scalpel, more controversial in the case of knowledge-contextualism—is not at all to our present purpose. For while it would be crass to see them as involving anything comparable to simple ambiguity in 'sharp' or 'knows,' they do involve that the truth-conditions of ascriptions of sharpness and knowledge are so affected by contextual or other relevant parameters that *there is no single content* respectively affirmed and denied by the surgeon's claim and that of his assistant, or—to cut a long story short—by G. E. Moore's claim that he knows he has a hand and the skeptical claim that he does not. These views might naturally, if perhaps a little loosely, be described as involving relativism about sharpness, or knowledge. But true relativism is relativism about *truth*. It is *not* the thesis that the content of a certain kind of ascription can vary as a function of varying standards, or contexts, or other parameters. That's a thesis that, applied to our present problem, simply gives up on the attempt to satisfy Contradiction and so holds out no comfort to the Ordinary View. True relativism is the thesis—to repeat—that *after* the truth-conditions of an utterance have been settled, there can be relativity in the question whether they are satisfied. It is a thesis that engages at the level of content, rather than at the level of speech-acts. Or if it is not, then it's merely a slightly more sophisticated cousin of the simple indexical relativist proposal I canvassed at the start—a variant which holds that while a statement on which a dispute of inclination is targeted is indeed not an ellipsis for something which explicitly mentions some parametric standard or perspective, etc., it is nevertheless something whose content is implicitly fixed by reference to such a parameter, so that—as before—Tim and I will have no genuine conflict of opinion about rhubarb. A true relativist accommodation of the Ordinary View must demand that it is the very same proposition that Tim affirms and that I deny—and at the same time that neither the affirmation nor the denial need be mistaken, with this a point which the antagonists themselves can coherently take on board. The latter point is entirely unproblematical if it is not really the same proposition that is involved. What the relativist has to explain, in contrast, is how to maintain the point alongside the claim that there is a single proposition affirmed and denied respectively. What is the relevant notion of propositional identity, and how is it possible rationally to affirm the truth of such a proposition consistently with allowing that someone else's denial of it is also true?

It is not, it seems to me, at all straightforward to see that the demanded notion of relative truth—relative truth at the level of propositions—is fully intelligible. But the difficulties are especially daunting if we essay to think of truth as *correspondence*, in a robust sense of correspondence with calls for an internal relation between a proposition, conceived as an articulated abstract entity, and some correspondingly articulated aspect of non-propositional reality. On any such picture of truth and truth-conferral, it seems impossible to make room for the additional parameter which relativism posits; the internal structural relationship between propositions and the things that make them true or false is so conceived as to be essentially dyadic. It's like the congruence in form between a head-and-shoulders sculpture and the model who posed for it. No doubt the former may be an accurate representation, or not, relative to the conventions of representation, but we are looking for something to illuminate an alleged relativity which bites *after* the conventions of representation have been fixed. And we draw a blank. The unavoidable conclusion seems to be that, while particular such conventions may allow of degrees of accuracy in representation, the degree to which there is accuracy is something which supervenes entirely upon the respective physiognomies of the statue and the sitter. There is no place for a third term in the relation.[9]

If that is correct, the immediate lesson to draw is merely the unremarkable one that to attempt to think of truth—propositional truth—relativistically is to foreclose on thinking of it as correspondence. That's an objection to relativism only if it's impossible to think of truth in any other viable way. Suppose on the contrary that, at least in some regions of thought, truth may satisfyingly be construed as consisting in some kind of coherence relation, with coherence an internal, analytic relationship, fixed by the content of the propositions among which it obtains. Let it be proposed, for example, that the truth of a proposition consists in its participation within a maximal, coherent system of propositions incorporating some specified base class of propositions, B. Then depending on the choice of B, a proposition may be true or not—may be a member of the relevant maximal set of coherent propositions or not—even after its content is fully fixed. Such a conception of truth may only locally have any attraction at all—one might, for example, think of truth in pure set theory along such lines—but it provides at least a prima facie model of how a truth predicate for propositions may intelligibly be conceived as relative.[10]

No such coherentist model is presumably wanted for the notion of truth that is to engage disputes of taste and other matters of inclination. Still, the example suggests that once one begins to think of truth along the kind of pluralist lines that a number of philosophers, myself included, have canvassed in recent work,[11] it may be possible to come closer to a stable working-out of true relativism than one might otherwise suspect.[12] I'll conclude by outlining one specific suggestion in that direction.

VIII. RELATIVISM AND IDEALIZED ASSERTIBILITY

Assertibility[13] is manifestly a relative notion: a statement may be assertible relative to one state of information and not to another. Might notions of truth arrived at by idealization of assertibility retain this, or a kindred, relativity?

There are two principal such proposed idealizations to be found in the literature. The first, in the Peircean tradition and associated with Hilary Putnam's latterly renounced 'internal realism,' idealizes on the state of information: what is true is what is assertible in a state of information incorporating all possible relevant data for the proposition in question. It's obvious that this proposal, whatever we might want to say pro- or anti- the credentials of the resulting truth predicate, holds out no interesting prospect of relativism, since the whole point of the idealization involved is that it is supposed to ensure *convergence*. Either a proposition is assertible at the relevant Peircean limit of information gathering—in which case it is true *simpliciter*—or, even at the limit, its credentials are matched by a rival, in which case it is neither assertible nor—for internal realism—true.

Matters may turn out interestingly differently, however, if the idealization assumes the form proposed in the notion of *superassertibility*.[14] Superassertibility is the property not of being assertible in some ideal—perhaps limiting—state of information, but of being assertible in some ordinary, accessible state of information and then remaining so no matter what additions or improvements are made to it. When superassertibility for a given class of statements is taken to be truth, then truth is held to consist not in assertibility at some ideal limit of information gathering but in enduring assertibility over indefinite improvements. Does superassertibility offer the prospect of an interesting relativity? More specifically: can this happen—that *in a single world* one thinker, Hero, is in position to accept P, and another, Heroine, is in position to accept not-P, and that each can retain their respective situations no matter what improvements or enlargements are made to their states of information?

Well, not if Hero's and Heroine's respective bodies of information allow of *pooling*, and if it is determinate and unique what the resulting pooled state of information should be, and determinate whether it supports P, or not-P, or neither. But those conditions may not all be met. When Hero and Heroine bring their respective bodies of information together, it may be that there is more than one equally rationally defensible way for accommodating the components into a unified state, each may be involving some discards, with none superior to the others in virtue of the number or kind of discards involved or the quality of the information remaining. It may also happen that some of the resulting enlarged states of information continue to warrant acceptance of P, and others acceptance of not-P. And once granted to be possible at all, it's difficult to see how to exclude the thought that such a situation might persist indefinitely. In that case, superassertibility would be relative to a starting point, an initial basis for acceptance or rejection. If one were satisfied there were no other obstacles to the identification of truth with superassertibility over the region of discourse in question that would be a kind of relativity of truth.

However, the kind of case which is our main focus—disputes of taste—is marked by the following peculiarity: that the basic form of assertibility condition for statements of the relevant kind is given by a subject's finding herself in a certain type of *non-cognitive* affective state: liking the taste of rhubarb, for instance. The basic form of assertibility condition, that is to say, for the impersonal statement—about the vegetable—coincides with that for the self-ascription of a subjective state that is not conceived—at least not by anyone attracted to the Ordinary View—as a cognitive response. In that case, Hero and Heroine may respectively be in a position to assert P and to assert not-P, not because they possess differing initial information bases but just by virtue of differing in their non-cognitive responses to things—and because these responses are non-cognitive, there will be no clear sense to the idea of 'pooling' their respective starting points and determining what is warranted by the result. Of course, there is such a thing as enlarging one's information by the addition of the datum that others do not share a particular non-cognitive response. But if that datum is not treated per se as a defeater, then there will be no immediate threat to the superassertibility of the original claim.

Much more would need to be said if a satisfying proposal in this direction is to be developed. In particular, if a content is to be associated with the impersonal statement—"Rhubarb is delicious"—contrasting with that of a subjective report, then something has to be said about how the contrast between the two is sustained. Presumably such an account will give central place to asymmetries in the conditions of defeat, with the assertibility of, for example, "I relish eating rhubarb," surviving in circumstances where that of "Rhubarb is delicious" is lost. It's hard to envisage how the story might plausibly go without some kind of play with intersubjective accord: what purposes could be served by our having the impersonal form of statement if one could seldom reliably encourage expectations in an audience about their own affective states and responses? Still, if one's own tastes are not too idiosyncratic—if enough of a constituency goes along with them—then that may be enough to license a claim, even if significantly many may, with the same license, dissent from it. And in that case there may be theoretical advantages in representing the situation as one in which conflicting claims are each true relative to varying parameters of taste, with truth construed as superassertibility on the basis of a notion of assertibility grounded on the relevant non-cognitive affect.

Such a proposal looks to be promisingly placed to handle Faultlessness and Sustainability. But matters may seem less clear with Contradiction—the claim that genuinely incompatible opinions are involved: how exactly does the proposal promise a better accommodation of the Ordinary View in this respect than the kind of position, illustrated by the examples of the blunt scalpel and knowledge-attributions when construed along contextualist lines, which effectively diagnoses disputes of inclination as illusory? What can be said, in the spirit of the superassertibilist-relativist proposal, to support the idea that it is the *same* content that, as it may be, is superassertible for Tim but not for me?

To think of truth in some area of discourse as constituted by superassertibility no doubt leaves considerable latitude when it comes to theorizing about propositional content. I shall not here attempt such a theory. However, if Tim and I do have an understanding in common of the proposition that rhubarb is delicious, as it occurs in our respective affirmation and denial, it would be natural to locate the commonality in a shared conception of basic, sufficient—if defeasible—grounds for accepting the proposition (one's enjoying rhubarb, presumably) and a shared conception of the consequences of regarding it as correct. Among the latter might be, for example, the desirability of regular harvesting of one's rhubarb crop when in season, a high ranking for choosing a dessert in a German restaurant identified to one as rhubarb crumble, a high priority assigned to the rhubarb patch in the reorganization of the vegetable garden, and so on. Commonality of understanding will involve that my negative view, by contrast, will lead to corresponding low priorities and opposed choices. This is the pre-theoretic background against which it seems intuitive to say that Tim and I have genuinely conflicting views about a single proposition. An explicit theory subserving the point would be one in the broad tradition deriving from

Gentzen's work on the logical constants, which locates the individuation of content in canonical grounds and consequences.

Against this kind of background, it's salient that the situation contrasts with the case of the rejected scalpel. Baldly, suitable grounds for the attribution of sharpness that the surgeon denies would be quite different to those sufficient for the attribution of sharpness that the orderly affirms. When the latter asserts that the scalpel is (dangerously) sharp he is not challenging the surgeon's judgment that it is not—as indeed the surgeon is not challenging the orderly's judgment that great care is necessary in handling it and preparing it for sharpening and sterilization. But more: each can quite coherently accept and, in various ways, appropriately *act on* the other's claim while still maintaining his own—surely a conclusive consideration in favor of the point that different, and compatible, contents are involved. By contrast, that Tim and I are involved in genuine disagreement is borne out by the fact that we agree about the, loosely described, consequences of each other's views and then sustain our disagreement through our respective acceptance or rejection of those consequences and the courses of action involved. Tim orders the crumble; I don't. Tim designs his vegetable patch in a certain way; I don't.[15] Rational action on either of the views excludes rational action on the other.

So here's the package: Tim and I are in genuine disagreement about whether rhubarb is delicious. Our opinions are incompatible. And the common understanding, necessary to ground that incompatibility, is based on a common conception of the assertibility conditions of the claim—that, absent defeating considerations, it may be asserted just if one relishes eating rhubarb—and on a shared conception of a range of consequences, both analytical and practical, which attend its correctness. Our disagreement can be faultless because it can be based on our respectively perfectly proper responses to our respective non-cognitive propensities. And it can be sustainable because—precisely—neither claim has been defeated nor has to be defeasible. Finally, the Simple Deduction is blocked in exactly the way prefigured: when truth is conceived as superassertibility relative to a subject's non-cognitive responses, the supposition that P is true will be answerable to the corresponding responses of a tacitly understood constituency of subjects; and it will implicate a mistake in the opinion of one who takes it that not-P is true only if one's opinion is properly held answerable to the responses of the same constituency.

If all this is soundly conceived, then a relativism about truth, fashioned along the indicated lines, may be the natural companion of non-cognitivist conceptions of competence in particular regions of discourse. But here I must be content merely to have outlined the approach.

This sort of relativism is compatible with the existence of some moral requirements that apply to everyone. Were everyone to share a given commitment, it would be possible that a moral requirement be universally applicable. Still, all it would take for such a moral requirement to fail of its universal scope would be the alteration of a commitment on someone's part, and that introduces a kind of contingency that strikes many as deeply worrying.

As a moral realist, I am one of the worried. Though *moral realism* is a term of art, and, like any other philosophical 'ism,' is liable to be understood somewhat differently by different users, I think that the following captures the core of what is commonly meant by the term. Moral realism is the doctrine that there are true moral claims, and that such claims, when true, are not made true by virtue of being endorsed by any actual or idealized human beings. Nor are moral claims true, when they are, because of being endorsed, implied or entailed by norms that are constructed from our evaluative attitudes. The basic principles that specify our moral duties, or dictate the conditions of moral value, are not vulnerable to alteration based on the attitudes of those to whom they apply.

There are many forms of moral realism, and many forms of moral relativism. Realistic doctrines are sorted largely by whether they conceive of moral facts as part and parcel of a wholly naturalistic world, or whether they allow for a *sui generis* realm of normativity, within which moral facts find a home. Relativistic doctrines can be distinguished from one another on the basis of what it is that they take morality to be relative *to*. The most important forms of relativism, it seems to me, will all endorse the master argument that appears above. I allow that some may not, but in what follows, I will restrict my attention to those that do. If moral realism is true, these theories must be false. For these forms of relativism all make the content of moral requirements, and so the truth of claims that specify the existence of moral requirements, dependent on the attitudes of the agents to whom they apply. Realism cannot allow that. And so we have a nice challenge to moral realism, one presented by the master argument for moral relativism.

Because the master argument is valid, the only way to resist it (if one is so inclined) is to undermine one or both of its premises. I find the first premise quite attractive, and am pleased to be able to agree with moral relativists on this point. And so it is the second premise—the one that records the contingency of moral requirements on personal commitments—that I will have to reject. Other realists endorse the opposite strategy, and abandon the rational authority of morality (premise 1) as a way of vindicating the contingency recorded in premise 2. For reasons that I won't go into here, I find that route less than ideal. So my goal will be to do what I can to undermine the second premise of the master argument.

For purposes of assessing this argument, I intend to understand *commitments*, and their objects, very broadly. They include one's short- and long-term desires and cares, one's attachments, what one wants or aims at, what one takes an interest in, one's projects and goals, and the objects of one's passions and longings.

It will be useful to have a term for the view that receives expression in the second premise. Following common philosophical parlance, let us call this *practical instrumentalism* (henceforth, just *instrumentalism*). It is the view that the only reasons there can be are so-called *hypothetical reasons*, i.e., reasons to do things that are in some way ancillary to the achievement of one's commitments (cares, desires, wants, goals, etc.).

If instrumentalism is true, then there can be no *categorical reasons*. Categorical reasons, as I will define them here, are reasons that obtain independently of their relation to an agent's commitments. I believe that there are categorical reasons for action. I will offer two arguments on their behalf. I do not think that any of their premises can be plausibly denied.

If I am right, then we will have excellent grounds for rejecting the second premise of the master argument. That would not, of course, show that moral relativism, in any of its forms, is false. But it would suffice to undermine perhaps the most powerful argument available in its defense. That is work enough for a day.

II

Both of my arguments for categorical reasons, and against instrumentalism, begin by directing our attention to a familiar sort of example: that of the dedicated, successful immoralist. Imagine a person who is very sharp, very cunning, but also deeply malicious. His happiness is directly proportioned to the misery he wreaks. His top priority in life is to cause pain and suffering, even if, as he knows, such conduct will likely bring an early death, or a long incarceration. We intuitively regard such a person as (at the least) morally obligated to desist from the cruel treatment he longs to impose. Don't we also believe that there are excellent reasons for him to so refrain—namely, all of those considerations that constitute the wrongness of his actions? The reasons to refrain from cruelty are (at the least) the very considerations that make his actions wrong in the first place.

Consider an experienced torturer working on behalf of an authoritarian government. Such a person not only endorses the legitimacy of the regime, but takes active pleasure in breaking his victims. His greatest joy is stripping the last vestiges of dignity from those who initially resist his demands. At a given session, as he is about to apply the electrodes, he pauses to consider the merits of his action. He sees that doing so will get him what he most wants, and will frustrate none of his desires. He proceeds accordingly.

Consider a different case, one in which a person can very easily rescue another. A child has strayed from her parents on a busy city street, and is about to toddle into the path of a car that will surely kill her. The bystander sees what is happening. He need only reach an arm down to the child to save her from an awful death. Rather than doing so, he watches in delight as the child is destroyed by an oncoming car.

If there were nothing to be said against these actions and omissions—no considerations that opposed, extinguished or overturned the case these agents might make for their cruel conduct—then it is hard to see how their actions could be wrong. But they obviously are wrong. And the sorts of considerations just mentioned—those directly relevant to matters of justification (and, in this particular context, those that indict the agent's cruelty)—are precisely what reasons are. Reasons are, by definition, considerations that favor or oppose, that make something appropriate, legitimate, or justified (or the reverse). So, if we think that there is a plausible story to tell about why the dedicated evildoer is wrong for indulging his inclinations, then we are committed to there being reasons for him to refrain. And this despite the fact that, by hypothesis, he's got no commitments that would be furthered by his doing so.

But surely, some will say, the moral monster has *some* commitments that will be furthered were he to refrain from cruelty. And that shows that he will, after all, have some reason to refrain. But we've no grounds for thinking this a categorical reason. Whatever reasons he has to desist will stem straightforwardly from his aversion to jail, or his desire to avoid the potential harms inflicted by his vengeful victims, etc.

Two fairly obvious points should be mentioned here. First, even if all real people in the real world do have at least some ends that would be served by avoiding cruelty, we can imagine a possible world in which our misanthrope does not. The instrumentalist's rejection of categorical reasons is meant to express a necessary truth—reasons must further what an agent cares about—and so is vulnerable if there are possible contexts in which this truth fails to obtain. In the scenario I am imagining, the ruthless immoralist has no commitments that would be served were he to refrain from his cruelty. But there are, nevertheless, excellent reasons for him to so refrain—namely, and at the very least, all of the considerations that make his proposed actions immoral.

Moreover, we would not want to make the case against cruelty be dependent on an instrumental link with this man's goals. Suppose, for instance, that our torturer wanted to avoid the censure that he would earn were his actions publicized. The best way to minimize his risk is to stop doing what he does. Though this, let us grant, does provide him a reason to stop, it isn't the only, or nearly the strongest, reason to do so. The cruelties he perpetrates are opposed by a host of considerations that make no mention of his aims. These considerations are reasons—reasons to refrain from deliberately inflicting misery. And these reasons will, first and foremost, mention the suffering of his victims, and the absence of their consent to his treatment. If the immoralist's aversion to being found out enters into it at all, it is only in a subordinate role, as a consideration that may supply an additional reason to refrain from his actions, one that is likelier than the others to motivate him to do the right thing.

Here is the argument in a nutshell:

(1) A reason, by definition, is a consideration that favors, justifies, legitimizes or makes appropriate (or the reverse).

(2) Some such considerations bear no instrumental link to an agent's ends.

(3) Therefore, there are some reasons that bear no instrumental link to an agent's ends.

(4) Therefore, there are categorical reasons.

I hope that the definition expressed in premise (1), though obviously not a reductive one, is nevertheless uncontroversial. It's meant to be broad enough to be acceptable both to fans and to critics of categorical reasons. Where they will part company is with regard to premise (2). I have tried to reveal its attractions with the example of the dedicated evildoer. So long as we think—as all of us do—that there are genuine considerations to oppose his cruelty, and also think that such considerations obtain independently of his commitments, then premise (2) is secure. That would be enough to establish the existence of categorical reasons.

Instrumentalists will likely charge that premise (2) begs the question. It is true that the considerations offered in support of the premise, together with the definition expressed in premise (1), entail the falsity of practical instrumentalism. But that cannot be a fatal flaw. Rather, it is a requirement of any logically valid argument whose conclusion vindicates the existence of categorical reasons.

Still, the instrumentalist may claim that the examples and considerations that support premise (2) are insufficiently independent of the conclusion being argued for. An ideal argument is one that is not only logically valid, but one whose premises can find support from those who are as yet uncommitted on the matter at hand. If the only reason to endorse a premise is that one already accepts the conclusion it is meant to support, then the premise is question-begging. The instrumentalist will likely insist that the only ones willing to ratify premise (2) are those who are already committed to rejecting instrumentalism.

Now I don't think that instrumentalists are right about that. But before saying why, we might undertake a brief excursus on the matter of begging questions. Begging a question is sometimes unavoidable. In ethics, the likeliest scenarios are ones in which one is advancing fundamental normative or evaluative commitments. It is hard to avoid begging a question if one encounters someone who denies that pain is ever bad, or denies that there is anything immoral about humiliating vulnerable innocents. Perhaps the only way to avoid a petitio in these circumstances is to show that one's interlocutor is contradicting himself. This is the fond hope of Kantians and others—to show that those with patently immoral sensibilities are in some way undercutting their own commitments and displaying some internal incoherence.

Perhaps the Kantians are right. It would be lovely were it so. But let us pursue other possibilities, ones that do not vindicate the existence of categorical reasons by attributing a contradiction to those who refuse to acknowledge them. On this alternative line, those who oppose our basic normative and evaluative commitments can coherently reject the claims we hold so dear. Any defense of our deepest commitments will have to come from the sorts of bolstering considerations that are involved in revealing a belief to be situated within a network of mutually supporting beliefs. But such a defense will not be able to avoid the charge of begging the question. The other beliefs we enlist on behalf of our original claim may be no more persuasive to opponents than the position originally in need of support.

Unless we can reveal a contradiction in our opponent's position, we may have to beg a question somewhere. The most likely point is, as I have said, with regard to our fundamental normative and evaluative commitments. And we are certainly in the neighborhood, when considering an endorsement (or rejection) of categorical reasons.

This is not yet to concede that this first argument is question-begging. But what if it were? There is independent reason for thinking that question-begging claims and arguments are ones that agents may sometimes be justified in believing. I am justified in believing myself to be conscious, even if others regard me as an unthinking automaton whose protestations are merely programmed behaviors. If I am imprisoned on false charges, I am justified in believing myself innocent, even if all publicly available evidence convinces everyone else of the justice of the sentence. If, having cried "Wolf!" once too many times, my next cry is unheeded and disbelieved, I am nonetheless justified in believing that there is such a beast before me, if I see it approaching and ready to attack.

In each of these cases, we can easily imagine that any evidence that I bring to bear to substantiate my claim will be taken as confirming the hypotheses of the doubters who surround me. The credibility of my testimony will be invariably rejected, as it is expressive of a conclusion that the skeptics will not accept. In this context, anything I say on my behalf is bound to be question-begging. But I am nevertheless justified in regarding my supporting beliefs, and the claims they seek to vindicate, as eminently plausible.

I don't say that our belief in the existence of considerations that oppose the actions of the immoralist is as epistemically secure as the contested beliefs in the examples just given. That is not the point of introducing them. Rather, the examples are designed to show that some question-begging claims are credible and justifiably held. So even if the various beliefs that condemn the actions of the immoralist beg the question against the instrumentalist, such beliefs might be epistemically justified.

To pursue this path, we would need to distinguish between those question-begging beliefs that are, and those that are not, justifiably held. I don't intend to embark on such a discussion, because I do not believe that the considerations that support premise (2) are, in fact, question-begging.

I don't believe that only those already convinced of the existence of categorical reasons will find these considerations compelling. What is true is that dedicated instrumentalists will find something to resist. I submit that those who have yet to develop a considered view about the existence of categorical reasons will find the considerations that support the second premise natural and highly plausible. They won't need convincing that there is something to be said against the torturer's actions, and something to be said in favor of easily preventing a child from being needlessly killed. They will then discover that such considerations, when conjoined with an uncontroversial definition of reasons, entail the existence of categorical reasons. The only ones who will deny the appeal of such considerations are those whose theoretical commitments already require them to do so. That such sensibilities are offended is not enough to undermine any success this first argument may enjoy.

III

A second argument on behalf of categorical reasons also relies on our views about the dedicated immoralist, but shifts the focus to matters of responsibility and blameworthiness. Consider those who freely commit themselves to blowing up civilians in crowded areas. Such people are (with perhaps rare exceptions) highly capable of assessing options, gathering information to discover how best to pursue their chosen goals, and taking the needed steps to ensure that their goals are met. They are not insane. They are genuine agents, responsible for their deeds. They are as blameworthy as agents can be.

We would rescind our condemnation of such people were they literally compelled to do what they did. We would mitigate the blame were we to discover that they had been coerced or manipulated into doing what they had done. But on the assumption that the killers have autonomously elected to proceed in their undertaking, then they are, at the very least, rightly subject to blame.

One is blameworthy for an action only if there is some reason to refrain from committing it. Because the killers are blameworthy for their deeds, there is a reason that opposes their actions. Since this reason does not depend on the ends that the killers happen to have, the reason is a categorical one. That they have violated or ignored it is the basis of their blameworthiness.

We have here the makings of a second argument for categorical reasons:

(1) If one is blameworthy for doing something, then there is a reason not to do it.

(2) Autonomous fanatics are blameworthy for their killings.

(3) Therefore there is a reason for these fanatics not to perpetrate such killings.

(4) Such a reason, by hypothesis, is neither the content of one of the fanatic's commitments, nor instrumental in securing or protecting one of his commitments.

(5) Therefore, such a reason applies to the fanatic independently of his commitments.

(6) Therefore, there is at least one categorical reason.

There are only three premises to the argument, and I think that they are each highly plausible. Premise (4) is a stipulation that comports with the relevant possibilities, and should be granted by all parties to the debate. It is easy to conjure situations in which perfect instrumentally rational deliberation, begun from a fanatic's existing commitments, would generate no consideration that opposed his deadly undertakings.

Premise (1) seems to me a conceptual truth. If no reasons oppose an action, then those who commit the action are not blameworthy for what they have done. Being deserving of blame entails that one has (at the least) ignored a relevant consideration that opposes the action that one has performed. If one has complied with all relevant and applicable reasons, then there is no room for criticism.

And if there is nothing criticizable about an agent's actions, then the person is not properly blameworthy for his behavior. So a person is blameworthy for an action only if there is some reason that stands against it. That is what the first premise says.

Now consider premise (2). It can be supported thus: if *any* agents are blameworthy for their actions, surely those who are bent on evil are among them. This is so whether the immoralists are doing evil for its own sake, or doing what is in fact evil, all the while characterizing their actions to themselves as ones that are aimed at a good. An autonomous, rational fanatic is the perfect exemplar of the blameworthy agent. His consistency is no proof against criticism. His intelligence and cunning, his ability to select appropriate means to his chosen ends, render him more, rather than less, liable to blame. The standard exculpation conditions do not apply here. The dedicated evildoers are not compelled to act as they do, but have chosen their path and have ruthlessly pursued it in the absence of compulsion, coercion, necessity or factual ignorance.

As far as I can tell, there are only three ways to try to falsify the second premise. The first asserts that fanatics are immune from blame, because their existing commitments will prevent them from seeing the reasons that oppose their misdeeds. If they cannot see these reasons, then they are not blameworthy for ignoring them. The second way to reject premise (2) is to deny the existence of autonomous fanatics. The third is to deny that anyone is blameworthy for anything.

The first criticism of premise (2) acknowledges that there can be autonomous fanatics. It acknowledges that some agents are blameworthy for their misdeeds. But it denies that autonomous fanatics are among them. According to this line of argument, such fanatics are blameless, because flawless reasoning on the basis of their existing commitments will not lead such agents to acknowledge the reasons that oppose their misdeeds. They cannot recognize the error of their ways, since (by hypothesis) none of their commitments will be served by refraining from their evil conduct. And if they cannot recognize their error, then they are free of blame for committing it.

Let us concede a point that is in fact debatable, namely, that deliberative rationality is a matter entirely of identifying means to one's endorsed ends. In that case, rational fanatics cannot recognize the existence of reasons to refrain from cruelty, since such reasons, by hypothesis, are not instrumental to their ends. But their inability to appreciate the existence or force of such reasons does not immunize them from blame, if they are blameworthy for having endorsed their ends in the first place.

To see this point, imagine a person who has promised another to meet him at a certain place and time, but then, through her culpable negligence, finds that it is impossible to fulfill the promise. This inability does not cancel her liability to blame. So, too, if the fanatic's prior culpable choices are rendering him unable to see the merits of refraining from his actions, then his inability to appreciate these considerations does not immunize him from blame.

The question thus devolves to one about whether the fanatic's initial choices to ally himself with evil ends are choices that he is blameworthy for. And why wouldn't they be? I am not imagining a person who has been brainwashed or neurologically manipulated, but someone who makes choices that are as unco-erced and as informed as those of anyone with more ordinary moral preferences. As far as I can see, the only reason to suspend blame here is because one is supposing that no one's choices are blameworthy. Such a view may be true. But so long as we are willing to blame anyone for the choices that he makes, then we should be prepared to blame the fanatic for his. And that means that his subsequent choices and actions, even if they are endorsed by his instrumentally rational deliberations, are ones for which he is blameworthy. That is just what premise (2) states.

A second criticism of premise (2) claims that autonomous fanatics are not blameworthy for their actions, because there can be no such thing as an autono-mous fanatic. This criticism, sometimes heard in Kantian corners, strikes me as highly implausible. If the claim is more than an instance of a wholesale denial of personal autonomy, then there must be some special reason that agents are unable to autonomously elect evil, though they are able to freely attach themselves to the good. But what could this special reason be? The evil, recall, need not be concep-tualized as such—the autonomous fanatic may tell himself that what he is doing is good, and be a dedicated evildoer nonetheless. And he may surely pursue what he really cares about in the absence of coercion, and in possession of relevantly full information. Certainly, absent clear and compelling argument, we are warranted in abiding by the general maxim that anything apparently conceivable is possible. It seems that we can conceive of the autonomous fanatic. Thus absent a very strong argument to the contrary, we are right to suppose that such fanatics can exist.

A last basis for rejecting premise (2) comes from the assertion that no one is blameworthy for anything. This might be true. If so, my second argument is unsound. I can't say anything here to falsify this potential criticism. All I can do is to express the conviction, shared by almost everyone, that at least some people are rightly blameworthy for their poor choices and actions. The examples used to substantiate this conviction seem to me more compelling than any of the prem-ises employed in arguments to defeat them.

Because my second argument rests in part on this undefended conviction, it is best to conceive of its conclusion conditionally: *if* anyone is blameworthy for any of her choices, then there are categorical reasons. We get to this conclusion by means of a conceptual truth (premise 1), an uncontroversial statement of possibilities (premise 4), and a highly plausible premise (2) that expresses a deeply commonsensical assessment of evildoing.

IV

The most powerful kind of philosophical criticism is one that reveals a contradiction in its target. I have not presented such a criticism of practical instrumentalism, because I do not believe that instrumentalism entails a contradiction. Nor must instrumentalists exemplify any kind of practical inconsistency in behavior or commitment. Most defenders of categorical reasons, following Kant, have tried to sustain such charges. Their vindication would be welcome news for friends of categorical reasons. But I am not optimistic about this most direct route to instrumentalism's refutation.

If a view is not internally contradictory, then any successful criticism of it must proceed by adducing nonconclusive but highly plausible reasons, cogently put together to make a strong, albeit defeasible, case. That is what I have tried to do here. Of course, what counts as a plausible reason is relative to antecedent beliefs and commitments. If one is already devoted to instrumentalism, then one will find the considerations I have offered less plausible than anyone else. But that does not distinguish the instrumentalist from (say) the skeptic about other minds. Such people can have internally consistent views, and will regard with great suspicion the supporting evidence introduced by their critics. Still, for those not antecedently wedded to this skepticism, the falsifying evidence can be compelling.

I think that the very same thing is true of practical instrumentalism. We cannot prove that there are categorical reasons. But when we vividly contemplate a world without them, one in which there is literally no consideration that stands against the actions of a torturer, and none in favor of easily rescuing a child from imminent death, most of us will find that instrumentalism has as much appeal as the various sorts of skepticism that we take seriously only in the study.

V

I have tried to show that practical instrumentalism is false. If I have succeeded, then we have excellent reason for thinking that the master argument for moral relativism is unsound. That argument sought to show that all moral requirements are contingent on personal commitments, by assuming that such require-ments entail excellent reasons for action, and combining that assumption with the instrumentalist claim that reasons for action depend for their existence on personal commitments.

There are forms of moral relativism that do not make moral requirements contingent upon personal commitments. And there are arguments, other than the master argument, for the sort of moral relativism that insists on this kind of contingency. So it's not as if we've managed to undermine moral relativism in one fell swoop; the moral realist is hardly able to rest easy at this stage. But it does seem that a great deal of the philosophical motivations underlying common forms of moral relativism can be traced to this master argument, or a variation thereof. To that extent, and to the extent that my criticisms of instrumentalism are on target, we have less reason than we might have thought to succumb to relativistic temptations.

NOTE

Many thanks to audiences at the University of Michigan, Edinburgh University, North-ern Illinois University, the University of Arkansas-Fayetteville, and Union College for their acute comments on earlier versions of this paper.

Relativism, Culture, and Understanding | **PART IV**

Anti Anti-Relativism | **24**

CLIFFORD GEERTZ

A scholar can hardly be better employed than in destroying a fear. The one I want to go after is cultural relativism. Not the thing itself, which I think merely there, like Transylvania, but the dread of it, which I think unfounded. It is unfounded because the moral and intellectual consequences that are commonly supposed to flow from relativism—subjectivism, nihilism, incoherence, Machiavellianism, ethical idiocy, esthetic blindness, and so on—do not in fact do so and the promised rewards of escaping its clutches, mostly having to do with pasteurized knowledge, are illusory.

To be more specific, I want not to defend relativism, which is a drained term anyway, yesterday's battle cry, but to attack anti-relativism, which seems to me broadly on the rise and to represent a streamlined version of an antique mistake. Whatever cultural relativism may be or originally have been (and there is not one of its critics in a hundred who has got that right), it serves these days largely as a specter to scare us away from certain ways of thinking and toward others. And, as the ways of thinking away from which we are being driven seem to me to be more cogent than those toward which we are being propelled, and to lie at the heart of the anthropological heritage, I would like to do something about this. Casting out demons is a praxis we should practice as well as study

My through-the-looking-glass title is intended to suggest such an effort to counter a view rather than to defend the view it claims to be counter to. The analogy I had in mind in choosing it—a logical one, I trust it will be understood, not in any way a substantive one—is what, at the height of the cold war days (you remember them) was called 'anti anti-communism.' Those of us who strenuously opposed the obsession, as we saw it, with the Red Menace were thus denominated by those who, as they saw it, regarded the Menace as the primary fact of contemporary political life, with the insinuation—wildly incorrect in the vast majority of cases—that, by the law of the double negative, we had some secret affection for the Soviet Union.

Again, I mean to use this analogy in a formal sense; I don't think relativists are like communists, anti-relativists are like anti-communists, and that anyone (well . . . hardly anyone) is behaving like McCarthy. One could construct a similar parallelism using the abortion controversy. Those of us who are opposed to increased legal restrictions on abortion are not, I take it, pro-abortion, in the sense that we think abortion a wonderful thing and hold that the greater the abortion rate the greater the well-being of society; we are 'anti anti-abortionists' for quite other reasons I need not rehearse. In this frame, the double negative simply doesn't work in the usual way; and therein lies its rhetorical attractions. It enables one to reject something without thereby committing oneself to what it rejects. And this is precisely what I want to do with anti-relativism.

So lumbering an approach to the matter, explaining and excusing itself as it goes, is necessary because, as the philosopher-anthropologist John Ladd has remarked, "all the common definitions of . . . relativism are framed by opponents of relativism . . . they are absolutist definitions."[1] (Ladd, whose immediate focus is Edward Westermarck's famous book, is speaking of 'ethical relativism' in particular, but the point is general: for 'cognitive relativism,' think of Israel Schemer's attack on Thomas Kuhn, for 'aesthetic relativism,'[2] Wayne Booth's on Stanley Fish.)[3] And, as Ladd also says, the result of this is that relativism, or anything that at all looks like relativism under such hostile definitions, is identified with nihilism.[4] To suggest that 'hard rock' foundations for cognitive, esthetic, or moral judgments may not, in fact, be available, or anyway that those one is being offered are dubious, is to find oneself accused of disbelieving in the existence of the physical world, thinking pushpin as good as poetry, regarding Hitler as just a fellow with unstandard tastes, or even, as I myself have recently been—God save the mark—"[having] no politics at all."[5] The notion that someone who does not hold your views holds the reciprocal of them, or simply hasn't got any, has, whatever its comforts for those afraid reality is going to go away unless we believe very hard in it, not conduced to much in the way of clarity in the anti-relativist discussion, but merely far too many people spending far too much time describing at length what it is they do *not* maintain than seems in any way profitable.

All this is of relevance to anthropology because, of course, it is by way of the idea of relativism, grandly ill-defined, that it has most disturbed the general intellectual peace. From our earliest days, even when theory in anthropology—evolutionary, diffusionist, or *elementargedankenisch*—was anything but relativistic, the message that we have been thought to have for the wider world has been that, as they see things differently and do them otherwise in Alaska or the D'Entrecasteaux, our confidence in our own seeings and doings and our resolve to bring others around to sharing them are rather poorly based. This point, too, is commonly ill-understood. It has not been anthropological theory, such as it is, that has made our field seem to be a massive argument against absolutism in thought, morals, and esthetic judgment; it has been anthropological data: customs, crania, living floors, and lexicons. The notion that it was Boas, Benedict, and Melville J. Herskovits, with a European assist from Westermarck, who infected our field with the relativist virus, and Kroeber, Kluckhohn, and Redfield, with a similar assist from Lévi-Strauss, who have labored to rid us of it, is but another of the myths that bedevil this whole discussion. After all, Montaigne could draw relativistic, or relativistic-looking, conclusions from the fact, as he heard it, that the Caribs didn't wear breeches;[6] he did not have to read *Patterns of Culture*.[7] Even earlier on, Herodotus, contemplating "certain Indians of the race called Callatians," among whom men were said to eat their fathers, came, as one would think he might, to similar views.[8]

The relativist bent, or more accurately the relativist bent anthropology, so often induces in those who have much traffic with its materials, is thus in some sense implicit in the field as such; in cultural anthropology perhaps particularly, but in much of archeology, anthropological linguistics, and physical anthropology as well. One cannot read too long about Nayar matriliny, Aztec sacrifice, the Hopi verb, or the convolutions of the hominid transition and not begin at least to consider the possibility that, to quote Montaigne again, "each man calls barbarism whatever is not his own practice . . . for we have no other criterion of reason than the example and idea of the opinions and customs of the country we live in."[9] That notion, whatever its problems, and however more delicately expressed, is not likely to go entirely away unless anthropology does.

It is to this fact, progressively discovered to be one as our enterprise has advanced and our findings grown more circumstantial, that both relativists and anti-relativists have, according to their sensibilities, reacted. The realization that news from elsewhere about ghost marriage, ritual destruction of property, initiatory fellatio, royal immolation, and (Dare I say it? Will he strike again?) nonchalant adolescent sex, naturally inclines the mind to an "other beasts other mores" view of things has led to arguments, outraged, desperate, and exultant by turns, designed to persuade us either to resist that inclination in the name of reason, or to embrace it on the same grounds. What looks like a debate about the broader implications of anthropological research is really a debate about how to live with them.

Once this fact is grasped, and 'relativism' and 'anti-relativism' are seen as general responses to the way in which what Kroeber once called the centrifugal impulse of anthropology—distant places, distant times, distant species . . . distant grammars—affects our sense of things, the whole discussion comes rather better into focus. The supposed conflict between Benedict's and Herskovits's call for tolerance and the intolerant passion with which they called for it turns out not to be the simple contradiction so many amateur logicians have held it to be, but the expression of a perception, caused by thinking a lot about Zunis and Dahomeys, that, the world being so full of a number of things, rushing to judgment is more than a mistake, it's a crime. Similarly, Kroeber's and Kluckhohn's pan-cultural verities—Kroeber's were mostly about messy creatural matters like delirium and menstruation, Kluckhohn's about messy social ones like lying and killing within the in-group—turn out not to be just the arbitrary, personal obsessions they so much look like, but the expression of a much vaster concern, caused by thinking a lot about *anthropos* in general, that if something isn't anchored everywhere nothing can be anchored anywhere. Theory here—if that is what these earnest advices as to how we must look at things if we are to be accounted decent should be called—is rather more an exchange of warnings than an analytical debate. We are being offered a choice of worries.

What the relativists, so-called, want us to worry about, is provincialism—the danger that our perceptions will be dulled, our intellects constricted, and our sympathies narrowed by the over-learned and overvalued acceptances of our own society. What the anti-relativists, self-declared, want us to worry about, and worry about and worry about, as though our very souls depended upon it, is a kind of spiritual entropy, a heat death of the mind, in which everything is as significant, thus as insignificant, as everything else: anything goes, to each his own, you pays your money and you takes your choice, I know what I like, not in the south, *tout comprendre, c'est tout pardonner.*

As I have already suggested, I myself find provincialism altogether the more real concern so far as what actually goes on in the world. (Though even there, the thing can be overdone: "You might as well fall flat on your face," one of Thurber's marvelous 'morals' goes, "as lean too far over backward.") The image of vast numbers of anthropology readers running around in so cosmopolitan a frame of mind as to have no views as to what is and isn't true, or good, or beautiful, seems to me largely a fantasy. There may be some genuine nihilists out there, along Rodeo Drive or around Times Square, but I doubt very many have become such as a result of an excessive sensitivity to the claims of other cultures; and at least most of the people I meet, read, and read about, and indeed I myself, are all too committed to something or other, usually parochial. "'Tis the eye of childhood that fears a painted devil": anti-relativism has largely concocted the anxiety it lives from.

II

But surely I exaggerate? Surely anti-relativists, secure in the knowledge that rattling gourds cannot cause thunder, and that eating people is wrong, cannot be so excitable? Listen, then, to William Gass, novelist, philosopher, *precieux*, and pop-eyed observer of anthropologists' ways:

Anthropologists or not, we all used to call them 'natives'—those little, distant, jungle and island people—and we came to recognize the unscientific snobbery in that. Even our more respectable journals could show them naked without offense, because their pendulous or pointed breasts were as inhuman to us as the udder of a cow. Shortly we came to our senses and had them dress. We grew to distrust our own point of view, our local certainties, and embraced relativism, although it is one of the scabbier whores; and we went on to endorse a nice equality among cultures, each of which was carrying out its task of coalescing, conversing, and structuring some society. A large sense of superiority was one of the white man's burdens, and that weight, released, was replaced by an equally heavy sense of guilt.

No more than we might expect a surgeon to say "Dead and good riddance" would an anthropologist exclaim, stepping from the culture just surveyed as one might shed a set of working clothes, "What a lousy way to live!" Because, even if the natives were impoverished, covered with dust and sores; even if they had been trodden on by stronger feet till they were flat as a path; even if they were rapidly dying off; still, the observer could remark how frequently they smiled, or how infrequently their children fought, or how serene they were. We can envy the Zuni their peaceful ways and the Navaho their 'happy heart.'

It was amazing how mollified we were to find that there was some functional point to food taboos, infibulation, or clitoridectomy; and if we still felt morally squeamish about human sacrifice or headhunting, it is clear we were still squeezed into a narrow modern European point of view, and had no sympathy, and didn't—couldn't—understand. Yet when we encountered certain adolescents among indolent summery seaside tribes who were allowed to screw without taboo, we wondered whether this enabled them to avoid the stresses of our own youth, and we secretly hoped it hadn't.

Some anthropologists have untied the moral point of view, so sacred to Eliot and Arnold and Emerson, from every mooring (science and art also float away on the stream of Becoming), calling any belief in objective knowledge 'fundamentalism,' as if it were the same as benighted Biblical literalism; and arguing for the total mutability of man and the complete sociology of what under such circumstances could no longer be considered knowledge but only *doxa* or 'opinion.'[10]

This overheated vision of 'the anthropological point of view,' rising out of the mists of caricatured arguments ill-grasped to start with (it is one of Gass's ideas that Mary Douglas is some sort of skeptic, and Benedict's satire, cannier than his, has escaped him altogether), leaves us with a fair lot to answer for. But even from within the profession, the charges, though less originally expressed, as befits a proper science, are hardly less grave. Relativism (the position that all assessments are assessments relative to some standard or other, and standards derive from cultures), I. C. Jarvie remarks:

has these objectionable consequences: namely, that by limiting critical assessment of human works it disarms us, dehumanizes us, leaves us unable to enter into communicative interaction: that is to say, unable to criticize cross-culturally, cross-subculturally: ultimately, relativism leaves no room for criticism at all ... Behind relativism nihilism looms.[11]

More in front, scarecrow and leper's bell, it sounds like, than behind: certainly none of us, clothed and in our right minds, will rush to embrace a view that so dehumanizes us as to render us incapable of communicating with anybody. The heights to which this 'beware of the scabby whore who will cut off your critical powers' sort of thing can aspire is indicated, to give one last example, by Paul Johnson's ferocious new book on the history of the world since 1917, *Modern Times*, which, opening with a chapter called "A Relativistic World"[12] (Hugh Thomas's review of the book in the *TLS* was more aptly entitled, "The Inferno of Relativism"),[13] accounts for the whole modern disaster—Lenin and Hitler, Amin,

do not involve other people as victims; for instance, extreme narcissism, suicide, obsessiveness, incest, and exclusive mutual admiration societies. "It is an unnatural life" we say, meaning that its center has been misplaced. Further examples, which do involve victimizing others, are redirected aggression, the shunning of cripples, ingratitude, vindictiveness, parricide. All these things are *natural* in that there are well-known impulses toward them, which are parts of human nature. . . . But redirected aggression and so on can properly be called *unnatural* when we think of nature in the fuller sense, not just as an assembly of parts, but as an organized whole. They are parts, which will ruin the shape of that whole if they are allowed in any sense to take it over.[21]

Aside from the fact that it legitimates one of the more popular sophisms of intellectual debate nowadays, asserting the strong form of an argument and defending the weak one (sadism is natural as long as you don't bite too deep), this little game of concept juggling (natural may be unnatural when we think of nature 'in the fuller sense') displays the basic thesis of all such Human Nature arguments. Virtue (cognitive, esthetic, and moral alike) is to vice as fitness is to disorder, normality to abnormality, well-being to sickness. The task for man, as for his lungs or his thyroid, is to function properly. Shunning cripples can be dangerous to your health.

Or as Stephen Salkever, a political scientist and follower of Midgeley's, puts it:

Perhaps the best developed model or analogue for an adequate functionalist social science is that provided by medicine. For the physician, physical features of an individual organism become intelligible in the light of a basic conception of the problems confronting this self-directed physical system and in the light of a general sense of healthy or well-functioning state of the organism relative to those problems. To understand a patient is to understand him or her as being more or less healthy relative to some stable and objective standard of physical well-being, the kind of standard the Greeks called *arete*. This word is now ordinarily translated 'virtue,' but in the political philosophy of Plato and Aristotle it refers simply to the characteristic or definitive excellence of the subject of any functional analysis.[22]

Again, one can look almost anywhere within anthropology these days and find an example of the revival of this 'it all comes down to' (genes, species being, cerebral architecture, psychosexual constitution) cast of mind. Shake almost any tree and a selfish altruist or a biogenetic structuralist is likely to fall out.

But it is better, I think, or at least less disingenuous, to have for an instance neither a sitting duck nor a self-destructing artifact. And so let me examine, very briefly, the views, most especially the recent views, of one of our most experienced ethnographers and influential theorists, as well as one of our most formidable polemicists: Melford Spiro. Purer cases, less shaded and less circumspect, and thus all the better to appall you with, could be found. But in Spiro we are at least not dealing with some marginal phenomenon—a Morris or an Ardrey—easily dismissed as an enthusiast or a popularizer, but with a major figure at, or very near, the center of the discipline.

Spiro's more important recent forays into 'down deep' in the *Homo* anthropology—his rediscovery of the Freudian family romance, first in his own material on the kibbutz and then in Malinowski's on the Trobriands—are well known and will be, I dare say, as convincing or unconvincing to their readers as psychoanalytic theory of a rather orthodox sort is in general. But my concern is, again, less with that than with the Here Comes Everyman anti-relativism he develops on the basis of it. And to get a sense for that, a recent article of his summarizing his advance from past confusions to present clarities will serve quite well. Called "Culture and Human Nature," it catches a mood and a drift of attitude much more widely spread than its rather beleaguered, no longer avant-garde theoretical perspective.[23]

Spiro's paper is, as I mentioned, again cast in the "when a child I spake as a child but now that I am grown I have put away childish things" genre so prominent in the anti-relativist literature generally. (Indeed, it might better have been titled, as another southern California–based anthropologist—apparently relativism seems a clear and present danger out that way—called the record of his deliverance, "Confessions of a Former Cultural Relativist.")[24]

Spiro begins his apologia with the admission that when he came into anthropology in the early 1940s, he was preadapted by a Marxist background and too many courses in British philosophy to a radically environmentalist view of man, one that assumed a tabula rasa view of mind, a social determinist view of behavior, and a cultural relativist view of, well … culture, and then traces his field trip history as a didactic, parable for our times, narrative of how he came not just to abandon these ideas but to replace them by their opposites. In Ifaluk, he discovered that a people who showed very little social aggression could yet be plagued by hostile feelings. In Israel, he discovered that children "raised in [the] totally communal and cooperative system" of the kibbutz and socialized to be mild, loving and noncompetitive, nevertheless resented attempts to get them to share goods and when obliged to do so grew resistant and hostile. And in Burma, he discovered that a belief in the impermanence of sentient existence, Buddhist nirvana and nonattachment, did not result in a diminished interest in the immediate materialities of daily life:

In short, [my field studies] convinced me that many motivational dispositions are culturally invariant [and] many cognitive orientations [are so] as well. These invariant dispositions and orientations stem ... from panhuman biological and cultural constants, and they comprise that universal human nature which, together with received anthropological opinion, I had formerly rejected as yet another ethnocentric bias.[25]

Whether or not a portrait of peoples from Micronesia to the Middle East as angry moralizers deviously pursuing hedonic interests will altogether still the suspicion that some ethnocentric bias yet clings to Spiro's view of universal human nature remains to be seen. What doesn't remain to be seen, because he is quite explicit about them, are the kinds of ideas, noxious products of a noxious relativism, such a recourse to medical functionalism is designed to cure us of:

[The] concept of cultural relativism ... was enlisted to do battle against racist notions in general, and the notion of primitive mentality, in particular.... [But] cultural relativism was also used, at least by some anthropologists, to perpetuate a kind of inverted racism. That is, it was used as a powerful tool of cultural criticism, with the consequent derogation of Western culture and of the mentality which it produced. Espousing the philosophy of primitivism ... the image of primitive man was used ... as a vehicle for the pursuit of personal utopian quests, and/or as a fulcrum to express personal discontent with Western man and Western society. The strategies adopted took various forms, of which the following are fairly representative. (1) Attempts to abolish private property, or inequality, or aggression in Western societies have a reasonably realistic chance of success since such states of affairs may be found in many primitive societies. (2) Compared to at least some primitives, Western man is uniquely competitive, warlike, intolerant of deviance, sexist, and so on. (3) Paranoia is not necessarily an illness, because paranoid thinking is institutionalized in certain primitive societies; homosexuality is not deviant because homosexuals are the cultural cynosures of some primitive societies; monogamy is not viable because polygamy is the most frequent form of marriage in primitive societies. (336)

Aside from adding a few more items to the list, which promises to be infinite, of unoptional abominations, it is the introduction of the idea of 'deviance,' conceived as a departure from an inbuilt norm, like an arrhythmic heartbeat, not as a statistical oddity, like fraternal polyandry, that is the really critical move amid all this huffing and puffing about 'inverted racism,' 'utopian quests,' and 'the philosophy of primitivism.' For it is through that idea, The Lawgiver's Friend, that Midgeley's transition between the natural natural (aggression, inequality) and the unnatural natural (paranoia, homosexuality) gets made. Once that camel's nose has been pushed inside, the tent—indeed, the whole riotous circus crying all its booths—is in serious trouble.

Just how much trouble can perhaps be more clearly seen from Robert Edgerton's companion piece to Spiro's in the same volume, "The Study of Deviance, Marginal Man or Everyman?"[26] After a useful, rather eclectic, review of the study of deviance in anthropology, psychology, and sociology, including again his own quite interesting work with American retardates and African intersexuals, Edgerton too comes, rather suddenly as a matter of fact—a cartoon light bulb going on—to the conclusion that what is needed to make such research genuinely productive is a context-independent conception of human nature—one in which "genetically encoded potentials for behavior that we all share" are seen to "underlie (our universal) propensity for deviance." Man's 'instinct' for self-preservation, his flight/fight mechanism, and his intolerance of boredom are instanced; and, in an argument I, in my innocence, had thought gone from anthropology, along with euhemerism and primitive promiscuity, it is suggested that, if all goes well on the science side, we may, in time, be able to judge not just individuals but entire societies as deviant, inadequate, failed, unnatural:

> More important still is our inability to test any proposition about the relative adequacy of a society. Our relativistic tradition in anthropology has been slow to yield to the idea that there could be such a thing as a deviant society, one that is contrary to human nature. . . . Yet the idea of a deviant society is central to the alienation tradition in sociology and other fields and it poses a challenge for anthropological theory. Because we know so little about human nature . . . we cannot say whether, much less how, any society has failed. . . . Nevertheless, a glance at any urban newspaper's stories of rising rates of homicide, suicide, rape and other violent crimes should suffice to suggest that the question is relevant not only for theory, but for questions of survival in the modern world. (470)

With this the circle closes; the door slams. The fear of relativism, raised at every turn like some mesmeric obsession, has led to a position in which cultural diversity, across space and over time, amounts to a series of expressions, some salubrious, some not, of a settled, underlying reality, the essential nature of man, and anthropology amounts to an attempt to see through the haze of those expressions to the substance of that reality. A sweeping, schematic, and content-hungry concept, conformable to just about any shape that comes along, Wilsonian, Lorenzian, Freudian, Marxian, Benthamite, Aristotelian ("one of the central features of Human Nature," some anonymous genius is supposed to have remarked, "is a separate judiciary"), becomes the ground upon which the understanding of human conduct, homicide, suicide, rape . . . the derogation of Western culture, comes definitively to rest. Some gods from some machines cost, perhaps, rather more than they come to.

IV

About that other conjuration The Human Mind, held up as a protective cross against the relativist Dracula, I can be somewhat more succinct: for the general pattern, if not the substantial detail, is very much the same. There is the same effort to promote a privileged language of 'real' explanation ('nature's own vocabulary,' as Richard Rorty, attacking the notion as scientist fantasy, has put it);[27] and the same wild dessensus as to just which language—Shannon's? Saussure's? Piaget's?—that in fact is. There is the same tendency to see diversity as surface and universality as depth. And there is the same desire to represent one's interpretations not as constructions brought to their objects—societies, cultures, languages—in an effort, somehow, somewhat to comprehend them, but as quiddities of such objects forced upon our thought.

There are, of course, differences as well. The return of Human Nature as a regulative idea has been mainly stimulated by advances in genetics and evolutionary theory, that of The Human Mind by ones in linguistics, computer science, and cognitive psychology. The inclination of the former is to see moral relativism as the source of all our ills; that of the latter is to pin the blame on conceptual relativism. And a partiality for the tropes and images of therapeutic discourse (health and illness, normal and abnormal, function and dysfunction) on the one side is matched by a penchant for those of epistemological discourse (knowledge and opinion, fact and illusion, truth and falsity) on the other. But they hardly count, these differences, against the common impulse to final analysis, we have now arrived at Science, explanation. Wiring your theories into something called The Structure of Reason is as effective a way to insulate them from history and culture as building them into something called The Constitution of Man.

So far as anthropology as such is concerned, however, there is another difference, more or less growing out of these, which, while also (you should excuse the expression) more relative than radical, does act to drive the two sorts of discussions in somewhat divergent, even contrary, directions, namely, that where the Human Nature tack leads to bringing back one of our classical conceptions into the center of our attention—'social deviance'—the Human Mind tack leads to bringing back another—'primitive (*sauvage*, primary, preliterate) thought.'

The anti-relativist anxieties that gather in the one discourse around the enigmas of conduct gather in the other around those of belief.

More exactly, they gather around 'irrational' (or 'mystical,' 'prelogical,' 'affective' or, particularly nowadays, 'noncognitive') beliefs. Where it has been such unnerving practices as headhunting, slavery, caste, and foot binding, which have sent anthropologists rallying to the grand old banner of Human Nature under the impression that only thus could taking a moral distance from them be justified, it has been such unlikely conceptions. as witchcraft substance, animal tutelaries, god kings, and (to foreshadow an example I will be getting to in a moment) a dragon with a golden heart and a horn at the nape of its neck which have sent them rallying to that of The Human Mind under the impression that only thus could adopting an empirical skepticism with respect to them be defended. It is not so much how the other half behaves that is so disquieting, but—what is really rather worse—how it thinks.

There are, again, a fairly large number of such rationalist or neorationalist perspectives in anthropology of varying degrees of purity, cogency, coherence, and popularity, not wholly consonant one with another. Some invoke formal constancies, usually called cognitive universals; some, developmental constancies, usually called cognitive stages; some, operational constancies, usually called cognitive processes. Some are structuralist, some are Jungian, some are Piagetian, some look to the latest news from MIT, Bell Labs, or Carnegie-Mellon. All are after something steadfast: Reality reached, Reason saved from drowning.

What they share, thus, is not merely an interest in our mental functioning. Like an interest in our biological makeup, that is uncontroversially A Good Thing, both in itself and for the analysis of culture; and if not all the supposed discoveries in what is coming to be called, in an aspiring sort of way, 'cognitive science' turn out in the event genuinely to be such, some doubtless will, and will alter significantly not only how we think about how we think but how we think about what we think. What, beyond that, they share, from Lévi-Strauss to Rodney Needham, something of a distance, and what is not so uncontroversially beneficent, is a foundationalist view of Mind. That is, a view which sees it—like 'The Means of Production' or 'Social Structure' or 'Exchange' or 'Energy' or 'Culture' or 'Symbol' in other, bottom-line, the-buck-stops-here approaches to social theory (and of course like Human Nature)—as the sovereign term of explanation, the light that shines in the relativist darkness.

That it is the fear of relativism, the anti-hero with a thousand faces, that provides a good part of the impetus to neo-rationalism, as it does to neo-naturalism, and serves as its major justification, can be conveniently seen from the excellent new collection of anti-relativist exhortations—plus one unbuttoned relativist piece marvelously designed to drive the others to the required level of outrage—edited by Martin Hollis and Steven Lukes, *Rationality and Relativism*.[28] A product of the so-called rationality debate that Evans-Pritchard's chicken stories,[29] among other things, seem to have induced into British social science and a fair part of British philosophy ("Are there absolute truths that can be gradually approached over time through rational processes? Or are all modes and systems of thought equally valid if viewed from within their own internally consistent frames of reference?"),[30] the book more or less covers the Reason in Danger! waterfront. "The temptations of relativism are perennial and pervasive," the editors' introduction opens, like some Cromwellian call to the barricades: "[The] primrose path to relativism ... is paved with plausible contentions."[31]

The three anthropologists in the collection all respond with enthusiasm to this summons to save us from ourselves. Ernest Gellner argues that the fact that other people do not believe what we, The Children of Galileo, believe about how reality is put together is no argument against the fact that what we believe is not the correct, 'One True Vision.'[32] And especially as others, even Himalayans, seem to him to be coming around, he thinks it almost certain that it is. Robin Horton argues for a 'cognitive common core,' a culturally universal, only trivially variant, 'primary theory' of the world as filled with middle-sized, enduring objects, interrelated in terms of a 'push-pull' concept of causality, five spatial dichotomies (left/right, above/below, etc.), a temporal trichotomy (before/at the same time/after) and two categorical distinctions (human/nonhuman, self/other), the existence of which insures that "Relativism is bound to fail whilst Universalism may, some day, succeed."[33]

But it is Dan Sperber, surer of his rationalist ground (Jerry Fodor's computational view of mental representations) than either of these, and with a One True Vision of his own ("there is no such thing as a non-literal fact"), who develops the most vigorous attack.[34] Relativism, though marvelously mischievous (it makes "ethnography ... inexplicable, and psychology immensely difficult"), is not even an indefensible position, it really doesn't qualify as a position at all. Its ideas are semi-ideas, its beliefs semi-beliefs, its propositions semi-propositions. Like the gold-hearted dragon, with the horn at the base of his neck, that one of his elderly Dorze informants innocently, or perhaps not quite so innocently, invited him to track down and kill (wary of nonliteral facts, he declined), such 'relativist slogans' as "peoples of different cultures live in different worlds" are not, in fact, factual beliefs. They are half-formed and indeterminate representations, mental stopgaps, that result when, less circumspect than computers, we try to process more information than our inherent conceptual capacities permit. Useful, sometimes, as place holders until we can get our cognitive powers up to speed, occasionally fun to toy with while we are waiting, even once in a while "sources of suggestion in [genuine] creative thinking," they are not, these academic dragons with plastic hearts and no horn at all, matters even their champions take as true, for they do not really understand, nor can they, what they mean. They are hand-wavings—more elaborate or less—of a, in the end, conformist, false-profound, misleading, 'hermeneutico-psychedelic,' self-serving sort:

> The best evidence against relativism is . . . the very activity of anthropologists, while the best evidence for relativism [is] in the writings of anthropologists. . . . In retracing their steps [in their works], anthropologists transform into unfathomable gaps the shallow and irregular cultural boundaries they had not found so difficult to cross [in the field], thereby protecting their own sense of identity, and providing their philosophical and lay audience with just what they want to hear. (180)

In short, whether in the form of hearty common sense (never mind about liver gazing and poison oracles, we have after all got things more or less right), wistful ecumenicalism (despite the variations in more developed explanatory schemes, juju or genetics, at base everyone has more or less the same conception of what the world is like), or aggressive scientism (there are things which are really ideas, such as 'propositional attitudes' and 'representational beliefs,' and there are things that only look like ideas, such as "there's a dragon down the road" and "peoples of different cultures live in different worlds"), the resurrection of The Human Mind as the still point of the turning world defuses the threat of cultural relativism by disarming the force of cultural diversity. As with Human Nature, the deconstruction of otherness is the price of truth. Perhaps, but it is not what either the history of anthropology, the materials it has assembled, or the ideals that have animated it would suggest; nor is it only relativists who tell their audiences what they would like to hear. There are some dragons—'tigers in red weather'—that deserve to be looked into.

V

Looking into dragons, not domesticating or abominating them, nor drowning them in vats of theory, is what anthropology has been all about. At least, that is what it has been all about, as I, no nihilist, no subjectivist, and possessed, as you can see, of some strong views as to what is real and what is not, what is commendable and what is not, what is reasonable and what is not, understand it. We have, with no little success, sought to keep the world off balance; pulling out rugs, upsetting tea tables, setting off firecrackers. It has been the office of others to reassure; ours to unsettle. Australopithecines, Tricksters, Clicks, Megaliths—we hawk the anomalous, peddle the strange, Merchants of astonishment.

We have, no doubt, on occasion, moved too far in this direction and transformed idiosyncrasies into puzzles, puzzles into mysteries, and mysteries into humbug. But such an affection, for what doesn't fit and won't comport, reality out of place, has connected us to the leading theme of the cultural history of 'Modern Times.' For that history has indeed consisted of one field of thought after another having to discover how to live on without the certainties that launched it. Brute fact, natural law, necessary truth, transcendent beauty, immanent authority, unique revelation, even the in-here self facing the out-there world have all come under such heavy attack as to seem by now lost simplicities of a less strenuous past. But science, law, philosophy, art, political theory, religion, and the stubborn insistences of common sense have contrived nonetheless to continue. It has not proved necessary to revive the simplicities.

It is, so I think, precisely the determination not to cling to what once worked well enough and got us to where we are and now doesn't quite work well enough and gets us into recurrent stalemates that makes a science move. As long as there was nothing around much faster than a marathon runner, Aristotle's physics worked well enough, Stoic paradoxes notwithstanding. So long as technical instrumentation could get us but a short way down and a certain way out from our sense-delivered world, Newton's mechanics worked well enough, action-at-a-distance perplexities notwithstanding. It was not relativism—Sex, The Dialectic and The Death of God—that did in absolute motion, Euclidean space, and universal causation. It was wayward phenomena, wave packets and orbital leaps, before which they were helpless. Nor was it Relativism—Hermeneutico-Psychedelic Subjectivism—that did in (to the degree they *have* been done in) the Cartesian *cogito*, the Whig view of history, and "the moral point of view so sacred to Eliot and Arnold and Emerson." It was odd actualities—infant betrothals and nonillusionist paintings—that embarrassed their categories.

In this move away from old triumphs become complacencies, one-time breakthroughs transformed to roadblocks, anthropology has played, in our day, a vanguard role. We have been the first to insist on a number of things: that the world does not divide into the pious and the superstitious; that there are sculptures in jungles and paintings in deserts; that political order is possible without centralized power and principled justice without codified rules; that the norms of reason were not fixed in Greece, the evolution of morality not consummated in England. Most important, we were the first to insist that we see the lives of others through lenses of our own grinding and that they look back on ours through ones of their own. That this led some to think the sky was falling, solipsism was upon us, and intellect, judgment, even the sheer possibility of communication had all fled is not surprising. The repositioning of horizons and the decentering of perspectives has had that effect before. The Bellarmines you have always with you; and as someone has remarked of the Polynesians, it takes a certain kind of mind to sail out of the sight of land in an outrigger canoe.

But that is, at least at our best and to the degree that we have been able, what we have been doing. And it would be, I think, a large pity if, now that the distances we have established and the elsewheres we have located are beginning to bite, to change our sense of sense and our perception of perception we should turn back to old songs and older stories in the hope that somehow only the superficial need alter and that we shan't fall off the edge of the world. The objection to anti-relativism is not that it rejects an it's-all-how-you-look-at-it approach to knowledge or a when-in-Rome approach to morality, but that it imagines that they can only be defeated by placing morality beyond culture and knowledge beyond both. This, speaking of things, which must need be so, is no longer possible. If we wanted home truths, we should have stayed at home.

NOTES

1. Jon Ladd, "The Poverty of Absolutism," in *Edward Westermarck: Essays on His Life and Works*, ed. Timothy Stroup (Helsinki: Societas Philosophica Fennica, 1982), 158–180.

2. I. Schemer, *Science and Subjectivity* (Indianapolis: Bobbs-Merrill, 1967).

3. W. Booth, "A New Strategy for Establishing a Truly Democratic Criticism," *Daedalus* 112 (1983):193–214.

4. Ladd, "Poverty of Absolutism," 158.

5. P. Rabinow, "Humanism as Nihilism: The Bracketing of Truth and Seriousness in American Cultural Anthropology," in *Social Science as Moral Inquiry*, ed. N. Haan, R. M. Bellah, P. Rabinow, and W. M. Sullivan (New York: Columbia University Press, 1983), 70.

6. P. Villey, ed., *Les Essais de Michel de Montaigne* (Paris: Universitaires de France, 1978), 202–214.

7. Ruth Benedict, *Patterns of Culture* (New York: Houghton Mifflin, 1934).

8. Herodotus, *History of Herodotus*, bk. 3, ed. George Rawlinson, Henry Crewicke, et al. (New York: Appleton, 1859–1861), chap. 38.

9. Villey, *Essais de Michel de Montaigne*, 205, cited in T. Todorov, "Montaigne, Essays in Reading," in *Yale French Studies*, ed. Gerard Defaux (New Haven, Conn.: Yale Univer-

sity Press, 1983), 64:44. See Todorov for a general discussion of Montaigne's relativism from a position similar to mine.

10. W. Gass, "Culture, Self, and Style," *Syracuse Scholar* 2 (1981): 54–68, esp. 53–54.

11. I. C. Jarvie, "Rationalism and Relativism," *British Journal of Sociology* 34 (1983): 44–60, esp. 46.

12. P. Johnson, *Modern Times: The World from the Twenties to the Eighties* (New York: Harper & Row, 1983).

13. H. Thomas, "The Inferno of Relativism," *Times Literary Supplement*, July 8, 1983, 718.

14. Johnson, *Modern Times*, 48.

15. G. W. Stocking Jr., "Afterword: A View from the Center," *Ethnos* 47 (1982): 172–186, 176.

16. L. Tiger and J. Sepher, *Women in the Kibbutz.* (New York: Harcourt Brace Jovanovich Harvest, 1975), 16.

17. W. Empson, *Collected Poems* (New York: Harcourt, Brace & World, 1955), cited to opposite purposes in C. Kluckhohn, "Education, Values and Anthropological Relativity," in *Culture and Behavior*, ed. Clyde Kluckhohn (New York: Free Press, 1962), 292–293.

18. For materialism, see M. Harris, *The Rise of Anthropological Theory* (New York: Crowell, 1968); for 'science' and 'The Big Ditch,' see E. Gellner, *Spectacles and Predicaments* (Cambridge: Cambridge University Press, 1979); for 'literacy,' see J. Goody, *The Domestication of the Savage Mind* (Cambridge: Cambridge University Press, 1977); for 'inter-theoretic competition,' see R. Horton, "Tradition and Modernity Revisited," in *Rationality and Relativism*, ed. M. Hollis and S. Lukes (Cambridge, Mass.: MIT Press, 1982), 201–260; for 'the Cartesian conception of knowledge,' see ibid.; cf. B. Williams, *Descartes: The Project of Pure Enquiry* (Harmondsworth: Penguin, 1978); for Popper, from whom all these blessings flow, see *Conjectures and Refutations: The Growth of Scientific Knowledge* (London: Routledge and Kegan Paul, 1963), and *Objective Knowledge: An Evolutionary Approach* (Oxford: Clarendon Press, 1972).

19. I. Lakatos, *The Methodology of Scientific Research* (Cambridge: Cambridge University Press, 1976).

20. M. Midgeley, *Beast and Man: The Roots of Human Nature* (Ithaca, N.Y.: Cornell University Press, 1978), xiv–xv; emphasis in original.

21. Ibid., 79–80. The 'monotony' example occurs in a footnote ("Monotony is itself an abnormal extreme").

22. S. Salkever, "Beyond Interpretation: Human Agency and the Slovenly Wilderness," in Haan et al., *Social Science as Moral Inquiry*, 195–217, esp. 210.

23. M. Spiro, "Culture and Human Nature," in *The Making of Psychological Anthropology*, ed. G. Spindler (Berkeley: University of California Press, 1978), 330–360.

24. H. Baggish, "Confessions of a Former Cultural Relativist," in *Anthropology*, ed. E. Angeloni (Guilford, Conn.: Dushkin, 1983–1984). For another troubled discourse on 'the relativism problem' from that part of the world ("I set out what I think a reasonable point of view to fill the partial void left by ethical relativism, which by the 1980s, seems more often to be repudiated than upheld"), see E. Hatch, *Culture and Morality: The Relativity of Values in Anthropology* (New York: Columbia University Press, 1983), 12.

25. Spiro, "Culture and Human Nature," 349–350.

26. R. Edgerton, "The Study of Deviance, Marginal Man or Everyman," in Spindler, *Making of Psychological Anthropology*, 444–471.

27. Richard Rorty, "Method and Morality," in Haan et al., *Social Science as Moral Inquiry*; cf. Rorty, *Philosophy and the Mirror of Nature* (Princeton, N.J.: Princeton University Press, 1979).

28. S. Lukes, "Relativism in Its Place," in Hollis and Lukes, *Rationality and Relativism*, 261–305. There are also some more moderate, split-the-difference pieces by Ian Hacking, Charles Taylor, and Lukes, but only the first of these seems genuinely free of cooked-up alarms.

29. B. Wilson, *Rationality* (Oxford: Blackwell, 1970); F. A. Hanson, "*Anthropoiogie und die Rationalitätsdebatte*," in *Der Wissenschaftler und das Irrationale*, vol. 1, ed. H. P. Duerr (Frankfurt am Main: Syndikat, 1981).

30. The parenthetical quotations are from the book jacket, which, for once, reflects the contents.

31. M. Hollis and S. Lukes, eds., *Rationality and Relativism* (Cambridge, Mass.: MIT Press, 1982), 1.

32. E. Gellner, "Relativism and Universals," in Hollis and Lukes, *Rationality and Relativism*, 181–200.

33. Horton, "Tradition and Modernity Revisited," 260.

34. D. Sperber, "Apparently Irrational Beliefs," in Hollis and Lukes, *Rationality and Relativism*, 149–180.

Solidarity or Objectivity?

25

RICHARD RORTY

There are two principal ways in which reflective human beings try, by placing their lives in a larger context, to give sense to those lives. The first is by telling the story of their contribution to a community. This community may be the actual historical one in which they live, or another actual one, distant in time or place, or a quite imaginary one, consisting perhaps of a dozen heroes and heroines selected from history or fiction or both. The second way is to describe themselves as standing in immediate relation to a nonhuman reality. This relation is immediate in the sense that it does not derive from a relation between such a reality and their tribe, or their nation, or their imagined band of comrades. I shall say that stories of the former kind exemplify the desire for solidarity, and that stories of the latter kind exemplify the desire for objectivity. Insofar as a person is seeking solidarity, he or she does not ask about the relation between the practices of the chosen community and something outside that community. Insofar as he seeks objectivity, he distances himself from the actual persons around him not by thinking of himself as a member of some other real or imaginary group, but rather by attaching himself to something which can be described without reference to any particular human beings.

The tradition in Western culture which centers around the notion of the search for Truth, a tradition which runs from the Greek philosophers through the Enlightenment, is the clearest example of the attempt to find a sense in one's existence by turning away from solidarity to objectivity. The idea of Truth as something to be pursued for its own sake, not because it will be good for oneself, or for one's real or imaginary community, is the central theme of this tradition. It was perhaps the growing awareness by the Greeks of the sheer diversity of human communities which stimulated the emergence of this ideal. A fear of parochialism, of being confined within the horizons of the group into which one happens to be born, a need to see it with the eyes of a stranger, helps produce the skeptical and ironic tone characteristic of Euripides and Socrates. Herodotus' willingness to take the barbarians seriously enough to describe their customs in detail may have been a necessary prelude to Plato's claim that the way to transcend skepticism is to envisage a common goal of humanity—a goal set by human nature rather than by Greek culture. The combination of Socratic alienation and Platonic hope gives rise to the idea of the intellectual as someone who is in touch with the nature of things, not by way of the opinions of his community, but in a more immediate way.

Plato developed the idea of such an intellectual by means of distinctions between knowledge and opinion, and between appearance and reality. Such distinctions conspire to produce the idea that rational inquiry should make visible a realm to which nonintellectuals have little access, and of whose very existence they may be doubtful. In the Enlightenment, this notion became concrete in the adoption of the Newtonian physical scientist as a model of the intellectual. To most thinkers of the eighteenth century, it seemed clear that the access to Nature which physical science had provided should now be followed by the establishment of social, political, and economic institutions which were in accordance with Nature. Ever since, liberal social thought has centered around social reform as made possible by objective knowledge of what human beings are like—not knowledge of what Greeks or Frenchmen or Chinese are like, but of humanity as such. We are the heirs of this objectivist tradition, which centers round the assumption that we must step outside our community long enough to examine it in the light of something which transcends it, namely, that which it has in common with every other actual and possible human community. This tradition dreams of an ultimate community, which will have transcended the distinction between the natural and the social, which will exhibit a solidarity, which is not parochial because it is the expression of an ahistorical human nature. Much of the rhetoric of contemporary intellectual life takes for granted that the goal of scientific inquiry into man is to understand 'underlying structures', or, 'culturally invariant factors', or 'biologically determined patterns.'

Those who wish to ground solidarity in objectivity—call them 'realists'—have to construe truth as correspondence to reality. So they must construct a metaphysics which has room for a special relation between beliefs and objects which will differentiate true from false beliefs. They also must argue that there are procedures of justification of belief which are natural and not merely local. So they must construct an epistemology which has room for a kind of justification which is not merely social but natural, springing from human nature itself, and made possible by a link between that part of nature and the rest of nature. On their view, the various procedures which are thought of as providing rational justification by one or another culture may, or may not, really *be* rational. For to be truly rational, procedures of justification *must* lead to the truth, to correspondence to reality, to the intrinsic nature of things.

By contrast, those who wish to reduce objectivity to solidarity—call them 'pragmatists'—do not require either a metaphysics or an epistemology. They view truth as, in William James' phrase, what it is good for *us* to believe. So they do not need an account of a relation between beliefs and objects called 'correspondence', nor an account of human cognitive abilities which ensures that our species is capable of entering into that relation. They see the gap between truth and justification not as something to be bridged by isolating a natural and transcultural sort of rationality, which can be used to criticize certain cultures and praise others, but simply as the gap between the actual good and the possible better. From a pragmatist point of view, to say that what is rational for us now to believe may not be *true*, is simply to say that somebody may come up with a better idea. It is to say that there is always room for improved belief, since new evidence, or new hypotheses, or a whole new vocabulary, may come along.[1] For pragmatists, the desire for objectivity is not the desire to escape the limitations of one's community, but simply the desire for as much intersubjective agreement as possible, the desire to extend the reference of 'us' as far as we can. Insofar as pragmatists make a distinction between knowledge and opinion, it is simply the distinction between topics on which such agreement is relatively easy to get and topics on which agreement is relatively hard to get.

'Relativism' is the traditional epithet applied to pragmatism by realists. Three different views are commonly referred to by this name. The first is the view that every belief is as good as every other. The second is the view that 'true' is an equivocal term, having as many meanings as there are procedures of justification. The third is the view that there is nothing to be said about either truth or rationality apart from descriptions of the familiar procedures of justification which a given society—*ours*—uses in one or another area of inquiry. The pragmatist holds the ethnocentric third view. But he does not hold the self-refuting first view, nor the eccentric second view. He thinks that his views are better than the realists', but he does not think that his views correspond to the nature of things. He thinks that the very flexibility of the word 'true'—the fact that it is merely an expression of commendation—insures its univocity. The term 'true,' on his account, means the same in all cultures, just as equally flexible terms like 'here,' 'there,' 'good,' 'bad,' 'you,' and 'me' mean the same in all cultures. But the identity of meaning is, of course, compatible with diversity of reference, and with diversity of procedures for assigning the terms. So he feels free to use the term 'true' as a general term of commendation in the same way as his realist opponent does—and in particular to use it to commend his own view.

However, it is not clear why 'relativist' should be thought an appropriate term for the ethnocentric third view, the one which the pragmatist *does* hold. For the pragmatist is not holding a positive theory which says that something is relative to something else. He is, instead, making the purely *negative* point that we should drop the traditional distinction between knowledge and opinion, construed as the distinction between truth as correspondence to reality and truth as a commendatory term for well-justified beliefs. The reason that the realist calls this negative claim 'relativistic' is that he cannot believe that anybody would seriously deny that truth has an intrinsic nature. So when the pragmatist says that there is nothing to be said about truth save that each of us will commend as true those beliefs which he or she finds good to believe, the realist is inclined to interpret this as one more positive theory about the nature of truth: a theory according to which truth is simply the contemporary opinion of a chosen individual or group. Such a theory would, of course, be self-refuting. But the pragmatist does not have a theory of truth, much less a relativistic one. As a partisan of solidarity, his account of the value of cooperative human inquiry has only an ethical base, not an epistemological or metaphysical one. Not having *any* epistemology, *a fortiori* he does not have a relativistic one.

The question of whether truth or rationality has an intrinsic nature, of whether we ought to have a positive theory about either topic, is just the question of whether our self-description ought to be constructed around a relation to human nature or around a relation to a particular collection of human beings, whether we should desire objectivity or solidarity. It is hard to see how one could choose between these alternatives by looking more deeply into the nature of knowledge, or of man, or of nature. Indeed, the proposal that this issue might be so settled begs the question in favor of the realist, for it presupposes that knowledge, man, and nature *have* real essences which are relevant to the problem at hand. For the pragmatist, by contrast, 'knowledge' is, like 'truth,' simply a compliment paid to the beliefs which we think so well justified that, for the moment, further justification is not needed. An inquiry into the nature of knowledge can, on his view, only be a socio-storical account of how various people have tried to reach agreement on what to believe.

This view which I am calling 'pragmatism' is almost, but not quite, the same as what Hilary Putnam, in his recent *Reason, Truth and History*, calls "the internalist conception of philosophy."[2] Putnam defines such a conception as one which gives up the attempt at a God's-eye view of things, the attempt at contact with the nonhuman which I have been calling 'the desire for objectivity.' Unfortunately, he accompanies his defense of the anti-realist views I am recommending with a polemic against a lot of the other people who hold these views; e.g., Kuhn, Feyerabend, Foucault, and myself. We are criticized as 'relativists.' Putnam presents 'internalism' as a happy *via media* between realism and relativism. He speaks of "the plethora of relativistic doctrines being marketed today" (119) and in particular of "the French philosophers" as holding "some fancy mixture of cultural relativism and 'structuralism'" (x). But when it comes to criticizing these doctrines all that Putnam finds to attack is the so-called incommensurability thesis: viz. "terms used in another culture cannot be equated in meaning or reference with any terms or expressions *we* possess" (114). He sensibly agrees with Donald Davidson in remarking that this thesis is self-refuting. Criticism of this thesis, however, is destructive of, at most, some incautious passages in some early writings by Feyerabend. Once this thesis is brushed aside, it is hard to see how Putnam himself differs from most of those he criticizes.

Putnam accepts the Davidsonian point that, as he puts it, "the whole justification of an interpretative scheme . . . is that it renders the behavior of others at least minimally reasonable by *our* lights" (114). It would seem natural to go on from this to say that we cannot get outside the range of those lights, that we cannot stand on neutral ground illuminated only by the natural light of reason. But Putnam draws back from this conclusion. He does so because he construes the claim that we cannot do so as the claim that the range of our thought is restricted by what he calls 'institutionalized norms,' publicly available criteria for settling of arguments, including philosophical arguments. He rightly says that there are no such criteria, arguing that the suggestion, that there are, is as self-refuting as the 'incommensurability thesis.' He is, I think, entirely right in saying that the notion that philosophy is or should become such an application of explicit criteria contradicts the very idea of philosophy.[3] One can gloss Putnam's point by saying that 'philosophy' is precisely what a culture becomes capable of when it ceases to define itself in terms of explicit rules, and becomes sufficiently leisured and civilized to rely on inarticulate know-how, to substitute *phronesis* for codification, and conversation with foreigners for conquest of them.

But to say that we cannot refer every question to explicit criteria institutionalized by our society does not speak to the point which the people whom Putnam calls 'relativists' are making. One reason these people are pragmatists is precisely that they share Putnam's distrust of the positivistic idea that rationality is a matter of applying criteria.

Such a distrust is common, for example, to Kuhn, Mary Hesse, Wittgenstein, Michael Polanyi, and Michael Oakeshott. Only someone who did think of rationality in this way would dream of suggesting that 'true' means something different in different societies. For only such a person could imagine that there was anything to pick out to which one might make 'true' relative. Only if one shares the logical positivists' idea that we all carry around things called 'rules of language' which regulate what we say when, will one suggest that there is no way to break out of one's culture.

In the most original and powerful section of his book, Putnam argues that the notion that "rationality ... is defined by the local cultural norms" is merely the demonic counterpart of positivism. It is, as he says, "a scientistic theory inspired by anthropology as positivism was a scientistic theory inspired by the exact sciences." By 'scientism' Putnam means the notion that rationality consists in the application of criteria (126). Suppose we drop this notion, and accept Putnam's own Quinean picture of inquiry as the continual reweaving of a web of beliefs rather than as the application of criteria to cases. Then the notion of 'local cultural norms' will lose its offensively parochial overtones. For now to say that we must work by our own lights, that we must be ethnocentric, is merely to say that beliefs suggested by another culture must be tested by trying to weave them together with beliefs we already have. It is a consequence of this holistic view of knowledge, a view shared by Putnam and those he criticizes as 'relativists,' that alternative cultures are not to be thought of on the model of alternative geometries. Alternative geometries are irreconcilable because they have axiomatic structures, and contradictory axioms. They are *designed* to be irreconcilable. Cultures are not so designed, and do not have axiomatic structures. To say that they have 'institutionalized norms' is only to say, with Foucault, that knowledge is never separable from power—that one is likely to suffer if one does not hold certain beliefs at certain times and places. But such institutional backups for beliefs take the form of bureaucrats and policemen, not of 'rules of language' and 'criteria of rationality.' To think otherwise is the Cartesian fallacy of seeing axioms where there are only shared habits, of viewing statements, which summarize such practices as if they reported constraints enforcing such practices. Part of the force of Quine and Davidson's attack on the distinction between the conceptual and the empirical is that the distinction between different cultures does not differ in kind from the distinction between different theories held by members of a single culture. The Tasmanian aborigines and the British colonists had trouble communicating, but this trouble was different only in extent from the difficulties in communication experienced by Gladstone and Disraeli. The trouble in all such cases is just the difficulty of explaining why other people disagree with us, of reweaving our beliefs so as to fit the fact of disagreement together with the other beliefs we hold. The same Quinean arguments, which dispose of the positivists' distinction between analytic and synthetic truth dispose of the anthropologists' distinction between the intercultural and the intracultural.

On this holistic account of cultural norms, however, we do not need the notion of a universal transcultural rationality which Putnam invokes against those whom he calls 'relativists.' Just before the end of his book, Putnam says that once we drop the notion of a God's-eye point of view we realize that:

> We can only hope to produce a more rational *conception* of rationality or a better *conception* of morality if we operate from *within* our tradition (with its echoes of the Greek agora, of Newton, and so on, in the case of rationality, and with its echoes of scripture, of the philosophers, of the democratic revolutions, and so on ... in the case of morality). We are invited to engage in a truly human dialogue. (216)

With this I entirely agree, and so, I take it, would Kuhn, Hesse, and most of the other so-called relativists—perhaps even Foucault. But Putnam then goes on to pose a further question, "Does this dialogue have an ideal terminus?" Is there a *true* conception of rationality, an ideal morality, even if all we ever have are our *conceptions* of these? I do not see the point of this question. Putnam suggests that a negative answer—the view that 'there is only the dialogue'—is just another form of self-refuting relativism. But, once again, I do not see how a claim that something does not exist can be construed as a claim that something is relative to something else. In the final sentence of his book, Putnam says that "The very fact that we speak of our different conceptions as different conceptions of *rationality* posits a *Grenzbegriff*, a limit-concept of ideal truth." But what is such a posit supposed to do, except to say that from God's point of view the human race is heading in the right direction? Surely Putnam's 'internalism' should forbid him to say anything like that. To say that *we* think we're heading in the right direction is just to say, with Kuhn, that we can, by hindsight, tell the story of the past as a story of progress. To say that we still have a long way to go, that our present views should not be cast in bronze, is too platitudinous to require support by posit-ing limit-concepts. So it is hard to see what difference is made by the difference between saying "there is only the dialogue" and saying "there is also that to which the dialogue converges."

I would suggest that Putnam here, at the end of the day, slides back into the scientism he rightly condemns in others. For the root of scientism, defined as the view that rationality is a matter of applying criteria, is the desire for objectivity, the hope that what Putnam calls 'human flourishing' has a transhistorical nature. I think that Feyerabend is right in suggesting that until we discard the metaphor of inquiry, and human activity generally, as converging rather than proliferating, as becoming more unified rather than more diverse, we shall never be free of the motives which once led us to posit gods. Positing *Grenzbegriffe* seems merely a way of telling ourselves that a nonexistent God would, if he did exist, be pleased with us. If we could ever be moved solely by the desire for solidarity, setting aside the desire for objectivity altogether, then we should think of human progress as making it possible for human beings to do more interesting things and be more interesting people, not as heading towards a place which has somehow been pre-pared for humanity in advance. Our self-image would employ images of making rather than finding, the images used by the Romantics to praise poets rather than the images used by the Greeks to praise mathematicians. Feyerabend seems to me right in trying to develop such a self-image for us, but his project seems misdescribed, by himself as well as by his critics, as 'relativism.'[4]

Those who follow Feyerabend in this direction are often thought of as nec-essarily enemies of the Enlightenment, as joining in the chorus, which claims that the traditional self-descriptions of the Western democracies are bankrupt, that they somehow have been shown to be 'inadequate' or 'self-deceptive.' Part of the instinctive resistance to attempts by Marxists, Sartreans, Oakeshottians, Gadamerians, and Foucauldians to reduce objectivity to solidarity is the fear that our traditional liberal habits and hopes will not survive the reduction. Such feel-ings are evident, for example, in Habermas' criticism of Gadamer's position as relativistic and potentially repressive, in the suspicion that Heidegger's attacks on realism are somehow linked to his Nazism, in the hunch that Marxist attempts to interpret values as class interests are usually just apologies for Leninist takeovers, and in the suggestion that Oakeshott's skepticism about rationalism in politics is merely an apology for the status quo.

I think that putting the issue in such moral and political terms, rather than in epistemological or metaphilosophical terms, makes clearer what is at stake. For now the question is not about how to define words like 'truth' or 'rationality' or 'knowledge' or 'philosophy,' but about what self-image our society should have of itself. The ritual invocation of the 'need to avoid relativism' is most compre-hensible as an expression of the need to preserve certain habits of contemporary European life. These are the habits nurtured by the Enlightenment, and justified by it in terms of an appeal of Reason, conceived as a transcultural human ability to correspond to reality, a faculty whose possession and use is demonstrated by obedience to explicit criteria. So the real question about relativism is whether these same habits of intellectual, social, and political life can be justified by a conception of rationality as criterionless muddling through, and by a pragmatist conception of truth.

I think that the answer to this question is that the pragmatist cannot justify these habits without circularity, but then neither can the realist. The pragmatists' justification of toleration, free inquiry, and the quest for undistorted communi-cation can only take the form of a comparison between societies which exemplify these habits and those which do not, leading up to the suggestion that nobody who has experienced both would prefer the latter. It is exemplified by Winston Churchill's defense of democracy as the worst form of government imaginable, except for all the others, which have been tried so far. Such justification is not by reference to a criterion, but by reference to various detailed practical advantages. It is circular only in that the terms of praise used to describe liberal societies will be drawn from the vocabulary of the liberal societies themselves. Such praise has to be in *some* vocabulary, after all, and the terms of praise current in primitive or theocratic or totalitarian societies will not produce the desired result. So the pragmatist admits that he has no ahistorical standpoint from which to endorse the habits of modern democracies he wishes to praise. These consequences are just what partisans of solidarity expect. But among partisans of objectivity they give rise, once again, to fears of the dilemma formed by ethnocentrism on the one hand and relativism on the other. Either we attach a special privilege to our own community, or we pretend an impossible tolerance for every other group.

I have been arguing that we pragmatists should grasp the ethnocentric horn of this dilemma. We should say that we must, in practice, privilege our own group, even though there can be no noncircular justification for doing so. We must insist that the fact that nothing is immune from criticism does not mean that we have a duty to justify everything. We Western liberal intellectuals should accept the fact that we have to start from where we are, and that this means that there are lots of views which we simply cannot take seriously. To use Neurath's familiar analogy, we can *understand* the revolutionary's suggestion that a sail-able boat can't be made out of the planks which make up ours, and that we must simply abandon ship. But we cannot take his suggestion seriously. We cannot take it as a rule for action, so it is not a live option. For some people, to be sure, the option *is* live. These are the people who have always hoped to become a New Being, who have hoped to be converted rather than persuaded. But we—the liberal Rawlsian searchers for consensus, the heirs of Socrates, the people who wish to link their days dialectically each to each—cannot do so. Our community—the community of the liberal intellectuals of the secular modern West—wants to be able to give a *post factum* account of any change of view. We want to be able, so to speak, to justify ourselves to our earlier selves. This preference is not built into us by human nature. It is just the way *we* live now.[5]

This lonely provincialism, this admission that we are just the historical moment that we are, not the representatives of something ahistorical, is what makes traditional Kantian liberals like Rawls draw back from pragmatism.[6] 'Relativism,' by contrast, is merely a red herring. The realist is, once again, projecting his own habits of thought upon the pragmatist when he charges him with relativism. For the realist thinks that the whole point of philosophical thought is to detach oneself from any particular community and look down at it from a more universal standpoint. When he hears the pragmatist repudiating the desire for such a standpoint he cannot quite believe it. He thinks that everyone, deep down inside, *must* want such detachment. So he attributes to the pragmatist a perverse form of his own attempted detachment, and sees him as an ironic, sneering aesthete who refuses to take the choice between communities seriously, a mere 'relativist.' But the pragmatist, dominated by the desire for solidarity, can only be criticized for taking his own community *too* seriously. He can only be criticized for ethnocentrism, not for relativism. To be ethnocentric is to divide the human race into the people to whom one must justify one's beliefs and the others. The first group—one's ethnos—comprises those who share enough of one's beliefs to make fruitful conversation possible. In this sense, everybody is ethnocentric when engaged in actual debate, no matter how much realist rhetoric about objectivity he produces in his study.[7]

What is disturbing about the pragmatist's picture is not that it is relativistic but that it takes away two sorts of metaphysical comfort to which our intellectual tradition has become accustomed. One is the thought that membership in our biological species carries with it certain 'rights,' a notion which does not seem to make sense unless the biological similarities entail the possession of something nonbiological, something which links our species to a nonhuman reality and thus gives the species moral dignity. This picture of rights as biologically transmitted is so basic to the political discourse of the Western democracies that we are troubled by any suggestion that 'human nature' is not a useful moral concept. The second comfort is provided by the thought that our community cannot wholly die. The picture of a common human nature oriented towards correspondence to reality as it is in itself comforts us with the thought that even if our civilization is destroyed, even if all memory of our political or intellectual or artistic community is erased, the race is fated to recapture the virtues and the insights and the achievements which were the glory of that community. The notion of human nature as an inner structure which leads all members of the species to converge to the same point, to recognize the same theories, virtues, and works of art as worthy of honor, assures us that even if the Persians had won, the arts and sciences of the Greeks would sooner or later have appeared elsewhere. It assures us that even if the Orwellian bureaucrats of terror rule for a thousand years the achievements of the Western democracies will someday be duplicated by our remote descendants. It assures us that 'man will prevail,' that something reasonably like *our* worldview, *our* virtues, *our* art, will bob up again whenever human beings are left alone to cultivate their inner natures. The comfort of the realist picture is the comfort of saying not simply that there is a place prepared for our race in our advance, but also that we now know quite a bit about what that place looks like. The inevitable ethnocentrism to which we are all condemned is thus as much a part of the realist's comfortable view as of the pragmatists' uncomfortable one.

The pragmatist gives up the first sort of comfort because he thinks that to say that certain people have certain rights is merely to say that we should treat them in certain ways. It is not to give a *reason* for treating them in those ways. As to the second sort of comfort, he suspects that the hope that something resembling *us* will inherit the earth is impossible to eradicate, as impossible as eradicating the hope of surviving our individual deaths through some satisfying transfiguration. But he does not want to turn this hope into a theory of the nature of man. He wants solidarity to be our *only* comfort, and to be seen not to require metaphysical support.

My suggestion that the desire for objectivity is in part a disguised form of the fear of the death of our community echoes Nietzsche's charge that the philosophical tradition, which stems from Plato, is an attempt to avoid facing up to contingency, to escape from time and chance. Nietzsche thought that realism was to be condemned not only by arguments from its theoretical incoherence, the sort of argument we find in Putnam and Davidson, but also on practical, pragmatic grounds. Nietzsche thought that the test of human character was the ability to live with the thought that there was no convergence. He wanted us to be able to think of truth as, "a mobile army of metaphors, metonyms, and anthropomorphisms—in short a sum of human relations, which have been enhanced, transposed, and embellished poetically and rhetorically and which after long use seem firm, canonical, and obligatory to a people."[8] Nietzsche hoped that eventually there might be human beings who could and did think of truth in this way, but who still liked themselves, who saw themselves as *good* people for whom solidarity was *enough*.[9]

I think that pragmatism's attack on the various structure-content distinctions, which buttress the realist's notion of objectivity, can best be seen as an attempt to let us think of truth in this Nietzschean way, as entirely a matter of solidarity. That is why I think we need to say, despite Putnam, that "there is only the dialogue," only *us*, and to throw out the last residues of the notion of 'transcultural rationality.' But this should not lead us to repudiate, as Nietzsche sometimes did, the elements in our movable host which embody the ideas of Socratic conversation, Christian fellowship, and Enlightenment science. Nietzsche ran together his diagnosis of philosophical realism as an expression of fear and resentment with his own resentful idiosyncratic idealizations of silence, solitude, and violence. Post-Nietzschean thinkers like Adorno, Heidegger, and Foucault have run together Nietzsche's criticisms of the metaphysical tradition, on the one hand, with his criticisms of bourgeois civility, of Christian love, and of the nineteenth century's hope that science would make the world a better place to live, on the other. I do not think that there is any interesting connection between these two sets of criticisms. Pragmatism seems to me, as I have said, a philosophy of solidarity rather than of despair. From this point of view, Socrates' turn away from the gods, Christianity's turn from an Omnipotent Creator to the man who suffered on the Cross, and the Baconian turn from science as contemplation of eternal truth to science as instrument of social progress, can be seen as so many preparations for the act of social faith which is suggested by a Nietzschean view of truth.[10]

The best argument we partisans of solidarity have against the realistic partisans of objectivity is Nietzsche's argument that the traditional Western metaphysico-epistemological way of firming up our habits simply isn't working anymore. It isn't doing its job. It has become as transparent a device as the postulation of deities who turn out, by a happy coincidence, to have chosen *us* as their people. So the pragmatist suggestion that we substitute a 'merely' ethical foundation for our sense of community—or, better, that we think of our sense of community as having no foundation except shared hope and the trust created by such sharing—is put forward on practical grounds. It is *not* put forward as a corollary of a metaphysical claim that the objects in the world contain no intrinsically action-guiding properties, nor of an epistemological claim that we lack a faculty of moral sense, nor of a semantic claim that truth is reducible to justification. It is a suggestion about how we might think of ourselves in order to avoid the kind of resentful belatedness—characteristic of the bad side of Nietzsche—which now characterizes much of high culture. This resentment arises from the realization, which I referred to at the beginning of this essay, that the Enlightenment's search for objectivity has often gone sour.

The rhetoric of scientific objectivity, pressed too hard and taken too seriously, has led us to people like B. F. Skinner, on the one hand, and people like Althusser, on the other—two equally pointless fantasies, both produced by the attempt to be 'scientific' about our moral and political lives. Reaction against scientism led to attacks on natural science as a sort of false god. But there is nothing wrong with science, there is only something wrong with the attempt to divinize it, the attempt characteristic of realistic philosophy. This reaction has also led to attacks on liberal social thought of the type common to Mill and Dewey and Rawls as a mere ideological superstructure, one which obscures the realities of our situation and represses attempts to change that situation. But there is nothing wrong with liberal democracy, nor with the philosophers who have tried to enlarge its scope. There is only something wrong with the attempt to see their efforts as failures to achieve something which they were not trying to achieve—a demonstration of the 'objective' superiority of our way of life over all other alternatives. There is, in short, nothing wrong with the hopes of the Enlightenment, the hopes which created the Western democracies. The value of the ideals of the Enlightenment is, for us pragmatists, just the value of some of the institutions and practices which they have created. In this essay, I have sought to distinguish these institutions and practices from the philosophical justifications for them provided by partisans of objectivity, and to suggest an alternative justification.

NOTES

1. This attitude toward truth, in which the consensus of a community rather than a relation to a nonhuman reality is taken as central, is associated not only with the American pragmatic tradition but with the work of Popper and Habermas. Habermas' criticisms of lingering positivist elements in Popper parallel those made by Deweyan holists of the early logical empiricists. It is important to see, however, that the pragmatist notion of truth common to James and Dewey is not dependent upon either Peirce's notion of an 'ideal end of inquiry' nor on Habermas' notion of an 'ideally free community.' For criticism of these notions, which in my view are insufficiently ethnocentric, see my "Pragmatism, Davidson, and Truth," in *Truth and Interpretation: Perspectives on the Philosophy of Donald Davidson*, ed. Ernest LePore (New York: Blackwell, 1986), and "Habermas and Lyotard on Postmodernity," *Praxis International* 4, no. 1 (1984): 32–44.

2. Hilary Putnam, *Reason, Truth, and History* (Cambridge: Cambridge University Press, 1981), 49–50.

3. Ibid., 113.

4. See, for example, Paul Feyerabend, *Science in a Free Society* (London: New Left Books, 1978), 9, where Feyerabend identifies his own view with 'relativism' (in the old and simple sense of Protagoras). This identification is accompanied by the claim that "'Objectively' there is not much to choose between antisemitism and humanitarianism." I think Feyerabend would have served himself better by saying that the scare-quoted word 'objectively' should simply be dropped from use, together with the traditional philosophical distinctions between scheme and content [...] which buttress the subjective-objective distinction, than by saying that we may keep the word and use it to say the sort of thing Protagoras said. What Feyerabend is really against is the correspondence theory of truth, not the idea that some views cohere better than others.

5. This quest for consensus is opposed to the sort of quest for authenticity which wishes to free itself from the opinion of our community. See, for example, Vincent Descombes' account of Deleuze in *Modern French Philosophy* (Cambridge: Cambridge University Press, 1980), 153: "Even if philosophy is essentially demystificatory, philosophers often fail to produce authentic critiques; they defend order, authority, institutions, 'decency,' everything in which the ordinary person believes." On the pragmatist or ethnocentric view I am suggesting, all that critique can or should do is play off elements in 'what the ordinary person believes' against other elements. To attempt to do more than this is to fantasize rather than to converse. Fantasy may, to be sure, be an incentive to more fruitful conversation, but when it no longer fulfills this function it does not deserve the name of 'critique.'

6. In *A Theory of Justice* (Cambridge, Mass.: Harvard University Press, 1971), Rawls seemed to be trying to retain the authority of Kantian 'practical reason' by imagining a social contract devised by choosers 'behind a veil of ignorance'—using the 'rational self-interest' of such choosers as a touchstone for the ahistorical validity of certain social institutions. Much of the criticism to which that book was subjected, e.g., by Michael Sandel in *Liberalism and the Limits of Justice* (Cambridge: Cambridge University Press, 1982), has centered on the claim that one cannot escape history in this way. In the meantime, however, Rawls has put forward a metaethical view which drops the claim to ahistorical validity. See his "Kantian Constructivism in Moral Theory," *Journal of Philosophy* 77, no. 9 (1980): 515–572, and "Justice as Fairness: Political not Metaphysical," *Philosophy and Public Affairs* 14, no. 3 (1985): 223–251. Concurrently, T. M. Scanlon has urged that the essence of a 'contractualist' account of moral motivation is better understood as the desire to justify one's action to others than in terms of 'rational self-interest.' See Scanlon, "Contractualism and Utilitarianism," in *Utilitarianism and Beyond*, ed. A. Sen and B. Williams (Cambridge: Cambridge University Press, 1982). Scanlon's emendation of Rawls leads in

the same direction as Rawls' later work, since Scanlon's use of the notion of 'justification to others on grounds they could not reasonably reject' chimes with the 'constructivist' view that what counts for social philosophy is what can be justified to a particular historical community, not to 'humanity in general.' On my view, the frequent remark that Rawls' rational choosers look remarkably like twentieth-century American liberals is perfectly just, but not a criticism of Rawls. It is merely a frank recognition of the ethnocentrism which is essential to serious, nonfantastical thought. I defend this view in "Postmodernist Bourgeois Liberalism," *Journal of Philosophy*, Eightieth Annual Meeting of the American Philosophical Association, Eastern Division, 80, no. 10, pt. 1 (1983): 583–589.

7. In an important paper called "The Truth in Relativism," included in his *Moral Luck* (Cambridge: Cambridge University Press, 1981), Bernard Williams makes a similar point in terms of a distinction between 'genuine confrontation' and 'notional confrontation.' The latter is the sort of confrontation which occurs, asymmetrically, between us and primitive tribes people. The belief-systems of such people do not present, as Williams puts it, 'real options' for us, for we cannot imagine going over to their view without 'self-deception or paranoia.' These are the people whose beliefs on certain topics overlap so little with ours that their inability to agree with us raises no doubt in our minds about the correctness of our own beliefs. Williams' use of 'real option' and 'notional confrontation' seems to me very enlightening, but I think he turns these notions to purposes they will not serve. Williams wants to defend ethical relativism, defined as the claim that when ethical confrontations are merely notional 'questions of appraisal do not genuinely arise.' He thinks they *do* arise in connection with notional confrontations between, e.g., Einsteinian and Amazonian cosmologies (142). This distinction between ethics and physics seems to me an awkward result to which Williams is driven by his unfortunate attempt to find *something* true in relativism, an attempt which is a corollary of his attempt to be 'realistic' about physics. On my (Davidsonian) view, there is no point in distinguishing between true sentences which are 'made true by reality' and true sentences which are 'made true by us,' because the whole idea of 'truth-makers' needs to be dropped. So I would hold that there is *no* truth in relativism, but this much truth in ethnocentrism: we cannot justify our beliefs (in physics, ethics, or any other area) to everybody, but only to those whose beliefs overlap ours to some appropriate extent. (This is not a theoretical problem about 'untranslatability,' but simply a practical problem about the limitations of argument; it is not that we live in different worlds than the Nazis or the Amazonians, but that conversion from or to their point of view, though possible, will not be a matter of inference from previously shared premises.)

8. Nietzsche, "On Truth and Lie in an Extra-Moral Sense," in *The Portable Nietzsche*, ed. and trans. Walter Kaufmann (New York: Viking, 1954), 46–47.

9. Sabina Lovibond, *Realism and Imagination in Ethics* (Minneapolis: University of Minnesota Press, 1983), 158: "An adherent of Wittgenstein's view of language should

equate that goal with the establishment of a language-game in which we could partici-pate ingenuously, while retaining our awareness of it as a specific historical formation. A community in which such a language-game was played would be one . . . whose members understood their own form of life and yet were not embarrassed by it."

10. See Hans Blumenberg, *The Legitimation of Modernity* (Cambridge, Mass.: MIT Press, 1982), for a story about the history of European thought which, unlike the stories told by Nietzsche and Heidegger, sees the Enlightenment as a definitive step forward. For Blumenberg, the attitude of 'self-assertion,' the kind of attitude which stems from a Baconian view of the nature and purpose of science, needs to be distinguished from 'self-foundation,' the Cartesian project of grounding such inquiry upon ahistorical crite-ria of rationality. Blumenberg remarks, pregnantly, that the 'historicist' criticism of the optimism of the Enlightenment, criticism which began with the Romantics' turn back to the Middle Ages, undermines self-foundation but not self-assertion.

26

Relativism, Power, and Philosophy

ALASDAIR MACINTYRE

I

It was Anthony Collins, the friend of John Locke, who remarked that, had it not been for the Boyle Lecturers' annual demonstrations of the existence of God, few people would ever have doubted it.[1] It may have been a similar spirit of argumentative contrariness that led me to begin to appreciate fully both the strength and the importance of the case to be made out in favor of at least one version of relativism only after reading some recent philosophical root and branch dismissals of relativism as such.[2] But of course, I ought not to have been such a late-comer to that appreciation. For relativism, like skepticism, is one of those doctrines that have by now been refuted a number of times too often. Nothing is perhaps a surer sign that a doctrine embodies some not to be neglected truth than that in the course of the history of philosophy it should have been refuted again and again. Genuinely refutable doctrines only need to be refuted once.

Originally published as Alasdair Chalmers MacIntyre, "Relativism, Power, and Philosophy," *Proceedings and Addresses of the* American *Philosophical Association* 59:1 (September 1985): 5–22, copyright granted by American Philosophical Association, all rights reserved.

Philosophical doctrines that are not susceptible of genuine refutation fall into at least two classes. There are some to which, in the light of the rational justification that can be provided for them, we owe simple assent. But there are others to which our assent is or ought to be accorded only with a recognition that what they present is a moment in the development of thought which has to be, if possible, transcended; and this even although we may as yet lack adequate grounds for believing ourselves able to transcend them. Skepticism is one such doctrine; and relativism is another. But no doctrine can be genuinely transcended until we understand what is to be said in its favor. And a first step towards understanding this in the case of relativism must be to show that the purported refutations have largely missed its point and so been misdirected.

It is not that there is nothing to be learned from them. From them we can certainly learn how to formulate relativism in a way that does not gratuitously entangle it with error. So we can learn from Socrates' encounter with the formulations of Protagoras in the *Theatetus*[3] that relativists must be careful not to allow themselves to be trapped into making some type of universal self-referential claim. Such a claim, by denying to all doctrines whatsoever the predicates 'is true' and 'is false,' unless these are radically reinterpreted to mean no more than 'seems true to such and such persons' and 'seems false to such and such persons,' turns the interesting assertion that relativism is true into the uninteresting assertion that relativism seems true to relativists. And we can learn from Hegel's critique of Kant that relativists must be careful to avoid framing their theses in a way that presupposes the legitimacy of some version of what has come to be called the scheme-content distinction, that is, the distinction between some concept or conceptual scheme on the one hand and on the other an entirely preconceptual world or given waiting to be rescued from in one version blindness, in another nakedness, by being conceptualized.[4]

Yet it is important to be precise about what we have to learn from these refutations of particular formulations of relativism; and it is important therefore not to abstract for formulaic use what we take to be the essence of some refutation from the context in which such as Plato or Hegel embedded it and from which it drew its peculiar force. So we are perhaps entitled to express a certain polite surprise when a contemporary philosopher who has shown both assiduity and ingenuity in trying to make credible the view that 'is true' says no more than is said by 'seems true to such and such persons, namely *us*,' asserts that if there were any contemporary relativists, one could use against them some variant of what he calls the "arguments Socrates used against Protagoras."[5] The surprise derives from our remembering that the premises from which Plato derived Socrates' refutation of Protagoras' version of relativism also entailed the necessary failure of any reinterpretative reduction of 'is true' to 'seems true to such and such persons.' From these premises the one conclusion is not available without the other.

The same kind of polite surprise is warranted when another distinguished contemporary philosopher, having repeated the substance of Hegel's demonstration of the illegitimacy of any dualism which tears apart conceptual schemes on the one hand and the world on the other, concludes to the necessary incoherence of the very idea of a conceptual scheme.[6] It was, after all, Hegel who gave its canonical form both to the idea of a conceptual scheme and to that of alternative and incompatible conceptual schemes and he did so without ever violating his own ban on the illegitimate dualist scheme/content and scheme/world distinctions.[7] Nor was Hegel alone in this; the same could be said of his predecessor, Vico,[8] and of his successor, R. G. Collingwood.[9]

We need, then, in order to capture the truth in relativism, a formulation of that doctrine which has learnt from both Plato and Hegel: it must avoid Protagorean self-trivializing by giving its due to the Platonic distinction between 'is true' and 'seems true to such and such persons'; and in any appeal that it makes to the idea of alternative conceptual schemes, it must be careful to follow Hegel in leaving no opening for any scheme/content or scheme/world distinction.

II

'Relativism,' as I am going to use that expression, names one kind of conclusion to enquiry into a particular class of problems. Those questions arise in the first place for people who live in certain highly specific types of social and cultural situation; but this is not to say that they are not distinctively philosophical questions. They are indeed examples of questions which *both* are inescapable for certain ordinary agents and language-users *and* have the characteristic structure of philosophical problems. It is perhaps unsurprising that they have been overlooked by those recent philosophers who want to make a sharp dichotomy between the realm of philosophical theorizing and that of everyday belief because they suppose both that it is philosophers themselves who largely generate philosophical problems by their own misconceptions and that everyday life cannot be apt to suffer from types of disorder which require specifically philosophical diagnosis.

This attitude is perhaps a symptom of a certain lack of sociological imagination, of too impoverished a view of the types of social and institutional circumstance which generate philosophical problems. What then are the social and institutional circumstances which generate the cluster of problems to which some version of relativism can be a rational response?

They are the social and institutional circumstances of those who inhabit a certain type of frontier or boundary situation. Consider the predicament of someone who lives in a time and place where he or she is a full member of two linguistic communities, speaking one language, Zuni, say, or Irish, exclusively to the older members of his or her family and village and Spanish or English, say, to those from the world outside, who seek to engage him or her in a way of life in the exclusively Spanish- or English-speaking world. Economic and social circumstance may enforce on such a person a final choice between inhabiting the one linguistic community and inhabiting the other; and in some times and places this is much more than a choice between two languages, at least in any narrowly conceived sense of 'language.' For a language may be so used, and both Irish and Zuni have in some past periods been so used, that to share in its use is to presuppose one cosmology rather than another, one relationship of local law and custom to cosmic order rather than another, one justification of particular relationships of individual to community and of both to land and to landscape rather than another. In such a language even the use of proper names may on occasion have such presuppositions.

If, for example, I speak in Irish, even today, let alone three hundred years ago, of Doire Colmcille—of Doire in modern Irish—the presuppositions and implications of my utterance are quite other than if I speak in English of Londonderry. But, it may be asked, are these not simply two names of one and the same place? The answer is first that no proper name of place or person names any place or person *as such*; it names *in the first instance* only *for* those who are members of some particular linguistic and cultural community, by identifying places and persons in terms of the scheme of identification shared by, and perhaps partially constitutive of, that community. The relation of a proper name to its bearer cannot be elucidated without reference to such identifying functions.[10] And secondly that 'Dore Colmcille' names—embodies a communal intention of naming—a place with a continuous identity ever since it became, in fact, St. Columba's oak grove in 546 and that 'Londonderry' names a settlement made only in the seventeenth century and is a name whose use presupposes the legitimacy of that settlement and of the use of the English language to name it. Notice that the name '*Doire Colmcille*' is as a name untranslatable; you can translate the Gaelic expression '*doire Colmcille*' by the English expression 'St. Columba's oak grove'; but that cannot be the translation of a place name, for it is not itself the name of any place. And what is true of the relationship of '*Doire Colmcille*' in Irish to 'Londonderry' in English holds equally of the relationship of the names of the Zuni villages in the sixteenth century, such as '*It wan a*,' to the Spanish name for them as the Seven Cities of Cibola.[11]

To this the response may be that although there may, as a matter of contingent historical fact, be certain kinds of association attaching to the use of '*Doire Colmcille*' rather than 'Londonderry' or vice versa, the use of the name merely *qua* name carries with it no presuppositions concerning political or social legitimacy. And it might be thought that this could be shown by appeal to the fact that some ignorant stranger might use the name Londonderry in order to ask the way and in identifying the place on the map at which he or she wished to arrive would have shown that one *can* use the name for purposes of identification without any such presupposition. But such a stranger is only able now to use a name which has indeed been made available to those outside its primary community of use because the members of the primary community use or used it as they do, and that stranger's secondary use of the name is therefore parasitic upon its uses by the primary community. Moreover such secondary non-presupposition-laden uses do not thereby become names freed from any specific social context of use. They are very specifically names-as-used-by-strangers-or-tourists. Philosophers of logic have sometimes treated the way in which such names are used by strangers or tourists as exemplifying some essential core naming relation, a concept about which I shall have to say something later on in the argument; for the moment I note only that in so doing such philosophers have obscured the difference between the type of natural language in which the standard uses of a variety of expressions commit the user to an expression of a shared, communal belief and the type of natural language in which this is so minimally or not at all.

In the type of frontier or boundary situation which I have been describing both languages—the Irish of, say, 1700 and the English of the plantation settlements of the same date, or the Zuni Shiwi language of, say, 1540 and the Spanish of the *conquistadores*—are at the former end of this spectrum of natural-languages-in-use. Thus what the bilingual speaker in both members of one of these pairs is going to have to choose between, in deciding to spend his or her life within one linguistic community rather than the other, is also to some substantial degree alternative and incompatible sets of beliefs and ways of life. Moreover each of these sets of beliefs and ways of life will have internal to it its own specific modes of rational justification in key areas and its own correspondingly specific warrants for claims to truth.

It is not that the beliefs of each such community cannot be represented in any way at all in the language of the other; it is rather that the outcome in each case of rendering those beliefs sufficiently intelligible to be evaluated by a member of the other community involves characterizing those beliefs in such a way that they are bound to be rejected; will be from the other theft; what is from the one point of view an original act of acquisition, of what had so far belonged to nobody and therefore of what had remained available to become only now someone's private property, will be from the other point of view the illegitimate seizure of what had so far belonged to nobody because it is what *cannot* ever be made into private property—for example, common land. The Spaniards brought alien concepts of ownership deriving from Roman, feudal and canon law to their transactions with the Indians; the English brought concepts of individual property rights recognized by English common law decisions to Ireland at a time when there was certainly a translation for the Latin '*jus*' in Irish, but none for the expression 'a right' (understood as something that attaches not to status, role or function, but to individuals as such).

It will not, at this point, be helpful to remark either that in both these pairs of linguistic communities a great many other beliefs were, of course, shared by members of both communities, or that in particular, no one had ever had any difficulty in translating "Snow is white" from one language to the other. There are indeed large parts of every language that are translatable into every other; and there are types of routine or routinizable social situations which are reproduced in many—some perhaps even in all—cultures. And the project of matching types of sentence-in-use to types of routinizable situation reproduced in many cultures, and of both to the habits of assenting to or dissenting from the uses of such sentences, will doubtless, if actually carried through rather than merely projected, lay bare the relationship between these facts and the type and range of translatability that hold in consequence of that relationship. But the suspicion which I have gradually come to entertain about this type of project is that what can be expected from it is perhaps not so much an adequate semantics for natural languages or a theory of truth in such languages as a series of excellent Phrase Books for Travelers. For it is precisely those features of languages mastery of which *cannot* be acquired from such phrase books which generate untranslatability between languages.

What are those features? They include a power to extrapolate from uses of expressions learned in certain types of situations to the making and understanding of new and newly illuminating uses. The availability of this power to the members of a whole linguistic community of the type which I have been characterizing depends in part upon their shared ability to refer and allude to a particular common stock of canonical texts, texts which define the literary and linguistic tradition which members of that community inhabit. For it is by allusion to such texts that linguistic innovation and extrapolation proceed; what those texts provide are both shared exemplars from which to extrapolate and shared exemplars of the activity of extrapolation.

It is characteristically poets and saga reciters who, in such societies, make and continually remake these at first oral, and then written texts; only poetic narrative is memorable in the required way and, as we should have learned from Vico,[12] it is the linguistic capacities and abilities provided by poetry and saga which make later forms of prose possible. Concepts are first acquired and understood in terms of poetic images and the movement of thought from the concreteness and particularity of the imaged to the abstractness of the conceptual never completely leaves that concreteness and particularity behind. Conceptions of courage and of justice, of authority, sovereignty and property, of what understanding is and what failure to understand is, all these will continue to be elaborated from exemplars to be found in the socially recognized canonical texts. And this will still be the case when prose supplements poetry, when law books are added to myth and epic and when dramatic works are added to both. The consequence is that when two such distinct linguistic communities confront one another, each with its own body of canonical texts, its own exemplary images and its own tradition of elaborating concepts in terms of these, but each also lacking a knowledge of, let alone linguistic capacities informed by, the tradition of the other community, each will represent the beliefs of the other within its own discourse in abstraction from the relevant tradition and so in a way that ensures misunderstanding. From each point of view certain of the key concepts and beliefs of the other, just because they are presented apart from that context of inherited texts from which they draw their conceptual life, will necessarily appear contextless and lacking in justification.

Here we confront one more instance of the hermeneutic circle. The initial inability of the members of each linguistic community to translate certain parts of the language of the other community into their own is a barrier to knowledge of the tradition embodied in the uses of that language; but lack of knowledge of the tradition is itself sufficient to preclude accurate translation of those parts of the alien language. And once again the fact that certain other parts of the two languages may translate quite easily into each other provides no reason at all for skepticism about partial untranslatability. The sentences-in-use which are the untranslatable parts of this type of language-in-use are not in fact capable of being logically derived from, constructed out of, reduced to, or otherwise rendered into the sentences-in-use which comprise the translatable part of the same language-in-use. Nor should this surprise us. One of the marks of a genuinely adequate knowledge of two quite different languages by one and the same person is that person's ability to discriminate between those parts of each language which are translatable into the other and those which are not. Some degree of partial untranslatability marks the relationship of every language to every other.

Notice that this recognition of untranslatability never entails an acknowledgment of some necessary limit to understanding. Conversely, that we can understand completely what is being said in some language other than our own never entails that we can translate what we understand. And it is this ability both to understand and to recognize the partial untranslatability of what is understood which combines with the specific social, conceptual and linguistic characteristics of the type of boundary situation which I have identified to create the predicament of the bilingual speaker who in that type of situation has to choose between membership in one or other of the two rival linguistic communities.

Remember that the contingent features of that speaker's situation make this not only a choice between languages, but between two mutually incompatible conceptualizations of natural and social reality; and it is not only a choice between two mutually incompatible sets of beliefs, but one between sets of beliefs so structured that each has internal to it its own standards of truth and justification. Moreover this choice has to be made with only the limited linguistic and conceptual resources afforded by the two languages in question. What constraints do these limits impose?

They exclude the possibility of appeal to some neutral or independent standard of rational justification to justify the choice of one set of beliefs, one way of life, one linguistic community rather than the other. For the only standards of truth and justification made available within the two communities are those between which a choice has to be made. And the only resources afforded for the members of each community to represent the concepts, beliefs and standards of the other ensure that from the point of view of each its own concepts, beliefs and standards will be vindicated and those of its rival found wanting.

Here then two rival conceptual schemes do confront one another. For those culturally and linguistically able to inhabit only one of them no problem arises. But for our imagined person who has the abilities to understand both, but who must choose to inhabit only one, the nature of the choice is bound, if he or she is adequately reflective, to transform his or her understanding of truth and of rational justification. For he or she will not be able to find application for the concepts of truth and justification which are independent of the standards of one community or the other. There is no access to any subject-matter which is not conceptualized in terms that already presuppose the truth of one set of claims rather than the other. Hegel's proscription of any appeal to an extra-conceptual reality is not being infringed. Each community, using its own criteria of *sameness* and *difference*, recognizes that it is one and the same subject-matter about which they are advancing their claim; incommensurability and incompatibility are not incompatible.

The only way to characterize adequately the predicament thus created for our imaginary person is in the idiom which Plato provided. For that person will now have to reinterpret the predicates 'is true' and 'is justified' so that to apply them will in future claim no more than would be claimed by 'seems true to this particular community' or 'seems justified to this particular community.' Rational choice will have transformed our imaginary person into a relativist. But why call this a predicament? Because in so reinterpreting these predicates our imaginary Zuni or Irish person will have, without in the least intending to, separated him- or herself effectively from both contending communities. For no sixteenth- or seventeenth-century community was able to understand itself relativistically.

To all this the reply may well be: So what? Even if it is conceded that I have provided a defensible version of relativism, and even if it is allowed that our imaginary person did, in certain times and places, have real counterparts, Irish or Zuni or whatever, what of it? That kind of relativism was imposed by the contingencies of their historical, social, and linguistic circumstances; contingencies which deprived our imaginary person and his or her real counterparts of the linguistic and conceptual resources necessary to avoid or refute relativism. But *we*, it may be suggested, do have those resources, so what is the relevance of your philosophical figment to *us*?

Just this is, of course, the question. Is it indeed the case that, if we were to specify the linguistic and conceptual resources that would have to be provided to enable our imaginary person to overcome the particular contingent limitations of his or her situation, we should have shown how relativism can be avoided or refuted? If we succeed in transforming this imaginary person, so that he or she becomes just like us, will the relativization of the predicates of truth and justification no longer be forced upon him or her, or indeed ourselves? To these questions I therefore turn, but before turning I want to enquire briefly what will be at stake in giving one kind of answer to them rather than another.

III

The same considerations, which ensure that someone compelled to choose between the claims of two rival linguistic communities, in the type of circumstance that I have described, will be unable to appeal to any neutral, independent standard of rational justification by which to judge between their competing claims, also ensure that more generally the members of any two such communities will have to conduct their relationship with members of the other community without resort to any such appeal. But where there is no resort to such standards, human relationships are perforce relationships of will and power unmediated by rationality. I do not mean that, where there is no resort to such standards, each of the contending parties in such communal relationships will necessarily act unreasonably, that is unreasonably from its own particular point of view as to what constitutes unreason. But it is just that point of view that in their transactions each community will be trying to impose upon the other. And when it becomes reasonable from the point of view of one of the contending parties to impose their will by force upon the other in the name of their own idiosyncratic conception of reasonableness, that is what they will do.

So it was with the Spanish in their relationships with the Zuni, so it has been with the English in their relationships with the Irish. And one instrument of such force is the imposition of one's own language at the expense of the other's. But can it ever be otherwise? Only if the relativism which emerged as the only rational attitude to the competing claims of two such antagonistic communities turns out not to be the last word on all relationships between rival human communities; only, that is, if linguistic and conceptual resources can indeed be supplied, so that that relativism can be avoided or circumvented. For only in cases where that relativism does not have the last word does the possibility open up of substituting, for a politics in which the exercise of power is unmediated by rationality, a politics in which the exercise of power is both mediated and tempered by appeal to standards of rational justification independent of the particularism of the contending parties.

I am not, of course, suggesting that the identification and formulation of such nonrelativist standards of truth and justification is ever by itself sufficient to overcome a politics of unmediated will and power, in the conflicts that occur within communities, let alone in the conflicts that occur between communities. And I am not suggesting that force may not, on occasion, be used to serve the purposes of genuine practical rationality as well as those of idiosyncratic and one-sided reasonableness. I *am* claiming that it is only in those forms of human relationship in which it is possible to appeal to impersonal standards of judgment, neutral between competing claims and affording the best type of rational justification both relevant and available, that the possibility opens up of unmasking and dethroning arbitrary exercises of power, tyrannical power within communities and imperialist power between communities. Plato was once again right: the argument against the tyrant and the argument against relativized predicates of truth and justification require the same premises.

This would, of course, be denied by our contemporary post-Nietzschean anti-Platonists. But even they, on occasion, inadvertently provide support for this thesis. Perhaps the most cogent, because the most systematic, exposition of the view that all attempts to appeal to would-be impersonal standards of truth and rational justification must fail to provide any effective alternative to established distributions of power, just because every such attempt and appeal itself operates according to the laws of some institutionalized distribution of power, is that of Michel Foucault in his earlier writings. So Foucault can write about the politics of truth and the political economy of truth in a way that treats all appeals to truth and to rational justification as themselves particularist forms of power inextricably associated with other forms of imposition—and constraint.[13] But Foucault cannot articulate this view either generally or in his detailed institutional studies without presupposing a radical incommensurability thesis, a thesis that indeed only seems to emerge as a conclusion from his studies because it *was* presupposed from the outset. And that thesis is entitled to our assent, if and only if the version of relativism which I have described does have the last word.

So it turns out that how we understand the politics of power depends in crucial part upon the answers that we give to certain philosophical questions. Janice Moulton[14] and Robert Nozick[15] have both recently suggested that philosophy has been damaged by an excessive use of adversarial and antagonistic idioms. We speak too readily, they think, of winning and losing arguments, of others being forced to acknowledge our conclusions and so on; and insofar as such idioms obscure the need for the cooperative virtues in philosophical activity, they are certainly right. Nonetheless, the language of antagonism has one important positive function. It signals to us that philosophy, like all other institutionalized human activities, is a milieu of conflict. And the conflicts of philosophy stand in a number of often complex and often indirect relationships to a variety of other conflicts. The complexity, the indirectness and the variety all help to conceal from us that even the more abstract and technical issues of our discipline—issues concerning naming, reference, truth and translatability—may on occasion be as crucial in their political or social implications as are theories of the social contract or of natural right. The former no less than the latter have implications for the nature and limitations of rationality in the arenas of political society. All philosophy, one way or another, is political philosophy.

Sometimes philosophy fares better by our forgetting this, at least temporarily, but we can scarcely avoid bearing it in mind in returning to the question to which the present argument has led: what other resources would our imaginary person in his or her sixteenth- or seventeenth-century boundary situation have had to possess, what resources that he or she lacked would we have to possess, if we are to be able to appeal to standards of judgment in respect of truth and rational justification which do not relativize these predicates to the conceptual scheme of one particular cultural and linguistic community?

IV

A necessary first step out of the relativistic predicament would be the learning of some third language, a language of a very different kind from the two available to our imaginary person so far. Such a third language, if it was to provide the needed resources, would have to be a language with two central characteristics. First its everyday use must be such that it does *not* presuppose allegiance to either of the two rival sets of beliefs between which our imaginary person has to choose or indeed, so far as possible, to any other set of beliefs which might compete for allegiance with those two. And secondly it must be able to provide the resources for an accurate representation of the two competing schemes of belief, including that in the tradition of each community which provides that background for its present beliefs, without which they cannot be fully intelligible nor their purported justification adequately understood. What kind of language-in-use would this be?

One central feature that it would have to possess, if it were to satisfy the first of these two conditions, can be illustrated by considering how its use of proper names, for example of place-names, would contrast with that of the languages in terms of which the problem has so far been framed. For in this third language the relationship of a name to what is named will have to be specifiable, so far as possible, independently of any particular scheme of identification embodying the beliefs of some particular community. Names in consequence will have to have become detached from those descriptions which, within some given and presupposed context deemed by the beliefs of some particular community, uniquely identify person or place. Particular proper names will have ceased to be equivalent to, and, in virtue of that loss of equivalence, will have ceased to have the same sense as, particular definite descriptions. Names of places will have become equally available for any user to employ whatever his or her beliefs. Names having been Fregean will have become by a process of social change Kripkean.[16]

The immediate response of most philosophical logicians will once again be to say that I have in so characterizing these changes confused the essential function of naming with its merely contingent accompaniments. But it is just this notion of a single essential naming relationship or function that I reject; just as we have learned that meaning is not a unitary notion, so we ought also to have learned that there are multifarious modes of identifying, picking out, referring to, calling towards, in, or up and the like, all of which connect a name and a named, but there is no single core relation of name to named for theories of reference to be theories of. Or rather, if there were to be such a relation, it would be what Russell said it was, and it is notorious that Russell's characterization of that relation entails that there is indeed a class of proper names, but that none of the expressions which we have hitherto called names is among them.[17]

A second feature of this type of language will be the absence of texts which are canonical for its common use. Allusion and quotation will have become specialized devices and the literate will have been divorced from the literary. For texts, whether oral or written, embody and presuppose beliefs and this type of language is, so far as possible, *qua* language-in-use, neutral between competing systems of beliefs. What it will provide are resources for the representation of an indefinite variety of systems of beliefs, most of them originally at home in very different types of linguistic community by means of a variety of devices which enable those who construct such representations to do so in a way that is quite independent of their own commitments. What kind of devices are these? Where the text is in a foreign language, translation will be supplemented both by paraphrase and by scholarly gloss.[18] Words as common as '*polis*' and '*dikaiosune*' in fifth-century ancient Greek cannot be translated in any strict sense into twentieth-century English or French or German—examples, it will have been obvious at once, of this type of language—but their use can be quite adequately elucidated. The traditions that appealed to canonical texts can now become matter for successful historical enquiry and the relevant texts embodying those traditions can be established, edited and translated or otherwise elucidated. The belief-system of any and every culture, or of almost any and every culture, can thus be accurately represented within our own. But certain features of the resulting stock of representations need to be taken into account.

One concerns the asymmetry of this representation relation. From the fact that we in modern English or some other modern language, with our academic resources, can accurately represent the belief-system or part of the belief-system of another culture, it does not follow that the corresponding part of our belief-system can be represented in the language-in-use of that other culture. Using modern English, Charles H. Kahn has shown how the Homeric uses of the verb *eimi* can be accurately and adequately represented.[19] But his explanation of why certain types of translation or paraphrase would be a misrepresentation, namely that, for example, the English verb 'exist' has emerged from a history whose first stage was the transition to classical Greek and which was then informed successively by classical Latin poetic usage, by medieval Latin philosophical usage and finally by some essentially modern preoccupations, so that we just cannot use 'exist' to translate or to explicate the characteristic and varying features of Homeric uses of *eimi*, has as a consequence that it would not have been possible within the Homeric linguistic community to represent accurately the modern English uses of 'exist.' And what is true of the relationship of archaic Greek to modern English would be equally true of the relationship to modern English of seventeenth-century Irish or sixteenth-century Zuni. But from this fact we might be tempted to draw a mistaken conclusion.

Return to the condition of our imaginary person once poised between sixteenth-century Zuni and Spanish, or seventeenth-century Irish and English, but now, presumably some three hundred years older, considering whether to address his other problems instead in twentieth-century English or French or whatever. Since such a person can provide him- or herself with such an adequate degree of neutral representation of both systems of belief in a modern language, but cannot represent adequately or neutrally in either of his or her earlier languages either the systems of belief of the rival linguistic communities who spoke those languages or the standpoints afforded by twentieth-century English or French for the provision of such representation, it might seem that the only rational course for such a person is to conduct his or her enquiry from now on in one of the modern languages, thus escaping from some at least of the limitations imposed on his or her earlier condition, the very limitations which enforced relativist conclusions. But it is just at this point that a second feature of the representations of schemes of belief in specifically modern natural languages presents a crucial difficulty.

The only way in which our frustrated relativist can hope to transcend the limitations which imposed that relativism is by formulating in the language that he or she can now speak, one of the languages of modernity, an impersonal and neutral standard of rational justification in the light of which the claims of the competing belief-systems can be evaluated. But what he or she will in fact learn from acquiring this new language is that it is a central feature of the culture whose language it is that rationally founded agreement as to the nature of the justification required is not to be obtained. Rational justification within the context of such cultures becomes an essentially contested concept and this for a number of distinct, but related types of reason.

One arises from the nature of the historical process which made the language of modernity what it is. A central feature of that process had to be, I have already argued, the detachment of the language-in-use from any particular set of canonical texts; and an early stage in that history was the gradual accumulation in the culture of so many different, heterogeneous and conflicting bodies of canonical texts from so many diverse parts of the cultural past that every one of them had to forego any exclusive claim to canonical status and thereby, it soon became apparent, any claim to canonical status at all. So the accumulation of Greek, Hebrew and Latin texts at the Renaissance proved only a prologue not only to the annexation of Chinese, Sanskrit, Mayan and Old Irish texts, and to the bestowal of equal status upon texts in European vernacular languages from the thirteenth to the nineteenth centuries, but also to the discovery of a wide range of preliterate cultures, the whole finally to be assembled in that modern liberal arts college museum of academic culture, whose introductory tour is provided by those Great Books courses which run from Gilgamesh to Saul Bellow via Confucius, Dante, Newton, Tristram Shandy,[20] and Margaret Mead.

What the history that culminates in this kind of educational gallimaufry produced along the way was a large and general awareness of the wide range of varying and conflicting types of justificatory argument used to support various types of contending belief, and also of the wide range of varying and conflicting theoretical accounts of rational justification available to support their use. The consequence was a multiplication of rival standpoints concerning a wide range of subject-matters, none of them able to provide the resources for their own final vindication and the overthrow of their competitors. So within philosophy foundationalists war with coherentists and both with skeptics and perspectivists; while conceptions of truth as empirical adequacy contend against a variety of mutually incompatible realisms and both against truth conceived as disclosure. Within the academic study of literature, controversies—over the nature of interpretation and about the justification not only of particular interpretations of particular texts but even of what it is that such interpretations are interpretations of—parody philosophical debate in both idiom and interminability. And psychology has happily accommodated numbers of mutually incompatible schools of thought, each with its own idiosyncratic account of justification, ever since it became an independent academic discipline.

Where the dominant institutions and modes of thought in our larger political society sanction and even encourage disagreement, as upon theological questions, it is widely accepted that in the debates between contending modes of justification there can be no rational conclusion. But even where those same institutions and modes of thought prescribe a large measure of agreement, as in the natural sciences, not only do non-scientific modes of thought such as astrology (which happens to have its own well-organized and far from unsophisticated standards of justification) continue to flourish alongside the sciences, but it remains impossible to secure agreement on why the key transitions in the past history of our culture from prescientific thought to scientific, and from one mode of scientific thought to another, were or are rationally justified. So incommensurability as a feature of the history of the natural sciences has continually been rediscovered and recharacterized from a variety of justificatory standpoints: by Gaston Bachelard in the context of the French debates of the 1920s; by Michael Polanyi in such a way as to warrant a blend of fideism and realism; by Thomas

Kuhn in a way designed to undermine logical empiricism; by Paul Feyerabend in an anarchist mode; and by Ian Hacking in an historical thesis about 'styles of thought.'

The multiplicity of mutually irreconcilable standpoints concerning justification is one that each of us tends to recognize easily and even scornfully in other academic professions. But from within our own profession each of us characteristically views and describes the situation only from the specific point of view of his or her own commitments, judging the success and failure of other points of view from the standpoint afforded by standards of justification internal to our own; and by so doing we render our overall cultural situation invisible, at least for most of the time. That this should be the case, that we should tend to be guilty of this kind of one-sidedness, is scarcely surprising. It says no more about us than that we are, sociologically at least, normal human beings. The danger of contemporary anti-relativism however is that it suggests that what is in fact a contingent social condition whose limitations it is important for us to overcome is in fact a necessary condition of rational social existence. For anti-relativism pictures us first as necessarily inhabiting our own conceptual scheme, our own *Weltanschauung* ("*Whose* conceptual scheme, whose *Weltanschaung* but our own could we be expected to inhabit?" is the rhetorical question that is sometimes posed) and secondly as necessarily acquiring whatever understanding we may possess of the conceptual schemes and *Weltanschaung* of others by a process of translation so conceived that any intelligible rendering of the concepts and beliefs of the others must represent them as in all central respects similar to our own.

What I have tried to suggest by contrast is that when we learn the languages of certain radically different cultures, it is in the course of discovering what is untranslatable in them, and why, that we not only learn how to occupy alternative viewpoints, but in terms of those viewpoints to frame questions to which under certain conditions a version of relativism is the inescapable answer. And in so doing we are also able to learn how to view our own peculiarly modern standpoint from a vantage point outside itself. For consider now the view of that modern standpoint afforded to our imaginary person who had hoped to remedy the deficiencies of his or her particular type of premodern language by learning to speak one of the languages of modernity.

Where in his or her premodern language he or she was unable to free him- or herself from the limitations of the justificatory schemes built into and presupposed by each particular language-in-use, and so was unable to discover a set of neutral and independent standards of rational justification, by appeal to which his or her choice of allegiance to the beliefs and way of life of one community rather than the other could be made, he or she now speaks a language the use of which is free from such commitments. But the culture which is able to make such a language available is so only because it is a culture offering, for the relevant kinds of controversial subject-matter, all too many heterogeneous and incompatible schemes of rational justification. And every attempt to advance sufficient reasons for choosing any one such scheme over its rivals must always turn out to presuppose the prior adoption of that scheme itself or of some other. For without such a prior pre-rational commitment, no reason will count as a good reason.

Hence, our imaginary person whose acquisition of one of the natural languages of modernity—twentieth-century English or French or whatever—was to rescue him or her from the relativism imposed by his or her previous condition cannot find here any more than there, albeit for very different reasons, any genuinely neutral and independent standard of rational justification. And it remains only to recognize that if our imaginary sixteenth- or seventeenth-century person, knowing both the languages that he or she then knew and subsequently learning our own, would be unable to avoid relativistic conclusions, then we in turn by learning his or her languages, or languages like them, and so learning both to imagine and to understand ourselves from the standpoint of such an external observer would have to reach the same conclusions. Relativism after all turns out to be so far immune to refutation, even by us.

V

It does not follow that relativism cannot be transcended. We may be tempted to think so by noticing that the version of relativism which resists refutation is itself a relativized relativism, since what my arguments show, if they succeed, are that relativism is inescapable from certain particular points of view—one of which happens to be that which most people in modern societies such as ours take to be their own. And this may seem to provide additional confirmation, if such is still needed, that there is after all no mode of thought, enquiry or practice which is not from some particular point of view, and whose judgments do not therefore take place on the basis of what Edmund Burke called prejudices, prejudgments. But it does not follow, as we might suppose if we did concede the last word to relativism, that we are thereby condemned to or imprisoned within our own particular standpoint, able to controvert that of others only by appealing to standards which already presuppose the standpoint of our own prejudices. Why not?

Begin from a fact which, at this stage, can be little more than suggestive. It is that those natural languages in which philosophy became a developed form of enquiry, so later generating from itself first the natural and then the social sciences, were in the condition neither on the one hand of sixteenth- and seventeenth-century Zuni and Irish nor in that of the natural languages of modernity. The Attic Greek of the fifth and fourth centuries, the Latin of the twelfth to fourteenth centuries, the English, French, German and Latin of the seventeenth and eighteenth centuries were each of them neither as relatively presupposition-less in respect of key beliefs as the languages of modernity were to become, nor as closely tied in their use to the presuppositions of one single closely knit set of beliefs as some premodern languages are and have been. Consider in this respect the difference between Attic and Homeric Greek or that between mature philo-sophical Latin after Augustine and Jerome and the Latin that had preceded the discoveries by Lucretius and Cicero that they could only think certain Greek thoughts in Latin if they radically neologized. Such languages-in-use, we may note, have a wide enough range of canonical texts to provide to some degree alternative and rival modes of justification, but a narrow enough range so that the debate between these modes is focused and determinate. What emerges within the conceptual schemes of such languages is a developed problematic, a set of debates concerning a body of often interrelated problems, problems canonical for those inhabiting that particular scheme, by reference to work upon which rational progress, or failure to achieve such progress, is evaluated. Each such problematic is, of course, internal to some particular conceptual scheme embod-ied in some particular historical tradition with its own given starting-point, its own prejudices. To become a philosopher always involved learning to inhabit such a tradition, a fact not likely to be obvious to those brought up from infancy within one, but very obvious to those brought up outside any such. It is no acci-dent for example that for Irish speakers to become philosophers, they had first to learn Greek and Latin, like Johannes Scotus Erigena in the ninth century.

The development of a problematic within a tradition characteristically goes through certain well-marked stages—not necessarily, of course, the same stages in every tradition—among them periods in which progress, as judged by the standards internal to that particular tradition, falters or fails, attempt after attempt to solve or resolve certain key problems or issues proves fruitless and the tradition appears, again by its own standards, to have degenerated. Charac-teristically, if not universally, at this stage contradictions appear that cannot be resolved within the particular tradition's own conceptual framework; that is to say, there can be drawn from within the tradition equally well-grounded support for incompatible positions; at the same time enquiries tend to become diverse and particularized and to lose any overall sense of direction; and debates about realism may become fashionable.[21] And what the adherents of such a tradition may have to learn in such a period is that their tradition lacks the resources to explain its own failing condition. They are all the more likely to learn that if they encounter some other standpoint, conceptually richer and more resourceful, which *is* able to provide just such an explanation.

So it was, for example, when Galilean and Newtonian natural philosophy turned out to provide a more adequate explanation by its own standards not only of nature than scholasticism had afforded, but also of why late medieval scholastic enquiries had been only able to proceed so far and no further. Scholasticism's successes and more importantly its frustrations and limitation, judged by scholasticism's own standards of success and failure rather than by any later standards, only became intelligible in the light afforded by Galileo and Newton.

That the theoretical standpoint of Galileo or Newton may have been incommensurable with that of the scholastics is not inconsistent with this recognition of how the later physical tradition transcended the limitations of the earlier. And it is, of course, not only within the history of natural philosophy that this kind of claim can be identified and sometimes vindicated. Such a claim is implicit in the relationship of some of the medieval theistic Aristotelians to Aristotle in respect of theology and of Dante's *Commedia* to the *Aeneid* in respect of poetic imagination.

These examples direct our attention to a central characteristic of theoretical and practical rationality. Rationality, understood within some particular tradition with its own specific conceptual scheme and problematic, as it always has been and will be, nonetheless requires qua rationality a recognition that the rational inadequacies of that tradition from its own point of view, and every tradition must from the point of view of its own problematic view itself as to some degree inadequate—may at any time prove to be such that perhaps only the resources provided by some quite alien tradition—far more alien, it may be, than Newton was to the scholastics—will enable us to identify and to understand the limitations of our own tradition; and this provision may require that we transfer our allegiance to that hitherto alien tradition. It is because such rationality requires this recognition that the key concepts embodied in rational theory and practice within any tradition which has a developed problematic, including the concepts of truth and rational justification, cannot be defined exclusively in terms of or collapsed into those conceptions of them that are presently at home within the modes of theory and practice of the particular conceptual scheme of that tradition, or even some idealized version of those conceptions: the Platonic distinction between 'is true' and 'seems true to such and such person' turns out within such traditions to survive the recognition of the truth in relativism.

It is only from the standpoint of a rationality thus characterized, and that is to say from the standpoint of a tradition embodying such a conception of rationality, that a rejoinder can be made to those post-Nietzschean theories according to which rational argument, enquiry and practice always express some interest of power and are indeed the masks worn by some will to power. And in this respect there is a crucial difference between rationality thus understood and the rationality characteristic of the Enlightenment and of its heirs. Ever since the Enlightenment our culture has been far too hospitable to the all too plainly self-interested belief that, whenever we succeed in discovering the rationality of other and alien cultures and traditions, by making their behavior intelligible and by understanding their languages, what we will also discover is that in essentials they are just like us. Too much in recent and contemporary anti-relativism continues to express this Enlightenment point of view and thereby makes more plausible than they ought to be those theories which identify every form of rationality with some form of contending power. What can liberate rationality from this identification is precisely an acknowledgement, only possible from within a certain kind of tradition, that rationality requires a readiness on our part to accept, and indeed to welcome, a possible future defeat of the forms of theory and practice in which it has up till now been taken to be embodied within our own tradition, at the hands of some alien and perhaps even as yet largely unintelligible tradition of thought and practice; and this is an acknowledgement of which the traditions that we inherit have too seldom been capable.

NOTES

My colleagues John Compton, John Post, Charles Scott and Harry Teloh subjected an earlier version of this address to rigorous and constructive criticism. A different kind of debt is to Brian Friel's play *Translations* (London: Faber & Faber, 1981) and to my former colleague Dennis Tedlock's translations of narrative poetry of the Zuni Indians, *Finding the Centre: The Art of the Zuni Storyteller* (Lincoln: University of Nebraska Press, 1978), which threw a very different light on problems of translation from that afforded by most recent philosophical writing.

1. Anthony Collins, "An Answer to Mr. Clarke's Third Defence of his Letter to Mr. Dodwell," in Samuel Clarke, *The Works of Samuel Clarke, D. D.* (London: John and Paul Knapton, 1738), 3:883.

2. Most notably by Richard Rorty, "Pragmatism, Relativism, and Irrationalism," *Proceedings and Addresses of the American Philosophical Association* 53 (1980): 719–738, reprinted in *Consequences of Pragmatism* (Minneapolis: University of Minnesota Press, 1982), 160–175; and Donald Davidson, "On the Very Idea of a Conceptual Scheme,"

Proceedings and Addresses of the American Philosophical Association 47 (1974): 5–20, reprinted in *Inquiries into Truth and Interpretation* (Oxford: Clarendon, 1984), 183–198, and in *Expressing Evaluations*, The 1982 Lindley Lecture at the University of Kansas (Lawrence: University Press of Kansas, 1984) (this volume, chap. 8).

3. Plato, *Theaetetus*, 152a–179b, esp. 170e–171c.

4. See, for example, in the first part of the *Enzyklopädie der Philosophischen Wissenschaften* (1817), trans. William Wallace as *The Logic of Hegel* (Oxford: Oxford University Press, 1873), sec. 44; and "Remark: The Thing-in-Itself of Transcendental Idealism," appended to chap. 1, A(b) of sec. 2, bk. 2 of Hegel's *Science of Logic* (London: Allen & Unwin, 1969), which is A. V. Miller's translation of the *Wissenschaft der Logik* (1812).

5. Rorty, "Pragmatism, Relativism, and Irrationalism," 167.

6. Davidson argues in "On the Very Idea of a Conceptual Scheme" that the scheme-content distinction involves the notion of a relationship between a language or conceptual scheme, on the one hand, and, on the other, "something neutral and common that lies outside all schemes" (*Inquiries into Truth and Interpretation*, 190) and that the only relationships possible between a language or conceptual scheme and such a something are those of the scheme organizing, systematizing or dividing whatever it is, or of it fitting or accounting for whatever it is. Davidson then shows that spelling out these relationships involves characterizing what was allegedly neutral and common, so that it is neither, but a subject-matter which "we will have to individuate according to familiar principles," so that any language which enables us to speak of it "must be a language very like our own" (192). Hegel argues conversely in the passages cited in note 5 that if we deny to such a something or other those characteristics that it must lack if it is to be genuinely prior to all categorization, as what is "neutral and common" (Davidson's expression) must be, it will turn out to be nothing at all. And in the context of a different discussion, after pointing out that what is alleged to be beyond all conceptualization by reason of its particularity "*cannot be reached* by language. In the actual attempt to say it, it would therefore crumble away," in Georg Wilhelm Friedrich Hegel, *Phanomenologie des Geistes* (1807), para. 110, in *Phenomenology of Spirit*, trans. A. V. Miller (Oxford: Clarendon Press, 1977), he points out that in characterizing the whatever it is we find ourselves individuating according to familiar principles, anticipating Davidson very precisely.

7. One example of Hegel's treatment of rival conceptual schemes is found in the *Phanomenologie*, VI, B, II, as "*Der Kampf der Aufklärung mit dem Aberglauben.*"

8. For Vico, who gave us the first genuinely historical treatment of conceptual schemes, see especially bk. 4, sec. 1–11 of the *Principi di Scienza Nuova* (1744), trans. T. G. Bergin and H. Fisch as *The New Science of Giambattista Vico* (Ithaca, N.Y.: Cornell University Press, 1948).

9. It was, of course, Collingwood's anti-realism, already spelled out in *Speculum Mentis* (Oxford: Clarendon Press, 1924), that committed him to rejection of any version

of the scheme-context distinction. For his treatment of alternative conceptual schemes, see especially the *Essay on Metaphysics* (Oxford: Clarendon Press, 1940).

10. Paul Zipp in "About Proper Names," *Mind* 86 (1977): 319–332, draws attention to the importance of attending "to the relevant anthropological and linguistic date." An exemplary study is Robin Fox, "Structure of Personal Names on Tory Island," *Man* (1963), reprinted as "Personal Names," in *Encounter with Anthropology* (New York: Harcourt Brace Jovanovich, 1973).

11. On the first encounters of the Zuni with the Spaniards, see F. H. Cushing, "Outlines of Zuni Creation Myths," in *13th Annual Report of the Bureau of Ethnology* (Washington, D.C., 1896), 326–333, and on the way places are located and the middle place named, 367–373.

12. Vico, *Principi di Scienza Nuova*, 34–36, for example.

13. See, for an introduction, chaps. 5, 6 (both originally in Michel Foucault, *Microfisica del potere* [Turin: Einaudi, 1977]) of *Power/Knowledge: Selected Interviews and Other Writings, 1972–1977*, ed. Colin Gordon (New York: Pantheon Books, 1980). Chapter 5 is translated by Kate Soper; chapter 6, by Colin Gordon.

14. Janice Moulton, "A Paradigm of Philosophy: The Adversary Method," in *Discovering Reality: Feminist Perspectives on Epistemology, Metaphysics, Methodology, and Philosophy of Science*, ed. S. Harding and M. B. Hintikka (Dordrecht: Reidel, 1983).

15. Robert Nozick, *Philosophical Explanations* (Cambridge, Mass.: Harvard University Press, 1981), 4–8.

16. What has to be supplied here is an account of how one and the same proper name can be used in a variety of ways which connect it to one and the same bearer.

17. Bertrand Russell, "The Philosophy of Logical Atomism," in *Logic and Knowledge: Essays, 1901–1950*, ed. R. C. Marsh (London: Allen & Unwin, 1956), 200–203; originally published in *The Monist* (1918).

18. John Wallace, "Translation Theories and the Decipherment of Linear B," *Theory and Decision* 11 (1979): 153–237.

19. Charles H. Hahn, *The Verb 'Be' in Ancient Greek*, pt. 6 of J. W. M. Verhaar, ed., *The Verb 'Be' and Its Synonyms: Philosophical and Grammatical Studies*, Foundations of Language Supplement Series, vol. 16 (Dordrecht: Reidel, 1973).

20. Laurence Sterne, *The Life and Opinions of Tristram Shandy* (London: J. Dodsley, 1768).

21. Neither realism nor anti-realism should be thought of as mistakes (or truths) generated by philosophers reflecting upon the sciences from some external standpoint. They are in fact primarily moments in the self-interpretation of the sciences. And the growth of debates about realism characteristically is a symptom of the inability of scientists to give a cogent account to themselves of the status of their enquiries.

27

Internal Criticism and Indian Rationalist Traditions

MARTHA C. NUSSBAUM AND AMARTYA SEN

I. INTRODUCTION

This paper has two closely related aims. The first is to diagnose some problems of emphasis and interpretation that have arisen in attempts to describe the values of a particular society, namely, India. The second is to investigate some general methodological and philosophical issues that are raised by any attempt to describe and assess the values of a traditional society. Both projects were originally motivated by the desire to find a philosophical and conceptual framework within which to discuss some urgent problems that arise in the course of 'development,' especially economic development. It was originally prepared for a project at the World Institute for Development Economics Research (WIDER) that was concerned with analyzing the relationship among value, technology, and development. The project was based on the important recognition that values cannot be treated, as they often are in the literature on 'economic development,' as purely instrumental objects in promoting development. Indeed, the very idea of

Martha C. Nussbaum and Amartya Sen, "Internal Criticism and Indian Rationalist Traditions," was originally published in *Relativism: Interpretation and Confrontation*, edited by Michael Krausz, and published by Notre Dame University Press, 1989, pp. 299–325. Reprinted here with permission of the authors. All rights reserved.

development—whether seen from within a culture or in the stylized impersonal context of development economics—is inevitably based on a particular class of values, in terms of which progress is judged and development is measured.

There are two distinct issues involved in recognizing the importance of the 'value-relativity' of the concept of development. The first is the elementary but far-reaching fact that without some idea of ends that are themselves external to the development process and in terms of which the process may be assessed, we cannot begin to say what changes are to count as development. In judging development in the context of a culture the values that are supported and are sustainable in that culture provide an essential point of reference. The need for internal criticism and rational assessment of the values of a culture—to be discussed presently (section IV)—does not undermine the essentiality of the cultural reference or eliminate the fact of the value-relativity of the concept of development.

The second issue concerns the possible undermining of traditional values that may result from the process of change. The WIDER project has been particularly concerned with the impact of imported technology on traditional values, but the problem is, of course, relevant in many other contexts as well. This 'undermining' may take two rather different forms, which have to be distinguished. It could be the case that the *objects of valuation* that a particular traditional value system treasures—such as a particular lifestyle—may become more difficult to obtain and sustain as a result of material change. The other way that the values may be 'undermined' is a weakening of the hold of those *values themselves* on the subjects.

To illustrate the difference, the use of modern technology may make it hard to lead a life of free, unrouted work, and this would, in one sense, 'undermine' a traditional value that attaches importance to spontaneity of the kind rejected by the use of the new technology. The other sense of 'undermining' the value in question is to make people turn against valuing that type of spontaneity altogether. The two processes, which we may respectively call 'object failure' and 'value rejection,' are undoubtedly related to each other (for one thing, 'sour grapes' are common enough),[1] but they raise rather different evaluative problems, neither of which can subsume the other.

When values are unchanged but the objects valued (such as states of affairs, activities, and so on) become unachievable (that is, when there is object failure), there is a clear and palpable loss *within* the unchanging frame of reference. The importance that is attached to that loss cannot be independent of the assessment of that value, but there is no denial of the immediacy of the loss. In the case, on the other hand, of value rejection the frame of reference itself ceases to be stationary, and whether there is any loss in this or not cannot be ascertained automatically on the basis of *either* the subsequent *or* the antecedent values. The *process* of rejection is important here. Was the rejection based on, or would it be supported by, a reasoned and involved internal critique? A reasoned critical rejection of old values on the basis of, say, new facts or new knowledge or new understanding of old facts must command respect. Indeed, such value rejection may often show the power and reach of an appropriate internal critique (see sections IV and V).

Aside from the conceptual and evaluative complications involved in this problem, there are also difficult substantive issues in characterizing the values of a culture. The identification of values may itself be difficult, and there is, in addition, the further problem of determining what values are to be regarded as central. The lives of human beings are guided by a variety of valuational presumptions and attitudes, and some things are valued more fundamentally than others. Indeed, some values are basically instrumental to achieving other valuable things, and this instrumentality may either be immediately seen or be ascertainable on the basis of probing and deliberative analysis.[2] The undermining of some values subscribed to in a community may be a matter of great moment in a way the undermining of some other—more instrumental or less deeply held—values need not be.

The problem of identification of values and diagnosis of central values is further compounded by the diversity that may well exist within a community. Various divergent traditions may survive side by side within the same country and indeed even in the same locality. Determining what the 'basic' traditional values are (the undermining of which, especially through object failure, would involve a loss) may not be a trivial, or even a simple, question. Since no culture is fully static, there is also the problem of valuational dynamics and evolution, and the issue of centrality is not independent of that problem either.

The substantive issue with which our discussion is concerned relates to certain standard diagnoses of the fundamental nature of Indian culture and the identification of the central values in that tradition, the undermining of which is particularly feared by cultural conservationists (section II). This essay will examine some biases in the common reading of Indian traditions and cultures in this context (section III), arguing, in particular, that there has been an overemphasis on the mystical and religious aspects of Indian society and a relative neglect of the more 'rationalistic' and 'analytical' features.

Much of our discussion, however, is concerned with methodological rather than substantive issues (sections IV–V). Understanding a culture and its central values is a demanding exercise, raising difficult problems of observation and evidence, on the one hand, and of interpretation and assessment, on the other.

Indeed, the paper's substantive propositions regarding the nature of Indian culture and its misdescriptions are put forward here with some hesitation and tentativeness in recognition of the difficulty of these methodological problems. We shall say little here about problems of evidence and description, which are plain enough from the paper's substantive sections. But we shall describe an approach to rational critical assessment, one that has Aristotelian roots, and we shall examine its power and reach.

II. RELIGION, MYSTICISM, AND THE NONRATIONAL

The importance of religion in Indian society can scarcely be denied. Religious values and practices differ between groups. Furthermore, given the nature of Hinduism, the majority religion in India, the religious beliefs are frequently of a kind that can be described as being more mystical than corresponding religious beliefs in many other cultures, though the ranking of mysticism is an inherently ambiguous exercise.

In understanding the values of a culture, it is tempting to take a rapid jump from one aspect of the lives that many people lead to a characterization of the 'essence' of that culture. What may be called the 'more mystical than thou' interpretation of the nature of Indian culture undoubtedly draws part of its strength from such an exercise. The interpretation is, however, also much assisted by a particular reading of the intellectual contributions of India to the world of thought, imagination, and creativity. The sheer volume of religious literature in India far exceeds that of all other countries, perhaps even all of them put together. Given the religious interpretation of Indian philosophy (on which more presently), the massive contribution of philosophical ideas coming from India is also typically seen in a very special light, emphasizing their nonanalytical aspects.

There are, of course, many scholarly studies of other aspects of Indian civilization, and there is no dearth of expertise on other areas of Indian culture and thought, but as a broad generalization of how India is widely viewed in terms of its alleged values and culture there is much truth in this more mystical imaging. Aside from the role of this image in the assessment of Indian culture, it also has a clear bearing on the alarm with which the undermining of 'traditional' Indian values is often viewed in the context of economic development. Modern technology and science tend to be hostile to mysticism, and to that extent it might well be thought that something exceptionally valuable is being threatened by the expansion of modern technology and science occurring in India. The issue, thus, relates directly to the central question in the WIDER research project on technology and values.[3]

The special imaging of India is not new. In the last few centuries, with the so-called expansion of Europe, the common Western perception of India has been, to a great extent, based on looking for contrasts, with differences, rather than similarities, tending to be emphasized in the Western 'discovery of India.' This has gone hand in hand with recognizing certain very elementary points of similarity on basic and gross matters (rather than those involving sophistication of emotions or thought). For example, Rudyard Kipling could unhesitatingly assert, "Oh, East is East, and West is West, and never the twain shall meet," and in the same verse go on to say:

> But there is neither East nor West,
> nor Border, nor Breed, nor Birth,
> When two strong men stand face to face,
> though they come from the ends of earth! (*The Ballad of East and West*)

The 'macho' values may thus be shared between the 'East' and the 'West,' which for Kipling did not really differ much from India and Britain respectively, but on less elementary matters Kipling would not accept any diminution of the East-West gulf.

The image of the 'mystical East,' and specifically India, is not a matter only of popular conception but has a good deal of following in the typical Indologist's summary view of Indian intellectual history. In this respect, there is also no real gulf between the things that the Western scholars have typically tended to emphasize in Indian culture and what Indian Indologists have themselves most often highlighted. This close correspondence may not, however, be particularly remarkable, since approaches to 'cultural summarizing' are generally quite 'infectious,' and, no less importantly, modern Indian scholarship is greatly derivative from the West. There is nothing odd in the fact that this dependence extends even to the understanding of the 'essence' of Indian culture itself. It is nevertheless a matter of some descriptive importance to recognize that the more mystical overall view of Indian traditions is largely *shared* in Western and Indian professional perceptions.

In their eminently useful 'sourcebook' of Indian philosophy, Radhakrishnan and Moore give expression to the standard view of Indian philosophy when they say, "the chief mark of Indian philosophy in general is its concentration upon the spiritual."[4] This is not based on ignoring nonspiritual parts of Indian thinking altogether (indeed Radhakrishnan and Moore include in their sourcebook extensive excerpts from the atheistic and materialistic 'Cārvāka' school) (227–249). It is based rather on seeing these departures as aberrations, which are 'relatively minor' (xxiii).

This simple view of the nature of Indian philosophy is rather rarely challenged. Bimal Matilal, one of the few major challengers, puts the problem thus in answer to the criticism that he has been 'leaning over backwards' to 'show the analytic nature of Indian philosophy': "Too often the term Indian philosophy is identified with a subject that is presented as mystical and non-argumentative, that is at best poetic and at worst dogmatic. A corrective to this view is long overdue."[5]

In fact, the origins of the dominant view of Indian philosophy go back many centuries. For example, already in 1690, John Locke felt rather superior on this score in his *Essay Concerning Human Understanding*:

> Had the poor Indian Philosopher (who imagined that the earth also wanted something to bear it Up) but thought of this word substance he needed not to have been at the trouble to find an elephant to support it, and a tortoise to support his elephant; the word substance would have done it effectively.[6]

> The Indian before mentioned who, saying that the world was supported by a great elephant, was asked what the elephant rested on; to which his answer was, a great tortoise; but being again pressed to know what gave support to the broad-backed tortoise, replied, *something he knows not what*. (chap. 23, 2)

The parable does of course come from an old religious myth in India, but as Matilal notes, "it would be impossible to find a text in classical Indian philosophy where the elephant-tortoise device is put forward as a philosophical explanation of the support of the earth."[7]

III. PLURALITIES AND DIVISIONS

There is, in fact, a peculiar contrast between the enormous variety in traditional Indian culture and the simple concentration on mysticism and nonrationality in the typical image of India. The contrast is not, however, one of nonintersecting contrariness. The mystical and the nonrational do, in fact, exist plentifully in Indian intellectual history and social practice. The problem relates, not to the *inclusion* of these elements in the conventional image of India, but to the almost total *exclusion* of all other elements, which also belong to the Indian traditions.[8]

aim is to help, and that aim can never be completely separated from a concern for the patient's own sense of the better and the worse. Suppose the heavenly doctor comes down from the rim of heaven and announces, "See this condition of body which you, poor old women, find intolerably painful and crippling? Well, that's what health is, as I have discovered by consulting the sort of knowledge that resides in true being. You children here: you say that you are hungry; you cry. But this too is health; and you will be making cognitive progress if you learn to see things this way." Our first reaction may be that this 'doctor' is sadistic and callous. But the important point here is that he *cannot be right*.

Health does not have an existence in heaven, apart from people and their lives. It is not a being apart from becoming. People can indeed go wrong about their health in many ways. They can think they are doing well when they are not. They can also think they are doing badly when they are really well. But the *sense* of that claim is that the scientist or doctor could *show* them something about their condition, which, were they to listen and eventually to understand, would convince them—in terms of a general idea of health and human activity about which they both agree—that their initial judgment had been wrong. Perhaps not all actual individuals will be convinced by the medical truth, but for it to *be* medical truth it seems to be necessary, at the least, that individuals who are in some way representative, attentive, who have scrutinized the alternatives in the right way, should be convinced. This does not, of course, mean that the therapist cannot alter people's ideas concerning what health is at the level of more concrete specification. One of her main tasks will frequently be to produce a concrete specification of this vague end, telling us its elements; and this specification may well clash with the patient's prereflective specification. But the challenge of medicine always is to come back to people's desires and needs and sense of value. It must deliver to them a life that will, in the end, be accepted as a flourishing existence, or else nothing has been accomplished.

So much, Aristotle claims, is true of ethical value. We do not inquire in a vacuum. Our conditions and ways of life, and the hopes, pleasures, pains, and evaluations that are a part of these, cannot be left out of the inquiry without making it pointless and incoherent. We do not stand on the rim of heaven and look 'out there' for truth; if we did, we would not find the right thing. Ethical truth is in and of human life; it can be seen only from the point of view of immersion. He illustrates the point with an example. Some people have suggested that the good life comes to human beings simply by luck or by nature; our own voluntary striving and activity contribute nothing. But, says Aristotle, if we hold this view up against the deepest values and beliefs of the people with whom we are concerned, we are entitled to reject it—and to reject it *as false*—on the grounds that its acceptance would clash so deeply with these values that we would consider such a life to be not worth the living. Here, as in the medical case, we want to say not only that we would be pragmatically justified in rejecting the dismal proposal. We want to say that it must be false as a view of value for these people—just as the view must be false that an intolerable crippling condition of body is what human health is. The ethical good, like health, is a notion whose meaning cannot be understood except in relation to the creature in question, *and* in relation to the nature of their antecedent values and ways of life.[21]

Are we, then, entitled to speak of 'truth' here? John Rawls, developing a somewhat similar account of ethical inquiry,[22] has concluded that we are not. We ought to jettison the notion of truth, once we see that the search for the best account in ethics has these pragmatic elements. Aristotle does, however, speak of truth, and for good reason. Rawls is deeply impressed by a contrast between the human sciences and the natural sciences; and he refers sympathetically to a view like Plato's about truth in the natural sciences. Aristotle holds that *all* truth is in some sense internal and value-laden. And recent work in the philosophy of sciences has given support to his position. Detachment in any area yields not objectivity but incoherence. All truth is seen from somewhere; if we try to see from outside of human life, we see nothing at all. Supporting this position, Hilary Putnam has recently argued that once we have the correct understanding of scientific truth, we will see that there is just as much, and the same sort of, truth and objectivity in ethics as in science. And he argues, with Aristotle, that this really is *truth*, and an 'internal realism,' not a collapse into idealism or subjectivism.[23]

Aristotle has further arguments defending the claim that an internal inquiry can yield truth and objectivity. He gives us an account of the practical achievements of an internal inquiry that show us how it can in fact achieve a degree of clarity, ordering, and societal consensus that entitle us to claim that we have moved beyond the superficial desires of the participants to a deeper and more objective level. That movement, he holds, is what truth in ethics is all about. He does not dispute Plato's claim that many desires that people feel are bad guides to ethical truth—because they can be deformed by conditions of injustice and deprivation, because they frequently express superficial interests that are at odds even with a deeper level of need and value in that same person. But he thinks that the way to circumnavigate these obstacles is not Plato's way of disregarding the people's values altogether; it is to conduct a reflective dialectical examination that will take the people's views very seriously and then move them toward the recognition and the clarification of what actually are, for them, the most central values. Most of the time, we talk carelessly and somewhat 'randomly' about our values. And yet it may sometimes be very important to us (as it is in connection with many of our practical purposes) to become clearer about our values and also to reach some sort of societal agreement about them. Aristotle insists that these two goals—individual clarification and communal attunement—can be achieved together by a cooperative critical discourse that insists upon the philosophical virtues of orderliness, deliberateness, and precision:

Concerning all these things, we must try to seek conviction through arguments, using the traditional beliefs as our witnesses and standards. For it would be best of all if all human beings could come into an evident communal agreement with what we shall say, but, if not, that all should agree in some way. And this they will do if they are led carefully until they shift their position. For everyone has something of his own to contribute to the truth, and it is from these that we go on to give a sort of demonstration about these things. For from what is said truly but not clearly, as we advance we will also get clarity, always moving from what is usually said in a jumbled fashion to a more perspicuous view. There is a difference in every inquiry between arguments that are said in a philosophical way and those that are not. Hence we must not think that it is superfluous for the political person to engage in the sort of reflection that makes perspicuous not only the 'that' but also the 'why': for this is the contribution of the philosopher in each area.[24]

Here again Aristotle insists, against the Platonist approach, on the fundamental internality of the reflective process that assesses values: the 'witnesses' and 'standards' of the process are the 'appearances,' or the shared beliefs, and each participant has something to contribute to the truth. And yet, the process does not give us back a simple repetition of what each person thought at the start. This is so because when we scrutinize what we think, we will notice inconsistencies and unclarities that we do not notice when we simply talk and act without reflecting. When the deliberative process confronts the reflecting participant with all of the alternative views on a topic, leads him or her through a thorough imaginative exploration of each, and shows how each choice bears on many others that this person wishes to make in a consistent way—then many unconsidered positions may be modified. And yet this modification, if it takes place, will take place, not as imposition from without, but as a discovery about that person's own values that are the deepest and the most central. This is self-discovery and discovery of one's own traditions.

Aristotle believes that agreement *among* people will be enhanced by this self-clarifying procedure. For much disagreement results from ambiguous and vague statement of positions, and much more from a pressing of one idea to the neglect of other related considerations. The effort to develop a position that is consistent over many issues frequently leads to the dropping of immoderate claims on a single issue. But his method also relies upon the fact that the parties engaged in the procedure identify themselves as social beings (not as isolated units)—beings connected to one another by a network of relations, political, cognitive, emotional (and the political relation is best understood, he believes, as having emotional dimensions). Thus they conceive of the goal of the reflective process as the finding of a view according to which they can live together in community—a shared and shareable view of value. And so they are frequently willing to move away from a personal claim, even when narrow consistency does not force them to do so, in order to bring themselves into harmony with the views and claims of others—achieving the larger sort of self-consistency that is the internal harmony of the political and relational self.

This process is viewed not in any simple way as the transcending or sacrificing of self; it is a further part of the discovery of self, since the self is understood in its very nature to be a relational entity, and its own ends are understood as shared ends. We emphasize this, since it seems clear that to conceive of the person as fundamentally relational does transform the way in which numerous familiar problems of social and political choice will be stated. And it offers a promising way of reformulating the goals and procedures of the reflective process—one that will also harmonize well with conceptions of selfhood, individuality, and community that are in fact held by many people in developing nations. In Western society they are less widely held, and it has been forcefully argued that they are held by women far more frequently than by men.[25] So we are saying that the most promising account of the reflective assessment of values may be one that departs from *some* traditional norms of Western rationality (though this departure is suggested by Aristotle's criticisms of Plato, therefore by an internal criticism of this tradition by other aspects of itself).

In three other important ways, the Aristotelian process departs from the norms that are frequently defended in contemporary ethical and social theory. This is not the place to go into these in detail, but they need to be mentioned, or the relationship of our process to its political aim will be misunderstood.[26]

i. *Noncommensurability.* The procedure insists on treating each of the values involved as a qualitatively distinct item, not reducible to any other item, not conceivable as simply a certain quantity of something else. This commitment to the qualitative integrity of each value is one of the greatest advantages of this procedure over other approaches that might be used (e.g., in some of the literature on development economics) in assessing traditional cultures.[27]

ii. *Essentiality of the Particular.* This procedure insists that evaluative choices cannot be well made unless we confront contexts of choice, and the items in them, as particulars (in this connection, one of us has spoken of 'the priority of the particular').[28] Universal rules and other ethical generalizations have worth only insofar as they correctly summarize particulars; they are rules of thumb and cannot, in general, take precedence over concrete perceptions. Correct choice is understood, not as the application of rules that have independent validity to cases, but as an improvisatory perceiving, guided by rules but responsible above all to what is newly seen. This seems to us, again, to have considerable importance for the issues involved in the WIDER project. For if reflection and choice are understood in this way, it becomes vastly more difficult to overlook the complex and individual history of a culture and its people. These historical idiosyncrasies become of high ethical relevance and must be confronted. And they will best be confronted, the procedure tells us, by a person who is experienced in that culture, immersed, and not detached. For only that sort of person will be in a position to *see* all the particular factors that bear upon choice in a complex and historically rich context.

iii. *Essential Role of Emotions and Imagination.* The procedure is immersed in another way: it insists that intellect cannot work well apart from the emotions and the imagination. Many conceptions of rationality, including Plato's, regard these elements of the personality as intrusions and not aids in the valuational process. This means, among other things, that it is vastly easier for them to commend a reflection that is detached and lacking in concrete experience of the culture being evaluated. The Aristotelian insists that a correct 'perception' of value cannot be reached at all by the intellect acting alone and, therefore, not without the kind of experienced connectedness that would enable the person to feel and respond to, as well as intellectually apprehend, the values with which he or she is confronted. Their meaning can be seen only through and in such responses. The emotions are cognitive; they indicate to us where importance is to be found.

We want to put the problem of rational assessment of the values of a culture in this general perspective. In understanding what types of problems are involved in assessing various effects of economic development and in appraising different kinds of social change we cannot simply assume that there are given lists of 'good' changes and 'bad' ones, as is often taken for granted (e.g., 'modernizing' is good, or—alternatively—'preserving tradition' is desirable). We have to see the nature of that identification as itself a dynamic process requiring internal and immersed critical appraisal and involving emotional and imaginative responses to the challenges involved.

Given the nature of this evaluative process, it might look as if such critical work can never come from people who do not belong to that culture. This is not quite correct, but it is important for an outsider to get enough understanding of the culture in question to be able to satisfy the requirement that the critique be internal and immersed in the ways discussed earlier. The problem of understanding can be a serious one even for members of that culture itself, since even they may not have direct experience of all the relevant alternatives. The Aristotelian procedure would recommend various ways of closing this gap as a part of the critical exercise. There are, of course, very many different means of acquiring knowledge and understanding of a traditional culture. It is particularly important in this context to emphasize the relevance of turning to history, and also to literature, including stories—formal and informal. In stories a traditional culture tells about itself. By studying them the 'critical subject' not merely discovers the values that are cherished in that culture but is also initiated into an activity of imagination and emotion that can enable her to *see* these values.[29] The discussion in the two preceding sections has pointed to some of the issues involved in this inquiry and to some types of literature that might be particularly relevant. The important additional point to emphasize here is that a valid procedure calls for the use of literature, not so much for detached intellectual judgment, but primarily for involved and responsive understanding and evaluation.

The critical process discussed here, though internal, can frequently lead to criticism of traditional values, and indeed to the rejection of some of them. There are contradictory beliefs entertained, and reflection may lead to reassertion of some and rejection of others. There is also recognition of the beliefs held by others and an understanding of their values, aims, and predicaments. Deeper reflection may lead to the rejection of many things people superficially believe and say. Even an internal critique—not only an external one—can go against practices that may give the appearance of uncompromising conviction.

Many different types of unsustainable values can be illustrated. To take but one example, consider the following example from Aristotle himself. He records—accurately enough—that in traditional Greek thought such great importance is attached to honor and to the avoidance of shame that people frequently say, and at some level think they believe, that honor is the main end in human life. He argues very persuasively that a deeper and broader survey of beliefs will reveal that honor actually is not valuable apart from excellent action: that honor won by bad deeds or by erroneous attribution of good deeds is not prized at all, and that when honor is prized, it is so as the fitting cultural sign that an excellent action has been performed. This seems to be, in fact, a perceptive and deep reading of tradition—more correct *as description* than many ancient (and modern) descriptions of Greek values. In a certain sense, however, it is also a genuine criticism of tradition, in that people really did say these things and did act on them in social life. This is the way in which an inquiry that is descriptive—but reflectively descriptive—can also have real critical force.

V. LIMITS AND REACH

There are some special features of the outlined view of a valuational procedure that should be noted as being potentially problematic. In this section, two of them are taken up. First, human beings are seen in a particular way in this approach. They are seen essentially as social creatures whose deep aim is to live in a community with others and to share with others a conception of value. This belief plays a regulative role in the entire process and is clearly at a different level from the values that are assessed by the process described (using the regulative value). Another regulative value is the commitment to a tradition of rational argumentation—especially to standards of consistency and clarity. These are, in fact, among the deepest held traditional values in ancient Athenian culture. But they need not be always accepted. (The latter requirement is, for example, not so clearly accepted even in all parts of ancient Greek culture, for example in Sparta, though the Athenian endorsement was largely shared by some others, say, Ionians.)

Those who see the Indian tradition as geared to unreasoned mysticism and uncritical synthesizing (a view that is commonly held but was challenged in earlier sections of this essay) would possibly see in the role of these regulative values—especially in the assumption of a rational tradition—a proof of the inappropriateness of the Aristotelian procedure for Indian use. But the tradition of rational argument is, in fact, one part of the Indian heritage also and has a long history of strong endorsement (see section III). The difficulty that might have to be faced concerns the existence of some traditions within the plurality of Indian culture, which would seem to have no such commitment. But even in those cases it is not obvious that a reasoned *defense* can be sustained any more than a reasoned *criticism* can be made. Indeed, as Aristotle has argued elsewhere, a good case can be made for considering a commitment to noncontradiction to be constitutive at a very basic level of *all* human thought and speech.[30] The absence of this commitment in the culture would be problematic not merely for the procedure discussed here but for any kind of critical procedure—except a purely 'external' one in which the values of that culture are rejected or endorsed by critical (rational) commentators *from outside*. The regulative values are, thus, rather crucial for the entire exercise of internal assessment, to which the motivation underlying the WIDER project in question is committed (no less than we are).

Second, we have a very important set of issues to face about the boundaries of the cultural unit that is to be described in each case. We have spoken of a rational criticism of culture that proceeds by utilizing material internal to the culture itself. But what, after all, is 'a culture'? Does all of India have a single culture, and, if so, in what sense? (Does all of the United States?) It is quite easy to see why a member of a certain *part* of a culture could feel resentful of a criticism that comes from another part—from, for example, another religious tradition with different ethical beliefs. Members of two subgroups may well not agree on what are the deepest values. Will not a procedure that decides in favor of one or another set of values seem arbitrary and unfair? We all know in our own political lives the sense of indignation that comes when one discovers that the values of a group whose entire way of life seems completely alien to us have been imposed upon all by a procedure that pretends to fairness. It takes extreme goodwill and long traditions of respect for the deliberative procedures involved not to refuse the result directly. Will not India raise comparable and far greater problems? The Aristotelian procedure says nothing about the value of toleration or about protection of the right to diverse choices of good. These values need to be incorporated into the procedure as regulative, and it will take a lot of thought to decide exactly how and where to do this.

There is a similar problem at the other end. Suppose the culture under survey shows widespread agreement—traditionally and now—on certain value or values. Does this really suffice to make the value or values justified according to our procedure? Or are we entitled to appeal to a larger community—a plurality of related societies, say—for a rational criticism of that entire culture? This is often an urgent question, especially where issues of sexism, racism, and religious intolerance are concerned. We can identify many groups at many times in human history who have held beliefs about female inferiority. Sometimes these views are lightly held, so that they would not survive the process of reflective scrutiny. Frequently they are opposed by other internal values, such as belief in the equal rights of each human individual. And frequently it is true that a richer and more imaginative (and correspondingly more involved or compassionate) look at women's lives will go far to alter perceptions and engender internal criticisms. But this need not invariably happen.[31]

However, the limits of internal criticism are not always easy to define. Any culture is a part of a bigger plurality to which it belongs. The values and traditions of the others may be known and discussed (or *can be* known and discussed) without making criticism based on that understanding in any sense 'external.' An internal critique cannot ignore internal facts but does not preclude response to other societies and to an extended plurality of cultures. Values of one part of that plurality can, thus, enter in an integral way in an internal critique in another part, since the knowledge of culture A by culture B is as much a part of the internal reality of culture B—indeed more directly so—as it is of culture A.

It is this admissibility of cross-cultural reference that makes the scope of internal critiques a good deal wider than might be at first imagined. It also makes the phenomenon of value rejection, which was discussed in the first section of this essay, have a more inclusive class of possible causal antecedents than responses to changes occurring primarily inside the economy or society in question. Sustainability of values in a world not cut up into self-contained bits is a more exacting critical test—within the general structure of *internal* criticism— than it is in a world within which information or influence does not travel. While it should not be taken for granted, as Elster has rightly argued (in *Sour Grapes*), that subsequent values are necessarily more important than antecedent values, it is nevertheless difficult not to have respect for subsequent values that are arrived at on the basis of an internal critique in response to enhanced information and understanding (including *inter alia* those about the workings and achievements of other societies and cultures).

Cross-cultural linkages have importance in several different ways. The coverage of principles of justice and equality defended in a society can leave out some groups within that society when it stands largely in isolation, but the same society may find that exclusion to be unviable when less exclusive formats in other societies are known and understood here. The exclusion of slaves in one society, untouchables in another, and women in still another may be much harder to sustain when other societies show the way to different types of social arrangements. This genesis of value rejection can be seen to be a part of an internal process in which facts of knowledge, understanding, and response play a crucial part.

Another respect in which cross-cultural links may be important is in the terms of the requirements of well-being of each person whose interests may command attention. It is possible to think of the well-being of a person as being a matter of his or her ability to do this or be that—what has been called the person's 'capabilities.'[32] It has been argued that there is some basic similarity in the list of capabilities sought in different parts of the world, even when the commodity bundles associated with the same capabilities may differ (for example, the ability to appear in public without shame, which may be valued in different cultures in much the same way, may nevertheless have quite different commodity or action requirements in one culture vis-à-vis another).[33] Intercultural linkages help, on the one hand, to identify and endorse the valuation of these basic, *generally* formulated, capabilities, and, on the other, they may also tend to reduce the differences of *specific* forms of commodities and actions needed for the realization of those capabilities in the respective culture.

Coming back to the question of the position of women, which is important both as an illustration and as a case on its own, the issue of linkages is important in several distinct respects. First, linkages make it hard for women to be excluded from consideration of justice and equality in one society when they are not so excluded in others.[34] Second, in highlighting the congruence in valuing certain basic capabilities (e.g., the ability to be well nourished, to be free from avoidable morbidity or premature mortality, to be free to occupy positions of power and influence) the more 'open' perspective places certain parameters inescapably in the focus of attention, and they have to be taken into account in judging the position of women as well (rather than judging their well-being or advantage in some specially limited way, such as by the test as to whether women are 'happy' with their place in life).[35] Third, as the *forms* of free actions of women in one society influence what is accepted in another, even the differences in the specific *forms* of free action may be revised.

These issues, which may be practically quite important, are to be seen, not as matters of external critique, but as parts of an internal critique when the influences operate *through* internal response to things learned from elsewhere. For example, in criticizing the position of women in, say, today's Iran, reference to freedom enjoyed by women elsewhere is no more external than reference to the position of women in Iran's own past if the challenge to the present arrangements comes through criticisms from within, based on responding to conditions at another time or at another place.

The limits of an internal critique can be as wide as the varieties of information that affect the reflection and aspirations of members of the culture in question. The demand for internality of criticism insists that criticism cannot come altogether from outside, but it need not insist on a narrow or exclusive list of the influences that can 'count' in the dynamics of a society's internal critique. Internal criticism can have a long reach.

VI. CONCLUDING REMARKS

In this paper, we have been concerned with both substantive and methodological issues. On substantive matters our general conclusion regarding the often-aired conservationist worries about the undermining of Indian culture due to the spread of modern science and technology is that they may well be, to a great extent, seriously misleading. It is arguable that these worries are based on drawing alarmist inferences from an overly narrow and biased view of the nature of Indian culture, and also on ignoring the legitimacy, power, and reach of possible internal criticism of parts of the old tradition in the light of new information and understanding. The descriptive and evaluative problems raised by the phenomenon of value rejection (as opposed to object failure) call for a reexamination of the nature of Indian culture and of the requirements of internal criticism.

NOTES

1. Jon Elster, *Sour Grapes* (Cambridge: Cambridge University Press, 1983).

2. On this, see Amartya Sen, *Collective Choice and Social Welfare* (San Francisco: Holden-Day, 1970; Amsterdam: North-Holland, 1979), chap. 5.

3. Stephen A. Marglin and Frederique Apffel Marglin, "Project Guidelines: Development and Technological Transformation in Traditional Societies, Alternative Approaches" (Helsinki: WIDER, 1986).

4. S. Radhakrishnan and S. A. Moore, eds., *A Sourcebook in Indian Philosophy* (Princeton, N.J.: Princeton University Press, 1957), xxiii. Among the other characteristics that Radhakrishnan and Moore identify are: "the intimate relationship of philosophy and life"; "the introspective attitude to reality"; the alleged feature that "most Indian philosophy is idealistic in one form or another"; that "intuition is accepted as the only method through which the ultimate can be known"; "acceptance of authority"; and a "synthetic approach" (xxiii–xxviii).

5. B. K. Matilal, *Perception: An Essay on Classical Indian Theories of Knowledge* (Oxford: Clarendon Press, 1986), 4–5. Among the earlier disputations there are the Marxist critiques by Debiprasad Chattopadhyaya, *Lokayata: A Study of Ancient Indian Materialism* (New Delhi: People's Publishing House, 1959), and *Indian Atheism: A Marxist Analysis* (Calcutta: Manisha, 1959).

6. John Locke, *An Essay Concerning Human Understanding* (1690), bk. 2, chap. 13, 19.

7. Matilal, *Perception*, 4.

8. The specifically 'Hindu' form of much of the interpretation of Indian culture is itself a very serious limitation, both because of the size and importance of other religious communities—especially Islam—in undivided India (and indeed even in India *after* the partition) and also because of the influence of Islamic civilization and values on Hindu culture. The latter has been extensively discussed in Kshiti Mohan Sen, *Hindu O Mushalmāner Jukto Shādhonā* (Bengali; Calcutta, 1950), and *Hinduism* (Harmondsworth: Penguin Books, 1960), esp. chaps. "Medieval Mysticism in India" and "The Bauls of Bengal."

9. Matilal, *Perception*; see also B. K. Matilal and J. L. Shaw, eds., *Analytical Philosophy in Comparative Perspective: Exploratory Essays in Current Theories and Classical Indian Theories of Meaning and Reference* (Dordrecht: Reidel, 1985).

10. As a matter of some interest, as far as influence abroad is concerned, the two main religions that India helped in spreading abroad were Buddhism (through the efforts

of Asoka and later ones) and Islam, which went to Southeast Asian countries (such as Indonesia), not from the Arab world, but from India (in particular Gujarat).

11. A. Murray, *Reason and Society in the Middle Ages*, rev. ed. (Oxford: Clarendon Press, 1985), 168. Murray's own analysis is concerned with showing that "the pattern of the numerals adoption will reflect, not any foreign technological bombardment, but native aspirations and pressures" (ibid.). It is arguable that this perspective may be relevant not merely in understanding the impact of Eastern technology on the West but also the converse. See also section V.

12. Ian Hacking relates the development of sampling and probability theory in India to the presence of "an advanced merchant system," in *The Emergence of Probability* (Cambridge: Cambridge University Press, 1975), 8.

13. Buddha's critical views of 'personal identity' have also received some serious philosophical analysis and support recently. See Derek Parfit, *Reasons and Persons* (Oxford: Clarendon Press, 1984), chaps. 12, 13, and appendix J.

14. Madhava Acharya, *The Sarva-Darsana Samgraha or Review of Different Systems of Hindu Philosophy*, trans. R. B. Cowell and A. E. Gough (New Delhi: Cosmo, 1976). Radhakrishnan and Moore also provide partial translations of some other documents related to this tradition, in particular *Sarvasiddhāntasaṃgraha*, by Saṃkara; the seventh-century treatise *Tattvopaplavasiṃha* (highly polemical "against all of the other schools of Indian Philosophy"); and the ancient play *Prabodha-candrodaya* (literally translated, *The Moonrise of Intellect*) with characters expounding materialist views.

15. On this, see Ranajit Guha, "On Some Aspects of Historiography of Colonial India," in *Subaltern Studies 1*, ed. R. Guha (New Delhi: Oxford University Press, 1982).

16. Martha Nussbaum, "Therapeutic Arguments: Epicurus and Aristotle," in *The Norms of Nature*, ed. M. Schofield and G. Striker (Cambridge: Cambridge University Press, 1986), and "Nature, Function, and Capability: Aristotle on Political Distribution" [read to the Oberlin Philosophy Colloquium, April 1986] (Helsinki: WIDER, 1987).

17. On this passage (*Nicomachean Ethics*, 1145 b I ff.) and Aristotle's method in both science and ethics see Martha Nussbaum, *The Fragility of Goodness* (Cambridge: Cambridge University Press, 1986), chap. 8 (which is much the same as her "Saving Aristotle's Appearances," in *Language and Logos*, eds. M. Schofield and M. Nussbaum [Cambridge: Cambridge University Press, 1982]).

18. Nussbaum, *Fragility of Goodness*, chap. 8; G. E. L. Owen, "*Tithenai ta Phainomena*," in G. E. L. Owen, *Logic, Science, and Dialectic: Collected Essays on Greek Philosophy*, ed. Martha Craven Nussbaum (London: Duckworth, 1986).

19. This contrast is developed at greater length in Martha Craven Nussbaum, *The Therapy of Desire: Theory and Practice in Hellenistic Ethics*, The Martin Classical Lectures (Princeton, N.J.: Princeton University Press, 1994). For the account of Plato, see also Nussbaum, *Fragility of Goodness*, chap. 5.

20. Matilal, *Perception*.

21. Again, this argument is developed with full textual references in Nussbaum, *Therapy of Desire*.

22. J. Rawls, "Kantian Constructivism in Ethical Theory: Dewey Lectures 1980," *Journal of Philosophy* 77 (1980), and *A Theory of Justice* (Cambridge, Mass.: Harvard University Press, 1971), 46–53.

23. H. Putnam, *Reason, Truth, and History* (Cambridge: Cambridge University Press, 1981), and, especially, *The Many Faces of Realism*, The Carus Lectures (LaSalle, Ill.: Open Court, 1987). For a more detailed development of some aspects of Aristotle's position, see Nussbaum, "Non-Relative Virtues: An Aristotelian Approach" [WIDER Working Paper], in *Ethical Theory: Character and Virtue*, ed. Peter A. French, Theodore E. Uehling Jr., and Howard K. Wettstein, Midwest Studies in Philosophy, vol. 13 (Notre Dame, Ind.: University of Notre Dame Press, 1988).

24. Aristotle, *Eudemian Ethics*, 1216a, 26–39; also see Nussbaum, "Therapeutic Arguments."

25. See, for example, Carol Gilligan, *In a Different Voice: Psychological Theory and Women's Development* (Cambridge, Mass.: Harvard University Press, 1985).

26. All these points are given a detailed discussion in Martha Nussbaum, "The Discernment of Perception: An Aristotelian Conception of Private and Public Morality," *Proceedings of Boston Area Colloquium in Ancient Philosophy* (1985): 151–201.

27. Nussbaum, "Discernment of Perception," and "Plato on Commensurability and Desire," *Proceedings of the Aristotelian Society*, supplementary volume 84 (1984): 55–80; Amartya Sen, "Plural Utility," *Proceedings of the Aristotelian Society* 80 (1980): 193–197.

28. Nussbaum, "Discernment of Perception"; *Fragility of Goodness*, chap. 10; "Perceptive Equilibrium: Literary Theory and Ethical Theory," *Logos* 8 (1987): 55–83; and "Moral Attention and the Moral Task of Literature," in *Philosophy and the Question of Literature*, ed. A. Cascardi (Baltimore: Johns Hopkins University Press, 1987). A shorter version of the last was previously published as "'Finely Aware and Richly Responsible': Moral Attention and the Moral Task of Literature," *Journal of Philosophy* 82 (1985): 516–529.

29. Nussbaum, "Moral Attention and the Moral Task of Literature."

30. Nussbaum, "Saving Aristotle's Appearances"; H. Putnam, "There Is at Least One a priori Truth," *Erkenntnis* 13 (1978): 153–170, reprinted in Putnam, *Realism and Reason: Philosophical Papers* (Cambridge: Cambridge University Press, 1983), 3:98–114.

31. Aristotle's infamous remarks concerning women and slaves are a case in point, though their superficiality shows some evidence of lack of reflection.

32. The position argued in Amartya Sen, "Equality of What?" in *Tanner Lectures on Human Values*, vol. 1, ed. S. McMurrin (Cambridge: Cambridge University Press, 1980), reprinted in *Choice, Welfare, and Measurement* (Oxford: Blackwell, 1982), and "Well-Being, Agency, and Freedom: The Dewey Lectures 184," *Journal of Philosophy* 82 (1985): 169–221.

33. The point goes back to Adam Smith, *An Inquiry into the Nature and Causes of the Wealth of Nations* (1776). On this see Amartya Sen, *Resources, Values, and Development* (Oxford: Blackwell, 1984), and, in some form, to Aristotle himself, on which (and for some further explorations of the Aristotelian perspective), see Nussbaum, "Nature, Function, and Capability."

34. One could certainly ask whether Aristotle's views on women could have survived critical reflection armed with the information and understanding of social arrangements that have emerged since his times.

35. On this, see Amartya Sen, *Commodities and Capabilities* (Amsterdam: North-Holland, 1985), and "Well-Being, Agency and Freedom."

Phenomenological Rationality and the Overcoming of Relativism

28

JITENDRA N. MOHANTY

Instead of first developing the phenomenological concept of rationality, and then applying that concept in the task of overcoming relativism, I will, in this article, follow the reverse order: I will first show that relativism can be overcome from within phenomenology and then draw some morals about the type of rationality this procedure of overcoming relativism illustrates. I turn now to the first task.

I. PHENOMENOLOGY AND RELATIVISM

In the early years of the phenomenological movement, it appeared as though relativism had been, once for all, overcome. The elaborate and widely ramified critique of psychologism was also taken to be, by implication, a critique of all relativism and a defense not merely of the idea of pure logic but also of the possibility of arriving at essential, and so nonrelative, truths about all sorts of things: religion, law, art, and society, to mention only some.

Jitendra N. Mohanty, "Phenomenological Rationality and the Overcoming of Relativism," was originally published in *Relativism: Interpretation and Confrontation* (Notre Dame, Ind.: Notre Dame University, 1989), pp. 326–338. Reprinted here with permission of the author. All rights reserved.

Such is, however, the fate of phenomenology that relativistic implications appear to disrupt its essentialism from within. This occurs in various ways, some of which I will recall.[1] First of all, the purely descriptive, nonreductionist approach to phenomena inevitably led to a pluralism, which refused to be rounded off within, or for the sake of, a system. Consider, for example, space: purely descriptively, you have sacred space and profane space,[2] space as experienced in a familiar setting, and space that is threatening and strange (in an unfamiliar setting), space as experienced in walking or in dancing, in listening to music, or in looking at a painting.[3] How are you to bring these data under a common 'essence'? All those ethnological data, which seemingly promote relativisms, would find their places within such a descriptive phenomenology. The very idea of one objective world, of one moral theory, even of one life-world would be threatened by such descriptive phenomenology.

Second, as essentialism in phenomenology imperceptibly yielded to meaning-constitution, and as the given data for descriptive research were found to have been preconstituted by meaning-conferring, and thus interpretive acts, the possibility of very different, often radically different, interpretations of the same hyletic data, and so of the constitution of incommensurable objectivities, came to the fore. The transition to the relativism of alternate conceptual frameworks did not require a long step. In fact, all that was needed was another premise: namely, that every interpretive act presupposes, and is already embedded in, an interpretive framework (a step Edmund Husserl, perhaps, never could take).

Third, as phenomenology, in its attempt to be *radical*, reached the seemingly ultimate ground of the *life-world* that is prior to, and also the point of departure for, all theoretical constituting acts, it also found itself confronted with the same specter of relativism which it had faced early during the purely descriptive program. For if life-world is truly to be *life-world* and not a theoretical posit, then one must recognize that there is not one life-world, but, in fact, there are many life-worlds. Here, again, ethnology finds itself useful for phenomenology. A primitive tribal community of New Guinea certainly does not have the same lifeworld as the present-day New Yorker. Whose life-world was Alfred Schütz describing?

I believe that a sound philosophy, phenomenological or not, must be able to overcome relativism. But I also believe that the early phenomenologist's optimism that relativism had been disposed of was too hasty. If relativism is to be overcome, one cannot just begin by 'refuting it'; one must be able to 'go through' it as far as one can and *then* go beyond it. In other words, the journey has to be long and understanding, and the overcoming has to be from within relativism. In this essay, I will briefly follow such a path, in its barest outline, and toward the end indicate its bearing on moral philosophy.

II. 'ALTERNATE CONCEPTUAL FRAMEWORKS'/
'RADICALLY DIFFERENT WORLDS': SOME ATTEMPTS AT REFUTATIONS

If Husserl rejected relativism as incoherent, Donald Davidson, in a well-known paper, has sought to demonstrate that the talk of alternate conceptual frameworks (which, as I pointed out, emerges from within descriptive as well as constitutive phenomenology) is unintelligible.[4] But Davidson's aim is not merely to show that the idea of a conceptual scheme as alternate to ours makes no sense but also to prove the far more radical thesis that the very talk of a conceptual framework is unintelligible. As a consequence, he insists, the very distinction between conceptual scheme and uninterpreted data must also be given up. To give up that distinction would amount to giving up all transcendental arguments, and so all foundationalist transcendental philosophies—to give up, in other words, the project of legitimizing the application of a conceptual framework, the *quaestio juris* of the Kantian philosophy.

I will not presently comment upon the claim that Davidson has given a transcendental argument to prove the impossibility of all transcendental arguments. My present concern is to what extent he succeeds in showing the impossibility of a radical relativism of conceptual frameworks or of their correlative worlds. Davidson's argument runs somewhat like this. To speak of alternate conceptual schemes is to speak of *radically* different schemes in the sense that they must have to be mutually untranslatable. If there are alternate conceptual schemes, they must be embodied in languages, which are not translatable to ours. But it is this claim which Davidson finds unacceptable, especially because any such conceptual scheme could be true without making any sense to us. For Davidson, a theory of meaning is indeed reducible to a theory of truth, so that the notion of truth cannot be divorced from that of translation (if the Tarskian Convention T embodies our best intuitions about 'truth'). It therefore could make no sense to speak of a conceptual scheme as being true but untranslatable. Now, of course we are not obliged to accept Donaldson's premise that the Tarskian Convention T does indeed embody our best intuition about truth, or his other assumption that a theory of meaning is reducible to a theory of truth (which is consequent upon denying the Frege-Husserl semantics to which I am committed). Nevertheless, we have to take into account Davidson's point that an alternate conceptual scheme or talk about a radically different world, being untranslatable to our home language, would make no sense. In order to bring out the nature of this argument and assess its value, I will compare it with an argument by Husserl, which seemingly is to the same effect, that is, a denial of radically different worlds.

The argument occurs in Husserl's writings at various places. I will recall three such places. First, in §48 of the *Ideas* I, Husserl writes:

What is perceivable by *one* Ego must *in principle* be conceivable by *every* Ego. And though *as a matter of fact* it is not true that everyone stands or can stand in a relation of empathy of inward understanding of every other one, . . . yet in point of principle there exist *essential possibilities for the setting up of an understanding*. . . . If there are worlds or real things at all, the empirical motivations which constitute them must be *able* to reach into my experience, and that of every single Ego.[5]

In §60 of the *Cartesian Meditations*, Husserl asks: "Is it *conceivable* (to me) that two or more separate *pluralities of monads*, i.e., pluralities *not in communion*, coexist, each of which accordingly constitute *a world of its own*, so that together they constitute two worlds?" To this question he answers: "Manifestly, instead of being a conceivability, that is a pure absurdity ... the two worlds are then necessarily mere 'surrounding worlds,' ... and mere aspects of a single objective world, which is *common* to them. For indeed, the two intersubjectivities are not absolutely isolated. As imagined by me, each of them is in necessary communion with me ... as the constitutive primal monad relative to them." "Actually therefore," Husserl concludes, "there *can* exist only a single community of monads" (vol. 1, 166ff.).

Finally, in a fragment dating from 1921, now included in the second intersubjectivity volume (vol. 45, 91–101), Husserl discusses the same issue in greater detail. He sets out to prove that if there are several subjects, they must necessarily be able to be in a possible communicative state (*Kommerzium*) and therefore constitute a common world. By the common world he means one spatio-temporal world in which the subjects as corporeal beings apprehend each other as 'other' subjects. Apprehension of the other subject's body (*Leib*), which is necessary for apprehending the other as a subject, requires being in the same spatio-temporal system. Furthermore, if there is to be a plurality of subjects, this plurality must be, in principle, experienceable as a plurality. Every experience or presentation of such a plurality points to a possible subject. Such a subject must be in *Ein Uhlungszusammenhang* (i.e., belong to an interconnection of empathetic understanding with the others). Therefore, such a subject and the others, that is, the plurality of subjects we hypothesized, must belong to one common world.

These arguments are in part intended to prove that there must be one space and time, that is, one spatio-temporal world for all subjects, although each subject may have its own *Mit-Welt* [experienced world]. For otherwise (1) these subjects would not apprehend each other as subjects; (2) the plurality of subjects that is hypothesized will not be apprehended *as a plurality* by any possible subject, and so the hypothesization would be meaningless; and (3) the positing of a world that is for only one subject will be meaningless for another unless the latter can experience the world as his. The argument can be generalized to prove the unity of the world in a sense that goes beyond the thesis of one space and one time.

Compare Husserl's arguments with Davidson's. Davidson's argument insists on translatability, for the ideas of translatability, meaningfulness, and truth cannot be separated. If there is to be another conceptual framework, or talk of another world, any such must be translatable to mine, our home language; if it is, then it is not an alternate conceptual scheme, not a description of another radically different world. Husserl's argument insists on 'Vorstellbarkeit.' The other subject must be presentable along with his body to any of the others, to me, to start with. The other's world (regarded initially as being radically different) must be experienceable by me. And the plurality of subjects (each *ex hypothesis* with its own world) must be presentable to someone as a plurality. Otherwise, each of these locutions (that there is another subject, another world, a plurality of subjects) would make no sense to me but so also to any of the others. Both Davidson and Husserl are making a similar demand upon the relativist: The talk of alternate schemes or worlds can make sense only if such a scheme is translatable to ours, that is, home language; the talk of a world would make sense only if it is *experienceable* by me or by us (who already share a common world). It might appear that the idea of translatability is free from that subjectivism which attaches to the idea of experienceability, but the fault of subjectivism is mitigated to the point of being totally harmless when what is required is experienceability by any subject whatsoever. Likewise, the requirement of translatability to *our* home language may appear to be chauvinistic, but this is removed by requiring that all alternate schemes should be mutually translatable.

What is dissatisfying with this way of overcoming relativism—Davidson's or Husserl's—is that *it again takes a short cut.* It is impatient with relativism, even as an initial truth. In fact, one suspects whether the 'refutation' does not beg the issue. What I, on the other hand, want to begin with is a recognition of the fact that a certain cultural pluralism (and an associated thesis of pluralism of worlds) is one of the desiderata of modern ways of thinking. An unadulterated monistic conception of the world—be it the conception of the world of antiquity or of modern science—has simply no future. Richard Rorty has complained that transcendental philosophies have sought to legitimize a favored representation of the world.[6] We simply cannot start today with any such favored representation in the same way as Kant started from the world of which Euclidean geometry and Newtonian physics held good. If we are to find a way out of relativism, it can only be *after* the phenomenon of relativism has been granted its initial recognition. But where can we go from there? What path lies open for us?

III. ANOTHER HUSSERLIAN PATH

Two suggestions of Husserlian thinking have been mentioned by me and then set aside. One was to insist on essence of 'world,' even if there are many worlds. This essence, which is to be a 'formal essence' after all, is given by a formal ontology. What was threatened at the level of contents is thereby gained only at the level of form. The other was to tie the significance of any locution about alternate worlds to experienceability by *me*, and, in the long run, by any and every ego. This delivers a common intersubjective world at the level of contents, but, not unlike Davidson's, appears to beg the issue, and is no less impatient with the phenomenon of relativism than the first, the eidetic move.

But the same Husserlian thinking provides us with another, and to my mind, more promising lead: this is the famed principle of noesis-noema correlation. In order to bring out how this can help us here, let me recall a distinction that Davidson draws in the paper referred to earlier. The talk of many different worlds, Davidson points out, is ambiguous as between (1) talking about the many possible worlds from the same point of view; and (2) talking about them as though they are but the same world seen from many different points of view. "P. F. Strawson's many imagined worlds are seen (or heard)—anyway described—from the same point of view, Thomas Kuhn's one world is seen from different points of view."[7] Davidson has no quarrel with the former sort of concept, and so with the Leibnizian talk of many possible worlds. Nor does Husserl have anything against such locution. "Naturally Leibniz is right," Husserl writes, "that infinitely many monads and groups of monads are conceivable, that it does not follow that all these possibilities are compossible; and, again, when he says that infinitely many worlds might have been 'created,' but not two or more at once, since they are incompossible."[8]

What Davidson wants to rule out is the possibility of describing the same world from radically different points of view, where these points of view are mutually incommensurable, and their descriptions mutually untranslatable. In fact, what he ends up by proving—what was the ruling intention all along—is that there is *no point of view* on the world, no conceptual scheme by which it is interpreted. There can only be different languages in which to describe the world, and these languages are mutually translatable.

Obviously, Husserl's rejection of relativism in the sense of the thesis that there are mutually incommensurable worlds can amount neither to the thesis that we cannot speak of many possible worlds any two of which are jointly incompossible, nor to the thesis that we cannot describe the same world from many different points of view. The notion of point of view, of interpretive framework, is not ruled out by Husserl. What he is rejecting is the *actuality* (not possibility) of many incommensurable worlds. So although it appeared a little while ago as though both Husserl and Davidson were attacking the same thesis, it indeed now seems that Husserl does in fact envisage that the same world must be describable from many different points of view. What he was rejecting is the thesis that each of these descriptions is *a* world. It is rather a world-noema. The different world-noemata can nevertheless be of one and the same world and therefore must be, in the long run, commensurable.

I do not think anyone would want to deny that there are different points of view from which one and the same thing can be perceived, thought of, talked about. But to say that there are *radically* different points of view such that the descriptions they generate are totally incommensurable is quite another thing, and I deny this. Between the view that there are such incommensurable worlds (or, untranslatable languages, totally unintelligible conceptual schemes) and the view that all talk of possible nonactual worlds involves nothing more than 'redistribution of truth-values' over sentences in our present languages 'in various systematic ways' there must be an intermediate position which I want to adopt. In order to formulate such a position I will proceed through several steps. First, I will indicate how the principle of noesis-noema correlation applies to the problem at hand. Second, I will distinguish between two levels of discourse: internal and external. I will, in effect, insist upon the relevance of the idea of transcendental ego to this issue. Finally, I will make a distinction between 'person' and 'subject.'

(1) Let us view each world as a noematic structure. To each such structure there would correspond an entire nexus of interpretive acts on the part of the community for which such a world obtains. We may then speak of a noesis-noema correlation that is itself nonrelativistic. If the essentialism was a shortcut and also too formalistic a step, and the tying of all meaningfulness to experience-ability by *any* ego too liberal (inasmuch it permits every one to be an insider to every world), the present manner of isolating invariant noesis-noema correlation structure overcomes relativism by taking seriously the phenomena on which relativism is founded. The next step would be this: just as the identity of an object is constituted by the system of noemata through which 'one and the same' object is presented, so also in the case under consideration the one world—not in the sense of the totality of all worlds, but in the sense of that whose versions they all are—may be looked upon as that regulative concept which not

only orders the various quasi-incommensurable worlds but also delineates the path that shall lead us out of a possibly hopeless chaos toward communication and understanding.

On the intermediate position I am seeking to formulate, each world-noema is different from any other, it embodies a unique point of view, but it also 'overlaps' and 'intersects' some other world-noemata—thus making transition from one to the other *theoretically* possible. (Although W^1 and W^3 would appear to be utterly distinct, their distinction is mediated by W^2 with which both 'overlap.') Translatability is a deceptive concept in any case. If you can adhere to a very strict concept of translatability, no 'radical translation' between any two languages is possible. And yet with a less strict concept we do translate. Every language can say—as Gadamer has stated—what is said in any other, but *in its own way* This 'way' alone is what is untranslatable.

(2) To get clear about the situation, let us distinguish between two levels of discourse: the internal and external. At the internal level there are 'radically' different worlds, conceptual frameworks, languages, such that for the *person* who naively lives *within* his own, the others are 'bare others,' at most 'interesting,' but still 'do not make sense.' Translatability and intelligibility are at most ideals, but they were never meant to work out. Translation, understanding, and communication take place within a common, shared world. At this level there is a home language and a home 'life-world.'

However, if I am to be able to speak of alternate conceptual schemes, I must be able to translate the others into mine, or mine into the others'. Languages (and schemes) must be mutually translatable. But when I assert this, I am taking, not the 'internal' standpoint, but rather the 'external' standpoint, from which stance any language is as good as any other; none is *mine*. All possible worlds are then spread out before my gaze; none is more my own than any other. I am then a transcendental ego. The transcendental ego is no standpoint: all possible standpoints are arraigned before his look. The transcendental ego has no *home* language.

Thus the empirical person living in his world, speaking his language, using his conceptual scheme, sharing in his tradition, is subject to a point of view of his own, of his community. But he does not, in his prereflective naivety, know that he sees the world from a standpoint. He lives in, perceives, knows the world, the only world that is there for him. That, however, he is subject to a perspective, a standpoint, a conceptual framework, is brought out by reflection (and the reflection may be occasioned by a great variety of circumstances). But to be able to survey all possible points of view, conceptual frameworks, languages objectively—as making sense to each other; therefore, as commensurable and mutually translatable—one needs to take up a stance, which is none other than that of a transcendental ego.

The thesis of relativity of worlds is an initial response of reflection. But this thesis of relativity has to be limited by the thesis of the common horizon within which these standpoints are after all possible. The *one* world is not the common *content* to which the different world-noemata provide different conceptual schemes. The many worlds are then neither gotten by 'redistribution of truth-values' for sentences in the home language, nor are they different conceptualizations of one and the same preexistent world. They are noemata *of* one world, but the one world is also *being* constituted through them—always under the threat of being broken down.

IV. THE 'WORLD OF PHYSICS'

It is not my intention to identify this concept of one world of which the many worlds are noemata with the world of physics or the Kantian Nature. There is no doubt, though, that the world of physics does indeed lay claim to this status. For me it is but another such noematic structure. The expression 'world of physics' is ambiguous. For one thing, it means the world of scientific entities. In another sense it means the world of experienceable things and events determined and governed by laws of physics, and for whose explanation the scientific entities are posited as theoretical constructs. Nature, as Kant understood it, is the world of physics in the second sense. Kant, as is well known, regarded Nature in this sense as constructed out of simple, atomic, discrete sense impressions. I basically agree with the Kantian point of view. However, since I reject the Humean-Kantian conception of 'impression', I regard the Kantian Nature as constructed rather out of the many prescientific *worlds* in which we, with our prescientific interests, find ourselves. Any such world is a sedimented structure of meanings inherited from the past. I will not, in this essay, develop the broad stages of the process by which the scientific-objective world emerges, with its imperious claim to be the world-in-itself, out of the prescientific worlds. It claims to be the world as it is in itself, when all human subjectivity is removed from the scene. Paradoxically, however, science itself gives rise to a new tradition, and like all traditions, this one also is constituted by sedimentation of meaning structures. What is important for my present concern is that in my view the world of physics is a higher order noematic structure, founded upon prescientific noemata, claiming to supersede their validity-claims, but with no more than its own validity-claim. The appeal to science, then, with a view to overcome relativism is futile.

V. TWO CLARIFICATIONS

In my attempt to find a way out of relativism I have made use of two strategies. One of them is the idea of overlapping of noemata. The other is that of translatability. In this section I will briefly clarify these two as I want them to be understood.

(1) The basic idea of overlapping of noemata is Husserl's, but my present use of it was first *suggested* to me by Michael Dummett's use of the principle of 'conservative extension' with a view to make communication possible between classical and intuitionistic logics. Let W and W^1 be two world-noemata such that they are furthest removed from each other in the sense that any communication between them seems impossible. In such a case, what I postulate is that there will always be a series of Ws such that (a) every succeeding member of the series overlaps the preceding member, and (b) the first member of the series will overlap W and the final member will overlap W^1 (figure 28.1).

Nothing in this guarantees that there is only one such series. There may be in fact many different ways of linking W and W^1. But in any case the result would be the same: there would be in principle a way of establishing communication between W and W^1. In conceiving of such a series of overlapping noemata, I am of course assuming that each W is *not* a fully holistic system; if it were so, it would just be impossible for it to share part of its contents with another W.

(2) By insisting that any language is translatable to any other, I may be taken to be begging the issue. However, that would be the case only if we take 'translatability' in a static sense. In this static sense we ascribe translatability or the lack of it to two languages L^1 and L^2 when each is regarded as a completed totality. We freeze the growing process that a language is and want to find out if one such frozen system is translatable or not to another such. It is in this sense that I take Davidson to be insisting on translatability. My use of it, however, is different. I take it that as L^1 is translated into L^2, or vice versa, in this process both L^1 and L^2

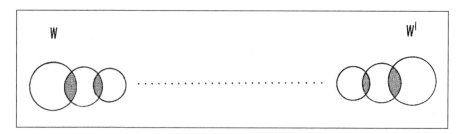

Figure 28.1

undergo transformation. They both end up enriched. Translation in this sense changes both the languages. One cannot arrest L^1 at its present stage of growth and demand L^2 to be translated into it, or vice versa. Like interpersonal communication, translation enriches both. In this sense, then, mutual translatability is a regulative ideal that we can hardly dispense with: languages have to grow toward its realization.

VI. THE 'TRANSCENDENTAL EGO,' IMPERSONALITY, AND OBJECTIVITY

Since I have characterized the point of view of the transcendental ego as that of an outsider, a few words need to be added to avoid misunderstanding on this score. It has wrongly been held by many that the point of view of transcendental ego yields a fully objective, and objectively determinate, world, such as the world of physics. However, it is not without significance that in Husserl's thinking the idea of transcendental ego and the idea of noesis-noema correlation are closely interlinked. From the stance of the transcendental ego, all are not objects, but rather all objects are meaning-structures. What we have then is not one impersonal description of the world in which personal or communal interpretations do not figure at all. What we have is rather an array of noesis-noema correlations, an array of worlds and morals, each having its own validity-claim and its origin in interpreting and evaluating acts. Thus the transcendental ego is antimonistic: it respects pluralism and is tolerant of diversities. In this sense transcendental thinking, instead of being committed to a favored representation of the world, shall respect limitless diversities of interpretations.

The overcoming of relativism that phenomenology should espouse cannot consist in that *violent* act by which one validity-claim imperiously supersedes all others but shall rather consist in that gentle and tolerant view which recognizes that unity is always in the process of being achieved by communication and is just too fragile to be sustained by any violence. The world-in-itself is rather a regulative idea that guides communication and translation. To elevate any world, scientific or religious, to the status of absolute is to fall into the trap of relativistic arguments: the 'other' would remain unconvinced, and communication and internal criticism would be closed off.

After indicating how phenomenology can overcome relativism, I propose to use the preceding argument as a case study for eliciting a few lessons about the peculiar nature of phenomenological rationality.

First of all, it is clear that phenomenological rationality is *not* the formal-mathematical rationality which finds expression in the formalism of logic, semantics, formal ontology, and mathematics. The formal-mathematical rationality is empty, the universality that is accomplished pays the price of abstracting from all contents. But while not eschewing this empty formalism, phenomenology does not simply turn away from it. Rather, it recognizes its role as an incipient formal ontology and proceeds to the concrete domain of consciousness wherein these forms come into being through a constructive and constitutive rationality.

At the other end from formal-mathematical rationality is the anthropological, local, cultural rationality which sustains relativisms of all sorts and which resists attempts to impose universality *ab extra*. There is an initial validity of the claim of each such 'system' of the local standpoint, the conceptual framework of each culture, to be autonomous, refusing absorption into a larger scheme of things.

But the phenomenological rationality rejects as much that empty formal universality as this concrete particularity. Using a Hegelian jargon, one may say that what phenomenology is after is rather a concrete universality.

The search for essences and essential structures—so inalienably linked with the idea of phenomenology—holds out hopes for reaching such a concrete universality. The rationality that manifests itself in essential structures of phenomena is not however typically phenomenological; it is rather basically Greek, and to the extent phenomenology exhibits it, it is a participant in the grand tradition inherited from the Greeks. Two serious difficulties vitiate the quest for essences: for one thing, the method employed—construed as a method for discovering essences—is hopelessly circular; for another, an essence characterizes a thing only under a certain description and not under another (recall W. V. O. Quine's famous example of a bicyclist mathematician).

The truly phenomenological rationality, then, exhibits itself in the next move from here onward: in the suspension of the first-order truth claims and in transforming the concern with essences (formal or material) to concern with *meanings*. The local anthropological systems, then, reveal themselves as meaning-structures, or complex noemata. Universality is *not* imposed *ab extra* on the plurality of such noemata but is permitted to emerge through the process of overlapping among such noemata. It is in this idea of 'overlapping' and 'emergence' of identity, rather than its imposition through a metaphysical essentialism (as through political absolution), that rationality is seen in operation.

I will conclude by drawing attention to two features of this process. Here, in the first place, there is no opposition between diversity and unity. Unity is being worked out rather than being a preexistent metaphysical entity. The process is gentle and tolerant rather than violent and imperious. In the second place, the rationality that underlies this process is a reconciliation between the perceptual and the communicative models. In perception we find the origin of the idea of overlapping noemata; in conversation we find the origin of the idea of conservative extension. Phenomenological rationality lies perched between the two.

NOTES

An early version of this paper was read at the meetings of the German Phenomenological Society in Trier, Germany, June 1985, and appears in German in *Vernwift und Kontingenz*, ed. Wolfgang Orth (Freiburg: Karl Alber, 1986).

1. David Carr has shown this well in his unpublished essay with the same title as my present essay.

2. Mircea Eliade has emphasized this distinction in his numerous studies on the phenomenology of religion.

3. Erwin W. Straus, *Phenomenological Psychology* (New York: Basic Books, 1966).

4. D. Davidson, "On the Very Idea of Conceptual Scheme," *Proceedings of the American Philosophical Association* 19 (1973–1974): 5–20 (this volume, chap. 8).

5. Edmund Husserl, *Husserliana: Gesammelte Werke*, 3/1:102ff.

6. R. Rorty, *Philosophy and the Mirror of Nature* (Princeton, N.J.: Princeton University Press, 1979).

7. Davidson, "On the Very Idea of Conceptual Scheme," 9.

8. Husserl, *Husserliana*, 1:167.

Understanding and Ethnocentricity

29

CHARLES TAYLOR

|

[I have argued that] we ought to turn to look at what we *do* when we theorize; that when we do we see that theories serve more than descriptive and explanatory purposes, they also serve to *define* ourselves; and that such self-definition *shapes* practice. But if all this is true, I argued, then the use of theory as self-definition also has to be borne in mind when we come to explain, when we practice, social science.

For even though theory may be serving us, the social scientists, simply as an instrument of explanation, the agents whose behavior we are trying to explain will be using (the same or another) theory, or prototheory, to define themselves. So that whether we are trying to validate a theory as self-definition, or establish it as an explanation, we have to be alive to the way that understanding shapes practice, disrupts, or facilitates it.

Reprinted from Charles Taylor, "Understanding and Ethnocentricity," *Philosophy and the Human Sciences: Philosophical Papers* 2 (Cambridge: Cambridge University Press, 1985), pp. 116–133. Reprinted with the permission of Cambridge University Press.

But this raises a number of questions about the relation between the scientist's explanatory theory and the self-definitions of his subjects. Suppose they offer very different, even incompatible, views of the world and of the subjects' action? Does the scientist have the last word? Can he set the worldview of his subjects aside as erroneous? But to condemn this worldview does he not have to stand outside it, and is this external stance compatible with understanding their self-definitions?

We come here to one of the main issues of the debate around *verstehende* social science. And this had to arise. Because in fact, my thesis amounts to an alternative statement of the main proposition of interpretive social science, that an adequate account of human action must make the agents more understandable. On this view, it cannot be a sufficient objective of social theory that it just predict, or allow us to derive, the actual pattern of social or historical events, and the regularities which occur in it, described in whatever language admits of unambiguous verification. A satisfactory explanation must also make sense of the agents.

This is not to say, of course, that it must show their action as making sense. For it very often does not. Frequently they are confused, malinformed, contradictory in their goals and actions. But in identifying the contradictions, confusions, etc., we make sense of what they did. And this means that we come to see how as agents—i.e., beings who act, have purposes, desires—they came to do what they did, and to bring about what befell.

Now my argument has been converging onto a similar conclusion. For my contention has been that social theory has to take subjects as agents of self-definition, whose practice is shaped by their understanding. And this is just an alternative way of stating the thesis that we have to give an account of them as agents, and that we cannot do this unless we understand them, that is, grasp their self-understanding. The opposing ideal of a verifiable, predictive science, on the model of the natural sciences, is, I have argued, a chimera.

I hope that the above discussion may help us to set aside two common misapprehensions about interpretive social science. The first is that what it demands of us is empathy with our subjects. But this is to miss the point. Empathy may certainly be useful in coming to have the understanding we seek; but it is not what understanding consists in. Science is a form of discourse, and what we want is an account, which sets out the significance of action and situation. What we are crucially looking for, therefore, is the right language in which we can make this clear. I will say more on this shortly.

The second misapprehension is the one evoked by my questions above. It is to the effect that understanding the agent involves adopting his point of view; or, to speak in terms of language, describing and accounting for what he does in his own terms, or those of his society and time. This is the thesis which has been associated (rightly or wrongly) with the name of Peter Winch.[1] Taken strictly, it would seem to make social science rather unilluminating, and in some circumstances next to impossible. It would make it unilluminating, since in many cases actors are confused, misinformed, have contradictory purposes, and their language may reflect this. Simply recovering their self-description may cast no light at all on what was going on. Indeed, the starting point of our scientific effort may be that we find something perplexing in their action as they understood it. And in the limit case where we are dealing with a so-called primitive society, that is, one which is pre-scientific, which has not yet produced a discourse of reflective theory, a scientific account in their terms would be quite impossible.

But this kind of demand has nothing to do with interpretive social science as I have been expounding it here. On the contrary, in the normal case what is demanded of a theoretical account is that it makes the agent's doings clearer than they were to him. And this may easily involve challenging what he sees/saw as the normal language of self-description. [. . .] But the need to challenge the agent's self-descriptions does not take away in the least from the requirement that we understand him as an agent. Understanding someone cannot simply mean adopting his point of view, for otherwise a good account could never be the basis of more clairvoyant practice.

There is, however, an important truth, which underlies this confusion. And that is that making sense of agents does require that we *understand* their self-descriptions. We may, indeed often must, take account of their confusion, malinformation, illusion; but we make sense of them if we grasp *both* how they see things *and* what is wrong, lacunary [*sic*], contradictory in this. Interpretive social science cannot bypass the agent's self-understanding.

We might distinguish the two theses in this way: interpretive social science requires that we master the agent's self-description in order to identify our *explananda*; but it by no means requires that we couch our *explanantia* in the same language. On the contrary, it generally demands that we go beyond it. The false assimilation of interpretive science with adopting the agent's point of view does place exactly this crippling restriction on the *explanantia*. But if, on the other hand, we attempt to bypass his self-descriptions even in picking out our *explananda*, we have put paid to any attempt to make sense of him.

Now there is a strong temptation to bypass these self-descriptions, which is felt particularly by those who accept natural sciences as the model for social science. We can easily see why this is so, if we examine what is involved here.

so on, which we are trying to explain. There is no way to finesse the requirement of understanding. Our Marxist or other historian convinces us he has explained the detail when he can give a convincing interpretation of it in his canonical terms. But to give a convincing interpretation, one has to show that one has understood what the agent is doing, feeling here. His action/feeling/aspirations/outlook in his terms constitutes our *explanandum*.

In the end, there is no way to finesse understanding if we are to give a convincing account of the explanatory significance of our theory. I hope it will be evident that this applies not only to functionalist theories, but to any attempt to identify what agents are doing in 'scientific' language, be it that of holistic functionalism, or of individual utility-maximization, or whatever.

II

What I have been trying to show is that although there is a strong temptation to bypass agents' self-descriptions arising from the strong pull of the natural science model, any attempt to do this is stultifying, and leads to an account which cannot be adequately validated.

The view, which I am defending here, which I can call the interpretive view, or the *verstehen* view, or the thesis that social theories are about practices, has to be marked off from two other conceptions. One is the original enemy, the natural science model, which I have been arguing against all along. And the other is a false ally, the view that misconstrues interpretation as adopting the agent's point of view. Let me call this 'the incorrigibility thesis,' just to give it a name, because in requiring that we explain each culture or society in its own terms, it rules out an account which shows them up as wrong, confused or deluded. Each culture on this view is incorrigible.

The interpretive view, I want to argue, avoids the two equal and opposite mistakes: on one hand, of ignoring self-descriptions altogether, and attempting to operate in some neutral scientific language; on the other hand, of taking these descriptions with ultimate seriousness, so that they become incorrigible. Social theory in general, and political theory especially, is very much in the business of correcting common sense understanding. It is of very little use unless it goes beyond, unless it frequently challenges and negates what we think we are doing, saying, feeling, aiming at. But its criterion of success is that it makes us as agents more comprehensible, that it makes sense of what we feel, do, aim at. And this it cannot do without getting clear on what we think about our action and feeling. That is, after all, what offers the puzzle which theory tries to resolve. And so there is no way of showing that some theory has actually explained *us* and *our* action until it can be shown to make sense of what we did under *our* description (where this emphatically does *not* mean, let me repeat, showing how what we did made sense). For otherwise, we may have an interesting, speculative rational reconstruction (like the functional theory above), but no way of showing that it actually *explains* anything.

But it might still be thought that I have been too quick with the incorrigibility thesis. It does not just come from a confusion of *explananda* and *explanantia*. There is also a serious moral point. Social science aspires not just to understand a single society, but to be universal. In principle, social scientists strive to understand not just their own society and culture but foreign ones. Indeed, the discipline of anthropology is concerned with virtually nothing else.

In this context, to insist blithely that social science has the task of correcting our common sense understanding—a demand, which may sound properly radical when it comes to understanding our own culture may be to encourage dangerous illusions when it comes to understanding other cultures. One of the striking faults of transcultural and comparative social science has been its tendency to ethnocentrism. At the outset, it was European students who interpreted other societies in terms derived from European culture, very often at the cost of extreme distortion, and frequently also in an unflattering light. Now students from other cultures are also engaged, but the difficulties and dangers are still present. Some have been even tempted to despair of any cross-cultural understanding.

In this situation, it might be argued, to speak of social science, as correcting everyday understanding is to invite scientists of a dominant culture to 'correct' the self-understandings of the less dominant ones by substituting their own. What is really going on then becomes simply what *we* can recognize in our own terms; and their self-descriptions are wrong to the extent that they deviate from ours. Transcultural study becomes a field for the exercise of ethnocentric prejudice.

No one can doubt that this has happened. We have only to think of theories like that of James G. Frazer, which portrayed primitive magic as a kind of early and largely mistaken technology, to see how distorted our perspective can be.

It is in face of this tendency that the incorrigibility thesis seems to have a lot going for it. For it seems guaranteed against ethnocentricity. Indeed, one could easily come to believe that it is the only real safeguard against it. We understand each culture in its own terms, and we never can fall into the error of misunderstanding one according to the categories of another. This seems to be the message that emerges from Peter Winch's very persuasive "Understanding a Primitive Society."[3]

From this point of view, the interpretive thesis may seem especially vulnerable. At least the natural science model can make a claim for neutrality, by looking for a scientific language, which is outside all cultures, and thus can hope to be non-culture-relative. But the *verstehen* view, while not allowing for such neutral languages, nevertheless sets us the task of challenging and going beyond other people's self-understanding. But if not in their terms, how else can we understand them but in our own? Aren't we unavoidably committed to ethnocentricity?

No, I want to argue, we are not. The error in this view is to hold that the language of a cross-cultural theory has to be either theirs or ours. If this were so, then any attempt at understanding across cultures would be faced with an impossible dilemma: either accept incorrigibility, or be arrogantly ethnocentric. But as a matter of fact, while challenging their language of self-understanding, we may also be challenging ours. Indeed, what I want to argue is that there are times where we cannot question the one properly without also questioning the other.

In fact, it will almost always be the case that the adequate language in which we can understand another society is not our language of understanding, or theirs, but rather what one could call a language of perspicuous contrast. This would be a language in which we could formulate both their way of life and ours as alternative possibilities in relation to some human constants at work in both. It would be a language in which the possible human variations would be so formulated that both our form of life and theirs could be perspicuously described as alternative such variations. Such a language of contrast might show their language of understanding to be distorted or inadequate in some respects, or it might show ours to be so (in which case, we might find that understanding them leads to an alteration of our self-understanding, and hence our form of life—a far from unknown process in history); or it might show both to be so.

This notion of a language of perspicuous contrast is obviously very close to Hans-Georg Gadamer's conception of the 'fusion of horizons' and owes a great deal to it. An excellent example of an illuminating theory in comparative politics, which uses such a language (or languages), is Montesquieu's. The contrast with despotism was, of course, not an unqualified success, because it was not based on a real understanding of the alien (Turkish or Persian) society. But Montesquieu's contrast between monarchy and republic brought about a great deal of understanding of modern society precisely by placing it relative to (at least the traditional image of) republican society in a language of perspicuous contrast.

This conception of contrast clearly avoids the pitfalls of the incorrigibility thesis. Our account does not have to be in the language of understanding of the agents' society, but rather in the language of contrast. And the agents' language clearly is not taken as incorrigible. At the same time, we are not committed to an ethnocentric course. This much has been learned from the arguments of Winch and others, that the other society may be incomprehensible in our terms; that is, in terms of our self-understanding.

And our conception is also superior to the natural science model. For it can accept the validity of the *verstehen* thesis. In fact, allegedly neutral scientific languages, by claiming to avoid understanding, always end up being unwittingly ethnocentric. The supposedly neutral terms in which other people's actions are identified: the functions of functional theory, or the maximization-descriptions of various consequentialist accounts of individual action, all reflect the stress on instrumental reason in our civilization since the seventeenth century. To see them everywhere is really to distort the action, beliefs, and so on, of alien societies in an ethnocentric way. A good example is the theory of development dominant until recently in American political science. This was based on the notion that certain functions were being performed by all political systems, only in different ways by different structures. But these functions, for example interest-aggregation and articulation, are only clearly identifiable in advanced industrial society, where the political process is played out through the articulation of individual and group interests. This identification of functions pre-supposes a degree of individuation, which is not present everywhere. The importance of understanding another people's language of self-understanding is precisely that it can protect us against this kind of ethnocentric projection.

We can see how the three approaches—the natural science model, the incorrigibility thesis and the interpretative view—relate if we take a well-discussed example. This is the question of how to account for the exotic practices of primitive societies; for instance their magic. This is the issue taken up by Winch in his "Understanding a Primitive Society" (307–324).

Very crudely put, there are two families of position on this issue. The traditional view of earlier Western anthropology, going back to Frazer, is to see magic as a kind of proto-science/technology, an attempt by primitive people to master their environment, to do what we do better by modern science and technology. This view naturally gave grounds for criticizing the factual beliefs seen as implicit in the magical practices, for instance the belief in magical powers and spirits.

This theory is naturally congenial to proponents of a 'neutral' scientific language. It allows us a way of identifying what these people are doing, at least what general category their actions fit in, transculturally. At least to get this far, we do not need to grasp their self-understanding in all its peculiarity.

In contrast to this, the rival view is influenced by the incorrigibility thesis or by other similar doctrines. It holds that identifying these practices as a proto-technology is an ethnocentric howler. Rather we have to understand what is going on here as a quite different practice, which may have no corresponding activity in our society. The various rituals of magic are thought to have a 'symbolic' or 'expressive' function, rather than being intended to get things done in the world.[4] The tribe dances to recover its sense of the important meanings it lives by in face of the challenge of drought, rather than seeing the dance as a mechanism to bring on rain—the way we see seeding clouds, for instance.

We can see that this view puts the magical practices beyond the strictures of our modern science and technology. The tribe is not making a factual error about what causes precipitation, they are doing something quite different which cannot be judged in these terms; indeed, should not be judged at all, since this is just their form of life, the way that they face the human constants of birth, death, marriage, drought, plenty, etc. There may be nothing quite corresponding to it in our society. We have to understand it in its own terms; and it is the height of ethnocentric gaucherie to judge it in terms of one of our practices, which are all quite incommensurable with it. To come to grips with it we need understanding.

Now the view I am defending here would disagree with both these approaches. Perhaps somewhat paradoxically, it would accuse both of them of sharing an ethnocentric assumption: that the tribe's practice must be *either* proto-science/technology *or* the integration of meaning through symbolism. For it is a signal feature of our civilization that we have separated these two, and sorted them out. Even our pre-modern forebears of four centuries ago might have found this a little difficult to understand. If we examine the dominant pre-seventeenth-century worldviews, such as the conceptions of the correspondences that were so important in the High Renaissance, it is clear that what we would consider two quite independent goals—understanding what reality is like, and putting ourselves in tune with it—were not separated, nor separable. For us, these are goals which we pursue respectively through science, and (for some of us perhaps) poetry, or music, or flights into the wilderness, or whatever.

But if your conception of man as rational animal is of a being who can understand the rational order of things, and if (following Plato) we hold that understanding this order is necessarily loving it, hence being in tune with it, then it is not so clear how understanding the world and getting in tune with it can be separated. For the terms in which we get in tune with it, and lay bare the significance of things, must be those in which we present it as rational order. And since it is rational order, these will be the most perspicuous terms of understanding. On the other side, to step beyond the conceptual limits of attunement to the world, to cease to see it as a rational order, to adopt, say, a

Democritan perspective on it, must be to step beyond the conceptual limits of perspicuous understanding.

I am reminding us of this bit of our past only to illustrate what it can be like not to have sorted out two goals, which we now consider quite distinct and incombinable. We do this because the seventeenth-century revolution in science involved, inter alia, sorting these out and rigorously separating them. This has been the basis for our spectacular progress in natural science of the last three centuries.

So the hypothesis I put forward is that the way to understand the magical practices of some primitive societies might be to see them not through the disjunction, either proto-technology or expressive activity, but rather as partaking of a mode of activity in which this kind of clear separation and segregation is not yet made. Now identifying these two possibilities—respectively, the fusion and the segregation of the cognitive or manipulative on one hand, and the symbolic or integrative on the other—amounts to finding a language of perspicuous contrast. It is a language which enables us to give an account of the procedures of both societies in terms of the same cluster of possibilities.

Unlike the neutralist account, it does not involve projecting our own gamut of activities onto the agents of the other society. It allows for the fact that their range of activities may be crucially different from ours, that they may have activities which have no correspondent in ours; which in fact they turn out to do. But unlike the incorrigibility view, it does not just accept that their particular activities will be incommensurable with ours, and must somehow be understood on their own terms or not at all. On the contrary, it searches for a language of perspicuous contrast in which we can understand their practices in relation to ours.

This means that their self-understanding is not incorrigible. We avoid criticizing them on irrelevant grounds. We do not see them as just making a set of scientific/technological errors. But we can criticize them. For the separation perspective has in *certain respects* shown its undoubted superiority over the fusion perspective. It is infinitely superior for the understanding of the natural world. Our immense technological success is proof of this. It may be that we are inferior to the primitives in other respects, for example our integration with our world, as some contemporaries would hold. But this is something which the language of contrast should help us to assess more clear-headedly. It certainly contributes to our understanding, whatever the verdict, because we can see how the modern scientific perspective is an historic achievement and not the perennial human mode of thought.

This example was meant to show how the interpretive approach, far from leading to ethnocentrism, ought properly understood to bring about the exact opposite, because it will frequently be the case that we cannot understand another society until we have understood ourselves better as well. This will be so wherever the language of perspicuous contrast, which is adequate to the case, also forces us to re-describe what we are doing. In the above example, it forces us to see the separation of knowledge of and attunement with the cosmos as something we have brought about, one possibility among others, and not as the inescapable framework of all thought. We are always in danger of seeing our ways of acting and thinking as the only conceivable ones. That is exactly what ethnocentricity consists in. Understanding other societies ought to wrench us out of this; it ought to alter our self-understanding. It is the merit of the interpretive view that it explains how this comes about, when it does.

As a matter of fact, in the world encounter of cultures over the last four centuries, there has been a great deal of alteration in self-understanding through meeting with others. Only it has been very unevenly distributed. It was the societies who were less powerful who felt the full force of the constraint to alter their traditional terms of understanding. The dominant culture, the European, was for a while afforded the luxury of ethnocentricity. Power can allow itself illusions.

But as the world moves towards a new equilibrium of power, a new kind of mutual understanding ought also to be possible unless the different parties are again tempted to flee from it into the convenient illusions of scientific or religious infallibility. In so far as a new mutual understanding involves a new self-understanding—and this can be disturbing—the temptations to flee may be all too pressing.

III

I have tried to present a view here of social and political theories as theories about practice. In this they are to be sharply contrasted with the theories which have developed in the natural sciences. The temptation to assimilate the two is very strong in our civilization, partly because of the signal success of the natural sciences, partly because they seem to promise a degree of technological control over things, which we often long for in society.

But to yield to this temptation is to fall into a distorted conception of what we are doing in social science. And this has a cost. We generate not only bogus explanations and specious knowledge, but we also encourage ourselves to look for technological solutions to our deepest social problems, which are frequently aggravated by our misguided attempts to manipulate their parameters.

I have tried to argue that learning to situate our social theorizing among our *practices* can free us from these misconceptions. It can enable us to understand better what it is to validate a theory. We can see how explaining another involves understanding him. And at the same time, it can give us some insight into the complex relations that bind explanation and self-definition, and the understanding of self and other.

In this paper, I have tried to get to the root of the intellectual and moral malaise, which we feel in theorizing about very different societies. If explanation demands understanding, then how can we ever be confident that we have explained what goes on in another society? But more, if the account is to make sense to us, how can it avoid being critical? And what gives us this right to declare that others are wrong about themselves? The moral malaise in particular makes us want to flee into a supposedly neutral social science, or into a debilitating relativism.

My contention has been that there is no cause to lose our nerve. Understanding is inseparable from criticism, but this in turn is inseparable from self-criticism. Seeing this, of course, may give us an even stronger motive to panic and take refuge in a bogus objectivity, but it ought to discredit decisively the justifying grounds for this move.

This brings to the fore another facet of the interweaving of explanation and self-definition which has been implicit in much of the above discussion. What I have been trying to sketch above is the way in which understanding another society can make us challenge our self-definitions. It can force us to this, because we cannot get an adequate explanatory account of them until we understand their self-definitions, and these may be different enough from ours to force us to extend our language of human possibilities.

But what this also shows is the way in which explanatory sciences of society are logically and historically dependent on our self-definitions. They are logically dependent, because a valid account, I have argued, must take the subject as an agent. But this points also to an historical dependence: within any given culture, the languages of social science are developed out of and nourished by the languages of self-definition, which have grown within it. The idea of a science which could ignore culture and history, which could simply bypass the historically developed languages of political and social self-understanding, has been one of the great recurring illusions of modern Western civilization.

Supposedly independent and culture-transcendent theories of politics turn out to be heavily dependent on certain parochial Western forms of political culture. For instance, a conception of the political system as responding to the demands generated by individuals or partial groups within society is obviously heavily dependent for whatever plausibility it may possess on the individualist

practices of modern Western politics, within which government institutions figure mainly as instruments. If we did not have an institutional and political life in
which negotiation and brokerage between individual and group interests played
such a large and legitimately accepted role, there would not even be a surface
case for explaining our political life by these theories.

But the fact that our practices are of this kind is itself dependent on the self-
definitions of an individualist kind, which have grown in our civilization; and
these in turn have been fed by the atomist-instrumentalist theories which bulk so
large in modern thought. So that contemporary political science has a large unacknowledged, and hence also undischarged, debt to modern political theory.

The self-definitions, in other words, give the explanatory theory some fit,
which is far from saying that the fit is perfect. On the contrary, the vice of these
individualist theories is that they ignore important other sides of Western political reality, those that are bound up with the practices of self-rule, and our self-
understanding as citizen republics. It can be argued that these are as fundamental
and integral to our reality as the practices captured in atomist-instrumentalist
theories. And these, of course, have been explored and further defined in other
traditions of political theory, for example the tradition of civic humanism, or from
a revolutionary perspective, Marxist or anarchist theory. The practice of Western
society today is partly shaped by the definitions these theories have provided.
And they have correspondingly offered the bases of critical political science.

Thus, the supposedly culture-free political science, which models its independence of history on the paradigm of natural science, is in fact deeply rooted
in Western culture. What is worse, its roots are in one of the warring tendencies
in Western political culture. So that it is not only unaware of its origins, but
also deeply and unconsciously partisan. It weighs in on behalf of atomist and
instrumentalist politics against the rival orientations to community and citizen
self-rule.

But when one comes to comparative politics, the distortion is even greater.
The supposedly culture-free model is applied to societies in which nothing closely
analogous to the atomist-instrumentalist politics of the West exists, and the result
is both unilluminating and tendentious. That is, nothing very much is explained
in the politics of these non-Western societies, while the theory insinuates the
norm of instrumentalist good function as the unquestionable *telos* of development. The confused model of value-free, culture-transcendent science hides
from its practitioners both their ethnocentrism and their norm setting. In fact
they are unconsciously setting for non-Western society a goal which no Western
society would consent to for a minute. Because in fact, in Western politics, instrumentalist politics has been tempered and counter-balanced and controlled by the

politics of citizen participation. Indeed, the fact that this equilibrium is now under threat is, I believe, the source of a major crisis in Western society.

But the influence of inappropriate, Western and pseudo-universal models over the social science of some non-Western countries exemplified, I would argue, by the impact of American behaviorism on Indian political science—is due to more than historic relations of unequal political power. If we take this impact as an example, it is closely bound up, I should want to claim, with a failure to appreciate that an illuminating political science of Indian society would have to be based on Indian self-definitions.

But this failure itself is due to the relative absence in traditional Indian thought of self-definitions of *politics*, by which I mean something like: the practices by which people contribute, cooperatively or in struggle, to shape the way power and authority are exercised in their lives. As Ashis Nandy has argued, there is a traditional Indian reflection on statecraft, focused on non-moral and non-responsible uses of power;[5] and there are conceptions of the proper order of things, even with a specific place for political power, if we follow Louis Dumont.[6] But politics as a realm of activity with its own intrinsic norms, its own specific good or fulfillments, had no place in this tradition.

This is not surprising. This notion of politics, it could be argued, was invented in the West, more specifically, by the Greeks. And this was itself no accident, in that the Greeks had developed practices of participation in power that few other peoples had. Traditional India, one could say, did not need the concept of a practice it did not possess.

But politics exist in contemporary India. There are practices by which people contribute to shape the incidence of power, whatever inequalities and exclusions may mar the democratic process. Contemporary India thus does need a concept of this kind. But if I am right, this is one thing that cannot be provided ready-made from outside. An appropriate concept—or concepts—of politics in India will only arise through an articulation of the self-definitions of people engaged in the practices of politics in India. That is, after all, how the few notions of politics, which offer us any insight at all, arose in the West. It is, I believe, the only path by which such concepts can arise. And it follows from what I argued above that this would not just be of relevance to India. A more appropriate political science for this society would transform comparative politics. It would put the challenge of developing an adequate theoretical language in which very different practices of politics, Indian and Western, could be compared in an illuminating way. To achieve such a language would in turn transform the understanding each of our societies has of itself. The international community of scholars has potentially a great deal to gain from work in India.

NOTES

1. Peter Winch, *The Idea of a Social Science* (London: Routledge and Paul, 1958), and "Understanding a Primitive Society," *American Philosophical Quarterly* 1 (1964): 307–324.

2. G. A. Cohen, *Karl Marx's Theory of History: A Defence* (Oxford: Oxford University Press, 1978).

3. Winch, "Understanding a Primitive Society."

4. J. H. M. Beattie, "On Understanding Ritual," in *Rationality*, ed. Bryan Wilson (Oxford: Oxford University Press, 1970).

5. Ashis Nandy, "The Making and Unmaking of Political Cultures in India," in *At the Edge of Psychology: Essays in Politics and Culture* (Delhi: Oxford University Press, 1980).

6. Louis Dumont, *Homo Hierarchicus: An Essay on the Caste System* (Paris: Gallimard, 1966).

KWAME ANTHONY APPIAH

People disagree with one another, within and across cultures, all the time.[1] One source of disagreement is that they come from places with different cultural backgrounds. Another is that they have different evidence—even when they have the same cultural background—because they have taken different paths through the world. If relativism about some subject matter were just the descriptive claim that people disagree and their disagreements are correlated with—and so 'relative' to—differences in culture and experience, the view would be simply banal. The descriptive fact of widespread disagreement is an anthropological commonplace. Indeed, I am tempted to say that the interesting fact is the odd range of things on which we agree.

The factual claim that there are cultural correlations among the extensive disagreements that people have with one another is not the only boring claim we might dub 'relativism.' Obvious and boring *normative* truths characterize our disagreements also. The normative thesis that people are entitled to different views, since they have had different experiences, is dull. If you have not seen the picture painted on the other side of the elephant, you have every reason not to think that it is there. I, looking at that picture, have every reason to think that it *is* there. If my parents and teachers taught me that the earth is five thousand years old and you learned that it was billions of years old—and that was the extent of our evidence—we would reasonably hold different views. For each of us to think otherwise would be unreasonable.

So is there an interesting version of relativism? I think many relativisms can be conceived; I do not intend to collect and classify them all. My interest here is in varieties of moral relativism. So my question, more exactly, is this: What interesting claims do moral relativists make about the reasonableness of moral disagreement?

Consider the case where two people, Kwame and Anthony, one Ghanaian, one English, disagree about whether homosexuality is wrong. This is the sort of case where people who call themselves relativists often suggest that Kwame's options and Anthony's are different and depend on the different moral frameworks of their different cultures. As a descriptive matter, each may hold the view he does in some sense because it is the standard view where he grew up. So far, so boring. What does relativism have to offer? One possibility is just the claim that each of them is right, according to the standards of his culture. So, when Kwame says, "Homosexuality is wrong," and Anthony says, "No, it isn't," each of them might be saying something true. That looks like a straightforward contradiction. So, to begin, we might want to offer the relativist this fallback position: Don't you want to say that each is saying something that is true-for-*him*?

Now, since true-for-Kwame and true-for-Anthony are different properties, to say that "Homosexuality is wrong" is true-for-Kwame and not true-for Anthony is not contradictory on its face. To make sense of this proposal, however, you have to know how to interpret talk of things being true-for-people, and, in particular, what the connection is between being true-for-A and just being true. Presumably there had better be no difference *for A* between being true and being true-for-A. The gap between truth and truth for X only arises from other perspectives. *I* can see a difference between something being true-for-you and it being true. But the difference disappears from your perspective; though you can see a difference between what is true (or, equivalently-for-you, true-for-you) and what is true-for-me.

This settlement will face an important difficulty, however, when, as with Kwame and Anthony, the judgment we are considering is moral. To think of homosexuality as (morally) wrong is to think, among other things, that it would be better for everyone not to engage in homosexual acts and better for everyone not just to avoid them but also to believe that they are wrong. This is the practical meaning of the idea that moral judgments are universalizable. Other things being equal, the wrongness of homosexual acts gives me reasons to try to persuade you not to engage in them if you are inclined to. I also have reason to try to persuade you not just to avoid such acts but also to judge that they would be wrong. If I do, you will have reasons not only to abstain from homosexual sex, but also to try to persuade others to abstain from the acts and to judge them wrong. You will also be inclined to persuade others that they are wrong. So if it is true-for-me that the act is wrong, then I have a reason to want it to be true-for-you, and I have a reason not just to try to stop you acting on your belief that homosexual acts are okay but to try to stop you from having the belief at all. If the judgment is moral, then, I cannot rest at the thought that the judgment that homosexuality is wrong is true-for-me but not for you. It would be difficult to make moral sense of the idea that it is true-for-you that homosexual acts are okay but that you should nevertheless not engage in them.

So even if moral relativism can be made sense of theoretically, it faces a difficulty in practice. If I think that a moral claim that is true-for-me is false-for-you, the fact that it is false-for-you leaves me still convinced that you should act as if it were true—and not just true-for-me but also true-for-you. The relativism gives me no reason to live and let live, no reason to accept that you might live by one standard and I by another.

Of course, there may be moral claims that have a relativity built into them that we *can* accept. Anthony might think that people ought to act, in matters of sex, as their consciences dictate. Then he will think that Kwame should avoid homosexual acts just because he conscientiously (though mistakenly) believes them to be wrong. But he will not take it to be true-for-Kwame that homosexual acts are wrong. Homosexual acts will not be wrong, though there is a sense in which they are wrong for Kwame (and all those who conscientiously believe them to be wrong). Still an act being wrong for Kwame in this sense will still leave Anthony convinced that it would be better if Kwame did not have the mistaken belief that makes the act wrong for him. In Kwame's cognitive situation, avoiding homosexual acts is the best thing for him to do; but it would be better if he were in the cognitive situation of one who recognizes that these acts are not, in themselves, wrong. Once he realized that, Anthony thinks, Kwame would have no moral reason to avoid them.

Now many relativists will think that there is nothing Anthony can do to rationally persuade Kwame that he is wrong about homosexuality. They will say that there is still a truth in relativism, even if the arguments I have just offered mean we cannot make much sense of the idea that a moral claim is true-for-one-person and not for another. That truth is that there are no rationally compelling reasons for people to change their mind about morality. Once Kwame and Anthony have moral views, there is nothing to which either can appeal to give the other a good reason to believe what he himself believes. This view is held by some relativists because they are anti-realists about morality: they think no independent moral reality constrains our views. They think we cannot appeal to features of the world to persuade one another about morality. Another reason is that some are committed to a version of prescriptivism; they think that to believe that X is right is to have a pro-attitude of some sort to X, and they think that, in the end, the only rational constraints on such attitudes are constraints of consistency.

I think what we should say about arguments such as these is not clear. But they strike me essentially as arguments from premises about how things are as a matter of metaphysical of psychological fact to conclusions about how things ought to be. I share Hume's belief that we ought to be careful when we see such slides from metaphysical 'is' to moral 'ought.' I suggest we start, instead, from a moral premise—that it is better to treat one another's moral beliefs as responsive to reasons, because to treat a person's moral views as bare facts about them, ungrounded in reasons, is to treat them with disrespect. If you think that, then the relativist claim that we can only evaluate moral beliefs from within shared frameworks will lead you to wonder if you can treat people from other cultures with respect. Relativism of this sort looks like it will lead not to tolerance—as relativists sometimes claim—but to contempt. I argue that, even if the form of relativism that claims that moral disagreements across cultures are—at least sometimes—rationally irresolvable is true, it does not, in practice, undermine the point of discussing normative issues with people from other cultures.

We should begin by noting that our vocabulary of evaluation is multifarious. Some terms—good, bad—are, as philosophers put it, rather 'thin.' They express approval or disapproval, but their application is otherwise rather unconstrained: good soil, good argument, good guy. Much of our language of evaluation, however, is much 'thicker.' To apply the concept of 'rudeness,' for example, you have to think of the act you are criticizing as a breach of good manners or as lacking the appropriate degree of concern for the feelings of others. Thin concepts appear to be universal; we are not the only people who have the concepts of right and wrong, good and bad. Every society has terms that correspond to these thin concepts. Even thick concepts such as rudeness are ubiquitous. But some even thicker concepts are distinctive of particular societies.

For example, people everywhere have ideas about responsibility to one's children. But who are your children? I grew up in two societies, each of which conceived of family in quite different ways. Because these societies—Akan society in Ghana and the English world of my mother's kin—have been in touch with one another for several centuries, these differences are diminishing, but important distinctions remain.

Consider the Akan idea of the *abusua*, a group of people related by common ancestry, who have relations of love and obligation to one another. The closer in time your shared ancestors, roughly speaking, the stronger the bonds. Sounds, in short, like a family. But an *abusua* and a family have important differences. Membership in an *abusua* depends only on who your mother is; your father is irrelevant. If you are a woman, then your children are in your *abusua*, and so are the descendants of your daughters, and their daughters, on to the end of time. Membership in the *abusua* is shared like mitochondrial DNA, passing only through women. So I am in the same *abusua* as my sister's children but not in the same one as my brother's children. Since I am not related to my father through a woman, he is not a member of my *abusua* either.

The Akan conception of the family is what anthropologists call *matrilineal*. A hundred years ago in Asante, in most lives, your mother's brother—your senior maternal uncle or *wofa*—would have played the role a father would have been expected to play in England. He was responsible, with the child's mother, for making sure that his sister's children were fed, clothed, and educated. Many married women lived with their brothers, visiting their husbands regularly. Men took an interest in their children, but their obligations to their children were relatively less demanding, rather like being an English uncle.

These are different ways of organizing family life. Which one makes sense to you will depend, in good measure, on the concepts with which you grew up. As long as a society has a way of assigning responsibilities for children that works, it would be odd to say that one way was the right way of doing it, and all the others wrong. Most Americans feel, rightly, that a father delinquent in child support payments is doing something wrong. Many Akans would feel the same about a delinquent *wofa*. Once you understand the two systems, you will likely agree with both judgments, and not because you've given up any of your basic moral commitments. Good parenting epitomizes thin, universal values. But their expression is highly particular, thickly enmeshed with local customs and expectations and the facts of social arrangements. Disagreements like these—about who has the primary responsibility for the welfare of children—are consistent with thinking that each society can recognize the reasons the other has for doing what it does.

Other local values scarcely correspond to anything an American might recognize. My father, for example, would not eat animals killed in the forest. He told us that when he once ate venison by accident in England, his skin broke out in a rash. Had you asked him why he would not eat bush meat, though, he would not have mentioned an allergy. He would have told you—if he thought it was any of your business—that it was *akyiwadee* for him, because he was of the clan of the Bush Cow. Etymologically *akyiwadee* means something like 'a thing you turn your back on,' and, if you had to guess at a translation of it, you would presumably suggest 'taboo,' a word that came into English from a Polynesian language, where it was used to refer to things that people of certain groups strenuously avoided. In Ghanaian English, too, we translate *akyiwadee* as 'taboo.'

Now, I make no claim that my non-Akan readers cannot learn what *akyiwadee* means—I hope you mostly grasp its usage based on the little I have already said. If you read a little Akan anthropology, you would soon know enough to grasp the concept. Even then, this is not likely to become an idea that plays any role in your day-to-day thinking. You avoid some acts that you might loosely call taboo, the prohibition on incest, for example. But you do not think incest is to be avoided because it is taboo, but that it is taboo *because* we can cite good reasons not to do it.

I have deliberately not used the word 'moral' to describe these taboos. They are values: they guide acts, thoughts, and feelings. They are unlike what we would think of as moral values, however, in at least three ways. First, they do not always apply to everybody. Only members of the Bush Cow clan have the obligation to avoid bush meat. Second, people who break taboos are polluted, even if their action is accidental, whereas with an offense against morality, lack of intention counts as a substantial defense. Oedipus was no better off for having broken the incest taboo unknowingly. A final difference between taboos and moral demands is that breaches of them pollute mostly *you*: they are not fundamentally about how you should treat others; they dictate how you should keep yourself (ritually) clean.

Taboos are thickly enmeshed in all sorts of customs and factual beliefs (including the existence of irascible ancestors and shrine gods), and one response to such alien values is just to dismiss them as primitive and irrational. But if that is what they are, then the primitive and the irrational are pervasive outside Ghana, too. Indeed, that kind of repugnance is surely universal: that is one reason why it is not difficult to grasp. Many Americans eat pigs but will not eat cats. It would be hard to make the case that cats are, say, dirtier or more intelligent than pigs. Most American meat eaters who refuse to eat cats have only the defense that the very thought of it fills them with disgust.

Some things you touch make you feel polluted, dirty; eating them would nauseate you. You will run off to wash your hands or wash out your mouth if you come into contact with them. Mostly we defend these responses as rational: cockroaches, rats, and others' saliva or vomit may actually carry diseases, we say; cats and dogs taste horrible. Yet these reactions are not really explained by the stories we tell. Flies carry most of the same risks as cockroaches but usually produce less 'pollution.' People are disgusted by the idea of drinking orange juice that has had a cockroach in it, even if they know that the cockroach was rigorously cleansed of all bacteria by being autoclaved in advance.[2]

Psychologists (notably Paul Rozin, who did some of those experiments with cockroaches in orange juice) think that this tendency to disgust is a fundamental human trait, one evolved in us because distinguishing between what you will and will not eat is a crucial cognitive task for an omnivorous species like ours. Disgust goes with nausea, because it is a response that developed to deal with food that we should avoid. But that capacity for disgust, like all our natural capabilities, can be enhanced by culture. Is this tendency to disgust the *same* one that makes some men in many cultures feel polluted when they learn they have shaken hands with a menstruating woman, or that makes most Americans squirm in disgust at the thought of incest? I don't think we know yet. The pervasiveness of these taboo responses does suggest that they draw on something deep in human nature.

Many people in the United States, secular and religious, think that the attitudes of some of their contemporaries toward some sexual acts—masturbation, homosexuality, and even consensual adult incest—are versions of the taboos found in other cultures. In the so-called Holiness Code, at the end of Leviticus, eating animals that have died of natural causes requires you to wash yourself and your clothes. Priests, 'the sons of Aaron,' learn that if they touch people or 'any swarming thing' that is polluting, they must bathe and wait until sunset before they can eat the 'sacred donations.' The same chapters proscribe the consuming of blood, bodily self-mutilation (though not male circumcision), and seeing one's relatives naked, while prescribing detailed rules for some kinds of sacrifice. For most modern Christians, these regulations are parts of Jewish law from which Christ freed them. But the famous proscription against a man 'lying with a man as with a woman' is found alongside these passages, along with commands to avoid incest and bestiality, which most Christians still endorse.[3]

Akan people largely accept now that others do not feel the power of our taboos; we know that they may have their own. Most important, these local values do not stop us from also recognizing, as we do, kindness, generosity, and compassion, or cruelty, stinginess, and inconsiderateness—virtues and vices recognized widely among other human societies.

Most of our evaluative language is 'open-textured': two people who both know what the words mean can reasonably disagree about whether they apply in a particular case.[4] Grasping what the words mean does not give you a rule that will definitively decide whether it applies in every case.

Several years ago an international parliament of religious leaders issued a "Universal Declaration of a Global Ethic." Their exhortations had the quality of those horoscopes that seem wonderfully precise while being vague enough to suit all comers. "We must not commit any kind of sexual immorality": a fine sentiment, unless we do not agree about what counts as sexual immorality. "We must put behind us all forms of domination and abuse": but societies that, by our lights, subject women to domination and abuse are unlikely to recognize themselves by that description. They are convinced that they are protecting women's honor and chastity.

So it goes with our most central values. Is it cruel to spank children to teach them how to behave? We could, no doubt, argue our way to one position or the other on the issue. If we ended up disagreeing, it would not be because one of us did not understand the value at stake; it would be because applying value terms to new cases requires judgment and discretion. Often part of our understanding of these terms is that their applications are *meant* to be debated. They are, to use another piece of philosopher's jargon, *essentially contestable*. For many concepts, as W. B. Gallie wrote when he introduced the term, "proper use inevitably involves endless disputes about their proper use on the part of users."[5] Evaluative language aims to shape not only our acts but also our thoughts and our feelings. When we describe past acts with words like 'courageous' and 'cowardly,' 'cruel' and 'kind,' we are shaping what people think and feel about what was done—and shaping our understanding of our moral language. Because that language is open-textured and essentially contestable, even people who share a moral vocabulary have plenty to contest.

There is yet a third way of disagreeing about values. Even if we share a value language, and even if we agree on how to apply it to a particular case, we can disagree about the weight to give to different values. Confucius, for example, in the *Analects*, says that a son should respect his parents. A *chün tzu* (often translated as a gentleman) should be generous to those who have done well by him and avoid vindictiveness toward those who have done him injury. He should avoid avarice and not let self-interest get in the way of doing what is right. He should be courageous, wise, and keep his word. Summarized in this, no doubt, simplistic way, Confucius may sound banal. But because we share these values with him does not mean that we will always agree with him about what we ought to think and feel. He placed a lot more weight on obedience to authority, for example, than most of us would. As a result, sometimes Confucius might respond to the demands on the many values we both recognize differently than we would.

Such conflicts among shared values can take place within a single society—indeed, within a single human heart. Hegel famously said that tragedy involved the clash not between good and evil but between two goods. Agamemnon, as commander of the Greek army, had to choose between the interests of the Trojan expedition and his devotion to his wife and daughter. Such dilemmas are a mainstay of imaginative fiction, but clashes among our values, if usually less exalted, are an everyday occurrence.

Consider criminal punishment. No reasonable person thinks that punishing innocent people is good. But we all know that human institutions are imperfect, that our knowledge is always fallible, and that juries are not free from prejudice. So we know that—sometimes—innocent people will be punished. That would seem like an argument for abandoning criminal punishment; but we also think that punishing the guilty is desirable, especially to deter future crime. So we may be unable to agree on how to strike the balance between avoiding the injustice of punishing the innocent and other values, even though we agree on what other values are at stake such as the security of people and property, justice, and retribution. The legal scholar Charles Black argued that 'caprice and mistake' are inevitable in capital trials and that killing an innocent person was too important a mistake to risk.[6] Many proponents of capital punishment believe punishing those who deserve to die is important—important enough that we must, regretfully, accept that we will sometimes kill an innocent. Not to do the right thing in the cases where we punish the guilty, they think, would be a greater wrong. We can find people on either side of the capital punishment debate who share the same values but weigh them differently.

We have identified three kinds of disagreement about values: we can fail to share a vocabulary of evaluation; we can give the same vocabulary different interpretations; and we can give the same values different weights. These problems seem more likely to arise if the discussion involves people from different societies. Mostly we share evaluative language with our neighbors, you might think. Whereas evaluation is essentially contestable, the range of disagreement will usually be wider—will it not?—when people from different places try to come to a shared evaluation. You and I may not always agree about what is polite. Still, *politeness* is what we are disagreeing about. Other societies will have words that behave roughly like our word 'polite' and will have something like the idea of 'good manners,' but an extra level of difference will arise when this thick vocabulary of evaluation is embedded in different ways of life. Finally, we know that one way in which societies differ is in the relative weight they place on different values.

In much of the Mediterranean world, men believe that their honor is tied up with the chastity of their sisters, daughters, and wives. Men in the United States also feel shamed or dishonored when their wives or daughters are raped. But unless they come from one of those honor-based societies, they are not likely to think that the solution is to repudiate the woman. Family honor is not as important to us now as it clearly is, and was, to others. So you might conclude that cross-cultural conversations about values are bound to end in disagreement; indeed, you might fear that they would inflame conflict, not create understanding.

This conclusion, I think, is wrong for at least two reasons. First, we can agree about *what* to do even when we do not agree *why* we should do it. Second, we exaggerate the role of reasoned argument in reaching or failing to reach agreements about values. Let me explain.

The Akan, you will no doubt be glad to hear, shun incest between brothers and sisters and parents and children as *akyiwadee*. You can agree with the Akan *that* incest is wrong, even if you do not accept their explanation of *why* it is wrong. If my interest is in discouraging theft, I need not worry that one person might avoid stealing because of belief in the Golden Rule, another because of a conception of personal integrity, or others because they believe God frowns on it. Value language helps shape common responses of thought, action, and feeling. But when the issue is *what* to do, differences in what we think and feel can fall away. We know from our own family lives that conversation does not start with agreement on principles. Who but someone in the grip of a terrible theory would want to insist on an agreement on principles before discussing which movie to see, what to have for dinner, or when to go to bed?

Our political coexistence depends on being able to agree about practices while disagreeing about their justification. For many years, in medieval Spain under the Moors and later in the Ottoman Near East, Jews and Christians of various denominations lived under Muslim rule. This modus vivendi was possible only because the communities did not have to agree on a set of universal values. In seventeenth-century Holland, starting roughly during the time of Rembrandt, the Sephardic Jewish community began to be increasingly integrated into Dutch society, and a great deal of intellectual and social exchange transpired between Christian and Jewish communities. Christian toleration of Jews did not depend on express agreement on fundamental values. These historical examples of religious toleration should remind us of the most obvious fact about our own society: that we agree about many institutions and practices without agreeing as to why.

Americans share a willingness to be governed under the United States Constitution. But that does not require anyone to agree to any particular claims or values. The Bill of Rights tells us, "Congress shall make no law respecting an establishment of religion, or prohibiting the free exercise thereof," yet we do not need to agree on what values underlie our acceptance of the First Amendment's treatment of religion. Is it religious toleration as an end in itself? Or a Protestant commitment to the sovereignty of the individual conscience? Is it prudence, which recognizes that trying to force religious conformity on people only leads to civil discord? Or skepticism that any religion has it right? Is it to protect the government from religion, or religion from the government? Or some combination of these, or other, aims?

Cass Sunstein has written eloquently that the American understanding of constitutional law is a set of what he calls "incompletely theorized agreements."[7] Most people will agree that for the Congress to pass laws banning mosques would be wrong, for example, without agreeing exactly as to why. Many of us would, no doubt, mention the First Amendment (even though we do not agree about what values it embodies). But others would ground their judgment not in any particular law but in a conception, say, of democracy or in the equal citizenship of Muslims, neither of which is explicitly mentioned in the Constitution. There is no agreed-upon answer—the point is that there does not need to be one. We can live together without agreeing on what the values are that make it good to live together; we can agree about what to do in most cases, without agreeing about why it is right. I do not want to overstate the point. No doubt there are widely shared values that help Americans live together in amity. But we do not live together successfully because we have a shared theory of value or a shared story as to how to bring 'our' values to bear in each case.

So, what makes conversation across cultures worthwhile is not that we are likely to come to a reasoned agreement about values. We might change our minds, but the reasons we exchange in our conversations will seldom do much to persuade others who do not share our fundamental evaluative judgments. The same holds for factual judgments, by the way. The essential idea here is not that there is no moral or factual reality but that we have a very hard time looking for it.

We offer judgments, after all, rarely because we have applied well-considered principles to a set of facts and then deduced a conclusion. Our justifications for what we have done—or what we plan to do—are typically construed after the event, being rationalizations of what we have decided intuitively. A good deal of what we intuitively take to be right, we take to be right because we are accustomed to it. If you live in a society where children are spanked, you will probably spank your children. You will believe that it is a good way to teach them right from wrong and that, despite the temporary suffering caused by a beating, they will end up better off for it. You will point to the wayward child and say, sotto voce, that his parents do not know how to discipline him; you will mean that they do not beat him enough. You will also, no doubt, recognize that some people spank their children too hard or too often. So you will recognize that beating a child can sometimes be cruel. Faced with someone who thinks all spanking is wrong, you are likely to be simply flummoxed.

I am not celebrating this argumentative impasse. I am not happy about the poverty of reasoning in much discussion within and across cultures. But a large part of what we do we do because it *is* just what we do. You get up in the morning at eight-thirty. Why *that* time? You have coffee and cereal every morning for breakfast. Why not porridge? Reasoning—by which I mean the public act of exchanging stated justifications—becomes salient not when we are going on in the usual way but when we are thinking about change. Regarding change, what moves people is often not an argument from a principle, not a long discussion about values, but just a gradually acquired new way of seeing things.

Just a couple of generations ago, in most of the industrialized world, most people thought that, ideally, middle-class women should be housewives and mothers. If they had extra time, they could engage in charitable work or entertain one another; a few might engage in the arts, writing novels, painting, performing in music, theater, and dance. But society offered little place for them in the 'learned professions'—as lawyers or doctors, priests or rabbis. If they were to enter academia, they would teach young children and probably remain unmarried. They were not likely to make their way in politics, except perhaps at the local level. They were not welcome in science. How much of the shift away from these assumptions is the result of arguments? The significant part of the shift was just the consequence of our getting used to new ways of doing things. The arguments that kept the old pattern in place were not—to put it mildly—terribly good. If the *reasons* for the old sexist way of doing things had been the problem, the women's movement could have been dispensed in a couple of weeks. Some people still believe that the ideal life for any woman is homemaking. More believe it is an honorable option. Still, the vast majority of Westerners at the turn of the new millennium would be appalled at the idea of trying to force women back into these roles. Arguments mattered for the women who made the women's movement and the men who responded to them. This I do not mean to deny. But their greatest achievement has been to change our habits. During the 1950s, if a college-educated woman wanted to go to law school or business school, the natural response was "Why?" Now the natural response is "Why not?" We have gotten used to gender equality.

I am urging that we should discuss normative questions with people in other places not because that will bring us to agreement but because it will help us get used to one another. If that is the aim, then all these opportunities for disagreement about values need not put us off. Understanding one another may be difficult, but it certainly does not require agreement. If agreement is not the only thing worth having, then the difficulties relativists claim there are for finding agreement may not matter very much.

NOTES

1. The central arguments of this chapter are from my *Cosmopolitanism: Ethics in a World of Strangers* (New York: Norton, 2006).

2. Paul Rozin, "Food Is Fundamental, Fun, Frightening, and Far-reaching," *Social Research* 66 (1999): 9–30. Thanks to John Haidt for a discussion of these issues.

3. Leviticus 18:22 and 20:13, in Robert Alter, trans., *The Five Books of Moses* [Pentateuch] (New York: Norton, 2004).

4. H. L. A. Hart, *The Concept of Law* (Oxford: Clarendon Press, 1997), chap. 6. Hart borrowed the idea from F. Waismann, who thought it to be an irreducible feature of language. The example of the bylaw about vehicles in the park is in Hart, "Positivism and the Separation of Law and Morals," *Harvard Law Review* 71 (1958): 593–629.

5. W. B. Gallie, "Essentially Contested Concepts," *Proceedings of the Aristotelian Society* 56 (1956): 169.

6. Charles L. Black Jr., *Capital Punishment: The Inevitability of Caprice and Mistake*, 2nd ed. (New York: Norton, 1981).

7. Cass R. Sunstein, "Incompletely Theorized Agreements," *Harvard Law Review* 108 (1995): 1733–1772.

Relativism, Persons, and Practices 31

AMÉLIE OKSENBERG RORTY

|

To put it bluntly, the controversy over cultural relativism, whether it be construed as a controversy about cross-cultural interpretation or about cross-cultural evaluation, is the kind of dispute that gives intellectuals a bad name among sensible people. Both sides are so bent on exaggeration that they seem to be displacing the real issues that divide them. The claims of relativists and their opponents are, when sanely and modestly construed, each plausible and mutually compatible. When those claims are globally extended and exaggerated—with relativists denying the possibility of cross-cultural understanding and their opponents denying the possibility of systematic untranslatability—they are indeed incompatible; but then they are also wildly implausible. Any sensible, widely traveled, multilingual person knows that in matters of translation, as in other practical matters, there is nothing resembling certainty or proof: the correctness or adequacy of an interpretation cannot be conclusively or uncontrovertibly established. Sometimes there is unexpectedly subtle and refined communication across radically

Amélie Oksenberg Rorty, "Relativism, Persons, and Practices," was originally published in *Relativism: Interpretation, and* Confrontation, edited by Michael Krausz, and published by Notre Dame University Press, 1989, pp. 418–440. Reprinted here with permission of the author. All rights reserved.

different cultures; sometimes there is insurmountable bafflement and systematic misunderstanding between relatively close cultures. For the most part, however, we live in the interesting intermediate grey area of partial success and partial failure of interpretation and communication. That grey area is to be found at home among neighbors as well as abroad among strangers, and it is to be found between the self of yesterday and the self of tomorrow.

What, if anything, is really at stake in the controversy? And why do the parties to the dispute energetically inflate their claims beyond plausibility, deflecting attention from what might really divide them?

First, relativists are quite right to insist that even such dramatically basic activities as birth, copulation, and death, such basic processes as eating and sleeping, physical growth and physical decay, are intentionally described in ways that affect phenomenological experience. Events and processes are encompassed and bounded, articulated and differentiated, within the web of a culture's conceptual and linguistic categories; their meaning is formed by its primary practices and sacred books, songs and rituals. Even the conceptions of social practices and meaning are sufficiently culturally specific so that it is tendentious to refer to conceptions of culture practices, as if *culture* or *practice* were Platonic forms, waiting to be conceptualized this way or that. Indeed the very practices of interpretation and evaluation are themselves culturally variable.

But nothing follows from this about the impossibility of cross-cultural interpretation, communication, or evaluation, particularly among cultures engaged in practical interactions with one another. The core truth of relativism—the intentionality of practice and experience—does not entail that successful communication and justified evaluation require strict identity of meaning. There are, furthermore, basic culturally invariant psychophysical and biosocial salience markers that set the focus and boundaries of attention, however variously these foci may be identified, interpreted, or evaluated.

Second, antirelativists with a strong realist bent rightly insist that there are events and facts—some of them intentionally described by reference to social practices—whose truth is not culturally determined. However they may be articulated or conceptualized, radical changes take place at birth and death; however they may be evaluated or integrated with other activities, eating and sleeping have specific organic effects. Shylock's plaintive "If you cut me, do I not bleed?" must be acknowledged, even if the connotations of the Elizabethan expressions 'cut' and 'bleed' cannot be captured in Ladino or Italian. Though there are dramatic variations in the criteria for, and the evaluation of, health and illness, and even in the experience of pain, specific chemicals tend on the whole to produce specific bodily changes, some impeding and others enhancing vital bodily functioning.

Realist-minded antirelativists are also right to claim that, in the nature of the case, social life has certain crucial nodes or foci of attention and concern: a society establishes patterns or modes of governance, of decision making and arbitration; it has patterns and modes of producing food and raising children; it has ways of dealing with transitions between life and death, with growth and aging. Since we are the sorts of creatures for whom everything is significant, creatures who also attempt to find regularities, if not laws, we endow these nodes and foci of social concern with meaning. It is an open empirical question—one which cannot be settled to everyone's satisfaction—whether these social nodes exhibit significant regularities.

But it doesn't follow from this that there are basic culturally neutral referential expressions or that distinctive cultures must in the end assign the same significance to cross-cultural facts or events. The core truths of antirelativism do not entail that there is a reductive foundational basis for interpretation, or universal standards for all types of evaluation. Antirelativists can acknowledge that the significance of social life—and sometimes even the determination of what is important to a culture's life—is so culturally specific that it is sometimes difficult to identify such foci or nodes across cultures. (If the 'legal system' of a culture is entirely absorbed in what another culture would regard as 'religious life' it is tendentious to compare legal systems as if one were comparing different varieties of the same species or variations on the same theme.) Empirical investigation determines whether—or how—specific kinds of intentional descriptions of such nodal foci are phenomenologically, and sometimes even physiologically, self-fulfilling.

Third, relativism and antirelativism are, when modestly formulated, perfectly compatible. Relativism need not foreclose the possibility of successful cross-cultural interpretation, communication, or evaluation; antirelativism need not foreclose the possibility of radical cross-cultural incomprehension and misinterpretation.

Sometimes it is helpful to remind ourselves of obvious, banal, Philistine truths.

(1) Most cultures are composed of intersecting networks of subcultures, each with distinctive practices, forming linguistic subcommunities. The directness of interpretation and evaluation among a culture's subcultures is, like that between cultures, partly a function of the extent to which their practices and experiences overlap. 'Sharing a history' is not sufficient for direct interpretation and communication: the length and indirectness of an interpretive chain depend on the extent to which subcultures share experiences and perspectives on that history. (Did Southern slaves share a history with their owners in 1860? Did Manchester mill hands share a history with factory owners?) When tasks and practices are

radically differentiated by gender, status, age, or roles, interpretation and communication are correspondingly attenuated. The evaluation of practices and performances across groups becomes increasingly perspectively slanted.

(2) The success of difficult, subtle interpretation and communication often depends on the temperament, the talent, and the preoccupations of the individuals involved. To be sure, everything—including hostility—is grist for the interpreter, but on the whole a nonthreatening demeanor is more likely to elicit cooperative, culturally typical speech and behavior than an intrusive one. Though gestures, intonation patterns, silences, and facial expressions themselves differ culturally, talented and skilled observers of such expressive behavior are advantaged in interpreting and communicating. Besides the interpretive advantages of temperament and talent there are those of experience. A recently bereaved anthropologist might, without sentimental projection, be in a better position to give a subtle explanation of culturally variable mourning behavior than an angry adolescent boy who shares the mourner's language.

(3) There are distinctive types, levels, and degrees of communication, each with distinctive criteria for success.

(a) 'Good enough' communication for interactive situations and practices does not require strict identity of connotative meaning. In political negotiations and mercantile exchange, for instance, it is enough that the parties recognize the suitability of the other's contributions to be willing to continue the exchange. Such communication can be practically successful without being subtly shaded.

(b) 'Good enough translation'—even of highly allusive poetry—does not require a word-by-word or phrase-by-phrase synonymy. The sense and meaning can be conveyed to the satisfaction of bilingualists by a network of analogous connotative associations. Sometimes this is achieved by indirection, sometimes by verbosity. Here, as elsewhere, there are trade-offs for distinctive criteria of success. The poignant sense of untranslatability—of lost meaning—does not argue for incomprehensibility: a translator might be able to fabricate a 'missing verse' good enough to fool a discerning native literary critic.

(c) 'Good enough explanation' need not involve elegant or precise translation. An interpreter's explanation of the etiology and function of native speech and practice can sometimes require lengthy, elaborate, and sometimes indirect translation into the original language.

(4) Our own neighbors are often the true but opaque audience for crosscultural evaluation. In condemning or praising the practices of cultures that do not interact with our own, we are often implicitly considering whether to adopt analogous practices ourselves. In evaluating the practices of cultures with which

we are interacting, our concerns are directed largely to their effects on the area of intersection. In a way most evaluations are not intended to hit their direct objects: they are presented as considerations in a practical deliberation rather than as contextless conclusions to be registered in the Book of the World. Their declarative form is meant to enhance their rhetorical force.

Since the core truths of relativism are compatible with those of its alleged opponents, what is at stake in keeping the debate alive? The electrical charge of controversy carries the baggage of personal and cultural psychology, with both parties speaking to central but archaic desires and convictions. One item on the hidden agenda is the horror of being judged or evaluated, mixed with the pleasure of judging and evaluating. The relativist voices our conviction that only our intimates have the right to evaluate us, along with the certainty that those who judge us harshly have failed to understand us. The antirelativist voices our conviction that we could, given time and cooperation, understand anybody, and that anybody should be able to understand us, if he would but take the time and if we choose to help him. (So if he doesn't understand us, either he didn't try hard enough or we chose to remain opaque.)

There is another, more philosophically respectable philosophic issue at stake. It is not surprising that the relativism controversy should have arisen in the wake of logical positivism. Strong versions of relativism have their roots in the seed bed that hybridized, cross-fertilized theories of truth with theories of meaning. The antirelativist reaction is, in part at least, an attempt to secure an independent ground for the evaluation of truth-claims. It rests on the view that while meaning points to the direction for verification, it cannot determine truth. It is for this reason that a good deal of the relativism controversy centered on two related issues: whether there are culture-neutral referential expressions and whether radical translation is susceptible to verification.

One of the reasons that generalized debates about relativism are ill-conceived is that they treat cross-cultural interpretations and evaluations as reports of speakers' beliefs, truth-claims requiring verification and validation. But such interpretations and evaluations are generally located within a set of specific practices and activities. They involve determining whether to continue or modify a practice, whether to imitate or import the practices or institutions of another culture. Contemporary Chinese attempts to evaluate the economic structures of the West are, for instance, focused on the issue of determining the consequences of such importation *for China*. Not unreasonably, their interest in our practices takes the form "What does it mean for the Chinese? Is it good for us?" When cross-cultural interpretations and evaluations are phrased in objective terms, as if they were part of a theoretical investigation, they are not on that account judgments of goodness or rightness *überhaubt*; nor are they attempts to determine whether a particular cultural conception conforms to a Platonic idea. Even assessments of justice are placed within the context of a specific set of practices. Like intracultural evaluators, cross-cultural evaluators want to determine whether another culture's various conceptions of persons (for instance) is bound to a system of practices that could or should be avoided or imitated. Such investigations are submerged and highly particular, contextual, practical investigations, guided by specific own concerns.

II

There is a philosophical dream, a dream that moral and political ideals are not only grounded in and explained by human nature, but that fundamental moral and political principles can be derived from the narrower conditions that define persons. Though sometimes bold and wild dreamers do go so far, this dream does not usually express a metaphysical wish that could be satisfied by analyzing the conditions for reflective subjectivity or the psycho linguistic conditions for the reflexivity of first-person attributions. More commonly, the dream is that the normative political principles concerning rights and moral principles regarding respect can be derived from what is essential to the concept of a person.

The strongest version of this dream attempts to use the (initially value-neutral) concept of a person to derive specific rights, principles, and obligations; a somewhat more modest version of the dream attempts to use the concept of a person to set constraints on such rights, principles, and obligations; a yet weaker version makes the two notions—the concept of a person and the delineation of moral and political rights—mutually explicative. But all versions of this dream press for *one* concept of a person, whose various components form a harmonious structure that could provide adjudication among competing normative claims about what does or does not fall within the domain of the rights and obligations of persons. The press for one well-structured concept that allocates priorities among its various conditions is a press for a decision procedure to settle disagreements about, and conflicts among, competing values and obligations.

But there is no such thing as *the* concept of a person, not only for the obvious historical reason that there have been dramatically discontinuous changes in the characterization of *persons*—though that is true—but for the equally obvious anthropological-cultural reason that the moral and legal practices heuristically treated as analogous across cultures in fact differ so dramatically that they capture 'the concept' of person only at a vacuously vague level—though that is also true.

Social and political conceptions of persons—conceptions of their powers, rights, and limits, the criteria for their individuation and continued identity— derive from conceptions of primary, privileged activities, the activities which are thought to express human excellences and tasks. Attributes believed to be required for performing such primary activities are designated as the essential identificatory properties of persons. The significant powers and limitations of persons in a society focused on spiritual and meditational activity are, for instance, radically different from those attributed to persons in a society focused on political participation or on scientific advancement; both differ from the properties thought essential to persons in societies focused on military or civic glory. The philosophic problems concerning the identities of persons vary correspondingly: when Descartes treats scientific demonstration as the primary activity, the ego became mind, and the philosophical problems concerning persons shift to those involving the analysis of the relation between private and public interests in rights; when the self is defined by its economic activity, the philosophic problems focus on issues of rational choice. Moral and political principles cannot be derived from 'the' concept of personhood because that concept is socially and politically constructed: the defining characteristics of persons are set by the primary practices and privileged actions. The norms and ideals embedded in these practices also set the rules and principles that govern just social and political associations. The two—the normic criteria for personhood and the principles of justice—are coordinate. A culture's concept of a person is one way in which the norms that govern its moral and political principles are expressed; its moral and political principles are the articulation of some of the strands in the normative concept of a person.

The various functions performed by our contemporary concept of persons do not hang together: there is some overlap, but also some tension. Indeed the various functions that 'the' notion plays are so related that various attempts to structure them in a taxonomic order express quite different norms and ideals. Disagreements about primary values and goods reappear as disagreements about the priorities and relations among the various functions the concept plays, disagreements about what is essential to persons. Not only does each of the functions bear a different relation to the class of persons and human beings, but each also has a different contrast class.

These are some of the functions we—inheritors of the Judeo-Christian-Renaissance-Enlightenment-Romantic traditions—want the concept to play:

(1) The attribution should give us objective grounds for being taken seriously, with respect ... and on grounds that we cannot lose with illness, poverty, villainy, inanity, or senility. On this view, the idea of person is an insurance policy.

Some think of the insurance as assuring us rights; others think of it as assuring us a certain kind of regard, to be treated as ends rather than merely as means, our activities centrally rational (or at least reasonable) and good willed (or at least well-intentioned), interpreted by an extension of the principle of charity. For some the special status of persons is justified by some set of properties: persons should be respected because they are capable of critical rationality, or because they are free inventors of their lives, or because they have divinely donated souls, or because they can be harmed, frustrated in living out their life-plans. (Cf. sections 3–5 below.) For others the special status of persons cannot be grounded by any essential properties either (a) because respect or rights are not *grounded* in the concept of a person (they are not *derived* from that concept but are necessarily part of it) or (b) because the grounds for such respect or rights consist of a range of social or political goods rather than the nature of persons.

(Among the Hellenes, the contrast class for this notion was the class of slaves and barbarians. Among Christians, the contrast class is that of unsouled beings. For Kantians the contrast class is that of nonrational beings, incapable of understanding the laws of nature and unable to act freely from the idea of the laws of morality. This conception of the class of persons intersects but is not identical with, nor subsumed within, the class of human beings: Martians and dolphins might be persons, as might intrapsychic homunculi.)

(2) Sometimes the respect and rights of persons are assured by law: the concept of a person is treated as primarily a legal concept. The legal concept of a person is meant to assure:

(a) *Liability*. This is a retrospective function, defined by the conditions for presumptive agency: bodily continuity, memory, *mens rea*. (The contrast class: those with defective conditions for agency: e.g., the insane, the senile.)

(b) *Legally Defined Responsibility*. This is a prospective and regionalized function that defines specific duties and obligations. Such responsibilities are often institutionally defined: sometimes the legal person's duties and responsibilities are contractually fixed, with explicitly articulated sanctions for default or violation; sometimes the obligations are defined informally by commonly accepted practices and sanctions. In such cases, liability is carried by the legal entity rather than by the individuals—for example, trustees, corporations, guardians, boards of directors, banks—who act as its officers. (The contrast class: minors; [once, and still in some places] women.)

(c) *Specifically Defined Citizen Rights and Duties*. This is a function that empowers a specifically designated class of individuals to act and speak on behalf of the State. They are, as Hobbes put it, its 'artificial persons.' Polities accord specific rights and duties of participation in decision making, representation, governance. Indeed, this is one way political systems differ: by the different ways they distribute the power and the right to act or speak in the person of the State, as an agent of one of its constitutive institutions. As the frontispiece of Hobbes' *Leviathan* graphically demonstrates, the king of an absolute monarchy is the embodied Person of the State. If the State is composed of families or clans, rather than of individuals, those families or clans are the person-citizens of the State, and their heads or elders speak and act for them. Similarly, the representatives of state-defined political institutions (the judiciary, the legislative body, city officials) act in the person of the State: their decisions personify the official acts of the State. When the pope speaks *ex cathedra*, he speaks as the Personification of the Church; the voice of Parliament is the voice of the people; citizens—"We the People"—casting votes on public issues or selecting their representatives, are expressing the views of the Person(s) of the State. Even though their rights and welfare are under the legal protection of the State, the disenfranchised— etymologically, the unfree—are the subjects or wards of the State rather than citizen-persons entitled to act or speak as the Person of the State. Whether the class of citizen-persons coincides with or is a subset of the class of those who are legally liable is, of course, a political and even an ideological issue. (The contrast class is usually under contention: aliens, slaves, exiles, fetuses.)

Neither the Kantian regulative principle of respect nor the Christian idea of the immortal soul has any necessary connection with the legal function of the idea of person. Respect for the person does not entail any particular legal rights; nor does the assurance of legal personhood assure social or moral respect. Furthermore, each of the distinctive legal *personae* might well select different grounds for the attribution of personhood. For instance, an individual can claim some citizen rights (the right of *habeas corpus*, for instance) without satisfying the conditions for liability. Nor need a legal person be accorded all the rights of citizenship: universities do not, as such, vote or receive social security. The conditions for prospective responsibility are regional and relativised: whether an individual or a group is designated a legal person is characteristically a political, and sometimes an ideological, issue.

Some legal theorists have argued that no single concept of a person can— or should—be used to derive the wide variety of legislative and judicial policies required to give appropriately differentiated treatment to the varieties of legal *personae*.[1] They maintain that moral and legal practices contextualize and regionalize the status of a person: a fetus is, for example, accorded the status of a legal person in some contexts and for some issues but not for others; a corporation has the legal status of a person for some purposes, for others not. We should, they hold, draw our inclusionary and exclusionary classes contextually, following our sense of what is morally and judicially appropriate rather than attempting to derive our legal practices from a sharply—and, they suggest, arbitrarily—defined class of persons. ("First come the practices of right and wrong, and then come definitions and classifications.") The question of whether there are several distinctive legal concepts of a person, each with its own pragmatically defined domain, or whether there is one concept, with distinctive pragmatic applications, is an idle question, since neither legal theory nor legal practice are affected by the answer.

There are, of course, dramatic cultural variations in the criteria for agency, variations in the legal conditions that define persons. The class of liable and responsible persons can, for instance, exclude individuals in favor of groups of individuals (clans or families); or the heads of such groups (the chief patriarch); intrapsychic homunculi, daemonic possessors. It can be treated as an all-or-none classification or as a matter of degrees. It is often difficult to determine how to diagnose such cultural variation: Do these differences represent disagreements about the proper analysis of the concept of a person? Do some cultures lack the concept or do they have an analogue? Do some cultures lack what we consider a legal system or do they rather locate their legal system in a different network of institutions? There may be no fact of the matter: exigencies of theory construction rather than ontology may determine whether we can legitimately project our concept of a legal person to analogous bearers of liability and responsibility, or whether we should decline the attribution to individuals whose agency is defined within radically different schemes of liability and responsibility.

(3) The idea of a person is also the idea of an autonomous agent, capable of self-defined and self-defining choices. There are at least two versions of this idea.

(a) The first is primarily negative and defensive, concentrating on the desire to fend off external interference: "*Noli me tangere*," or in Amerispeak: "Don't tread on me, buddy."

(b) The second is primarily positive and constructive, concentrating on capacities for self-determination.

Both the negative and the positive version come in two varieties:

(a) One emphasizes critical rationality and independent evaluation: a person is essentially capable of stepping back from her beliefs and desires to evaluate their rationality and appropriateness; she is also capable (at the very least) of attempting to form and modify her beliefs and desires, her actions, on the basis of her rational evaluations. (The contrast class: the mindless, the nonrational, the dissociated.)

(b) The other emphasizes imaginative creativity. Because their decisions and actions are intentionally identified, and because they have latitude in transforming, improvising, and inventing their intentions, persons can, in a number of significant ways, form the worlds in which they live. There are two dimensions on which such formations take place: the political and the visionary-poetic.

(i) Since the social and political domain is constructed, it can be reconstructed, if only a piece at a time. To be a person is to participate actively in public life, forming or at least modifying the social and political policies and institutions that significantly and effectively shape life. (The contrast class: the masses, whose opinions and actions can be manipulated.)

(ii) By choosing or constructing systems of values, persons create the categories that structure and interpret their world, that form their ambitions, hopes, and fears. Since they determine what is important and significant, their interpretations structure both what they see and what they do. (The contrast class: the dependent, the fearful, the timid, the unimaginative.)

These differences mark differences in two faces or moments in Enlightenment political theory. The first stance is defensive: it is designed to protect the person from what is perceived as tyrannical or unjust political or epistemic authority. This concept of a person stresses negative liberty and minimal government. There is some correlation, but no necessary connection, between the defensive boundary conception of the free person and the conception of the person whose critical, rational capacities are primarily exercised in scientific discovery or poetic creativity and only secondarily in defense against error.

Although the Enlightenment concept of a person began with the Christian conception of a person as defined by his free will, his capacity to affirm or deny God's law, autonomy shifted from the freedom of the will to the rational power of independent critical judgments of truth and falsity. When the old order loses its authority, the emphasis on persons as autonomous judges preserving and protecting individual boundaries is replaced by an emphasis on autonomous legislators generating new social structures and practices. Negative liberty gives way to positive liberty; minimal government gives way to a government charged with the formation of citizen values. Protection against error gives way to the power of constructing a systematic science, and eventually to the power of the imagination in constructing a world through poetic language. There is some correlation, but no necessary connection, between the concept of a person as a constructive, self-determining legislator and the conception of a person as primarily an inventive creator. The movement from the earlier defensive to the later constructive conceptions of persons correlates in a very rough way with the movement from early Cartesian Enlightenment conceptions of the independent inquiring rational self, free of the claims of dogmatic doctrine, to late Enlightenment Romanticism, with its emphasis on positive liberty, political reform, and poetic creativity.

The conception of persons as deserving respect is sometimes grounded on the conception of a person as capable of self-definition. But of course both the rationality and the creativity version of the self-defining person (in their negative and positive forms) make individual claims to personhood empirically contingent. If claims to respect are based on the capacities for autonomy, we are in deep trouble. Constitutional and sociopolitical contingencies affect the likelihood of an individual actually, rather than notionally or potentially, developing her capacities for critical rationality; similar contingencies determine whether she is actually (rather than notionally) capable of creative self-determination. Has the individual been well nourished and nurtured, well educated and well formed? Or has she suffered irreparable traumas that make autonomy practically impossible? *Logical* or *notional* possibility is not helpful here: aardvarks, baboons, and caterpillars might notionally be capable of autonomy. It might seem as if this concept of a person provides grounds for normative political claims. Precisely because certain kinds of political structures are required to actualize otherwise only notional claims to personhood, there is a prima facie obligation to structure political systems in such a way as to allow the best development of the capacities for critical self-determination. Unfortunately, many extra premises are required to substantiate this claim, premises about the primary and the proper functions of the obligations of political systems. The obligation cannot follow solely from the requirements for personhood.

(This conception of the class of persons intersects but is not identical with, or subsumed within, the class of biologically defined human beings. The contrast class is composed of all those incapable of self-correcting and self-legislating critical reflexivity.)

Christianity is, for once, surprisingly open and generous. If part of the point of the concept of a person is to assure respect, it is wiser not to rest one's hopes on such fragile and vulnerable capacities as those for autonomy or creativity. Maybe a divinely assured immortal soul—or even just a divinely assured soul, immortal or not—would provide more secure grounds for respect. To be sure, standardly conditions for rationality and autonomy are regulative rather than empirical: we might take comfort in the principle that every rational being *ought* to be treated with respect. But it takes unusually good luck to get that regulative principle realized under hard and harsh circumstances, just when it is most needed. Respect may be well-grounded without being well-assured. (What is the recourse of the unrespected when they most require it? Moral indignation? Righteousness in the eyes of history—itself a politically variable matter—is not reliably effective in assuring entitlements.)

More recently the Christian conception of persons as endowed with a free will capable of affirming or denying God's law has been redefined: the rights of persons are accorded to all those capable of suffering, those whose naturally formed life history can be harmed, shortened, frustrated. Whether the sentient are self-consciously aware of the natural shapes of their lives, whether they form plans and expectations (the transformation of the idea of the will as legislator) matters less than the fact that their lives can be painful or unfulfilled. It is the sheer fact of sentience that qualifies an individual to the rights of persons.[2]

(4) Social persons are identified by their mutual interactions, by the roles they enact in the dynamic dramas of their shared lives. There are several varieties of this conception.

(a) The idea of a *dramatis persona* as the bearer of roles in a dramatic unfolding of action has its source in the theater. A persona is the mask of an actor, cast to play a part in developing a narrative or a plot. Essentially meshed with others, a person's scope and directions are defined by her role in a complex course of events involving the interactions of agents whose varied intentions modify the outcomes—and indeed sometimes the directions—of one another's projects. While the dramatic conception of a person has no necessary connection with the concept of a person as entitled to respect, or with that of a self-defining individual, it bears some kinship to the idea of a person as an agent, as the source of liable and responsible action. When *dramatis personae* are, in principle, able to predict their effects on one another's lives, their intentions can carry moral or legal weight. (The contrast class: whatever is inert, without the power of intentional action. Since inanimate objects and events—volcanoes, wars, famines—can forward or redirect dramatic action, they are sometimes personified, but they are accounted persons only if intentional action is attributed to them.)

(b) Some psychologists introduce a normative notion of a person as capable of taking Others seriously, capable of entering into mutually affective and effective relations. To be a person is to acknowledge the reality of Others, living in a commonly constructed world, actively and cooperatively sharing practices. Some psychologists attempt to connect the sociability with the respect-based conditions for persons, attempting to treat these as mutually supportive conditions.[3] But there is no necessary connection between the two conditions. On the one hand, respect might be grounded in the idea of (a divinely donated) soul, whose sociability is contingent on the identity and roles assigned to it; on the other, some conceptions of sociability might valorize a type of intimacy that minimizes respect—across-individual—boundaries. Such a manifestly culture-bound concept of an ideal person can readily conflict with the (equally culture-bound) concept of an ideal person as capable of radical autonomy. (The contrast class: dissociated personalities, psychopaths.)

(c) There is a presumptively ontological, prepsychological version of the concept of a person as essentially formed by its relations to others. It is the conception of a person as constituted, formed, by 'The Look of the Other.' According to this theory, consciousness is initially unreflective, without a sense of self; it acquires an image of itself—an image that comes to form the person's somatic sense of herself—by seeing itself mirrored in the eyes of Others. We form one another's identities by the act of mutual mirroring, mutual regard. A person's life is constructed from, and constituted by, such interactive formative relations. Though there may be normative claims about how we *ought* to regard one another, the conception of a person as interactively emergent neither entails nor is entailed by the conception of a person as entitled to respect or to specific legal rights. (The contrast class: nonconscious beings, beings incapable of self-conscious reflection.)

(d) Associated but not identical with the psychological condition is the honorific attribution of personhood. Some individuals are accounted *real* persons: "She's a real *Mensch!*" But although the capacities for autonomy (rationality or creativity) might be ingredient in the qualifications for being a *real* person, in contrast to the usual humanoid lump, they are not sufficient. Indeed a zealot of the concept of a person as an autonomous creator might well straightaway be disqualified as a real *Mensch*-person. On this view—to be sure a view not widely shared as definitory of the concept of a person—a *real* person is generally distinguished by fortitude and reliability, by a sense of presence, of style and individuality, often combined with compassion and a humorous sense of proportion, an ironic recognition of human frailty and finitude. (The contrast class: the psychopath, the creep, the jerk, the whine, the brute, the Neanderthal.)

(5) The concept of a person is also used to sketch the norms for the appropriate shape and structure of a life. Those who identify persons by a characteristic life history or life plan require an account of a standard—or maybe not so standard!—shaping of a life, one that goes beyond biologically determined patterns of maturation and aging. This concept of a person originally derives from the Christian conception of a soul whose life and choices move her toward salvation or damnation; it is a descendant of the picture of a person as the constructor of a fate. The emphasis shifts: the person is first identified as the *author* of the story, then by the sheer *activity* of story construction, and then simply by the emergent content of the narrative.[4]

There are two versions of this focus.

(a) The *Realist 'Fact of the Matter' Version.* On this view, a culture could be mistaken: it can malform and misdirect lives, and it can misunderstand the processes by which it shapes characteristic life stories. Real alienation and malformation are possible, probably common, and often denied in good faith.

(b) The *'It's All Up to Us' Version.*

(i) It is all up to those who are individual free spirits.

(ii) It is all up to us as members of a community, forming a system of practices that define lives.

While this conception of a person is compatible with the conception that defines persons as autonomous, it neither entails nor is entailed by that conception. A person's life story need not be autonomously constructed; nor need it provide grounds for respect. Even more dramatically, the conditions for autonomy need have no bearing on the shape and events of life histories, which are, after all, contingent and heteronomous. In a Kantian framework, for example, the conditions for autonomy are purely intellectual: they neither affect nor can be affected by the contingent narrative of a life. Nor need the possibility of reflective subjectivity be essential to the construction of a life story: a life can have the shape of a well-formed narrative, without its subject experiencing anything like first-person inner subjectivity. It is the convenience of theory construction rather than of brute ontology that determines whether the life-story condition for personhood requires further qualification.

As it stands, the life-story concept of a person seems to allow any subject of a narrative life story to qualify even if that subject is not conscious of itself as a subjective center of experience. An individual might have a life story without being subjectively aware of it, and certainly without being self-consciously reflective about herself shaping it. Yet if the unadorned life-story condition of personhood allows mice and mountains to qualify as persons, the additional requirement of active subjective reflection seems too strong: it appears to disqualify individuals who might, on moral or political grounds, qualify as persons. The capacities for active subjective reflection—for constructing life plans—might turn out to be consequences of, rather than presuppositions for, an individual qualifying as a social and political person. (The contrast class of the weak version of persons, as characterized by life stories, is difficult to define. Everything temporal can be construed as having a life story, even a life story with a normative form. This criterion allows squirrels, a particular patch of pachysandra, and the Mediterranean basin to qualify as persons because they have life stories with a beginning, middle, and end. The contrast class of the stronger version, with the additional condition that persons must be capable of reflecting on, if not actively forming, a life story or a life plan, is equally difficult to define. Who has the capacity for the automonous construction of a life plan? Should the class include individuals who in principle might acquire the capacities for reflective agency, for constructing and following a life plan, if they could be accorded the status of persons? How are such counterfactual claims evaluated in holistic systems?)

(6) The biological conception of an individual is sometimes taken to provide the foundation or basic structure of the concept of a person. Biologists want a concept that will provide:

(a) the unit of genetic individuation, and

(b) conatus: the determination of growth and immunology, the energy and direction of action, reaction and defense.

Persons are, among other things, self-sustainers and self-starters. The biological account of organic independence provides the practical origin of the more far-reaching notion of autonomy. But the concept of an organic individual does not necessarily provide a sharp distinction between human beings and other species, let alone between persons and other sorts of organic entities. Whether there is a subclass, a variety of human beings that can be designated as persons by virtue of a special set of standardly inheritable properties is a matter for empirical determination. If rationality marks the class of persons, are the various properties and capacities that constitute rationality biologically fixed, genetically coded? How do the conditions for reflective critical rationality described by Kant and Frankfurt function in the organism's system of action and reaction, expansion and defense? If self-determination marks the class of persons, are the various properties and traits that constitute an individual's capacity for self-determination biologically fixed, genetically coded? How do the various capacities for creature self-definition affect a person's constitution? We are a long way from having a reasonable speculative theory, let alone a sound research program, connecting the moral, political, and legal notions of persons with the biological notion of a reproductive, self-sustaining, defensively structured organism. (The contrast class: inanimate entities.)

It has been argued that just as women and blacks were once excluded from the class of persons on presumptively biological grounds, so too we are now misled by superficial speciesism to exclude dolphins and mammals. But we are a long way from an account of the criteria for appropriate classification: What formally identical or analogous constitutional structures qualify nonhumans as person? Why should baboons but not robots qualify? Or, Martians but not Crustaceans? While empirical considerations are relevant (Do dolphins have central nervous systems?), they cannot settle the questions of whether corporations and robots only qualify as persons by metaphorical courtesy, while dolphins and chimpanzees qualify as full members by an appropriate, corrective extension of the class. (When is a batch of wires a central nervous system and when is it only an analogue? When is an analogue good enough? When is it all too good? When does behavioral similarity qualify for literal attribution? What are the criteria for identifying biologically based behavioral similarity?) Both the arguments for excluding corporations and the left hemisphere of the brain and the arguments for including robots and Martians depend on normatively charged conceptual analyses. Since similarities and differences can be found wholesale, some other sets of considerations are required to select the features that demarcate the class of persons. What considerations select the capacity to feel pain rather than those for rational thought as the criteria for the class? Indeed, because the classification has significant political and social consequences, we should not be surprised to discover that conceptual analyses of biological functions—particularly those presumed to affect intentional agency—are strongly, though often only implicitly and unself-consciously guided by moral intuitions, ideology, and taste. Controversies among sociobiologists about drawing relevant analogies between humans and other animals—their hierarchy or altruistic behavior, their protection of property—should make us suspicious about attempts to support policies concerning the rights of persons on what are allegedly purely empirical, biological considerations. (The contrast class: inanimate objects.)

(7) Psycho metaphysicians have a notion of the elusive, ultimate subject of experience, the *I* that cannot be reduced to an object, even though it can treat itself objectively, as the focus of introspection and investigation.[5] But this *I* can be diachronically discontinuous: the subject of sequential experiences need not be strictly identical. And even synchronic subjects of experiences need not be united: every aspect of a complex act of awareness could, in principle, have its own subject. The subject who is aware of the acute pain of loss need not be identical with the subject who is at the same time aware of the shifting pattern of light on the leaves of a tree. Or, at any rate, the transcendental unity of apperception (if there is such a thing) does not necessarily provide specific closure to what is, and what is not, included within the bounds of such a presumptive unity. The limits of the domain of experience cannot be set by the subject of a transcendental unity of apperception without circularity.

In any case, there are a number of distinctive construals of subjectivity as the condition for personhood, and while each has quite different consequences for the concept, none has any necessary consequences for morality or for political or legal theory. The *I*, which is the subject of experience, serves as the contrastive notion, but the various contrasts are not isomorphic. The person as the *I*, the subject of experience, has been identified with the interior or internal perspective in contrast to the external; the subjective in contrast to the objective; the subject-of-experiences in contrast with its experiences; with rationality and the will in contrast to causality and desire; with spontaneity and creativity in contrast to the conditioned; with the decision maker and agent in contrast to the predictor and observer; with the knower or interpreter in contrast to the known or interpreted; with reflective consciousness in contrast to the content of reflection; with mind in contrast to body.

Although each of these marks quite a different contrast, each is guided by the intuition that persons are capable of bearing a unique reflexive, reflective relation to themselves, a relation that somehow shapes them. Persons are sometimes characterized as capable of having a distinctive set of experiences—ego-oriented attitudes of anxiety, remorse, pride, guilt—which originally give rise to the idea of the self. But the reflective *I* can reject or identify with *these* ego-oriented attitudes as easily as it can with its body or its habits. It is no more identical with any set of 'existential attitudes' than it is with any of its more externally defined attributes. The *act* of reflecting on an attribute or attitude, asking "Is that *me*?" ('putting the self in question'), is always different from the attitude or attribute itself, even if the attitude reveals—as anxiety is said to do—the precarious position of the *I* as the act of self-constituting reflection. Being anxious is one thing; being the act that identifies with anxiety is another; both are different from something-perhaps-a-nothing-I-know-not-what, or a simple soul beyond experience, or a pure act of reflection that constitutes itself. All these—different as they are from one another—are far from the original starting point of the *I* as a being whose experience, and especially its experience of itself, is *sui generis*. None of these reflexive attitudes carries specific political, legal, or moral consequences. In *Notes from Underground*, Dostoyevsky's dramatic explorations of the subterranean destructiveness of the endlessly ironic self-mirroring self-consciousness demonstrate that even rational, self-critical reflexivity can assure neither sociability nor morality, and it can destroy self-respect. (The contrast class: objects; those incapable of self-conscious reflection.)

III

The variety of functions that the concept of a person plays—the variety of conceptions of persons we have sketched—cannot plausibly be combined in a single concept. At most, one might settle for a heterogeneous class, defined by a disjunction of heterogeneous conditions. Even if some rough construction of a denominator common to all these notions and functions were proposed, that conception would be so general that it could not fulfill—nor could it generate—the various functions performed by the various regional and substantively rich conceptions.

But this stark conclusion seems premature. Perhaps we can characterize persons by attempting some sort of synthesis of our various conditions: *a person is a unit of agency, a unit which is (a) capable of being directed by its conception of its own identity and by what is important to that identity and (b) capable of acting with others in a common world. A person is an interactive member of a community, reflexively sensitive to the contexts of her activity, a critically reflective inventor of the story line of her life.* Surely, this is a parody of a characterization. The conditions only cohere if one does not look too closely. Crucially, it is not clear whether these conditions are conjunctive or whether they are nested. After all, the conditions for strong autonomy might well on occasion conflict with those for strong sociability. The conditions of critical rationality might well on occasion conflict with those of poetic creativity. The conditions for personhood—and indeed the class of those qualifying as persons—are quite different if critical rationality dominates over sociability rather than sociability over the capacities for critical rationality. Societies, which weight them differently, differ dramatically, and sometimes ideological or political issues determine the weighting and priority of the various conditions.

Might the metaphysical notion of a person be primary, in a way that would settle these questions of priority? Primary to what? A universalistic metaphysical notion can constrain, but it cannot select or determine the priorities among competing politically and ideologically defined persons. If the metaphysical idea of a person is rich and robust enough to generate political consequences, it is already charged and directed toward those consequences. If it stands neutrally above those consequences, it is unlikely to be rich enough to do the work done by the various (strands in the) concepts of *persons.* The concept of the referent of first-person attributions, or the concept of the subject of experience, *might* be a precondition for the political or moral uses of the concept of a person. But even that is questionable: it is not conceptually necessary that the bearer of rights be capable of reflexive first-person attributions.

The notion of a human being is a notion of a biologically defined entity; the notion of a person is, however, normatively and sometimes ideologically charged. It expresses a view about what is important, valuable about being creatures like us, in having this or that set of significant traits and properties. Such creatures need not belong to our biological species. Martians or super robots could be persons; organically organized families and clans might qualify, as could intrapsychic daemons, homunculi, or consciences. For some, this designates a natural kind: there is a fact of the matter about what ought to be important and significant to us. For others, we are that natural kind whose primary attributes are plastic: within limits we are self-legislatively self-defining, even self-constructing creatures.

But even those who think of persons as self-defining creators of their identities do not agree about the extension of this class. For some, self-determination is a matter of individual volition; for others, only historical communities with self-perpetuating practices can be considered self-determining. For some, *every* individual, no matter how pathetically malformed, however constitutionally or socially deprived or deformed, is equally the creator of the story that is her life. No matter what story she tells about her life, that story is her life as a person. For others, only Nietzschean free, self-creating individual spirits, the solitary ones who transcend the herd and the conventions of the herd, are capable of self-definition. For others, only cultural and political communities can define or create themselves: individual persons are self-legislating only as members of a community defined by shared interactive practices, which define the boundaries and the essential traits of persons. On this view, the definition of persons is implicit in the practices that express and reproduce the community's cultural forms, especially the practices of parenting and education, the distribution of legal and political power.

These reflections on 'the' concept of a person seem unsatisfactory: all we have is a whining complaint (mis)inspired by vulgar forms of Wittgensteinianism, mock innocently shifting the burden of analysis. Instead of dispatching yet another vexed philosophic issue, counseling Quixotic philosophers to stop looking for a nonexistent essential definition of persons, we should perhaps more modestly end with an account of the many different reasons we have wanted, and perhaps needed, the notion of a person. These are, after all, honorable desires, as philosophic desires go. We have, in a sketchy way, explored some of the reasons that philosophers and legal-political theorists want the concept: those reasons are given by the heterogeneous list of functions—some of them rhetorical—that the concept has played. The Procrustean tactic of cutting limbs to fit an arbitrarily, if elegantly, designed form neither illuminates nor gains anything: it limits rather than enhances an understanding of the various functions of 'the' concept.

It is, of course, possible to legislate one central notion of a person and fend off strong contending candidates for definition. Such legislation might express a moral or an ideological victory; if it is widely accepted, it might even succeed in being a culturally self-fulfilling prophecy. But it would not on that account alone constitute an insightful illumination into the nature of persons.

Such legislation about the essential character of persons expresses rather than grounds or legitimates our moral and legal principles. But, significantly, the deep fissures and conflicts that are central to moral experience, and that make their way into the complexities of legal practice, are reintroduced among, and even sometimes within, the various functions of the concepts of persons. We do not even have the luxury of assuring ourselves that at least 'the' concept of the person is coordinate with 'the' concepts of moral and legal practices. At best we can say that the tensions and conflicts that are at the heart of moral and legal practices are reflected in, and sometimes clarified by, tensions and conflicts in conceptions of persons.

Why then is there such a metaphysical longing for *one* concept? (Or is it a longing for *one* metaphysical concept?) Perhaps the explanation is that the various functions the concept plays are each *unifying* functions: *the* locus of liability; *the* subject of experience; *the* autonomous critical reflector or creator. Since these various functions are unifying functions, there might be a strong temptation to look for the unified source of these various unifying functions. But this is an elementary error, on a par with illicitly extracting and then detaching an existential quantifier from its proper nested location. A desire for unity cannot by itself perform the conjuring trick of pulling one rabbit out of several hats: a transcendental unity of the concept of person, unifying the *variety* of distinct, independently (unifying) functions that each regional concept plays.

Our reflections leave our conclusions open: we might conclude either that there is no such thing as the concept of personhood, that there are only highly regionalized functions that seemed, erroneously, to be subsumable in a structured concept? Or we might conclude that the various functions of the concept are sometimes at odds, that the concept of a person cannot function to provide decision procedures for resolving conflicts among competing claims for rights and obligations because it embeds and expresses just those conflicts. Nothing hangs on the choice between these conclusions because neither political practice nor philosophic theory is affected by the outcome. For all practices and theoretical purposes it does not matter whether the concept of a person has multiple and sometimes conflicting functions, or whether there is no single concept which can be characterized as *the* concept of a person. Since *the* concept(s) of a person is not foundational, it does not matter whether we deny that there is a concept of a person or conclude there is a concept with multiple and sometimes conflicting functions.

Another metaphysical longing remains unsatisfied. But of course that does not mean that we shall be freed of metaphysical longing, or even of this particular metaphysical longing.

IV

The desire to discover a culturally or contextually neutral concept of persons—one that is independent of the range of practices in which 'persons' function—rests on the desire to provide a nontendentious way of evaluating those practices. Critics and reformers must, of course, attend to whatever facts of the matter—empirical or conceptual—might affect practices. Sometimes, when those facts undetermine the specification or justification of a practice, the holism of a culture helps to close the gap. A reform may be justified—or shown untenable—by reference to other, deeply embedded practices. But sometimes even holism fails to close the gap. When that happens, critics and defenders alike attempt to turn to what they present as neutral, extracultural principles to arbitrate their differences. It is remarkable how quickly and surely all sides of disputes manage to find extracultural principles to justify their positions, as against those of their opponents. The 'justifications' of practices are often further articulations, specifications, and determinations of the general features of the practice. These further articulations are by no means merely emotive expressions or blind existential choices. They are cognitive, conceptual, and, above all, systematic formulations of practices. Specifying and justifying practices are themselves practices: the primary models, principles, and criteria for justification are themselves derived from the primary activities that are central to a culture. The criteria and procedures for justification in a culture whose central activities center around common-law juridical practices differ from those focused on the primacy of mathematical demonstrations; both differ from the primary models of justification that derive from Talmudic or Koranic commentary.

Is this a capitulation to relativism, a retreat from the high ground that judges the entire controversy to be ill-conceived? Not at all. Contextualism is perfectly compatible with realism; a sober modesty about justification and proof is compatible with a denial of skepticism. Once a context of interpretation or justification is specified, context-independent facts of the matter set constraints on truth conditions. Uncertainty remains, as it does in all practical and empirical contexts where there is no final, uncontestable demonstration of the adequacy or inadequacy of an interpretation. Cross-cultural influence or interaction can, of course, involve mistaken interpretations, interpretations that are sometimes profoundly and systematically mistaken. In such cases the actions and interactions based on mistaken interpretations tend to fail, usually visibly. But such interpretations are also corrigible. When communication fails, interested interlocutors usually persist in trying to understand and to make themselves understood. It is persistent interaction rather than the assurance of independent context-neutral principles of demonstration that supports successful communication.

NOTES

I am grateful to Christopher Gill, Adam Morton, and other participants in a conference held at Aberystwyth in June 1985. An earlier and shorter version of this essay appeared as "Persons as Rhetorical Categories," *Social Research* 54, no. 1 (1987): 55–72. Another shorter version appeared as "Persons and Personae," in *Persons and Human Beings*, ed. Christopher Gill (New York: Oxford University Press, 1988), and in *Mind in Action*, ed. Amélie Rorty (Boston: Beacon Press, 1988). I am also grateful to Michael Krausz for his encouragement, patience, and suggestions.

1. Charles Baron, "The Concept of Person in the Law," in *Defining Human Life: Medical, Legal, and Ethical Implications*, ed. M. W. Shaw and A. E. Doudera (Washington, D.C.: AUPHA Press, 1983); Richard Tur, "The 'Person' in Law," in *Persons and Personality*, ed. Arthur Peacocke and Grant Gillett (Oxford: Blackwell, 1987).

2. Karl Capek, *War with the Newts* (London: Unwin, 1985); Peter Singer, *Animal Liberation* (New York: Avon Books, 1977).

3. H. Kohut, *The Restoration of the Self* (New York: International Universities Press, 1977).

4. Jerome Bruner, *Actual Minds, Possible Worlds* (Cambridge, Mass.: Harvard University Press, 1986).

5. Thomas Nagel, *The View from Nowhere* (New York: Oxford University Press, 1986).

Relativism and Poststructuralism

DAVID COUZENS HOY

I. INTRODUCTION

Anglophone critics often charge the continental tradition of philosophy with harboring relativism. I will provisionally define relativism as the view that nothing is absolutely true or right. In this paper, I focus on the question whether relativism can be attributed to 'poststructuralism.' Poststructuralism is a label applied in North America to certain intellectual imports from Europe. Although poststructuralism stems from the German hermeneutical movement, it is largely 'made in France.'

The poststructuralists include principally, Jacques Derrida, Michel Foucault, and Gilles Deleuze. From the North American perspective, poststructuralism starts in 1962, with Deleuze's important early book on Friedrich Nietzsche (a precursor of the alleged relativism). In that book, Deleuze is concerned to show that Nietzsche represents a viable alternative to Georg Wilhelm Friedrich Hegel. If Hegel's dialectical method had been the preoccupation of continental philosophers before Deleuze's critique of dialectics in this book, after it, Nietzsche's genealogical method becomes the paradigm for the poststructuralist period of philosophy. Whether that movement is over now, or whether it was only an American misperception of European fashions, is currently a matter of intense debate, mainly because of sharp critiques of poststructuralism by more recent philosophers such as Slavoj Žižek. This debate we are seeing in continental philosophy today is likely to become a deep tectonic shift that will rearrange the philosophical landscape and present us with a different set of problems and thinkers to discuss in the future.

Among the motivations for welcoming this shift in continental philosophy away from poststructuralism is the fear of relativism. Poststructuralism inherits from hermeneutics specific tenets that smack of relativism. These tenets include such epistemological claims such as that truth is internal to an interpretation or that knowledge depends on the context of understanding. Poststructuralism shares the hermeneutical critique of the Kantian view of knowledge as the subjective representation of objective reality. Thus, Martin Heidegger, the major hermeneutical philosopher to have an influence on poststructuralism, rejects the subject-object distinction and offers an alternative account of understanding and interpretation. On this account, human beings do not stand over against the world, but are beings actively engaged in the world. 'World' in this tradition means most generally, the way things 'show up.' What the world is even depends on how we understand and interpret it.

This last sentence brings out why these philosophies are accused of relativism. Traditionally, philosophers think of the world as being mind-independent. Insofar as the hermeneutical and poststructuralist philosophers argue that what counts as the world is a function of how it is understood, rather than saying that the world determines whether the understanding is correct, they court relativism. Furthermore, not only are epistemological dangers here, but also worries about how to deal with norms and values. Ethical relativism in particular and normative relativism in general are also implicated.

The basic tenet of hermeneutics since Heidegger and Hans-Georg Gadamer has been that everything is a matter of interpretation. The question that often arises and that the continental tradition has had difficulty in resolving is what makes some interpretations better than others. One possible answer is that interpretations that open up possibilities for human development are better than those that narrow down possibilities. This response only pushes the hard question one step further back, however, for someone is bound to ask, how do we distinguish between good and bad possibilities? What makes some possibilities better than others?

Philosophers have wrestled with various answers to these questions. Possibilities are ruled out if they are restrictive rather than enabling (John Stuart Mill), sickly rather than healthful (Nietzsche), reactive rather than active (Deleuze), inauthentic rather than authentic (early Heidegger), closing off rather than opening up (later Heidegger). Obviously these terms are normative, and none can claim to be definitive—not surprising if everything is a matter of interpretation. If one says this, however, one should also recognize that this claim is also a matter of interpretation.

This hermeneutical position is not paradoxical, however, and it does not fall into relativism. At minimum, we should distinguish kinds of positions instead of subsuming them all under one label. One such position is epistemological relativism, which maintains that all knowledge is relative to the standpoint of the knower. But that claim itself is not relative. Thus, we have a paradox because the claim that all knowledge is relative is itself not relative. Epistemological relativism should not be pinned on hermeneutics because it is precisely a thesis about what can be *known*, whereas hermeneutics is concerned with understanding and interpretation. Ontological pluralism stands in contrast to this paradoxical relativism. This view is closer to hermeneutics insofar as hermeneutics holds that different interpretations of what there is exist. If the world is infinitely complex, we have no reason to think that finally one all-encompassing interpretation of everything exists. More than one interpretation of an infinitely complex world is always possible.

Note that ontological pluralism is compatible with realism. The realist could be a monist and maintain that the world is one. If the world is also infinitely complex, different plausible interpretations of it can exist. We need not think that there are as many worlds as there are interpretations. A philosophical stance can be pluralistic about interpretations at the same time that it is monistic about the world. But given the plurality of interpretations, the monist is going to be hard pressed to justify the ontological assertion that the world is one. The pluralist will push the monist to explain *one what*?

In return, pluralists reject monism about the world because they find no use for the notion of *the* world. Pluralists then have to face the question, what is interpretation about? If the pluralist responds that it is about different 'domains of inquiry' or 'objects of interpretation,' the danger is that interpretations will simply talk past one another because they will be talking about different things. Missing the mark will result from not knowing what the interpretation is aiming at. Thus, if pluralists reject monism about the world, they must explain why pluralism is a better interpretation of interpretation than monism, and how it separates good interpretations from bad ones. So both the pluralist and the monist face hard questions.

To sort out the different sides, let me start the discussion over again by distinguishing interpretation-pluralism (IP) and interpretation-monism (IM) from world-pluralism (WP) and world-monism (WM). IP holds that a plurality of good interpretations is possible. IM holds that there is one best interpretation.

WM holds that there is one world. WP avoids the philosophical idea of *the* world on the grounds that it does no work. There would seem to be four possible combinations of these positions: (1) IP and WP; (2) IP and WM; (3) IM and WM; and (4) IM and WP. In this chapter, I am particularly interested in the arguments for the first two. No philosopher among those whom I know well holds the last of these (IM/WP). The third is perhaps the most widely shared of the four and thus deserves a few words.

II. IM/WM MONISM

Those who are monistic in the third sense would generally not distinguish between interpretation and world. A monist who holds that the world is one (and not infinitely complex) would probably also maintain that it could be captured by the best interpretation. What makes an interpretation the best on this view is that it captures the world. Insofar as there is no further question about whether it is correct, it is already said to be more than an interpretation, since it represents all the possible knowledge about what there is.

I do not accept this ideal because it contains some unjustifiable assumptions. Let me briefly mention three of these. First, IM/WM posits the idea that the world is 'represented' in the interpretation. On my view, interpretations do not 'represent' the world so much as allow it to show up. This is not necessarily to say that the interpretation 'makes up' the world. The world is not simply a fiction or a social construction. Second, in addition to the idea of interpretation as representation, IM/WM assumes that giving a complete description of things is a viable goal. I do not see, however, what sense it makes to talk of giving a complete description of anything. More predicates could always be applied, and we usually limit our descriptions to those predicates we consider significant. But 'significance' is itself a matter of interpretation. Third, monists generally assume that knowledge is more than interpretation. On their view, interpretation is at best a subset of knowledge, and confirmed interpretations become knowledge. Pluralists, in contrast, maintain that knowledge is a subset of interpretation. Moreover, acceptable knowledge is whatever the ruling interpretation generally permits.

III. TWO PLURALISMS

Although more could be said about the assumptions behind the position that links IM and WM, let me turn to the two positions that most interest me here.

Is an IP that combines with WM better able to avoid relativism than an IP that combines with WP? Prima facie, IP/WM might seem to be less relativistic than IP/WP insofar as it can accommodate realism. The world is no longer relative to an interpretation, even if it shows up only in some interpretation or other. The IP/WM theorist can thus believe that the interpretation is right as far as it goes, because it captures genuine aspects of the way the world really is.

The IP/WP theorist will say in response that no difference exists between the two views because an interpretation determines what accounts for features being features of the world. To put the claim in terms of descriptions, the IP/WP theorist says that insofar as actions are only understandable and interpretable under a description, if the interpretation changes the description, the reality is changed as well. This view has two versions. One is 'interpretive voluntarism,' which maintains that the interpreter can change descriptions at will. The other position, 'interpretive non-voluntarism,' holds that the way the interpreter sees the world is not a matter of choice, but a consequence of how the world shows up for the interpreter. I adhere to the second position if only because I believe that we do not want our interpretations of the world to be the result of a voluntaristic rewriting. How we do see the world is different from how we might like to see the world. Thinking does *not* make it so. Insofar as these attitudes represent nascent idealism and nominalism, neither IP nor WP is the equivalent of idealism or nominalism.

The value of these distinctions depends on whether they capture some real philosophical differences. Let me therefore fit some philosophers' names to these abstract labels with the admission that the philosophers themselves might be unlikely to accept them. The IM/WM position has many candidates. These include Husserl (who sees philosophy as aspiring to rigorous science), Jügen Habermas (when he was theorizing the ideal speech situation), and Alexander Nehamas (whose exemplary discussions of monism first focused my thinking about pluralism). Candidates for the IP/WP position are harder to identify, but they would seem to me to include Nelson Goodman, Gadamer, Nietzsche, and Foucault. I discuss the problem of classifying Derrida below.

Other philosophers are more difficult to pigeonhole in this scheme. I found no good candidate for the IM/WP label. Possibly the bill could be filled by a metaphysician holding that there are rigid designators that feature necessarily in the one right interpretation of all possible worlds. Let me leave this position aside, however, so that I can focus on the philosophers who figure in the poststructuralist tradition, particularly Derrida and Foucault.

IV. JACQUES DERRIDA

If the contrast between IM/WM and IP/WP was most interesting during the 1980s when Habermas was raising issues about modernity and postmodernity, then I see the contrast between IP/WP and IP/WM as more interesting today. Jacques Derrida's development will show why. In his lectures on modernity, Habermas clearly views Derrida as a dangerous relativist of the postmodern, IP/WP variety.[1] Whether Derrida then changes his tone simply because of this critique or for other reasons is moot. Clearly, however, Derrida wants to distance himself from relativism. So that no one will accuse him of relativism again, in his later writings, he goes so far as to affirm that he is not opposed to universalism and that not everything is deconstructible. Justice, for instance, is not deconstructible, Derrida argues, even if concrete law is. Justice is unconditional, and relativists are allergic to unconditionals. Derrida's later celebration of certain unconditionals is thus a move toward universalism.

With this move, Derrida most emphatically distances himself from relativism. Indeed, he becomes irate when an interviewer asks him what he thinks about Hilary Putnam's charge that he, like W. V. O. Quine, believes in the indeterminacy of meaning. Putnam knows that believing in indeterminacy does not make one a relativist, because Quine was not one. Quine can appeal to molecular motion or to a basic behaviorism as a rock bottom level that blocks relativism. For Putnam, Derrida has no similar resource for evading relativism. This remark incenses Derrida who responds to the question whether this is a misunderstanding of his work as follows:

If I wanted to be brutal I would say yes, this is a radical misunderstanding. I am shocked by the debate around this question of relativism. What is relativism? Are you a relativist simply because you say, for instance, that the other is the other, and that every other is other than the other? ... No, relativism is a doctrine, which has its own history in which there are only points of view with no absolute necessity, or no references to absolutes. That is the *opposite* to what I have to say. Relativism is, in classical philosophy, a way of referring to the absolute and denying it; it states that there are only cultures and that there is no pure science or truth. I have never said such a thing. Neither have I ever used the word 'relativism.'[2]

Derrida then also denies having ever said that there is *indeterminacy* of meaning. He suggests that Putnam may have confused his notion of the undecidability of meaning with Quine's notion of the indeterminacy of meaning. For Derrida, undecidability requires very definite determinations of meaning so that we can judge that no adequate grounds exist for deciding between two possible meanings. An example is the Greek word *'pharmakon*,' the meaning of which in Plato's text is supposedly undecidable between cure and poison.

If relativism is the view that interpretation can make anything into whatever the interpreter wants, then Derrida was never a relativist, not even early on. He vents as follows about this way of reading him: "Usually they charge me with saying that the text means anything, a charge made even in academic circles, not only in the media. If I were saying such a stupid thing, why would that be of any interest? Who would be interested in that, starting with me?" (79) If Derrida were simply admitting to the need for universalistic discourse, I would definitely classify him as a WM theorist. When he adds, however, the following remarks about the complexity of the text, where the text is always the analogue for what I have been calling the world, he sounds more like a pluralist: "I would say that a text is complicated, there are many meanings struggling with one another, there are tensions, there are overdeterminations, there are equivocations; but this doesn't mean that there is indeterminacy. On the contrary, there is too much determinacy. That is the problem. So these charges really have to be interpreted" (79)

My schema helps in stating Derrida's position more precisely. In my terms, we can say that he is an interpretive pluralist of the IP variety. On my schema, however, one can be both a pluralist (about interpretations) and a monist (about the world). Insofar as the later Derrida posits universals in the ideal, he is thus a WM theorist as well, although a weaker one than the IM/WM sort. The later Derrida contrasts sharply with the early Derrida for whom deconstruction is a tool against the tyranny of the One (where the One is the metaphysical logos). The later Derrida is more cautious philosophically and willing to contemplate the universal as the goal of philosophy although not as its starting point—as an essence. "The universal projected in this way [when philosophy tries to liberate itself from its context of origin] is not a given, the way an essence would be; rather, it announces an infinite process of universalization."[3] He thus does not equate anti-essentialism and anti-universalism. Although he continues to be an anti-essentialist, he is emphatically not denying the aspirations of philosophy to a universal discourse, or rather, to a discourse of universals.

I therefore see the position of the early Derrida, or at least, of the early understanding of what Derrida is saying, as an IP/WP theory. The later Derrida then becomes more explicitly an IP/WM theorist insofar as he posits this 'infinite process of universalization.'

Regardless how committed Derrida is to universals, I do not want to suggest that he ever comes close to the strong monism of the IM/WM type. He will always be seen as a critic of the philosophical tradition, and of the monism built into the very idea of 'philosophy.' IM/WM is an idealization of philosophical discourse that goes back to the aspirations of the ancient Greeks for philosophy that would transcend its origins and be valid for everybody everywhere. Philosophy, in the sense of the monistic discourse that aspires to universal validity, must thus overcome its ethnocentric origins in Greece, and eventually Europe. Following both Husserl and Heidegger, Derrida sees philosophy as a "living contradiction" and a "paradox" insofar as it involves "the universal project of a will to deracination" (18) Despite his earlier insistence that texts always require contexts, he now argues that this process of deracination can overcome all contexts of origin, and thus that universalization triumphs over relativism. "If Greek philosophy is European at its point of departure, but if its vocation is indeed universal," Derrida thinks it follows that "it must ceaselessly liberate itself from relativism" (19) By relativism here he means all sorts of anti-universalistic leanings, including ethnocentrism, Eurocentrism, and the repressive colonialism of which he was a victim in his youth.

Does this interpretation turn Derrida into Habermas? Habermas is indeed a very strong IM/WM theorist when he is promoting his theory of communicative action. This occurred, however, about twenty years ago. In reminiscing about his change of relations with Habermas more recently, Derrida feels that Habermas's attacks on him in 1985 for being a 'postmodernist' were 'unjust.' (17) Later, however, he feels that they are on friendlier terms, with each understanding the other's position better. In fact, their political positions, Derrida observes, have been remarkably "allied, if not deeply identical" (17). I think that this convergence may be due to Derrida's own turn toward unconditional universals such as justice. The main difference separating them is that Habermas's universalism aspires to being a realizable condition. In contrast, Derrida's universalism is an 'infinite process' and thus can never be fully realized.

V. MICHEL FOUCAULT

If the interest has now moved from the conflict between strong monism (IM/WM) and strong pluralism (IP/WP) to the contrast between weak pluralism (IP/WM) and strong pluralism (IP/WP), that shift may be due to the ameliorative effects of aging on the major players in the modernist-postmodernist debates. I think that I could show a similar shift of interest in the Anglophone tradition by focusing on philosophers of the generation of Richard Rorty (the most clever pluralist in the history of philosophy, on a par with Nietzsche), Bernard Williams (Rorty's severest critic), or John Rawls (who was above such polemics, but who showed at the end that Hegel was as much of an influence on his later views as

Kant was on his early theory of justice). My space is restricted, however, so I shall confine my remaining remarks to Michel Foucault and Ian Hacking.

The question is, why not settle for saying that there is one world, but an infinitely complex one? Then one could be a monist about the world (WM) at the same time that one believed in a plurality of partial descriptions of it (IP). Ian Hacking suggested this idea in a seminar at UCLA in 1976, and I have always found it very powerful. He has also suggested reading the early Foucault's *The Archaeology of Knowledge*[4] not as a philosopher of science who denies truth but as a critical historian of science who thinks that what counts as true is internal to a discourse.[5] The historian of science explains the discursive conditions that allow certain statements or *énoncés* (Foucault later called them 'problematizations') even to 'come up for grabs' as possibly true or false. The archaeological Foucault thus neither affirms nor denies truth but spells out the conditions or procedures at play in a particular regime of knowledge. These conditions allow for certain statements to seem of central importance, while others are of lesser significance.

When Foucault then in *Discipline and Punish* (1975) turns from the archaeological method to Nietzschean genealogy, he is able to add a political dimension to the analysis.[6] The genealogical method is described as a way of talking about the 'history of the present,' that is, a history of how we have become who we are. Thus, like critical theory (as opposed to traditional theory of theory) for Max Horkheimer,[7] Foucault's genealogical method never aspires to more than revealing a contemporary subjectification or problematization. Once it makes visible the power relations that are effective only so long as they remain invisible, genealogy will have done its job. As Foucault was fond of saying, the task of genealogy is not to change the world but to prepare the world for change. Since the world can change, I take it that Foucault is best described, as Nietzsche is as well, as a strong pluralist of the IP/WP type.

From the Foucaultian point of view, holding on to the idea of one world because it could never be cashed in concretely is pointless. Even at the meta-level it does not do any work because interpretations delimit for themselves the ontological boundaries of their object domains. Richard Rorty sees the idea of the one world as a vestige of the metaphysical tradition that insists on the ultimate integration of everything into one science. Rorty maintains that this philosophical idea of *the* world is 'well lost.'[8] The contrast between Foucault's strong IP/WP pluralism and the later Derrida's weak IP/WM pluralism explains in part the difficulty they had in relating to each other while they were alive and the difficulty scholars have today of bringing them into meaningful dialogue with each other. I note, however, that toward the end of his life, Derrida was calling his method 'deconstructive genealogy.'[9]

VI. CONCLUSION: WHY PLURALISM IS NOT RELATIVISM

The burden of proof for this chapter is to explain the relation not of pluralism and monism but of pluralism and relativism. For both a strong monist (IM/WM) and a weak monist (IM/WP), of course, any form of pluralism will involve relativism. Pluralism, whether strong or weak, will not think of itself as relativism (although weak pluralism, IP/WM, will probably think of strong pluralism as relativism). So my question in this final section is why is strong pluralism (IP/WP) not a form of relativism, from its own point of view?

Let me start with the description of relativism that Richard J. Bernstein gives of relativism in his classic book, *Beyond Objectivism and Relativism*:

"In its strongest form, relativism is the basic conviction that when we turn to the examination of those concepts that philosophers have taken to be the most fundamental—whether it is the concept of rationality, truth, reality, right, the good, or norms—we are forced to recognize that in the final analysis all such concepts must be understood as relative to a specific conceptual scheme, theoretical framework, paradigm, form of life, society, or culture. Since the relativist believes that there is (or can be) a nonreducible plurality of such conceptual schemes, he or she challenges the claim that these concepts can have a determinate and univocal significance. For the relativist, there is no substantive overarching framework or single metalanguage by which we can rationally adjudicate or univocally evaluate competing claims of alternative paradigms. Thus, for example, when we turn to something as fundamental as the issue of criteria or standards of rationality, the relativist claims that we can never escape from the predicament of speaking of 'our' and 'their' standards of rationality—standards that may be 'radically incommensurable.' It is an illusion to think that there is something that might properly be labeled '*the* standards of rationality,' standards that are genuinely universal and that are not subject to historical or temporal change."[10]

For my money, if the terms 'pluralism' or 'pluralist' in either sense (IP/WP or IP/WM) were substituted for every occurrence of 'relativism' or 'relativist,' Bernstein's description for me would not be a description of relativism. On the contrary, it would come very close not only to a fine statement of what pluralism is but also to the preferable philosophical view overall. Of course, I would make some modifications here and there to avoid traps such as the scheme-content distinction (which surely leads to relativism) that Bernstein has carefully hidden in the thickets. Saying this allows me to focus the question why prefer that the term 'pluralism' replace 'relativism'?

First, relativism has no critical bite, whereas pluralism does. Relativism cannot criticize any competing view, since it comes down to asserting 'anything goes.' (Nihilism is the related view in practical philosophy that 'nothing matters.') Relativism is not simply two interpretations 'talking past one another.' Relativism is the inability to commensurate between competing interpretations. Pluralism, in contrast, does envision the possibility of commensurating between competing discourses. It does not think that every interpretation is correct. Pluralism is the view that more than one interpretation can possibly be true. But it may also say that no given interpretation ever completely captures its entire domain. There is always 'more to say.'

Second, we should recognize a Heideggerian distinction between interpretation in the ontic sense when used as a count noun and interpretation in a deeper sense that Donald Davidson calls radical interpretation where interpretation cannot be used as a count noun.[11] Thinking of interpretation as countable, even if only in the sense of 'one' or 'many,' is not the same as the underlying phenomenon of interpretation in the sense of skillful engagement in the world. The experience of flow is not necessary to understand this sense, which is similar to the difference between 'a' language and language. Language is the ability to communicate or triangulate with another speaker on some worldly feature, and it is what makes possible the natural languages that can be distinguished from one another and counted as separate systems.

Third, in our experience, we cannot distinguish the way the world shows up for us, the *context* of interpretation, from the *contents* of interpretation. Nevertheless, context and content are *conceptually* different in a significant way. Unlike contents, contexts are not right or wrong, true or false. They are appropriate or inappropriate, seemly or unseemly, elegant or far-fetched, plausible or implausible. The criteria for what counts as good interpretation are often built into the interpretation itself. Insofar as understanding is always self-understanding, then, the interpretation that reflects on and illuminates its own conditions and assumptions is better than one that does not.

I conclude, therefore, that pluralism is not relativism because it does have the conceptual means to say what makes some interpretations better than others. Whereas relativism says that no way to say if one interpretation is better than another exists, I have indicated in the previous paragraph at least one way that pluralism has an explicit criterion for better interpretation. If I had space, I would develop further the idea that pluralism insists on the corrigibility of understanding and on the constant need to revise interpretations, which are never fixed and closed. Whereas the relativistic insistence on the incommensurability of vocabularies leaves interpretations unable to say whether they are even talking about the same thing, pluralism keeps open the possibility of contesting competing readings and of commensurating disagreements. For now, however, I have said enough to spark competing interpretations of interpretation that will disagree substantially with what I have argued here. But then, this is to be expected insofar as disagreement is, after all, not the death but the life of interpretation.

NOTES

I am grateful to Michael Krausz for his helpful comments and distinctions as well as his hermeneutical subtlety.

1. Jürgen Habermas, *The Philosophical Discourse of Modernity: Twelve Lectures*, trans. Frederick G. Lawrence (Cambridge, Mass.: MIT Press, 1987).

2. Jacques Derrida, "Hospitality, Justice and Responsibility: A Dialogue with Jacques Derrida," in *Questioning Ethics: Debates in Contemporary Continental Philosophy*, ed. Richard Kearney and Mark Dooley (New York: Routledge, 1999), 78, emphasis added.

3. Jacques Derrida and Elisabeth Roudinesco, *For What Tomorrow . . . A Dialogue*, trans. Jeff Fort (Stanford, Calif.: Stanford University Press, 2004), 18.

4. Michel Foucault, *L'Archéologie du savoir* (Paris: Gallimard, 1969).

5. Ian Hacking, "The Archaeology of Foucault," in *Foucault: A Critical Reader*, ed. David Couzens Hoy (Oxford: Blackwell, 1986), 27–40.

6. Michel Foucault, *Surveiller et punir: naissance de la prison* (Paris: Gallimard, 1975).

7. See my debate with Thomas McCarthy about Max Horkheimer's epoch-making essay, "Traditional and Critical Theory," in *Critical Theory*, ed. David Couzens Hoy and Thomas McCarthy (Oxford: Blackwell, 1994), esp. chap. 4.

8. Richard Rorty, "The World Well Lost," in *Consequences of Pragmatism (Essays: 1972–1980)* (Minneapolis: University of Minnesota Press, 1982), 3–18.

9. David Couzens Hoy, "Postscript: On Deconstructive Genealogy," in *Critical Resistance: From Poststructuralism to Post-Critique* (Cambridge, Mass.: MIT Press, 2004), 227–239.

10. Richard J. Bernstein, *Beyond Objectivism and Relativism: Science, Hermeneutics, and Praxis* (Oxford: Blackwell, 1983), 8.

11. David Couzens Hoy and Christoph Durt, "What Subjectivity Isn't," in *The Hermeneutic Davidson*, ed. Jeff Malpas (Cambridge, Mass.: MIT Press, forthcoming); David Couzens Hoy, "Post-Cartesian Interpretation: Hans-Georg Gadamer and Donald Davidson," in *The Philosophy of Hans-Georg Gadamer*, ed. Lewis E. Hahn (Peru, Ill.: Open Court, 1997), 111–128.

Lorraine Code

I. FEMINISM AND RELATIVISM

Feminist epistemologists are uneasily situated vis-à-vis vexed questions about relativism. The mission of post-positivist Anglo-American epistemology has been to establish necessary and sufficient conditions for the existence of knowledge in general. Its singularity of purpose is compromised if it speaks from or to specific interests, for its aim of producing, a priori, normative analyses of knowledge, impartially acquired and adjudicated, requires transcending, abstracting from such interests. Discursively—rhetorically—Anglo-American mainstream epistemology has staked out its domain so as to require its practitioners to disavow relativist tendencies. Hence, ritualistically, many self-identified *feminist* epistemologists establish the parameters of their projects by insisting that their goals and methods do not entail relativism; evaluations of their achievements address how well they make good those avowals. Even the most nuanced feminist analyses, committed to exposing the exclusionary, oppressive implications of 'pure,' 'universal' knowledge claims 'from nowhere,' often affirm that their historicizing or situating 'the epistemological project' does not, after all, consign them to the non-place of relativism.[1] These avowals are neither disingenuous nor self-deceived.

My question is why identification as a relativist marks a philosopher as a pariah—to propose that feminists have a strategic advantage in 'coming out' as relativists after all. An acknowledgment of the relativistic implications of feminist epistemology would make space for reassessing the stark conceptions of relativism that have prompted critics to target a caricatured, hyperbolic relativism that no self-respecting relativist would endorse. Refusing to contain epistemology within the dichotomies that sustain this construal, requiring contorted apologetics from theorists who defy it, a relativist acknowledgment would encourage case-by-case deliberation about degrees of relativism according to the tenor of each inquiry, without unraveling the whole (epistemic) garment by pulling one thread.[2]

Oversimplified analyses routinely caution that the specter of relativism has haunted philosophy since the ancient Greeks. Citing the Protagorean dictum "man is the measure of all things, of the things that are, that they are, and of the things that are not, that they are not," relativism's opponents derive the bleakest consequences, representing it as an 'anything goes' position for which all 'truths' are idiosyncratically relative. In the post-positivist epistemic imaginary, relativism eschews appeals to evidence, denies all bases for adjudicating among rival knowledge claims, all distinctions between knowledge and opinion or whimsy. For such (putative) relativists, according to their opponents, nothing holds fast, there are no common grounds, foundations, or objective truths, and relativism is self-refuting. It is impossible to demonstrate the truth of its principles, for, *ex hypothesi*, any demonstration must be relative. The only options are tolerance of every would-be knowledge claim, however bizarre, or collapse into epistemic anarchy, symbolized by the mute figure of Cratylus, reduced to finger waggling by his conviction that everything is in flux—neither communication nor knowledge is possible. Cratylus becomes the negative exemplar in a cautionary tale depicting the dangers of stepping onto this slippery slope down which every relativist must slide. Clifford Geertz remarks, "What the anti-relativists ... want ... us to worry about, and worry about and worry about, as though our very souls depended upon it, is a kind of spiritual entropy, a heat death of the mind, in which everything is as significant, thus as insignificant, as everything else."[3] Thus anti-relativist Paul Boghossian challenges: "Why this fear of knowledge? Whence this felt need to protect against its deliverances?"[4] His contention is that relativism and constructivism thrive where a curiously impersonal *fear of knowledge* prevails.

Has this specter haunted philosophy ever since Protagoras? Granted, Western philosophers have persistently attempted to establish foundations for knowledge, thereby refuting skepticism, which—in its nihilistic, neo-Cartesian guise—is aligned with relativism.

But, historically, relativism did not shadow these projects as doggedly as it has in the mid- to late-twentieth century, when relativists reemerged as exemplars of irrationality, bearers of the sins of unknowing positivists and neo-positivists who sought to banish relativists from places where knowledge is produced and validated. Warning against a slide into relativism became a strategy for silencing any suggestion that situations, subjectivities, or interests figure integrally in the making, and *should* figure in the adjudication, of knowledge claims. Here I focus on relativism as it surfaces in the 'grammar' of post-positivist epistemology, with which feminists must contend.

Anglo-American anti-relativists assume a grammatical fixity, a discursive hegemony, for a conception of relativism born more of their ideological commitments than of the 'real-world' effects of working as a relativist. Borrowing Michel Foucault's terms, a proscription of relativism has become an 'anonymous, historical rule,' one of 'the conditions of operation' of discursive practices constitutive of epistemological legitimacy.[5] Such condemnations mask their investment in preserving privileged ways of knowing while consigning others to oblivion. They silence intimations that 'universalism,' or 'anti-relativism,' are politically inflected, not 'purely' epistemological requirements, that they attach to specifically located conceptions of knowledge, not to 'natural,' 'necessary,' or universal conceptions. (Efforts to preserve foundationalism against post-modern critiques illustrate the interests anti-relativism serves.)

Characterizing the issue as *grammatical* does not cast it as merely semantic. It appeals to Wittgenstein's sense of 'grammar,' where "Grammar tells what kind of object anything is" within a form of life, a domain of inquiry.[6] The prevailing grammar casts the anxiety relativism occasions as "a philosophical disease" produced by a "one-sided diet," which "nourishes one's thinking with only one kind of example" (§593); a "bump ... the understanding has got by running its head up against the limits of language" (§119). Ray Monk writes of Wittgenstein's war work at Guy's Hospital, where doctors were investigating an effect of injury they called 'wound shock,' a term they struggled to define precisely enough to achieve the requisite explanatory power. Only when they abandoned 'shock' for the open-ended terminology of 'injury' or 'trauma' could the research proceed. The *term* 'shock' had inhibited inquiry; the doctors were running their heads up against the redundant—bewitching—question of whether *these* symptoms provided evidence of shock. For Wittgenstein, the problem recalled Heinrich Hertz's attempts to define 'force,' which required investigators (in Hertz's view) to ask 'illegitimate questions.' Hence, Hertz proposed re-describing Newtonian physics without invoking 'force.' Monk quotes Wittgenstein, "In my way of doing philosophy, its whole aim is to give an expression such a form that certain disquietudes disappear."[7]

Analogously, I propose a diagnosis of the 'philosophical disease' with which relativistic anxieties have infected epistemology. A 'one-sided diet' of dislocated, monologic examples—simple perceptual propositions, 'elementary' propositions of physical science, easily verified or falsified regardless of context—has demarcated a rhetorical domain that limits meaningful epistemological discourse to such propositions or multiples thereof. Rules for correct utterance maintain a carefully guarded space for determining necessary and sufficient conditions for justifiable knowledge claims; inquirers are beset with disquietude lest they overstep the boundaries and slide into relativism. In Foucauldian language, anti-relativism produces "a system of control in the production of [epistemic] discourse" that requires practitioners "to conform to [an] activity of limitation and exclusion ... proposing an ideal truth as a law of discourse, and an immanent rationality as the principle of ... behaviour."[8] To undo these constraints, epistemologists have to transgress the boundaries they hold in place, rearticulate relativism to dispel the disquietude, and defy the strictures that threaten excommunication.

In short, reasons the threat of relativism seems so dire derive from the presuppositions and prohibitions that structure hegemonic epistemological practice, not from the 'natural' dictates of reason and the logic of inquiry or the practical consequences of occupying a relativist position. Exposing the effects these disciplinary presuppositions generate reveals how empiricist, positivist, and rationalist principles, classical and modern, have, albeit unwittingly, contributed to erasing or discrediting women's knowledge, the knowledge of the 'unlettered,' and knowledge produced by people of races, hues, classes, and cultures that diverge from those of standard epistemology makers. It urges epistemologists to reconsider how relativism and constructivism, responsibly engaged and wisely articulated, afford release from a fear different from that against which Boghossian warns; a fear of the absolutism, rigidity, and dogma that have generated the dominant social-political-epistemic imaginary of the Western world.[9] The grammar of epistemology has restricted the honorific label 'knowledge' to products of the epistemic labors of white, educated, propertied men who occupy positions of power from which they claim the authority to make and evaluate public knowledge. Whether women or other Others would 'know differently' remains moot; but fears of relativism preclude addressing it with the seriousness it merits.

By contrast with projects of determining formal, a priori, necessary and sufficient conditions for knowledge in general, many epistemologists, following 'the naturalistic turn,' have sought to examine and explicate epistemic *practices*—to understand how people can, do, and should achieve knowledge within the symbolic, cultural, social, and other structures and institutions they inhabit.[10] The effects of a theoretical project and its openness to modification when practice reveals its shortcomings have become as worthy of epistemic attention as the logical possibilities epistemologists are wont to endorse. Yet ritual gestures of obeisance that countering the relativist threat has required complicate processes of assessing what it would mean, in practice, to *be* a relativist. Dispelling such disquietude could begin by reestablishing continuities between the formal concerns of epistemologists and the multiple modalities of everyday knowledge seeking: a move naturalist, feminist, and anti-racist epistemologists have made, variously, without descending into incoherence.

II. FALSE DICHOTOMIES?

Feminist and other postcolonial critiques of epistemology and genealogies of reason, rationality, objectivity, and knowledge have exposed binary oppositions that produce and maintain hegemonic, epistemic ideals. The reason/emotion, theory/practice, fact/value, mind/body, culture/nature, objective/subjective dichotomies and their analogues, and their alignment with the male/female dichotomy, are familiar to feminist theorists, as are their evaluative implications: the positive valuation of each first term, the negative valuation of the second. Feminists and other Others have contested these oppositions, casting them as contrasts not dichotomies, negotiating ways of refusing identification with either side. Yet even those who deconstruct pivotal epistemic terms (objectivity, value-neutrality, reason), resist essentialism across a range of conceptual constructs (women, intuition, nature), and argue for situated, locally sensitive epistemology remain caught in a net cast by the most rigid and reductive conception of relativism in circulation. Even epistemologists who evade traditional dichotomies are constrained by second-order dichotomies, for which relativism is *opposed to* rationality, realism, and objectivism:[11] oppositions more pertinent to an outmoded 'grammar' of relativism than to practical consequences of avowing or avoiding it. When relativism is imagined as precluding rationality, objectivity, or realism, it counts as a position no sane inquirer could support. No epistemologist worth her *or his* salt would come out as irrational, subjectivist, anti-realist.

For *feminists*, such dangers present urgent reasons for resisting relativism. Those who refuse the traditional first-order dichotomies are reminded daily of their power. Neither can epistemologists easily reject them without residue. Feminism's detractors invoke them as exclusionary principles to discredit feminist ventures onto epistemological territory, representing feminist research as 'preoccupied with practical matters,' 'too subjective,' 'overly emotional,' or 'merely political.' They are products of a history where women—persistently, across racial, cultural, class, and other 'differences'—are typed and stereotyped as irrational, incapable of abstract thought, unable to cope with 'reality' (despite

edge and revalue putatively superseded truths. Simple examples include renewed interest in Goethe's color theory and the readiness of allopathic medical practitioners to incorporate 'alternatives' such as indigenous medicine, acupuncture, or naturopathy into their practice.

In my reconstruction of the grammar of relativism and the totalizing consequences its critiques (grammatically) entail, would-be knowers could position themselves as relativists in some areas and not others, as my physics example shows. Feminists are rightly wary of how relativism is conflated with an irrationalism that has long been women's lot. Hence, resistance may be strategically prudent in inquiries committed to preserving a particular relation to, a voice within, standard epistemological debates, taking a stance in relation to power. A 'strategic universalism' analogous to the 'strategic essentialism' some feminists advocate might be required. Just as feminists unite in pro-choice marches, strategically affirming coalitions around otherwise contested issues of female identity, so they might unite across epistemic differences (relativist stances) should circumstances require. The issue is to determine what relation is reasonable for the excluded and silenced to preserve with hegemonic universalist epistemology. It cannot be answered 'from nowhere.'

Even feminist principles are relative to their time and place, and contextually mutable. Consider how feminist affirmations of sisterhood and struggles for equality have yielded to contestations of equality as a goal, and celebrations of difference. It is not that early liberal second-wave feminists worked with primitive understandings, or 'got it wrong.' The sheer numbers of women mobilized in the name of the sisterhood of women attest to the truth in their time, and the pragmatic efficacy of their (revisable) convictions. Glossing over truths that inspired them diminishes the foremothers who made feminist debates possible. Epistemologists have not told universal truths of a constant, coherent 'human nature,' but truths whose persuasiveness derives from the lives of those 'brightest and best of the sons of the morning' who found them pertinent to their aspirations and interests. Bedazzled by their achievements, they did not recognize the epistemic norms governing their practice as a function of *their* social setting, which differently situated members of the allegedly homogeneous human race were structurally inhibited from emulating.

Even this claim is too stark with its residual colonialist presumption that 'differently situated' people would opt for emulation if they could. It reiterates a universalist credo, erases any thought that 'others' might not want to conform to those ideals. In sum, acknowledging this degree of specificity makes denials of relativism disempowering and superfluous, for it inhibits feminism's self-critical orientation. Although the relativism I advocate is a refusal, it is more active than reactive: it clears the ground, seeks new possibilities, stands as a reminder of the irrational reductivism of the old ways despite their claims to universal truth and justice.

III. VARIETIES OF RELATIVISM

Although relativism takes multiple forms, I use the term promiscuously to cover cultural, historical, linguistic, and epistemological (judgmental) relativism. Cultural and historical relativism (perspectivism) sit more easily with feminists than epistemological relativism. Yet I have advocated a relativist stance *tout court*, before considering how it might be modified or mitigated in diverse situations. Perspectivism preserves tight connections with the universalist tradition: it allows a knower to stand outside, as a spectator. More radical relativism is participatory, located within the situations and circumstances to be known, neither requiring nor assuming transcendence.

Feminists and other Others are wary of imperialistic claims to universal sameness: of ethnocentrism, androcentrism, classism, Eurocentrism, and other 'centrisms' that silently shape Western culture: and of the homogenizing effects of early second-wave feminism's celebration of white female solidarity. They are likewise aware of the coercive, reductive effects of positivistic social science. Such sensitivities recommend a measure of cultural and historical relativism. No practicing feminist, now, would presume to speak for or about women of other cultures, races, classes, or historical periods as though they were 'just like us,' especially since 'we' cannot claim homogeneity. When such imperialist risks are acute, even relativism's opponents may concede that anti-relativism constrains understanding (*Verstehen*) and empathy, which are increasingly pertinent to feminist and other postcolonial theory.

Anti-relativism sustains the often coercive view that everyone sees everything in the same way, that we are identically and equally constrained and enabled by 'real world' circumstances; equally able to transcend everyday particularities. It fosters (non-empathic) incredulity at the idea that anyone would be dissatisfied with formal equality provisions or seek to preserve 'nonfunctional' aspects of their culture and tradition. Still, even feminists keenly aware of the imperialist effects of false universalism may balk at endorsing epistemological relativism. I have considered reasons for their reluctance.

Cultural and historical relativism are respectable feminist positions, according well with recognitions of historical, racial, cultural, class, and other specificities. The assumption is that their effects can be contained. Epistemological—judgmental—relativism is another story. Sandra Harding maintains, "even if embracing judgmental relativism could make sense in anthropology and other social sciences, it appears absurd as an epistemological stance in physics or biology," for "no reasonable standards can or could in principle be found for adjudicating between one culture's claim that the earth is flat and another culture's that the earth is round."[21] If such were its inevitable consequence, feminists, with other epistemologists, would have to resist relativism. Insisting that so fundamental a question is, in principle, undecidable would cast them among the naive and ignorant, insuring their membership in a group to which women have long been consigned. It would count, retrogressively, as proof that women cannot grasp the simplest truths. If relativism commits feminists to holding that violence against women, homophobia, racism, the dangers of environmental pollution, and inequities in female-male salaries and employment opportunities are merely notional, no feminist could responsibly be a relativist.

The alternatives demand attention. My contention is that places where knowledge claims demand unequivocal assent are the exceptions not the rule in early-twenty-first-century societies. It is impossible, even in such cases, to know whether assent will hold forever. Just as rejecting relativism acknowledges the impressive achievements of science and technology, doing so also reaffirms their unchallengeable place in industrial capitalist societies and the dubious agendas their venerable status endorses. Although repudiating relativism secures a place for feminists within authoritative scientific discourse, it reinforces the reductive, exclusionary effects of scientificity. Although it preserves feminists from conceding that flat-earthers might be right, it commits them to endorsing scientific medicine against naturopathy or midwifery, behaviorism against folk psychology, apolitical conceptions of biology against demonstrations of the politics of biology that feminist and other research has produced. A relativist can engage the apparently 'contradictory' findings of these conflicting systems, can resist forced choices.

Harding's worry that judgmental relativism would immobilize knowledge projects recalls the nihilism of the pronouncement, "If God does not exist, everything is permitted." Anti-relativists fear just such a consequence: if there are no absolute stopping places where interpretation and inquiry terminate in "*the truth of the matter*," then every conclusion is as good as any other. Yet the location Harding chooses as her stopping place—physics—is one she herself has disqualified, contending that "'physics' is a bad model [even] for physics" (chap. 4). The mythologized 'physics' which for post-positivists is the epitome of human cognitive achievement bears scant resemblance to what physicists *do* in practice. Not even physics can be modeled on 'physics.'

Oddly, in repudiating relativism, Harding appeals to physics after all: her distinction between judgmental/epistemological relativism and sociological-cultural-historical relativism posits a residual foundation where perspectives converge. Despite having characterized physics as a myth, and physics-as-practice as anomalous among intellectual projects, she returns to physics (with biology) to demonstrate the falsity of epistemological relativism. My appeal to the consensus that physicists and other scientists sometimes achieve emphasizes its rarity and temporal specificity.

In practice, the secularization of Western societies (where god may indeed be dead) has not resulted in everything being permitted: questions of permission and prohibition are as fiercely debated as ever, case by case, according to principles with significant, if not universal, force. Some questions have proven to be decidable for action-guiding purposes, on empirical grounds as functionally viable as members of the Vienna Circle wished; but their successes are rarely universalizable as the 'unity of science' project promised. The random location of these successes urges a reversal: an experiment with taking relativism of some degree (determined case by case) as the norm, and its opposites as the exception.

The question of how an avowed relativist could refute her opponents remains unanswered: anti-relativists will insist there is no way. But a surprising feature of anti-relativism, pertinent to this argument, is that it neglects an aspect of human lives—appropriately homogenized—that feminists and other post-positivists emphasize: people talk to one another, not only when they can assume a common ground but to negotiate across differences, establish commonalities. Anti-relativism—even feminist anti-relativism—reclaims the monologic utterance, the isolated truth claim uttered into a void by an abstract individual relying solely on his resources and singly accountable for their deliverances. Anti-relativism underestimates the deliberative, negotiative, cooperative, contestatory aspects of knowledge production, suppressing the situatedness whose recognition informs feminist and other postcolonial projects. It makes too little of how knowledge claims are produced, negotiated, validated, or discredited in ongoing discussion, some of which relies on sedimented truths about the shape of the earth, some of which contests apparently sedimented truths about women's rational inferiority to men, or about rape as not a serious form of harm. Which truths will withstand discussion and critique will not be apparent *before the fact*—despite the successes of theoretical physics and mathematics in producing truths that apparently hold ubiquitously and univocally, for now.

In negotiation, people succeed in working out relative and universal dimensions of knowledge and reality, not once and for all, but continuously, not always in perfect agreement, but with enough accord to enable them to 'go on.' They set aside differences and eschew certain agreed injustices to dislodge the self-certainty of unchallenged practices and assumptions, in self-contained communities or more widespread discussion. It involves moving about the epistemic terrain. In some places, simple empirical techniques are appropriate: learning about medium-sized material objects, learning which medicines and foods are effective for people in certain circumstances. There are numerous seemingly stable points, both mundane and esoteric. Scientifically informed technology, to which people entrust their lives, works more often than not: its reliability is impressive. Yet also in discussion and negotiation of the private, intimate kind, and in pressure groups, political coalitions, academic settings, workplaces, and the media, it emerges that the most secure, apparently universal assurances of 'science' are not just wrong but slanted, culpably partial. Relativism keeps that partiality on the conversational agenda. It shifts the discursive emphasis to make fixity and finality the exceptions, and partiality the rule, as the burden of proof shifts to places where finality and perfect objectivity are claimed, away from seemingly aberrant instances where relativism has to be eradicated.

Some claims may be immune to challenge: Harding's flat earth example may be one, as may other practical and commonsensical expectations that shape the lives of privileged members of prosperous societies. But focusing on the disempowering consequences of undecidability for seemingly incontestable (and practically necessary) truths repeats the problem Wittgenstein diagnoses: it relies on one-sided examples that make relativism ridiculous, and dangerous. It invokes a double standard: relativism cannot be true *because of* the ludicrous consequences it entails; but objectivism must be true *despite* the ludicrous (assimilationist, reductive) consequences it entails. The totalizing consequences of the old absolutisms must give way to textured readings in certain areas: there appears to be no problem. But the totalizing consequences of relativism are just that: there is everything wrong with them. In my view, there are no good reasons to generalize from the fabric of apparent certainty such examples yield to the universalist positions that have claimed hegemony and silenced relativism, no reasons to assume homogeneity across the physical and social world. Affirmations of relativism reject the Procrustean tradition of requiring practices to conform to theory, to return to practices in making and testing theories. They are risky, but feminists would do well to take this risk.

Some philosophers think similarly about positivism in its behaviorist garb, seeing it as a bold experiment. They propose treating people as if they were unknowable, as if they were opaque, yet manipulable, quantifiable. What kind of knowledge would be possible? I propose a radical reversal in an experiment just as bold: suppose 'we' run for now with relativism, assume relativism is viable, and may be true. We might encounter examples where it could not be true: the flat earth could be one; knowing 'medium-sized hardware' might be another. At other times, a boldly affirmed relativism would sound a cautionary note against totalizing impulses, as Paul Feyerabend does in characterizing relativism as 'a weapon against intellectual tyranny.'[22]

Recognizing the totalizing consequences of anti-relativism and the anxiety relativism produces, Cornel West observes:

> After the philosophical smoke clears, the crucial task is to pursue social and hetero-geneous genealogies ... accounts of the emergence, development, sustenance, and decline of vocabularies, discourses, and (non-discursive) practices in the natural and human sciences against the background of dynamic changes in specific (and often coexisting) modes of production, political conflicts, cultural configurations, and personal turmoil.[23]

In a period of dynamic social change, when the world is evolving in ways that will differ radically from anything 'we' have known, relativism demands a new hearing. Occupying a relativist position amounts, initially, to refusing the exclusions and prohibitions that have shaped the epistemology of the Anglo-American mainstream. Some of those constraints may prove strategically viable, but the reversal, I urge, would draw such a conclusion only after, not before, the fact. Its riskiness, its daring, recommends relativism as a revisionary position.

NOTES

1. Donna Haraway condemns relativism as a "way of being nowhere while claiming to be everywhere equally" ("Situated Knowledges," in *Simians, Cyborgs, and Women: The Reinvention of Nature* [New York: Routledge, 1991], 191). Sandra Harding contends that feminist standpoint epistemologies "call for recognition of a historical or sociological or cultural relativism—but not for a judgmental or epistemological relativism" (*Whose Science? Whose Knowledge?: Thinking from Women's Lives* [Ithaca, N.Y.: Cornell University Press, 1991], 142); Helen Longino cautions: "Loosening up the experiential/theoretical boundary need not ... and should not lead us to unbridled relativism" (*Science as Social Knowledge: Values and Objectivity in Scientific Inquiry* [Princeton, N.J.: Princeton University Press, 1990], 221); Lynn Hankinson Nelson resists relativism with the claim that "we can and should distinguish between beliefs and theories that are warranted and those that are not" (*Who Knows: From Quine to Feminist Empiricism* [Philadelphia:

Temple University Press, 1990], 40), implying that for a relativist such distinctions are not possible.

2. Several essays in *Science and Other Cultures: Issues in Philosophies of Science and Technology*, ed. Robert Figueroa and Sandra Harding (New York: Routledge, 2003), can be read as contributors to just such deliberation.

3. Clifford Geertz, "Anti Anti-Relativism," in *Relativism: Interpretation and Confrontation*, ed. Michael Krausz (Notre Dame, Ind.: University of Notre Dame Press, 1989), 15 (this volume, chap. 24).

4. Paul Boghossian, *Fear of Knowledge: Against Relativism and Constructivism* (Oxford: Clarendon Press, 2006), 130.

5. Michael Foucault, "Discourse on Language," in *The Archaeology of Knowledge and the Discourse on Language*, trans. A. M. Sheridan Smith (New York: Pantheon, 1972), 117.

6. Ludwig Wittgenstein, *Philosophical Investigations*, trans. G. E. M. Anscombe (Oxford: Blackwell, 1968), §373.

7. Ray Monk, *Ludwig Wittgenstein: The Duty of Genius* (London: Jonathan Cape, 1990), 446.

8. Foucault, "Discourse on Language," 224, 227.

9. Lorraine Code, review of *Fear of Knowledge: Against Relativism and Constructivism*, by Paul Boghossian, *International Studies in the Philosophy of Science* 22, no. 1 (2008): 97–100.

10. W. V. O. Quine, "Epistemology Naturalized" and "Natural Kinds," in *Naturalizing Epistemology*, 2nd ed., ed. Hilary Kornblith (Cambridge, Mass.: MIT Press, 1994); Lorraine Code, "What Is Natural About Epistemology Naturalized?" *American Philosophical Quarterly* 33, no. 1 (1996): 1–22, and *Ecological Thinking: The Politics of Epistemic Location* (New York: Oxford University Press, 2006).

11. For classic discussions of these dichotomies, see Richard Bernstein, *Beyond Objectivism and Relativism* (Philadelphia: University of Pennsylvania Press, 1983); Martin Hollis and Steven Lukes, eds., *Rationality and Relativism* (Cambridge, Mass.: MIT Press, 1982); and Anne Seller, "Realism versus Relativism: Toward a Politically Adequate Epistemology," in *Feminist Perspectives in Philosophy*, ed. Morwenna Griffiths and Margaret Whitford (Bloomington: Indiana University Press, 1988).

12. I use 'universalist,' 'objectivist,' 'realist,' 'foundational' and 'absolute' not as interchangeable terms, *supra*, and as a quasi-Wittgensteinian family of terms that map some labels relativists and anti-relativists have assigned to the putative default opposition to relativistic stances. See also Michael Krausz, "Mapping Relativisms," this volume, chap. 1.

13. An allusion to the title of Richard Rorty's *Philosophy and the Mirror of Nature* (Princeton, N.J.: Princeton University Press, 1980).

14. Kathleen Lennon, "Feminist Epistemology as Local Epistemology," *Proceedings of the Aristotelian Society*, supplementary volume 71 (1997): 37.

15. Haraway, "Situated Knowledges."

16. Lennon, "Feminist Epistemology as Local Epistemology," 187.

17. According to Boghossian, "The difficulty lies in understanding why such generalized applications of social construction have come to tempt so many" (*Fear of Knowledge*, 130). For a persuasive counter-story to Boghossian's, see Michael Williams, "Why (Wittgensteinian) Contextualism Is Not Relativism," *Episteme: A Journal of Social Epistemology* 4, no. 1 (2007): 93–114.

18. James F. Harris, *Against Relativism: A Philosophical Defense of Method* (LaSalle, Ill.: Open Court, 1992).

19. Joseph Rouse, *How Scientific Practices Matter: Reclaiming Philosophical Naturalism* (Chicago: University of Chicago Press, 2002), 146–159.

20. I owe this formulation to Jack Meiland, "Concepts of Relative Truth," *The Monist* 60 (1977): 564–574. See also his "On the Paradox of Cognitive Relativism," *Metaphilosophy* 11, no. 2 (1980): 115–126.

21. Harding, *Whose Science? Whose Knowledge?* 139.

22. Paul Feyerabend, "Notes on Relativism," in *Farewell to Reason* (London: Verso, 1987), 19.

23. Cornel West, *The American Evasion of Philosophy: A Genealogy of Pragmatism* (Madison: University of Wisconsin Press, 1987), 208.

Contributors

Kwame Anthony Appiah is Laurance S. Rockefeller University Professor of Philosophy with a cross-appointment at the University Center for Human Values at Princeton University.

Maria Baghramian is associate professor and co-director of the Postgraduate Programme in Cognitive Science at University College, Dublin.

Akeel Bilgrami is Johnsonian Professor of Philosophy and director of the Heyman Center for the Humanities at Columbia University.

Simon Blackburn is professor of philosophy at the University of Cambridge.

Paul A. Boghossian is professor of philosophy at New York University.

Nancy Cartwright is professor of philosophy at the London School of Economics and the University of California, San Diego.

Lorraine Code is Distinguished Research Professor in Philosophy and Social and Political Thought at York University, Canada.

Donald Davidson (1917–2003) was Slusser Professor of Philosophy at the University of California, Berkeley.

Catherine Z. Elgin is professor of the philosophy of education at Harvard University.

Clifford Geertz (1926–2006) was professor emeritus of anthropology at the Princeton Institute for Advanced Study.

Nelson Goodman (1906–1998) was professor emeritus of philosophy at Harvard University.

Gilbert Harman is Stuart Professor of Philosophy at Princeton University.

David Couzens Hoy is professor of philosophy and director of graduate studies at the University of California, Santa Cruz.

Michael Krausz is Milton C. Nahm Professor of Philosophy at Bryn Mawr College.

David Lyons is professor of philosophy and professor of law at Boston University.

John MacFarlane is associate professor of philosophy at the University of California, Berkeley.

Alasdair MacIntyre is Rev. John A. O'Brien Senior Research Professor in the Department of Philosophy and Permanent Senior Research Fellow in the Center for Ethics and Culture at the University of Notre Dame. He is also professor emeritus at Duke University.

Maurice Mandelbaum (1908–1987) was Andrew Mellon Professor of Philosophy at Johns Hopkins University.

Joseph Margolis is Laura H. Carnell Professor of Philosophy at Temple University.

Jitendra N. Mohanty is professor emeritus of philosophy at Temple University.

Thomas Nagel is University Professor of Philosophy and Law at New York University.

Martha C. Nussbaum is Ernst Freund Distinguished Service Professor of Law and Ethics at the University of Chicago.

Hilary Putnam is Cogan University Professor Emeritus of Philosophy at Harvard University.

Amélie Oksenberg Rorty is lecturer in the Department of Social Medicine at Harvard University.

Richard Rorty (1931–2007) was professor of comparative literature and, by courtesy, of philosophy at Stanford University.

Alan Ryan is warden of New College, Oxford, and professor of politics at the University of Oxford.

Amartya Sen is Lamont University Professor in Philosophy and Economics at Harvard University.

Russ Shafer-Landau is professor of philosophy at the University of Wisconsin, Madison.

Harvey Siegel is professor of philosophy at the University of Miami.

Gopal Sreenivasan is professor of philosophy at Duke University.

Charles Taylor is professor emeritus of political science and philosophy at McGill University and Board of Trustees Professor of Law and Philosophy at Northwestern University.

David Wiggins is Wykeham Professor Emeritus of Logic at Oxford University.

Bernard Williams (1929–2003) was White's Professor of Moral Philosophy at Oxford University, Deutsch Professor of Philosophy at the University of California, Berkeley, and fellow of All Souls College, Oxford.

Crispin Wright is professor of logic and metaphysics at the University of St. Andrews, and Global Distinguished Professor at New York University.

David B. Wong is Susan Fox Beischer and George D. Beischer Professor of Philosophy at Duke University.

Index

opinion, 101, 337, 373, 376, 441; anthropological, 383; authenticity and, 406n.5; differences of, 152, 153, 259, 283, 321n.6, 331; diversity of, 36, 47n.15; knowledge and, 385, 394–396, 537; manipulation and, 511; truth vs., 115, 152, 153, 306, 334, 338–341, 343, 347, 351, 352
oppression, 541, 542
options, real, 5, 248–252, 285, 407
Ordinary View, 331
overdetermination, 530

Pānini, 437
paranoia, 249, 383, 384, 407
particles, fundamental, 9, 272, 274
Peirce, Charles Sanders, 220, 221, 349, 405; "The Fixation of Belief," 220
perception, 8, 25, 40, 57, 58, 62, 65, 66, 73, 142, 149, 440, 450, 469; ethical generalizations not precedent over concrete, 447; perception of, 390
perseverance, 14, 143, 284, 285, 311, 312, 314, 319, 322
persons, 9, 12, 14, 506–508, 515–519, 521, 543; artificial, 508; as citizens, 509; contextually neutral concept of, 522; as creators of identity, 520; defining characteristics of, 9, 26, 506, 507, 510, 511, 514, 515; free will and, 513; human beings and, 508, 512; legal, 509; politically and ideologically defined, 519; respect and, 508, 512; rights of, 257, 513; social construction of, 2; weak version of, 515
perspectives, 18, 33, 38, 44–46, 61, 62, 93, 324, 346, 347, 386, 485, 546; Confucian, 259; Democritan, 482; decentering of, 8, 390; distorted, 478; external vs. internal, 37, 517; fusion vs. separation, 482; on human nature, 378, 379; impersonal, 260, 261; 'open,' 452; personal, 7, 326; reasons and, 327; of relativists, 34; sharability of, 169, 503. See also conceptual schemes; reference frames; standpoint

phenomenology, 9, 46, 327, 457, 458, 459, 467, 468
physics, 21, 45, 62, 67, 90, 92, 95, 273, 389, 407, 461, 465, 467, 538, 547, 548
Piaget, Jean, 385, 386
Plato, 2, 33–35, 46, 183, 185, 187, 209, 381, 394, 403, 410, 411, 417, 418, 441, 442, 446, 481; Cratylus, 47n.6; Phaedrus, 441; Republic, 441; Theaetetus, 33
plausibility, 118, 484, 502
pluralism, 10, 17, 60, 254–266, 274, 276–280, 458, 467, 527, 534, 354; cultural, 461; interpretation vs. world, 526–533; moral, 176; ontological, 526; weak vs. strong, 533
Poincaré, Jules Henri, 64, 74
points of view, 18, 58, 62, 63, 69, 72, 140, 141, 196, 210, 215, 235, 326, 424, 425, 529; adaptation of, to understand someone, 472; alternative/competing, 41, 144, 413–416, 418; conversion from or to, 407n.7; detached, 324, 326; God's-eye, 399; incoherent assertions that reflect no, 135, 327; incommensurable, 245; moral, 376, 389; outside system or scheme, 37, 147; possibility of describing same world from radically different, 462–464; possible worlds considered from same, 462; relativity of, 54, 60, 63, 93, 196, 209, 210, 214, 215, 217, 277, 440, 443. See also standpoints
Polanyi, Michael, 398, 423
politics, 21, 42, 46, 164, 165, 247, 373, 400, 418, 419, 485, 486, 547; analysis of, 437; comparative, 479, 485, 486; culture-transcendent theories of, 484
polymorphism, 25, 262
Popper, Karl, 49n.37
positivism, 64, 72, 398, 505, 546, 549
possible worlds, 102, 108, 112, 126, 144, 359, 462–464, 528
Postmodernism, 2, 32, 37, 38, 43, 45, 46, 174, 405, 529, 531
poststructuralism, 2, 30, 524–535
power, 46, 164, 195, 452, 483, 543, 545;

CPSIA information can be obtained
at www.ICGtesting.com
Printed in the USA
LVOW04s0031140416

483411LV00004B/10/P